# Table of Contents

Y0-BQZ-192

# Executive Summary

# Executive Summary

Effective rule of law reduces corruption, combats poverty and disease, and protects people from injustices large and small. It is the foundation for communities of peace, opportunity, and equity – underpinning development, accountable government, and respect for fundamental rights.

The World Justice Project (WJP) joins efforts to produce reliable data on rule of law through the *WJP Rule of Law Index® 2016*, the sixth report in an annual series, which measures rule of law based on the experiences and perceptions of the general public and in-country experts worldwide. We hope this annual publication, anchored in actual experiences, will help identify strengths and weaknesses in each country under review and encourage policy choices that strengthen the rule of law.

The *WJP Rule of Law Index 2016* presents a portrait of the rule of law in each country by providing scores and rankings organized around eights factors: constraints on government powers, absence of corruption, open government, fundamental rights, order and security, regulatory enforcement, civil justice, and criminal justice. A ninth factor, informal justice, is measured but not included in aggregated scores and rankings. These factors are intended to reflect how people experience rule of law in everyday life.

The country scores and rankings for the *WJP Rule of Law Index 2016* are derived from more than 110,000 households and 2,700 expert surveys in 113 countries and jurisdictions. The *Index* is the world's most comprehensive data set of its kind and the only to rely solely on primary data, measuring a nation's adherence to the rule of law from the perspective of how ordinary people experience it. These features make the *Index* a powerful tool that can help identify strengths and weaknesses in each country, and help to inform policy debates, both within and across countries, that advance the rule of law.

# Rule of Law Around the World: Scores and Rankings

The table below presents the scores and rankings of the *WJP Rule of Law Index 2016*. Scores range from 0 to 1 (with 1 indicating strongest adherence to the rule of law). Scoring is based on answers drawn from a representative sample of 1,000 respondents in the three largest cities per country and a set of in-country legal practitioners and academics. Tables organized by region and income group, along with disaggregated data for each factor, can be found in the "Scores and Rankings" section of this report. The methodology used to compute the scores and determine the mapping of survey questions to the conceptual framework is available in the "Methodology" section of the *WJP Rule of Law Index* website (worldjusticeproject.org/methodology).

| COUNTRY/ JURISDICTION | SCORE | GLOBAL RANKING | RANK CHANGE[1] |
|---|---|---|---|
| Afghanistan | 0.35 | 111 | 1 ▲ |
| Albania | 0.5 | 72 | 9 ▼ |
| Antigua & Barbuda | 0.67 | 29 | — |
| Argentina | 0.55 | 51 | 12 ▲ |
| Australia | 0.81 | 11 | 1 ▼ |
| Austria | 0.83 | 7 | — |
| Bahamas | 0.61 | 38 | — |
| Bangladesh | 0.41 | 103 | 1 ▲ |
| Barbados | 0.67 | 28 | — |
| Belarus | 0.54 | 57 | 2 ▲ |
| Belgium | 0.79 | 13 | 3 ▲ |
| Belize | 0.47 | 82 | 5 ▼ |
| Bolivia | 0.4 | 104 | 1 ▲ |
| Bosnia & Herzegovina | 0.56 | 50 | 1 ▼ |
| Botswana | 0.58 | 45 | 6 ▼ |
| Brazil | 0.55 | 52 | 3 ▲ |
| Bulgaria | 0.54 | 53 | 1 ▲ |
| Burkina Faso | 0.48 | 79 | 10 ▲ |
| Cambodia | 0.33 | 112 | 2 ▼ |
| Cameroon | 0.37 | 109 | 1 ▼ |
| Canada | 0.81 | 12 | 2 ▲ |
| Chile | 0.68 | 26 | — |
| China | 0.48 | 80 | 2 ▲ |
| Colombia | 0.51 | 71 | 1 ▲ |
| Costa Rica | 0.68 | 25 | — |
| Cote d'Ivoire | 0.46 | 87 | — |
| Croatia | 0.61 | 39 | 3 ▲ |
| Czech Republic | 0.75 | 17 | 3 ▲ |
| Denmark | 0.89 | 1 | — |
| Dominica | 0.6 | 40 | — |
| Dominican Republic | 0.47 | 85 | 7 ▼ |
| Ecuador | 0.45 | 91 | 3 ▼ |
| Egypt | 0.37 | 110 | 13 ▼ |
| El Salvador | 0.49 | 75 | 8 ▼ |
| Estonia | 0.79 | 14 | 1 ▲ |
| Ethiopia | 0.38 | 107 | 5 ▼ |
| Finland | 0.87 | 3 | 1 ▲ |
| France | 0.72 | 21 | 3 ▼ |
| Georgia | 0.65 | 34 | 1 ▼ |

| COUNTRY/ JURISDICTION | SCORE | GLOBAL RANKING | RANK CHANGE[1] |
|---|---|---|---|
| Germany | 0.83 | 6 | 2 ▲ |
| Ghana | 0.58 | 44 | 2 ▼ |
| Greece | 0.6 | 41 | — |
| Grenada | 0.66 | 31 | — |
| Guatemala | 0.44 | 97 | 1 ▼ |
| Guyana | 0.49 | 76 | — |
| Honduras | 0.42 | 102 | 1 ▼ |
| Hong Kong SAR, China | 0.77 | 16 | 1 ▲ |
| Hungary | 0.57 | 49 | 3 ▼ |
| India | 0.51 | 66 | 3 ▲ |
| Indonesia | 0.52 | 61 | 1 ▲ |
| Iran | 0.47 | 86 | 13 ▲ |
| Italy | 0.64 | 35 | 1 ▼ |
| Jamaica | 0.57 | 47 | 3 ▲ |
| Japan | 0.78 | 15 | 2 ▼ |
| Jordan | 0.59 | 42 | 7 ▲ |
| Kazakhstan | 0.5 | 73 | 2 ▲ |
| Kenya | 0.43 | 100 | 5 ▼ |
| Kyrgyzstan | 0.47 | 83 | 2 ▲ |
| Lebanon | 0.46 | 89 | 10 ▼ |
| Liberia | 0.45 | 94 | — |
| Macedonia, FYR | 0.54 | 54 | 1 ▼ |
| Madagascar | 0.45 | 90 | 3 ▲ |
| Malawi | 0.51 | 69 | 2 ▲ |
| Malaysia | 0.54 | 56 | 8 ▼ |
| Mexico | 0.46 | 88 | 2 ▲ |
| Moldova | 0.49 | 77 | 3 ▲ |
| Mongolia | 0.54 | 55 | 1 ▲ |
| Morocco | 0.53 | 60 | 5 ▲ |
| Myanmar | 0.43 | 98 | 5 ▼ |
| Nepal | 0.52 | 63 | 5 ▼ |
| Netherlands | 0.86 | 5 | — |
| New Zealand | 0.83 | 8 | 2 ▼ |
| Nicaragua | 0.42 | 101 | 1 ▼ |
| Nigeria | 0.44 | 96 | 11 ▲ |
| Norway | 0.88 | 2 | — |
| Pakistan | 0.38 | 106 | 3 ▲ |
| Panama | 0.52 | 62 | 3 ▼ |
| Peru | 0.51 | 65 | 8 ▲ |

| COUNTRY/ JURISDICTION | SCORE | GLOBAL RANKING | RANK CHANGE[1] |
|---|---|---|---|
| Philippines | 0.51 | 70 | 9 ▼ |
| Poland | 0.71 | 22 | 1 ▼ |
| Portugal | 0.71 | 23 | — |
| Republic of Korea | 0.73 | 19 | 8 ▼ |
| Romania | 0.66 | 32 | 4 ▲ |
| Russia | 0.45 | 92 | 6 ▼ |
| Senegal | 0.57 | 46 | — |
| Serbia | 0.5 | 74 | 4 ▲ |
| Sierra Leone | 0.45 | 95 | 3 ▲ |
| Singapore | 0.82 | 9 | — |
| Slovenia | 0.67 | 27 | 1 ▲ |
| South Africa | 0.59 | 43 | 1 ▲ |
| Spain | 0.7 | 24 | — |
| Sri Lanka | 0.51 | 68 | — |
| St. Kitts & Nevis | 0.66 | 30 | — |
| St. Lucia | 0.64 | 36 | — |
| St. Vincent & the Grenadines | 0.61 | 37 | — |
| Suriname | 0.53 | 59 | — |
| Sweden | 0.86 | 4 | 1 ▼ |
| Tanzania | 0.47 | 84 | 1 ▼ |
| Thailand | 0.51 | 64 | 2 ▲ |
| Trinidad & Tobago | 0.57 | 48 | — |
| Tunisia | 0.53 | 58 | 6 ▼ |
| Turkey | 0.43 | 99 | 8 ▼ |
| Uganda | 0.39 | 105 | 1 ▲ |
| Ukraine | 0.49 | 78 | 3 ▲ |
| United Arab Emirates | 0.66 | 33 | 2 ▼ |
| United Kingdom | 0.81 | 10 | 2 ▲ |
| United States | 0.74 | 18 | 1 ▲ |
| Uruguay | 0.72 | 20 | 2 ▲ |
| Uzbekistan | 0.45 | 93 | 1 ▼ |
| Venezuela | 0.28 | 113 | — |
| Vietnam | 0.51 | 67 | 7 ▼ |
| Zambia | 0.48 | 81 | 3 ▲ |
| Zimbabwe | 0.37 | 108 | 3 ▲ |

[1]The change in rankings was calculated by comparing the positions of the 102 countries measured in 2015 with the rankings of the same 102 countries in 2016, exclusive of the 11 new countries indexed in 2016.

The 11 new countries added to the *Index* are Antigua and Barbuda, The Bahamas, Barbados, Dominica, Grenada, Guyana, St. Kitts and Nevis, St. Lucia, St. Vincent and the Grenadines, Suriname, and Trinidad and Tobago.

# Country Specific Data and Online Tools

In addition to this written report, an interactive online platform for country-specific *WJP Rule of Law Index* data is available at data.worldjusticeproject.org.

The interactive data site invites viewers to browse each of the 113 country profiles and explore country scores for the eight aggregated factors of the rule of law: constraints on government powers, absence of corruption, open government, fundamental rights, order and security, regulatory enforcement, civil justice, and criminal justice.

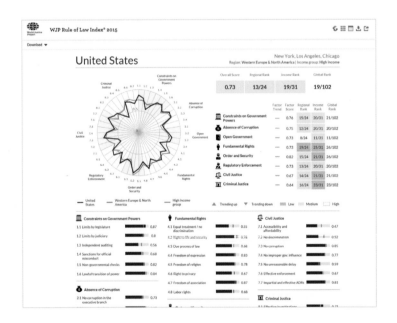

Discover each country's overall rule of law scores. The site features the *Index's* entire dataset, as well as global, regional, and income group rankings.

# The WJP Rule of Law Index®

# The WJP Rule of Law Index

The World Justice Project (WJP) is an independent, multidisciplinary organization working to advance the rule of law around the world. The rule of law provides the foundation for communities of peace, opportunity, and equity – underpinning development, accountable government, and respect for fundamental rights.

Where the rule of law is weak, medicines fail to reach health facilities, criminal violence goes unchecked, laws are applied unequally, and foreign investments are held back. Effective rule of law reduces corruption, improves public health, enhances education, alleviates poverty, and protects people from injustices and dangers large and small.

Strengthening the rule of law is a major goal of governments, donors, businesses, and civil society organizations around the world. To be effective, however, rule of law development requires clarity about the fundamental features of the rule of law, as well as an adequate basis for its evaluation and measurement. In response to this need, the World Justice Project has developed the *WJP Rule of Law Index*, a quantitative measurement tool that offers a comprehensive picture of the rule of law in practice.

The *WJP Rule of Law Index* presents a portrait of the rule of law in each country by providing scores and rankings organized around eight themes: constraints on government powers, absence of corruption, open government, fundamental rights, order and security, regulatory enforcement, civil justice, and criminal justice. A ninth factor, informal justice, is measured but not included in aggregated scores and rankings. These country scores and rankings are based on answers drawn from more than 110,000 households and 2,700 expert surveys in 113 countries and jurisdictions.

The *WJP Rule of Law Index 2016* is the sixth report in an annual series, and is the product of years of development, intensive consultation, and vetting with academics, practitioners, and community leaders from over 100 countries and 17 professional disciplines. The *Index* is intended for a broad audience of policy makers, civil society practitioners, academics, and others. The rule of law is not the rule of lawyers and judges: all elements of society are stakeholders. It is our hope that, over time, this diagnostic tool will help identify strengths and weaknesses in each country under review and encourage policy choices that strengthen the rule of law.

# Defining the Rule of Law

The rule of law is notoriously difficult to define and measure. A simple way of approaching it is in terms of some of the outcomes that the rule of law brings to societies – such as accountability, respect for fundamental rights, or access to justice – each of which reflects one aspect of the complex concept of the rule of law. The *WJP Rule of Law Index* seeks to embody these outcomes within a simple and coherent framework to measure the extent to which countries attain these outcomes *in practice* by means of performance indicators.

## Universal Principles of the Rule of Law

The WJP uses a working definition of the rule of law based on four universal principles, derived from internationally accepted standards. The rule of law is a system in which the following four universal principles are upheld:

1.  The government and its officials and agents as well as individuals and private entities are accountable under the law.

2.  The laws are clear, publicized, stable and just; are applied evenly; and protect fundamental rights, including the security of persons and property.

3.  The process by which the laws are enacted, administered, and enforced is accessible, fair, and efficient.

4.  Justice is delivered timely by competent, ethical, and independent representatives and neutrals who are of sufficient number, have adequate resources and reflect the makeup of the communities they serve.

The *WJP Rule of Law Index* captures adherence to the rule of law (as defined by the WJP's universal principles above) through a comprehensive and multi-dimensional set of outcome indicators, each of which reflects a particular aspect of this complex concept. The theoretical framework linking these outcome indicators draws on two main ideas pertaining to the relationship between the state and the governed: first, that the law imposes limits on the exercise of power by the state and its agents, as well as individuals and private entities. This is measured in factors 1, 2, 3, and 4 of the *Index*. Second, that the state limits the actions of members of society and fulfills its basic duties towards its population, so that the public interest is served, people are protected from violence and members of society have access to mechanisms to settle disputes and redress grievances. This is captured in factors 5, 6, 7, 8, and 9 of the *Index*. Although broad in scope, this framework assumes very little about the functions of the state, and when it does, it incorporates functions that are recognized by practically all societies, such as the provisions of justice or the guarantee of order and security.

The resulting set of indicators is also an effort to strike a balance between what scholars call a "thin" or minimalist conception of the rule of law that focuses on formal, procedural rules, and a "thick" conception that includes substantive characteristics, such as self-government and various fundamental rights and freedoms. Striking this balance between "thin" and "thick" conceptions of the rule of law enables the *Index* to apply to different types of social and political systems, including those which lack many of the features that characterize democratic nations, while including sufficient substantive characteristics to render the rule of law as more than merely a system of rules. Indeed, the *Index* recognizes that a system of positive law that fails to respect core human rights guaranteed under international law is at best "rule by law" and does not deserve to be called a rule of law system.

The *WJP Rule of Law Index* is comprised of nine factors further disaggregated into 47 specific sub-factors. These sub-factors are presented on page 13 and are described in detail in the section below.

### Factor 1: Constraints on Government Powers

Factor 1 measures the extent to which those who govern are bound by law. It comprises the means, both constitutional and institutional, by which the powers of the government and its officials and agents are limited and held accountable under the law. It also includes non-governmental checks on the government's power, such as a free and independent press.

Governmental checks take many forms; they do not operate solely in systems marked by a formal separation of powers, nor are they necessarily codified in law. What is essential, however, is that authority is distributed, whether by formal rules or by convention, in a manner that ensures that no single organ of government has the practical ability to exercise unchecked power.[1] This factor addresses the effectiveness of the institutional checks on government power by the legislature (1.1), the judiciary (1.2), and independent auditing and review agencies (1.3),[2] as well as the effectiveness of non-governmental oversight by the media and civil society (1.5), which serve an important role in monitoring government actions and holding officials accountable. The extent to which transitions of power occur in accordance with the law is also examined (1.6).[3] In addition to these checks, this factor also measures the extent to which government officials are held accountable for official misconduct (1.4).

### Factor 2: Absence of Corruption

Factor 2 measures the absence of corruption in a number of government agencies. The factor considers three forms of corruption: bribery, improper influence by public or private interests, and misappropriation of public funds or other resources. These three forms of corruption are examined with respect to government officers in the executive branch (2.1), the judiciary (2.2), the military and police (2.3), and the legislature (2.4), and encompass a wide range of possible situations in which corruption — from petty bribery to major kinds of fraud — can occur.

### Factor 3: Open Government

Factor 3 measures the openness of government defined as a government that shares information, empowers people with tools to hold the government accountable, and fosters citizen participation in public policy deliberations.

The factor measures whether basic laws and information in legal rights are publicized, and evaluates the quality of information published by the government (3.1). It also measures whether requests for information held by a government agency are properly granted (3.2). Finally it assesses the effectiveness of civic participation mechanisms –including the protection of freedoms of opinion and expression, assembly and association, and the right to petition (3.3), and whether people can bring specific complaints to the government (3.4).

---

[1] The *Index* does not address the further question of whether the laws are enacted by democratically elected representatives.

[2] This includes a wide range of institutions, from financial comptrollers and auditing agencies to the diverse array of entities that monitor human rights compliance (e.g. "Human Rights Defender", "Ombudsman", "People's Advocate", "Defensor del Pueblo", "Ouvidoria", "Human Rights Commissioner", "Oiguskantsler", "Mediateur de la Republique", "Citizen's Advocate", "Avocatul Poporului"). In some countries these functions are performed by judges or other state officials; in others, they are carried out by independent agencies.

[3] This sub-factor does not address the issue of whether transitions of political power take place through democratic elections. Rather, it examines whether the rules for the orderly transfer of power are actually observed. This sub-factor looks at the prevalence of electoral fraud and intimidation (for those countries in which elections are held), the frequency of coups d'etat, and the extent to which transition processes are open to public scrutiny

## Factor 4: Fundamental Rights

Factor 4 measures the protection of fundamental human rights. It recognizes that a system of positive law that fails to respect core human rights established under international law is at best "rule by law," and does not deserve to be called a rule of law system. Since there are many other indices that address human rights, and as it would be impossible for the *Index* to assess adherence to the full range of rights, this factor focuses on a relatively modest menu of rights that are firmly established under the Universal Declaration of Human Rights and are most closely related to rule of law concerns. Accordingly, Factor 4 encompasses adherence to the following fundamental rights: effective enforcement of laws that ensure equal protection (4.1),[4] the right to life and security of the person (4.2),[5] due process of law and the rights of the accused (4.3),[6] freedom of opinion and expression (4.4), freedom of belief and religion (4.5), the right to privacy (4.6), freedom of assembly and association (4.7), and fundamental labor rights, including the right to collective bargaining, the prohibition of forced and child labor, and the elimination of discrimination (4.8).[7]

## Factor 5: Order & Security

Factor 5 measures how well the society assures the security of persons and property. Security is one of the defining aspects of any rule of law society and a fundamental function of the state. It is also a precondition for the realization of the rights and freedoms that the rule of law seeks to advance. This factor includes three dimensions

that cover various threats to order and security: crime (5.1 particularly conventional crime),[8] political violence (5.2 including terrorism, armed conflict, and political unrest), and violence as a socially acceptable means to redress personal grievances (5.3 vigilante justice).

## Factor 6: Regulatory Enforcement

Factor 6 measures the extent to which regulations are fairly and effectively implemented and enforced. Regulations, both legal and administrative, structure behaviors within and outside of the government. Strong rule of law requires that these regulations and administrative provisions are enforced effectively (6.1) and are applied and enforced without improper influence by public officials or private interests (6.2). Additionally, strong rule of law requires that administrative proceedings are conducted in a timely manner, without unreasonable delays (6.4), that due process is respected in administrative proceedings (6.3), and that there is no expropriation of private property without adequate compensation (6.5).

This factor does not assess which activities a government chooses to regulate, nor does it consider how much regulation of a particular activity is appropriate. Rather, it examines how regulations are implemented and enforced. To facilitate comparisons, this factor considers areas that all countries regulate to one degree or another, such as public health, workplace safety, environmental protection, and commercial activity.

---

[4] The laws can be fair only if they do not make arbitrary or irrational distinctions based on economic or social status – the latter defined to include race, color, ethnic or social origin, caste, nationality, alienage, religion, language, political opinion or affiliation, gender, marital status, sexual orientation or gender identity, age, and disability. It must be acknowledged that for some societies, including some traditional societies, certain of these categories may be problematic. In addition, there may be differences both within and among such societies as to whether a given distinction is arbitrary or irrational. Despite these difficulties, it was determined that only an inclusive list would accord full respect to the principles of equality and non-discrimination embodied in the Universal Declaration of Human Rights and emerging norms of international law.

[5] Sub-factor 4.2 concerns police brutality and other abuses – including arbitrary detention, torture and extrajudicial execution – perpetrated by agents of the state against criminal suspects, political dissidents, members of the media, and ordinary people.

[6] This includes the presumption of innocence and the opportunity to submit and challenge evidence before public proceedings; freedom from arbitrary arrest, detention, torture and abusive treatment, and access to legal counsel and translators.

[7] Sub-factor 4.8 includes the four fundamental principles recognized by the ILO Declaration of Fundamental Principles and Rights at Work of 1998: 1) the freedom of association and the effective recognition of the right to collective bargaining, 2) the elimination of all forms of forced or compulsory labor, 3) the effective abolition of child labor, and 4) the elimination of discrimination in respect of employment and occupation.

[8] In this category, we include measures of criminal victimization, such as homicide, kidnapping, burglary, armed robbery, extortion, and fraud.

## Factor 7: Civil Justice

Factor 7 measures whether ordinary people can resolve their grievances peacefully and effectively through the civil justice system. The delivery of effective civil justice requires that the system be accessible and affordable (7.1), free of discrimination (7.2), free of corruption (7.3), and without improper influence by public officials (7.4). The delivery of effective civil justice also necessitates that court proceedings are conducted in a timely manner, not subject to unreasonable delays, and are effectively enforced (7.5 and 7.6). Finally, recognizing the value of Alternative Dispute Resolution mechanisms (ADRs), this factor also measures the accessibility, impartiality, and efficiency of mediation and arbitration systems that enable parties to resolve civil disputes (7.7).

## Factor 8: Criminal Justice

Factor 8 evaluates the criminal justice system. An effective criminal justice system is a key aspect of the rule of law, as it constitutes the conventional mechanism to redress grievances and bring action against individuals for offenses against society. Effective criminal justice systems are capable of investigating and adjudicating criminal offenses successfully and in a timely manner (8.1 and 8.2), through a system that is impartial and non-discriminatory (8.4), and that is free of corruption and improper government influence (8.5 and 8.6), all while ensuring that the rights of both victims and the accused are effectively protected (8.7).[9] The delivery of effective criminal justice also necessitates correctional systems that effectively reduce criminal behavior (8.3). Accordingly, an assessment of the delivery of criminal justice should take into consideration the entire system, including the police, the lawyers, prosecutors, judges, and prison officers.

## Factor 9: Informal Justice

Finally, Factor 9 concerns the role played in many countries by customary and 'informal' systems of justice – including traditional, tribal, and religious courts, and community-based systems – in resolving disputes. These systems often play a large role in cultures in which formal legal institutions fail to provide effective remedies for large segments of the population, or when formal institutions are perceived as remote, corrupt, or ineffective. This factor covers three concepts: whether these dispute resolution systems are timely and effective (9.1), whether they are impartial and free of improper influence (9.2), and the extent to which these systems respect and protect fundamental rights (9.3).[10]

---

[9] Sub-factor 8.7 includes the presumption of innocence and the opportunity to submit and challenge evidence before public proceedings, freedom from arbitrary arrest, detention, torture and abusive treatment, and access to legal counsel and translators.

[10] WJP has devoted significant effort to collecting data on informal justice in a dozen countries. Nonetheless, the complexities of these systems and the difficulties of measuring their fairness and effectiveness in a manner that is both systematic and comparable across countries, make assessments extraordinarily challenging. Although the WJP has collected data on this dimension, they are not included in the aggregated scores and rankings.

# The Nine Factors of the Rule of Law

### Factor 1: Constraints on Government Powers

1.1 Government powers are effectively limited by the legislature
1.2 Government powers are effectively limited by the judiciary
1.3 Government powers are effectively limited by independent auditing and review
1.4 Government officials are sanctioned for misconduct
1.5 Government powers are subject to non-governmental checks
1.6 Transition of power is subject to the law

### Factor 2: Absence of Corruption

2.1 Government officials in the executive branch do not use public office for private gain
2.2 Government officials in the judicial branch do not use public office for private gain
2.3 Government officials in the police and military do not use public office for private gain
2.4 Government officials in the legislative branch do not use public office for private gain

### Factor 3: Open Government

3.1 Publicized laws and government data
3.2 Right to information
3.3 Civic participation
3.4 Complaint mechanisms

### Factor 4: Fundamental Rights

4.1 Equal treatment and absence of discrimination
4.2 The right to life and security of the person is effectively guaranteed
4.3 Due process of law and the rights of the accused
4.4 Freedom of opinion and expression is effectively guaranteed
4.5 Freedom of belief and religion is effectively guaranteed
4.6 Freedom from arbitrary interference with privacy is effectively guaranteed
4.7 Freedom of assembly and association is effectively guaranteed
4.8 Fundamental labor rights are effectively guaranteed

### Factor 5: Order & Security

5.1 Crime is effectively controlled
5.2 Civil conflict is effectively limited
5.3 People do not resort to violence to redress personal grievances

### Factor 6: Regulatory Enforcement

6.1 Government regulations are effectively enforced
6.2 Government regulations are applied and enforced without improper influence
6.3 Administrative proceedings are conducted without unreasonable delay
6.4 Due process is respected in administrative proceedings
6.5 The government does not expropriate without lawful process and adequate compensation

### Factor 7: Civil Justice

7.1 People can access and afford civil justice
7.2 Civil justice is free of discrimination
7.3 Civil justice is free of corruption
7.4 Civil justice is free of improper government influence
7.5 Civil justice is not subject to unreasonable delay
7.6 Civil justice is effectively enforced
7.7 Alternative dispute resolution mechanisms are accessible, impartial, and effective

### Factor 8: Criminal Justice

8.1 Criminal investigation system is effective
8.2 Criminal adjudication system is timely and effective
8.3 Correctional system is effective in reducing criminal behavior
8.4 Criminal system is impartial
8.5 Criminal system is free of corruption
8.6 Criminal system is free of improper government influence
8.7 Due process of law and the rights of the accused

### Factor 9: Informal Justice

9.1 Informal justice is timely and effective
9.2 Informal justice is impartial and free of improper influence
9.3 Informal justice respects and protects fundamental rights

# The Rule of Law in Everyday Life

The rule of law affects all of us in our everyday lives. Although we may not be aware of it, the rule of law is profoundly important – and not just to lawyers or judges. It is the foundation for a system of rules to keep us safe, resolve disputes, and enable us to prosper. In fact, every sector of society is a stakeholder in the rule of law. Below are a few examples:

**Business environment.** Imagine an investor seeking to commit resources abroad. She would probably think twice before investing in a country where corruption is rampant, property rights are ill-defined, and contracts are difficult to enforce. Uneven enforcement of regulations, corruption, insecure property rights, and ineffective means to settle disputes undermine legitimate business and drive away both domestic and foreign investment.

**Public works.** Consider the bridges, roads, or runways we traverse daily — or the offices and buildings in which we live, work, and play. What if building codes governing their design and safety were not enforced, or if government officials and contractors employed low-quality materials in order to pocket the surplus? Weak regulatory enforcement and corruption decrease the security of physical infrastructures and waste scarce resources, which are essential to a thriving economy.

**Public health and environment.** Consider the implications of pollution, wildlife poaching, and deforestation for public health, the economy, and the environment. What if a company was pouring harmful chemicals into a river in a highly populated area and the environmental inspector turned a blind eye in exchange for a bribe? While countries around the world have laws to protect the public's health and the environment, these laws are not always enforced. Adherence to the rule of law is essential to effective enforcement of public health and environmental regulations and to hold government, businesses, civil society organizations, and communities accountable for protecting the environment without unduly constraining economic opportunities.

**Public participation.** What if residents of a neighborhood were not informed of an upcoming construction project commissioned by the government that would cause disruptions to their community? Or what if they did not have the opportunity to present their objections to the relevant government authorities prior to the start of the construction project? Being able to voice opinions about government decisions that directly impact the lives of ordinary people is a key aspect of the rule of law. Public participation ensures that all stakeholders have the chance to be heard and provide valuable input in the decision-making process.

**Civil Justice.** Imagine an individual having a dispute with another party. What if the system to settle the dispute and obtain a remedy was largely inaccessible, unreliable, or corrupt? Without a well-functioning justice system – a core element of the rule of law – individuals faced with a dispute have few options other than giving up or resorting to violence to settle the conflict.

# Measuring the Rule of Law

## This conceptual framework provides the basis for measuring the rule of law.

The scores and rankings of the 44 sub-factors (factors 1 through 8)[1] draw from two data sources collected by the World Justice Project in each country: 1) a general population poll (GPP) conducted by leading local polling companies using a representative sample of 1,000 respondents in the three largest cities,[2] and 2) qualified respondents' questionnaires (QRQs) consisting of closed-ended questions completed by in-country practitioners and academics with expertise in civil and commercial law, criminal justice, labor law, and public health. Taken together, these two data sources provide up-to-date firsthand information from a large number of people on their experiences and perceptions concerning their dealings with the government, the police, and the courts, as well as the openness and accountability of the state, the extent of corruption, and the magnitude of common crimes to which the general public is exposed.

These data are processed, normalized on a 0 to 1 scale, and aggregated from the variable level all the way up to the dimension level for each country, and then to an overall score and ranking using the data map and weights reported in the "Methodology" section of the *WJP Rule of Law Index* website. Finally, these scores are validated and cross-checked against qualitative and quantitative third-party sources to identify possible mistakes or inconsistencies within the data.

The WJP has produced the *Rule of Law Index* for each of the last six years. During this time, the number of countries covered has increased, and the surveys and indicators have evolved to better reflect the rule of law landscape of countries around the world. While this year's indicators are closely aligned with those used in the previous edition, new questions pertaining to open government and dispute resolution have been added to the surveys.[3] The *WJP Rule of Law Index 2016* report also includes 11 new

countries: Antigua and Barbuda, The Bahamas, Barbados, Dominica, Grenada, Guyana, St. Kitts and Nevis, St. Lucia, St. Vincent and the Grenadines, Suriname, and Trinidad and Tobago. In total, this year's report covers 113 countries and jurisdictions that account for more than 90 percent of the world's population.

The country scores and rankings presented in this report are based on data collected and analyzed during the second and third quarters of 2016, with the exception of general population data for countries indexed in 2015, which were gathered during the fall of 2014.

The scores and rankings have been organized into 113 country profiles, which are available at data.worldjusticeproject.org. Each of these profiles displays 1) the country's overall rule of law score and ranking; 2) the score of each of the eight dimensions of the rule of law as well as the global, regional, and income group rankings; 3) the score of each of the 44 sub-factors together with the average score of the country's region and the country's income group. A detailed description of the process by which data are collected and the rule of law is measured is available online at worldjusticeproject.org.

---

[1] Significant effort has been devoted during the last four years to collecting data on informal justice in a dozen countries. Nonetheless, the complexities of these systems and the difficulties of measuring their fairness and effectiveness in a manner that is both systematic and comparable across countries, make assessments extraordinarily challenging. Although the WJP has collected data on this dimension, they are not included in the aggregated scores and rankings.

[2] In order to achieve a representative sample in some Caribbean countries, nationally representative polls were conducted outside of the three largest cities using a sample of 500 respondents. Please see the "Methodology" section for a full explanation and polling methodology by country.

[3] Please see the "Methodology" section for a complete description of survey updates.

# The WJP Rule of Law Index Methodology in a Nutshell

## The production of the *WJP Rule of Law Index* may be summarized in eleven steps:

1. The WJP developed the conceptual framework summarized in the *Index's* 8 factors and 44 sub-factors, in consultation with academics, practitioners, and community leaders from around the world.

2. The *Index* team developed a set of five questionnaires based on the *Index's* conceptual framework, to be administered to experts and the general public. Questionnaires were translated into several languages and adapted to reflect commonly used terms and expressions.

3. The team identified, on average, more than 300 potential local experts per country to respond to the experts' questionnaires, and engaged the services of leading local polling companies to implement the household surveys.

4. Polling companies conducted pre-test pilot surveys of the general public in consultation with the *Index* team, and launched the final survey.

5. The team sent the questionnaires to local experts and engaged in continual interaction with them.

6. The *Index* team collected and mapped the data onto the 44 sub-factors with global comparability.

7. The *Index* team constructed the final scores using a five-step process:
   a. Codified the questionnaire items as numeric values.
   b. Produced raw country scores by aggregating the responses from several individuals (experts or general public).
   c. Normalized the raw scores.
   d. Aggregated the normalized scores into sub-factors and factors using simple averages.
   e. Produced the final rankings using the normalized scores.

8. The data were subject to a series of tests to identify possible biases and errors. For example, the *Index* team cross-checked all sub-factors against more than 60 third-party sources, including quantitative data and qualitative assessments drawn from local and international organizations.

9. A sensitivity analysis was conducted to assess the statistical reliability of the results.

10. To illustrate whether the rule of law in a country significantly changed over the course of the past year, a measure of change over time was produced based on the annual difference in the country-level factor scores, the standard errors of these scores (estimated from a set of 100 bootstrap samples), and the results of the corresponding t-tests.

11. The data were organized into country reports, tables, and figures to facilitate their presentation and interpretation.

---

*A detailed description of the process by which data are collected and the rule of law is measured is provided in the "Methodology" section of this report.

# Features of the Rule of Law Index

The *WJP Rule of Law Index* includes several features that set it apart from other indices and make it useful for a large number of countries:

### Rule of law in practice

The *Index* measures adherence to the rule of law by looking at policy outcomes (such as whether people have access to courts or whether crime is effectively controlled). This stands in contrast to efforts that focus on the laws on the books, or the institutional means by which a society may seek to achieve these policy outcomes.

### Comprehensive/Multi-dimensional

While other indices cover particular aspects of the rule of law, such as absence of corruption or human rights, they do not yield a full picture of rule of law compliance. The *WJP Rule of Law Index* is the only global instrument that looks at the rule of law comprehensively.

### Perspective of the ordinary people

The *WJP Rule of Law Index* puts people at its core by looking at a nation's adherence to the rule of law from the perspective of ordinary individuals who are directly affected by the degree of adherence to the rule of law in their societies. The *Index* examines practical, everyday situations, such as whether people can access public services and whether a dispute among neighbors can be resolved peacefully and cost-effectively by an independent adjudicator.

### New data anchored in actual experiences

The *Index* is the only comprehensive set of indicators on the rule of law that is based on primary data. The *Index's* scores are built from the assessments of local residents (1,000 respondents per country) and local legal experts, which ensure that the findings reflect the conditions experienced by the population, including marginalized sectors of society.

### Culturally competent

The *Index* has been designed to be applied in countries with vastly different social, cultural, economic, and political systems. No society has ever attained — let alone sustained — a perfect realization of the rule of law. Every nation faces the perpetual challenge of building and renewing the structures, institutions, and norms that can support and sustain a rule of law culture.

# Using the WJP Rule of Law Index

The *WJP Rule of Law Index* has been designed to offer a reliable and independent data source for policy makers, businesses, non-governmental organizations, and other constituencies to assess a nation's adherence to the rule of law as perceived and experienced by the average person, identify a nation's strengths and weaknesses in comparison to similarly situated countries, and track changes over time. The *Index* has been designed to include several features that set it apart from other indices and make it valuable for a large number of countries, thus providing a powerful resource that can inform policy debates both within and across countries. However, the *Index's* findings must be interpreted in light of certain inherent limitations.

1. The *WJP Rule of Law Index* does not identify priorities for reform and is not intended to establish causation or to ascertain the complex relationship among different rule of law dimensions in various countries.

2. The *Index's* rankings and scores are the product of a rigorous data collection and aggregation methodology. Nonetheless, as with all measures, they are subject to measurement error.

3. Given the uncertainty associated with picking a particular sample of respondents, standard errors have been calculated using bootstrapping methods to test whether the annual changes in the factor scores are statistically significant.

4. Indices and indicators are subject to potential abuse and misinterpretation. Once released to the public, they can take on a life of their own and be used for purposes unanticipated by their creators. If data are taken out of context, it can lead to unintended or erroneous policy decisions.

5. Rule of law concepts measured by the *Index* may have different meanings across countries. Users are encouraged to consult the specific definitions of the variables employed in the construction of the *Index*, which are discussed in greater detail in the "Methodology" section of the *WJP Rule of Law Index* website.

6. The *Index* is generally intended to be used in combination with other instruments, both quantitative and qualitative. Just as in the areas of health or economics, no single index conveys a full picture of a country's situation. Policymaking in the area of rule of law requires careful consideration of all relevant dimensions – which may vary from country to country – and a combination of sources, instruments, and methods.

7. Pursuant to the sensitivity analysis of the *Index* data conducted in collaboration with the Econometrics and Applied Statistics Unit of the European Commission's Joint Research Centre, confidence intervals have been calculated for all figures included in the *WJP Rule of Law Index*. These confidence intervals and other relevant considerations regarding measurement error are reported in Saisana and Saltelli (2015) and Botero and Ponce (2011).

# Scores and Rankings

# Rule of Law Around the World

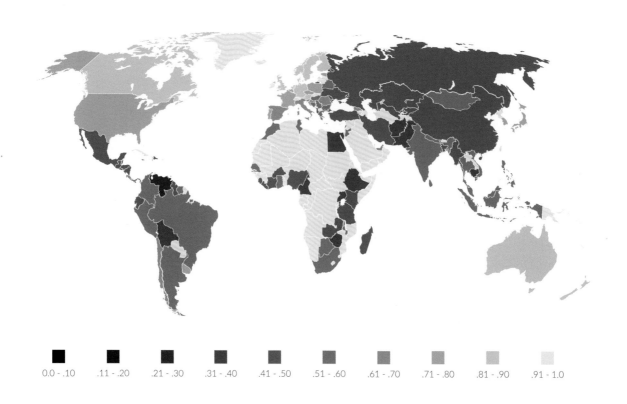

| ■ | ■ | ■ | ■ | ■ | ■ | ■ | ■ | ■ | ■ |
|---|---|---|---|---|---|---|---|---|---|
| 0.0 - .10 | .11 - .20 | .21 - .30 | .31 - .40 | .41 - .50 | .51 - .60 | .61 - .70 | .71 - .80 | .81 - .90 | .91 - 1.0 |

The *Rule of Law Index* measures a country's adherence to the rule of law from the perspective of how ordinary people experience it. The following pages in this section highlight the overall rule of law scores and rankings for 113 countries and jurisdictions, as well as scores and rankings by income, region, and each of the eight aggregated factors of the *Index*. This section also features an analysis of whether a country's primary rule of law factors experienced significant change over the past year.

| COUNTRY/ JURISDICTION | SCORE | GLOBAL RANKING |
|---|---|---|
| Denmark | 0.89 | 1 |
| Norway | 0.88 | 2 |
| Finland | 0.87 | 3 |
| Sweden | 0.86 | 4 |
| Netherlands | 0.86 | 5 |
| Germany | 0.83 | 6 |
| Austria | 0.83 | 7 |
| New Zealand | 0.83 | 8 |
| Singapore | 0.82 | 9 |
| United Kingdom | 0.81 | 10 |
| Australia | 0.81 | 11 |
| Canada | 0.81 | 12 |
| Belgium | 0.79 | 13 |
| Estonia | 0.79 | 14 |
| Japan | 0.78 | 15 |
| Hong Kong SAR, China | 0.77 | 16 |
| Czech Republic | 0.75 | 17 |
| United States | 0.74 | 18 |
| Republic of Korea | 0.73 | 19 |
| Uruguay | 0.72 | 20 |
| France | 0.72 | 21 |
| Poland | 0.71 | 22 |
| Portugal | 0.71 | 23 |
| Spain | 0.70 | 24 |
| Costa Rica | 0.68 | 25 |
| Chile | 0.68 | 26 |
| Slovenia | 0.67 | 27 |
| Barbados | 0.67 | 28 |
| Antigua & Barbuda | 0.67 | 29 |
| St. Kitts & Nevis | 0.66 | 30 |
| Grenada | 0.66 | 31 |
| Romania | 0.66 | 32 |
| United Arab Emirates | 0.66 | 33 |
| Georgia | 0.65 | 34 |
| Italy | 0.64 | 35 |
| St. Lucia | 0.64 | 36 |
| St. Vincent & the Grenadines | 0.61 | 37 |
| Bahamas | 0.61 | 38 |
| Croatia | 0.61 | 39 |
| Dominica | 0.60 | 40 |
| Greece | 0.60 | 41 |
| Jordan | 0.59 | 42 |
| South Africa | 0.59 | 43 |
| Ghana | 0.58 | 44 |
| Botswana | 0.58 | 45 |
| Senegal | 0.57 | 46 |
| Jamaica | 0.57 | 47 |
| Trinidad & Tobago | 0.57 | 48 |
| Hungary | 0.57 | 49 |
| Bosnia & Herzegovina | 0.56 | 50 |
| Argentina | 0.55 | 51 |
| Brazil | 0.55 | 52 |
| Bulgaria | 0.54 | 53 |
| Macedonia, FYR | 0.54 | 54 |
| Mongolia | 0.54 | 55 |
| Malaysia | 0.54 | 56 |
| Belarus | 0.54 | 57 |
| Tunisia | 0.53 | 58 |

| COUNTRY/ JURISDICTION | SCORE | GLOBAL RANKING |
|---|---|---|
| Suriname | 0.53 | 59 |
| Morocco | 0.53 | 60 |
| Indonesia | 0.52 | 61 |
| Panama | 0.52 | 62 |
| Nepal | 0.52 | 63 |
| Thailand | 0.51 | 64 |
| Peru | 0.51 | 65 |
| India | 0.51 | 66 |
| Vietnam | 0.51 | 67 |
| Sri Lanka | 0.51 | 68 |
| Malawi | 0.51 | 69 |
| Philippines | 0.51 | 70 |
| Colombia | 0.51 | 71 |
| Albania | 0.50 | 72 |
| Kazakhstan | 0.50 | 73 |
| Serbia | 0.50 | 74 |
| El Salvador | 0.49 | 75 |
| Guyana | 0.49 | 76 |
| Moldova | 0.49 | 77 |
| Ukraine | 0.49 | 78 |
| Burkina Faso | 0.48 | 79 |
| China | 0.48 | 80 |
| Zambia | 0.48 | 81 |
| Belize | 0.47 | 82 |
| Kyrgyzstan | 0.47 | 83 |
| Tanzania | 0.47 | 84 |
| Dominican Republic | 0.47 | 85 |
| Iran | 0.47 | 86 |
| Cote d'Ivoire | 0.46 | 87 |
| Mexico | 0.46 | 88 |
| Lebanon | 0.46 | 89 |
| Madagascar | 0.45 | 90 |
| Ecuador | 0.45 | 91 |
| Russia | 0.45 | 92 |
| Uzbekistan | 0.45 | 93 |
| Liberia | 0.45 | 94 |
| Sierra Leone | 0.45 | 95 |
| Nigeria | 0.44 | 96 |
| Guatemala | 0.44 | 97 |
| Myanmar | 0.43 | 98 |
| Turkey | 0.43 | 99 |
| Kenya | 0.43 | 100 |
| Nicaragua | 0.42 | 101 |
| Honduras | 0.42 | 102 |
| Bangladesh | 0.41 | 103 |
| Bolivia | 0.40 | 104 |
| Uganda | 0.39 | 105 |
| Pakistan | 0.38 | 106 |
| Ethiopia | 0.38 | 107 |
| Zimbabwe | 0.37 | 108 |
| Cameroon | 0.37 | 109 |
| Egypt | 0.37 | 110 |
| Afghanistan | 0.35 | 111 |
| Cambodia | 0.33 | 112 |
| Venezuela | 0.28 | 113 |

# Rule of Law Around the World By Region

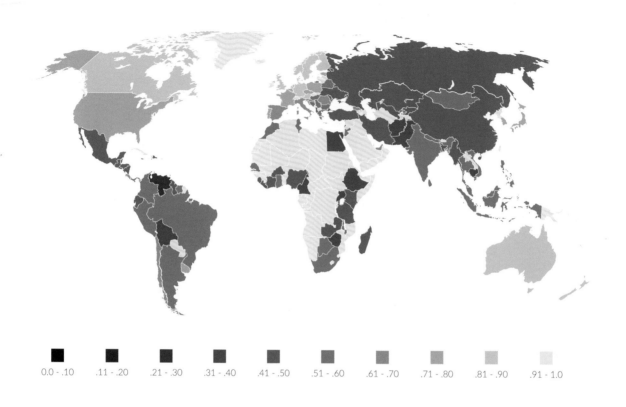

| | | | | | | | | | |
|---|---|---|---|---|---|---|---|---|---|
| ■ | ■ | ■ | ■ | ■ | ■ | ■ | ■ | ■ | ■ |
| 0.0 - .10 | .11 - .20 | .21 - .30 | .31 - .40 | .41 - .50 | .51 - .60 | .61 - .70 | .71 - .80 | .81 - .90 | .91 - 1.0 |

## East Asia & Pacific

| COUNTRY/ JURISDICTION | SCORE | GLOBAL RANKING |
|---|---|---|
| New Zealand | 0.83 | 8 |
| Singapore | 0.82 | 9 |
| Australia | 0.81 | 11 |
| Japan | 0.78 | 15 |
| Hong Kong SAR, China | 0.77 | 16 |
| Republic of Korea | 0.73 | 19 |
| Mongolia | 0.54 | 55 |
| Malaysia | 0.54 | 56 |
| Indonesia | 0.52 | 61 |
| Thailand | 0.51 | 64 |
| Vietnam | 0.51 | 67 |
| Philippines | 0.51 | 70 |
| China | 0.48 | 80 |
| Myanmar | 0.43 | 98 |
| Cambodia | 0.33 | 112 |

## Eastern Europe & Central Asia

| COUNTRY/ JURISDICTION | SCORE | GLOBAL RANKING |
|---|---|---|
| Georgia | 0.65 | 34 |
| Bosnia & Herzegovina | 0.56 | 50 |
| Macedonia, FYR | 0.54 | 54 |
| Belarus | 0.54 | 57 |
| Albania | 0.50 | 72 |
| Kazakhstan | 0.50 | 73 |
| Serbia | 0.50 | 74 |
| Moldova | 0.49 | 77 |
| Ukraine | 0.49 | 78 |
| Kyrgyzstan | 0.47 | 83 |
| Russia | 0.45 | 92 |
| Uzbekistan | 0.45 | 93 |
| Turkey | 0.43 | 99 |

## Latin America & Caribbean

| COUNTRY/ JURISDICTION | SCORE | GLOBAL RANKING |
|---|---|---|
| Uruguay | 0.72 | 20 |
| Costa Rica | 0.68 | 25 |
| Chile | 0.68 | 26 |
| Barbados | 0.67 | 28 |
| Antigua & Barbuda | 0.67 | 29 |
| St. Kitts & Nevis | 0.66 | 30 |
| Grenada | 0.66 | 31 |
| St. Lucia | 0.64 | 36 |
| St. Vincent & the Grenadines | 0.61 | 37 |
| Bahamas | 0.61 | 38 |
| Dominica | 0.60 | 40 |
| Jamaica | 0.57 | 47 |
| Trinidad & Tobago | 0.57 | 48 |
| Argentina | 0.55 | 51 |
| Brazil | 0.55 | 52 |
| Suriname | 0.53 | 59 |
| Panama | 0.52 | 62 |
| Peru | 0.51 | 65 |
| Colombia | 0.51 | 71 |
| El Salvador | 0.49 | 75 |
| Guyana | 0.49 | 76 |
| Belize | 0.47 | 82 |
| Dominican Republic | 0.47 | 85 |
| Mexico | 0.46 | 88 |
| Ecuador | 0.45 | 91 |
| Guatemala | 0.44 | 97 |
| Nicaragua | 0.42 | 101 |
| Honduras | 0.42 | 102 |
| Bolivia | 0.40 | 104 |
| Venezuela | 0.28 | 113 |

## Sub-Saharan Africa

| COUNTRY/ JURISDICTION | SCORE | GLOBAL RANKING |
|---|---|---|
| South Africa | 0.59 | 43 |
| Ghana | 0.58 | 44 |
| Botswana | 0.58 | 45 |
| Senegal | 0.57 | 46 |
| Malawi | 0.51 | 69 |
| Burkina Faso | 0.48 | 79 |
| Zambia | 0.48 | 81 |
| Tanzania | 0.47 | 84 |
| Cote d'Ivoire | 0.46 | 87 |
| Madagascar | 0.45 | 90 |
| Liberia | 0.45 | 94 |
| Sierra Leone | 0.45 | 95 |
| Nigeria | 0.44 | 96 |
| Kenya | 0.43 | 100 |
| Uganda | 0.39 | 105 |
| Ethiopia | 0.38 | 107 |
| Zimbabwe | 0.37 | 108 |
| Cameroon | 0.37 | 109 |

## EU, EFTA, & NA

| COUNTRY/ JURISDICTION | SCORE | GLOBAL RANKING |
|---|---|---|
| Denmark | 0.89 | 1 |
| Norway | 0.88 | 2 |
| Finland | 0.87 | 3 |
| Sweden | 0.86 | 4 |
| Netherlands | 0.86 | 5 |
| Germany | 0.83 | 6 |
| Austria | 0.83 | 7 |
| United Kingdom | 0.81 | 10 |
| Canada | 0.81 | 12 |
| Belgium | 0.79 | 13 |
| Estonia | 0.79 | 14 |
| Czech Republic | 0.75 | 17 |
| United States | 0.74 | 18 |
| France | 0.72 | 21 |
| Poland | 0.71 | 22 |
| Portugal | 0.71 | 23 |
| Spain | 0.70 | 24 |
| Slovenia | 0.67 | 27 |
| Romania | 0.66 | 32 |
| Italy | 0.64 | 35 |
| Croatia | 0.61 | 39 |
| Greece | 0.60 | 41 |
| Hungary | 0.57 | 49 |
| Bulgaria | 0.54 | 53 |

## Middle East & North Africa

| COUNTRY/ JURISDICTION | SCORE | GLOBAL RANKING |
|---|---|---|
| United Arab Emirates | 0.66 | 33 |
| Jordan | 0.59 | 42 |
| Tunisia | 0.53 | 58 |
| Morocco | 0.53 | 60 |
| Iran | 0.47 | 86 |
| Lebanon | 0.46 | 89 |
| Egypt | 0.37 | 110 |

## South Asia

| COUNTRY/ JURISDICTION | SCORE | GLOBAL RANKING |
|---|---|---|
| Nepal | 0.52 | 63 |
| India | 0.51 | 66 |
| Sri Lanka | 0.51 | 68 |
| Bangladesh | 0.41 | 103 |
| Pakistan | 0.38 | 106 |
| Afghanistan | 0.35 | 111 |

# Rule of Law Around the World By Income Group

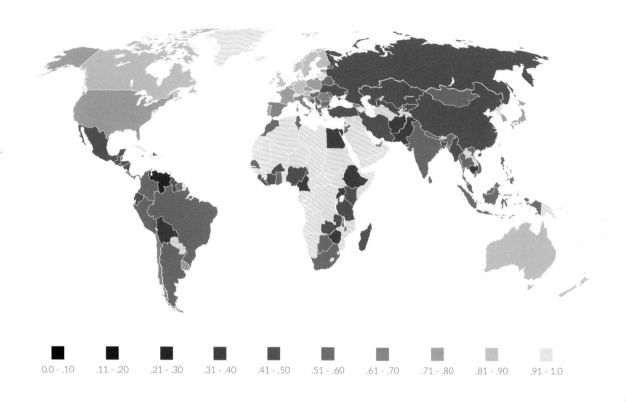

| 0.0 - .10 | .11 - .20 | .21 - .30 | .31 - .40 | .41 - .50 | .51 - .60 | .61 - .70 | .71 - .80 | .81 - .90 | .91 - 1.0 |

## Low Income

| COUNTRY/ JURISDICTION | SCORE | GLOBAL RANKING |
|---|---|---|
| Senegal | 0.57 | 46 |
| Nepal | 0.52 | 63 |
| Malawi | 0.51 | 69 |
| Burkina Faso | 0.48 | 79 |
| Tanzania | 0.47 | 84 |
| Madagascar | 0.45 | 90 |
| Liberia | 0.45 | 94 |
| Sierra Leone | 0.45 | 95 |
| Uganda | 0.39 | 105 |
| Ethiopia | 0.38 | 107 |
| Zimbabwe | 0.37 | 108 |
| Afghanistan | 0.35 | 111 |

## Lower Middle Income

| COUNTRY/ JURISDICTION | SCORE | GLOBAL RANKING |
|---|---|---|
| Ghana | 0.58 | 44 |
| Mongolia | 0.54 | 55 |
| Tunisia | 0.53 | 58 |
| Morocco | 0.53 | 60 |
| Indonesia | 0.52 | 61 |
| India | 0.51 | 66 |
| Vietnam | 0.51 | 67 |
| Sri Lanka | 0.51 | 68 |
| Philippines | 0.51 | 70 |
| El Salvador | 0.49 | 75 |
| Moldova | 0.49 | 77 |
| Ukraine | 0.49 | 78 |
| Zambia | 0.48 | 81 |
| Kyrgyzstan | 0.47 | 83 |
| Cote d'Ivoire | 0.46 | 87 |
| Uzbekistan | 0.45 | 93 |
| Nigeria | 0.44 | 96 |
| Guatemala | 0.44 | 97 |
| Myanmar | 0.43 | 98 |

## Lower Middle Income

| COUNTRY/ JURISDICTION | SCORE | GLOBAL RANKING |
|---|---|---|
| Kenya | 0.43 | 100 |
| Nicaragua | 0.42 | 101 |
| Honduras | 0.42 | 102 |
| Bangladesh | 0.41 | 103 |
| Bolivia | 0.40 | 104 |
| Pakistan | 0.38 | 106 |
| Cameroon | 0.37 | 109 |
| Egypt | 0.37 | 110 |
| Cambodia | 0.33 | 112 |

## Upper Middle Income

| COUNTRY/ JURISDICTION | SCORE | GLOBAL RANKING |
|---|---|---|
| Costa Rica | 0.68 | 25 |
| Grenada | 0.66 | 31 |
| Romania | 0.66 | 32 |
| Georgia | 0.65 | 34 |
| St. Lucia | 0.64 | 36 |
| St. Vincent & the Grenadines | 0.61 | 37 |
| Dominica | 0.60 | 40 |
| Jordan | 0.59 | 42 |
| South Africa | 0.59 | 43 |
| Botswana | 0.58 | 45 |
| Jamaica | 0.57 | 47 |
| Bosnia & Herzegovina | 0.56 | 50 |
| Argentina | 0.55 | 51 |
| Brazil | 0.55 | 52 |
| Bulgaria | 0.54 | 53 |
| Macedonia, FYR | 0.54 | 54 |
| Malaysia | 0.54 | 56 |
| Belarus | 0.54 | 57 |
| Suriname | 0.53 | 59 |
| Panama | 0.52 | 62 |
| Thailand | 0.51 | 64 |
| Peru | 0.51 | 65 |
| Colombia | 0.51 | 71 |
| Albania | 0.50 | 72 |
| Kazakhstan | 0.50 | 73 |
| Serbia | 0.50 | 74 |
| Guyana | 0.49 | 76 |
| China | 0.48 | 80 |
| Belize | 0.47 | 82 |
| Dominican Republic | 0.47 | 85 |
| Iran | 0.47 | 86 |
| Mexico | 0.46 | 88 |
| Lebanon | 0.46 | 89 |
| Ecuador | 0.45 | 91 |
| Russia | 0.45 | 92 |
| Turkey | 0.43 | 99 |
| Venezuela | 0.28 | 113 |

## High Income

| COUNTRY/ JURISDICTION | SCORE | GLOBAL RANKING |
|---|---|---|
| Denmark | 0.89 | 1 |
| Norway | 0.88 | 2 |
| Finland | 0.87 | 3 |
| Sweden | 0.86 | 4 |
| Netherlands | 0.86 | 5 |
| Germany | 0.83 | 6 |
| Austria | 0.83 | 7 |
| New Zealand | 0.83 | 8 |
| Singapore | 0.82 | 9 |
| United Kingdom | 0.81 | 10 |
| Australia | 0.81 | 11 |
| Canada | 0.81 | 12 |
| Belgium | 0.79 | 13 |
| Estonia | 0.79 | 14 |
| Japan | 0.78 | 15 |
| Hong Kong SAR, China | 0.77 | 16 |
| Czech Republic | 0.75 | 17 |
| United States | 0.74 | 18 |
| Republic of Korea | 0.73 | 19 |
| Uruguay | 0.72 | 20 |
| France | 0.72 | 21 |
| Poland | 0.71 | 22 |
| Portugal | 0.71 | 23 |
| Spain | 0.70 | 24 |
| Chile | 0.68 | 26 |
| Slovenia | 0.67 | 27 |
| Barbados | 0.67 | 28 |
| Antigua & Barbuda | 0.67 | 29 |
| St. Kitts & Nevis | 0.66 | 30 |
| United Arab Emirates | 0.66 | 33 |
| Italy | 0.64 | 35 |
| Bahamas | 0.61 | 38 |
| Croatia | 0.61 | 39 |
| Greece | 0.60 | 41 |
| Trinidad & Tobago | 0.57 | 48 |
| Hungary | 0.57 | 49 |

# The Eight Factors of the WJP Rule of Law Index

The following chart presents country performance on the eight aggregated factors of the *WJP Rule of Law Index*.

🏛 Constraints on Government Powers    💰 Absence of Corruption

🗄 Open Government    👤 Fundamental Rights

👥 Order & Security    ⚖ Regulatory Enforcement

⚖ Civil Justice    🏛 Criminal Justice

Top Tercile      Bottom Tercile

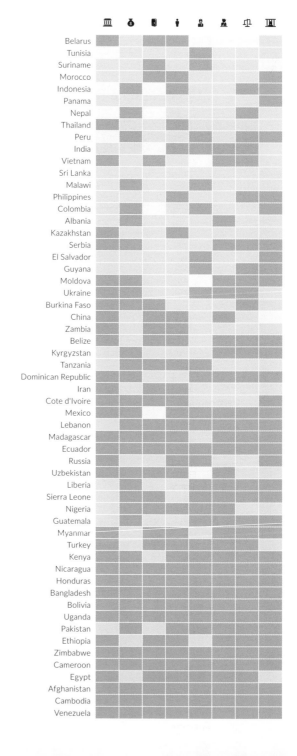

# Rule of Law Trends

The *WJP Rule of Law Index 2016* features analysis of whether a country's primary rule of law indicators experienced significant change over the past year. An arrow pointing up indicates a statistically significant improvement, while an arrow pointing down represents a statistically significant decline. A detailed explanation of these measures can be found in the "Methodology" section of this report.

🏛 Constraints on Government Powers     🏅 Absence of Corruption

📱 Open Government     👤 Fundamental Rights

👥 Order & Security     🗃 Regulatory Enforcement

⚖ Civil Justice     🏛 Criminal Justice

▼ Trending down     ▲ Trending up

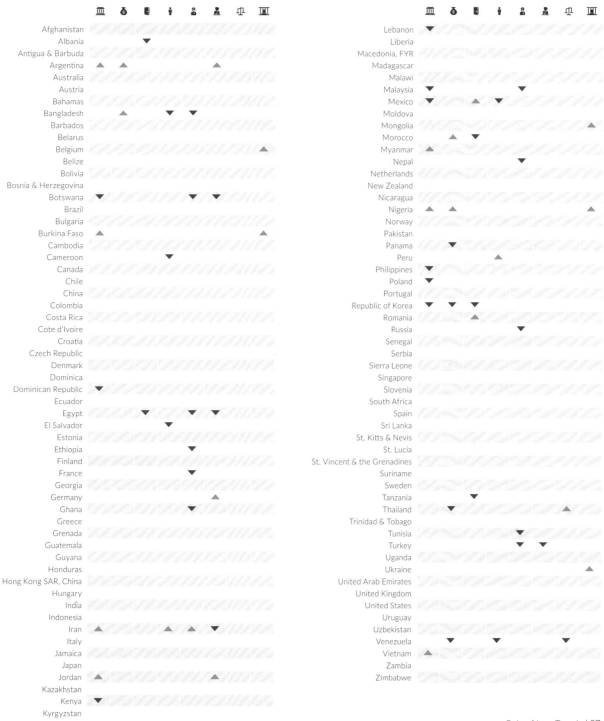

# Factor 1: Constraints on Government Powers ────────── 🏛

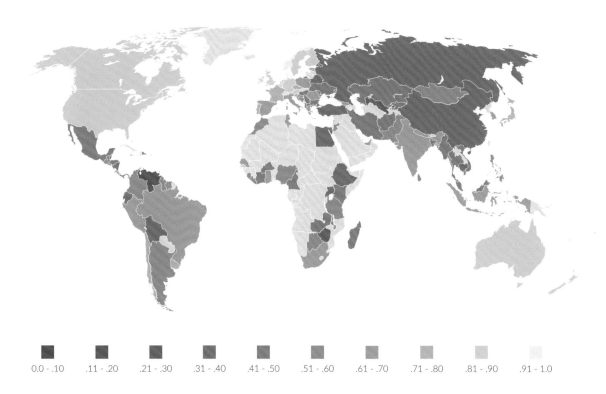

| 0.0 - .10 | .11 - .20 | .21 - .30 | .31 - .40 | .41 - .50 | .51 - .60 | .61 - .70 | .71 - .80 | .81 - .90 | .91 - 1.0 |

Factor 1 measures the effectiveness of the institutional checks on government power by the legislature, the judiciary, and independent auditing and review agencies, as well as the effectiveness of non-governmental oversight by the media and civil society, which serve an important role in monitoring government actions and holding officials accountable. This factor also measures the extent to which transitions of power occur in accordance with the law and whether government officials are held accountable for official misconduct.

| COUNTRY/ JURISDICTION | SCORE | GLOBAL RANKING |
|---|---|---|
| Denmark | 0.93 | 1 |
| Norway | 0.91 | 2 |
| Finland | 0.89 | 3 |
| Netherlands | 0.89 | 4 |
| Sweden | 0.88 | 5 |
| New Zealand | 0.86 | 6 |
| Austria | 0.86 | 7 |
| United Kingdom | 0.85 | 8 |
| Germany | 0.85 | 9 |
| Canada | 0.84 | 10 |
| Australia | 0.83 | 11 |
| Belgium | 0.83 | 12 |
| United States | 0.81 | 13 |
| Portugal | 0.80 | 14 |
| Estonia | 0.80 | 15 |
| Uruguay | 0.79 | 16 |
| Costa Rica | 0.78 | 17 |
| France | 0.77 | 18 |
| Czech Republic | 0.76 | 19 |
| Singapore | 0.75 | 20 |
| Japan | 0.74 | 21 |
| Chile | 0.73 | 22 |
| Spain | 0.70 | 23 |
| Italy | 0.70 | 24 |
| Hong Kong SAR, China | 0.70 | 25 |
| Romania | 0.69 | 26 |
| Republic of Korea | 0.68 | 27 |
| Poland | 0.68 | 28 |
| Ghana | 0.67 | 29 |
| Senegal | 0.67 | 30 |
| St. Kitts & Nevis | 0.67 | 31 |
| Barbados | 0.66 | 32 |
| Indonesia | 0.64 | 33 |
| Jamaica | 0.64 | 34 |
| India | 0.64 | 35 |
| Greece | 0.64 | 36 |
| St. Lucia | 0.64 | 37 |
| Antigua & Barbuda | 0.64 | 38 |
| Tunisia | 0.64 | 39 |
| Nepal | 0.63 | 40 |
| Grenada | 0.63 | 41 |
| Peru | 0.63 | 42 |
| Georgia | 0.62 | 43 |
| Trinidad & Tobago | 0.62 | 44 |
| United Arab Emirates | 0.61 | 45 |
| Slovenia | 0.61 | 46 |
| South Africa | 0.61 | 47 |
| Brazil | 0.61 | 48 |
| Bahamas | 0.60 | 49 |
| Croatia | 0.60 | 50 |
| Philippines | 0.59 | 51 |
| Argentina | 0.59 | 52 |
| Morocco | 0.57 | 53 |
| St. Vincent & the Grenadines | 0.57 | 54 |
| Bosnia & Herzegovina | 0.57 | 55 |
| Dominica | 0.57 | 56 |
| Malawi | 0.57 | 57 |
| Liberia | 0.56 | 58 |

| COUNTRY/ JURISDICTION | SCORE | GLOBAL RANKING |
|---|---|---|
| Panama | 0.56 | 59 |
| Botswana | 0.55 | 60 |
| Nigeria | 0.54 | 61 |
| Jordan | 0.53 | 62 |
| Colombia | 0.53 | 63 |
| Mongolia | 0.53 | 64 |
| Guatemala | 0.53 | 65 |
| Sri Lanka | 0.53 | 66 |
| Guyana | 0.53 | 67 |
| Albania | 0.53 | 68 |
| Suriname | 0.52 | 69 |
| Sierra Leone | 0.52 | 70 |
| Tanzania | 0.52 | 71 |
| Pakistan | 0.52 | 72 |
| Lebanon | 0.51 | 73 |
| El Salvador | 0.51 | 74 |
| Kyrgyzstan | 0.50 | 75 |
| Myanmar | 0.50 | 76 |
| Kenya | 0.50 | 77 |
| Malaysia | 0.50 | 78 |
| Zambia | 0.50 | 79 |
| Bulgaria | 0.49 | 80 |
| Vietnam | 0.49 | 81 |
| Thailand | 0.47 | 82 |
| Mexico | 0.47 | 83 |
| Serbia | 0.46 | 84 |
| Burkina Faso | 0.46 | 85 |
| Madagascar | 0.46 | 86 |
| Hungary | 0.46 | 87 |
| Ukraine | 0.45 | 88 |
| Cote d'Ivoire | 0.45 | 89 |
| Belize | 0.45 | 90 |
| Kazakhstan | 0.44 | 91 |
| Honduras | 0.44 | 92 |
| Dominican Republic | 0.44 | 93 |
| Iran | 0.44 | 94 |
| Moldova | 0.43 | 95 |
| Macedonia, FYR | 0.43 | 96 |
| Afghanistan | 0.43 | 97 |
| Bangladesh | 0.43 | 98 |
| Cameroon | 0.41 | 99 |
| Russia | 0.40 | 100 |
| Uganda | 0.40 | 101 |
| Bolivia | 0.39 | 102 |
| Ecuador | 0.39 | 103 |
| China | 0.38 | 104 |
| Belarus | 0.36 | 105 |
| Ethiopia | 0.35 | 106 |
| Nicaragua | 0.32 | 107 |
| Turkey | 0.32 | 108 |
| Cambodia | 0.31 | 109 |
| Egypt | 0.31 | 110 |
| Uzbekistan | 0.30 | 111 |
| Zimbabwe | 0.26 | 112 |
| Venezuela | 0.18 | 113 |

# Factor 2: Absence of Corruption

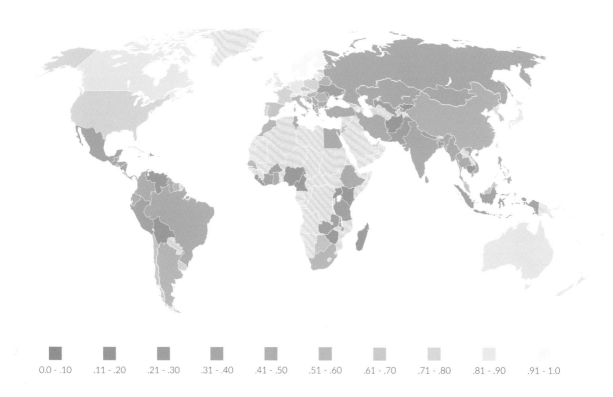

| 0.0 - .10 | .11 - .20 | .21 - .30 | .31 - .40 | .41 - .50 | .51 - .60 | .61 - .70 | .71 - .80 | .81 - .90 | .91 - 1.0 |

Factor 2 measures the absence of corruption in government. The factor considers three forms of corruption: bribery, improper influence by public or private interests, and misappropriation of public funds or other resources. These three forms of corruption are examined with respect to government officers in the executive branch, the judiciary, the military, police, and the legislature.

| COUNTRY/ JURISDICTION | SCORE | GLOBAL RANKING | | COUNTRY/ JURISDICTION | SCORE | GLOBAL RANKING |
|---|---|---|---|---|---|---|
| Denmark | 0.96 | 1 | | Belize | 0.48 | 59 |
| Singapore | 0.93 | 2 | | Tunisia | 0.47 | 60 |
| Norway | 0.92 | 3 | | Thailand | 0.47 | 61 |
| Finland | 0.92 | 4 | | Guyana | 0.46 | 62 |
| Sweden | 0.91 | 5 | | Brazil | 0.45 | 63 |
| New Zealand | 0.90 | 6 | | Sri Lanka | 0.45 | 64 |
| Netherlands | 0.88 | 7 | | Panama | 0.45 | 65 |
| Hong Kong SAR, China | 0.85 | 8 | | Egypt | 0.45 | 66 |
| Austria | 0.84 | 9 | | Vietnam | 0.45 | 67 |
| Germany | 0.84 | 10 | | Ethiopia | 0.44 | 68 |
| Canada | 0.83 | 11 | | India | 0.44 | 69 |
| Australia | 0.83 | 12 | | Myanmar | 0.44 | 70 |
| Japan | 0.83 | 13 | | Kazakhstan | 0.43 | 71 |
| United Kingdom | 0.82 | 14 | | Bosnia & Herzegovina | 0.43 | 72 |
| United Arab Emirates | 0.80 | 15 | | El Salvador | 0.42 | 73 |
| Belgium | 0.78 | 16 | | Ecuador | 0.42 | 74 |
| Estonia | 0.78 | 17 | | Serbia | 0.41 | 75 |
| Uruguay | 0.77 | 18 | | Ghana | 0.41 | 76 |
| France | 0.74 | 19 | | Colombia | 0.41 | 77 |
| United States | 0.73 | 20 | | Russia | 0.41 | 78 |
| Poland | 0.73 | 21 | | Bulgaria | 0.41 | 79 |
| Georgia | 0.73 | 22 | | Mongolia | 0.41 | 80 |
| Portugal | 0.72 | 23 | | Zambia | 0.40 | 81 |
| Barbados | 0.70 | 24 | | Tanzania | 0.39 | 82 |
| Chile | 0.70 | 25 | | Nepal | 0.38 | 83 |
| Grenada | 0.69 | 26 | | Indonesia | 0.38 | 84 |
| Costa Rica | 0.69 | 27 | | Cote d'Ivoire | 0.38 | 85 |
| Spain | 0.69 | 28 | | Burkina Faso | 0.38 | 86 |
| St. Lucia | 0.68 | 29 | | Nicaragua | 0.37 | 87 |
| Czech Republic | 0.68 | 30 | | Lebanon | 0.36 | 88 |
| St. Kitts & Nevis | 0.68 | 31 | | Ukraine | 0.36 | 89 |
| St. Vincent & the Grenadines | 0.67 | 32 | | Malawi | 0.36 | 90 |
| Jordan | 0.66 | 33 | | Peru | 0.36 | 91 |
| Antigua & Barbuda | 0.66 | 34 | | Honduras | 0.36 | 92 |
| Republic of Korea | 0.65 | 35 | | Dominican Republic | 0.34 | 93 |
| Dominica | 0.65 | 36 | | Bangladesh | 0.34 | 94 |
| Bahamas | 0.64 | 37 | | Guatemala | 0.34 | 95 |
| Botswana | 0.62 | 38 | | Uzbekistan | 0.33 | 96 |
| Malaysia | 0.61 | 39 | | Pakistan | 0.33 | 97 |
| Slovenia | 0.60 | 40 | | Albania | 0.33 | 98 |
| Italy | 0.60 | 41 | | Mexico | 0.32 | 99 |
| Croatia | 0.57 | 42 | | Nigeria | 0.30 | 100 |
| Suriname | 0.56 | 43 | | Sierra Leone | 0.30 | 101 |
| Romania | 0.55 | 44 | | Madagascar | 0.30 | 102 |
| South Africa | 0.55 | 45 | | Bolivia | 0.29 | 103 |
| Greece | 0.55 | 46 | | Zimbabwe | 0.29 | 104 |
| Jamaica | 0.55 | 47 | | Moldova | 0.28 | 105 |
| Senegal | 0.55 | 48 | | Kyrgyzstan | 0.28 | 106 |
| Trinidad & Tobago | 0.54 | 49 | | Uganda | 0.27 | 107 |
| Morocco | 0.54 | 50 | | Kenya | 0.26 | 108 |
| Belarus | 0.52 | 51 | | Liberia | 0.26 | 109 |
| China | 0.52 | 52 | | Venezuela | 0.25 | 110 |
| Hungary | 0.51 | 53 | | Cambodia | 0.24 | 111 |
| Argentina | 0.51 | 54 | | Cameroon | 0.24 | 112 |
| Macedonia, FYR | 0.50 | 55 | | Afghanistan | 0.23 | 113 |
| Philippines | 0.48 | 56 | | | | |
| Iran | 0.48 | 57 | | | | |
| Turkey | 0.48 | 58 | | | | |

# Factor 3: Open Government

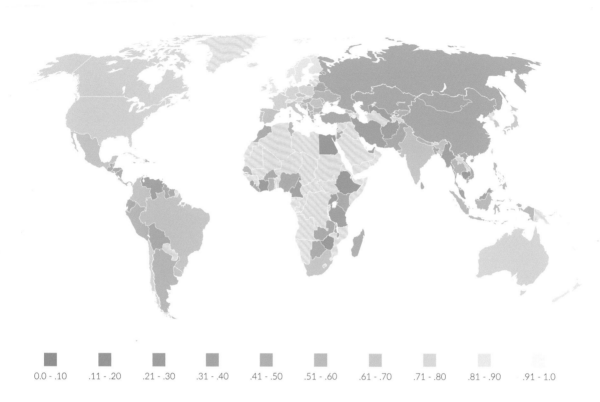

| | | | | | | | | | |
|---|---|---|---|---|---|---|---|---|---|
| 0.0 - .10 | .11 - .20 | .21 - .30 | .31 - .40 | .41 - .50 | .51 - .60 | .61 - .70 | .71 - .80 | .81 - .90 | .91 - 1.0 |

Factor 3 measures whether basic laws and information in legal rights are publicized, and assesses the quality of information published by the government. It also measures whether requests for information held by a government agency are properly granted. Finally, it evaluates the effectiveness of civic participation mechanisms and whether people can bring specific complaints to the government.

| COUNTRY/<br>JURISDICTION | SCORE | GLOBAL<br>RANKING |
|---|---|---|
| Norway | 0.87 | 1 |
| Denmark | 0.86 | 2 |
| Finland | 0.85 | 3 |
| Netherlands | 0.85 | 4 |
| Sweden | 0.84 | 5 |
| New Zealand | 0.84 | 6 |
| United Kingdom | 0.84 | 7 |
| Estonia | 0.81 | 8 |
| Canada | 0.80 | 9 |
| Germany | 0.79 | 10 |
| Australia | 0.78 | 11 |
| United States | 0.78 | 12 |
| France | 0.77 | 13 |
| Austria | 0.75 | 14 |
| Belgium | 0.73 | 15 |
| Poland | 0.72 | 16 |
| Chile | 0.72 | 17 |
| Uruguay | 0.70 | 18 |
| Costa Rica | 0.69 | 19 |
| Czech Republic | 0.69 | 20 |
| Japan | 0.68 | 21 |
| Republic of Korea | 0.68 | 22 |
| Spain | 0.68 | 23 |
| Singapore | 0.67 | 24 |
| Romania | 0.67 | 25 |
| Portugal | 0.67 | 26 |
| Hong Kong SAR, China | 0.66 | 27 |
| India | 0.66 | 28 |
| Slovenia | 0.66 | 29 |
| Colombia | 0.64 | 30 |
| Georgia | 0.63 | 31 |
| Italy | 0.63 | 32 |
| Brazil | 0.62 | 33 |
| Mexico | 0.61 | 34 |
| South Africa | 0.61 | 35 |
| Croatia | 0.59 | 36 |
| Indonesia | 0.58 | 37 |
| Moldova | 0.58 | 38 |
| Jamaica | 0.58 | 39 |
| Bulgaria | 0.58 | 40 |
| Panama | 0.58 | 41 |
| Greece | 0.57 | 42 |
| Argentina | 0.57 | 43 |
| Serbia | 0.56 | 44 |
| Macedonia, FYR | 0.56 | 45 |
| Peru | 0.56 | 46 |
| Grenada | 0.56 | 47 |
| Trinidad & Tobago | 0.55 | 48 |
| Kyrgyzstan | 0.55 | 49 |
| Ukraine | 0.55 | 50 |
| Ghana | 0.55 | 51 |
| Nepal | 0.54 | 52 |
| Bosnia & Herzegovina | 0.54 | 53 |
| Dominican Republic | 0.54 | 54 |
| Hungary | 0.52 | 55 |
| Barbados | 0.52 | 56 |
| Thailand | 0.52 | 57 |
| Senegal | 0.52 | 58 |

| COUNTRY/<br>JURISDICTION | SCORE | GLOBAL<br>RANKING |
|---|---|---|
| St. Lucia | 0.52 | 59 |
| Tunisia | 0.51 | 60 |
| El Salvador | 0.51 | 61 |
| Antigua & Barbuda | 0.51 | 62 |
| Philippines | 0.51 | 63 |
| Malawi | 0.50 | 64 |
| Dominica | 0.50 | 65 |
| Guatemala | 0.49 | 66 |
| Russia | 0.49 | 67 |
| Botswana | 0.49 | 68 |
| St. Vincent & the Grenadines | 0.49 | 69 |
| Kenya | 0.49 | 70 |
| Sri Lanka | 0.48 | 71 |
| Liberia | 0.48 | 72 |
| Kazakhstan | 0.48 | 73 |
| Mongolia | 0.48 | 74 |
| Guyana | 0.47 | 75 |
| Morocco | 0.47 | 76 |
| Honduras | 0.46 | 77 |
| St. Kitts & Nevis | 0.46 | 78 |
| Pakistan | 0.46 | 79 |
| Madagascar | 0.46 | 80 |
| Bahamas | 0.45 | 81 |
| Burkina Faso | 0.45 | 82 |
| Albania | 0.45 | 83 |
| Bangladesh | 0.45 | 84 |
| Ecuador | 0.45 | 85 |
| Suriname | 0.45 | 86 |
| Belize | 0.45 | 87 |
| Bolivia | 0.44 | 88 |
| China | 0.44 | 89 |
| Belarus | 0.43 | 90 |
| Zambia | 0.43 | 91 |
| Vietnam | 0.43 | 92 |
| Lebanon | 0.43 | 93 |
| Jordan | 0.43 | 94 |
| Nigeria | 0.43 | 95 |
| Turkey | 0.42 | 96 |
| Nicaragua | 0.41 | 97 |
| Sierra Leone | 0.40 | 98 |
| Afghanistan | 0.40 | 99 |
| Uganda | 0.39 | 100 |
| Tanzania | 0.39 | 101 |
| United Arab Emirates | 0.39 | 102 |
| Cote d'Ivoire | 0.37 | 103 |
| Cameroon | 0.35 | 104 |
| Malaysia | 0.35 | 105 |
| Iran | 0.34 | 106 |
| Myanmar | 0.33 | 107 |
| Venezuela | 0.32 | 108 |
| Uzbekistan | 0.31 | 109 |
| Zimbabwe | 0.30 | 110 |
| Ethiopia | 0.27 | 111 |
| Cambodia | 0.24 | 112 |
| Egypt | 0.23 | 113 |

# Factor 4: Fundamental Rights

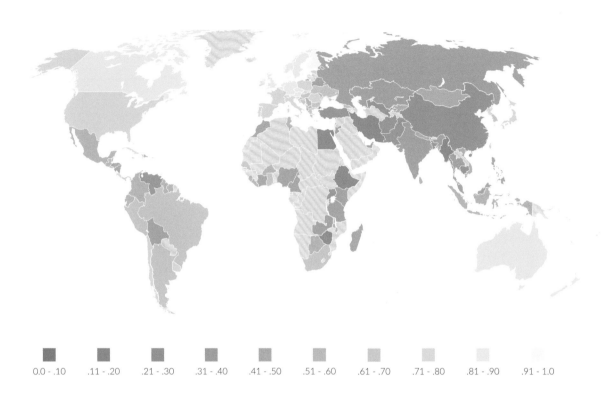

| | | | | | | | | | |
|---|---|---|---|---|---|---|---|---|---|
| 0.0 - .10 | .11 - .20 | .21 - .30 | .31 - .40 | .41 - .50 | .51 - .60 | .61 - .70 | .71 - .80 | .81 - .90 | .91 - 1.0 |

Factor 4 measures the protection of fundamental human rights, including effective enforcement of laws that ensure equal protection, the right to life and security of the person, due process of law and the rights of the accused, freedom of opinion and expression, freedom of belief and religion, the right to privacy, freedom of assembly and association, and fundamental labor rights, including the right to collective bargaining, the prohibition of forced and child labor, and the elimination of discrimination.

| COUNTRY/ JURISDICTION | SCORE | GLOBAL RANKING |
| --- | --- | --- |
| Denmark | 0.92 | 1 |
| Finland | 0.92 | 2 |
| Norway | 0.89 | 3 |
| Austria | 0.88 | 4 |
| Sweden | 0.88 | 5 |
| Netherlands | 0.86 | 6 |
| Germany | 0.85 | 7 |
| Belgium | 0.84 | 8 |
| Canada | 0.82 | 9 |
| New Zealand | 0.82 | 10 |
| Czech Republic | 0.81 | 11 |
| United Kingdom | 0.81 | 12 |
| Australia | 0.81 | 13 |
| Uruguay | 0.80 | 14 |
| Estonia | 0.80 | 15 |
| Barbados | 0.79 | 16 |
| Costa Rica | 0.79 | 17 |
| Portugal | 0.79 | 18 |
| Slovenia | 0.77 | 19 |
| Spain | 0.77 | 20 |
| United States | 0.75 | 21 |
| Chile | 0.75 | 22 |
| Japan | 0.75 | 23 |
| France | 0.75 | 24 |
| Antigua & Barbuda | 0.74 | 25 |
| Poland | 0.74 | 26 |
| St. Kitts & Nevis | 0.74 | 27 |
| Romania | 0.73 | 28 |
| St. Lucia | 0.73 | 29 |
| Italy | 0.72 | 30 |
| St. Vincent & the Grenadines | 0.71 | 31 |
| Republic of Korea | 0.70 | 32 |
| Hong Kong SAR, China | 0.70 | 33 |
| Croatia | 0.69 | 34 |
| Argentina | 0.69 | 35 |
| Singapore | 0.69 | 36 |
| Dominica | 0.68 | 37 |
| Grenada | 0.68 | 38 |
| Georgia | 0.68 | 39 |
| Bahamas | 0.67 | 40 |
| Greece | 0.65 | 41 |
| Bosnia & Herzegovina | 0.65 | 42 |
| Ghana | 0.65 | 43 |
| Peru | 0.64 | 44 |
| Bulgaria | 0.64 | 45 |
| Jamaica | 0.63 | 46 |
| Ukraine | 0.63 | 47 |
| South Africa | 0.63 | 48 |
| Panama | 0.63 | 49 |
| Hungary | 0.62 | 50 |
| Senegal | 0.62 | 51 |
| Brazil | 0.61 | 52 |
| Trinidad & Tobago | 0.61 | 53 |
| Mongolia | 0.60 | 54 |
| Albania | 0.60 | 55 |
| Dominican Republic | 0.60 | 56 |
| Serbia | 0.58 | 57 |
| Malawi | 0.58 | 58 |

| COUNTRY/ JURISDICTION | SCORE | GLOBAL RANKING |
| --- | --- | --- |
| Moldova | 0.58 | 59 |
| El Salvador | 0.57 | 60 |
| Sierra Leone | 0.57 | 61 |
| Tunisia | 0.57 | 62 |
| Burkina Faso | 0.56 | 63 |
| Liberia | 0.56 | 64 |
| Colombia | 0.55 | 65 |
| Guatemala | 0.55 | 66 |
| Macedonia, FYR | 0.54 | 67 |
| Vietnam | 0.54 | 68 |
| Kyrgyzstan | 0.54 | 69 |
| Guyana | 0.54 | 70 |
| Suriname | 0.53 | 71 |
| Nepal | 0.53 | 72 |
| Sri Lanka | 0.52 | 73 |
| Indonesia | 0.52 | 74 |
| Mexico | 0.51 | 75 |
| Ecuador | 0.51 | 76 |
| Lebanon | 0.51 | 77 |
| Botswana | 0.51 | 78 |
| Belize | 0.51 | 79 |
| Bolivia | 0.50 | 80 |
| India | 0.50 | 81 |
| Jordan | 0.50 | 82 |
| Philippines | 0.50 | 83 |
| Madagascar | 0.49 | 84 |
| Belarus | 0.48 | 85 |
| Tanzania | 0.48 | 86 |
| Kenya | 0.47 | 87 |
| Thailand | 0.47 | 88 |
| Nigeria | 0.46 | 89 |
| United Arab Emirates | 0.46 | 90 |
| Morocco | 0.45 | 91 |
| Kazakhstan | 0.45 | 92 |
| Nicaragua | 0.45 | 93 |
| Cote d'Ivoire | 0.45 | 94 |
| Zambia | 0.45 | 95 |
| Honduras | 0.44 | 96 |
| Russia | 0.44 | 97 |
| Malaysia | 0.44 | 98 |
| Cameroon | 0.43 | 99 |
| Afghanistan | 0.40 | 100 |
| Pakistan | 0.39 | 101 |
| Uganda | 0.39 | 102 |
| Cambodia | 0.39 | 103 |
| Uzbekistan | 0.36 | 104 |
| Turkey | 0.34 | 105 |
| Bangladesh | 0.34 | 106 |
| Venezuela | 0.33 | 107 |
| China | 0.32 | 108 |
| Myanmar | 0.30 | 109 |
| Egypt | 0.29 | 110 |
| Ethiopia | 0.29 | 111 |
| Iran | 0.29 | 112 |
| Zimbabwe | 0.28 | 113 |

# Factor 5: Order & Security

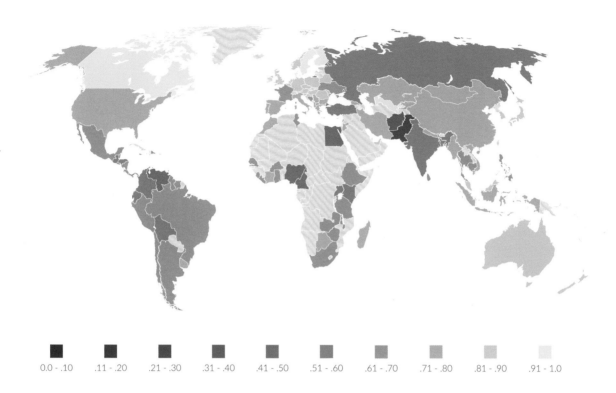

| | | | | | | | | | |
|---|---|---|---|---|---|---|---|---|---|
| 0.0 - .10 | .11 - .20 | .21 - .30 | .31 - .40 | .41 - .50 | .51 - .60 | .61 - .70 | .71 - .80 | .81 - .90 | .91 - 1.0 |

Factor 5 measures various threats to order and security
including conventional crime, political violence, and violence
as a means to redress personal grievances.

| COUNTRY/ JURISDICTION | SCORE | GLOBAL RANKING |
|---|---|---|
| Singapore | 0.93 | 1 |
| Finland | 0.93 | 2 |
| Sweden | 0.92 | 3 |
| Denmark | 0.92 | 4 |
| Uzbekistan | 0.91 | 5 |
| Canada | 0.91 | 6 |
| Austria | 0.90 | 7 |
| Norway | 0.90 | 8 |
| Japan | 0.90 | 9 |
| Czech Republic | 0.89 | 10 |
| Hong Kong SAR, China | 0.89 | 11 |
| United Arab Emirates | 0.89 | 12 |
| Australia | 0.87 | 13 |
| Germany | 0.87 | 14 |
| New Zealand | 0.86 | 15 |
| Hungary | 0.86 | 16 |
| United Kingdom | 0.85 | 17 |
| Estonia | 0.85 | 18 |
| Poland | 0.85 | 19 |
| Netherlands | 0.85 | 20 |
| Belgium | 0.84 | 21 |
| Romania | 0.84 | 22 |
| Republic of Korea | 0.83 | 23 |
| Slovenia | 0.83 | 24 |
| Croatia | 0.82 | 25 |
| Malaysia | 0.82 | 26 |
| St. Kitts & Nevis | 0.82 | 27 |
| Antigua & Barbuda | 0.82 | 28 |
| Belarus | 0.81 | 29 |
| Moldova | 0.81 | 30 |
| United States | 0.80 | 31 |
| Mongolia | 0.79 | 32 |
| Grenada | 0.79 | 33 |
| Jordan | 0.79 | 34 |
| Vietnam | 0.79 | 35 |
| Spain | 0.79 | 36 |
| Georgia | 0.78 | 37 |
| Barbados | 0.78 | 38 |
| Portugal | 0.77 | 39 |
| Kazakhstan | 0.76 | 40 |
| China | 0.76 | 41 |
| Albania | 0.75 | 42 |
| Greece | 0.75 | 43 |
| Dominica | 0.75 | 44 |
| St. Vincent & the Grenadines | 0.75 | 45 |
| Kyrgyzstan | 0.75 | 46 |
| Bulgaria | 0.74 | 47 |
| Macedonia, FYR | 0.74 | 48 |
| Nepal | 0.74 | 49 |
| Morocco | 0.73 | 50 |
| Madagascar | 0.73 | 51 |
| Uruguay | 0.73 | 52 |
| Myanmar | 0.73 | 53 |
| Serbia | 0.73 | 54 |
| Indonesia | 0.73 | 55 |
| Bahamas | 0.72 | 56 |
| St. Lucia | 0.72 | 57 |
| Italy | 0.72 | 58 |

| COUNTRY/ JURISDICTION | SCORE | GLOBAL RANKING |
|---|---|---|
| Iran | 0.72 | 59 |
| Botswana | 0.71 | 60 |
| Cote d'Ivoire | 0.71 | 61 |
| Ghana | 0.70 | 62 |
| Bosnia & Herzegovina | 0.70 | 63 |
| Thailand | 0.70 | 64 |
| Belize | 0.70 | 65 |
| Costa Rica | 0.68 | 66 |
| Chile | 0.68 | 67 |
| Sri Lanka | 0.68 | 68 |
| Burkina Faso | 0.67 | 69 |
| Zambia | 0.67 | 70 |
| Zimbabwe | 0.67 | 71 |
| Trinidad & Tobago | 0.67 | 72 |
| Panama | 0.67 | 73 |
| Senegal | 0.67 | 74 |
| Brazil | 0.67 | 75 |
| Ethiopia | 0.67 | 76 |
| Philippines | 0.67 | 77 |
| Sierra Leone | 0.66 | 78 |
| Nicaragua | 0.66 | 79 |
| Ukraine | 0.65 | 80 |
| Cambodia | 0.65 | 81 |
| Tanzania | 0.64 | 82 |
| Lebanon | 0.64 | 83 |
| Peru | 0.64 | 84 |
| Suriname | 0.64 | 85 |
| Jamaica | 0.64 | 86 |
| Guyana | 0.64 | 87 |
| Tunisia | 0.63 | 88 |
| France | 0.63 | 89 |
| El Salvador | 0.63 | 90 |
| South Africa | 0.63 | 91 |
| Malawi | 0.62 | 92 |
| Argentina | 0.62 | 93 |
| Mexico | 0.61 | 94 |
| Dominican Republic | 0.61 | 95 |
| Liberia | 0.61 | 96 |
| Ecuador | 0.60 | 97 |
| Turkey | 0.59 | 98 |
| Guatemala | 0.59 | 99 |
| Bangladesh | 0.58 | 100 |
| Bolivia | 0.58 | 101 |
| Russia | 0.56 | 102 |
| Honduras | 0.56 | 103 |
| India | 0.56 | 104 |
| Uganda | 0.56 | 105 |
| Colombia | 0.55 | 106 |
| Kenya | 0.51 | 107 |
| Egypt | 0.49 | 108 |
| Nigeria | 0.48 | 109 |
| Venezuela | 0.48 | 110 |
| Cameroon | 0.47 | 111 |
| Afghanistan | 0.34 | 112 |
| Pakistan | 0.29 | 113 |

# Factor 6: Regulatory Enforcement

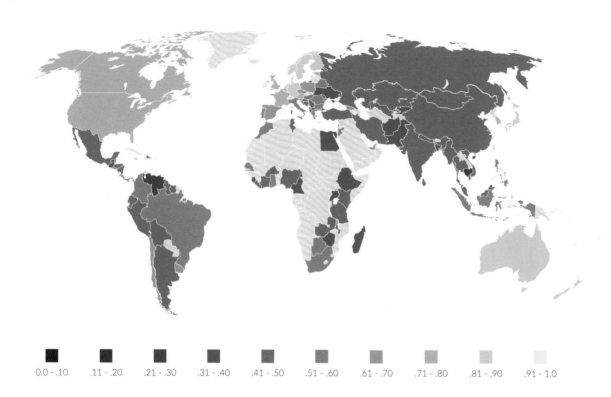

| 0.0 - .10 | .11 - .20 | .21 - .30 | .31 - .40 | .41 - .50 | .51 - .60 | .61 - .70 | .71 - .80 | .81 - .90 | .91 - 1.0 |

Factor 6 measures the extent to which regulations are effectively implemented and enforced without improper influence by public officials or private interests. It also includes whether administrative proceedings are conducted in a timely manner without unreasonable delays and whether due process is respected in administrative proceedings. This factor also addresses whether the government respects the property rights of people and corporations.

| COUNTRY/ JURISDICTION | SCORE | GLOBAL RANKING |
|---|---|---|
| Singapore | 0.90 | 1 |
| Netherlands | 0.88 | 2 |
| Norway | 0.86 | 3 |
| Sweden | 0.85 | 4 |
| Germany | 0.85 | 5 |
| Denmark | 0.85 | 6 |
| Finland | 0.83 | 7 |
| New Zealand | 0.82 | 8 |
| Australia | 0.82 | 9 |
| Japan | 0.82 | 10 |
| Austria | 0.80 | 11 |
| Hong Kong SAR, China | 0.80 | 12 |
| Canada | 0.79 | 13 |
| United Kingdom | 0.79 | 14 |
| Estonia | 0.78 | 15 |
| Belgium | 0.77 | 16 |
| Republic of Korea | 0.75 | 17 |
| France | 0.72 | 18 |
| United States | 0.71 | 19 |
| Uruguay | 0.69 | 20 |
| United Arab Emirates | 0.68 | 21 |
| Czech Republic | 0.68 | 22 |
| Costa Rica | 0.67 | 23 |
| Spain | 0.67 | 24 |
| St. Kitts & Nevis | 0.66 | 25 |
| Chile | 0.66 | 26 |
| Poland | 0.62 | 27 |
| Georgia | 0.62 | 28 |
| Slovenia | 0.62 | 29 |
| Barbados | 0.61 | 30 |
| Portugal | 0.60 | 31 |
| Botswana | 0.59 | 32 |
| Jordan | 0.58 | 33 |
| Grenada | 0.58 | 34 |
| Italy | 0.57 | 35 |
| Romania | 0.57 | 36 |
| St. Lucia | 0.56 | 37 |
| Senegal | 0.56 | 38 |
| Ghana | 0.56 | 39 |
| Greece | 0.56 | 40 |
| Morocco | 0.54 | 41 |
| Brazil | 0.54 | 42 |
| Trinidad & Tobago | 0.54 | 43 |
| St. Vincent & the Grenadines | 0.54 | 44 |
| South Africa | 0.54 | 45 |
| Antigua & Barbuda | 0.54 | 46 |
| Jamaica | 0.54 | 47 |
| Belarus | 0.53 | 48 |
| Panama | 0.52 | 49 |
| Dominica | 0.52 | 50 |
| Colombia | 0.52 | 51 |
| Bulgaria | 0.51 | 52 |
| Indonesia | 0.51 | 53 |
| Hungary | 0.51 | 54 |
| Philippines | 0.51 | 55 |
| Thailand | 0.50 | 56 |
| Kazakhstan | 0.50 | 57 |
| Sri Lanka | 0.50 | 58 |

| COUNTRY/ JURISDICTION | SCORE | GLOBAL RANKING |
|---|---|---|
| Bosnia & Herzegovina | 0.50 | 59 |
| Iran | 0.50 | 60 |
| Croatia | 0.50 | 61 |
| Peru | 0.50 | 62 |
| El Salvador | 0.50 | 63 |
| Tunisia | 0.49 | 64 |
| Cote d'Ivoire | 0.49 | 65 |
| Guyana | 0.48 | 66 |
| Nepal | 0.48 | 67 |
| Argentina | 0.47 | 68 |
| Bahamas | 0.47 | 69 |
| Macedonia, FYR | 0.47 | 70 |
| Russia | 0.47 | 71 |
| Mongolia | 0.47 | 72 |
| Suriname | 0.47 | 73 |
| Malaysia | 0.47 | 74 |
| Nicaragua | 0.46 | 75 |
| Ecuador | 0.46 | 76 |
| India | 0.46 | 77 |
| Serbia | 0.46 | 78 |
| Malawi | 0.45 | 79 |
| China | 0.45 | 80 |
| Uzbekistan | 0.45 | 81 |
| Burkina Faso | 0.45 | 82 |
| Zambia | 0.45 | 83 |
| Turkey | 0.44 | 84 |
| Mexico | 0.44 | 85 |
| Albania | 0.44 | 86 |
| Myanmar | 0.44 | 87 |
| Belize | 0.43 | 88 |
| Nigeria | 0.43 | 89 |
| Bolivia | 0.43 | 90 |
| Vietnam | 0.43 | 91 |
| Kenya | 0.43 | 92 |
| Tanzania | 0.42 | 93 |
| Honduras | 0.41 | 94 |
| Dominican Republic | 0.41 | 95 |
| Lebanon | 0.41 | 96 |
| Moldova | 0.41 | 97 |
| Liberia | 0.41 | 98 |
| Bangladesh | 0.40 | 99 |
| Ukraine | 0.40 | 100 |
| Guatemala | 0.39 | 101 |
| Madagascar | 0.38 | 102 |
| Cameroon | 0.38 | 103 |
| Kyrgyzstan | 0.38 | 104 |
| Uganda | 0.37 | 105 |
| Afghanistan | 0.36 | 106 |
| Sierra Leone | 0.35 | 107 |
| Zimbabwe | 0.35 | 108 |
| Pakistan | 0.34 | 109 |
| Egypt | 0.33 | 110 |
| Ethiopia | 0.31 | 111 |
| Cambodia | 0.28 | 112 |
| Venezuela | 0.21 | 113 |

# Factor 7: Civil Justice

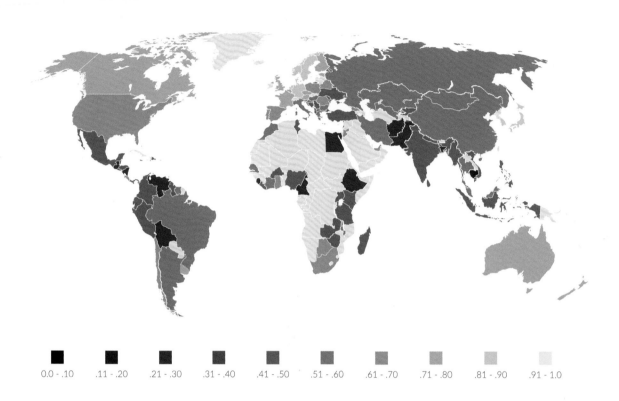

| 0.0 - .10 | .11 - .20 | .21 - .30 | .31 - .40 | .41 - .50 | .51 - .60 | .61 - .70 | .71 - .80 | .81 - .90 | .91 - 1.0 |

Factor 7 measures whether civil justice systems are accessible and affordable, free of discrimination, corruption, and improper influence by public officials. It examines whether court proceedings are conducted without unreasonable delays, and if decisions are enforced effectively. It also measures the accessibility, impartiality, and effectiveness of alternative dispute resolution mechanisms.

| COUNTRY/ JURISDICTION | SCORE | GLOBAL RANKING |
| --- | --- | --- |
| Netherlands | 0.88 | 1 |
| Germany | 0.86 | 2 |
| Norway | 0.85 | 3 |
| Singapore | 0.85 | 4 |
| Denmark | 0.84 | 5 |
| Japan | 0.82 | 6 |
| Sweden | 0.81 | 7 |
| Republic of Korea | 0.81 | 8 |
| Austria | 0.80 | 9 |
| Finland | 0.80 | 10 |
| New Zealand | 0.78 | 11 |
| Hong Kong SAR, China | 0.77 | 12 |
| Estonia | 0.77 | 13 |
| Australia | 0.77 | 14 |
| Belgium | 0.76 | 15 |
| United Kingdom | 0.75 | 16 |
| Uruguay | 0.73 | 17 |
| Czech Republic | 0.73 | 18 |
| Canada | 0.72 | 19 |
| Grenada | 0.72 | 20 |
| Antigua and Barbuda | 0.72 | 21 |
| St. Kitts and Nevis | 0.71 | 22 |
| France | 0.71 | 23 |
| Barbados | 0.68 | 24 |
| United Arab Emirates | 0.68 | 25 |
| Portugal | 0.66 | 26 |
| Poland | 0.66 | 27 |
| United States | 0.65 | 28 |
| Spain | 0.65 | 29 |
| Belarus | 0.65 | 30 |
| Romania | 0.65 | 31 |
| Chile | 0.64 | 32 |
| Slovenia | 0.64 | 33 |
| St. Lucia | 0.63 | 34 |
| Jordan | 0.63 | 35 |
| Botswana | 0.62 | 36 |
| Bahamas | 0.62 | 37 |
| Costa Rica | 0.62 | 38 |
| Georgia | 0.61 | 39 |
| Dominica | 0.61 | 40 |
| Ghana | 0.61 | 41 |
| Trinidad and Tobago | 0.61 | 42 |
| South Africa | 0.61 | 43 |
| Greece | 0.57 | 44 |
| Bulgaria | 0.57 | 45 |
| Italy | 0.57 | 46 |
| Senegal | 0.57 | 47 |
| Argentina | 0.57 | 48 |
| Malaysia | 0.56 | 49 |
| St. Vincent and the Grenadines | 0.56 | 50 |
| Macedonia, FYR | 0.56 | 51 |
| Iran | 0.55 | 52 |
| Kazakhstan | 0.55 | 53 |
| Jamaica | 0.54 | 54 |
| Mongolia | 0.54 | 55 |
| Malawi | 0.54 | 56 |
| Morocco | 0.53 | 57 |
| Brazil | 0.53 | 58 |

| COUNTRY/ JURISDICTION | SCORE | GLOBAL RANKING |
| --- | --- | --- |
| Thailand | 0.53 | 59 |
| Croatia | 0.53 | 60 |
| Hungary | 0.52 | 61 |
| China | 0.52 | 62 |
| Russia | 0.52 | 63 |
| Uzbekistan | 0.51 | 64 |
| Suriname | 0.51 | 65 |
| Cote d'Ivoire | 0.51 | 66 |
| Zambia | 0.50 | 67 |
| Tanzania | 0.50 | 68 |
| Bosnia and Herzegovina | 0.50 | 69 |
| Colombia | 0.50 | 70 |
| Tunisia | 0.49 | 71 |
| Panama | 0.48 | 72 |
| Guyana | 0.48 | 73 |
| Albania | 0.48 | 74 |
| Nigeria | 0.48 | 75 |
| El Salvador | 0.48 | 76 |
| Lebanon | 0.48 | 77 |
| Ukraine | 0.47 | 78 |
| Belize | 0.47 | 79 |
| Vietnam | 0.47 | 80 |
| Burkina Faso | 0.47 | 81 |
| Moldova | 0.46 | 82 |
| Serbia | 0.46 | 83 |
| Zimbabwe | 0.46 | 84 |
| Dominican Republic | 0.46 | 85 |
| Turkey | 0.46 | 86 |
| Philippines | 0.45 | 87 |
| Liberia | 0.45 | 88 |
| Ecuador | 0.44 | 89 |
| Peru | 0.44 | 90 |
| Kenya | 0.43 | 91 |
| Indonesia | 0.43 | 92 |
| India | 0.43 | 93 |
| Kyrgyzstan | 0.43 | 94 |
| Honduras | 0.43 | 95 |
| Sri Lanka | 0.42 | 96 |
| Uganda | 0.42 | 97 |
| Myanmar | 0.42 | 98 |
| Nepal | 0.41 | 99 |
| Madagascar | 0.41 | 100 |
| Mexico | 0.41 | 101 |
| Sierra Leone | 0.40 | 102 |
| Bangladesh | 0.39 | 103 |
| Egypt | 0.38 | 104 |
| Ethiopia | 0.37 | 105 |
| Pakistan | 0.37 | 106 |
| Nicaragua | 0.37 | 107 |
| Bolivia | 0.35 | 108 |
| Cameroon | 0.35 | 109 |
| Afghanistan | 0.34 | 110 |
| Guatemala | 0.33 | 111 |
| Venezuela | 0.29 | 112 |
| Cambodia | 0.19 | 113 |

# Factor 8: Criminal Justice

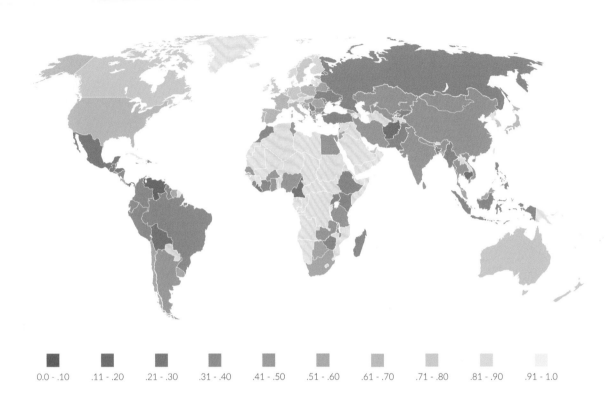

| | | | | | | | | | |
|---|---|---|---|---|---|---|---|---|---|
| 0.0 - .10 | .11 - .20 | .21 - .30 | .31 - .40 | .41 - .50 | .51 - .60 | .61 - .70 | .71 - .80 | .81 - .90 | .91 - 1.0 |

Factor 8 measures whether the criminal investigation, adjudication, and correctional systems are effective, and whether the criminal justice system is impartial, free of corruption, free of improper influence, and protective of due process and the rights of the accused.

| COUNTRY/ JURISDICTION | SCORE | GLOBAL RANKING |
|---|---|---|
| Finland | 0.85 | 1 |
| Norway | 0.83 | 2 |
| Austria | 0.83 | 3 |
| Singapore | 0.83 | 4 |
| Denmark | 0.82 | 5 |
| Hong Kong SAR, China | 0.80 | 6 |
| Netherlands | 0.80 | 7 |
| Sweden | 0.79 | 8 |
| Germany | 0.77 | 9 |
| United Kingdom | 0.76 | 10 |
| Belgium | 0.76 | 11 |
| Australia | 0.75 | 12 |
| New Zealand | 0.75 | 13 |
| United Arab Emirates | 0.74 | 14 |
| Canada | 0.74 | 15 |
| Czech Republic | 0.73 | 16 |
| Republic of Korea | 0.71 | 17 |
| Antigua and Barbuda | 0.70 | 18 |
| Estonia | 0.70 | 19 |
| Poland | 0.69 | 20 |
| Japan | 0.68 | 21 |
| United States | 0.68 | 22 |
| Bahamas | 0.68 | 23 |
| Portugal | 0.67 | 24 |
| Slovenia | 0.66 | 25 |
| Grenada | 0.65 | 26 |
| France | 0.65 | 27 |
| St. Lucia | 0.64 | 28 |
| Italy | 0.64 | 29 |
| Spain | 0.63 | 30 |
| St. Vincent & the Grenadines | 0.62 | 31 |
| Barbados | 0.61 | 32 |
| Jordan | 0.59 | 33 |
| Uruguay | 0.58 | 34 |
| Romania | 0.58 | 35 |
| St. Kitts and Nevis | 0.58 | 36 |
| Chile | 0.58 | 37 |
| Georgia | 0.56 | 38 |
| Bosnia and Herzegovina | 0.56 | 39 |
| Dominica | 0.56 | 40 |
| Malaysia | 0.56 | 41 |
| Costa Rica | 0.55 | 42 |
| Hungary | 0.54 | 43 |
| Suriname | 0.54 | 44 |
| Croatia | 0.54 | 45 |
| South Africa | 0.52 | 46 |
| Botswana | 0.52 | 47 |
| Macedonia, FYR | 0.51 | 48 |
| Belarus | 0.51 | 49 |
| Greece | 0.51 | 50 |
| Vietnam | 0.50 | 51 |
| Sri Lanka | 0.49 | 52 |
| Mongolia | 0.48 | 53 |
| Ghana | 0.47 | 54 |
| China | 0.47 | 55 |
| Tunisia | 0.46 | 56 |
| Albania | 0.46 | 57 |
| Jamaica | 0.45 | 58 |

| COUNTRY/ JURISDICTION | SCORE | GLOBAL RANKING |
|---|---|---|
| Thailand | 0.45 | 59 |
| Nepal | 0.44 | 60 |
| Malawi | 0.44 | 61 |
| Uzbekistan | 0.44 | 62 |
| Egypt | 0.43 | 63 |
| Burkina Faso | 0.43 | 64 |
| Iran | 0.43 | 65 |
| Senegal | 0.43 | 66 |
| Argentina | 0.43 | 67 |
| Nigeria | 0.42 | 68 |
| Zambia | 0.42 | 69 |
| Bulgaria | 0.41 | 70 |
| India | 0.41 | 71 |
| Tanzania | 0.41 | 72 |
| Kazakhstan | 0.41 | 73 |
| Trinidad and Tobago | 0.40 | 74 |
| Turkey | 0.40 | 75 |
| Madagascar | 0.40 | 76 |
| Ukraine | 0.40 | 77 |
| Brazil | 0.39 | 78 |
| Moldova | 0.38 | 79 |
| Indonesia | 0.38 | 80 |
| Pakistan | 0.38 | 81 |
| Morocco | 0.37 | 82 |
| Cote d'Ivoire | 0.37 | 83 |
| Philippines | 0.36 | 84 |
| Zimbabwe | 0.36 | 85 |
| Ecuador | 0.36 | 86 |
| Sierra Leone | 0.36 | 87 |
| Kenya | 0.35 | 88 |
| Guyana | 0.35 | 89 |
| Peru | 0.34 | 90 |
| Colombia | 0.34 | 91 |
| Serbia | 0.34 | 92 |
| Uganda | 0.34 | 93 |
| Dominican Republic | 0.34 | 94 |
| El Salvador | 0.34 | 95 |
| Kyrgyzstan | 0.33 | 96 |
| Bangladesh | 0.33 | 97 |
| Russia | 0.33 | 98 |
| Ethiopia | 0.33 | 99 |
| Belize | 0.32 | 100 |
| Myanmar | 0.32 | 101 |
| Nicaragua | 0.32 | 102 |
| Lebanon | 0.31 | 103 |
| Cambodia | 0.30 | 104 |
| Cameroon | 0.30 | 105 |
| Guatemala | 0.29 | 106 |
| Panama | 0.29 | 107 |
| Mexico | 0.29 | 108 |
| Afghanistan | 0.28 | 109 |
| Liberia | 0.26 | 110 |
| Honduras | 0.25 | 111 |
| Bolivia | 0.24 | 112 |
| Venezuela | 0.13 | 113 |

# Country Profiles

# How to Read the Country Profiles

This section presents profiles for the 113 countries and jurisdictions included in the *WJP Rule of Law Index 2016* report. Each country profile presents the featured country's scores for each of the *WJP Rule of Law Index's* factors and sub-factors, and draws comparisons between the scores of the featured country and the scores of other indexed countries that share regional and income level similarities. The scores range between 0 and 1, where 1 signifies the highest score (high rule of law adherence) and 0 signifies the lowest score (low rule of law adherence). The country profiles consist of four sections, outlined below.

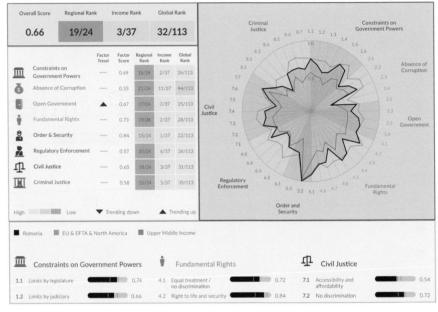

1. Displays the country's disaggregated scores for each of the sub-factors that compose the *WJP Rule of Law Index*. Each of the 44 sub-factors is represented by a gray line drawn from the center to the periphery of the circle. The center of the circle corresponds to the worst possible score for each sub-factor (0), and the outer edge of the circle marks the best possible score for each sub-factor (1).

   The featured country's scores are shown in purple. The average score of the country's region is represented with a yellow line. The average score of the country's income group is represented with a green line.

2. Displays the country's overall rule of law score, along with its overall global, income and regional ranks. The overall rule of law score is calculated by taking the simple average of the eight individual factors listed in the table in Section 3 of the country profile.

3. Displays the featured country's individual factor scores, along with the global, regional and income group rankings. The distribution of scores for the global rank, regional rank, and income rank is spread amongst three tiers — high, medium, and low as indicated by the color of the box in which the score is found.

   It also features upward and downward arrows to illustrate whether the rule of law in a country changed in the past year. Further information about the statistical procedure to construct these arrows can be found in the "Methodology" section of this report.

4. Presents the individual sub-factor scores underlying each of the factors listed in Section 3 of the country profile. The featured country's score is represented by the purple bar and labeled at the end of the bar. The average score of the country's region is represented by the yellow line. The average score of the country's income group is represented by the green line. Each sub-factor score is scaled between 0 and 1, where 1 is the highest score and 0 is the lowest score.

# Afghanistan

| | Overall Score | Regional Rank | Income Rank | Global Rank |
|---|---|---|---|---|
| | 0.35 | 6/6 | 12/12 | 111/113 |

| | Factor Trend | Factor Score | Regional Rank | Income Rank | Global Rank |
|---|---|---|---|---|---|
| Constraints on Government Powers | — | 0.43 | 5/6 | 9/12 | 97/113 |
| Absence of Corruption | — | 0.23 | 6/6 | 12/12 | 113/113 |
| Open Government | — | 0.40 | 6/6 | 8/12 | 99/113 |
| Fundamental Rights | — | 0.40 | 4/6 | 9/12 | 100/113 |
| Order & Security | — | 0.34 | 5/6 | 12/12 | 112/113 |
| Regulatory Enforcement | — | 0.36 | 5/6 | 9/12 | 106/113 |
| Civil Justice | — | 0.34 | 6/6 | 12/12 | 110/113 |
| Criminal Justice | — | 0.28 | 6/6 | 11/12 | 109/113 |

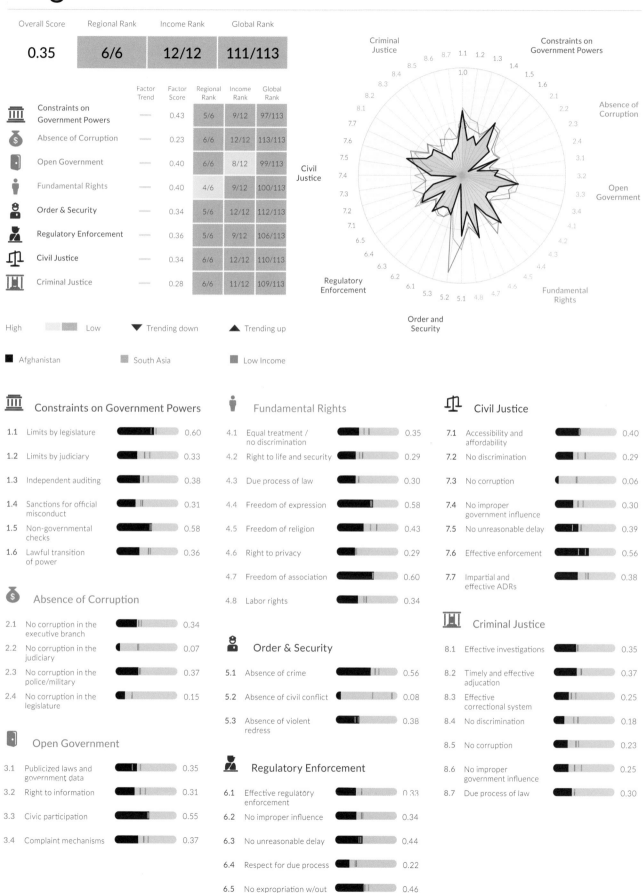

High    Low    ▼ Trending down    ▲ Trending up

■ Afghanistan    ■ South Asia    ■ Low Income

## Constraints on Government Powers

| 1.1 | Limits by legislature | 0.60 |
| 1.2 | Limits by judiciary | 0.33 |
| 1.3 | Independent auditing | 0.38 |
| 1.4 | Sanctions for official misconduct | 0.31 |
| 1.5 | Non-governmental checks | 0.58 |
| 1.6 | Lawful transition of power | 0.36 |

## Absence of Corruption

| 2.1 | No corruption in the executive branch | 0.34 |
| 2.2 | No corruption in the judiciary | 0.07 |
| 2.3 | No corruption in the police/military | 0.37 |
| 2.4 | No corruption in the legislature | 0.15 |

## Open Government

| 3.1 | Publicized laws and government data | 0.35 |
| 3.2 | Right to information | 0.31 |
| 3.3 | Civic participation | 0.55 |
| 3.4 | Complaint mechanisms | 0.37 |

## Fundamental Rights

| 4.1 | Equal treatment / no discrimination | 0.35 |
| 4.2 | Right to life and security | 0.29 |
| 4.3 | Due process of law | 0.30 |
| 4.4 | Freedom of expression | 0.58 |
| 4.5 | Freedom of religion | 0.43 |
| 4.6 | Right to privacy | 0.29 |
| 4.7 | Freedom of association | 0.60 |
| 4.8 | Labor rights | 0.34 |

## Order & Security

| 5.1 | Absence of crime | 0.56 |
| 5.2 | Absence of civil conflict | 0.08 |
| 5.3 | Absence of violent redress | 0.38 |

## Regulatory Enforcement

| 6.1 | Effective regulatory enforcement | 0.33 |
| 6.2 | No improper influence | 0.34 |
| 6.3 | No unreasonable delay | 0.44 |
| 6.4 | Respect for due process | 0.22 |
| 6.5 | No expropriation w/out adequate compensation | 0.46 |

## Civil Justice

| 7.1 | Accessibility and affordability | 0.40 |
| 7.2 | No discrimination | 0.29 |
| 7.3 | No corruption | 0.06 |
| 7.4 | No improper government influence | 0.30 |
| 7.5 | No unreasonable delay | 0.39 |
| 7.6 | Effective enforcement | 0.56 |
| 7.7 | Impartial and effective ADRs | 0.38 |

## Criminal Justice

| 8.1 | Effective investigations | 0.35 |
| 8.2 | Timely and effective adjudication | 0.37 |
| 8.3 | Effective correctional system | 0.25 |
| 8.4 | No discrimination | 0.18 |
| 8.5 | No corruption | 0.23 |
| 8.6 | No improper government influence | 0.25 |
| 8.7 | Due process of law | 0.30 |

# Albania

| | Overall Score | Regional Rank | Income Rank | Global Rank |
|---|---|---|---|---|
| | 0.50 | 5/13 | 24/37 | 72/113 |

| | Factor Trend | Factor Score | Regional Rank | Income Rank | Global Rank |
|---|---|---|---|---|---|
| Constraints on Government Powers | — | 0.53 | 3/13 | 19/37 | 68/113 |
| Absence of Corruption | — | 0.33 | 11/13 | 35/37 | 98/113 |
| Open Government | ▼ | 0.45 | 10/13 | 26/37 | 83/113 |
| Fundamental Rights | — | 0.60 | 4/13 | 16/37 | 55/113 |
| Order & Security | — | 0.75 | 6/13 | 9/37 | 42/113 |
| Regulatory Enforcement | — | 0.44 | 10/13 | 33/37 | 86/113 |
| Civil Justice | — | 0.48 | 8/13 | 28/37 | 74/113 |
| Criminal Justice | — | 0.46 | 5/13 | 17/37 | 57/113 |

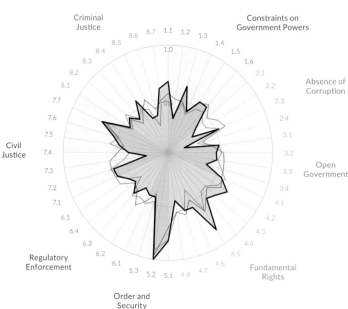

High ▮▮ Low    ▼ Trending down    ▲ Trending up

■ Albania    ▨ Eastern Europe & Central Asia    ▨ Upper Middle Income

---

## Constraints on Government Powers

| | | |
|---|---|---|
| 1.1 | Limits by legislature | 0.66 |
| 1.2 | Limits by judiciary | 0.32 |
| 1.3 | Independent auditing | 0.64 |
| 1.4 | Sanctions for official misconduct | 0.42 |
| 1.5 | Non-governmental checks | 0.56 |
| 1.6 | Lawful transition of power | 0.56 |

## Absence of Corruption

| | | |
|---|---|---|
| 2.1 | No corruption in the executive branch | 0.35 |
| 2.2 | No corruption in the judiciary | 0.27 |
| 2.3 | No corruption in the police/military | 0.53 |
| 2.4 | No corruption in the legislature | 0.16 |

## Open Government

| | | |
|---|---|---|
| 3.1 | Publicized laws and government data | 0.49 |
| 3.2 | Right to information | 0.46 |
| 3.3 | Civic participation | 0.47 |
| 3.4 | Complaint mechanisms | 0.38 |

## Fundamental Rights

| | | |
|---|---|---|
| 4.1 | Equal treatment / no discrimination | 0.56 |
| 4.2 | Right to life and security | 0.67 |
| 4.3 | Due process of law | 0.60 |
| 4.4 | Freedom of expression | 0.56 |
| 4.5 | Freedom of religion | 0.85 |
| 4.6 | Right to privacy | 0.56 |
| 4.7 | Freedom of association | 0.56 |
| 4.8 | Labor rights | 0.45 |

## Order & Security

| | | |
|---|---|---|
| 5.1 | Absence of crime | 0.82 |
| 5.2 | Absence of civil conflict | 1.00 |
| 5.3 | Absence of violent redress | 0.43 |

## Regulatory Enforcement

| | | |
|---|---|---|
| 6.1 | Effective regulatory enforcement | 0.43 |
| 6.2 | No improper influence | 0.39 |
| 6.3 | No unreasonable delay | 0.50 |
| 6.4 | Respect for due process | 0.41 |
| 6.5 | No expropriation w/out adequate compensation | 0.45 |

## Civil Justice

| | | |
|---|---|---|
| 7.1 | Accessibility and affordability | 0.53 |
| 7.2 | No discrimination | 0.54 |
| 7.3 | No corruption | 0.21 |
| 7.4 | No improper government influence | 0.38 |
| 7.5 | No unreasonable delay | 0.47 |
| 7.6 | Effective enforcement | 0.54 |
| 7.7 | Impartial and effective ADRs | 0.69 |

## Criminal Justice

| | | |
|---|---|---|
| 8.1 | Effective investigations | 0.43 |
| 8.2 | Timely and effective adjudication | 0.49 |
| 8.3 | Effective correctional system | 0.41 |
| 8.4 | No discrimination | 0.57 |
| 8.5 | No corruption | 0.35 |
| 8.6 | No improper government influence | 0.36 |
| 8.7 | Due process of law | 0.60 |

# Antigua & Barbuda

**Region:** Latin America & Caribbean
**Income Group:** High Income

| | Overall Score | Regional Rank | Income Rank | Global Rank |
|---|---|---|---|---|
| | 0.67 | 5/30 | 28/36 | 29/113 |

| | | Factor Trend | Factor Score | Regional Rank | Income Rank | Global Rank |
|---|---|---|---|---|---|---|
| 🏛 | Constraints on Government Powers | — | 0.64 | 8/30 | 30/36 | 38/113 |
| 💰 | Absence of Corruption | — | 0.66 | 9/30 | 28/36 | 34/113 |
| 📱 | Open Government | — | 0.51 | 17/30 | 33/36 | 62/113 |
| 👤 | Fundamental Rights | — | 0.74 | 5/30 | 24/36 | 25/113 |
| 👥 | Order & Security | — | 0.82 | 2/30 | 25/36 | 28/113 |
| 👷 | Regulatory Enforcement | — | 0.54 | 11/30 | 33/36 | 46/113 |
| ⚖ | Civil Justice | — | 0.72 | 3/30 | 20/36 | 21/113 |
| 🏛 | Criminal Justice | — | 0.70 | 1/30 | 18/36 | 18/113 |

High ▮ Low   ▼ Trending down   ▲ Trending up

■ Antigua & Barbuda   ▪ Latin America & Caribbean   ▪ High Income

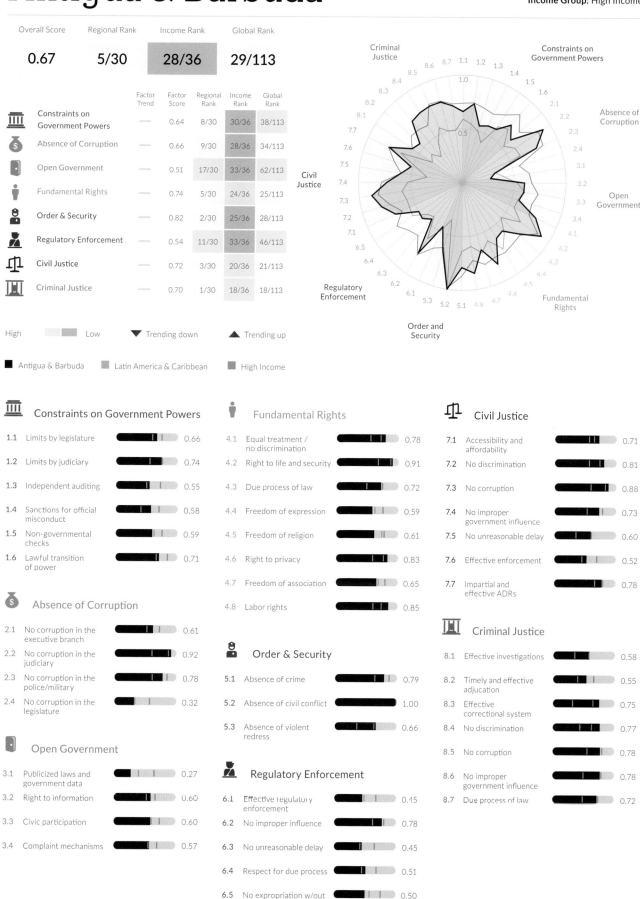

## 🏛 Constraints on Government Powers

| | | |
|---|---|---|
| 1.1 | Limits by legislature | 0.66 |
| 1.2 | Limits by judiciary | 0.74 |
| 1.3 | Independent auditing | 0.55 |
| 1.4 | Sanctions for official misconduct | 0.58 |
| 1.5 | Non-governmental checks | 0.59 |
| 1.6 | Lawful transition of power | 0.71 |

## 💰 Absence of Corruption

| | | |
|---|---|---|
| 2.1 | No corruption in the executive branch | 0.61 |
| 2.2 | No corruption in the judiciary | 0.92 |
| 2.3 | No corruption in the police/military | 0.78 |
| 2.4 | No corruption in the legislature | 0.32 |

## 📱 Open Government

| | | |
|---|---|---|
| 3.1 | Publicized laws and government data | 0.27 |
| 3.2 | Right to information | 0.60 |
| 3.3 | Civic participation | 0.60 |
| 3.4 | Complaint mechanisms | 0.57 |

## 👤 Fundamental Rights

| | | |
|---|---|---|
| 4.1 | Equal treatment / no discrimination | 0.78 |
| 4.2 | Right to life and security | 0.91 |
| 4.3 | Due process of law | 0.72 |
| 4.4 | Freedom of expression | 0.59 |
| 4.5 | Freedom of religion | 0.61 |
| 4.6 | Right to privacy | 0.83 |
| 4.7 | Freedom of association | 0.65 |
| 4.8 | Labor rights | 0.85 |

## 👥 Order & Security

| | | |
|---|---|---|
| 5.1 | Absence of crime | 0.79 |
| 5.2 | Absence of civil conflict | 1.00 |
| 5.3 | Absence of violent redress | 0.66 |

## 👷 Regulatory Enforcement

| | | |
|---|---|---|
| 6.1 | Effective regulatory enforcement | 0.45 |
| 6.2 | No improper influence | 0.78 |
| 6.3 | No unreasonable delay | 0.45 |
| 6.4 | Respect for due process | 0.51 |
| 6.5 | No expropriation w/out adequate compensation | 0.50 |

## ⚖ Civil Justice

| | | |
|---|---|---|
| 7.1 | Accessibility and affordability | 0.71 |
| 7.2 | No discrimination | 0.81 |
| 7.3 | No corruption | 0.88 |
| 7.4 | No improper government influence | 0.73 |
| 7.5 | No unreasonable delay | 0.60 |
| 7.6 | Effective enforcement | 0.52 |
| 7.7 | Impartial and effective ADRs | 0.78 |

## 🏛 Criminal Justice

| | | |
|---|---|---|
| 8.1 | Effective investigations | 0.58 |
| 8.2 | Timely and effective adjucation | 0.55 |
| 8.3 | Effective correctional system | 0.75 |
| 8.4 | No discrimination | 0.77 |
| 8.5 | No corruption | 0.78 |
| 8.6 | No improper government influence | 0.78 |
| 8.7 | Due process of law | 0.72 |

# Argentina

| | Overall Score | Regional Rank | Income Rank | Global Rank |
|---|---|---|---|---|
| | 0.55 | 14/30 | 13/37 | 51/113 |

| | | Factor Trend | Factor Score | Regional Rank | Income Rank | Global Rank |
|---|---|---|---|---|---|---|
| 🏛️ | Constraints on Government Powers | ▲ | 0.59 | 14/30 | 10/37 | 52/113 |
| 💰 | Absence of Corruption | ▲ | 0.51 | 15/30 | 16/37 | 54/113 |
| 📱 | Open Government | — | 0.57 | 9/30 | 11/37 | 43/113 |
| 👤 | Fundamental Rights | — | 0.69 | 9/30 | 5/37 | 35/113 |
| 👮 | Order & Security | | 0.62 | 22/30 | 30/37 | 93/113 |
| 🧑‍⚖️ | Regulatory Enforcement | ▲ | 0.47 | 19/30 | 23/37 | 68/113 |
| ⚖️ | Civil Justice | — | 0.57 | 12/30 | 12/37 | 48/113 |
| 🏛️ | Criminal Justice | — | 0.43 | 14/30 | 21/37 | 67/113 |

High ▢▢ Low ▼ Trending down ▲ Trending up

■ Argentina ▪ Latin America & Caribbean ▪ Upper Middle Income

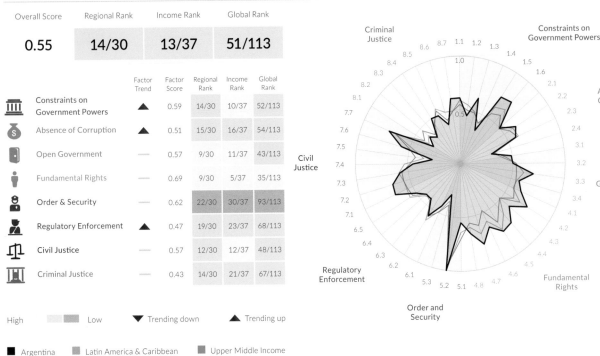

---

## 🏛️ Constraints on Government Powers

| | | |
|---|---|---|
| 1.1 | Limits by legislature | 0.61 |
| 1.2 | Limits by judiciary | 0.45 |
| 1.3 | Independent auditing | 0.63 |
| 1.4 | Sanctions for official misconduct | 0.34 |
| 1.5 | Non-governmental checks | 0.73 |
| 1.6 | Lawful transition of power | 0.75 |

## 💰 Absence of Corruption

| | | |
|---|---|---|
| 2.1 | No corruption in the executive branch | 0.50 |
| 2.2 | No corruption in the judiciary | 0.63 |
| 2.3 | No corruption in the police/military | 0.58 |
| 2.4 | No corruption in the legislature | 0.31 |

## 📱 Open Government

| | | |
|---|---|---|
| 3.1 | Publicized laws and government data | 0.49 |
| 3.2 | Right to information | 0.50 |
| 3.3 | Civic participation | 0.70 |
| 3.4 | Complaint mechanisms | 0.58 |

## 👤 Fundamental Rights

| | | |
|---|---|---|
| 4.1 | Equal treatment / no discrimination | 0.63 |
| 4.2 | Right to life and security | 0.75 |
| 4.3 | Due process of law | 0.61 |
| 4.4 | Freedom of expression | 0.73 |
| 4.5 | Freedom of religion | 0.75 |
| 4.6 | Right to privacy | 0.65 |
| 4.7 | Freedom of association | 0.78 |
| 4.8 | Labor rights | 0.66 |

## 👮 Order & Security

| | | |
|---|---|---|
| 5.1 | Absence of crime | 0.55 |
| 5.2 | Absence of civil conflict | 1.00 |
| 5.3 | Absence of violent redress | 0.30 |

## 🧑‍⚖️ Regulatory Enforcement

| | | |
|---|---|---|
| 6.1 | Effective regulatory enforcement | 0.43 |
| 6.2 | No improper influence | 0.57 |
| 6.3 | No unreasonable delay | 0.43 |
| 6.4 | Respect for due process | 0.43 |
| 6.5 | No expropriation w/out adequate compensation | 0.50 |

## ⚖️ Civil Justice

| | | |
|---|---|---|
| 7.1 | Accessibility and affordability | 0.68 |
| 7.2 | No discrimination | 0.67 |
| 7.3 | No corruption | 0.58 |
| 7.4 | No improper government influence | 0.45 |
| 7.5 | No unreasonable delay | 0.27 |
| 7.6 | Effective enforcement | 0.58 |
| 7.7 | Impartial and effective ADRs | 0.74 |

## 🏛️ Criminal Justice

| | | |
|---|---|---|
| 8.1 | Effective investigations | 0.30 |
| 8.2 | Timely and effective adjudication | 0.38 |
| 8.3 | Effective correctional system | 0.33 |
| 8.4 | No discrimination | 0.50 |
| 8.5 | No corruption | 0.49 |
| 8.6 | No improper government influence | 0.38 |
| 8.7 | Due process of law | 0.61 |

# Australia

Region: East Asia & Pacific
Income Group: High Income

| | Overall Score | Regional Rank | Income Rank | Global Rank |
|---|---|---|---|---|
| | 0.81 | 3/15 | 11/36 | 11/113 |

| | Factor Trend | Factor Score | Regional Rank | Income Rank | Global Rank |
|---|---|---|---|---|---|
| Constraints on Government Powers | — | 0.83 | 2/15 | 11/36 | 11/113 |
| Absence of Corruption | — | 0.83 | 4/15 | 12/36 | 12/113 |
| Open Government | — | 0.78 | 2/15 | 11/36 | 11/113 |
| Fundamental Rights | — | 0.81 | 2/15 | 13/36 | 13/113 |
| Order & Security | — | 0.87 | 4/15 | 12/36 | 13/113 |
| Regulatory Enforcement | — | 0.82 | 3/15 | 9/36 | 9/113 |
| Civil Justice | — | 0.77 | 6/15 | 14/36 | 14/113 |
| Criminal Justice | — | 0.75 | 3/15 | 12/36 | 12/113 |

High ▢ Low ▼ Trending down ▲ Trending up

■ Australia ▦ East Asia & Pacific ▦ High Income

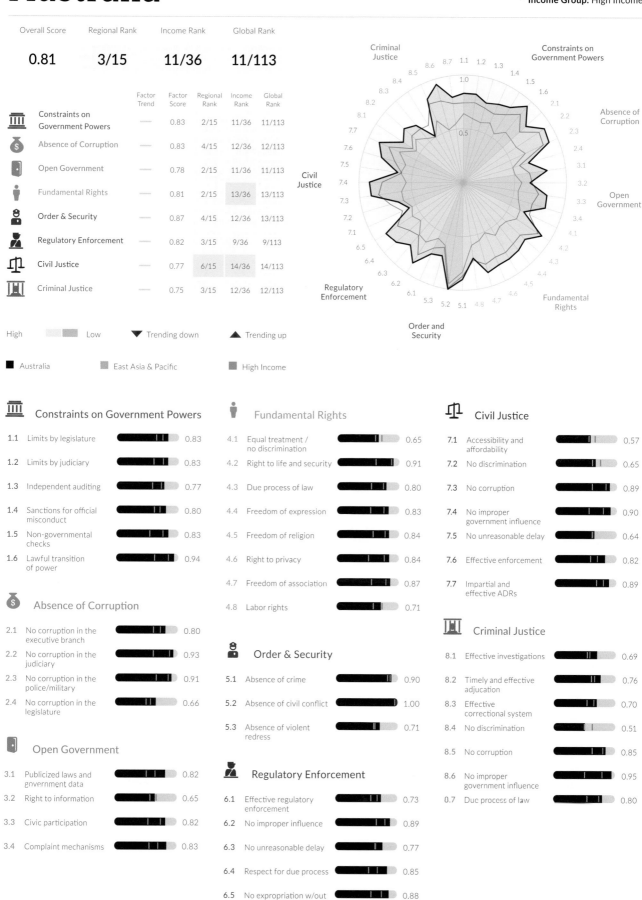

## Constraints on Government Powers

| | | |
|---|---|---|
| 1.1 | Limits by legislature | 0.83 |
| 1.2 | Limits by judiciary | 0.83 |
| 1.3 | Independent auditing | 0.77 |
| 1.4 | Sanctions for official misconduct | 0.80 |
| 1.5 | Non-governmental checks | 0.83 |
| 1.6 | Lawful transition of power | 0.94 |

## Absence of Corruption

| | | |
|---|---|---|
| 2.1 | No corruption in the executive branch | 0.80 |
| 2.2 | No corruption in the judiciary | 0.93 |
| 2.3 | No corruption in the police/military | 0.91 |
| 2.4 | No corruption in the legislature | 0.66 |

## Open Government

| | | |
|---|---|---|
| 3.1 | Publicized laws and government data | 0.82 |
| 3.2 | Right to information | 0.65 |
| 3.3 | Civic participation | 0.82 |
| 3.4 | Complaint mechanisms | 0.83 |

## Fundamental Rights

| | | |
|---|---|---|
| 4.1 | Equal treatment / no discrimination | 0.65 |
| 4.2 | Right to life and security | 0.91 |
| 4.3 | Due process of law | 0.80 |
| 4.4 | Freedom of expression | 0.83 |
| 4.5 | Freedom of religion | 0.84 |
| 4.6 | Right to privacy | 0.84 |
| 4.7 | Freedom of association | 0.87 |
| 4.8 | Labor rights | 0.71 |

## Order & Security

| | | |
|---|---|---|
| 5.1 | Absence of crime | 0.90 |
| 5.2 | Absence of civil conflict | 1.00 |
| 5.3 | Absence of violent redress | 0.71 |

## Regulatory Enforcement

| | | |
|---|---|---|
| 6.1 | Effective regulatory enforcement | 0.73 |
| 6.2 | No improper influence | 0.89 |
| 6.3 | No unreasonable delay | 0.77 |
| 6.4 | Respect for due process | 0.85 |
| 6.5 | No expropriation w/out adequate compensation | 0.88 |

## Civil Justice

| | | |
|---|---|---|
| 7.1 | Accessibility and affordability | 0.57 |
| 7.2 | No discrimination | 0.65 |
| 7.3 | No corruption | 0.89 |
| 7.4 | No improper government influence | 0.90 |
| 7.5 | No unreasonable delay | 0.64 |
| 7.6 | Effective enforcement | 0.82 |
| 7.7 | Impartial and effective ADRs | 0.89 |

## Criminal Justice

| | | |
|---|---|---|
| 8.1 | Effective investigations | 0.69 |
| 8.2 | Timely and effective adjudication | 0.76 |
| 8.3 | Effective correctional system | 0.70 |
| 8.4 | No discrimination | 0.51 |
| 8.5 | No corruption | 0.85 |
| 8.6 | No improper government influence | 0.95 |
| 0.7 | Due process of law | 0.80 |

# Austria

**Region:** EU & EFTA & North America
**Income Group:** High Income

| | Overall Score | Regional Rank | Income Rank | Global Rank |
|---|---|---|---|---|
| | 0.83 | 7/24 | 7/36 | 7/113 |

| | | Factor Trend | Factor Score | Regional Rank | Income Rank | Global Rank |
|---|---|---|---|---|---|---|
| 🏛 | Constraints on Government Powers | — | 0.86 | 6/24 | 7/36 | 7/113 |
| 💰 | Absence of Corruption | — | 0.84 | 6/24 | 9/36 | 9/113 |
| 🚪 | Open Government | — | 0.75 | 12/24 | 14/36 | 14/113 |
| 👤 | Fundamental Rights | — | 0.88 | 4/24 | 4/36 | 4/113 |
| 👥 | Order & Security | — | 0.90 | 5/24 | 6/36 | 7/113 |
| 👮 | Regulatory Enforcement | — | 0.80 | 7/24 | 11/36 | 11/113 |
| ⚖ | Civil Justice | — | 0.80 | 6/24 | 9/36 | 9/113 |
| 🏛 | Criminal Justice | — | 0.83 | 3/24 | 3/36 | 3/113 |

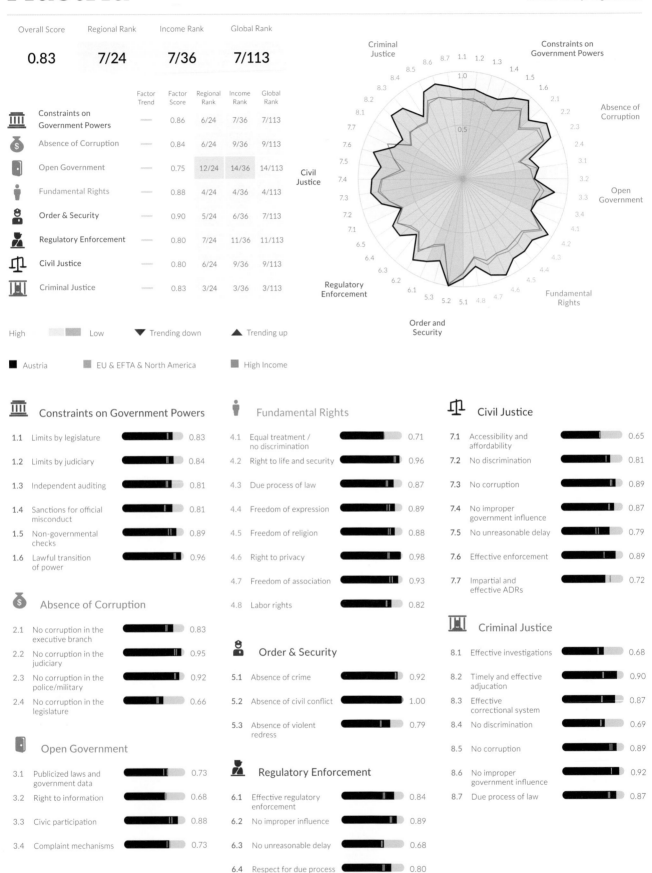

High ▬ Low   ▼ Trending down   ▲ Trending up

■ Austria    ▦ EU & EFTA & North America    ▬ High Income

## 🏛 Constraints on Government Powers

| | | |
|---|---|---|
| 1.1 | Limits by legislature | 0.83 |
| 1.2 | Limits by judiciary | 0.84 |
| 1.3 | Independent auditing | 0.81 |
| 1.4 | Sanctions for official misconduct | 0.81 |
| 1.5 | Non-governmental checks | 0.89 |
| 1.6 | Lawful transition of power | 0.96 |

## 💰 Absence of Corruption

| | | |
|---|---|---|
| 2.1 | No corruption in the executive branch | 0.83 |
| 2.2 | No corruption in the judiciary | 0.95 |
| 2.3 | No corruption in the police/military | 0.92 |
| 2.4 | No corruption in the legislature | 0.66 |

## 🚪 Open Government

| | | |
|---|---|---|
| 3.1 | Publicized laws and government data | 0.73 |
| 3.2 | Right to information | 0.68 |
| 3.3 | Civic participation | 0.88 |
| 3.4 | Complaint mechanisms | 0.73 |

## 👤 Fundamental Rights

| | | |
|---|---|---|
| 4.1 | Equal treatment / no discrimination | 0.71 |
| 4.2 | Right to life and security | 0.96 |
| 4.3 | Due process of law | 0.87 |
| 4.4 | Freedom of expression | 0.89 |
| 4.5 | Freedom of religion | 0.88 |
| 4.6 | Right to privacy | 0.98 |
| 4.7 | Freedom of association | 0.93 |
| 4.8 | Labor rights | 0.82 |

## 👥 Order & Security

| | | |
|---|---|---|
| 5.1 | Absence of crime | 0.92 |
| 5.2 | Absence of civil conflict | 1.00 |
| 5.3 | Absence of violent redress | 0.79 |

## 👮 Regulatory Enforcement

| | | |
|---|---|---|
| 6.1 | Effective regulatory enforcement | 0.84 |
| 6.2 | No improper influence | 0.89 |
| 6.3 | No unreasonable delay | 0.68 |
| 6.4 | Respect for due process | 0.80 |
| 6.5 | No expropriation w/out adequate compensation | 0.80 |

## ⚖ Civil Justice

| | | |
|---|---|---|
| 7.1 | Accessibility and affordability | 0.65 |
| 7.2 | No discrimination | 0.81 |
| 7.3 | No corruption | 0.89 |
| 7.4 | No improper government influence | 0.87 |
| 7.5 | No unreasonable delay | 0.79 |
| 7.6 | Effective enforcement | 0.89 |
| 7.7 | Impartial and effective ADRs | 0.72 |

## 🏛 Criminal Justice

| | | |
|---|---|---|
| 8.1 | Effective investigations | 0.68 |
| 8.2 | Timely and effective adjudication | 0.90 |
| 8.3 | Effective correctional system | 0.87 |
| 8.4 | No discrimination | 0.69 |
| 8.5 | No corruption | 0.89 |
| 8.6 | No improper government influence | 0.92 |
| 8.7 | Due process of law | 0.87 |

# Bahamas

| | Overall Score | Regional Rank | Income Rank | Global Rank |
|---|---|---|---|---|
| | 0.61 | 10/30 | 32/36 | 38/113 |

| | | Factor Trend | Factor Score | Regional Rank | Income Rank | Global Rank |
|---|---|---|---|---|---|---|
| 🏛 | Constraints on Government Powers | — | 0.60 | 13/30 | 34/36 | 49/113 |
| 💰 | Absence of Corruption | — | 0.64 | 11/30 | 30/36 | 37/113 |
| 🚪 | Open Government | — | 0.45 | 24/30 | 35/36 | 81/113 |
| 👤 | Fundamental Rights | — | 0.67 | 12/30 | 32/36 | 40/113 |
| 👮 | Order & Security | — | 0.72 | 8/30 | 32/36 | 56/113 |
| 🧑‍🏭 | Regulatory Enforcement | — | 0.47 | 20/30 | 36/36 | 69/113 |
| ⚖ | Civil Justice | — | 0.62 | 8/30 | 31/36 | 37/113 |
| 🏛 | Criminal Justice | — | 0.68 | 2/30 | 23/36 | 23/113 |

High ▢▢ Low   ▼ Trending down   ▲ Trending up

■ Bahamas   ▨ Latin America & Caribbean   ▨ High Income

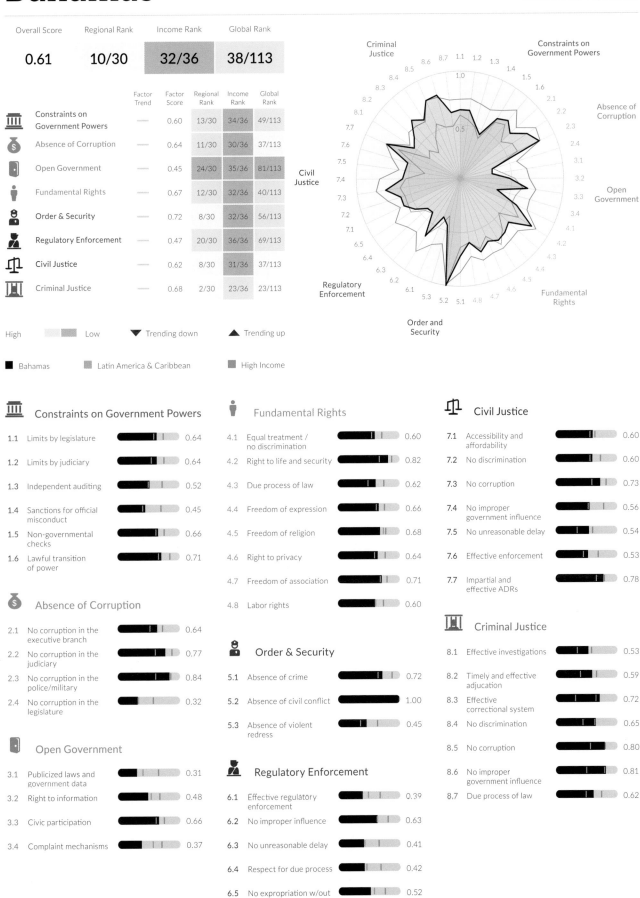

## 🏛 Constraints on Government Powers

| | | | |
|---|---|---|---|
| 1.1 | Limits by legislature | | 0.64 |
| 1.2 | Limits by judiciary | | 0.64 |
| 1.3 | Independent auditing | | 0.52 |
| 1.4 | Sanctions for official misconduct | | 0.45 |
| 1.5 | Non-governmental checks | | 0.66 |
| 1.6 | Lawful transition of power | | 0.71 |

## 💰 Absence of Corruption

| | | | |
|---|---|---|---|
| 2.1 | No corruption in the executive branch | | 0.64 |
| 2.2 | No corruption in the judiciary | | 0.77 |
| 2.3 | No corruption in the police/military | | 0.84 |
| 2.4 | No corruption in the legislature | | 0.32 |

## 🚪 Open Government

| | | | |
|---|---|---|---|
| 3.1 | Publicized laws and government data | | 0.31 |
| 3.2 | Right to information | | 0.48 |
| 3.3 | Civic participation | | 0.66 |
| 3.4 | Complaint mechanisms | | 0.37 |

## 👤 Fundamental Rights

| | | | |
|---|---|---|---|
| 4.1 | Equal treatment / no discrimination | | 0.60 |
| 4.2 | Right to life and security | | 0.82 |
| 4.3 | Due process of law | | 0.62 |
| 4.4 | Freedom of expression | | 0.66 |
| 4.5 | Freedom of religion | | 0.68 |
| 4.6 | Right to privacy | | 0.64 |
| 4.7 | Freedom of association | | 0.71 |
| 4.8 | Labor rights | | 0.60 |

## 👮 Order & Security

| | | | |
|---|---|---|---|
| 5.1 | Absence of crime | | 0.72 |
| 5.2 | Absence of civil conflict | | 1.00 |
| 5.3 | Absence of violent redress | | 0.45 |

## 🧑‍🏭 Regulatory Enforcement

| | | | |
|---|---|---|---|
| 6.1 | Effective regulatory enforcement | | 0.39 |
| 6.2 | No improper influence | | 0.63 |
| 6.3 | No unreasonable delay | | 0.41 |
| 6.4 | Respect for due process | | 0.42 |
| 6.5 | No expropriation w/out adequate compensation | | 0.52 |

## ⚖ Civil Justice

| | | | |
|---|---|---|---|
| 7.1 | Accessibility and affordability | | 0.60 |
| 7.2 | No discrimination | | 0.60 |
| 7.3 | No corruption | | 0.73 |
| 7.4 | No improper government influence | | 0.56 |
| 7.5 | No unreasonable delay | | 0.54 |
| 7.6 | Effective enforcement | | 0.53 |
| 7.7 | Impartial and effective ADRs | | 0.78 |

## 🏛 Criminal Justice

| | | | |
|---|---|---|---|
| 8.1 | Effective investigations | | 0.53 |
| 8.2 | Timely and effective adjudication | | 0.59 |
| 8.3 | Effective correctional system | | 0.72 |
| 8.4 | No discrimination | | 0.65 |
| 8.5 | No corruption | | 0.80 |
| 8.6 | No improper government influence | | 0.81 |
| 8.7 | Due process of law | | 0.62 |

# Bangladesh

| | Overall Score | Regional Rank | Income Rank | Global Rank |
|---|---|---|---|---|
| | 0.41 | 4/6 | 23/28 | 103/113 |

| | Factor Trend | Factor Score | Regional Rank | Income Rank | Global Rank |
|---|---|---|---|---|---|
| Constraints on Government Powers | — | 0.43 | 6/6 | 22/28 | 98/113 |
| Absence of Corruption | ▲ | 0.34 | 4/6 | 18/28 | 94/113 |
| Open Government | — | 0.45 | 5/6 | 17/28 | 84/113 |
| Fundamental Rights | ▼ | 0.34 | 6/6 | 26/28 | 106/113 |
| Order & Security | ▼ | 0.58 | 3/6 | 20/28 | 100/113 |
| Regulatory Enforcement | — | 0.40 | 4/6 | 21/28 | 99/113 |
| Civil Justice | — | 0.39 | 4/6 | 21/28 | 103/113 |
| Criminal Justice | — | 0.33 | 5/6 | 21/28 | 97/113 |

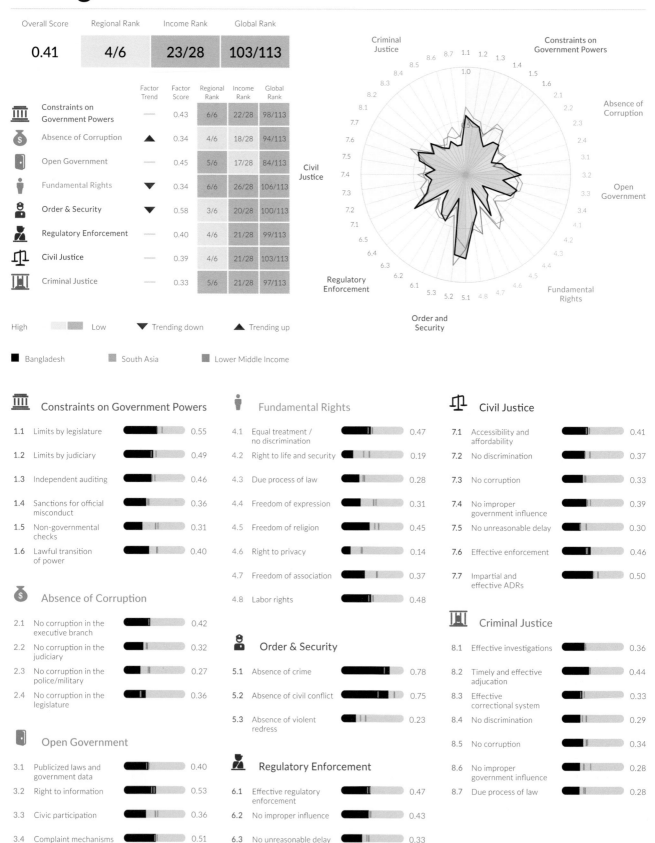

High ▮▮▮ Low    ▼ Trending down    ▲ Trending up

▮ Bangladesh    ▮ South Asia    ▮ Lower Middle Income

## Constraints on Government Powers

| | | |
|---|---|---|
| 1.1 | Limits by legislature | 0.55 |
| 1.2 | Limits by judiciary | 0.49 |
| 1.3 | Independent auditing | 0.46 |
| 1.4 | Sanctions for official misconduct | 0.36 |
| 1.5 | Non-governmental checks | 0.31 |
| 1.6 | Lawful transition of power | 0.40 |

## Absence of Corruption

| | | |
|---|---|---|
| 2.1 | No corruption in the executive branch | 0.42 |
| 2.2 | No corruption in the judiciary | 0.32 |
| 2.3 | No corruption in the police/military | 0.27 |
| 2.4 | No corruption in the legislature | 0.36 |

## Open Government

| | | |
|---|---|---|
| 3.1 | Publicized laws and government data | 0.40 |
| 3.2 | Right to information | 0.53 |
| 3.3 | Civic participation | 0.36 |
| 3.4 | Complaint mechanisms | 0.51 |

## Fundamental Rights

| | | |
|---|---|---|
| 4.1 | Equal treatment / no discrimination | 0.47 |
| 4.2 | Right to life and security | 0.19 |
| 4.3 | Due process of law | 0.28 |
| 4.4 | Freedom of expression | 0.31 |
| 4.5 | Freedom of religion | 0.45 |
| 4.6 | Right to privacy | 0.14 |
| 4.7 | Freedom of association | 0.37 |
| 4.8 | Labor rights | 0.48 |

## Order & Security

| | | |
|---|---|---|
| 5.1 | Absence of crime | 0.78 |
| 5.2 | Absence of civil conflict | 0.75 |
| 5.3 | Absence of violent redress | 0.23 |

## Regulatory Enforcement

| | | |
|---|---|---|
| 6.1 | Effective regulatory enforcement | 0.47 |
| 6.2 | No improper influence | 0.43 |
| 6.3 | No unreasonable delay | 0.33 |
| 6.4 | Respect for due process | 0.22 |
| 6.5 | No expropriation w/out adequate compensation | 0.58 |

## Civil Justice

| | | |
|---|---|---|
| 7.1 | Accessibility and affordability | 0.41 |
| 7.2 | No discrimination | 0.37 |
| 7.3 | No corruption | 0.33 |
| 7.4 | No improper government influence | 0.39 |
| 7.5 | No unreasonable delay | 0.30 |
| 7.6 | Effective enforcement | 0.46 |
| 7.7 | Impartial and effective ADRs | 0.50 |

## Criminal Justice

| | | |
|---|---|---|
| 8.1 | Effective investigations | 0.36 |
| 8.2 | Timely and effective adjucation | 0.44 |
| 8.3 | Effective correctional system | 0.33 |
| 8.4 | No discrimination | 0.29 |
| 8.5 | No corruption | 0.34 |
| 8.6 | No improper government influence | 0.28 |
| 8.7 | Due process of law | 0.28 |

# Barbados

**Region:** Latin America & Caribbean
**Income Group:** High Income

| | Overall Score | Regional Rank | Income Rank | Global Rank |
|---|---|---|---|---|
| | 0.67 | 4/30 | 27/36 | 28/113 |

| | Factor Trend | Factor Score | Regional Rank | Income Rank | Global Rank |
|---|---|---|---|---|---|
| Constraints on Government Powers | — | 0.66 | 5/30 | 28/36 | 32/113 |
| Absence of Corruption | — | 0.70 | 2/30 | 23/36 | 24/113 |
| Open Government | — | 0.52 | 14/30 | 32/36 | 56/113 |
| Fundamental Rights | — | 0.79 | 2/30 | 16/36 | 16/113 |
| Order & Security | — | 0.78 | 4/30 | 28/36 | 38/113 |
| Regulatory Enforcement | — | 0.61 | 5/30 | 28/36 | 30/113 |
| Civil Justice | — | 0.68 | 5/30 | 23/36 | 24/113 |
| Criminal Justice | — | 0.61 | 6/30 | 29/36 | 32/113 |

High ▬ Low   ▼ Trending down   ▲ Trending up

■ Barbados    Latin America & Caribbean    High Income

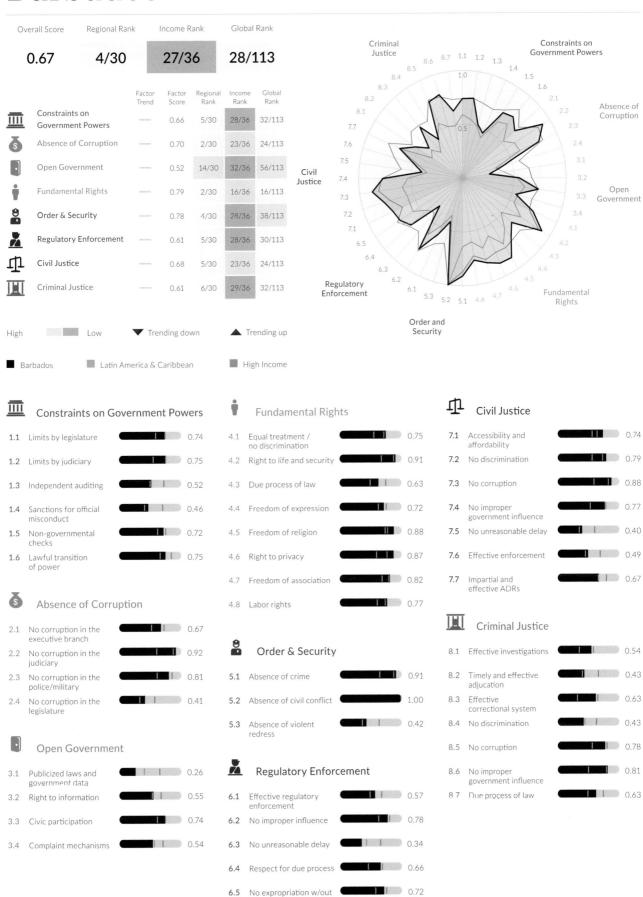

## Constraints on Government Powers

| | | |
|---|---|---|
| 1.1 | Limits by legislature | 0.74 |
| 1.2 | Limits by judiciary | 0.75 |
| 1.3 | Independent auditing | 0.52 |
| 1.4 | Sanctions for official misconduct | 0.46 |
| 1.5 | Non-governmental checks | 0.72 |
| 1.6 | Lawful transition of power | 0.75 |

## Absence of Corruption

| | | |
|---|---|---|
| 2.1 | No corruption in the executive branch | 0.67 |
| 2.2 | No corruption in the judiciary | 0.92 |
| 2.3 | No corruption in the police/military | 0.81 |
| 2.4 | No corruption in the legislature | 0.41 |

## Open Government

| | | |
|---|---|---|
| 3.1 | Publicized laws and government data | 0.26 |
| 3.2 | Right to information | 0.55 |
| 3.3 | Civic participation | 0.74 |
| 3.4 | Complaint mechanisms | 0.54 |

## Fundamental Rights

| | | |
|---|---|---|
| 4.1 | Equal treatment / no discrimination | 0.75 |
| 4.2 | Right to life and security | 0.91 |
| 4.3 | Due process of law | 0.63 |
| 4.4 | Freedom of expression | 0.72 |
| 4.5 | Freedom of religion | 0.88 |
| 4.6 | Right to privacy | 0.87 |
| 4.7 | Freedom of association | 0.82 |
| 4.8 | Labor rights | 0.77 |

## Order & Security

| | | |
|---|---|---|
| 5.1 | Absence of crime | 0.91 |
| 5.2 | Absence of civil conflict | 1.00 |
| 5.3 | Absence of violent redress | 0.42 |

## Regulatory Enforcement

| | | |
|---|---|---|
| 6.1 | Effective regulatory enforcement | 0.57 |
| 6.2 | No improper influence | 0.78 |
| 6.3 | No unreasonable delay | 0.34 |
| 6.4 | Respect for due process | 0.66 |
| 6.5 | No expropriation w/out adequate compensation | 0.72 |

## Civil Justice

| | | |
|---|---|---|
| 7.1 | Accessibility and affordability | 0.74 |
| 7.2 | No discrimination | 0.79 |
| 7.3 | No corruption | 0.88 |
| 7.4 | No improper government influence | 0.77 |
| 7.5 | No unreasonable delay | 0.40 |
| 7.6 | Effective enforcement | 0.49 |
| 7.7 | Impartial and effective ADRs | 0.67 |

## Criminal Justice

| | | |
|---|---|---|
| 8.1 | Effective investigations | 0.54 |
| 8.2 | Timely and effective adjucation | 0.43 |
| 8.3 | Effective correctional system | 0.63 |
| 8.4 | No discrimination | 0.43 |
| 8.5 | No corruption | 0.78 |
| 8.6 | No improper government influence | 0.81 |
| 8.7 | Due process of law | 0.63 |

# Belarus

**Region:** Eastern Europe & Central Asia
**Income Group:** Upper Middle Income

| | Overall Score | Regional Rank | Income Rank | Global Rank |
|---|---|---|---|---|
| | 0.54 | 4/13 | 18/37 | 57/113 |

| | | Factor Trend | Factor Score | Regional Rank | Income Rank | Global Rank |
|---|---|---|---|---|---|---|
| 🏛 | Constraints on Government Powers | — | 0.36 | 11/13 | 35/37 | 105/113 |
| 💰 | Absence of Corruption | — | 0.52 | 2/13 | 14/37 | 51/113 |
| 📱 | Open Government | — | 0.43 | 11/13 | 31/37 | 90/113 |
| 👤 | Fundamental Rights | — | 0.48 | 9/13 | 29/37 | 85/113 |
| 👮 | Order & Security | — | 0.81 | 2/13 | 3/37 | 29/113 |
| 💼 | Regulatory Enforcement | — | 0.53 | 2/13 | 12/37 | 48/113 |
| ⚖ | Civil Justice | — | 0.65 | 1/13 | 2/37 | 30/113 |
| ⚖ | Criminal Justice | — | 0.51 | 4/13 | 15/37 | 49/113 |

High ▭▭▭ Low     ▼ Trending down     ▲ Trending up

■ Belarus     ■ Eastern Europe & Central Asia     ■ Upper Middle Income

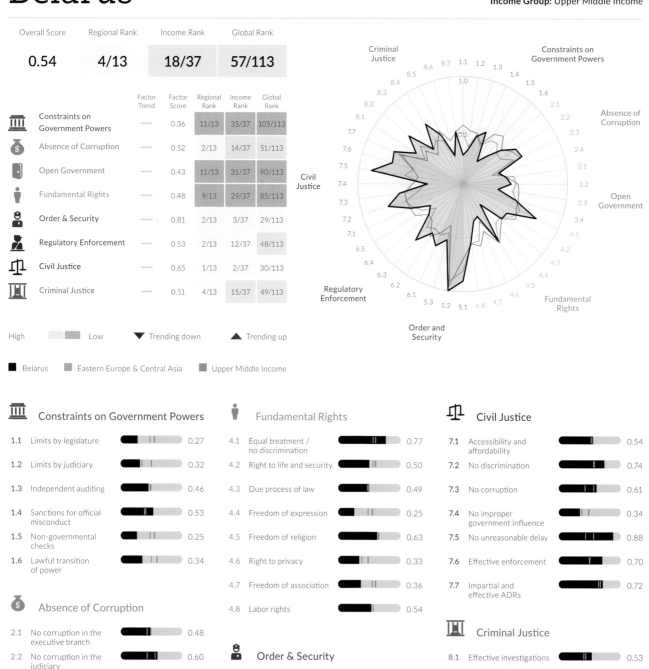

## 🏛 Constraints on Government Powers

| | | |
|---|---|---|
| 1.1 | Limits by legislature | 0.27 |
| 1.2 | Limits by judiciary | 0.32 |
| 1.3 | Independent auditing | 0.46 |
| 1.4 | Sanctions for official misconduct | 0.53 |
| 1.5 | Non-governmental checks | 0.25 |
| 1.6 | Lawful transition of power | 0.34 |

## 💰 Absence of Corruption

| | | |
|---|---|---|
| 2.1 | No corruption in the executive branch | 0.48 |
| 2.2 | No corruption in the judiciary | 0.60 |
| 2.3 | No corruption in the police/military | 0.62 |
| 2.4 | No corruption in the legislature | 0.36 |

## 📱 Open Government

| | | |
|---|---|---|
| 3.1 | Publicized laws and government data | 0.42 |
| 3.2 | Right to information | 0.46 |
| 3.3 | Civic participation | 0.34 |
| 3.4 | Complaint mechanisms | 0.52 |

## 👤 Fundamental Rights

| | | |
|---|---|---|
| 4.1 | Equal treatment / no discrimination | 0.77 |
| 4.2 | Right to life and security | 0.50 |
| 4.3 | Due process of law | 0.49 |
| 4.4 | Freedom of expression | 0.25 |
| 4.5 | Freedom of religion | 0.63 |
| 4.6 | Right to privacy | 0.33 |
| 4.7 | Freedom of association | 0.36 |
| 4.8 | Labor rights | 0.54 |

## 👮 Order & Security

| | | |
|---|---|---|
| 5.1 | Absence of crime | 0.90 |
| 5.2 | Absence of civil conflict | 1.00 |
| 5.3 | Absence of violent redress | 0.54 |

## 💼 Regulatory Enforcement

| | | |
|---|---|---|
| 6.1 | Effective regulatory enforcement | 0.63 |
| 6.2 | No improper influence | 0.54 |
| 6.3 | No unreasonable delay | 0.69 |
| 6.4 | Respect for due process | 0.43 |
| 6.5 | No expropriation w/out adequate compensation | 0.37 |

## ⚖ Civil Justice

| | | |
|---|---|---|
| 7.1 | Accessibility and affordability | 0.54 |
| 7.2 | No discrimination | 0.74 |
| 7.3 | No corruption | 0.61 |
| 7.4 | No improper government influence | 0.34 |
| 7.5 | No unreasonable delay | 0.88 |
| 7.6 | Effective enforcement | 0.70 |
| 7.7 | Impartial and effective ADRs | 0.72 |

## ⚖ Criminal Justice

| | | |
|---|---|---|
| 8.1 | Effective investigations | 0.53 |
| 8.2 | Timely and effective adjucation | 0.68 |
| 8.3 | Effective correctional system | 0.43 |
| 8.4 | No discrimination | 0.66 |
| 8.5 | No corruption | 0.50 |
| 8.6 | No improper government influence | 0.28 |
| 8.7 | Due process of law | 0.49 |

# Belgium

| | Overall Score | Regional Rank | Income Rank | Global Rank |
|---|---|---|---|---|
| | 0.79 | 10/24 | 13/36 | 13/113 |

| | | Factor Trend | Factor Score | Regional Rank | Income Rank | Global Rank |
|---|---|---|---|---|---|---|
| 🏛 | Constraints on Government Powers | — | 0.83 | 10/24 | 12/36 | 12/113 |
| 💰 | Absence of Corruption | — | 0.78 | 10/24 | 16/36 | 16/113 |
| 📱 | Open Government | — | 0.73 | 13/24 | 15/36 | 15/113 |
| 👤 | Fundamental Rights | — | 0.84 | 8/24 | 8/36 | 8/113 |
| 👤 | Order & Security | — | 0.84 | 14/24 | 20/36 | 21/113 |
| ⚖ | Regulatory Enforcement | — | 0.77 | 11/24 | 16/36 | 16/113 |
| ⚖ | Civil Justice | — | 0.76 | 9/24 | 15/36 | 15/113 |
| ⚖ | Criminal Justice | ▲ | 0.76 | 9/24 | 11/36 | 11/113 |

High ▬ Low    ▼ Trending down    ▲ Trending up

■ Belgium    ▨ EU & EFTA & North America    ▨ High Income

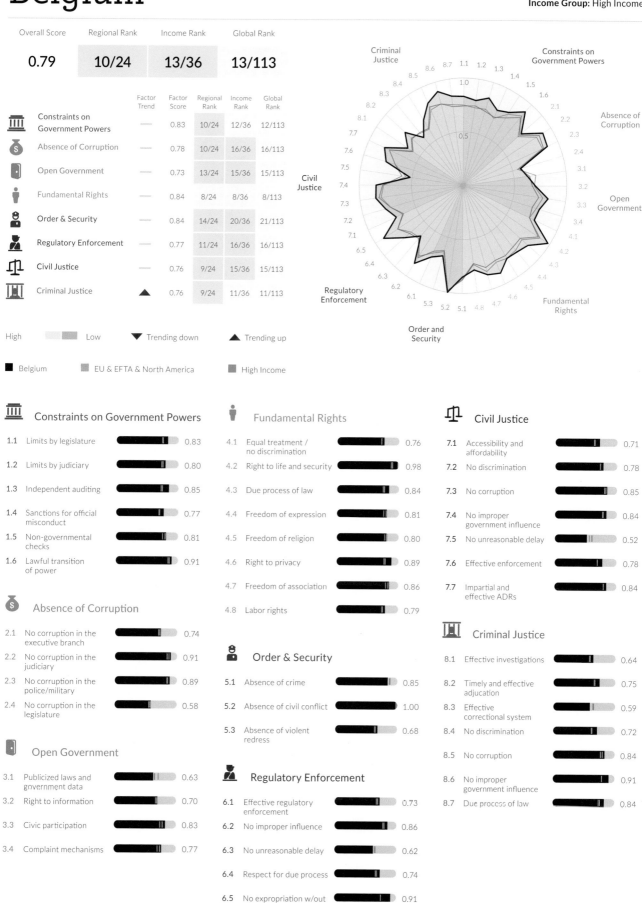

## 🏛 Constraints on Government Powers

| 1.1 | Limits by legislature | 0.83 |
|---|---|---|
| 1.2 | Limits by judiciary | 0.80 |
| 1.3 | Independent auditing | 0.85 |
| 1.4 | Sanctions for official misconduct | 0.77 |
| 1.5 | Non-governmental checks | 0.81 |
| 1.6 | Lawful transition of power | 0.91 |

## 💰 Absence of Corruption

| 2.1 | No corruption in the executive branch | 0.74 |
|---|---|---|
| 2.2 | No corruption in the judiciary | 0.91 |
| 2.3 | No corruption in the police/military | 0.89 |
| 2.4 | No corruption in the legislature | 0.58 |

## 📱 Open Government

| 3.1 | Publicized laws and government data | 0.63 |
|---|---|---|
| 3.2 | Right to information | 0.70 |
| 3.3 | Civic participation | 0.83 |
| 3.4 | Complaint mechanisms | 0.77 |

## 👤 Fundamental Rights

| 4.1 | Equal treatment / no discrimination | 0.76 |
|---|---|---|
| 4.2 | Right to life and security | 0.98 |
| 4.3 | Due process of law | 0.84 |
| 4.4 | Freedom of expression | 0.81 |
| 4.5 | Freedom of religion | 0.80 |
| 4.6 | Right to privacy | 0.89 |
| 4.7 | Freedom of association | 0.86 |
| 4.8 | Labor rights | 0.79 |

## 👤 Order & Security

| 5.1 | Absence of crime | 0.85 |
|---|---|---|
| 5.2 | Absence of civil conflict | 1.00 |
| 5.3 | Absence of violent redress | 0.68 |

## ⚖ Regulatory Enforcement

| 6.1 | Effective regulatory enforcement | 0.73 |
|---|---|---|
| 6.2 | No improper influence | 0.86 |
| 6.3 | No unreasonable delay | 0.62 |
| 6.4 | Respect for due process | 0.74 |
| 6.5 | No expropriation w/out adequate compensation | 0.91 |

## ⚖ Civil Justice

| 7.1 | Accessibility and affordability | 0.71 |
|---|---|---|
| 7.2 | No discrimination | 0.78 |
| 7.3 | No corruption | 0.85 |
| 7.4 | No improper government influence | 0.84 |
| 7.5 | No unreasonable delay | 0.52 |
| 7.6 | Effective enforcement | 0.78 |
| 7.7 | Impartial and effective ADRs | 0.84 |

## ⚖ Criminal Justice

| 8.1 | Effective investigations | 0.64 |
|---|---|---|
| 8.2 | Timely and effective adjudication | 0.75 |
| 8.3 | Effective correctional system | 0.59 |
| 8.4 | No discrimination | 0.72 |
| 8.5 | No corruption | 0.84 |
| 8.6 | No improper government influence | 0.91 |
| 8.7 | Due process of law | 0.84 |

# Belize

| | Overall Score | Regional Rank | Income Rank | Global Rank |
|---|---|---|---|---|
| | 0.47 | 22/30 | 29/37 | 82/113 |

| | Factor Trend | Factor Score | Regional Rank | Income Rank | Global Rank |
|---|---|---|---|---|---|
| Constraints on Government Powers | — | 0.45 | 24/30 | 27/37 | 90/113 |
| Absence of Corruption | — | 0.48 | 16/30 | 20/37 | 59/113 |
| Open Government | — | 0.45 | 27/30 | 29/37 | 87/113 |
| Fundamental Rights | — | 0.51 | 26/30 | 27/37 | 79/113 |
| Order & Security | — | 0.70 | 10/30 | 20/37 | 65/113 |
| Regulatory Enforcement | — | 0.43 | 25/30 | 34/37 | 88/113 |
| Civil Justice | — | 0.47 | 21/30 | 30/37 | 79/113 |
| Criminal Justice | — | 0.32 | 23/30 | 33/37 | 100/113 |

High ▢ Low    ▼ Trending down    ▲ Trending up

■ Belize    ▨ Latin America & Caribbean    ▨ Upper Middle Income

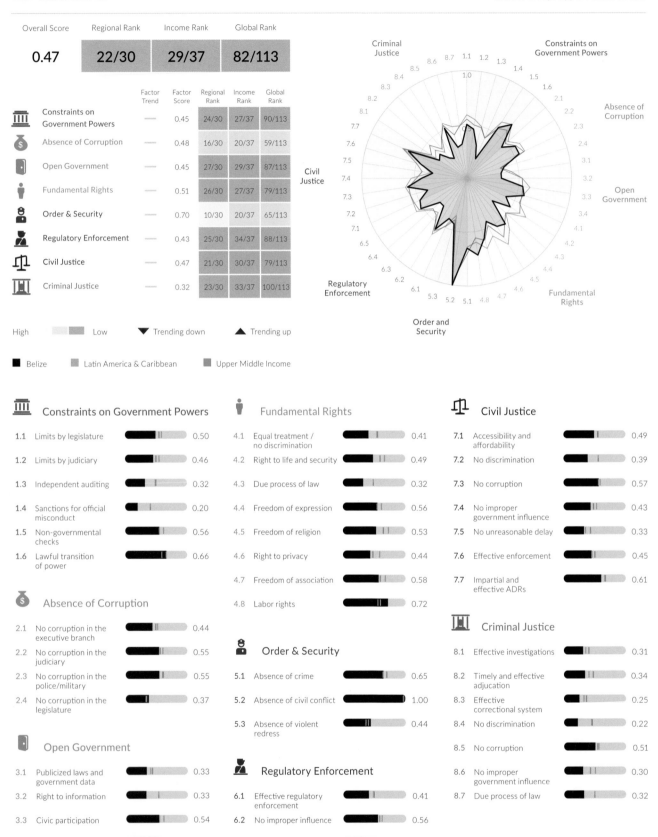

## Constraints on Government Powers

| | | |
|---|---|---|
| 1.1 | Limits by legislature | 0.50 |
| 1.2 | Limits by judiciary | 0.46 |
| 1.3 | Independent auditing | 0.32 |
| 1.4 | Sanctions for official misconduct | 0.20 |
| 1.5 | Non-governmental checks | 0.56 |
| 1.6 | Lawful transition of power | 0.66 |

## Absence of Corruption

| | | |
|---|---|---|
| 2.1 | No corruption in the executive branch | 0.44 |
| 2.2 | No corruption in the judiciary | 0.55 |
| 2.3 | No corruption in the police/military | 0.55 |
| 2.4 | No corruption in the legislature | 0.37 |

## Open Government

| | | |
|---|---|---|
| 3.1 | Publicized laws and government data | 0.33 |
| 3.2 | Right to information | 0.33 |
| 3.3 | Civic participation | 0.54 |
| 3.4 | Complaint mechanisms | 0.57 |

## Fundamental Rights

| | | |
|---|---|---|
| 4.1 | Equal treatment / no discrimination | 0.41 |
| 4.2 | Right to life and security | 0.49 |
| 4.3 | Due process of law | 0.32 |
| 4.4 | Freedom of expression | 0.56 |
| 4.5 | Freedom of religion | 0.53 |
| 4.6 | Right to privacy | 0.44 |
| 4.7 | Freedom of association | 0.58 |
| 4.8 | Labor rights | 0.72 |

## Order & Security

| | | |
|---|---|---|
| 5.1 | Absence of crime | 0.65 |
| 5.2 | Absence of civil conflict | 1.00 |
| 5.3 | Absence of violent redress | 0.44 |

## Regulatory Enforcement

| | | |
|---|---|---|
| 6.1 | Effective regulatory enforcement | 0.41 |
| 6.2 | No improper influence | 0.56 |
| 6.3 | No unreasonable delay | 0.34 |
| 6.4 | Respect for due process | 0.34 |
| 6.5 | No expropriation w/out adequate compensation | 0.52 |

## Civil Justice

| | | |
|---|---|---|
| 7.1 | Accessibility and affordability | 0.49 |
| 7.2 | No discrimination | 0.39 |
| 7.3 | No corruption | 0.57 |
| 7.4 | No improper government influence | 0.43 |
| 7.5 | No unreasonable delay | 0.33 |
| 7.6 | Effective enforcement | 0.45 |
| 7.7 | Impartial and effective ADRs | 0.61 |

## Criminal Justice

| | | |
|---|---|---|
| 8.1 | Effective investigations | 0.31 |
| 8.2 | Timely and effective adjudication | 0.34 |
| 8.3 | Effective correctional system | 0.25 |
| 8.4 | No discrimination | 0.22 |
| 8.5 | No corruption | 0.51 |
| 8.6 | No improper government influence | 0.30 |
| 8.7 | Due process of law | 0.32 |

# Bolivia

**Region:** Latin America & Caribbean
**Income Group:** Lower Middle Income

| | Overall Score | Regional Rank | Income Rank | Global Rank |
|---|---|---|---|---|
| | 0.40 | 29/30 | 24/28 | 104/113 |

| | | Factor Trend | Factor Score | Regional Rank | Income Rank | Global Rank |
|---|---|---|---|---|---|---|
| 🏛️ | Constraints on Government Powers | — | 0.39 | 27/30 | 24/28 | 102/113 |
| 💰 | Absence of Corruption | — | 0.29 | 29/30 | 23/28 | 103/113 |
| 📱 | Open Government | — | 0.44 | 28/30 | 18/28 | 88/113 |
| 👤 | Fundamental Rights | — | 0.5 | 27/30 | 12/28 | 80/113 |
| 👮 | Order & Security | — | 0.58 | 27/30 | 21/28 | 101/113 |
| 👷 | Regulatory Enforcement | — | 0.43 | 26/30 | 16/28 | 90/113 |
| ⚖️ | Civil Justice | — | 0.35 | 28/30 | 25/28 | 108/113 |
| ⚖️ | Criminal Justice | — | 0.24 | 29/30 | 28/28 | 112/113 |

High ▮▮▮ Low    ▼ Trending down    ▲ Trending up

■ Bolivia    ▨ Latin America & Caribbean    ▨ Lower Middle Income

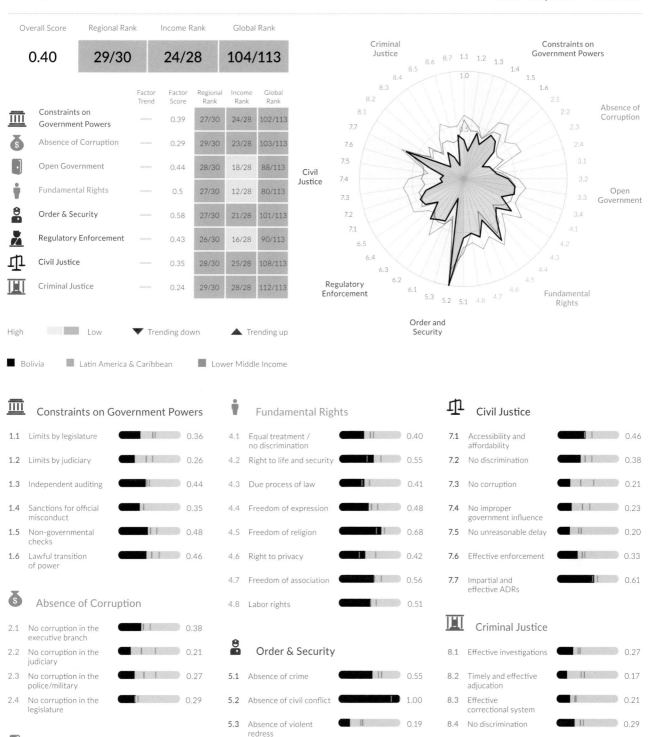

## 🏛️ Constraints on Government Powers

| | | |
|---|---|---|
| 1.1 | Limits by legislature | 0.36 |
| 1.2 | Limits by judiciary | 0.26 |
| 1.3 | Independent auditing | 0.44 |
| 1.4 | Sanctions for official misconduct | 0.35 |
| 1.5 | Non-governmental checks | 0.48 |
| 1.6 | Lawful transition of power | 0.46 |

## 💰 Absence of Corruption

| | | |
|---|---|---|
| 2.1 | No corruption in the executive branch | 0.38 |
| 2.2 | No corruption in the judiciary | 0.21 |
| 2.3 | No corruption in the police/military | 0.27 |
| 2.4 | No corruption in the legislature | 0.29 |

## 📱 Open Government

| | | |
|---|---|---|
| 3.1 | Publicized laws and government data | 0.32 |
| 3.2 | Right to information | 0.43 |
| 3.3 | Civic participation | 0.50 |
| 3.4 | Complaint mechanisms | 0.51 |

## 👤 Fundamental Rights

| | | |
|---|---|---|
| 4.1 | Equal treatment / no discrimination | 0.40 |
| 4.2 | Right to life and security | 0.55 |
| 4.3 | Due process of law | 0.41 |
| 4.4 | Freedom of expression | 0.48 |
| 4.5 | Freedom of religion | 0.68 |
| 4.6 | Right to privacy | 0.42 |
| 4.7 | Freedom of association | 0.56 |
| 4.8 | Labor rights | 0.51 |

## 👮 Order & Security

| | | |
|---|---|---|
| 5.1 | Absence of crime | 0.55 |
| 5.2 | Absence of civil conflict | 1.00 |
| 5.3 | Absence of violent redress | 0.19 |

## 👷 Regulatory Enforcement

| | | |
|---|---|---|
| 6.1 | Effective regulatory enforcement | 0.43 |
| 6.2 | No improper influence | 0.45 |
| 6.3 | No unreasonable delay | 0.49 |
| 6.4 | Respect for due process | 0.33 |
| 6.5 | No expropriation w/out adequate compensation | 0.44 |

## ⚖️ Civil Justice

| | | |
|---|---|---|
| 7.1 | Accessibility and affordability | 0.46 |
| 7.2 | No discrimination | 0.38 |
| 7.3 | No corruption | 0.21 |
| 7.4 | No improper government influence | 0.23 |
| 7.5 | No unreasonable delay | 0.20 |
| 7.6 | Effective enforcement | 0.33 |
| 7.7 | Impartial and effective ADRs | 0.61 |

## ⚖️ Criminal Justice

| | | |
|---|---|---|
| 8.1 | Effective investigations | 0.27 |
| 8.2 | Timely and effective adjucation | 0.17 |
| 8.3 | Effective correctional system | 0.21 |
| 8.4 | No discrimination | 0.29 |
| 8.5 | No corruption | 0.22 |
| 8.6 | No improper government influence | 0.13 |
| 8.7 | Due process of law | 0.41 |

# Bosnia & Herzegovina

**Region:** Eastern Europe & Central Asia
**Income Group:** Upper Middle Income

| Overall Score | Regional Rank | Income Rank | Global Rank |
|:---:|:---:|:---:|:---:|
| 0.56 | 2/13 | 12/37 | 50/113 |

| | Factor Trend | Factor Score | Regional Rank | Income Rank | Global Rank |
|---|:---:|:---:|:---:|:---:|:---:|
| 🏛 Constraints on Government Powers | — | 0.57 | 2/13 | 12/37 | 55/113 |
| 💰 Absence of Corruption | — | 0.43 | 6/13 | 26/37 | 72/113 |
| 🚪 Open Government | — | 0.54 | 7/13 | 16/37 | 53/113 |
| 🧍 Fundamental Rights | — | 0.65 | 2/13 | 9/37 | 42/113 |
| 👤 Order & Security | — | 0.70 | 10/13 | 18/37 | 63/113 |
| 👨‍💼 Regulatory Enforcement | — | 0.50 | 4/13 | 19/37 | 59/113 |
| ⚖ Civil Justice | — | 0.50 | 7/13 | 24/37 | 69/113 |
| 🏛 Criminal Justice | — | 0.56 | 2/13 | 7/37 | 39/113 |

High ▢ Low   ▼ Trending down   ▲ Trending up

■ Bosnia & Herzegovina   ■ Eastern Europe & Central Asia   ■ Upper Middle Income

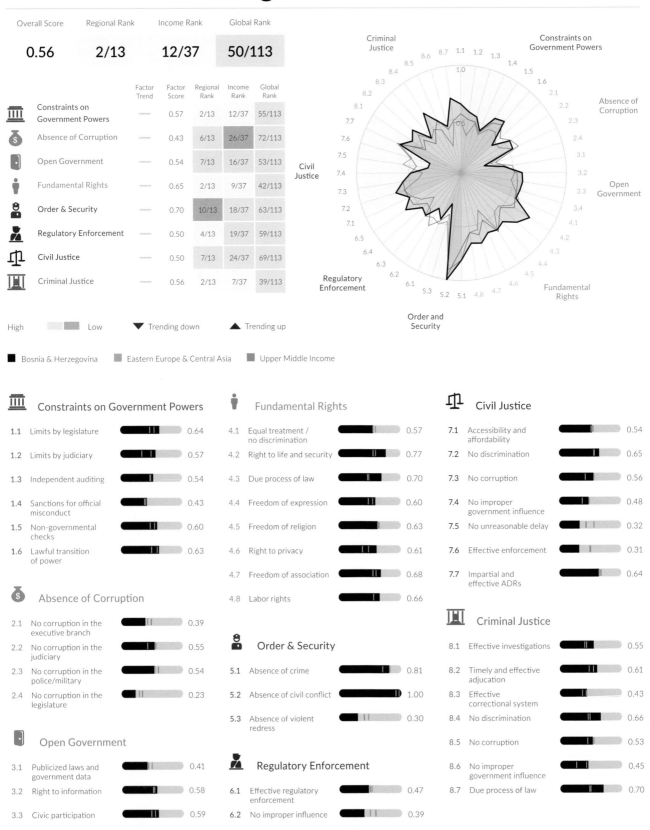

## 🏛 Constraints on Government Powers

| | | |
|---|---|---|
| 1.1 | Limits by legislature | 0.64 |
| 1.2 | Limits by judiciary | 0.57 |
| 1.3 | Independent auditing | 0.54 |
| 1.4 | Sanctions for official misconduct | 0.43 |
| 1.5 | Non-governmental checks | 0.60 |
| 1.6 | Lawful transition of power | 0.63 |

## 💰 Absence of Corruption

| | | |
|---|---|---|
| 2.1 | No corruption in the executive branch | 0.39 |
| 2.2 | No corruption in the judiciary | 0.55 |
| 2.3 | No corruption in the police/military | 0.54 |
| 2.4 | No corruption in the legislature | 0.23 |

## 🚪 Open Government

| | | |
|---|---|---|
| 3.1 | Publicized laws and government data | 0.41 |
| 3.2 | Right to information | 0.58 |
| 3.3 | Civic participation | 0.59 |
| 3.4 | Complaint mechanisms | 0.58 |

## 🧍 Fundamental Rights

| | | |
|---|---|---|
| 4.1 | Equal treatment / no discrimination | 0.57 |
| 4.2 | Right to life and security | 0.77 |
| 4.3 | Due process of law | 0.70 |
| 4.4 | Freedom of expression | 0.60 |
| 4.5 | Freedom of religion | 0.63 |
| 4.6 | Right to privacy | 0.61 |
| 4.7 | Freedom of association | 0.68 |
| 4.8 | Labor rights | 0.66 |

## 👤 Order & Security

| | | |
|---|---|---|
| 5.1 | Absence of crime | 0.81 |
| 5.2 | Absence of civil conflict | 1.00 |
| 5.3 | Absence of violent redress | 0.30 |

## 👨‍💼 Regulatory Enforcement

| | | |
|---|---|---|
| 6.1 | Effective regulatory enforcement | 0.47 |
| 6.2 | No improper influence | 0.39 |
| 6.3 | No unreasonable delay | 0.52 |
| 6.4 | Respect for due process | 0.49 |
| 6.5 | No expropriation w/out adequate compensation | 0.63 |

## ⚖ Civil Justice

| | | |
|---|---|---|
| 7.1 | Accessibility and affordability | 0.54 |
| 7.2 | No discrimination | 0.65 |
| 7.3 | No corruption | 0.56 |
| 7.4 | No improper government influence | 0.48 |
| 7.5 | No unreasonable delay | 0.32 |
| 7.6 | Effective enforcement | 0.31 |
| 7.7 | Impartial and effective ADRs | 0.64 |

## 🏛 Criminal Justice

| | | |
|---|---|---|
| 8.1 | Effective investigations | 0.55 |
| 8.2 | Timely and effective adjudication | 0.61 |
| 8.3 | Effective correctional system | 0.43 |
| 8.4 | No discrimination | 0.66 |
| 8.5 | No corruption | 0.53 |
| 8.6 | No improper government influence | 0.45 |
| 8.7 | Due process of law | 0.70 |

# Botswana

**Region:** Sub-Saharan Africa
**Income Group:** Upper Middle Income

| | Overall Score | Regional Rank | Income Rank | Global Rank |
|---|---|---|---|---|
| | 0.58 | 3/18 | 10/37 | 45/113 |

| | | Factor Trend | Factor Score | Regional Rank | Income Rank | Global Rank |
|---|---|---|---|---|---|---|
| 🏛 | Constraints on Government Powers | ▼ | 0.55 | 6/18 | 15/37 | 60/113 |
| 💰 | Absence of Corruption | — | 0.62 | 1/18 | 8/37 | 38/113 |
| 🗄 | Open Government | — | 0.49 | 5/18 | 22/37 | 68/113 |
| 👤 | Fundamental Rights | — | 0.51 | 8/18 | 26/37 | 78/113 |
| 👮 | Order & Security | ▼ | 0.71 | 2/18 | 17/37 | 60/113 |
| 👔 | Regulatory Enforcement | ▼ | 0.59 | 1/18 | 3/37 | 32/113 |
| ⚖ | Civil Justice | — | 0.62 | 1/18 | 6/37 | 36/113 |
| 🏛 | Criminal Justice | — | 0.52 | 2/18 | 13/37 | 47/113 |

High ▨ Low    ▼ Trending down    ▲ Trending up

■ Botswana    ▨ Sub-Saharan Africa    ▨ Upper Middle Income

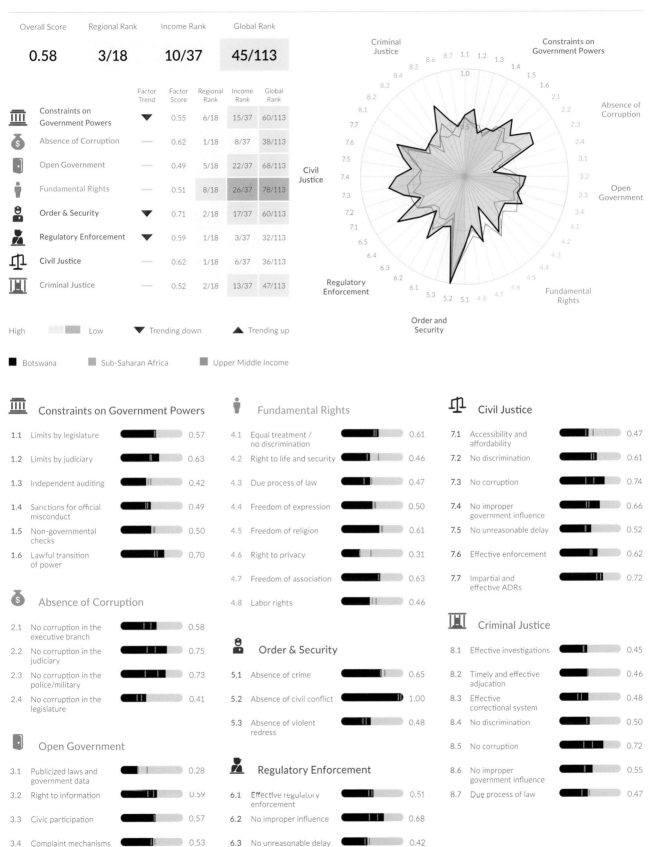

## 🏛 Constraints on Government Powers

| | | | |
|---|---|---|---|
| 1.1 | Limits by legislature | | 0.57 |
| 1.2 | Limits by judiciary | | 0.63 |
| 1.3 | Independent auditing | | 0.42 |
| 1.4 | Sanctions for official misconduct | | 0.49 |
| 1.5 | Non-governmental checks | | 0.50 |
| 1.6 | Lawful transition of power | | 0.70 |

## 💰 Absence of Corruption

| | | | |
|---|---|---|---|
| 2.1 | No corruption in the executive branch | | 0.58 |
| 2.2 | No corruption in the judiciary | | 0.75 |
| 2.3 | No corruption in the police/military | | 0.73 |
| 2.4 | No corruption in the legislature | | 0.41 |

## 🗄 Open Government

| | | | |
|---|---|---|---|
| 3.1 | Publicized laws and government data | | 0.28 |
| 3.2 | Right to information | | 0.59 |
| 3.3 | Civic participation | | 0.57 |
| 3.4 | Complaint mechanisms | | 0.53 |

## 👤 Fundamental Rights

| | | | |
|---|---|---|---|
| 4.1 | Equal treatment / no discrimination | | 0.61 |
| 4.2 | Right to life and security | | 0.46 |
| 4.3 | Due process of law | | 0.47 |
| 4.4 | Freedom of expression | | 0.50 |
| 4.5 | Freedom of religion | | 0.61 |
| 4.6 | Right to privacy | | 0.31 |
| 4.7 | Freedom of association | | 0.63 |
| 4.8 | Labor rights | | 0.46 |

## 👮 Order & Security

| | | | |
|---|---|---|---|
| 5.1 | Absence of crime | | 0.65 |
| 5.2 | Absence of civil conflict | | 1.00 |
| 5.3 | Absence of violent redress | | 0.48 |

## 👔 Regulatory Enforcement

| | | | |
|---|---|---|---|
| 6.1 | Effective regulatory enforcement | | 0.51 |
| 6.2 | No improper influence | | 0.68 |
| 6.3 | No unreasonable delay | | 0.42 |
| 6.4 | Respect for due process | | 0.57 |
| 6.5 | No expropriation w/out adequate compensation | | 0.77 |

## ⚖ Civil Justice

| | | | |
|---|---|---|---|
| 7.1 | Accessibility and affordability | | 0.47 |
| 7.2 | No discrimination | | 0.61 |
| 7.3 | No corruption | | 0.74 |
| 7.4 | No improper government influence | | 0.66 |
| 7.5 | No unreasonable delay | | 0.52 |
| 7.6 | Effective enforcement | | 0.62 |
| 7.7 | Impartial and effective ADRs | | 0.72 |

## 🏛 Criminal Justice

| | | | |
|---|---|---|---|
| 8.1 | Effective investigations | | 0.45 |
| 8.2 | Timely and effective adjucation | | 0.46 |
| 8.3 | Effective correctional system | | 0.48 |
| 8.4 | No discrimination | | 0.50 |
| 8.5 | No corruption | | 0.72 |
| 8.6 | No improper government influence | | 0.55 |
| 8.7 | Due process of law | | 0.47 |

# Brazil

**Region:** Latin America & Caribbean
**Income Group:** Upper Middle Income

| Overall Score | Regional Rank | Income Rank | Global Rank |
|---|---|---|---|
| 0.55 | 15/30 | 14/37 | 52/113 |

| | Factor Trend | Factor Score | Regional Rank | Income Rank | Global Rank |
|---|---|---|---|---|---|
| Constraints on Government Powers | — | 0.61 | 12/30 | 9/37 | 48/113 |
| Absence of Corruption | — | 0.45 | 18/30 | 23/37 | 63/113 |
| Open Government | — | 0.62 | 5/30 | 5/37 | 33/113 |
| Fundamental Rights | — | 0.61 | 16/30 | 15/37 | 52/113 |
| Order & Security | — | 0.67 | 15/30 | 23/37 | 75/113 |
| Regulatory Enforcement | — | 0.54 | 8/30 | 8/37 | 42/113 |
| Civil Justice | — | 0.53 | 15/30 | 19/37 | 58/113 |
| Criminal Justice | — | 0.39 | 16/30 | 25/37 | 78/113 |

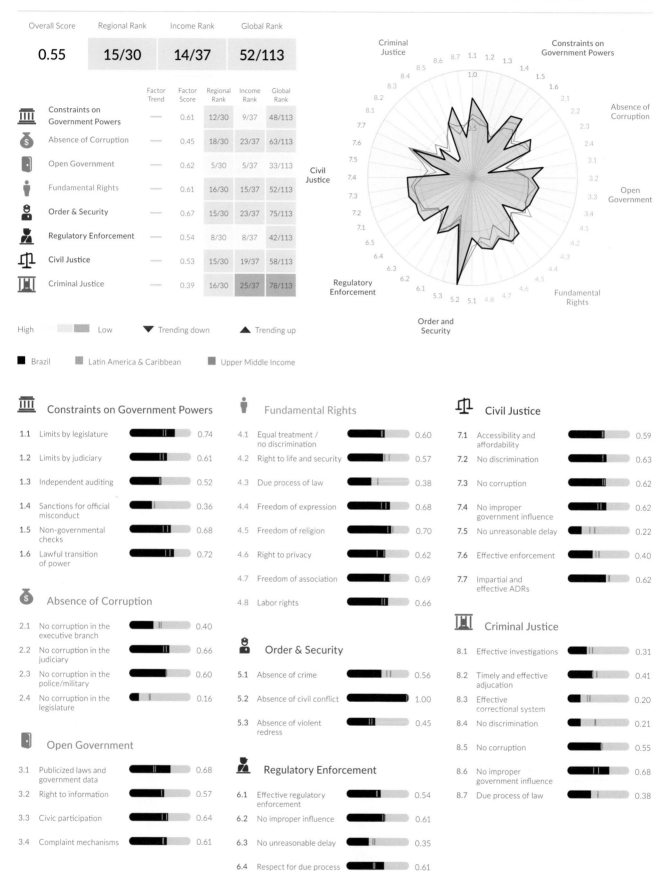

High ▬▬ Low   ▼ Trending down   ▲ Trending up

■ Brazil   ▨ Latin America & Caribbean   ▨ Upper Middle Income

## Constraints on Government Powers

| 1.1 | Limits by legislature | 0.74 |
|---|---|---|
| 1.2 | Limits by judiciary | 0.61 |
| 1.3 | Independent auditing | 0.52 |
| 1.4 | Sanctions for official misconduct | 0.36 |
| 1.5 | Non-governmental checks | 0.68 |
| 1.6 | Lawful transition of power | 0.72 |

## Absence of Corruption

| 2.1 | No corruption in the executive branch | 0.40 |
|---|---|---|
| 2.2 | No corruption in the judiciary | 0.66 |
| 2.3 | No corruption in the police/military | 0.60 |
| 2.4 | No corruption in the legislature | 0.16 |

## Open Government

| 3.1 | Publicized laws and government data | 0.68 |
|---|---|---|
| 3.2 | Right to information | 0.57 |
| 3.3 | Civic participation | 0.64 |
| 3.4 | Complaint mechanisms | 0.61 |

## Fundamental Rights

| 4.1 | Equal treatment / no discrimination | 0.60 |
|---|---|---|
| 4.2 | Right to life and security | 0.57 |
| 4.3 | Due process of law | 0.38 |
| 4.4 | Freedom of expression | 0.68 |
| 4.5 | Freedom of religion | 0.70 |
| 4.6 | Right to privacy | 0.62 |
| 4.7 | Freedom of association | 0.69 |
| 4.8 | Labor rights | 0.66 |

## Order & Security

| 5.1 | Absence of crime | 0.56 |
|---|---|---|
| 5.2 | Absence of civil conflict | 1.00 |
| 5.3 | Absence of violent redress | 0.45 |

## Regulatory Enforcement

| 6.1 | Effective regulatory enforcement | 0.54 |
|---|---|---|
| 6.2 | No improper influence | 0.61 |
| 6.3 | No unreasonable delay | 0.35 |
| 6.4 | Respect for due process | 0.61 |
| 6.5 | No expropriation w/out adequate compensation | 0.61 |

## Civil Justice

| 7.1 | Accessibility and affordability | 0.59 |
|---|---|---|
| 7.2 | No discrimination | 0.63 |
| 7.3 | No corruption | 0.62 |
| 7.4 | No improper government influence | 0.62 |
| 7.5 | No unreasonable delay | 0.22 |
| 7.6 | Effective enforcement | 0.40 |
| 7.7 | Impartial and effective ADRs | 0.62 |

## Criminal Justice

| 8.1 | Effective investigations | 0.31 |
|---|---|---|
| 8.2 | Timely and effective adjudication | 0.41 |
| 8.3 | Effective correctional system | 0.20 |
| 8.4 | No discrimination | 0.21 |
| 8.5 | No corruption | 0.55 |
| 8.6 | No improper government influence | 0.68 |
| 8.7 | Due process of law | 0.38 |

# Bulgaria

**Region:** EU & EFTA & North America
**Income Group:** Upper Middle Income

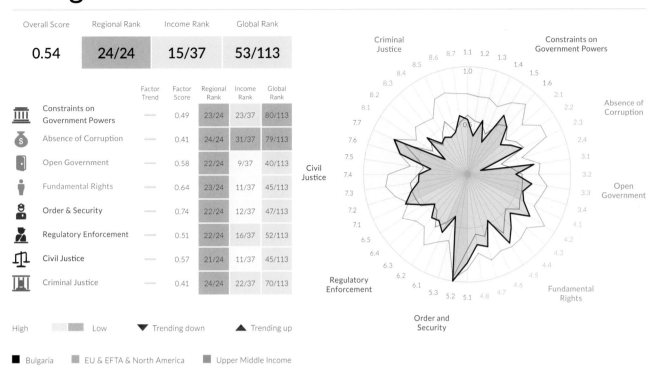

| | Overall Score | Regional Rank | Income Rank | Global Rank |
|---|---|---|---|---|
| | 0.54 | 24/24 | 15/37 | 53/113 |

| | | Factor Trend | Factor Score | Regional Rank | Income Rank | Global Rank |
|---|---|---|---|---|---|---|
| 🏛 | Constraints on Government Powers | — | 0.49 | 23/24 | 23/37 | 80/113 |
| 💲 | Absence of Corruption | — | 0.41 | 24/24 | 31/37 | 79/113 |
| 📱 | Open Government | — | 0.58 | 22/24 | 9/37 | 40/113 |
| 🧍 | Fundamental Rights | — | 0.64 | 23/24 | 11/37 | 45/113 |
| 👮 | Order & Security | — | 0.74 | 22/24 | 12/37 | 47/113 |
| 👷 | Regulatory Enforcement | — | 0.51 | 22/24 | 16/37 | 52/113 |
| ⚖ | Civil Justice | — | 0.57 | 21/24 | 11/37 | 45/113 |
| 🏛 | Criminal Justice | — | 0.41 | 24/24 | 22/37 | 70/113 |

High ▢▢▢ Low     ▼ Trending down     ▲ Trending up

■ Bulgaria     ■ EU & EFTA & North America     ■ Upper Middle Income

---

## 🏛 Constraints on Government Powers

| | | | |
|---|---|---|---|
| 1.1 | Limits by legislature | | 0.51 |
| 1.2 | Limits by judiciary | | 0.36 |
| 1.3 | Independent auditing | | 0.52 |
| 1.4 | Sanctions for official misconduct | | 0.33 |
| 1.5 | Non-governmental checks | | 0.65 |
| 1.6 | Lawful transition of power | | 0.58 |

## 💲 Absence of Corruption

| | | | |
|---|---|---|---|
| 2.1 | No corruption in the executive branch | | 0.42 |
| 2.2 | No corruption in the judiciary | | 0.50 |
| 2.3 | No corruption in the police/military | | 0.58 |
| 2.4 | No corruption in the legislature | | 0.13 |

## 📱 Open Government

| | | | |
|---|---|---|---|
| 3.1 | Publicized laws and government data | | 0.65 |
| 3.2 | Right to information | | 0.47 |
| 3.3 | Civic participation | | 0.63 |
| 3.4 | Complaint mechanisms | | 0.56 |

## 🧍 Fundamental Rights

| | | | |
|---|---|---|---|
| 4.1 | Equal treatment / no discrimination | | 0.60 |
| 4.2 | Right to life and security | | 0.72 |
| 4.3 | Due process of law | | 0.55 |
| 4.4 | Freedom of expression | | 0.65 |
| 4.5 | Freedom of religion | | 0.76 |
| 4.6 | Right to privacy | | 0.47 |
| 4.7 | Freedom of association | | 0.70 |
| 4.8 | Labor rights | | 0.66 |

## 👮 Order & Security

| | | | |
|---|---|---|---|
| 5.1 | Absence of crime | | 0.82 |
| 5.2 | Absence of civil conflict | | 1.00 |
| 5.3 | Absence of violent redress | | 0.41 |

## 👷 Regulatory Enforcement

| | | | |
|---|---|---|---|
| 6.1 | Effective regulatory enforcement | | 0.59 |
| 6.2 | No improper influence | | 0.51 |
| 6.3 | No unreasonable delay | | 0.53 |
| 6.4 | Respect for due process | | 0.42 |
| 6.5 | No expropriation w/out adequate compensation | | 0.52 |

## ⚖ Civil Justice

| | | | |
|---|---|---|---|
| 7.1 | Accessibility and affordability | | 0.66 |
| 7.2 | No discrimination | | 0.57 |
| 7.3 | No corruption | | 0.48 |
| 7.4 | No improper government influence | | 0.47 |
| 7.5 | No unreasonable delay | | 0.36 |
| 7.6 | Effective enforcement | | 0.68 |
| 7.7 | Impartial and effective ADRs | | 0.78 |

## 🏛 Criminal Justice

| | | | |
|---|---|---|---|
| 8.1 | Effective investigations | | 0.26 |
| 8.2 | Timely and effective adjudication | | 0.52 |
| 8.3 | Effective correctional system | | 0.38 |
| 8.4 | No discrimination | | 0.41 |
| 8.5 | No corruption | | 0.38 |
| 8.6 | No improper government influence | | 0.41 |
| 8.7 | Due process of law | | 0.55 |

# Burkina Faso

**Region:** Sub-Saharan Africa
**Income Group:** Low Income

| | Overall Score | Regional Rank | Income Rank | Global Rank |
|---|---|---|---|---|
| | 0.48 | 6/18 | 4/12 | 79/113 |

| | Factor Trend | Factor Score | Regional Rank | Income Rank | Global Rank |
|---|---|---|---|---|---|
| 🏛 Constraints on Government Powers | ▲ | 0.46 | 12/18 | 7/12 | 85/113 |
| 💰 Absence of Corruption | — | 0.38 | 9/18 | 5/12 | 86/113 |
| 🚪 Open Government | — | 0.45 | 9/18 | 6/12 | 82/113 |
| 🧍 Fundamental Rights | — | 0.56 | 6/18 | 4/12 | 63/113 |
| 🧑 Order & Security | — | 0.67 | 5/18 | 3/12 | 69/113 |
| 🧑‍🌾 Regulatory Enforcement | — | 0.45 | 7/18 | 4/12 | 82/113 |
| ⚖ Civil Justice | — | 0.47 | 10/18 | 4/12 | 81/113 |
| 🏛 Criminal Justice | ▲ | 0.43 | 5/18 | 3/12 | 64/113 |

High ▬ Low   ▼ Trending down   ▲ Trending up

■ Burkina Faso   ■ Sub-Saharan Africa   ■ Low Income

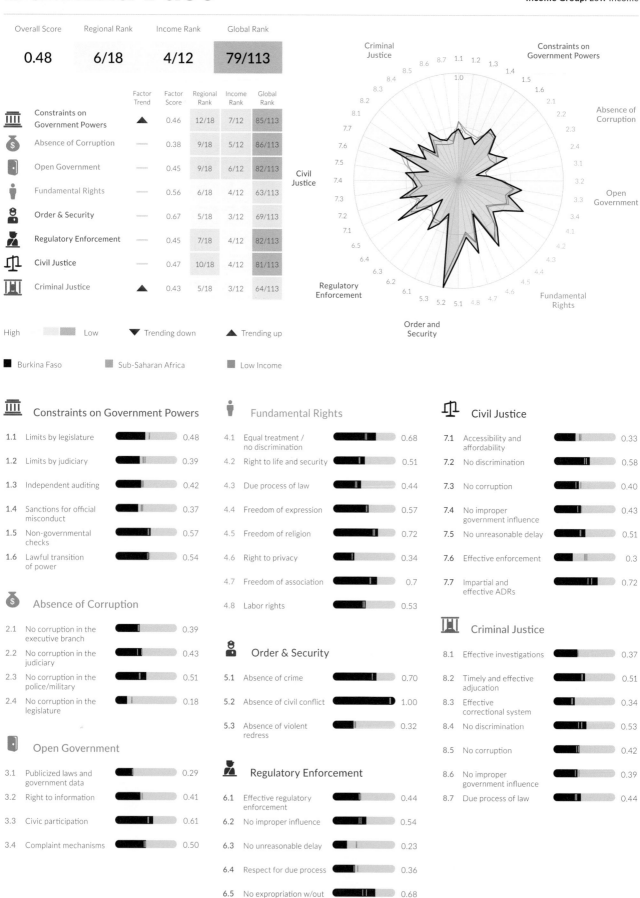

## 🏛 Constraints on Government Powers

| | | |
|---|---|---|
| 1.1 | Limits by legislature | 0.48 |
| 1.2 | Limits by judiciary | 0.39 |
| 1.3 | Independent auditing | 0.42 |
| 1.4 | Sanctions for official misconduct | 0.37 |
| 1.5 | Non-governmental checks | 0.57 |
| 1.6 | Lawful transition of power | 0.54 |

## 💰 Absence of Corruption

| | | |
|---|---|---|
| 2.1 | No corruption in the executive branch | 0.39 |
| 2.2 | No corruption in the judiciary | 0.43 |
| 2.3 | No corruption in the police/military | 0.51 |
| 2.4 | No corruption in the legislature | 0.18 |

## 🚪 Open Government

| | | |
|---|---|---|
| 3.1 | Publicized laws and government data | 0.29 |
| 3.2 | Right to information | 0.41 |
| 3.3 | Civic participation | 0.61 |
| 3.4 | Complaint mechanisms | 0.50 |

## 🧍 Fundamental Rights

| | | |
|---|---|---|
| 4.1 | Equal treatment / no discrimination | 0.68 |
| 4.2 | Right to life and security | 0.51 |
| 4.3 | Due process of law | 0.44 |
| 4.4 | Freedom of expression | 0.57 |
| 4.5 | Freedom of religion | 0.72 |
| 4.6 | Right to privacy | 0.34 |
| 4.7 | Freedom of association | 0.7 |
| 4.8 | Labor rights | 0.53 |

## 🧑 Order & Security

| | | |
|---|---|---|
| 5.1 | Absence of crime | 0.70 |
| 5.2 | Absence of civil conflict | 1.00 |
| 5.3 | Absence of violent redress | 0.32 |

## 🧑‍🌾 Regulatory Enforcement

| | | |
|---|---|---|
| 6.1 | Effective regulatory enforcement | 0.44 |
| 6.2 | No improper influence | 0.54 |
| 6.3 | No unreasonable delay | 0.23 |
| 6.4 | Respect for due process | 0.36 |
| 6.5 | No expropriation w/out adequate compensation | 0.68 |

## ⚖ Civil Justice

| | | |
|---|---|---|
| 7.1 | Accessibility and affordability | 0.33 |
| 7.2 | No discrimination | 0.58 |
| 7.3 | No corruption | 0.40 |
| 7.4 | No improper government influence | 0.43 |
| 7.5 | No unreasonable delay | 0.51 |
| 7.6 | Effective enforcement | 0.3 |
| 7.7 | Impartial and effective ADRs | 0.72 |

## 🏛 Criminal Justice

| | | |
|---|---|---|
| 8.1 | Effective investigations | 0.37 |
| 8.2 | Timely and effective adjudication | 0.51 |
| 8.3 | Effective correctional system | 0.34 |
| 8.4 | No discrimination | 0.53 |
| 8.5 | No corruption | 0.42 |
| 8.6 | No improper government influence | 0.39 |
| 8.7 | Due process of law | 0.44 |

# Cambodia

**Region:** East Asia & Pacific
**Income Group:** Lower Middle Income

| | Overall Score | Regional Rank | Income Rank | Global Rank |
|---|---|---|---|---|
| | 0.33 | 15/15 | 28/28 | 112/113 |

| | Factor Trend | Factor Score | Regional Rank | Income Rank | Global Rank |
|---|---|---|---|---|---|
| 🏛 Constraints on Government Powers | — | 0.31 | 15/15 | 26/28 | 109/113 |
| 💰 Absence of Corruption | — | 0.24 | 15/15 | 27/28 | 111/113 |
| 📱 Open Government | — | 0.24 | 15/15 | 27/28 | 112/113 |
| 👤 Fundamental Rights | — | 0.39 | 13/15 | 24/28 | 103/113 |
| 👤 Order & Security | — | 0.65 | 15/15 | 16/28 | 81/113 |
| 👷 Regulatory Enforcement | — | 0.28 | 15/15 | 28/28 | 112/113 |
| ⚖ Civil Justice | — | 0.19 | 15/15 | 28/28 | 113/113 |
| ⚖ Criminal Justice | — | 0.30 | 15/15 | 24/28 | 104/113 |

High ▮▮▮ Low          ▼ Trending down          ▲ Trending up

■ Cambodia          ▨ East Asia & Pacific          ▨ Lower Middle Income

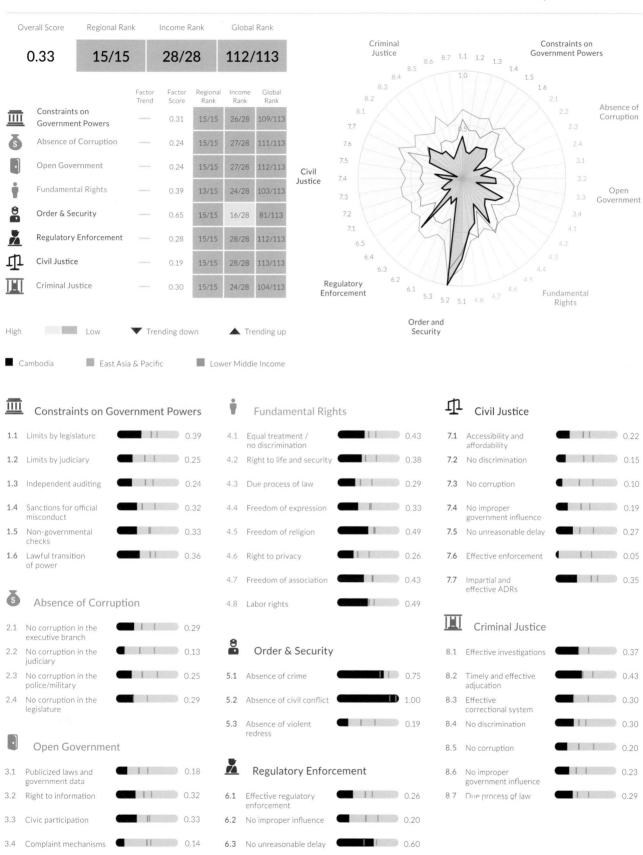

## 🏛 Constraints on Government Powers

| | | |
|---|---|---|
| 1.1 | Limits by legislature | 0.39 |
| 1.2 | Limits by judiciary | 0.25 |
| 1.3 | Independent auditing | 0.24 |
| 1.4 | Sanctions for official misconduct | 0.32 |
| 1.5 | Non-governmental checks | 0.33 |
| 1.6 | Lawful transition of power | 0.36 |

## 💰 Absence of Corruption

| | | |
|---|---|---|
| 2.1 | No corruption in the executive branch | 0.29 |
| 2.2 | No corruption in the judiciary | 0.13 |
| 2.3 | No corruption in the police/military | 0.25 |
| 2.4 | No corruption in the legislature | 0.29 |

## 📱 Open Government

| | | |
|---|---|---|
| 3.1 | Publicized laws and government data | 0.18 |
| 3.2 | Right to information | 0.32 |
| 3.3 | Civic participation | 0.33 |
| 3.4 | Complaint mechanisms | 0.14 |

## 👤 Fundamental Rights

| | | |
|---|---|---|
| 4.1 | Equal treatment / no discrimination | 0.43 |
| 4.2 | Right to life and security | 0.38 |
| 4.3 | Due process of law | 0.29 |
| 4.4 | Freedom of expression | 0.33 |
| 4.5 | Freedom of religion | 0.49 |
| 4.6 | Right to privacy | 0.26 |
| 4.7 | Freedom of association | 0.43 |
| 4.8 | Labor rights | 0.49 |

## 👤 Order & Security

| | | |
|---|---|---|
| 5.1 | Absence of crime | 0.75 |
| 5.2 | Absence of civil conflict | 1.00 |
| 5.3 | Absence of violent redress | 0.19 |

## 👷 Regulatory Enforcement

| | | |
|---|---|---|
| 6.1 | Effective regulatory enforcement | 0.26 |
| 6.2 | No improper influence | 0.20 |
| 6.3 | No unreasonable delay | 0.60 |
| 6.4 | Respect for due process | 0.15 |
| 6.5 | No expropriation w/out adequate compensation | 0.20 |

## ⚖ Civil Justice

| | | |
|---|---|---|
| 7.1 | Accessibility and affordability | 0.22 |
| 7.2 | No discrimination | 0.15 |
| 7.3 | No corruption | 0.10 |
| 7.4 | No improper government influence | 0.19 |
| 7.5 | No unreasonable delay | 0.27 |
| 7.6 | Effective enforcement | 0.05 |
| 7.7 | Impartial and effective ADRs | 0.35 |

## ⚖ Criminal Justice

| | | |
|---|---|---|
| 8.1 | Effective investigations | 0.37 |
| 8.2 | Timely and effective adjucation | 0.43 |
| 8.3 | Effective correctional system | 0.30 |
| 8.4 | No discrimination | 0.30 |
| 8.5 | No corruption | 0.20 |
| 8.6 | No improper government influence | 0.23 |
| 8.7 | Due process of law | 0.29 |

# Cameroon

**Region:** Sub-Saharan Africa
**Income Group:** Lower Middle Income

| | Overall Score | Regional Rank | Income Rank | Global Rank |
|---|---|---|---|---|
| | 0.37 | 18/18 | 26/28 | 109/113 |

| | | Factor Trend | Factor Score | Regional Rank | Income Rank | Global Rank |
|---|---|---|---|---|---|---|
| 🏛 | Constraints on Government Powers | — | 0.41 | 15/18 | 23/28 | 99/113 |
| 💰 | Absence of Corruption | — | 0.24 | 18/18 | 28/28 | 112/113 |
| 📱 | Open Government | — | 0.35 | 16/18 | 24/28 | 104/113 |
| 👤 | Fundamental Rights | ▼ | 0.43 | 15/18 | 22/28 | 99/113 |
| 🔒 | Order & Security | — | 0.47 | 18/18 | 27/28 | 111/113 |
| 🏗 | Regulatory Enforcement | — | 0.38 | 14/18 | 24/28 | 103/113 |
| ⚖ | Civil Justice | — | 0.35 | 18/18 | 26/28 | 109/113 |
| 🏛 | Criminal Justice | — | 0.30 | 17/18 | 25/28 | 105/113 |

High ▢ Low    ▼ Trending down    ▲ Trending up

■ Cameroon    ▨ Sub-Saharan Africa    ▨ Lower Middle Income

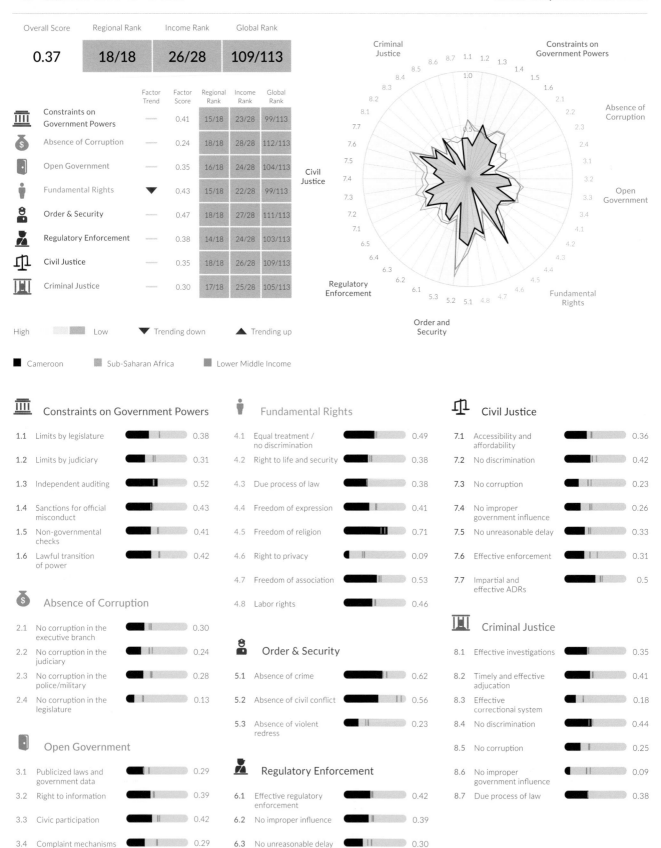

## 🏛 Constraints on Government Powers

| | | |
|---|---|---|
| 1.1 | Limits by legislature | 0.38 |
| 1.2 | Limits by judiciary | 0.31 |
| 1.3 | Independent auditing | 0.52 |
| 1.4 | Sanctions for official misconduct | 0.43 |
| 1.5 | Non-governmental checks | 0.41 |
| 1.6 | Lawful transition of power | 0.42 |

## 💰 Absence of Corruption

| | | |
|---|---|---|
| 2.1 | No corruption in the executive branch | 0.30 |
| 2.2 | No corruption in the judiciary | 0.24 |
| 2.3 | No corruption in the police/military | 0.28 |
| 2.4 | No corruption in the legislature | 0.13 |

## 📱 Open Government

| | | |
|---|---|---|
| 3.1 | Publicized laws and government data | 0.29 |
| 3.2 | Right to information | 0.39 |
| 3.3 | Civic participation | 0.42 |
| 3.4 | Complaint mechanisms | 0.29 |

## 👤 Fundamental Rights

| | | |
|---|---|---|
| 4.1 | Equal treatment / no discrimination | 0.49 |
| 4.2 | Right to life and security | 0.38 |
| 4.3 | Due process of law | 0.38 |
| 4.4 | Freedom of expression | 0.41 |
| 4.5 | Freedom of religion | 0.71 |
| 4.6 | Right to privacy | 0.09 |
| 4.7 | Freedom of association | 0.53 |
| 4.8 | Labor rights | 0.46 |

## 🔒 Order & Security

| | | |
|---|---|---|
| 5.1 | Absence of crime | 0.62 |
| 5.2 | Absence of civil conflict | 0.56 |
| 5.3 | Absence of violent redress | 0.23 |

## 🏗 Regulatory Enforcement

| | | |
|---|---|---|
| 6.1 | Effective regulatory enforcement | 0.42 |
| 6.2 | No improper influence | 0.39 |
| 6.3 | No unreasonable delay | 0.30 |
| 6.4 | Respect for due process | 0.35 |
| 6.5 | No expropriation w/out adequate compensation | 0.46 |

## ⚖ Civil Justice

| | | |
|---|---|---|
| 7.1 | Accessibility and affordability | 0.36 |
| 7.2 | No discrimination | 0.42 |
| 7.3 | No corruption | 0.23 |
| 7.4 | No improper government influence | 0.26 |
| 7.5 | No unreasonable delay | 0.33 |
| 7.6 | Effective enforcement | 0.31 |
| 7.7 | Impartial and effective ADRs | 0.5 |

## 🏛 Criminal Justice

| | | |
|---|---|---|
| 8.1 | Effective investigations | 0.35 |
| 8.2 | Timely and effective adjudication | 0.41 |
| 8.3 | Effective correctional system | 0.18 |
| 8.4 | No discrimination | 0.44 |
| 8.5 | No corruption | 0.25 |
| 8.6 | No improper government influence | 0.09 |
| 8.7 | Due process of law | 0.38 |

# Canada

| | Overall Score | Regional Rank | Income Rank | Global Rank |
|---|---|---|---|---|
| | 0.81 | 9/24 | 12/36 | 12/113 |

| | | Factor Trend | Factor Score | Regional Rank | Income Rank | Global Rank |
|---|---|---|---|---|---|---|
| 🏛️ | Constraints on Government Powers | — | 0.84 | 9/24 | 10/36 | 10/113 |
| 💰 | Absence of Corruption | — | 0.83 | 8/24 | 11/36 | 11/113 |
| 📱 | Open Government | — | 0.80 | 8/24 | 9/36 | 9/113 |
| 🧍 | Fundamental Rights | — | 0.82 | 9/24 | 9/36 | 9/113 |
| 👤 | Order & Security | — | 0.91 | 4/24 | 5/36 | 6/113 |
| 👷 | Regulatory Enforcement | — | 0.79 | 8/24 | 13/36 | 13/113 |
| ⚖️ | Civil Justice | — | 0.72 | 12/24 | 19/36 | 19/113 |
| 🏛️ | Criminal Justice | — | 0.74 | 10/24 | 15/36 | 15/113 |

High ▢ Low ▼ Trending down ▲ Trending up

■ Canada ▨ EU & EFTA & North America ■ High Income

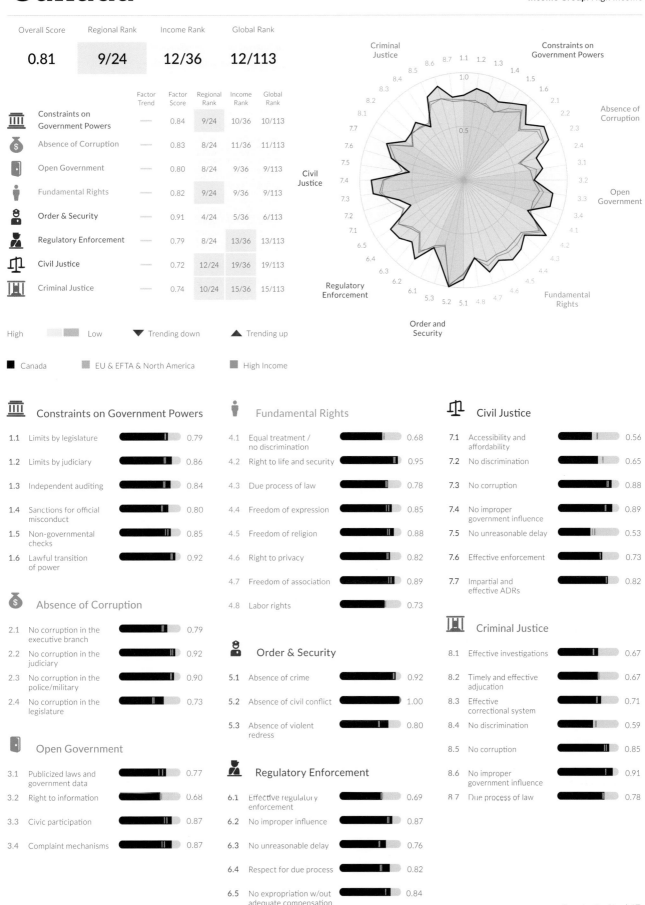

## 🏛️ Constraints on Government Powers

| 1.1 | Limits by legislature | 0.79 |
|---|---|---|
| 1.2 | Limits by judiciary | 0.86 |
| 1.3 | Independent auditing | 0.84 |
| 1.4 | Sanctions for official misconduct | 0.80 |
| 1.5 | Non-governmental checks | 0.85 |
| 1.6 | Lawful transition of power | 0.92 |

## 💰 Absence of Corruption

| 2.1 | No corruption in the executive branch | 0.79 |
|---|---|---|
| 2.2 | No corruption in the judiciary | 0.92 |
| 2.3 | No corruption in the police/military | 0.90 |
| 2.4 | No corruption in the legislature | 0.73 |

## 📱 Open Government

| 3.1 | Publicized laws and government data | 0.77 |
|---|---|---|
| 3.2 | Right to information | 0.68 |
| 3.3 | Civic participation | 0.87 |
| 3.4 | Complaint mechanisms | 0.87 |

## 🧍 Fundamental Rights

| 4.1 | Equal treatment / no discrimination | 0.68 |
|---|---|---|
| 4.2 | Right to life and security | 0.95 |
| 4.3 | Due process of law | 0.78 |
| 4.4 | Freedom of expression | 0.85 |
| 4.5 | Freedom of religion | 0.88 |
| 4.6 | Right to privacy | 0.82 |
| 4.7 | Freedom of association | 0.89 |
| 4.8 | Labor rights | 0.73 |

## 👤 Order & Security

| 5.1 | Absence of crime | 0.92 |
|---|---|---|
| 5.2 | Absence of civil conflict | 1.00 |
| 5.3 | Absence of violent redress | 0.80 |

## 👷 Regulatory Enforcement

| 6.1 | Effective regulatory enforcement | 0.69 |
|---|---|---|
| 6.2 | No improper influence | 0.87 |
| 6.3 | No unreasonable delay | 0.76 |
| 6.4 | Respect for due process | 0.82 |
| 6.5 | No expropriation w/out adequate compensation | 0.84 |

## ⚖️ Civil Justice

| 7.1 | Accessibility and affordability | 0.56 |
|---|---|---|
| 7.2 | No discrimination | 0.65 |
| 7.3 | No corruption | 0.88 |
| 7.4 | No improper government influence | 0.89 |
| 7.5 | No unreasonable delay | 0.53 |
| 7.6 | Effective enforcement | 0.73 |
| 7.7 | Impartial and effective ADRs | 0.82 |

## 🏛️ Criminal Justice

| 8.1 | Effective investigations | 0.67 |
|---|---|---|
| 8.2 | Timely and effective adjudication | 0.67 |
| 8.3 | Effective correctional system | 0.71 |
| 8.4 | No discrimination | 0.59 |
| 8.5 | No corruption | 0.85 |
| 8.6 | No improper government influence | 0.91 |
| 8.7 | Due process of law | 0.78 |

# Chile

| | Overall Score | Regional Rank | Income Rank | Global Rank |
|---|---|---|---|---|
| | 0.68 | 3/30 | 25/36 | 26/113 |

| | | Factor Trend | Factor Score | Regional Rank | Income Rank | Global Rank |
|---|---|---|---|---|---|---|
| 🏛 | Constraints on Government Powers | — | 0.73 | 3/30 | 21/36 | 22/113 |
| 💰 | Absence of Corruption | — | 0.70 | 3/30 | 24/36 | 25/113 |
| 📱 | Open Government | — | 0.72 | 1/30 | 17/36 | 17/113 |
| 👤 | Fundamental Rights | — | 0.75 | 4/30 | 21/36 | 22/113 |
| 👥 | Order & Security | — | 0.68 | 12/30 | 34/36 | 67/113 |
| 👷 | Regulatory Enforcement | — | 0.66 | 4/30 | 25/36 | 26/113 |
| ⚖ | Civil Justice | — | 0.64 | 6/30 | 29/36 | 32/113 |
| ⚖ | Criminal Justice | — | 0.58 | 9/30 | 32/36 | 37/113 |

High ▦ Low    ▼ Trending down    ▲ Trending up

■ Chile    ▦ Latin America & Caribbean    ▦ High Income

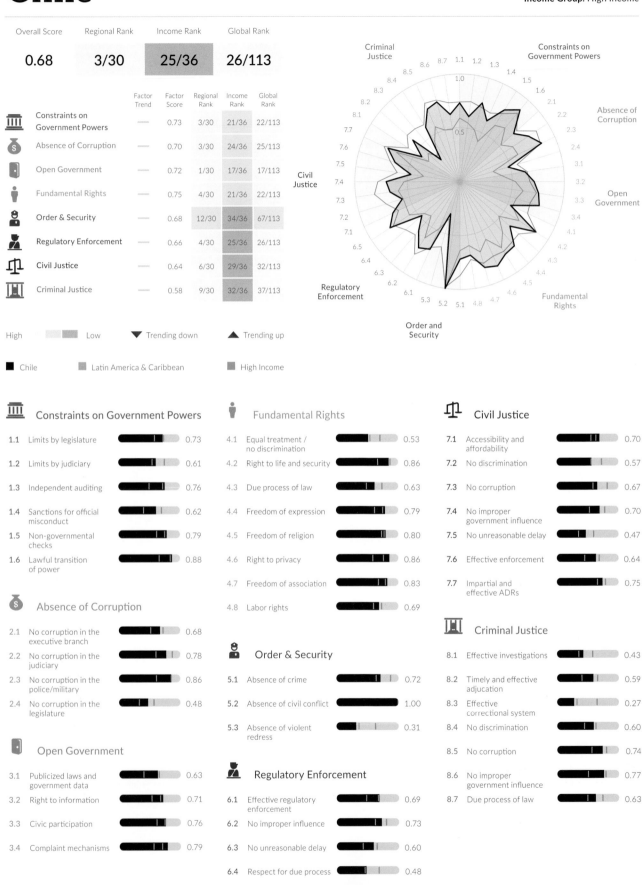

## 🏛 Constraints on Government Powers

| | | | |
|---|---|---|---|
| 1.1 | Limits by legislature | | 0.73 |
| 1.2 | Limits by judiciary | | 0.61 |
| 1.3 | Independent auditing | | 0.76 |
| 1.4 | Sanctions for official misconduct | | 0.62 |
| 1.5 | Non-governmental checks | | 0.79 |
| 1.6 | Lawful transition of power | | 0.88 |

## 💰 Absence of Corruption

| | | | |
|---|---|---|---|
| 2.1 | No corruption in the executive branch | | 0.68 |
| 2.2 | No corruption in the judiciary | | 0.78 |
| 2.3 | No corruption in the police/military | | 0.86 |
| 2.4 | No corruption in the legislature | | 0.48 |

## 📱 Open Government

| | | | |
|---|---|---|---|
| 3.1 | Publicized laws and government data | | 0.63 |
| 3.2 | Right to information | | 0.71 |
| 3.3 | Civic participation | | 0.76 |
| 3.4 | Complaint mechanisms | | 0.79 |

## 👤 Fundamental Rights

| | | | |
|---|---|---|---|
| 4.1 | Equal treatment / no discrimination | | 0.53 |
| 4.2 | Right to life and security | | 0.86 |
| 4.3 | Due process of law | | 0.63 |
| 4.4 | Freedom of expression | | 0.79 |
| 4.5 | Freedom of religion | | 0.80 |
| 4.6 | Right to privacy | | 0.86 |
| 4.7 | Freedom of association | | 0.83 |
| 4.8 | Labor rights | | 0.69 |

## 👥 Order & Security

| | | | |
|---|---|---|---|
| 5.1 | Absence of crime | | 0.72 |
| 5.2 | Absence of civil conflict | | 1.00 |
| 5.3 | Absence of violent redress | | 0.31 |

## 👷 Regulatory Enforcement

| | | | |
|---|---|---|---|
| 6.1 | Effective regulatory enforcement | | 0.69 |
| 6.2 | No improper influence | | 0.73 |
| 6.3 | No unreasonable delay | | 0.60 |
| 6.4 | Respect for due process | | 0.48 |
| 6.5 | No expropriation w/out adequate compensation | | 0.79 |

## ⚖ Civil Justice

| | | | |
|---|---|---|---|
| 7.1 | Accessibility and affordability | | 0.70 |
| 7.2 | No discrimination | | 0.57 |
| 7.3 | No corruption | | 0.67 |
| 7.4 | No improper government influence | | 0.70 |
| 7.5 | No unreasonable delay | | 0.47 |
| 7.6 | Effective enforcement | | 0.64 |
| 7.7 | Impartial and effective ADRs | | 0.75 |

## ⚖ Criminal Justice

| | | | |
|---|---|---|---|
| 8.1 | Effective investigations | | 0.43 |
| 8.2 | Timely and effective adjudication | | 0.59 |
| 8.3 | Effective correctional system | | 0.27 |
| 8.4 | No discrimination | | 0.60 |
| 8.5 | No corruption | | 0.74 |
| 8.6 | No improper government influence | | 0.77 |
| 8.7 | Due process of law | | 0.63 |

# China

**Region:** East Asia & Pacific
**Income Group:** Upper Middle Income

| | Overall Score | Regional Rank | Income Rank | Global Rank |
|---|---|---|---|---|
| | 0.48 | 13/15 | 28/37 | 80/113 |

| | | Factor Trend | Factor Score | Regional Rank | Income Rank | Global Rank |
|---|---|---|---|---|---|---|
| 🏛 | Constraints on Government Powers | — | 0.38 | 14/15 | 34/37 | 104/113 |
| 💰 | Absence of Corruption | — | 0.52 | 8/15 | 15/37 | 52/113 |
| 📱 | Open Government | — | 0.44 | 11/15 | 30/37 | 89/113 |
| 🧍 | Fundamental Rights | — | 0.32 | 14/15 | 36/37 | 108/113 |
| 🧑 | Order & Security | — | 0.76 | 10/15 | 8/37 | 41/113 |
| 🧑‍⚖️ | Regulatory Enforcement | — | 0.45 | 12/15 | 30/37 | 80/113 |
| ⚖️ | Civil Justice | — | 0.52 | 10/15 | 21/37 | 62/113 |
| 🏛 | Criminal Justice | — | 0.47 | 10/15 | 16/37 | 55/113 |

High ▬▬ Low    ▼ Trending down    ▲ Trending up

■ China    ▦ East Asia & Pacific    ▦ Upper Middle Income

## 🏛 Constraints on Government Powers

| | | |
|---|---|---|
| 1.1 | Limits by legislature | 0.58 |
| 1.2 | Limits by judiciary | 0.38 |
| 1.3 | Independent auditing | 0.46 |
| 1.4 | Sanctions for official misconduct | 0.48 |
| 1.5 | Non-governmental checks | 0.14 |
| 1.6 | Lawful transition of power | 0.21 |

## 💰 Absence of Corruption

| | | |
|---|---|---|
| 2.1 | No corruption in the executive branch | 0.48 |
| 2.2 | No corruption in the judiciary | 0.51 |
| 2.3 | No corruption in the police/military | 0.65 |
| 2.4 | No corruption in the legislature | 0.42 |

## 📱 Open Government

| | | |
|---|---|---|
| 3.1 | Publicized laws and government data | 0.42 |
| 3.2 | Right to information | 0.63 |
| 3.3 | Civic participation | 0.21 |
| 3.4 | Complaint mechanisms | 0.49 |

## 🧍 Fundamental Rights

| | | |
|---|---|---|
| 4.1 | Equal treatment / no discrimination | 0.45 |
| 4.2 | Right to life and security | 0.48 |
| 4.3 | Due process of law | 0.51 |
| 4.4 | Freedom of expression | 0.14 |
| 4.5 | Freedom of religion | 0.30 |
| 4.6 | Right to privacy | 0.22 |
| 4.7 | Freedom of association | 0.18 |
| 4.8 | Labor rights | 0.30 |

## 🧑 Order & Security

| | | |
|---|---|---|
| 5.1 | Absence of crime | 0.79 |
| 5.2 | Absence of civil conflict | 0.77 |
| 5.3 | Absence of violent redress | 0.71 |

## 🧑‍⚖️ Regulatory Enforcement

| | | |
|---|---|---|
| 6.1 | Effective regulatory enforcement | 0.5 |
| 6.2 | No improper influence | 0.54 |
| 6.3 | No unreasonable delay | 0.57 |
| 6.4 | Respect for due process | 0.23 |
| 6.5 | No expropriation w/out adequate compensation | 0.41 |

## ⚖️ Civil Justice

| | | |
|---|---|---|
| 7.1 | Accessibility and affordability | 0.59 |
| 7.2 | No discrimination | 0.43 |
| 7.3 | No corruption | 0.45 |
| 7.4 | No improper government influence | 0.23 |
| 7.5 | No unreasonable delay | 0.76 |
| 7.6 | Effective enforcement | 0.58 |
| 7.7 | Impartial and effective ADRs | 0.62 |

## 🏛 Criminal Justice

| | | |
|---|---|---|
| 8.1 | Effective investigations | 0.65 |
| 8.2 | Timely and effective adjudication | 0.65 |
| 8.3 | Effective correctional system | 0.37 |
| 8.4 | No discrimination | 0.40 |
| 8.5 | No corruption | 0.60 |
| 8.6 | No improper government influence | 0.11 |
| 8.7 | Due process of law | 0.51 |

# Colombia

**Region:** Latin America & Caribbean
**Income Group:** Upper Middle Income

| Overall Score | Regional Rank | Income Rank | Global Rank |
|---|---|---|---|
| 0.51 | 19/30 | 23/37 | 71/113 |

| | Factor Trend | Factor Score | Regional Rank | Income Rank | Global Rank |
|---|---|---|---|---|---|
| Constraints on Government Powers | — | 0.53 | 18/30 | 17/37 | 63/113 |
| Absence of Corruption | — | 0.41 | 22/30 | 29/37 | 77/113 |
| Open Government | — | 0.64 | 4/30 | 3/37 | 30/113 |
| Fundamental Rights | — | 0.55 | 20/30 | 19/37 | 65/113 |
| Order & Security | — | 0.55 | 29/30 | 36/37 | 106/113 |
| Regulatory Enforcement | — | 0.52 | 15/30 | 15/37 | 51/113 |
| Civil Justice | — | 0.50 | 17/30 | 25/37 | 70/113 |
| Criminal Justice | — | 0.34 | 20/30 | 29/37 | 91/113 |

High ▮▮▮ Low    ▼ Trending down    ▲ Trending up

■ Colombia    ▮ Latin America & Caribbean    ▮ Upper Middle Income

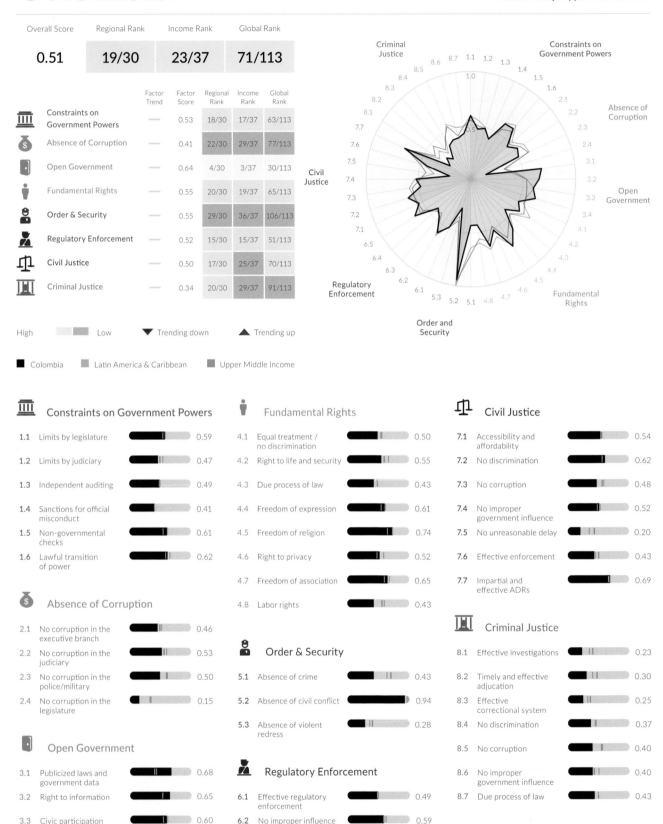

## Constraints on Government Powers

| | | |
|---|---|---|
| 1.1 | Limits by legislature | 0.59 |
| 1.2 | Limits by judiciary | 0.47 |
| 1.3 | Independent auditing | 0.49 |
| 1.4 | Sanctions for official misconduct | 0.41 |
| 1.5 | Non-governmental checks | 0.61 |
| 1.6 | Lawful transition of power | 0.62 |

## Absence of Corruption

| | | |
|---|---|---|
| 2.1 | No corruption in the executive branch | 0.46 |
| 2.2 | No corruption in the judiciary | 0.53 |
| 2.3 | No corruption in the police/military | 0.50 |
| 2.4 | No corruption in the legislature | 0.15 |

## Open Government

| | | |
|---|---|---|
| 3.1 | Publicized laws and government data | 0.68 |
| 3.2 | Right to information | 0.65 |
| 3.3 | Civic participation | 0.60 |
| 3.4 | Complaint mechanisms | 0.64 |

## Fundamental Rights

| | | |
|---|---|---|
| 4.1 | Equal treatment / no discrimination | 0.50 |
| 4.2 | Right to life and security | 0.55 |
| 4.3 | Due process of law | 0.43 |
| 4.4 | Freedom of expression | 0.61 |
| 4.5 | Freedom of religion | 0.74 |
| 4.6 | Right to privacy | 0.52 |
| 4.7 | Freedom of association | 0.65 |
| 4.8 | Labor rights | 0.43 |

## Order & Security

| | | |
|---|---|---|
| 5.1 | Absence of crime | 0.43 |
| 5.2 | Absence of civil conflict | 0.94 |
| 5.3 | Absence of violent redress | 0.28 |

## Regulatory Enforcement

| | | |
|---|---|---|
| 6.1 | Effective regulatory enforcement | 0.49 |
| 6.2 | No improper influence | 0.59 |
| 6.3 | No unreasonable delay | 0.46 |
| 6.4 | Respect for due process | 0.41 |
| 6.5 | No expropriation w/out adequate compensation | 0.63 |

## Civil Justice

| | | |
|---|---|---|
| 7.1 | Accessibility and affordability | 0.54 |
| 7.2 | No discrimination | 0.62 |
| 7.3 | No corruption | 0.48 |
| 7.4 | No improper government influence | 0.52 |
| 7.5 | No unreasonable delay | 0.20 |
| 7.6 | Effective enforcement | 0.43 |
| 7.7 | Impartial and effective ADRs | 0.69 |

## Criminal Justice

| | | |
|---|---|---|
| 8.1 | Effective investigations | 0.23 |
| 8.2 | Timely and effective adjucation | 0.30 |
| 8.3 | Effective correctional system | 0.25 |
| 8.4 | No discrimination | 0.37 |
| 8.5 | No corruption | 0.40 |
| 8.6 | No improper government influence | 0.40 |
| 8.7 | Due process of law | 0.43 |

# Costa Rica

**Region:** Latin America & Caribbean
**Income Group:** Upper Middle Income

| | Overall Score | Regional Rank | Income Rank | Global Rank |
|---|---|---|---|---|
| | 0.68 | 2/30 | 1/37 | 25/113 |

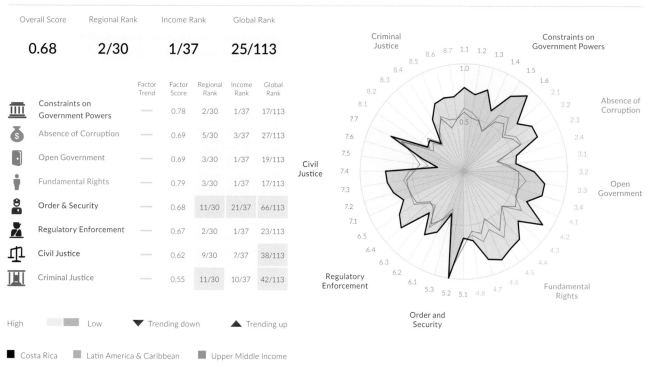

| | Factor Trend | Factor Score | Regional Rank | Income Rank | Global Rank |
|---|---|---|---|---|---|
| Constraints on Government Powers | — | 0.78 | 2/30 | 1/37 | 17/113 |
| Absence of Corruption | — | 0.69 | 5/30 | 3/37 | 27/113 |
| Open Government | — | 0.69 | 3/30 | 1/37 | 19/113 |
| Fundamental Rights | — | 0.79 | 3/30 | 1/37 | 17/113 |
| Order & Security | — | 0.68 | 11/30 | 21/37 | 66/113 |
| Regulatory Enforcement | — | 0.67 | 2/30 | 1/37 | 23/113 |
| Civil Justice | — | 0.62 | 9/30 | 7/37 | 38/113 |
| Criminal Justice | — | 0.55 | 11/30 | 10/37 | 42/113 |

High ▬▬ Low   ▼ Trending down   ▲ Trending up

■ Costa Rica   ■ Latin America & Caribbean   ■ Upper Middle Income

## Constraints on Government Powers

| | | |
|---|---|---|
| 1.1 | Limits by legislature | 0.78 |
| 1.2 | Limits by judiciary | 0.72 |
| 1.3 | Independent auditing | 0.79 |
| 1.4 | Sanctions for official misconduct | 0.62 |
| 1.5 | Non-governmental checks | 0.83 |
| 1.6 | Lawful transition of power | 0.93 |

## Absence of Corruption

| | | |
|---|---|---|
| 2.1 | No corruption in the executive branch | 0.68 |
| 2.2 | No corruption in the judiciary | 0.78 |
| 2.3 | No corruption in the police/military | 0.78 |
| 2.4 | No corruption in the legislature | 0.53 |

## Open Government

| | | |
|---|---|---|
| 3.1 | Publicized laws and government data | 0.51 |
| 3.2 | Right to information | 0.68 |
| 3.3 | Civic participation | 0.79 |
| 3.4 | Complaint mechanisms | 0.79 |

## Fundamental Rights

| | | |
|---|---|---|
| 4.1 | Equal treatment / no discrimination | 0.67 |
| 4.2 | Right to life and security | 0.91 |
| 4.3 | Due process of law | 0.70 |
| 4.4 | Freedom of expression | 0.83 |
| 4.5 | Freedom of religion | 0.85 |
| 4.6 | Right to privacy | 0.90 |
| 4.7 | Freedom of association | 0.85 |
| 4.8 | Labor rights | 0.65 |

## Order & Security

| | | |
|---|---|---|
| 5.1 | Absence of crime | 0.62 |
| 5.2 | Absence of civil conflict | 1.00 |
| 5.3 | Absence of violent redress | 0.41 |

## Regulatory Enforcement

| | | |
|---|---|---|
| 6.1 | Effective regulatory enforcement | 0.62 |
| 6.2 | No improper influence | 0.70 |
| 6.3 | No unreasonable delay | 0.51 |
| 6.4 | Respect for due process | 0.80 |
| 6.5 | No expropriation w/out adequate compensation | 0.74 |

## Civil Justice

| | | |
|---|---|---|
| 7.1 | Accessibility and affordability | 0.64 |
| 7.2 | No discrimination | 0.71 |
| 7.3 | No corruption | 0.75 |
| 7.4 | No improper government influence | 0.76 |
| 7.5 | No unreasonable delay | 0.26 |
| 7.6 | Effective enforcement | 0.42 |
| 7.7 | Impartial and effective ADRs | 0.78 |

## Criminal Justice

| | | |
|---|---|---|
| 8.1 | Effective investigations | 0.42 |
| 8.2 | Timely and effective adjucation | 0.44 |
| 8.3 | Effective correctional system | 0.34 |
| 8.4 | No discrimination | 0.57 |
| 8.5 | No corruption | 0.69 |
| 8.6 | No improper government influence | 0.71 |
| 8.7 | Due process of law | 0.70 |

# Cote d'Ivoire

| | Overall Score | Regional Rank | Income Rank | Global Rank |
|---|---|---|---|---|
| | 0.46 | 9/18 | 15/28 | 87/113 |

| | | Factor Trend | Factor Score | Regional Rank | Income Rank | Global Rank |
|---|---|---|---|---|---|---|
| 🏛 | Constraints on Government Powers | — | 0.45 | 14/18 | 19/28 | 89/113 |
| 💰 | Absence of Corruption | — | 0.38 | 8/18 | 14/28 | 85/113 |
| 📱 | Open Government | — | 0.37 | 15/18 | 23/28 | 103/113 |
| 👤 | Fundamental Rights | — | 0.45 | 13/18 | 19/28 | 94/113 |
| 👮 | Order & Security | — | 0.71 | 3/18 | 9/28 | 61/113 |
| 👨‍⚖ | Regulatory Enforcement | — | 0.49 | 5/18 | 8/28 | 65/113 |
| ⚖ | Civil Justice | — | 0.51 | 6/18 | 5/28 | 66/113 |
| ⚖ | Criminal Justice | — | 0.37 | 11/18 | 16/28 | 83/113 |

High ▭ Low     ▼ Trending down     ▲ Trending up

■ Cote d'Ivoire     ▨ Sub-Saharan Africa     ▨ Lower Middle Income

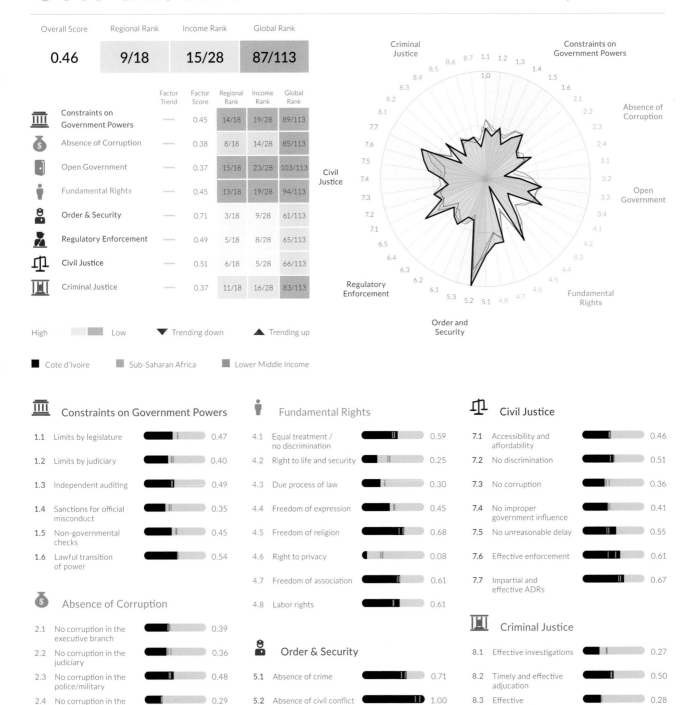

## 🏛 Constraints on Government Powers

| | | |
|---|---|---|
| 1.1 | Limits by legislature | 0.47 |
| 1.2 | Limits by judiciary | 0.40 |
| 1.3 | Independent auditing | 0.49 |
| 1.4 | Sanctions for official misconduct | 0.35 |
| 1.5 | Non-governmental checks | 0.45 |
| 1.6 | Lawful transition of power | 0.54 |

## 💰 Absence of Corruption

| | | |
|---|---|---|
| 2.1 | No corruption in the executive branch | 0.39 |
| 2.2 | No corruption in the judiciary | 0.36 |
| 2.3 | No corruption in the police/military | 0.48 |
| 2.4 | No corruption in the legislature | 0.29 |

## 📱 Open Government

| | | |
|---|---|---|
| 3.1 | Publicized laws and government data | 0.18 |
| 3.2 | Right to information | 0.33 |
| 3.3 | Civic participation | 0.54 |
| 3.4 | Complaint mechanisms | 0.42 |

## 👤 Fundamental Rights

| | | |
|---|---|---|
| 4.1 | Equal treatment / no discrimination | 0.59 |
| 4.2 | Right to life and security | 0.25 |
| 4.3 | Due process of law | 0.30 |
| 4.4 | Freedom of expression | 0.45 |
| 4.5 | Freedom of religion | 0.68 |
| 4.6 | Right to privacy | 0.08 |
| 4.7 | Freedom of association | 0.61 |
| 4.8 | Labor rights | 0.61 |

## 👮 Order & Security

| | | |
|---|---|---|
| 5.1 | Absence of crime | 0.71 |
| 5.2 | Absence of civil conflict | 1.00 |
| 5.3 | Absence of violent redress | 0.40 |

## 👨‍⚖ Regulatory Enforcement

| | | |
|---|---|---|
| 6.1 | Effective regulatory enforcement | 0.39 |
| 6.2 | No improper influence | 0.50 |
| 6.3 | No unreasonable delay | 0.46 |
| 6.4 | Respect for due process | 0.40 |
| 6.5 | No expropriation w/out adequate compensation | 0.68 |

## ⚖ Civil Justice

| | | |
|---|---|---|
| 7.1 | Accessibility and affordability | 0.46 |
| 7.2 | No discrimination | 0.51 |
| 7.3 | No corruption | 0.36 |
| 7.4 | No improper government influence | 0.41 |
| 7.5 | No unreasonable delay | 0.55 |
| 7.6 | Effective enforcement | 0.61 |
| 7.7 | Impartial and effective ADRs | 0.67 |

## ⚖ Criminal Justice

| | | |
|---|---|---|
| 8.1 | Effective investigations | 0.27 |
| 8.2 | Timely and effective adjucation | 0.50 |
| 8.3 | Effective correctional system | 0.28 |
| 8.4 | No discrimination | 0.43 |
| 8.5 | No corruption | 0.39 |
| 8.6 | No improper government influence | 0.40 |
| 8.7 | Due process of law | 0.30 |

# Croatia

| | Overall Score | Regional Rank | Income Rank | Global Rank |
|---|---|---|---|---|
| | 0.61 | 21/24 | 33/36 | 39/113 |

| | | Factor Trend | Factor Score | Regional Rank | Income Rank | Global Rank |
|---|---|---|---|---|---|---|
| 🏛 | Constraints on Government Powers | — | 0.60 | 22/24 | 35/36 | 50/113 |
| 💰 | Absence of Corruption | — | 0.57 | 20/24 | 33/36 | 42/113 |
| 📱 | Open Government | — | 0.59 | 21/24 | 28/36 | 36/113 |
| 🧍 | Fundamental Rights | — | 0.69 | 21/24 | 30/36 | 34/113 |
| 👮 | Order & Security | — | 0.82 | 17/24 | 23/36 | 25/113 |
| 🧑‍⚖ | Regulatory Enforcement | — | 0.50 | 24/24 | 35/36 | 61/113 |
| ⚖ | Civil Justice | — | 0.53 | 23/24 | 35/36 | 60/113 |
| 🏛 | Criminal Justice | — | 0.54 | 22/24 | 34/36 | 45/113 |

High ▨ Low    ▼ Trending down    ▲ Trending up

■ Croatia    ▨ EU & EFTA & North America    ▨ High Income

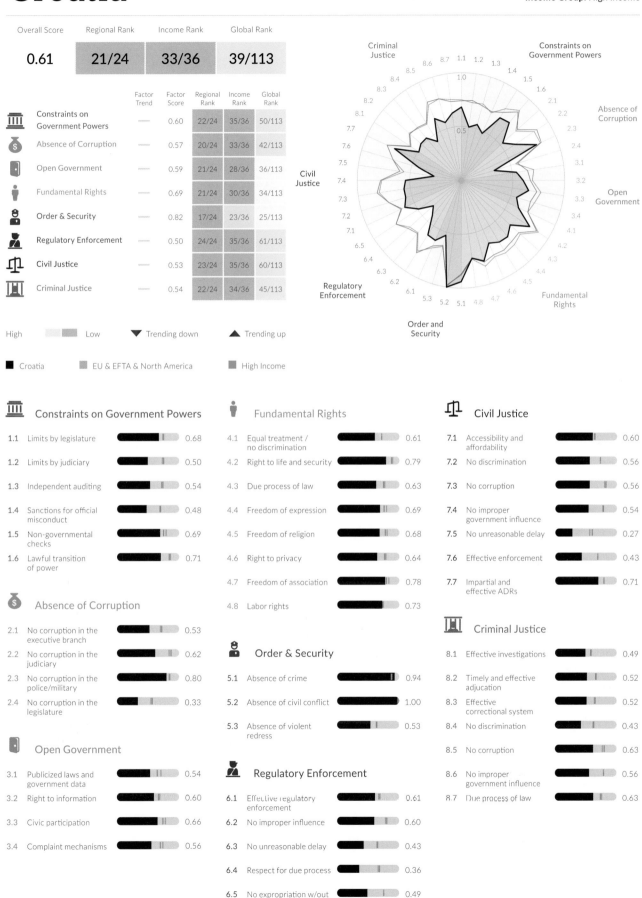

## 🏛 Constraints on Government Powers

| | | |
|---|---|---|
| 1.1 | Limits by legislature | 0.68 |
| 1.2 | Limits by judiciary | 0.50 |
| 1.3 | Independent auditing | 0.54 |
| 1.4 | Sanctions for official misconduct | 0.48 |
| 1.5 | Non-governmental checks | 0.69 |
| 1.6 | Lawful transition of power | 0.71 |

## 💰 Absence of Corruption

| | | |
|---|---|---|
| 2.1 | No corruption in the executive branch | 0.53 |
| 2.2 | No corruption in the judiciary | 0.62 |
| 2.3 | No corruption in the police/military | 0.80 |
| 2.4 | No corruption in the legislature | 0.33 |

## 📱 Open Government

| | | |
|---|---|---|
| 3.1 | Publicized laws and government data | 0.54 |
| 3.2 | Right to information | 0.60 |
| 3.3 | Civic participation | 0.66 |
| 3.4 | Complaint mechanisms | 0.56 |

## 🧍 Fundamental Rights

| | | |
|---|---|---|
| 4.1 | Equal treatment / no discrimination | 0.61 |
| 4.2 | Right to life and security | 0.79 |
| 4.3 | Due process of law | 0.63 |
| 4.4 | Freedom of expression | 0.69 |
| 4.5 | Freedom of religion | 0.68 |
| 4.6 | Right to privacy | 0.64 |
| 4.7 | Freedom of association | 0.78 |
| 4.8 | Labor rights | 0.73 |

## 👮 Order & Security

| | | |
|---|---|---|
| 5.1 | Absence of crime | 0.94 |
| 5.2 | Absence of civil conflict | 1.00 |
| 5.3 | Absence of violent redress | 0.53 |

## 🧑‍⚖ Regulatory Enforcement

| | | |
|---|---|---|
| 6.1 | Effective regulatory enforcement | 0.61 |
| 6.2 | No improper influence | 0.60 |
| 6.3 | No unreasonable delay | 0.43 |
| 6.4 | Respect for due process | 0.36 |
| 6.5 | No expropriation w/out adequate compensation | 0.49 |

## ⚖ Civil Justice

| | | |
|---|---|---|
| 7.1 | Accessibility and affordability | 0.60 |
| 7.2 | No discrimination | 0.56 |
| 7.3 | No corruption | 0.56 |
| 7.4 | No improper government influence | 0.54 |
| 7.5 | No unreasonable delay | 0.27 |
| 7.6 | Effective enforcement | 0.43 |
| 7.7 | Impartial and effective ADRs | 0.71 |

## 🏛 Criminal Justice

| | | |
|---|---|---|
| 8.1 | Effective investigations | 0.49 |
| 8.2 | Timely and effective adjudication | 0.52 |
| 8.3 | Effective correctional system | 0.52 |
| 8.4 | No discrimination | 0.43 |
| 8.5 | No corruption | 0.63 |
| 8.6 | No improper government influence | 0.56 |
| 8.7 | Due process of law | 0.63 |

# Czech Republic

| | Overall Score | Regional Rank | Income Rank | Global Rank |
|---|---|---|---|---|
| | 0.75 | 12/24 | 17/36 | 17/113 |

| | | Factor Trend | Factor Score | Regional Rank | Income Rank | Global Rank |
|---|---|---|---|---|---|---|
| 🏛️ | Constraints on Government Powers | — | 0.76 | 15/24 | 18/36 | 19/113 |
| 💰 | Absence of Corruption | — | 0.68 | 17/24 | 26/36 | 30/113 |
| 📱 | Open Government | — | 0.69 | 15/24 | 19/36 | 20/113 |
| 👤 | Fundamental Rights | — | 0.81 | 10/24 | 11/36 | 11/113 |
| 👮 | Order & Security | — | 0.89 | 7/24 | 9/36 | 10/113 |
| 🧑‍⚖️ | Regulatory Enforcement | — | 0.68 | 14/24 | 22/36 | 22/113 |
| ⚖️ | Civil Justice | — | 0.73 | 11/24 | 18/36 | 18/113 |
| ⚱️ | Criminal Justice | — | 0.73 | 11/24 | 16/36 | 16/113 |

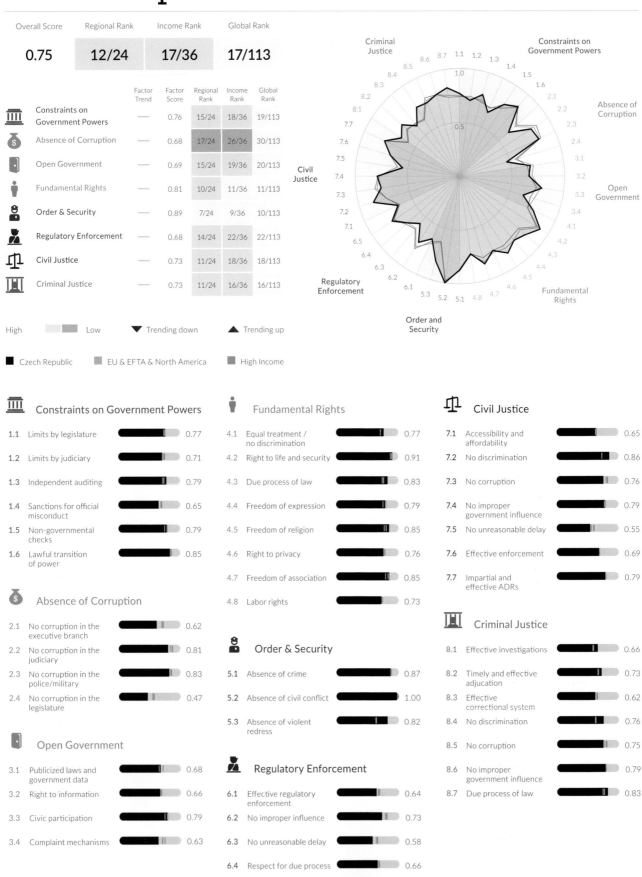

High  ▬▬  Low       ▼ Trending down       ▲ Trending up

■ Czech Republic    ■ EU & EFTA & North America    ■ High Income

## 🏛️ Constraints on Government Powers

| | | |
|---|---|---|
| 1.1 | Limits by legislature | 0.77 |
| 1.2 | Limits by judiciary | 0.71 |
| 1.3 | Independent auditing | 0.79 |
| 1.4 | Sanctions for official misconduct | 0.65 |
| 1.5 | Non-governmental checks | 0.79 |
| 1.6 | Lawful transition of power | 0.85 |

## 💰 Absence of Corruption

| | | |
|---|---|---|
| 2.1 | No corruption in the executive branch | 0.62 |
| 2.2 | No corruption in the judiciary | 0.81 |
| 2.3 | No corruption in the police/military | 0.83 |
| 2.4 | No corruption in the legislature | 0.47 |

## 📱 Open Government

| | | |
|---|---|---|
| 3.1 | Publicized laws and government data | 0.68 |
| 3.2 | Right to information | 0.66 |
| 3.3 | Civic participation | 0.79 |
| 3.4 | Complaint mechanisms | 0.63 |

## 👤 Fundamental Rights

| | | |
|---|---|---|
| 4.1 | Equal treatment / no discrimination | 0.77 |
| 4.2 | Right to life and security | 0.91 |
| 4.3 | Due process of law | 0.83 |
| 4.4 | Freedom of expression | 0.79 |
| 4.5 | Freedom of religion | 0.85 |
| 4.6 | Right to privacy | 0.76 |
| 4.7 | Freedom of association | 0.85 |
| 4.8 | Labor rights | 0.73 |

## 👮 Order & Security

| | | |
|---|---|---|
| 5.1 | Absence of crime | 0.87 |
| 5.2 | Absence of civil conflict | 1.00 |
| 5.3 | Absence of violent redress | 0.82 |

## 🧑‍⚖️ Regulatory Enforcement

| | | |
|---|---|---|
| 6.1 | Effective regulatory enforcement | 0.64 |
| 6.2 | No improper influence | 0.73 |
| 6.3 | No unreasonable delay | 0.58 |
| 6.4 | Respect for due process | 0.66 |
| 6.5 | No expropriation w/out adequate compensation | 0.77 |

## ⚖️ Civil Justice

| | | |
|---|---|---|
| 7.1 | Accessibility and affordability | 0.65 |
| 7.2 | No discrimination | 0.86 |
| 7.3 | No corruption | 0.76 |
| 7.4 | No improper government influence | 0.79 |
| 7.5 | No unreasonable delay | 0.55 |
| 7.6 | Effective enforcement | 0.69 |
| 7.7 | Impartial and effective ADRs | 0.79 |

## ⚱️ Criminal Justice

| | | |
|---|---|---|
| 8.1 | Effective investigations | 0.66 |
| 8.2 | Timely and effective adjudication | 0.73 |
| 8.3 | Effective correctional system | 0.62 |
| 8.4 | No discrimination | 0.76 |
| 8.5 | No corruption | 0.75 |
| 8.6 | No improper government influence | 0.79 |
| 8.7 | Due process of law | 0.83 |

# Denmark

**Region:** EU & EFTA & North America
**Income Group:** High Income

| Overall Score | Regional Rank | Income Rank | Global Rank |
|---|---|---|---|
| 0.89 | 1/24 | 1/36 | 1/113 |

|  |  | Factor Trend | Factor Score | Regional Rank | Income Rank | Global Rank |
|---|---|---|---|---|---|---|
| 🏛 | Constraints on Government Powers | — | 0.93 | 1/24 | 1/36 | 1/113 |
| 💰 | Absence of Corruption | — | 0.96 | 1/24 | 1/36 | 1/113 |
| 📱 | Open Government | — | 0.86 | 2/24 | 2/36 | 2/113 |
| 🧍 | Fundamental Rights | — | 0.92 | 1/24 | 1/36 | 1/113 |
| 👮 | Order & Security | — | 0.92 | 3/24 | 4/36 | 4/113 |
| 👷 | Regulatory Enforcement | — | 0.85 | 5/24 | 6/36 | 6/113 |
| ⚖ | Civil Justice | — | 0.84 | 4/24 | 5/36 | 5/113 |
| 🏛 | Criminal Justice | — | 0.82 | 4/24 | 5/36 | 5/113 |

High ▢ Low       ▼ Trending down       ▲ Trending up

■ Denmark       ▨ EU & EFTA & North America       ■ High Income

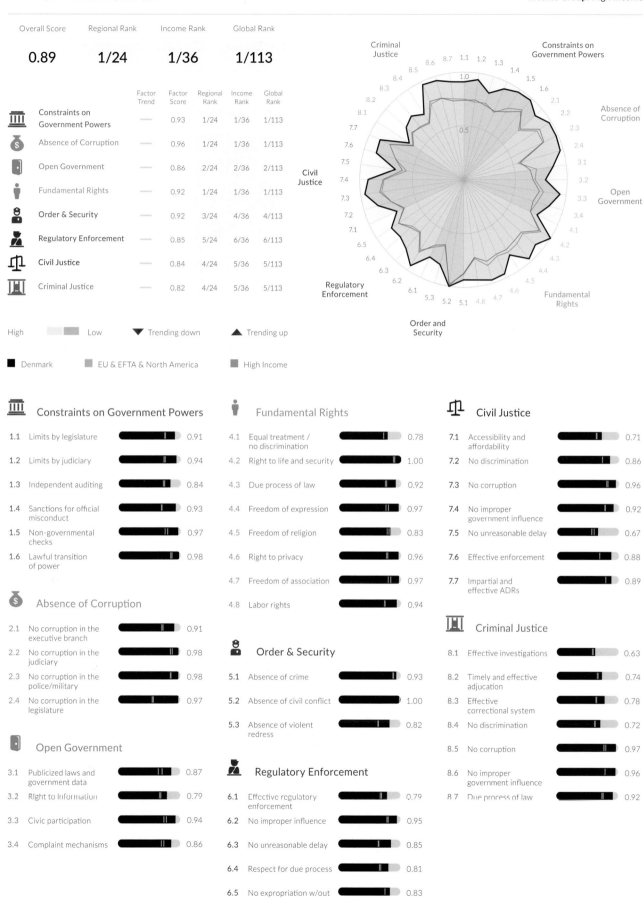

## 🏛 Constraints on Government Powers

| 1.1 | Limits by legislature | 0.91 |
|---|---|---|
| 1.2 | Limits by judiciary | 0.94 |
| 1.3 | Independent auditing | 0.84 |
| 1.4 | Sanctions for official misconduct | 0.93 |
| 1.5 | Non-governmental checks | 0.97 |
| 1.6 | Lawful transition of power | 0.98 |

## 💰 Absence of Corruption

| 2.1 | No corruption in the executive branch | 0.91 |
|---|---|---|
| 2.2 | No corruption in the judiciary | 0.98 |
| 2.3 | No corruption in the police/military | 0.98 |
| 2.4 | No corruption in the legislature | 0.97 |

## 📱 Open Government

| 3.1 | Publicized laws and government data | 0.87 |
|---|---|---|
| 3.2 | Right to information | 0.79 |
| 3.3 | Civic participation | 0.94 |
| 3.4 | Complaint mechanisms | 0.86 |

## 🧍 Fundamental Rights

| 4.1 | Equal treatment / no discrimination | 0.78 |
|---|---|---|
| 4.2 | Right to life and security | 1.00 |
| 4.3 | Due process of law | 0.92 |
| 4.4 | Freedom of expression | 0.97 |
| 4.5 | Freedom of religion | 0.83 |
| 4.6 | Right to privacy | 0.96 |
| 4.7 | Freedom of association | 0.97 |
| 4.8 | Labor rights | 0.94 |

## 👮 Order & Security

| 5.1 | Absence of crime | 0.93 |
|---|---|---|
| 5.2 | Absence of civil conflict | 1.00 |
| 5.3 | Absence of violent redress | 0.82 |

## 👷 Regulatory Enforcement

| 6.1 | Effective regulatory enforcement | 0.79 |
|---|---|---|
| 6.2 | No improper influence | 0.95 |
| 6.3 | No unreasonable delay | 0.85 |
| 6.4 | Respect for due process | 0.81 |
| 6.5 | No expropriation w/out adequate compensation | 0.83 |

## ⚖ Civil Justice

| 7.1 | Accessibility and affordability | 0.71 |
|---|---|---|
| 7.2 | No discrimination | 0.86 |
| 7.3 | No corruption | 0.96 |
| 7.4 | No improper government influence | 0.92 |
| 7.5 | No unreasonable delay | 0.67 |
| 7.6 | Effective enforcement | 0.88 |
| 7.7 | Impartial and effective ADRs | 0.89 |

## 🏛 Criminal Justice

| 8.1 | Effective investigations | 0.63 |
|---|---|---|
| 8.2 | Timely and effective adjucation | 0.74 |
| 8.3 | Effective correctional system | 0.78 |
| 8.4 | No discrimination | 0.72 |
| 8.5 | No corruption | 0.97 |
| 8.6 | No improper government influence | 0.96 |
| 8.7 | Due process of law | 0.92 |

# Dominica

| | Overall Score | Regional Rank | Income Rank | Global Rank |
|---|---|---|---|---|
| | 0.60 | 11/30 | 7/37 | 40/113 |

| | | Factor Trend | Factor Score | Regional Rank | Income Rank | Global Rank |
|---|---|---|---|---|---|---|
| 🏛 | Constraints on Government Powers | — | 0.57 | 16/30 | 13/37 | 56/113 |
| 💰 | Absence of Corruption | — | 0.65 | 10/30 | 7/37 | 36/113 |
| 📱 | Open Government | — | 0.50 | 18/30 | 20/37 | 65/113 |
| 👤 | Fundamental Rights | — | 0.68 | 10/30 | 6/37 | 37/113 |
| 👮 | Order & Security | — | 0.75 | 5/30 | 10/37 | 44/113 |
| 👷 | Regulatory Enforcement | — | 0.52 | 14/30 | 14/37 | 50/113 |
| ⚖ | Civil Justice | — | 0.61 | 10/30 | 9/37 | 40/113 |
| ⚖ | Criminal Justice | — | 0.56 | 10/30 | 8/37 | 40/113 |

High ▬▬ Low    ▼ Trending down    ▲ Trending up

■ Dominica    ▨ Latin America & Caribbean    ▨ Upper Middle Income

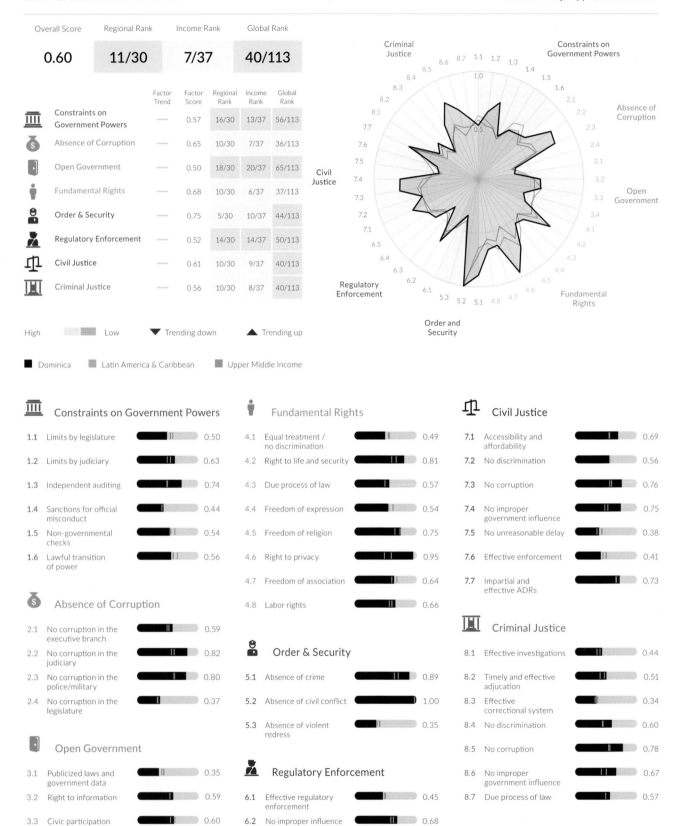

## 🏛 Constraints on Government Powers

| | | | |
|---|---|---|---|
| 1.1 | Limits by legislature | | 0.50 |
| 1.2 | Limits by judiciary | | 0.63 |
| 1.3 | Independent auditing | | 0.74 |
| 1.4 | Sanctions for official misconduct | | 0.44 |
| 1.5 | Non-governmental checks | | 0.54 |
| 1.6 | Lawful transition of power | | 0.56 |

## 💰 Absence of Corruption

| | | | |
|---|---|---|---|
| 2.1 | No corruption in the executive branch | | 0.59 |
| 2.2 | No corruption in the judiciary | | 0.82 |
| 2.3 | No corruption in the police/military | | 0.80 |
| 2.4 | No corruption in the legislature | | 0.37 |

## 📱 Open Government

| | | | |
|---|---|---|---|
| 3.1 | Publicized laws and government data | | 0.35 |
| 3.2 | Right to information | | 0.59 |
| 3.3 | Civic participation | | 0.60 |
| 3.4 | Complaint mechanisms | | 0.45 |

## 👤 Fundamental Rights

| | | | |
|---|---|---|---|
| 4.1 | Equal treatment / no discrimination | | 0.49 |
| 4.2 | Right to life and security | | 0.81 |
| 4.3 | Due process of law | | 0.57 |
| 4.4 | Freedom of expression | | 0.54 |
| 4.5 | Freedom of religion | | 0.75 |
| 4.6 | Right to privacy | | 0.95 |
| 4.7 | Freedom of association | | 0.64 |
| 4.8 | Labor rights | | 0.66 |

## 👮 Order & Security

| | | | |
|---|---|---|---|
| 5.1 | Absence of crime | | 0.89 |
| 5.2 | Absence of civil conflict | | 1.00 |
| 5.3 | Absence of violent redress | | 0.35 |

## 👷 Regulatory Enforcement

| | | | |
|---|---|---|---|
| 6.1 | Effective regulatory enforcement | | 0.45 |
| 6.2 | No improper influence | | 0.68 |
| 6.3 | No unreasonable delay | | 0.34 |
| 6.4 | Respect for due process | | 0.54 |
| 6.5 | No expropriation w/out adequate compensation | | 0.57 |

## ⚖ Civil Justice

| | | | |
|---|---|---|---|
| 7.1 | Accessibility and affordability | | 0.69 |
| 7.2 | No discrimination | | 0.56 |
| 7.3 | No corruption | | 0.76 |
| 7.4 | No improper government influence | | 0.75 |
| 7.5 | No unreasonable delay | | 0.38 |
| 7.6 | Effective enforcement | | 0.41 |
| 7.7 | Impartial and effective ADRs | | 0.73 |

## ⚖ Criminal Justice

| | | | |
|---|---|---|---|
| 8.1 | Effective investigations | | 0.44 |
| 8.2 | Timely and effective adjucation | | 0.51 |
| 8.3 | Effective correctional system | | 0.34 |
| 8.4 | No discrimination | | 0.60 |
| 8.5 | No corruption | | 0.78 |
| 8.6 | No improper government influence | | 0.67 |
| 8.7 | Due process of law | | 0.57 |

# Dominican Republic

**Region:** Latin America & Caribbean
**Income Group:** Upper Middle Income

| Overall Score | Regional Rank | Income Rank | Global Rank |
|---|---|---|---|
| 0.47 | 23/30 | 30/37 | 85/113 |

| | Factor Trend | Factor Score | Regional Rank | Income Rank | Global Rank |
|---|---|---|---|---|---|
| Constraints on Government Powers | ▼ | 0.44 | 26/30 | 29/37 | 93/113 |
| Absence of Corruption | — | 0.34 | 26/30 | 34/37 | 93/113 |
| Open Government | — | 0.54 | 13/30 | 17/37 | 54/113 |
| Fundamental Rights | — | 0.60 | 18/30 | 17/37 | 56/113 |
| Order & Security | — | 0.61 | 24/30 | 32/37 | 95/113 |
| Regulatory Enforcement | — | 0.41 | 28/30 | 35/37 | 95/113 |
| Civil Justice | — | 0.46 | 22/30 | 32/37 | 85/113 |
| Criminal Justice | — | 0.34 | 21/30 | 31/37 | 94/113 |

High ▢ Low   ▼ Trending down   ▲ Trending up

■ Dominican Republic   ▨ Latin America & Caribbean   ▨ Upper Middle Income

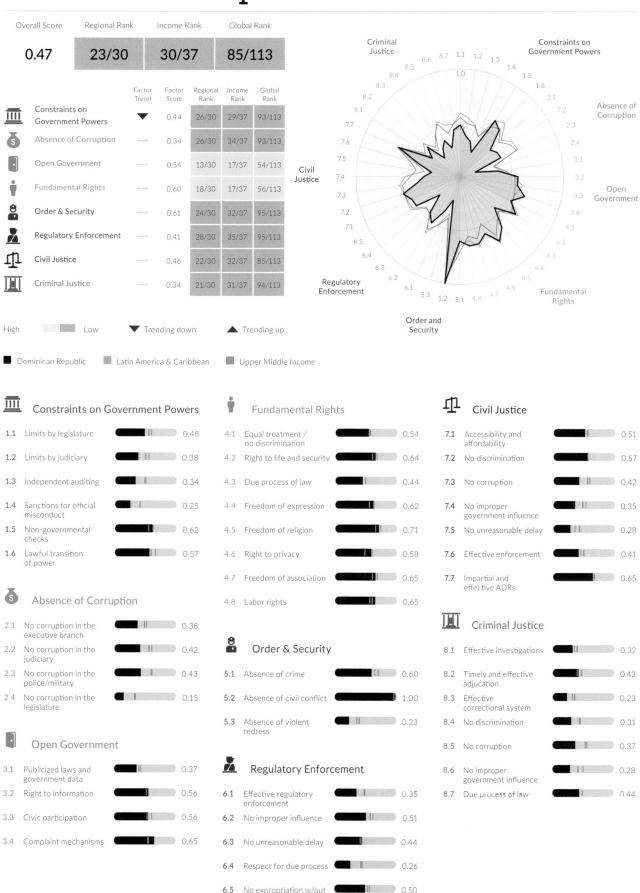

## Constraints on Government Powers

| | | |
|---|---|---|
| 1.1 | Limits by legislature | 0.48 |
| 1.2 | Limits by judiciary | 0.38 |
| 1.3 | Independent auditing | 0.34 |
| 1.4 | Sanctions for official misconduct | 0.25 |
| 1.5 | Non-governmental checks | 0.62 |
| 1.6 | Lawful transition of power | 0.57 |

## Absence of Corruption

| | | |
|---|---|---|
| 2.1 | No corruption in the executive branch | 0.38 |
| 2.2 | No corruption in the judiciary | 0.42 |
| 2.3 | No corruption in the police/military | 0.43 |
| 2.4 | No corruption in the legislature | 0.15 |

## Open Government

| | | |
|---|---|---|
| 3.1 | Publicized laws and government data | 0.37 |
| 3.2 | Right to information | 0.56 |
| 3.3 | Civic participation | 0.56 |
| 3.4 | Complaint mechanisms | 0.65 |

## Fundamental Rights

| | | |
|---|---|---|
| 4.1 | Equal treatment / no discrimination | 0.54 |
| 4.2 | Right to life and security | 0.64 |
| 4.3 | Due process of law | 0.44 |
| 4.4 | Freedom of expression | 0.62 |
| 4.5 | Freedom of religion | 0.71 |
| 4.6 | Right to privacy | 0.58 |
| 4.7 | Freedom of association | 0.65 |
| 4.8 | Labor rights | 0.65 |

## Order & Security

| | | |
|---|---|---|
| 5.1 | Absence of crime | 0.60 |
| 5.2 | Absence of civil conflict | 1.00 |
| 5.3 | Absence of violent redress | 0.23 |

## Regulatory Enforcement

| | | |
|---|---|---|
| 6.1 | Effective regulatory enforcement | 0.35 |
| 6.2 | No improper influence | 0.51 |
| 6.3 | No unreasonable delay | 0.44 |
| 6.4 | Respect for due process | 0.26 |
| 6.5 | No expropriation w/out adequate compensation | 0.50 |

## Civil Justice

| | | |
|---|---|---|
| 7.1 | Accessibility and affordability | 0.51 |
| 7.2 | No discrimination | 0.57 |
| 7.3 | No corruption | 0.42 |
| 7.4 | No improper government influence | 0.35 |
| 7.5 | No unreasonable delay | 0.28 |
| 7.6 | Effective enforcement | 0.41 |
| 7.7 | Impartial and effective ADRs | 0.65 |

## Criminal Justice

| | | |
|---|---|---|
| 8.1 | Effective investigations | 0.32 |
| 8.2 | Timely and effective adjudication | 0.42 |
| 8.3 | Effective correctional system | 0.23 |
| 8.4 | No discrimination | 0.31 |
| 8.5 | No corruption | 0.37 |
| 8.6 | No improper government influence | 0.28 |
| 8.7 | Due process of law | 0.44 |

# Ecuador

| | Overall Score | Regional Rank | Income Rank | Global Rank |
|---|---|---|---|---|
| | 0.45 | 25/30 | 34/37 | 91/113 |

| | | Factor Trend | Factor Score | Regional Rank | Income Rank | Global Rank |
|---|---|---|---|---|---|---|
| 🏛 | Constraints on Government Powers | — | 0.39 | 28/30 | 33/37 | 103/113 |
| 💰 | Absence of Corruption | — | 0.42 | 21/30 | 27/37 | 74/113 |
| 📱 | Open Government | — | 0.45 | 25/30 | 27/37 | 85/113 |
| 👤 | Fundamental Rights | — | 0.51 | 25/30 | 24/37 | 76/113 |
| 👮 | Order & Security | — | 0.60 | 25/30 | 33/37 | 97/113 |
| 👷 | Regulatory Enforcement | — | 0.46 | 23/30 | 28/37 | 76/113 |
| ⚖ | Civil Justice | — | 0.44 | 23/30 | 34/37 | 89/113 |
| 🏛 | Criminal Justice | — | 0.36 | 17/30 | 26/37 | 86/113 |

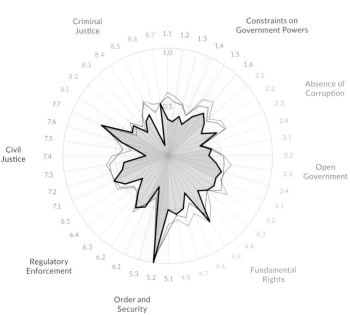

High ⬜⬜ Low      ▼ Trending down      ▲ Trending up

⬛ Ecuador      ⬛ Latin America & Caribbean      ⬛ Upper Middle Income

## 🏛 Constraints on Government Powers

| | | |
|---|---|---|
| 1.1 | Limits by legislature | 0.34 |
| 1.2 | Limits by judiciary | 0.32 |
| 1.3 | Independent auditing | 0.38 |
| 1.4 | Sanctions for official misconduct | 0.32 |
| 1.5 | Non-governmental checks | 0.43 |
| 1.6 | Lawful transition of power | 0.52 |

## 💰 Absence of Corruption

| | | |
|---|---|---|
| 2.1 | No corruption in the executive branch | 0.46 |
| 2.2 | No corruption in the judiciary | 0.38 |
| 2.3 | No corruption in the police/military | 0.51 |
| 2.4 | No corruption in the legislature | 0.32 |

## 📱 Open Government

| | | |
|---|---|---|
| 3.1 | Publicized laws and government data | 0.42 |
| 3.2 | Right to information | 0.39 |
| 3.3 | Civic participation | 0.46 |
| 3.4 | Complaint mechanisms | 0.53 |

## 👤 Fundamental Rights

| | | |
|---|---|---|
| 4.1 | Equal treatment / no discrimination | 0.50 |
| 4.2 | Right to life and security | 0.52 |
| 4.3 | Due process of law | 0.49 |
| 4.4 | Freedom of expression | 0.43 |
| 4.5 | Freedom of religion | 0.73 |
| 4.6 | Right to privacy | 0.38 |
| 4.7 | Freedom of association | 0.51 |
| 4.8 | Labor rights | 0.55 |

## 👮 Order & Security

| | | |
|---|---|---|
| 5.1 | Absence of crime | 0.50 |
| 5.2 | Absence of civil conflict | 1.00 |
| 5.3 | Absence of violent redress | 0.30 |

## 👷 Regulatory Enforcement

| | | |
|---|---|---|
| 6.1 | Effective regulatory enforcement | 0.52 |
| 6.2 | No improper influence | 0.57 |
| 6.3 | No unreasonable delay | 0.43 |
| 6.4 | Respect for due process | 0.32 |
| 6.5 | No expropriation w/out adequate compensation | 0.48 |

## ⚖ Civil Justice

| | | |
|---|---|---|
| 7.1 | Accessibility and affordability | 0.56 |
| 7.2 | No discrimination | 0.45 |
| 7.3 | No corruption | 0.42 |
| 7.4 | No improper government influence | 0.21 |
| 7.5 | No unreasonable delay | 0.28 |
| 7.6 | Effective enforcement | 0.46 |
| 7.7 | Impartial and effective ADRs | 0.69 |

## 🏛 Criminal Justice

| | | |
|---|---|---|
| 8.1 | Effective investigations | 0.40 |
| 8.2 | Timely and effective adjudication | 0.43 |
| 8.3 | Effective correctional system | 0.29 |
| 8.4 | No discrimination | 0.38 |
| 8.5 | No corruption | 0.42 |
| 8.6 | No improper government influence | 0.10 |
| 8.7 | Due process of law | 0.49 |

# Egypt

| | Overall Score | Regional Rank | Income Rank | Global Rank |
|---|---|---|---|---|
| | 0.37 | 7/7 | 27/28 | 110/113 |

| | | Factor Trend | Factor Score | Regional Rank | Income Rank | Global Rank |
|---|---|---|---|---|---|---|
| 🏛 | Constraints on Government Powers | — | 0.31 | 7/7 | 27/28 | 110/113 |
| 💰 | Absence of Corruption | — | 0.45 | 6/7 | 5/28 | 66/113 |
| 📱 | Open Government | ▼ | 0.23 | 7/7 | 28/28 | 113/113 |
| 👤 | Fundamental Rights | — | 0.29 | 6/7 | 28/28 | 110/113 |
| 👮 | Order & Security | ▼ | 0.49 | 7/7 | 25/28 | 108/113 |
| 👷 | Regulatory Enforcement | ▼ | 0.33 | 7/7 | 27/28 | 110/113 |
| ⚖ | Civil Justice | — | 0.38 | 7/7 | 22/28 | 104/113 |
| 🏛 | Criminal Justice | — | 0.43 | 4/7 | 7/28 | 63/113 |

High ▢ Low    ▼ Trending down    ▲ Trending up

■ Egypt    ▨ Middle East & North Africa    ▨ Lower Middle Income

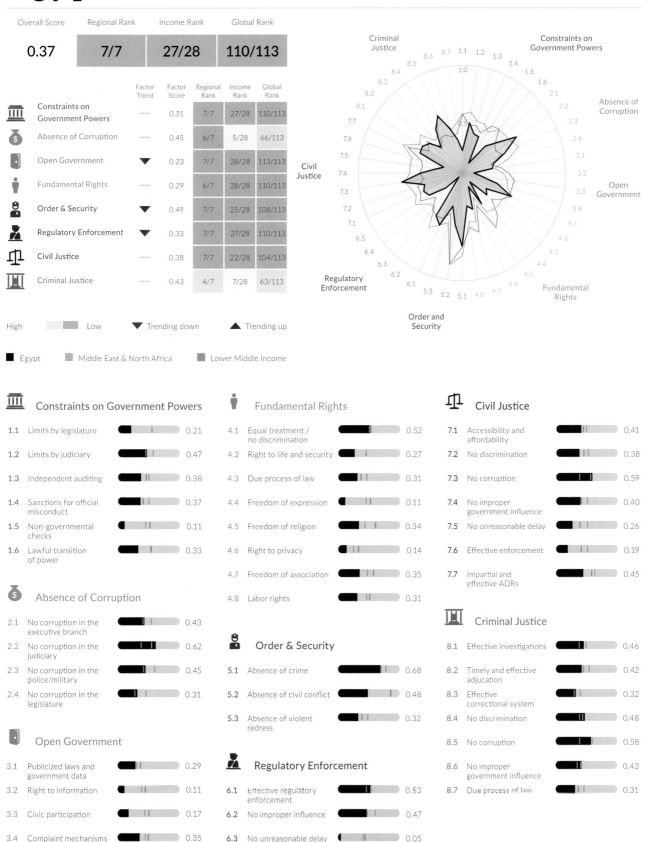

## 🏛 Constraints on Government Powers

| 1.1 | Limits by legislature | 0.21 |
|---|---|---|
| 1.2 | Limits by judiciary | 0.47 |
| 1.3 | Independent auditing | 0.38 |
| 1.4 | Sanctions for official misconduct | 0.37 |
| 1.5 | Non-governmental checks | 0.11 |
| 1.6 | Lawful transition of power | 0.33 |

## 💰 Absence of Corruption

| 2.1 | No corruption in the executive branch | 0.43 |
|---|---|---|
| 2.2 | No corruption in the judiciary | 0.62 |
| 2.3 | No corruption in the police/military | 0.45 |
| 2.4 | No corruption in the legislature | 0.31 |

## 📱 Open Government

| 3.1 | Publicized laws and government data | 0.29 |
|---|---|---|
| 3.2 | Right to information | 0.11 |
| 3.3 | Civic participation | 0.17 |
| 3.4 | Complaint mechanisms | 0.35 |

## 👤 Fundamental Rights

| 4.1 | Equal treatment / no discrimination | 0.52 |
|---|---|---|
| 4.2 | Right to life and security | 0.27 |
| 4.3 | Due process of law | 0.31 |
| 4.4 | Freedom of expression | 0.11 |
| 4.5 | Freedom of religion | 0.34 |
| 4.6 | Right to privacy | 0.14 |
| 4.7 | Freedom of association | 0.35 |
| 4.8 | Labor rights | 0.31 |

## 👮 Order & Security

| 5.1 | Absence of crime | 0.68 |
|---|---|---|
| 5.2 | Absence of civil conflict | 0.48 |
| 5.3 | Absence of violent redress | 0.32 |

## 👷 Regulatory Enforcement

| 6.1 | Effective regulatory enforcement | 0.53 |
|---|---|---|
| 6.2 | No improper influence | 0.47 |
| 6.3 | No unreasonable delay | 0.05 |
| 6.4 | Respect for due process | 0.21 |
| 6.5 | No expropriation w/out adequate compensation | 0.38 |

## ⚖ Civil Justice

| 7.1 | Accessibility and affordability | 0.41 |
|---|---|---|
| 7.2 | No discrimination | 0.38 |
| 7.3 | No corruption | 0.59 |
| 7.4 | No improper government influence | 0.40 |
| 7.5 | No unreasonable delay | 0.26 |
| 7.6 | Effective enforcement | 0.19 |
| 7.7 | Impartial and effective ADRs | 0.45 |

## 🏛 Criminal Justice

| 8.1 | Effective investigations | 0.46 |
|---|---|---|
| 8.2 | Timely and effective adjudication | 0.42 |
| 8.3 | Effective correctional system | 0.32 |
| 8.4 | No discrimination | 0.48 |
| 8.5 | No corruption | 0.58 |
| 8.6 | No improper government influence | 0.43 |
| 8.7 | Due process of law | 0.31 |

# El Salvador

**Region:** Latin America & Caribbean
**Income Group:** Lower Middle Income

| Overall Score | Regional Rank | Income Rank | Global Rank |
|---|---|---|---|
| 0.49 | 20/30 | 10/28 | 75/113 |

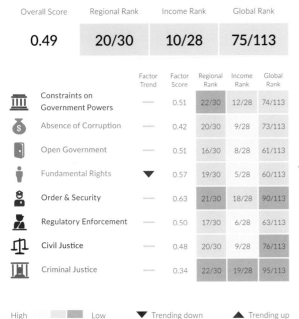

| | Factor Trend | Factor Score | Regional Rank | Income Rank | Global Rank |
|---|---|---|---|---|---|
| Constraints on Government Powers | — | 0.51 | 22/30 | 12/28 | 74/113 |
| Absence of Corruption | — | 0.42 | 20/30 | 9/28 | 73/113 |
| Open Government | — | 0.51 | 16/30 | 8/28 | 61/113 |
| Fundamental Rights | ▼ | 0.57 | 19/30 | 5/28 | 60/113 |
| Order & Security | — | 0.63 | 21/30 | 18/28 | 90/113 |
| Regulatory Enforcement | — | 0.50 | 17/30 | 6/28 | 63/113 |
| Civil Justice | — | 0.48 | 20/30 | 9/28 | 76/113 |
| Criminal Justice | — | 0.34 | 22/30 | 19/28 | 95/113 |

High Low ▼ Trending down ▲ Trending up

■ El Salvador ■ Latin America & Caribbean ■ Lower Middle Income

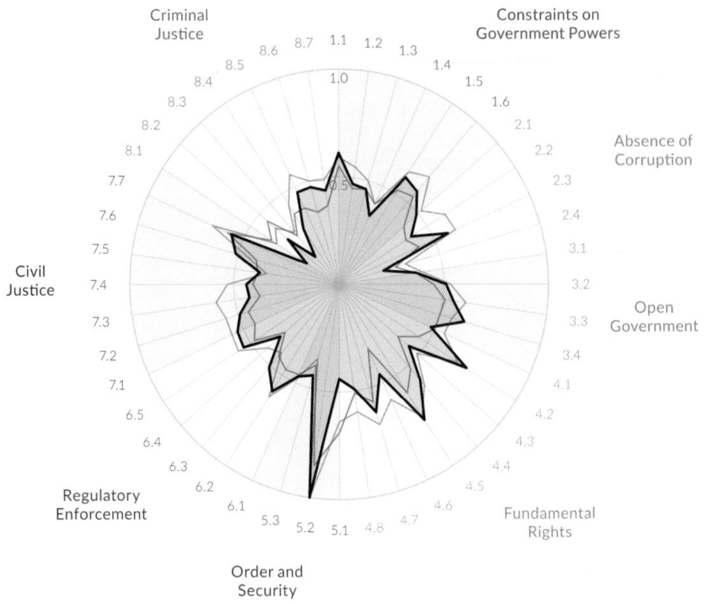


## Constraints on Government Powers

| | | |
|---|---|---|
| 1.1 | Limits by legislature | 0.61 |
| 1.2 | Limits by judiciary | 0.47 |
| 1.3 | Independent auditing | 0.46 |
| 1.4 | Sanctions for official misconduct | 0.35 |
| 1.5 | Non-governmental checks | 0.59 |
| 1.6 | Lawful transition of power | 0.57 |

## Absence of Corruption

| | | |
|---|---|---|
| 2.1 | No corruption in the executive branch | 0.49 |
| 2.2 | No corruption in the judiciary | 0.41 |
| 2.3 | No corruption in the police/military | 0.57 |
| 2.4 | No corruption in the legislature | 0.22 |

## Open Government

| | | |
|---|---|---|
| 3.1 | Publicized laws and government data | 0.37 |
| 3.2 | Right to information | 0.51 |
| 3.3 | Civic participation | 0.55 |
| 3.4 | Complaint mechanisms | 0.62 |

## Fundamental Rights

| | | |
|---|---|---|
| 4.1 | Equal treatment / no discrimination | 0.48 |
| 4.2 | Right to life and security | 0.72 |
| 4.3 | Due process of law | 0.44 |
| 4.4 | Freedom of expression | 0.59 |
| 4.5 | Freedom of religion | 0.75 |
| 4.6 | Right to privacy | 0.46 |
| 4.7 | Freedom of association | 0.62 |
| 4.8 | Labor rights | 0.49 |

## Order & Security

| | | |
|---|---|---|
| 5.1 | Absence of crime | 0.44 |
| 5.2 | Absence of civil conflict | 1.00 |
| 5.3 | Absence of violent redress | 0.44 |

## Regulatory Enforcement

| | | |
|---|---|---|
| 6.1 | Effective regulatory enforcement | 0.47 |
| 6.2 | No improper influence | 0.59 |
| 6.3 | No unreasonable delay | 0.51 |
| 6.4 | Respect for due process | 0.37 |
| 6.5 | No expropriation w/out adequate compensation | 0.54 |

## Civil Justice

| | | |
|---|---|---|
| 7.1 | Accessibility and affordability | 0.53 |
| 7.2 | No discrimination | 0.49 |
| 7.3 | No corruption | 0.43 |
| 7.4 | No improper government influence | 0.44 |
| 7.5 | No unreasonable delay | 0.38 |
| 7.6 | Effective enforcement | 0.51 |
| 7.7 | Impartial and effective ADRs | 0.56 |

## Criminal Justice

| | | |
|---|---|---|
| 8.1 | Effective investigations | 0.18 |
| 8.2 | Timely and effective adjucation | 0.32 |
| 8.3 | Effective correctional system | 0.17 |
| 8.4 | No discrimination | 0.31 |
| 8.5 | No corruption | 0.47 |
| 8.6 | No improper government influence | 0.47 |
| 8.7 | Due process of law | 0.44 |

# Estonia

**Region:** EU & EFTA & North America
**Income Group:** High Income

| Overall Score | Regional Rank | Income Rank | Global Rank |
|---|---|---|---|
| 0.79 | 11/24 | 14/36 | 14/113 |

| | | Factor Trend | Factor Score | Regional Rank | Income Rank | Global Rank |
|---|---|---|---|---|---|---|
| 🏛 | Constraints on Government Powers | — | 0.80 | 13/24 | 15/36 | 15/113 |
| 💰 | Absence of Corruption | — | 0.78 | 11/24 | 17/36 | 17/113 |
| 📱 | Open Government | — | 0.81 | 7/24 | 8/36 | 8/113 |
| 👤 | Fundamental Rights | — | 0.80 | 12/24 | 15/36 | 15/113 |
| 👮 | Order & Security | — | 0.85 | 11/24 | 17/36 | 18/113 |
| 🏗 | Regulatory Enforcement | — | 0.78 | 10/24 | 15/36 | 15/113 |
| ⚖ | Civil Justice | — | 0.77 | 8/24 | 13/36 | 13/113 |
| ⚖ | Criminal Justice | — | 0.70 | 12/24 | 19/36 | 19/113 |

High ▮▮ Low   ▼ Trending down   ▲ Trending up

■ Estonia    ▨ EU & EFTA & North America    ▨ High Income

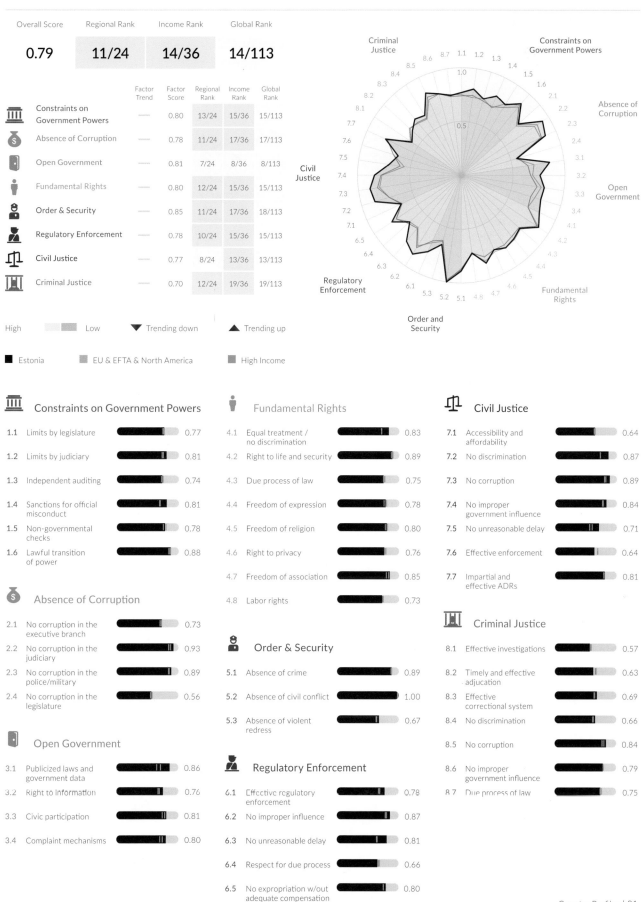

## 🏛 Constraints on Government Powers

| | | | |
|---|---|---|---|
| 1.1 | Limits by legislature | | 0.77 |
| 1.2 | Limits by judiciary | | 0.81 |
| 1.3 | Independent auditing | | 0.74 |
| 1.4 | Sanctions for official misconduct | | 0.81 |
| 1.5 | Non-governmental checks | | 0.78 |
| 1.6 | Lawful transition of power | | 0.88 |

## 💰 Absence of Corruption

| | | | |
|---|---|---|---|
| 2.1 | No corruption in the executive branch | | 0.73 |
| 2.2 | No corruption in the judiciary | | 0.93 |
| 2.3 | No corruption in the police/military | | 0.89 |
| 2.4 | No corruption in the legislature | | 0.56 |

## 📱 Open Government

| | | | |
|---|---|---|---|
| 3.1 | Publicized laws and government data | | 0.86 |
| 3.2 | Right to information | | 0.76 |
| 3.3 | Civic participation | | 0.81 |
| 3.4 | Complaint mechanisms | | 0.80 |

## 👤 Fundamental Rights

| | | | |
|---|---|---|---|
| 4.1 | Equal treatment / no discrimination | | 0.83 |
| 4.2 | Right to life and security | | 0.89 |
| 4.3 | Due process of law | | 0.75 |
| 4.4 | Freedom of expression | | 0.78 |
| 4.5 | Freedom of religion | | 0.80 |
| 4.6 | Right to privacy | | 0.76 |
| 4.7 | Freedom of association | | 0.85 |
| 4.8 | Labor rights | | 0.73 |

## 👮 Order & Security

| | | | |
|---|---|---|---|
| 5.1 | Absence of crime | | 0.89 |
| 5.2 | Absence of civil conflict | | 1.00 |
| 5.3 | Absence of violent redress | | 0.67 |

## 🏗 Regulatory Enforcement

| | | | |
|---|---|---|---|
| 6.1 | Effective regulatory enforcement | | 0.78 |
| 6.2 | No improper influence | | 0.87 |
| 6.3 | No unreasonable delay | | 0.81 |
| 6.4 | Respect for due process | | 0.66 |
| 6.5 | No expropriation w/out adequate compensation | | 0.80 |

## ⚖ Civil Justice

| | | | |
|---|---|---|---|
| 7.1 | Accessibility and affordability | | 0.64 |
| 7.2 | No discrimination | | 0.87 |
| 7.3 | No corruption | | 0.89 |
| 7.4 | No improper government influence | | 0.84 |
| 7.5 | No unreasonable delay | | 0.71 |
| 7.6 | Effective enforcement | | 0.64 |
| 7.7 | Impartial and effective ADRs | | 0.81 |

## ⚖ Criminal Justice

| | | | |
|---|---|---|---|
| 8.1 | Effective investigations | | 0.57 |
| 8.2 | Timely and effective adjucation | | 0.63 |
| 8.3 | Effective correctional system | | 0.69 |
| 8.4 | No discrimination | | 0.66 |
| 8.5 | No corruption | | 0.84 |
| 8.6 | No improper government influence | | 0.79 |
| 8.7 | Due process of law | | 0.75 |

# Ethiopia

**Region:** Sub-Saharan Africa
**Income Group:** Low Income

| Overall Score | Regional Rank | Income Rank | Global Rank |
|:---:|:---:|:---:|:---:|
| 0.38 | 16/18 | 10/12 | 107/113 |

| | Factor Trend | Factor Score | Regional Rank | Income Rank | Global Rank |
|---|:---:|:---:|:---:|:---:|:---:|
| Constraints on Government Powers | — | 0.35 | 17/18 | 11/12 | 106/113 |
| Absence of Corruption | — | 0.44 | 4/18 | 2/12 | 68/113 |
| Open Government | — | 0.27 | 18/18 | 12/12 | 111/113 |
| Fundamental Rights | — | 0.29 | 17/18 | 11/12 | 111/113 |
| Order & Security | ▼ | 0.67 | 9/18 | 6/12 | 76/113 |
| Regulatory Enforcement | — | 0.31 | 18/18 | 12/12 | 111/113 |
| Civil Justice | — | 0.37 | 17/18 | 11/12 | 105/113 |
| Criminal Justice | — | 0.33 | 16/18 | 10/12 | 99/113 |

High ▢ Low      ▼ Trending down      ▲ Trending up

■ Ethiopia      ■ Sub-Saharan Africa      ■ Low Income

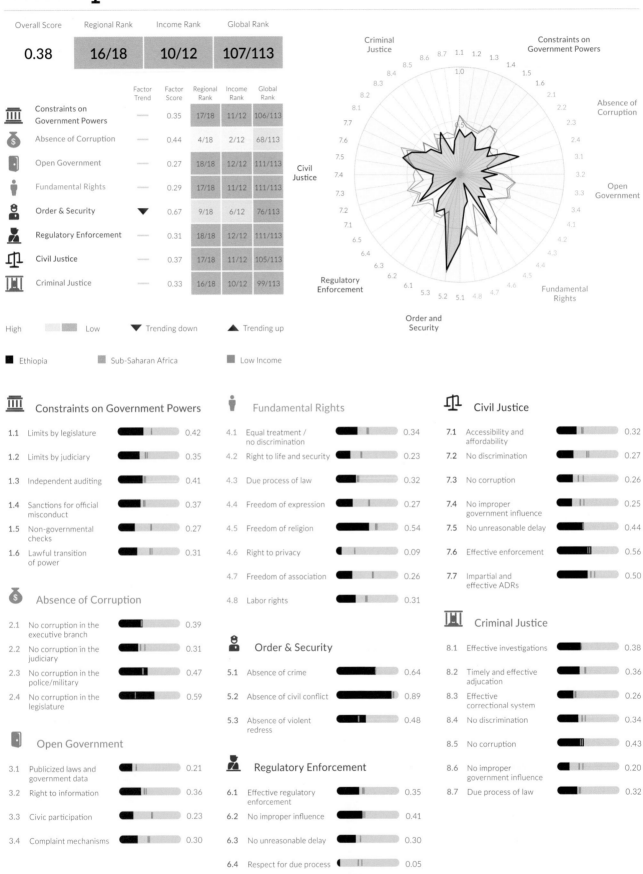

## Constraints on Government Powers

| | | |
|---|---|---|
| 1.1 | Limits by legislature | 0.42 |
| 1.2 | Limits by judiciary | 0.35 |
| 1.3 | Independent auditing | 0.41 |
| 1.4 | Sanctions for official misconduct | 0.37 |
| 1.5 | Non-governmental checks | 0.27 |
| 1.6 | Lawful transition of power | 0.31 |

## Absence of Corruption

| | | |
|---|---|---|
| 2.1 | No corruption in the executive branch | 0.39 |
| 2.2 | No corruption in the judiciary | 0.31 |
| 2.3 | No corruption in the police/military | 0.47 |
| 2.4 | No corruption in the legislature | 0.59 |

## Open Government

| | | |
|---|---|---|
| 3.1 | Publicized laws and government data | 0.21 |
| 3.2 | Right to information | 0.36 |
| 3.3 | Civic participation | 0.23 |
| 3.4 | Complaint mechanisms | 0.30 |

## Fundamental Rights

| | | |
|---|---|---|
| 4.1 | Equal treatment / no discrimination | 0.34 |
| 4.2 | Right to life and security | 0.23 |
| 4.3 | Due process of law | 0.32 |
| 4.4 | Freedom of expression | 0.27 |
| 4.5 | Freedom of religion | 0.54 |
| 4.6 | Right to privacy | 0.09 |
| 4.7 | Freedom of association | 0.26 |
| 4.8 | Labor rights | 0.31 |

## Order & Security

| | | |
|---|---|---|
| 5.1 | Absence of crime | 0.64 |
| 5.2 | Absence of civil conflict | 0.89 |
| 5.3 | Absence of violent redress | 0.48 |

## Regulatory Enforcement

| | | |
|---|---|---|
| 6.1 | Effective regulatory enforcement | 0.35 |
| 6.2 | No improper influence | 0.41 |
| 6.3 | No unreasonable delay | 0.30 |
| 6.4 | Respect for due process | 0.05 |
| 6.5 | No expropriation w/out adequate compensation | 0.45 |

## Civil Justice

| | | |
|---|---|---|
| 7.1 | Accessibility and affordability | 0.32 |
| 7.2 | No discrimination | 0.27 |
| 7.3 | No corruption | 0.26 |
| 7.4 | No improper government influence | 0.25 |
| 7.5 | No unreasonable delay | 0.44 |
| 7.6 | Effective enforcement | 0.56 |
| 7.7 | Impartial and effective ADRs | 0.50 |

## Criminal Justice

| | | |
|---|---|---|
| 8.1 | Effective investigations | 0.38 |
| 8.2 | Timely and effective adjucation | 0.36 |
| 8.3 | Effective correctional system | 0.26 |
| 8.4 | No discrimination | 0.34 |
| 8.5 | No corruption | 0.43 |
| 8.6 | No improper government influence | 0.20 |
| 8.7 | Due process of law | 0.32 |

# Finland

| | Overall Score | Regional Rank | Income Rank | Global Rank |
|---|---|---|---|---|
| | 0.87 | 3/24 | 3/36 | 3/113 |

| | | Factor Trend | Factor Score | Regional Rank | Income Rank | Global Rank |
|---|---|---|---|---|---|---|
| 🏛 | Constraints on Government Powers | — | 0.89 | 3/24 | 3/36 | 3/113 |
| 💰 | Absence of Corruption | — | 0.92 | 3/24 | 4/36 | 4/113 |
| 📱 | Open Government | — | 0.85 | 3/24 | 3/36 | 3/113 |
| 👤 | Fundamental Rights | — | 0.92 | 2/24 | 2/36 | 2/113 |
| 👮 | Order & Security | — | 0.93 | 1/24 | 2/36 | 2/113 |
| 📋 | Regulatory Enforcement | — | 0.83 | 6/24 | 7/36 | 7/113 |
| ⚖ | Civil Justice | — | 0.80 | 7/24 | 10/36 | 10/113 |
| ⛓ | Criminal Justice | — | 0.85 | 1/24 | 1/36 | 1/113 |

High ▬▬ Low    ▼ Trending down    ▲ Trending up

■ Finland    ▨ EU & EFTA & North America    ■ High Income

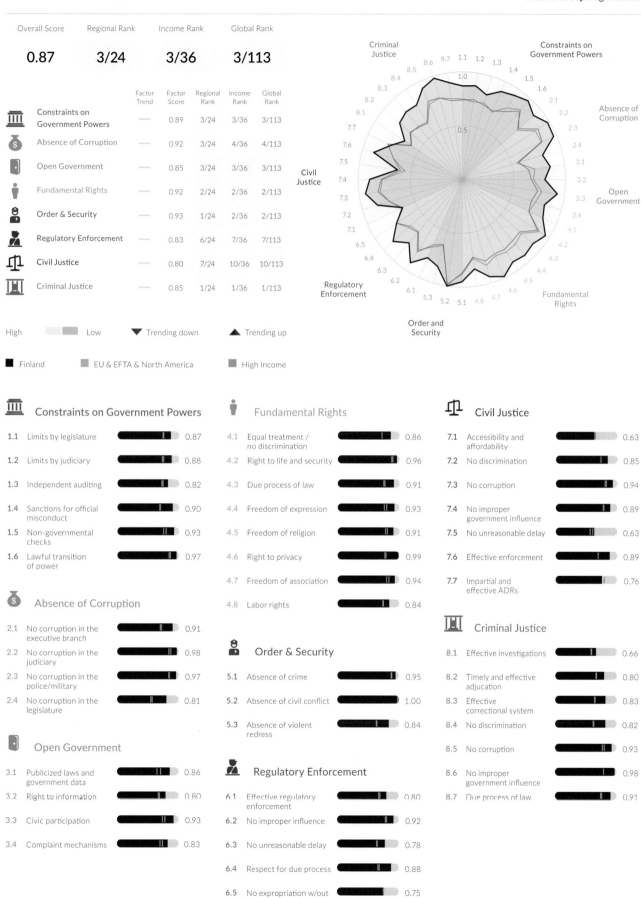

## 🏛 Constraints on Government Powers

| | | | |
|---|---|---|---|
| 1.1 | Limits by legislature | ▬ | 0.87 |
| 1.2 | Limits by judiciary | ▬ | 0.88 |
| 1.3 | Independent auditing | ▬ | 0.82 |
| 1.4 | Sanctions for official misconduct | ▬ | 0.90 |
| 1.5 | Non-governmental checks | ▬ | 0.93 |
| 1.6 | Lawful transition of power | ▬ | 0.97 |

## 💰 Absence of Corruption

| | | | |
|---|---|---|---|
| 2.1 | No corruption in the executive branch | ▬ | 0.91 |
| 2.2 | No corruption in the judiciary | ▬ | 0.98 |
| 2.3 | No corruption in the police/military | ▬ | 0.97 |
| 2.4 | No corruption in the legislature | ▬ | 0.81 |

## 📱 Open Government

| | | | |
|---|---|---|---|
| 3.1 | Publicized laws and government data | ▬ | 0.86 |
| 3.2 | Right to information | ▬ | 0.80 |
| 3.3 | Civic participation | ▬ | 0.93 |
| 3.4 | Complaint mechanisms | ▬ | 0.83 |

## 👤 Fundamental Rights

| | | | |
|---|---|---|---|
| 4.1 | Equal treatment / no discrimination | ▬ | 0.86 |
| 4.2 | Right to life and security | ▬ | 0.96 |
| 4.3 | Due process of law | ▬ | 0.91 |
| 4.4 | Freedom of expression | ▬ | 0.93 |
| 4.5 | Freedom of religion | ▬ | 0.91 |
| 4.6 | Right to privacy | ▬ | 0.99 |
| 4.7 | Freedom of association | ▬ | 0.94 |
| 4.8 | Labor rights | ▬ | 0.84 |

## 👮 Order & Security

| | | | |
|---|---|---|---|
| 5.1 | Absence of crime | ▬ | 0.95 |
| 5.2 | Absence of civil conflict | ▬ | 1.00 |
| 5.3 | Absence of violent redress | ▬ | 0.84 |

## 📋 Regulatory Enforcement

| | | | |
|---|---|---|---|
| 6.1 | Effective regulatory enforcement | ▬ | 0.80 |
| 6.2 | No improper influence | ▬ | 0.92 |
| 6.3 | No unreasonable delay | ▬ | 0.78 |
| 6.4 | Respect for due process | ▬ | 0.88 |
| 6.5 | No expropriation w/out adequate compensation | ▬ | 0.75 |

## ⚖ Civil Justice

| | | | |
|---|---|---|---|
| 7.1 | Accessibility and affordability | ▬ | 0.63 |
| 7.2 | No discrimination | ▬ | 0.85 |
| 7.3 | No corruption | ▬ | 0.94 |
| 7.4 | No improper government influence | ▬ | 0.89 |
| 7.5 | No unreasonable delay | ▬ | 0.63 |
| 7.6 | Effective enforcement | ▬ | 0.89 |
| 7.7 | Impartial and effective ADRs | ▬ | 0.76 |

## ⛓ Criminal Justice

| | | | |
|---|---|---|---|
| 8.1 | Effective investigations | ▬ | 0.66 |
| 8.2 | Timely and effective adjucation | ▬ | 0.80 |
| 8.3 | Effective correctional system | ▬ | 0.83 |
| 8.4 | No discrimination | ▬ | 0.82 |
| 8.5 | No corruption | ▬ | 0.93 |
| 8.6 | No improper government influence | ▬ | 0.98 |
| 8.7 | Due process of law | ▬ | 0.91 |

# France

**Region:** EU & EFTA & North America
**Income Group:** High Income

| | Overall Score | Regional Rank | Income Rank | Global Rank |
|---|---|---|---|---|
| | 0.72 | 14/24 | 21/36 | 21/113 |

| | | Factor Trend | Factor Score | Regional Rank | Income Rank | Global Rank |
|---|---|---|---|---|---|---|
| 🏛 | Constraints on Government Powers | — | 0.77 | 14/24 | 17/36 | 18/113 |
| 💰 | Absence of Corruption | — | 0.74 | 12/24 | 19/36 | 19/113 |
| 📱 | Open Government | — | 0.77 | 11/24 | 13/36 | 13/113 |
| 👤 | Fundamental Rights | — | 0.75 | 17/24 | 23/36 | 24/113 |
| | Order & Security | ▼ | 0.63 | 24/24 | 36/36 | 89/113 |
| ⚖ | Regulatory Enforcement | — | 0.72 | 12/24 | 18/36 | 18/113 |
| ⚖ | Civil Justice | — | 0.71 | 13/24 | 22/36 | 23/113 |
| ⚖ | Criminal Justice | — | 0.65 | 17/24 | 26/36 | 27/113 |

High ▬▬ Low ▼ Trending down ▲ Trending up

■ France  ■ EU & EFTA & North America  ■ High Income

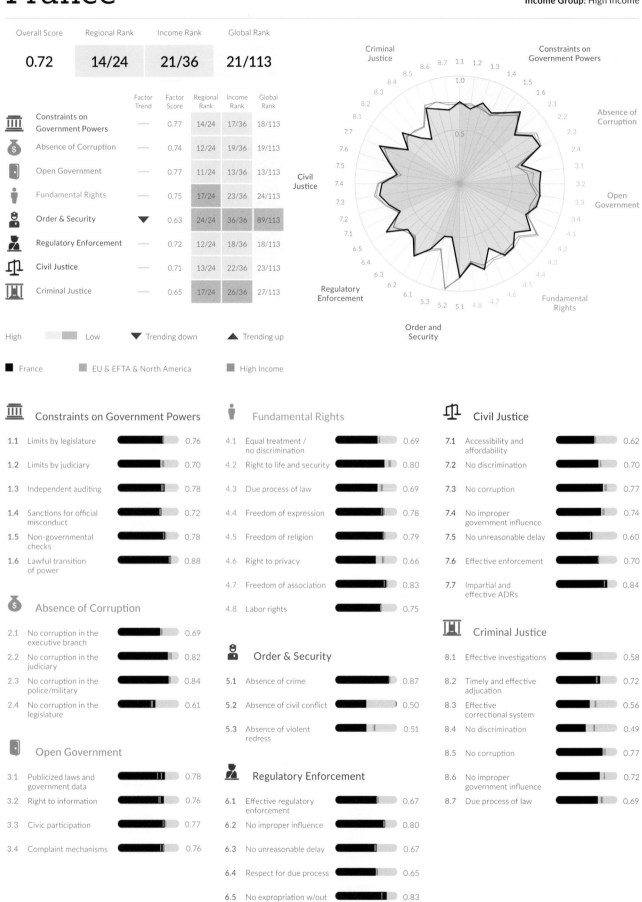

## 🏛 Constraints on Government Powers

| 1.1 | Limits by legislature | 0.76 |
|---|---|---|
| 1.2 | Limits by judiciary | 0.70 |
| 1.3 | Independent auditing | 0.78 |
| 1.4 | Sanctions for official misconduct | 0.72 |
| 1.5 | Non-governmental checks | 0.78 |
| 1.6 | Lawful transition of power | 0.88 |

## 💰 Absence of Corruption

| 2.1 | No corruption in the executive branch | 0.69 |
|---|---|---|
| 2.2 | No corruption in the judiciary | 0.82 |
| 2.3 | No corruption in the police/military | 0.84 |
| 2.4 | No corruption in the legislature | 0.61 |

## 📱 Open Government

| 3.1 | Publicized laws and government data | 0.78 |
|---|---|---|
| 3.2 | Right to information | 0.76 |
| 3.3 | Civic participation | 0.77 |
| 3.4 | Complaint mechanisms | 0.76 |

## 👤 Fundamental Rights

| 4.1 | Equal treatment / no discrimination | 0.69 |
|---|---|---|
| 4.2 | Right to life and security | 0.80 |
| 4.3 | Due process of law | 0.69 |
| 4.4 | Freedom of expression | 0.78 |
| 4.5 | Freedom of religion | 0.79 |
| 4.6 | Right to privacy | 0.66 |
| 4.7 | Freedom of association | 0.83 |
| 4.8 | Labor rights | 0.75 |

## 👮 Order & Security

| 5.1 | Absence of crime | 0.87 |
|---|---|---|
| 5.2 | Absence of civil conflict | 0.50 |
| 5.3 | Absence of violent redress | 0.51 |

## ⚖ Regulatory Enforcement

| 6.1 | Effective regulatory enforcement | 0.67 |
|---|---|---|
| 6.2 | No improper influence | 0.80 |
| 6.3 | No unreasonable delay | 0.67 |
| 6.4 | Respect for due process | 0.65 |
| 6.5 | No expropriation w/out adequate compensation | 0.83 |

## ⚖ Civil Justice

| 7.1 | Accessibility and affordability | 0.62 |
|---|---|---|
| 7.2 | No discrimination | 0.70 |
| 7.3 | No corruption | 0.77 |
| 7.4 | No improper government influence | 0.74 |
| 7.5 | No unreasonable delay | 0.60 |
| 7.6 | Effective enforcement | 0.70 |
| 7.7 | Impartial and effective ADRs | 0.84 |

## ⚖ Criminal Justice

| 8.1 | Effective investigations | 0.58 |
|---|---|---|
| 8.2 | Timely and effective adjucation | 0.72 |
| 8.3 | Effective correctional system | 0.56 |
| 8.4 | No discrimination | 0.49 |
| 8.5 | No corruption | 0.77 |
| 8.6 | No improper government influence | 0.72 |
| 8.7 | Due process of law | 0.69 |

# Georgia

| Overall Score | Regional Rank | Income Rank | Global Rank |
|---|---|---|---|
| **0.65** | **1/13** | **4/37** | **34/113** |

| | Factor Trend | Factor Score | Regional Rank | Income Rank | Global Rank |
|---|---|---|---|---|---|
| Constraints on Government Powers | — | 0.62 | 1/13 | 7/37 | 43/113 |
| Absence of Corruption | — | 0.73 | 1/13 | 1/37 | 22/113 |
| Open Government | — | 0.63 | 1/13 | 4/37 | 31/113 |
| Fundamental Rights | — | 0.68 | 1/13 | 8/37 | 39/113 |
| Order & Security | — | 0.78 | 4/13 | 6/37 | 37/113 |
| Regulatory Enforcement | — | 0.62 | 1/13 | 2/37 | 28/113 |
| Civil Justice | — | 0.61 | 2/13 | 8/37 | 39/113 |
| Criminal Justice | — | 0.56 | 1/13 | 6/37 | 38/113 |

High — Low   ▼ Trending down   ▲ Trending up

■ Georgia   ▨ Eastern Europe & Central Asia   ▨ Upper Middle Income

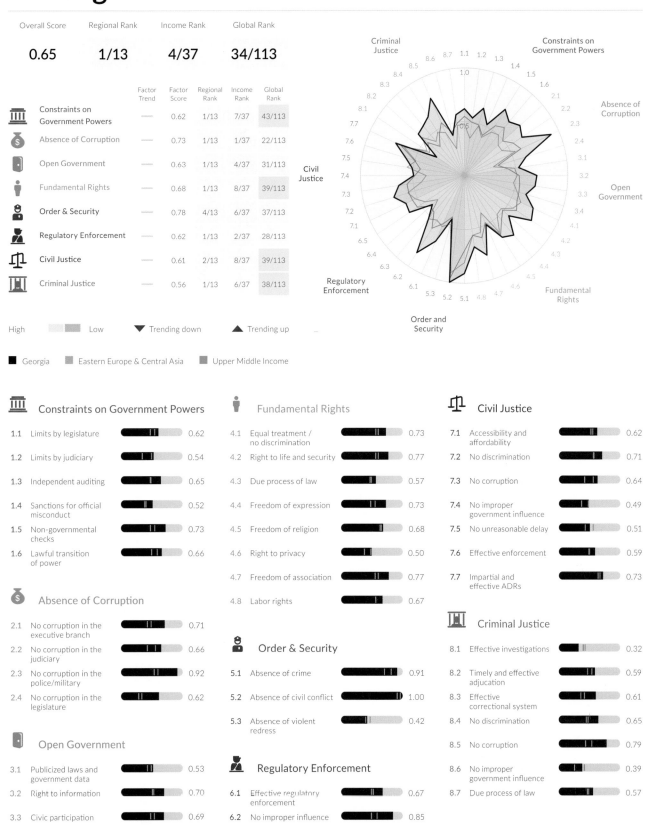

## Constraints on Government Powers

| | | |
|---|---|---|
| 1.1 | Limits by legislature | 0.62 |
| 1.2 | Limits by judiciary | 0.54 |
| 1.3 | Independent auditing | 0.65 |
| 1.4 | Sanctions for official misconduct | 0.52 |
| 1.5 | Non-governmental checks | 0.73 |
| 1.6 | Lawful transition of power | 0.66 |

## Absence of Corruption

| | | |
|---|---|---|
| 2.1 | No corruption in the executive branch | 0.71 |
| 2.2 | No corruption in the judiciary | 0.66 |
| 2.3 | No corruption in the police/military | 0.92 |
| 2.4 | No corruption in the legislature | 0.62 |

## Open Government

| | | |
|---|---|---|
| 3.1 | Publicized laws and government data | 0.53 |
| 3.2 | Right to information | 0.70 |
| 3.3 | Civic participation | 0.69 |
| 3.4 | Complaint mechanisms | 0.62 |

## Fundamental Rights

| | | |
|---|---|---|
| 4.1 | Equal treatment / no discrimination | 0.73 |
| 4.2 | Right to life and security | 0.77 |
| 4.3 | Due process of law | 0.57 |
| 4.4 | Freedom of expression | 0.73 |
| 4.5 | Freedom of religion | 0.68 |
| 4.6 | Right to privacy | 0.50 |
| 4.7 | Freedom of association | 0.77 |
| 4.8 | Labor rights | 0.67 |

## Order & Security

| | | |
|---|---|---|
| 5.1 | Absence of crime | 0.91 |
| 5.2 | Absence of civil conflict | 1.00 |
| 5.3 | Absence of violent redress | 0.42 |

## Regulatory Enforcement

| | | |
|---|---|---|
| 6.1 | Effective regulatory enforcement | 0.67 |
| 6.2 | No improper influence | 0.85 |
| 6.3 | No unreasonable delay | 0.53 |
| 6.4 | Respect for due process | 0.41 |
| 6.5 | No expropriation w/out adequate compensation | 0.63 |

## Civil Justice

| | | |
|---|---|---|
| 7.1 | Accessibility and affordability | 0.62 |
| 7.2 | No discrimination | 0.71 |
| 7.3 | No corruption | 0.64 |
| 7.4 | No improper government influence | 0.49 |
| 7.5 | No unreasonable delay | 0.51 |
| 7.6 | Effective enforcement | 0.59 |
| 7.7 | Impartial and effective ADRs | 0.73 |

## Criminal Justice

| | | |
|---|---|---|
| 8.1 | Effective investigations | 0.32 |
| 8.2 | Timely and effective adjudication | 0.59 |
| 8.3 | Effective correctional system | 0.61 |
| 8.4 | No discrimination | 0.65 |
| 8.5 | No corruption | 0.79 |
| 8.6 | No improper government influence | 0.39 |
| 8.7 | Due process of law | 0.57 |

# Germany

| | Overall Score | Regional Rank | Income Rank | Global Rank |
|---|---|---|---|---|
| | 0.83 | 6/24 | 6/36 | 6/113 |

| | | Factor Trend | Factor Score | Regional Rank | Income Rank | Global Rank |
|---|---|---|---|---|---|---|
| 🏛️ | Constraints on Government Powers | — | 0.85 | 8/24 | 9/36 | 9/113 |
| 💰 | Absence of Corruption | — | 0.84 | 7/24 | 10/36 | 10/113 |
| 🚪 | Open Government | — | 0.79 | 9/24 | 10/36 | 10/113 |
| 👤 | Fundamental Rights | — | 0.85 | 7/24 | 7/36 | 7/113 |
| 👮 | Order & Security | — | 0.87 | 8/24 | 13/36 | 14/113 |
| 🧑‍💼 | Regulatory Enforcement | ▲ | 0.85 | 4/24 | 5/36 | 5/113 |
| ⚖️ | Civil Justice | — | 0.86 | 2/24 | 2/36 | 2/113 |
| 🏛️ | Criminal Justice | — | 0.77 | 7/24 | 9/36 | 9/113 |

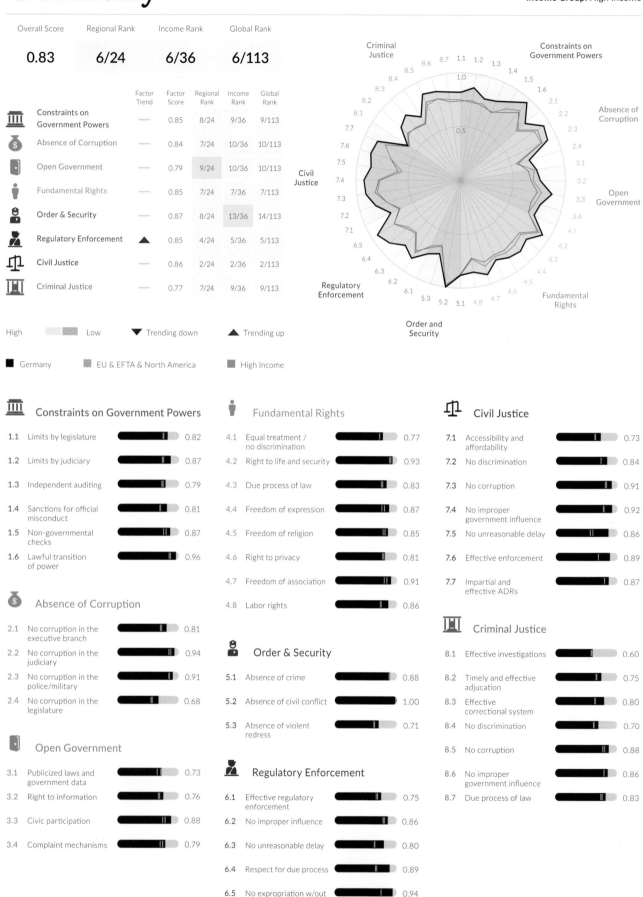

High ▣▣ Low   ▼ Trending down   ▲ Trending up

■ Germany   ▣ EU & EFTA & North America   ▣ High Income

## 🏛️ Constraints on Government Powers

| | | |
|---|---|---|
| 1.1 | Limits by legislature | 0.82 |
| 1.2 | Limits by judiciary | 0.87 |
| 1.3 | Independent auditing | 0.79 |
| 1.4 | Sanctions for official misconduct | 0.81 |
| 1.5 | Non-governmental checks | 0.87 |
| 1.6 | Lawful transition of power | 0.96 |

## 💰 Absence of Corruption

| | | |
|---|---|---|
| 2.1 | No corruption in the executive branch | 0.81 |
| 2.2 | No corruption in the judiciary | 0.94 |
| 2.3 | No corruption in the police/military | 0.91 |
| 2.4 | No corruption in the legislature | 0.68 |

## 🚪 Open Government

| | | |
|---|---|---|
| 3.1 | Publicized laws and government data | 0.73 |
| 3.2 | Right to information | 0.76 |
| 3.3 | Civic participation | 0.88 |
| 3.4 | Complaint mechanisms | 0.79 |

## 👤 Fundamental Rights

| | | |
|---|---|---|
| 4.1 | Equal treatment / no discrimination | 0.77 |
| 4.2 | Right to life and security | 0.93 |
| 4.3 | Due process of law | 0.83 |
| 4.4 | Freedom of expression | 0.87 |
| 4.5 | Freedom of religion | 0.85 |
| 4.6 | Right to privacy | 0.81 |
| 4.7 | Freedom of association | 0.91 |
| 4.8 | Labor rights | 0.86 |

## 👮 Order & Security

| | | |
|---|---|---|
| 5.1 | Absence of crime | 0.88 |
| 5.2 | Absence of civil conflict | 1.00 |
| 5.3 | Absence of violent redress | 0.71 |

## 🧑‍💼 Regulatory Enforcement

| | | |
|---|---|---|
| 6.1 | Effective regulatory enforcement | 0.75 |
| 6.2 | No improper influence | 0.86 |
| 6.3 | No unreasonable delay | 0.80 |
| 6.4 | Respect for due process | 0.89 |
| 6.5 | No expropriation w/out adequate compensation | 0.94 |

## ⚖️ Civil Justice

| | | |
|---|---|---|
| 7.1 | Accessibility and affordability | 0.73 |
| 7.2 | No discrimination | 0.84 |
| 7.3 | No corruption | 0.91 |
| 7.4 | No improper government influence | 0.92 |
| 7.5 | No unreasonable delay | 0.86 |
| 7.6 | Effective enforcement | 0.89 |
| 7.7 | Impartial and effective ADRs | 0.87 |

## 🏛️ Criminal Justice

| | | |
|---|---|---|
| 8.1 | Effective investigations | 0.60 |
| 8.2 | Timely and effective adjudication | 0.75 |
| 8.3 | Effective correctional system | 0.80 |
| 8.4 | No discrimination | 0.70 |
| 8.5 | No corruption | 0.88 |
| 8.6 | No improper government influence | 0.86 |
| 8.7 | Due process of law | 0.83 |

# Ghana

| | Overall Score | Regional Rank | Income Rank | Global Rank |
|---|---|---|---|---|
| | 0.58 | 2/18 | 1/28 | 44/113 |

| | | Factor Trend | Factor Score | Regional Rank | Income Rank | Global Rank |
|---|---|---|---|---|---|---|
| 🏛 | Constraints on Government Powers | — | 0.67 | 1/18 | 1/28 | 29/113 |
| 💰 | Absence of Corruption | — | 0.41 | 5/18 | 10/28 | 76/113 |
| 📱 | Open Government | — | 0.55 | 2/18 | 6/28 | 51/113 |
| 👤 | Fundamental Rights | — | 0.65 | 1/18 | 1/28 | 43/113 |
| 👮 | Order & Security | ▼ | 0.70 | 4/18 | 10/28 | 62/113 |
| 👷 | Regulatory Enforcement | — | 0.56 | 3/18 | 1/28 | 39/113 |
| ⚖ | Civil Justice | — | 0.61 | 2/18 | 1/28 | 41/113 |
| ⚖ | Criminal Justice | — | 0.47 | 3/18 | 4/28 | 54/113 |

High ▢ Low   ▼ Trending down   ▲ Trending up

■ Ghana   ■ Sub-Saharan Africa   ■ Lower Middle Income

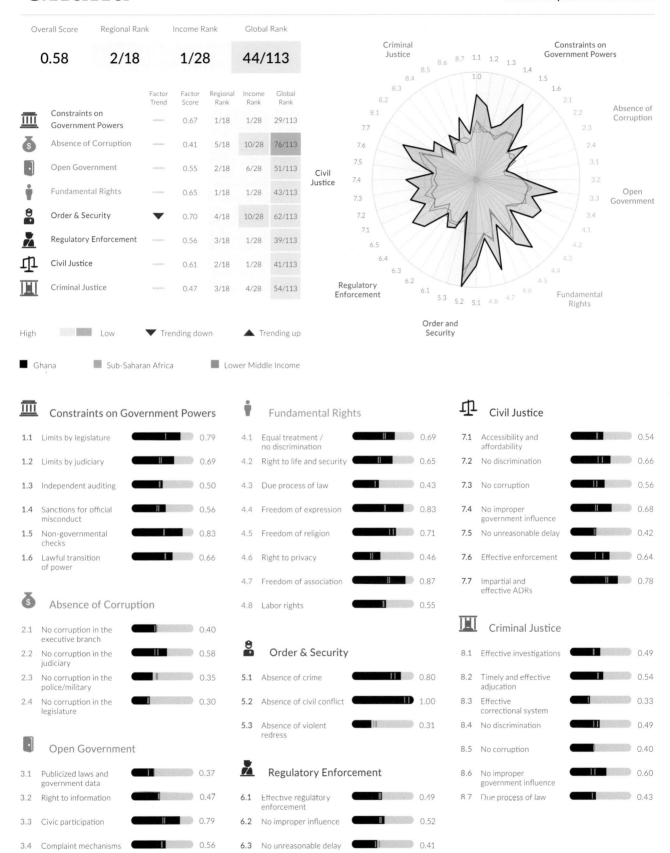

## 🏛 Constraints on Government Powers

| | | | |
|---|---|---|---|
| 1.1 | Limits by legislature | | 0.79 |
| 1.2 | Limits by judiciary | | 0.69 |
| 1.3 | Independent auditing | | 0.50 |
| 1.4 | Sanctions for official misconduct | | 0.56 |
| 1.5 | Non-governmental checks | | 0.83 |
| 1.6 | Lawful transition of power | | 0.66 |

## 💰 Absence of Corruption

| | | | |
|---|---|---|---|
| 2.1 | No corruption in the executive branch | | 0.40 |
| 2.2 | No corruption in the judiciary | | 0.58 |
| 2.3 | No corruption in the police/military | | 0.35 |
| 2.4 | No corruption in the legislature | | 0.30 |

## 📱 Open Government

| | | | |
|---|---|---|---|
| 3.1 | Publicized laws and government data | | 0.37 |
| 3.2 | Right to information | | 0.47 |
| 3.3 | Civic participation | | 0.79 |
| 3.4 | Complaint mechanisms | | 0.56 |

## 👤 Fundamental Rights

| | | | |
|---|---|---|---|
| 4.1 | Equal treatment / no discrimination | | 0.69 |
| 4.2 | Right to life and security | | 0.65 |
| 4.3 | Due process of law | | 0.43 |
| 4.4 | Freedom of expression | | 0.83 |
| 4.5 | Freedom of religion | | 0.71 |
| 4.6 | Right to privacy | | 0.46 |
| 4.7 | Freedom of association | | 0.87 |
| 4.8 | Labor rights | | 0.55 |

## 👮 Order & Security

| | | | |
|---|---|---|---|
| 5.1 | Absence of crime | | 0.80 |
| 5.2 | Absence of civil conflict | | 1.00 |
| 5.3 | Absence of violent redress | | 0.31 |

## 👷 Regulatory Enforcement

| | | | |
|---|---|---|---|
| 6.1 | Effective regulatory enforcement | | 0.49 |
| 6.2 | No improper influence | | 0.52 |
| 6.3 | No unreasonable delay | | 0.41 |
| 6.4 | Respect for due process | | 0.66 |
| 6.5 | No expropriation w/out adequate compensation | | 0.73 |

## ⚖ Civil Justice

| | | | |
|---|---|---|---|
| 7.1 | Accessibility and affordability | | 0.54 |
| 7.2 | No discrimination | | 0.66 |
| 7.3 | No corruption | | 0.56 |
| 7.4 | No improper government influence | | 0.68 |
| 7.5 | No unreasonable delay | | 0.42 |
| 7.6 | Effective enforcement | | 0.64 |
| 7.7 | Impartial and effective ADRs | | 0.78 |

## ⚖ Criminal Justice

| | | | |
|---|---|---|---|
| 8.1 | Effective investigations | | 0.49 |
| 8.2 | Timely and effective adjudication | | 0.54 |
| 8.3 | Effective correctional system | | 0.33 |
| 8.4 | No discrimination | | 0.49 |
| 8.5 | No corruption | | 0.40 |
| 8.6 | No improper government influence | | 0.60 |
| 8.7 | Due process of law | | 0.43 |

# Greece

**Region:** EU & EFTA & North America
**Income Group:** High Income

| | Overall Score | Regional Rank | Income Rank | Global Rank |
|---|---|---|---|---|
| | 0.60 | 22/24 | 34/36 | 41/113 |

| | Factor Trend | Factor Score | Regional Rank | Income Rank | Global Rank |
|---|---|---|---|---|---|
| Constraints on Government Powers | — | 0.64 | 20/24 | 29/36 | 36/113 |
| Absence of Corruption | — | 0.55 | 22/24 | 34/36 | 46/113 |
| Open Government | — | 0.57 | 23/24 | 29/36 | 42/113 |
| Fundamental Rights | — | 0.65 | 22/24 | 33/36 | 41/113 |
| Order & Security | — | 0.75 | 21/24 | 30/36 | 43/113 |
| Regulatory Enforcement | — | 0.56 | 21/24 | 31/36 | 40/113 |
| Civil Justice | — | 0.57 | 20/24 | 33/36 | 44/113 |
| Criminal Justice | — | 0.51 | 23/24 | 35/36 | 50/113 |

High ▬▬ Low     ▼ Trending down     ▲ Trending up

■ Greece     ■ EU & EFTA & North America     ■ High Income

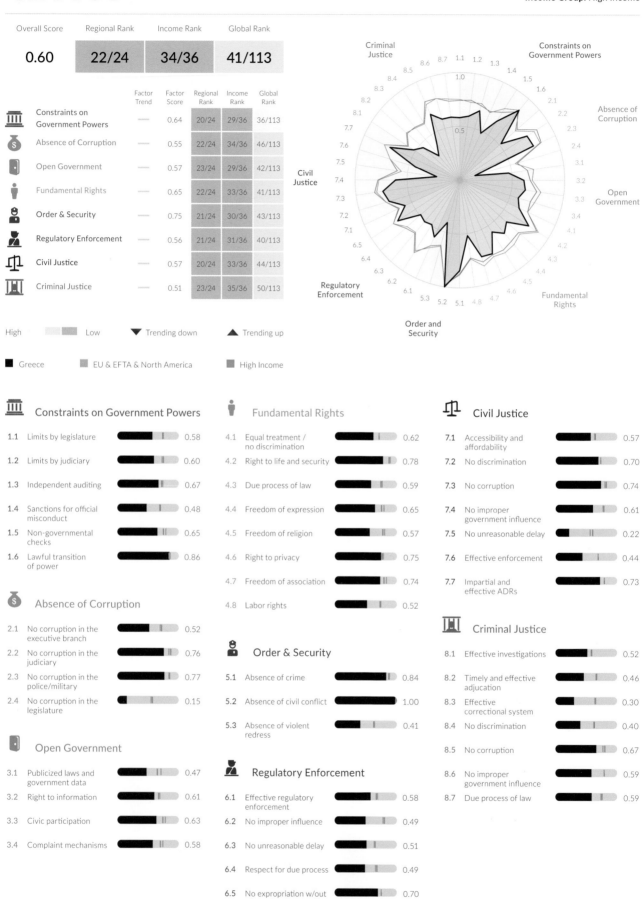

## Constraints on Government Powers

| | | |
|---|---|---|
| 1.1 | Limits by legislature | 0.58 |
| 1.2 | Limits by judiciary | 0.60 |
| 1.3 | Independent auditing | 0.67 |
| 1.4 | Sanctions for official misconduct | 0.48 |
| 1.5 | Non-governmental checks | 0.65 |
| 1.6 | Lawful transition of power | 0.86 |

## Absence of Corruption

| | | |
|---|---|---|
| 2.1 | No corruption in the executive branch | 0.52 |
| 2.2 | No corruption in the judiciary | 0.76 |
| 2.3 | No corruption in the police/military | 0.77 |
| 2.4 | No corruption in the legislature | 0.15 |

## Open Government

| | | |
|---|---|---|
| 3.1 | Publicized laws and government data | 0.47 |
| 3.2 | Right to information | 0.61 |
| 3.3 | Civic participation | 0.63 |
| 3.4 | Complaint mechanisms | 0.58 |

## Fundamental Rights

| | | |
|---|---|---|
| 4.1 | Equal treatment / no discrimination | 0.62 |
| 4.2 | Right to life and security | 0.78 |
| 4.3 | Due process of law | 0.59 |
| 4.4 | Freedom of expression | 0.65 |
| 4.5 | Freedom of religion | 0.57 |
| 4.6 | Right to privacy | 0.75 |
| 4.7 | Freedom of association | 0.74 |
| 4.8 | Labor rights | 0.52 |

## Order & Security

| | | |
|---|---|---|
| 5.1 | Absence of crime | 0.84 |
| 5.2 | Absence of civil conflict | 1.00 |
| 5.3 | Absence of violent redress | 0.41 |

## Regulatory Enforcement

| | | |
|---|---|---|
| 6.1 | Effective regulatory enforcement | 0.58 |
| 6.2 | No improper influence | 0.49 |
| 6.3 | No unreasonable delay | 0.51 |
| 6.4 | Respect for due process | 0.49 |
| 6.5 | No expropriation w/out adequate compensation | 0.70 |

## Civil Justice

| | | |
|---|---|---|
| 7.1 | Accessibility and affordability | 0.57 |
| 7.2 | No discrimination | 0.70 |
| 7.3 | No corruption | 0.74 |
| 7.4 | No improper government influence | 0.61 |
| 7.5 | No unreasonable delay | 0.22 |
| 7.6 | Effective enforcement | 0.44 |
| 7.7 | Impartial and effective ADRs | 0.73 |

## Criminal Justice

| | | |
|---|---|---|
| 8.1 | Effective investigations | 0.52 |
| 8.2 | Timely and effective adjudication | 0.46 |
| 8.3 | Effective correctional system | 0.30 |
| 8.4 | No discrimination | 0.40 |
| 8.5 | No corruption | 0.67 |
| 8.6 | No improper government influence | 0.59 |
| 8.7 | Due process of law | 0.59 |

# Grenada

**Region:** Latin America & Caribbean
**Income Group:** Upper Middle Income

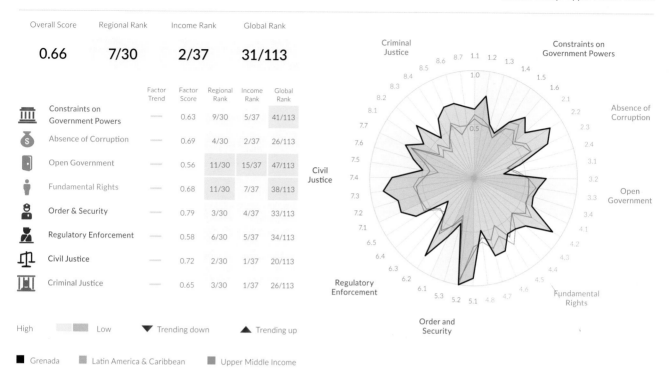

| | Overall Score | Regional Rank | Income Rank | Global Rank |
|---|---|---|---|---|
| | 0.66 | 7/30 | 2/37 | 31/113 |

| | Factor Trend | Factor Score | Regional Rank | Income Rank | Global Rank |
|---|---|---|---|---|---|
| Constraints on Government Powers | — | 0.63 | 9/30 | 5/37 | 41/113 |
| Absence of Corruption | — | 0.69 | 4/30 | 2/37 | 26/113 |
| Open Government | — | 0.56 | 11/30 | 15/37 | 47/113 |
| Fundamental Rights | — | 0.68 | 11/30 | 7/37 | 38/113 |
| Order & Security | — | 0.79 | 3/30 | 4/37 | 33/113 |
| Regulatory Enforcement | — | 0.58 | 6/30 | 5/37 | 34/113 |
| Civil Justice | — | 0.72 | 2/30 | 1/37 | 20/113 |
| Criminal Justice | — | 0.65 | 3/30 | 1/37 | 26/113 |

High ▢ Low   ▼ Trending down   ▲ Trending up

■ Grenada    ▨ Latin America & Caribbean    ▨ Upper Middle Income

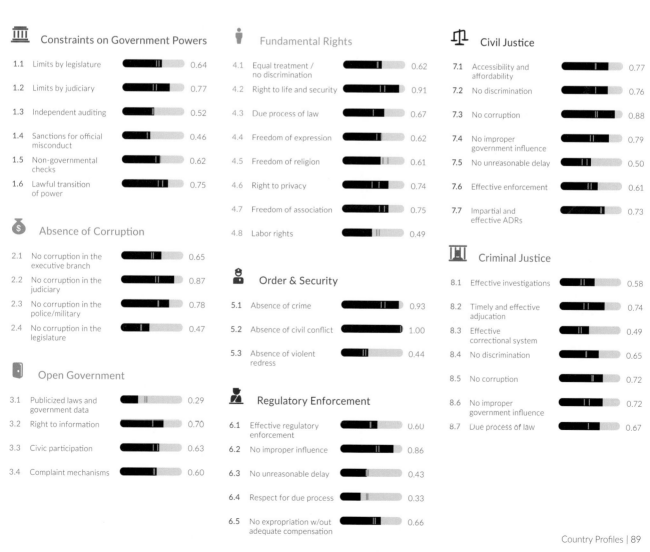

## Constraints on Government Powers

| | | |
|---|---|---|
| 1.1 | Limits by legislature | 0.64 |
| 1.2 | Limits by judiciary | 0.77 |
| 1.3 | Independent auditing | 0.52 |
| 1.4 | Sanctions for official misconduct | 0.46 |
| 1.5 | Non-governmental checks | 0.62 |
| 1.6 | Lawful transition of power | 0.75 |

## Absence of Corruption

| | | |
|---|---|---|
| 2.1 | No corruption in the executive branch | 0.65 |
| 2.2 | No corruption in the judiciary | 0.87 |
| 2.3 | No corruption in the police/military | 0.78 |
| 2.4 | No corruption in the legislature | 0.47 |

## Open Government

| | | |
|---|---|---|
| 3.1 | Publicized laws and government data | 0.29 |
| 3.2 | Right to information | 0.70 |
| 3.3 | Civic participation | 0.63 |
| 3.4 | Complaint mechanisms | 0.60 |

## Fundamental Rights

| | | |
|---|---|---|
| 4.1 | Equal treatment / no discrimination | 0.62 |
| 4.2 | Right to life and security | 0.91 |
| 4.3 | Due process of law | 0.67 |
| 4.4 | Freedom of expression | 0.62 |
| 4.5 | Freedom of religion | 0.61 |
| 4.6 | Right to privacy | 0.74 |
| 4.7 | Freedom of association | 0.75 |
| 4.8 | Labor rights | 0.49 |

## Order & Security

| | | |
|---|---|---|
| 5.1 | Absence of crime | 0.93 |
| 5.2 | Absence of civil conflict | 1.00 |
| 5.3 | Absence of violent redress | 0.44 |

## Regulatory Enforcement

| | | |
|---|---|---|
| 6.1 | Effective regulatory enforcement | 0.60 |
| 6.2 | No improper influence | 0.86 |
| 6.3 | No unreasonable delay | 0.43 |
| 6.4 | Respect for due process | 0.33 |
| 6.5 | No expropriation w/out adequate compensation | 0.66 |

## Civil Justice

| | | |
|---|---|---|
| 7.1 | Accessibility and affordability | 0.77 |
| 7.2 | No discrimination | 0.76 |
| 7.3 | No corruption | 0.88 |
| 7.4 | No improper government influence | 0.79 |
| 7.5 | No unreasonable delay | 0.50 |
| 7.6 | Effective enforcement | 0.61 |
| 7.7 | Impartial and effective ADRs | 0.73 |

## Criminal Justice

| | | |
|---|---|---|
| 8.1 | Effective investigations | 0.58 |
| 8.2 | Timely and effective adjudication | 0.74 |
| 8.3 | Effective correctional system | 0.49 |
| 8.4 | No discrimination | 0.65 |
| 8.5 | No corruption | 0.72 |
| 8.6 | No improper government influence | 0.72 |
| 8.7 | Due process of law | 0.67 |

# Guatemala

**Region:** Latin America & Caribbean
**Income Group:** Lower Middle Income

| | Overall Score | Regional Rank | Income Rank | Global Rank |
|---|---|---|---|---|
| | 0.44 | 26/30 | 18/28 | 97/113 |

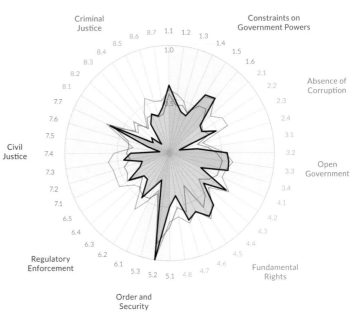

| | Factor Trend | Factor Score | Regional Rank | Income Rank | Global Rank |
|---|---|---|---|---|---|
| Constraints on Government Powers | — | 0.53 | 19/30 | 9/28 | 65/113 |
| Absence of Corruption | — | 0.34 | 27/30 | 19/28 | 95/113 |
| Open Government | — | 0.49 | 19/30 | 10/28 | 66/113 |
| Fundamental Rights | — | 0.55 | 21/30 | 7/28 | 66/113 |
| Order & Security | — | 0.59 | 26/30 | 19/28 | 99/113 |
| Regulatory Enforcement | — | 0.39 | 29/30 | 23/28 | 101/113 |
| Civil Justice | — | 0.33 | 29/30 | 27/28 | 111/113 |
| Criminal Justice | — | 0.29 | 25/30 | 26/28 | 106/113 |

High ▢ Low ▼ Trending down ▲ Trending up

■ Guatemala  ■ Latin America & Caribbean  ■ Lower Middle Income

## 🏛 Constraints on Government Powers

| | | |
|---|---|---|
| 1.1 | Limits by legislature | 0.63 |
| 1.2 | Limits by judiciary | 0.48 |
| 1.3 | Independent auditing | 0.40 |
| 1.4 | Sanctions for official misconduct | 0.38 |
| 1.5 | Non-governmental checks | 0.64 |
| 1.6 | Lawful transition of power | 0.67 |

## 💰 Absence of Corruption

| | | |
|---|---|---|
| 2.1 | No corruption in the executive branch | 0.39 |
| 2.2 | No corruption in the judiciary | 0.37 |
| 2.3 | No corruption in the police/military | 0.49 |
| 2.4 | No corruption in the legislature | 0.10 |

## 🚪 Open Government

| | | |
|---|---|---|
| 3.1 | Publicized laws and government data | 0.27 |
| 3.2 | Right to information | 0.55 |
| 3.3 | Civic participation | 0.57 |
| 3.4 | Complaint mechanisms | 0.58 |

## 🧍 Fundamental Rights

| | | |
|---|---|---|
| 4.1 | Equal treatment / no discrimination | 0.33 |
| 4.2 | Right to life and security | 0.64 |
| 4.3 | Due process of law | 0.43 |
| 4.4 | Freedom of expression | 0.64 |
| 4.5 | Freedom of religion | 0.70 |
| 4.6 | Right to privacy | 0.60 |
| 4.7 | Freedom of association | 0.65 |
| 4.8 | Labor rights | 0.40 |

## 🧑 Order & Security

| | | |
|---|---|---|
| 5.1 | Absence of crime | 0.50 |
| 5.2 | Absence of civil conflict | 1.00 |
| 5.3 | Absence of violent redress | 0.26 |

## 👷 Regulatory Enforcement

| | | |
|---|---|---|
| 6.1 | Effective regulatory enforcement | 0.34 |
| 6.2 | No improper influence | 0.49 |
| 6.3 | No unreasonable delay | 0.32 |
| 6.4 | Respect for due process | 0.32 |
| 6.5 | No expropriation w/out adequate compensation | 0.46 |

## ⚖ Civil Justice

| | | |
|---|---|---|
| 7.1 | Accessibility and affordability | 0.31 |
| 7.2 | No discrimination | 0.27 |
| 7.3 | No corruption | 0.44 |
| 7.4 | No improper government influence | 0.37 |
| 7.5 | No unreasonable delay | 0.09 |
| 7.6 | Effective enforcement | 0.22 |
| 7.7 | Impartial and effective ADRs | 0.62 |

## 🏛 Criminal Justice

| | | |
|---|---|---|
| 8.1 | Effective investigations | 0.18 |
| 8.2 | Timely and effective adjucation | 0.22 |
| 8.3 | Effective correctional system | 0.11 |
| 8.4 | No discrimination | 0.32 |
| 8.5 | No corruption | 0.40 |
| 8.6 | No improper government influence | 0.36 |
| 8.7 | Due process of law | 0.43 |

# Guyana

**Region:** Latin America & Caribbean
**Income Group:** Upper Middle Income

| Overall Score | Regional Rank | Income Rank | Global Rank |
|---|---|---|---|
| 0.49 | 21/30 | 27/37 | 76/113 |

| | Factor Trend | Factor Score | Regional Rank | Income Rank | Global Rank |
|---|---|---|---|---|---|
| Constraints on Government Powers | — | 0.53 | 20/30 | 18/37 | 67/113 |
| Absence of Corruption | — | 0.46 | 17/30 | 22/37 | 62/113 |
| Open Government | — | 0.47 | 21/30 | 25/37 | 75/113 |
| Fundamental Rights | — | 0.54 | 22/30 | 21/37 | 70/113 |
| Order & Security | — | 0.64 | 20/30 | 28/37 | 87/113 |
| Regulatory Enforcement | — | 0.48 | 18/30 | 22/37 | 66/113 |
| Civil Justice | — | 0.48 | 19/30 | 27/37 | 73/113 |
| Criminal Justice | — | 0.35 | 18/30 | 27/37 | 89/113 |

High ▮▮▮ Low    ▼ Trending down    ▲ Trending up

■ Guyana    ▨ Latin America & Caribbean    ▨ Upper Middle Income

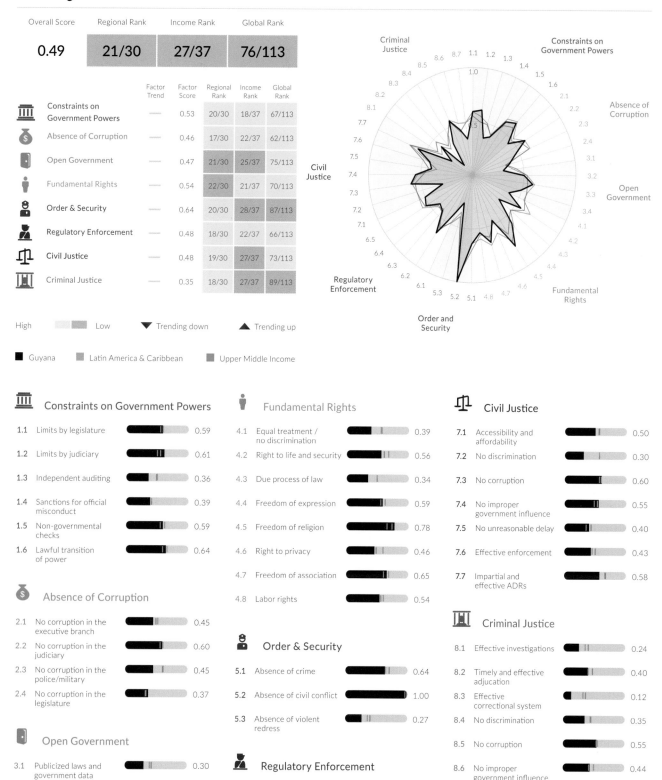

## Constraints on Government Powers

| | | |
|---|---|---|
| 1.1 | Limits by legislature | 0.59 |
| 1.2 | Limits by judiciary | 0.61 |
| 1.3 | Independent auditing | 0.36 |
| 1.4 | Sanctions for official misconduct | 0.39 |
| 1.5 | Non-governmental checks | 0.59 |
| 1.6 | Lawful transition of power | 0.64 |

## Absence of Corruption

| | | |
|---|---|---|
| 2.1 | No corruption in the executive branch | 0.45 |
| 2.2 | No corruption in the judiciary | 0.60 |
| 2.3 | No corruption in the police/military | 0.45 |
| 2.4 | No corruption in the legislature | 0.37 |

## Open Government

| | | |
|---|---|---|
| 3.1 | Publicized laws and government data | 0.30 |
| 3.2 | Right to information | 0.50 |
| 3.3 | Civic participation | 0.59 |
| 3.4 | Complaint mechanisms | 0.49 |

## Fundamental Rights

| | | |
|---|---|---|
| 4.1 | Equal treatment / no discrimination | 0.39 |
| 4.2 | Right to life and security | 0.56 |
| 4.3 | Due process of law | 0.34 |
| 4.4 | Freedom of expression | 0.59 |
| 4.5 | Freedom of religion | 0.78 |
| 4.6 | Right to privacy | 0.46 |
| 4.7 | Freedom of association | 0.65 |
| 4.8 | Labor rights | 0.54 |

## Order & Security

| | | |
|---|---|---|
| 5.1 | Absence of crime | 0.64 |
| 5.2 | Absence of civil conflict | 1.00 |
| 5.3 | Absence of violent redress | 0.27 |

## Regulatory Enforcement

| | | |
|---|---|---|
| 6.1 | Effective regulatory enforcement | 0.30 |
| 6.2 | No improper influence | 0.64 |
| 6.3 | No unreasonable delay | 0.44 |
| 6.4 | Respect for due process | 0.41 |
| 6.5 | No expropriation w/out adequate compensation | 0.53 |

## Civil Justice

| | | |
|---|---|---|
| 7.1 | Accessibility and affordability | 0.50 |
| 7.2 | No discrimination | 0.30 |
| 7.3 | No corruption | 0.60 |
| 7.4 | No improper government influence | 0.55 |
| 7.5 | No unreasonable delay | 0.40 |
| 7.6 | Effective enforcement | 0.43 |
| 7.7 | Impartial and effective ADRs | 0.58 |

## Criminal Justice

| | | |
|---|---|---|
| 8.1 | Effective investigations | 0.24 |
| 8.2 | Timely and effective adjucation | 0.40 |
| 8.3 | Effective correctional system | 0.12 |
| 8.4 | No discrimination | 0.35 |
| 8.5 | No corruption | 0.55 |
| 8.6 | No improper government influence | 0.44 |
| 8.7 | Due process of law | 0.34 |

# Honduras

| | Overall Score | Regional Rank | Income Rank | Global Rank |
|---|---|---|---|---|
| | 0.42 | 28/30 | 22/28 | 102/113 |

| | Factor Trend | Factor Score | Regional Rank | Income Rank | Global Rank |
|---|---|---|---|---|---|
| Constraints on Government Powers | — | 0.44 | 25/30 | 20/28 | 92/113 |
| Absence of Corruption | — | 0.36 | 25/30 | 17/28 | 92/113 |
| Open Government | — | 0.46 | 22/30 | 15/28 | 77/113 |
| Fundamental Rights | — | 0.44 | 29/30 | 21/28 | 96/113 |
| Order & Security | — | 0.56 | 28/30 | 22/28 | 103/113 |
| Regulatory Enforcement | — | 0.41 | 27/30 | 19/28 | 94/113 |
| Civil Justice | — | 0.43 | 25/30 | 18/28 | 95/113 |
| Criminal Justice | — | 0.25 | 28/30 | 27/28 | 111/113 |

High ▢▢▢ Low    ▼ Trending down    ▲ Trending up

■ Honduras    ■ Latin America & Caribbean    ■ Lower Middle Income

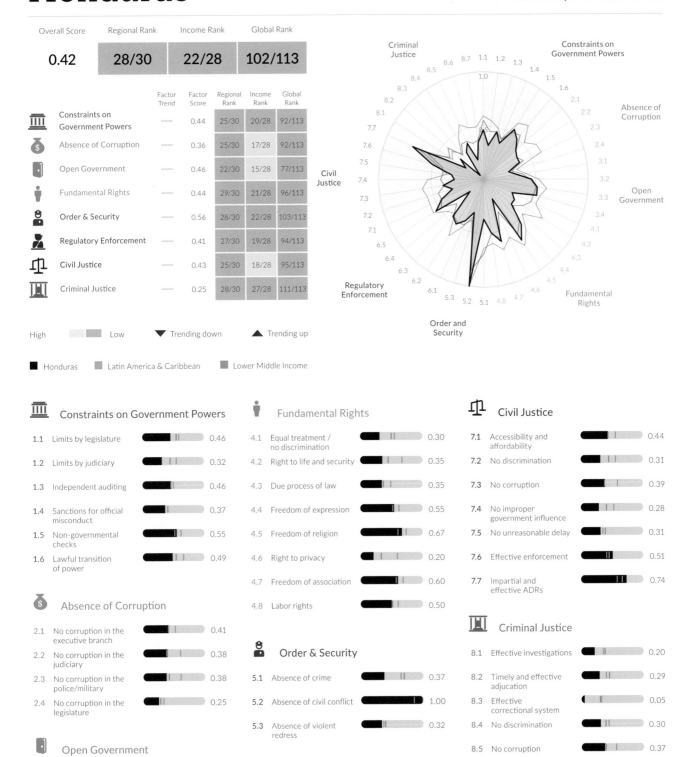

## Constraints on Government Powers

| | | |
|---|---|---|
| 1.1 | Limits by legislature | 0.46 |
| 1.2 | Limits by judiciary | 0.32 |
| 1.3 | Independent auditing | 0.46 |
| 1.4 | Sanctions for official misconduct | 0.37 |
| 1.5 | Non-governmental checks | 0.55 |
| 1.6 | Lawful transition of power | 0.49 |

## Absence of Corruption

| | | |
|---|---|---|
| 2.1 | No corruption in the executive branch | 0.41 |
| 2.2 | No corruption in the judiciary | 0.38 |
| 2.3 | No corruption in the police/military | 0.38 |
| 2.4 | No corruption in the legislature | 0.25 |

## Open Government

| | | |
|---|---|---|
| 3.1 | Publicized laws and government data | 0.32 |
| 3.2 | Right to information | 0.46 |
| 3.3 | Civic participation | 0.52 |
| 3.4 | Complaint mechanisms | 0.53 |

## Fundamental Rights

| | | |
|---|---|---|
| 4.1 | Equal treatment / no discrimination | 0.30 |
| 4.2 | Right to life and security | 0.35 |
| 4.3 | Due process of law | 0.35 |
| 4.4 | Freedom of expression | 0.55 |
| 4.5 | Freedom of religion | 0.67 |
| 4.6 | Right to privacy | 0.20 |
| 4.7 | Freedom of association | 0.60 |
| 4.8 | Labor rights | 0.50 |

## Order & Security

| | | |
|---|---|---|
| 5.1 | Absence of crime | 0.37 |
| 5.2 | Absence of civil conflict | 1.00 |
| 5.3 | Absence of violent redress | 0.32 |

## Regulatory Enforcement

| | | |
|---|---|---|
| 6.1 | Effective regulatory enforcement | 0.42 |
| 6.2 | No improper influence | 0.49 |
| 6.3 | No unreasonable delay | 0.45 |
| 6.4 | Respect for due process | 0.17 |
| 6.5 | No expropriation w/out adequate compensation | 0.54 |

## Civil Justice

| | | |
|---|---|---|
| 7.1 | Accessibility and affordability | 0.44 |
| 7.2 | No discrimination | 0.31 |
| 7.3 | No corruption | 0.39 |
| 7.4 | No improper government influence | 0.28 |
| 7.5 | No unreasonable delay | 0.31 |
| 7.6 | Effective enforcement | 0.51 |
| 7.7 | Impartial and effective ADRs | 0.74 |

## Criminal Justice

| | | |
|---|---|---|
| 8.1 | Effective investigations | 0.20 |
| 8.2 | Timely and effective adjucation | 0.29 |
| 8.3 | Effective correctional system | 0.05 |
| 8.4 | No discrimination | 0.30 |
| 8.5 | No corruption | 0.37 |
| 8.6 | No improper government influence | 0.19 |
| 8.7 | Due process of law | 0.35 |

# Hong Kong SAR, China

**Region:** East Asia & Pacific
**Income Group:** High Income

| | Overall Score | Regional Rank | Income Rank | Global Rank |
|---|---|---|---|---|
| | 0.77 | 5/15 | 16/36 | 16/113 |

| | | Factor Trend | Factor Score | Regional Rank | Income Rank | Global Rank |
|---|---|---|---|---|---|---|
| 🏛 | Constraints on Government Powers | — | 0.70 | 5/15 | 24/36 | 25/113 |
| 💰 | Absence of Corruption | — | 0.85 | 3/15 | 8/36 | 8/113 |
| 📱 | Open Government | — | 0.66 | 6/15 | 25/36 | 27/113 |
| 👤 | Fundamental Rights | — | 0.70 | 5/15 | 29/36 | 33/113 |
| 👥 | Order & Security | — | 0.89 | 3/15 | 10/36 | 11/113 |
| 👷 | Regulatory Enforcement | — | 0.80 | 5/15 | 12/36 | 12/113 |
| ⚖ | Civil Justice | — | 0.77 | 5/15 | 12/36 | 12/113 |
| ⚖ | Criminal Justice | — | 0.80 | 2/15 | 6/36 | 6/113 |

High ▮▮▮ Low    ▼ Trending down    ▲ Trending up

■ Hong Kong SAR, China    ▨ East Asia & Pacific    ▨ High Income

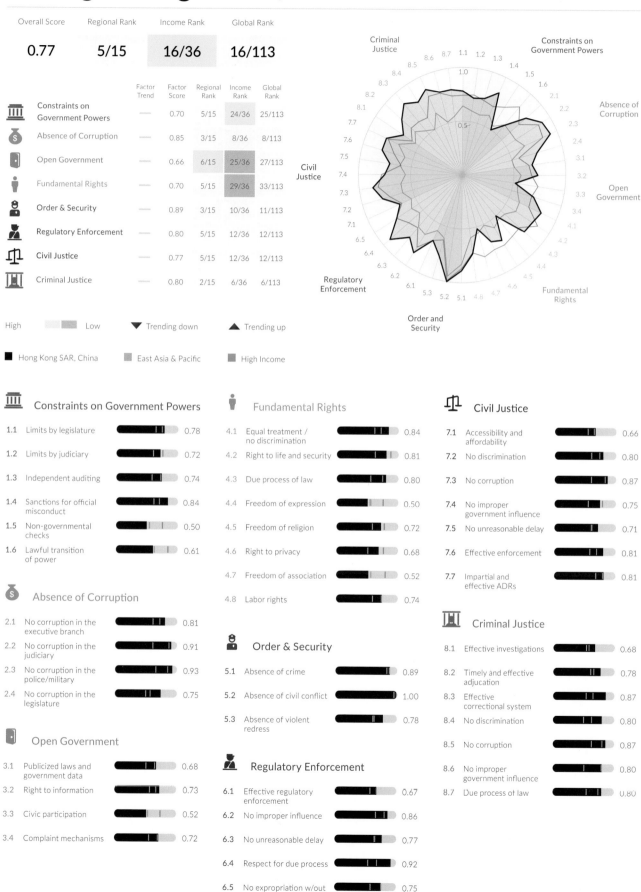

## 🏛 Constraints on Government Powers

| | | |
|---|---|---|
| 1.1 | Limits by legislature | 0.78 |
| 1.2 | Limits by judiciary | 0.72 |
| 1.3 | Independent auditing | 0.74 |
| 1.4 | Sanctions for official misconduct | 0.84 |
| 1.5 | Non-governmental checks | 0.50 |
| 1.6 | Lawful transition of power | 0.61 |

## 💰 Absence of Corruption

| | | |
|---|---|---|
| 2.1 | No corruption in the executive branch | 0.81 |
| 2.2 | No corruption in the judiciary | 0.91 |
| 2.3 | No corruption in the police/military | 0.93 |
| 2.4 | No corruption in the legislature | 0.75 |

## 📱 Open Government

| | | |
|---|---|---|
| 3.1 | Publicized laws and government data | 0.68 |
| 3.2 | Right to information | 0.73 |
| 3.3 | Civic participation | 0.52 |
| 3.4 | Complaint mechanisms | 0.72 |

## 👤 Fundamental Rights

| | | |
|---|---|---|
| 4.1 | Equal treatment / no discrimination | 0.84 |
| 4.2 | Right to life and security | 0.81 |
| 4.3 | Due process of law | 0.80 |
| 4.4 | Freedom of expression | 0.50 |
| 4.5 | Freedom of religion | 0.72 |
| 4.6 | Right to privacy | 0.68 |
| 4.7 | Freedom of association | 0.52 |
| 4.8 | Labor rights | 0.74 |

## 👥 Order & Security

| | | |
|---|---|---|
| 5.1 | Absence of crime | 0.89 |
| 5.2 | Absence of civil conflict | 1.00 |
| 5.3 | Absence of violent redress | 0.78 |

## 👷 Regulatory Enforcement

| | | |
|---|---|---|
| 6.1 | Effective regulatory enforcement | 0.67 |
| 6.2 | No improper influence | 0.86 |
| 6.3 | No unreasonable delay | 0.77 |
| 6.4 | Respect for due process | 0.92 |
| 6.5 | No expropriation w/out adequate compensation | 0.75 |

## ⚖ Civil Justice

| | | |
|---|---|---|
| 7.1 | Accessibility and affordability | 0.66 |
| 7.2 | No discrimination | 0.80 |
| 7.3 | No corruption | 0.87 |
| 7.4 | No improper government influence | 0.75 |
| 7.5 | No unreasonable delay | 0.71 |
| 7.6 | Effective enforcement | 0.81 |
| 7.7 | Impartial and effective ADRs | 0.81 |

## ⚖ Criminal Justice

| | | |
|---|---|---|
| 8.1 | Effective investigations | 0.68 |
| 8.2 | Timely and effective adjucation | 0.78 |
| 8.3 | Effective correctional system | 0.87 |
| 8.4 | No discrimination | 0.80 |
| 8.5 | No corruption | 0.87 |
| 8.6 | No improper government influence | 0.80 |
| 8.7 | Due process of law | 0.80 |

# Hungary

| | Overall Score | Regional Rank | Income Rank | Global Rank |
|---|---|---|---|---|
| | 0.57 | 23/24 | 36/36 | 49/113 |

| | | Factor Trend | Factor Score | Regional Rank | Income Rank | Global Rank |
|---|---|---|---|---|---|---|
| 🏛 | Constraints on Government Powers | — | 0.46 | 24/24 | 36/36 | 87/113 |
| 💰 | Absence of Corruption | — | 0.51 | 23/24 | 36/36 | 53/113 |
| 🚪 | Open Government | — | 0.52 | 24/24 | 31/36 | 55/113 |
| 🧍 | Fundamental Rights | — | 0.62 | 24/24 | 34/36 | 50/113 |
| 👤 | Order & Security | — | 0.86 | 9/24 | 15/36 | 16/113 |
| 👮 | Regulatory Enforcement | — | 0.51 | 23/24 | 34/36 | 54/113 |
| ⚖ | Civil Justice | — | 0.52 | 24/24 | 36/36 | 61/113 |
| 🏛 | Criminal Justice | — | 0.54 | 21/24 | 33/36 | 43/113 |

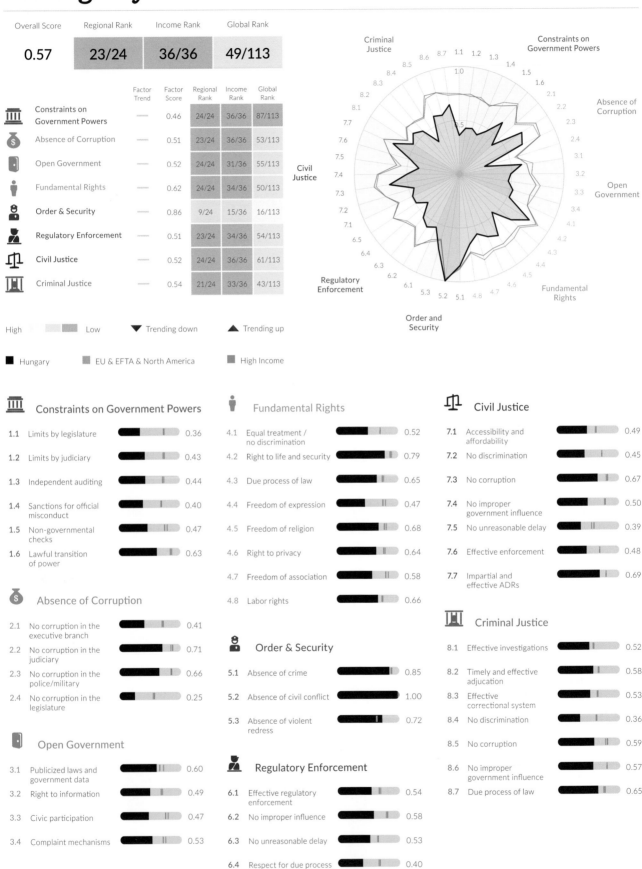

High ▬▬▬ Low   ▼ Trending down   ▲ Trending up

■ Hungary   ▨ EU & EFTA & North America   ▪ High Income

## 🏛 Constraints on Government Powers

| 1.1 | Limits by legislature | 0.36 |
|---|---|---|
| 1.2 | Limits by judiciary | 0.43 |
| 1.3 | Independent auditing | 0.44 |
| 1.4 | Sanctions for official misconduct | 0.40 |
| 1.5 | Non-governmental checks | 0.47 |
| 1.6 | Lawful transition of power | 0.63 |

## 💰 Absence of Corruption

| 2.1 | No corruption in the executive branch | 0.41 |
|---|---|---|
| 2.2 | No corruption in the judiciary | 0.71 |
| 2.3 | No corruption in the police/military | 0.66 |
| 2.4 | No corruption in the legislature | 0.25 |

## 🚪 Open Government

| 3.1 | Publicized laws and government data | 0.60 |
|---|---|---|
| 3.2 | Right to information | 0.49 |
| 3.3 | Civic participation | 0.47 |
| 3.4 | Complaint mechanisms | 0.53 |

## 🧍 Fundamental Rights

| 4.1 | Equal treatment / no discrimination | 0.52 |
|---|---|---|
| 4.2 | Right to life and security | 0.79 |
| 4.3 | Due process of law | 0.65 |
| 4.4 | Freedom of expression | 0.47 |
| 4.5 | Freedom of religion | 0.68 |
| 4.6 | Right to privacy | 0.64 |
| 4.7 | Freedom of association | 0.58 |
| 4.8 | Labor rights | 0.66 |

## 👤 Order & Security

| 5.1 | Absence of crime | 0.85 |
|---|---|---|
| 5.2 | Absence of civil conflict | 1.00 |
| 5.3 | Absence of violent redress | 0.72 |

## 👮 Regulatory Enforcement

| 6.1 | Effective regulatory enforcement | 0.54 |
|---|---|---|
| 6.2 | No improper influence | 0.58 |
| 6.3 | No unreasonable delay | 0.53 |
| 6.4 | Respect for due process | 0.40 |
| 6.5 | No expropriation w/out adequate compensation | 0.49 |

## ⚖ Civil Justice

| 7.1 | Accessibility and affordability | 0.49 |
|---|---|---|
| 7.2 | No discrimination | 0.45 |
| 7.3 | No corruption | 0.67 |
| 7.4 | No improper government influence | 0.50 |
| 7.5 | No unreasonable delay | 0.39 |
| 7.6 | Effective enforcement | 0.48 |
| 7.7 | Impartial and effective ADRs | 0.69 |

## 🏛 Criminal Justice

| 8.1 | Effective investigations | 0.52 |
|---|---|---|
| 8.2 | Timely and effective adjucation | 0.58 |
| 8.3 | Effective correctional system | 0.53 |
| 8.4 | No discrimination | 0.36 |
| 8.5 | No corruption | 0.59 |
| 8.6 | No improper government influence | 0.57 |
| 8.7 | Due process of law | 0.65 |

# India

**Region:** South Asia
**Income Group:** Lower Middle Income

| | Overall Score | Regional Rank | Income Rank | Global Rank |
|---|---|---|---|---|
| | 0.51 | 2/6 | 6/28 | 66/113 |

| | | Factor Trend | Factor Score | Regional Rank | Income Rank | Global Rank |
|---|---|---|---|---|---|---|
| 🏛 | Constraints on Government Powers | — | 0.64 | 1/6 | 3/28 | 35/113 |
| 💰 | Absence of Corruption | — | 0.44 | 2/6 | 7/28 | 69/113 |
| 🚪 | Open Government | — | 0.66 | 1/6 | 1/28 | 28/113 |
| 👤 | Fundamental Rights | — | 0.5 | 3/6 | 13/28 | 81/113 |
| 👮 | Order & Security | — | 0.56 | 4/6 | 23/28 | 104/113 |
| 👷 | Regulatory Enforcement | — | 0.46 | 3/6 | 11/28 | 77/113 |
| ⚖ | Civil Justice | — | 0.43 | 1/6 | 16/28 | 93/113 |
| ⚖ | Criminal Justice | — | 0.41 | 3/6 | 10/28 | 71/113 |

High ▢ Low   ▼ Trending down   ▲ Trending up

■ India   ▨ South Asia   ▨ Lower Middle Income

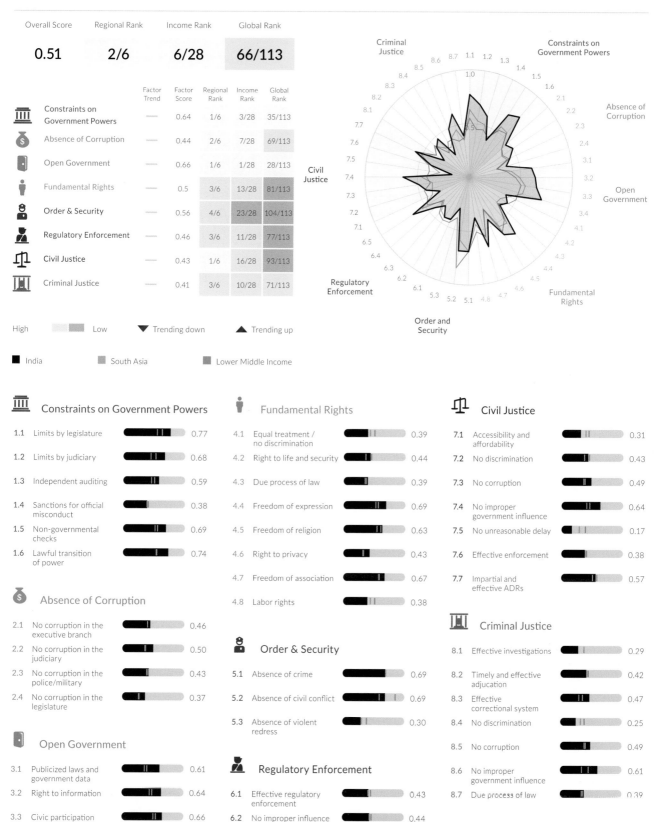

## 🏛 Constraints on Government Powers

| | | |
|---|---|---|
| 1.1 | Limits by legislature | 0.77 |
| 1.2 | Limits by judiciary | 0.68 |
| 1.3 | Independent auditing | 0.59 |
| 1.4 | Sanctions for official misconduct | 0.38 |
| 1.5 | Non-governmental checks | 0.69 |
| 1.6 | Lawful transition of power | 0.74 |

## 💰 Absence of Corruption

| | | |
|---|---|---|
| 2.1 | No corruption in the executive branch | 0.46 |
| 2.2 | No corruption in the judiciary | 0.50 |
| 2.3 | No corruption in the police/military | 0.43 |
| 2.4 | No corruption in the legislature | 0.37 |

## 🚪 Open Government

| | | |
|---|---|---|
| 3.1 | Publicized laws and government data | 0.61 |
| 3.2 | Right to information | 0.64 |
| 3.3 | Civic participation | 0.66 |
| 3.4 | Complaint mechanisms | 0.73 |

## 👤 Fundamental Rights

| | | |
|---|---|---|
| 4.1 | Equal treatment / no discrimination | 0.39 |
| 4.2 | Right to life and security | 0.44 |
| 4.3 | Due process of law | 0.39 |
| 4.4 | Freedom of expression | 0.69 |
| 4.5 | Freedom of religion | 0.63 |
| 4.6 | Right to privacy | 0.43 |
| 4.7 | Freedom of association | 0.67 |
| 4.8 | Labor rights | 0.38 |

## 👮 Order & Security

| | | |
|---|---|---|
| 5.1 | Absence of crime | 0.69 |
| 5.2 | Absence of civil conflict | 0.69 |
| 5.3 | Absence of violent redress | 0.30 |

## 👷 Regulatory Enforcement

| | | |
|---|---|---|
| 6.1 | Effective regulatory enforcement | 0.43 |
| 6.2 | No improper influence | 0.44 |
| 6.3 | No unreasonable delay | 0.35 |
| 6.4 | Respect for due process | 0.43 |
| 6.5 | No expropriation w/out adequate compensation | 0.64 |

## ⚖ Civil Justice

| | | |
|---|---|---|
| 7.1 | Accessibility and affordability | 0.31 |
| 7.2 | No discrimination | 0.43 |
| 7.3 | No corruption | 0.49 |
| 7.4 | No improper government influence | 0.64 |
| 7.5 | No unreasonable delay | 0.17 |
| 7.6 | Effective enforcement | 0.38 |
| 7.7 | Impartial and effective ADRs | 0.57 |

## ⚖ Criminal Justice

| | | |
|---|---|---|
| 8.1 | Effective investigations | 0.29 |
| 8.2 | Timely and effective adjucation | 0.42 |
| 8.3 | Effective correctional system | 0.47 |
| 8.4 | No discrimination | 0.25 |
| 8.5 | No corruption | 0.49 |
| 8.6 | No improper government influence | 0.61 |
| 8.7 | Due process of law | 0.39 |

# Indonesia

**Region:** East Asia & Pacific
**Income Group:** Lower Middle Income

| Overall Score | Regional Rank | Income Rank | Global Rank |
|---|---|---|---|
| 0.52 | 9/15 | 5/28 | 61/113 |

| | Factor Trend | Factor Score | Regional Rank | Income Rank | Global Rank |
|---|---|---|---|---|---|
| Constraints on Government Powers | — | 0.64 | 7/15 | 2/28 | 33/113 |
| Absence of Corruption | — | 0.38 | 14/15 | 13/28 | 84/113 |
| Open Government | — | 0.58 | 7/15 | 2/28 | 37/113 |
| Fundamental Rights | — | 0.52 | 9/15 | 11/28 | 74/113 |
| Order & Security | — | 0.73 | 12/15 | 8/28 | 55/113 |
| Regulatory Enforcement | — | 0.51 | 7/15 | 3/28 | 53/113 |
| Civil Justice | — | 0.43 | 13/15 | 15/28 | 92/113 |
| Criminal Justice | — | 0.38 | 12/15 | 13/28 | 80/113 |

High ▮▮▮ Low     ▼ Trending down     ▲ Trending up

■ Indonesia     ▦ East Asia & Pacific     ▦ Lower Middle Income

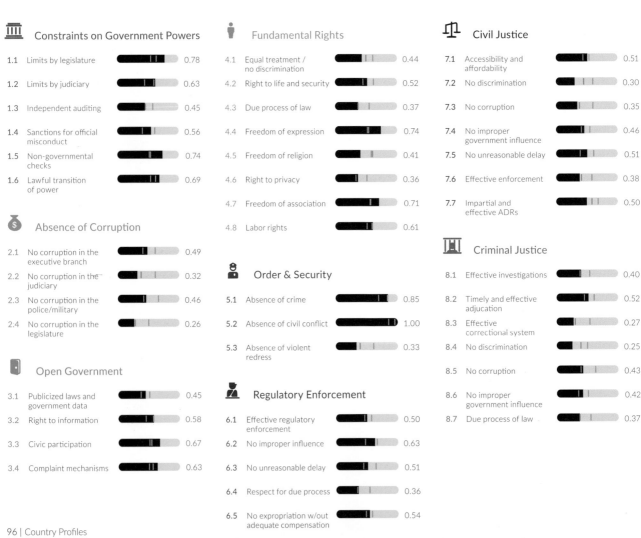

## Constraints on Government Powers

| | | |
|---|---|---|
| 1.1 | Limits by legislature | 0.78 |
| 1.2 | Limits by judiciary | 0.63 |
| 1.3 | Independent auditing | 0.45 |
| 1.4 | Sanctions for official misconduct | 0.56 |
| 1.5 | Non-governmental checks | 0.74 |
| 1.6 | Lawful transition of power | 0.69 |

## Absence of Corruption

| | | |
|---|---|---|
| 2.1 | No corruption in the executive branch | 0.49 |
| 2.2 | No corruption in the judiciary | 0.32 |
| 2.3 | No corruption in the police/military | 0.46 |
| 2.4 | No corruption in the legislature | 0.26 |

## Open Government

| | | |
|---|---|---|
| 3.1 | Publicized laws and government data | 0.45 |
| 3.2 | Right to information | 0.58 |
| 3.3 | Civic participation | 0.67 |
| 3.4 | Complaint mechanisms | 0.63 |

## Fundamental Rights

| | | |
|---|---|---|
| 4.1 | Equal treatment / no discrimination | 0.44 |
| 4.2 | Right to life and security | 0.52 |
| 4.3 | Due process of law | 0.37 |
| 4.4 | Freedom of expression | 0.74 |
| 4.5 | Freedom of religion | 0.41 |
| 4.6 | Right to privacy | 0.36 |
| 4.7 | Freedom of association | 0.71 |
| 4.8 | Labor rights | 0.61 |

## Order & Security

| | | |
|---|---|---|
| 5.1 | Absence of crime | 0.85 |
| 5.2 | Absence of civil conflict | 1.00 |
| 5.3 | Absence of violent redress | 0.33 |

## Regulatory Enforcement

| | | |
|---|---|---|
| 6.1 | Effective regulatory enforcement | 0.50 |
| 6.2 | No improper influence | 0.63 |
| 6.3 | No unreasonable delay | 0.51 |
| 6.4 | Respect for due process | 0.36 |
| 6.5 | No expropriation w/out adequate compensation | 0.54 |

## Civil Justice

| | | |
|---|---|---|
| 7.1 | Accessibility and affordability | 0.51 |
| 7.2 | No discrimination | 0.30 |
| 7.3 | No corruption | 0.35 |
| 7.4 | No improper government influence | 0.46 |
| 7.5 | No unreasonable delay | 0.51 |
| 7.6 | Effective enforcement | 0.38 |
| 7.7 | Impartial and effective ADRs | 0.50 |

## Criminal Justice

| | | |
|---|---|---|
| 8.1 | Effective investigations | 0.40 |
| 8.2 | Timely and effective adjudication | 0.52 |
| 8.3 | Effective correctional system | 0.27 |
| 8.4 | No discrimination | 0.25 |
| 8.5 | No corruption | 0.43 |
| 8.6 | No improper government influence | 0.42 |
| 8.7 | Due process of law | 0.37 |

# Iran

**Region:** Middle East & North Africa
**Income Group:** Upper Middle Income

| Overall Score | Regional Rank | Income Rank | Global Rank |
|---|---|---|---|
| 0.47 | 5/7 | 31/37 | 86/113 |

| | | Factor Trend | Factor Score | Regional Rank | Income Rank | Global Rank |
|---|---|---|---|---|---|---|
| 🏛 | Constraints on Government Powers | ▲ | 0.44 | 6/7 | 30/37 | 94/113 |
| 💰 | Absence of Corruption | — | 0.48 | 4/7 | 18/37 | 57/113 |
| 📱 | Open Government | — | 0.34 | 6/7 | 36/37 | 106/113 |
| 👤 | Fundamental Rights | ▲ | 0.29 | 7/7 | 37/37 | 112/113 |
| 👮 | Order & Security | ▲ | 0.72 | 4/7 | 16/37 | 59/113 |
| 🧑‍🌾 | Regulatory Enforcement | ▼ | 0.50 | 4/7 | 20/37 | 60/113 |
| ⚖ | Civil Justice | — | 0.55 | 3/7 | 16/37 | 52/113 |
| ⚖ | Criminal Justice | — | 0.43 | 5/7 | 20/37 | 65/113 |

High ▓▓ Low  ▼ Trending down  ▲ Trending up

■ Iran  ▓ Middle East & North Africa  ▓ Upper Middle Income

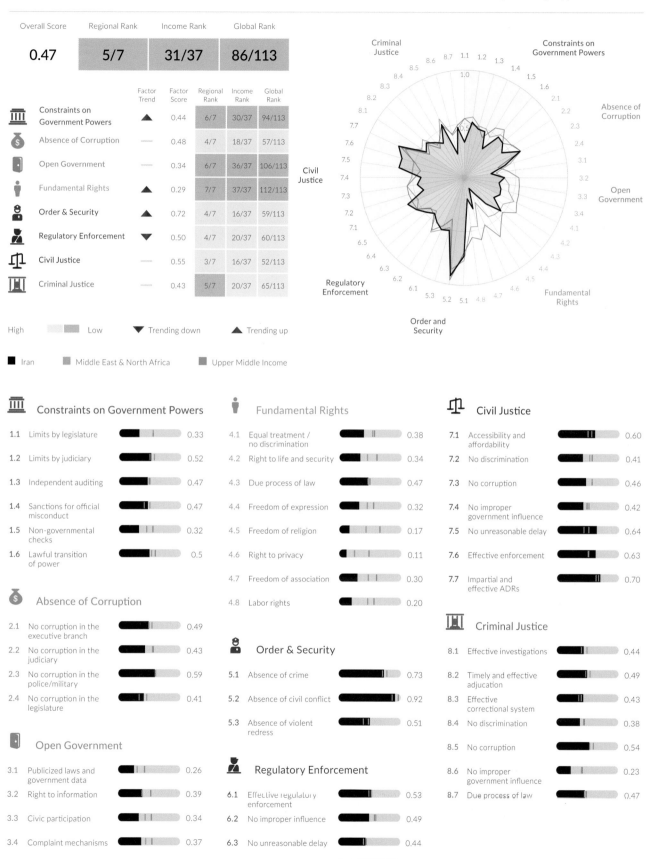

## 🏛 Constraints on Government Powers

| | | |
|---|---|---|
| 1.1 | Limits by legislature | 0.33 |
| 1.2 | Limits by judiciary | 0.52 |
| 1.3 | Independent auditing | 0.47 |
| 1.4 | Sanctions for official misconduct | 0.47 |
| 1.5 | Non-governmental checks | 0.32 |
| 1.6 | Lawful transition of power | 0.5 |

## 💰 Absence of Corruption

| | | |
|---|---|---|
| 2.1 | No corruption in the executive branch | 0.49 |
| 2.2 | No corruption in the judiciary | 0.43 |
| 2.3 | No corruption in the police/military | 0.59 |
| 2.4 | No corruption in the legislature | 0.41 |

## 📱 Open Government

| | | |
|---|---|---|
| 3.1 | Publicized laws and government data | 0.26 |
| 3.2 | Right to information | 0.39 |
| 3.3 | Civic participation | 0.34 |
| 3.4 | Complaint mechanisms | 0.37 |

## 👤 Fundamental Rights

| | | |
|---|---|---|
| 4.1 | Equal treatment / no discrimination | 0.38 |
| 4.2 | Right to life and security | 0.34 |
| 4.3 | Due process of law | 0.47 |
| 4.4 | Freedom of expression | 0.32 |
| 4.5 | Freedom of religion | 0.17 |
| 4.6 | Right to privacy | 0.11 |
| 4.7 | Freedom of association | 0.30 |
| 4.8 | Labor rights | 0.20 |

## 👮 Order & Security

| | | |
|---|---|---|
| 5.1 | Absence of crime | 0.73 |
| 5.2 | Absence of civil conflict | 0.92 |
| 5.3 | Absence of violent redress | 0.51 |

## 🧑‍🌾 Regulatory Enforcement

| | | |
|---|---|---|
| 6.1 | Effective regulatory enforcement | 0.53 |
| 6.2 | No improper influence | 0.49 |
| 6.3 | No unreasonable delay | 0.44 |
| 6.4 | Respect for due process | 0.49 |
| 6.5 | No expropriation w/out adequate compensation | 0.55 |

## ⚖ Civil Justice

| | | |
|---|---|---|
| 7.1 | Accessibility and affordability | 0.60 |
| 7.2 | No discrimination | 0.41 |
| 7.3 | No corruption | 0.46 |
| 7.4 | No improper government influence | 0.42 |
| 7.5 | No unreasonable delay | 0.64 |
| 7.6 | Effective enforcement | 0.63 |
| 7.7 | Impartial and effective ADRs | 0.70 |

## ⚖ Criminal Justice

| | | |
|---|---|---|
| 8.1 | Effective investigations | 0.44 |
| 8.2 | Timely and effective adjucation | 0.49 |
| 8.3 | Effective correctional system | 0.43 |
| 8.4 | No discrimination | 0.38 |
| 8.5 | No corruption | 0.54 |
| 8.6 | No improper government influence | 0.23 |
| 8.7 | Due process of law | 0.47 |

# Italy

**Region:** EU & EFTA & North America
**Income Group:** High Income

| | Overall Score | Regional Rank | Income Rank | Global Rank |
|---|---|---|---|---|
| | 0.64 | 20/24 | 31/36 | 35/113 |

| | | Factor Trend | Factor Score | Regional Rank | Income Rank | Global Rank |
|---|---|---|---|---|---|---|
| 🏛 | Constraints on Government Powers | — | 0.70 | 17/24 | 23/36 | 24/113 |
| 💰 | Absence of Corruption | — | 0.60 | 19/24 | 32/36 | 41/113 |
| 🚪 | Open Government | — | 0.63 | 20/24 | 27/36 | 32/113 |
| 👤 | Fundamental Rights | — | 0.72 | 20/24 | 27/36 | 30/113 |
| 👤 | Order & Security | — | 0.72 | 23/24 | 33/36 | 58/113 |
| 👮 | Regulatory Enforcement | — | 0.57 | 19/24 | 30/36 | 35/113 |
| ⚖ | Civil Justice | — | 0.57 | 22/24 | 34/36 | 46/113 |
| 🏛 | Criminal Justice | — | 0.64 | 18/24 | 27/36 | 29/113 |

High ▢▢▢ Low        ▼ Trending down        ▲ Trending up

■ Italy        ▨ EU & EFTA & North America        ▨ High Income

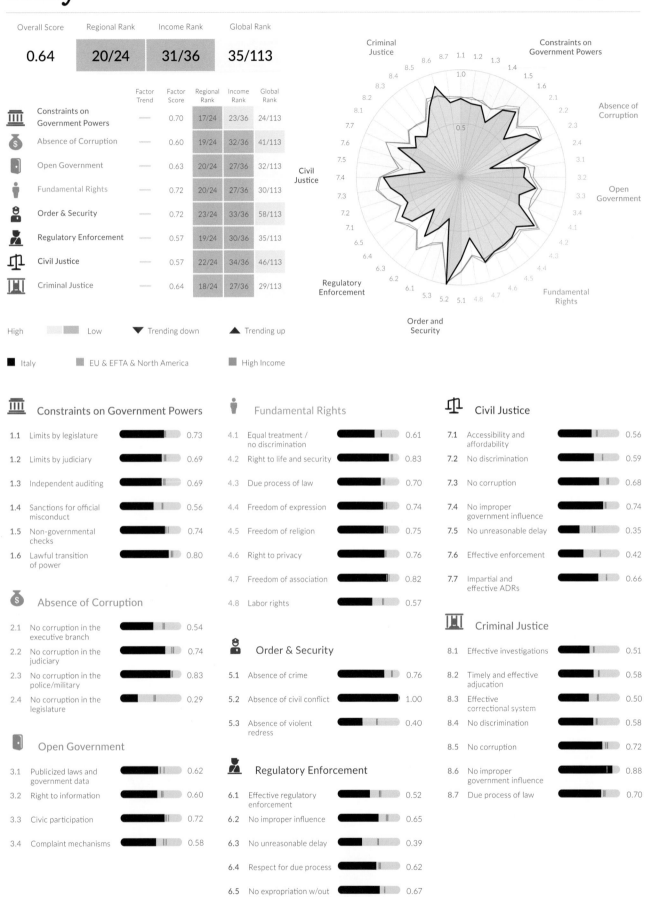

## 🏛 Constraints on Government Powers

| | | |
|---|---|---|
| 1.1 | Limits by legislature | 0.73 |
| 1.2 | Limits by judiciary | 0.69 |
| 1.3 | Independent auditing | 0.69 |
| 1.4 | Sanctions for official misconduct | 0.56 |
| 1.5 | Non-governmental checks | 0.74 |
| 1.6 | Lawful transition of power | 0.80 |

## 💰 Absence of Corruption

| | | |
|---|---|---|
| 2.1 | No corruption in the executive branch | 0.54 |
| 2.2 | No corruption in the judiciary | 0.74 |
| 2.3 | No corruption in the police/military | 0.83 |
| 2.4 | No corruption in the legislature | 0.29 |

## 🚪 Open Government

| | | |
|---|---|---|
| 3.1 | Publicized laws and government data | 0.62 |
| 3.2 | Right to information | 0.60 |
| 3.3 | Civic participation | 0.72 |
| 3.4 | Complaint mechanisms | 0.58 |

## 👤 Fundamental Rights

| | | |
|---|---|---|
| 4.1 | Equal treatment / no discrimination | 0.61 |
| 4.2 | Right to life and security | 0.83 |
| 4.3 | Due process of law | 0.70 |
| 4.4 | Freedom of expression | 0.74 |
| 4.5 | Freedom of religion | 0.75 |
| 4.6 | Right to privacy | 0.76 |
| 4.7 | Freedom of association | 0.82 |
| 4.8 | Labor rights | 0.57 |

## 👤 Order & Security

| | | |
|---|---|---|
| 5.1 | Absence of crime | 0.76 |
| 5.2 | Absence of civil conflict | 1.00 |
| 5.3 | Absence of violent redress | 0.40 |

## 👮 Regulatory Enforcement

| | | |
|---|---|---|
| 6.1 | Effective regulatory enforcement | 0.52 |
| 6.2 | No improper influence | 0.65 |
| 6.3 | No unreasonable delay | 0.39 |
| 6.4 | Respect for due process | 0.62 |
| 6.5 | No expropriation w/out adequate compensation | 0.67 |

## ⚖ Civil Justice

| | | |
|---|---|---|
| 7.1 | Accessibility and affordability | 0.56 |
| 7.2 | No discrimination | 0.59 |
| 7.3 | No corruption | 0.68 |
| 7.4 | No improper government influence | 0.74 |
| 7.5 | No unreasonable delay | 0.35 |
| 7.6 | Effective enforcement | 0.42 |
| 7.7 | Impartial and effective ADRs | 0.66 |

## 🏛 Criminal Justice

| | | |
|---|---|---|
| 8.1 | Effective investigations | 0.51 |
| 8.2 | Timely and effective adjucation | 0.58 |
| 8.3 | Effective correctional system | 0.50 |
| 8.4 | No discrimination | 0.58 |
| 8.5 | No corruption | 0.72 |
| 8.6 | No improper government influence | 0.88 |
| 8.7 | Due process of law | 0.70 |

# Jamaica

**Region:** Latin America & Caribbean
**Income Group:** Upper Middle Income

| | Overall Score | Regional Rank | Income Rank | Global Rank |
|---|---|---|---|---|
| | 0.57 | 12/30 | 11/37 | 47/113 |

| | | Factor Trend | Factor Score | Regional Rank | Income Rank | Global Rank |
|---|---|---|---|---|---|---|
| 🏛 | Constraints on Government Powers | — | 0.64 | 6/30 | 3/37 | 34/113 |
| 💰 | Absence of Corruption | — | 0.55 | 13/30 | 13/37 | 47/113 |
| 🚪 | Open Government | — | 0.58 | 7/30 | 8/37 | 39/113 |
| 👤 | Fundamental Rights | — | 0.63 | 14/30 | 12/37 | 46/113 |
| 👮 | Order & Security | — | 0.64 | 19/30 | 27/37 | 86/113 |
| 👷 | Regulatory Enforcement | — | 0.54 | 12/30 | 11/37 | 47/113 |
| ⚖ | Civil Justice | — | 0.54 | 14/30 | 18/37 | 54/113 |
| ⚖ | Criminal Justice | — | 0.45 | 13/30 | 18/37 | 58/113 |

High ▧ Low   ▼ Trending down   ▲ Trending up

■ Jamaica   ■ Latin America & Caribbean   ■ Upper Middle Income

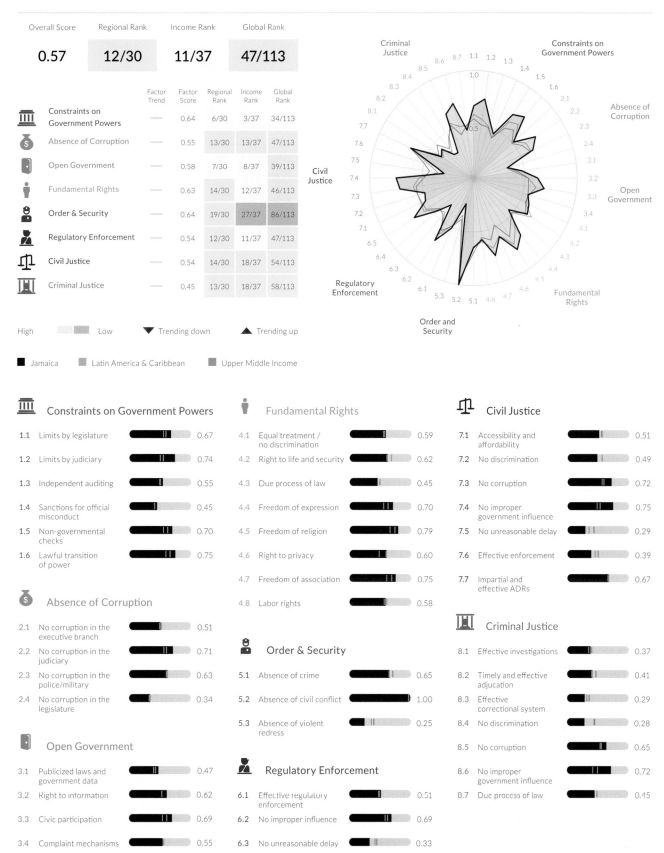

## 🏛 Constraints on Government Powers

| 1.1 | Limits by legislature | 0.67 |
|---|---|---|
| 1.2 | Limits by judiciary | 0.74 |
| 1.3 | Independent auditing | 0.55 |
| 1.4 | Sanctions for official misconduct | 0.45 |
| 1.5 | Non-governmental checks | 0.70 |
| 1.6 | Lawful transition of power | 0.75 |

## 💰 Absence of Corruption

| 2.1 | No corruption in the executive branch | 0.51 |
|---|---|---|
| 2.2 | No corruption in the judiciary | 0.71 |
| 2.3 | No corruption in the police/military | 0.63 |
| 2.4 | No corruption in the legislature | 0.34 |

## 🚪 Open Government

| 3.1 | Publicized laws and government data | 0.47 |
|---|---|---|
| 3.2 | Right to information | 0.62 |
| 3.3 | Civic participation | 0.69 |
| 3.4 | Complaint mechanisms | 0.55 |

## 👤 Fundamental Rights

| 4.1 | Equal treatment / no discrimination | 0.59 |
|---|---|---|
| 4.2 | Right to life and security | 0.62 |
| 4.3 | Due process of law | 0.45 |
| 4.4 | Freedom of expression | 0.70 |
| 4.5 | Freedom of religion | 0.79 |
| 4.6 | Right to privacy | 0.60 |
| 4.7 | Freedom of association | 0.75 |
| 4.8 | Labor rights | 0.58 |

## 👮 Order & Security

| 5.1 | Absence of crime | 0.65 |
|---|---|---|
| 5.2 | Absence of civil conflict | 1.00 |
| 5.3 | Absence of violent redress | 0.25 |

## 👷 Regulatory Enforcement

| 6.1 | Effective regulatory enforcement | 0.51 |
|---|---|---|
| 6.2 | No improper influence | 0.69 |
| 6.3 | No unreasonable delay | 0.33 |
| 6.4 | Respect for due process | 0.47 |
| 6.5 | No expropriation w/out adequate compensation | 0.68 |

## ⚖ Civil Justice

| 7.1 | Accessibility and affordability | 0.51 |
|---|---|---|
| 7.2 | No discrimination | 0.49 |
| 7.3 | No corruption | 0.72 |
| 7.4 | No improper government influence | 0.75 |
| 7.5 | No unreasonable delay | 0.29 |
| 7.6 | Effective enforcement | 0.39 |
| 7.7 | Impartial and effective ADRs | 0.67 |

## ⚖ Criminal Justice

| 8.1 | Effective investigations | 0.37 |
|---|---|---|
| 8.2 | Timely and effective adjudication | 0.41 |
| 8.3 | Effective correctional system | 0.29 |
| 8.4 | No discrimination | 0.28 |
| 8.5 | No corruption | 0.65 |
| 8.6 | No improper government influence | 0.72 |
| 8.7 | Due process of law | 0.45 |

Country Profiles | 99

# Japan

**Region:** East Asia & Pacific
**Income Group:** High Income

| | Overall Score | Regional Rank | Income Rank | Global Rank |
|---|---|---|---|---|
| | 0.78 | 4/15 | 15/36 | 15/113 |

| | | Factor Trend | Factor Score | Regional Rank | Income Rank | Global Rank |
|---|---|---|---|---|---|---|
| 🏛 | Constraints on Government Powers | — | 0.74 | 4/15 | 20/36 | 21/113 |
| 💰 | Absence of Corruption | — | 0.83 | 5/15 | 13/36 | 13/113 |
| 🚪 | Open Government | — | 0.68 | 3/15 | 20/36 | 21/113 |
| 👤 | Fundamental Rights | — | 0.75 | 3/15 | 22/36 | 23/113 |
| 👨‍💼 | Order & Security | — | 0.90 | 2/15 | 8/36 | 9/113 |
| 🧑‍💼 | Regulatory Enforcement | — | 0.82 | 4/15 | 10/36 | 10/113 |
| ⚖ | Civil Justice | — | 0.82 | 2/15 | 6/36 | 6/113 |
| 🏛 | Criminal Justice | — | 0.68 | 6/15 | 21/36 | 21/113 |

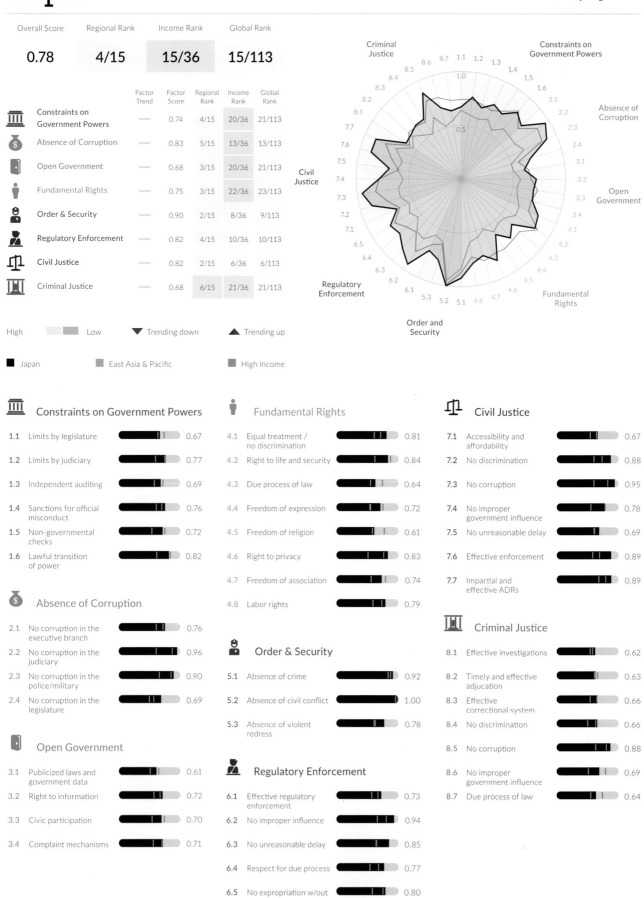

High ▢▢▢ Low   ▼ Trending down   ▲ Trending up

■ Japan   ▨ East Asia & Pacific   ▨ High Income

## 🏛 Constraints on Government Powers

| | | |
|---|---|---|
| 1.1 | Limits by legislature | 0.67 |
| 1.2 | Limits by judiciary | 0.77 |
| 1.3 | Independent auditing | 0.69 |
| 1.4 | Sanctions for official misconduct | 0.76 |
| 1.5 | Non-governmental checks | 0.72 |
| 1.6 | Lawful transition of power | 0.82 |

## 💰 Absence of Corruption

| | | |
|---|---|---|
| 2.1 | No corruption in the executive branch | 0.76 |
| 2.2 | No corruption in the judiciary | 0.96 |
| 2.3 | No corruption in the police/military | 0.90 |
| 2.4 | No corruption in the legislature | 0.69 |

## 🚪 Open Government

| | | |
|---|---|---|
| 3.1 | Publicized laws and government data | 0.61 |
| 3.2 | Right to information | 0.72 |
| 3.3 | Civic participation | 0.70 |
| 3.4 | Complaint mechanisms | 0.71 |

## 👤 Fundamental Rights

| | | |
|---|---|---|
| 4.1 | Equal treatment / no discrimination | 0.81 |
| 4.2 | Right to life and security | 0.84 |
| 4.3 | Due process of law | 0.64 |
| 4.4 | Freedom of expression | 0.72 |
| 4.5 | Freedom of religion | 0.61 |
| 4.6 | Right to privacy | 0.83 |
| 4.7 | Freedom of association | 0.74 |
| 4.8 | Labor rights | 0.79 |

## 👨‍💼 Order & Security

| | | |
|---|---|---|
| 5.1 | Absence of crime | 0.92 |
| 5.2 | Absence of civil conflict | 1.00 |
| 5.3 | Absence of violent redress | 0.78 |

## 🧑‍💼 Regulatory Enforcement

| | | |
|---|---|---|
| 6.1 | Effective regulatory enforcement | 0.73 |
| 6.2 | No improper influence | 0.94 |
| 6.3 | No unreasonable delay | 0.85 |
| 6.4 | Respect for due process | 0.77 |
| 6.5 | No expropriation w/out adequate compensation | 0.80 |

## ⚖ Civil Justice

| | | |
|---|---|---|
| 7.1 | Accessibility and affordability | 0.67 |
| 7.2 | No discrimination | 0.88 |
| 7.3 | No corruption | 0.95 |
| 7.4 | No improper government influence | 0.78 |
| 7.5 | No unreasonable delay | 0.69 |
| 7.6 | Effective enforcement | 0.89 |
| 7.7 | Impartial and effective ADRs | 0.89 |

## 🏛 Criminal Justice

| | | |
|---|---|---|
| 8.1 | Effective investigations | 0.62 |
| 8.2 | Timely and effective adjucation | 0.63 |
| 8.3 | Effective correctional system | 0.66 |
| 8.4 | No discrimination | 0.66 |
| 8.5 | No corruption | 0.88 |
| 8.6 | No improper government influence | 0.69 |
| 8.7 | Due process of law | 0.64 |

# Jordan

**Region:** Middle East & North Africa
**Income Group:** Upper Middle Income

| Overall Score | Regional Rank | Income Rank | Global Rank |
|:---:|:---:|:---:|:---:|
| 0.59 | 2/7 | 8/37 | 42/113 |

| | | Factor Trend | Factor Score | Regional Rank | Income Rank | Global Rank |
|---|---|:---:|:---:|:---:|:---:|:---:|
| 🏛️ | Constraints on Government Powers | ▲ | 0.53 | 4/7 | 16/37 | 62/113 |
| 💰 | Absence of Corruption | — | 0.66 | 2/7 | 6/37 | 33/113 |
| 📱 | Open Government | — | 0.43 | 4/7 | 33/37 | 94/113 |
| 👤 | Fundamental Rights | — | 0.50 | 3/7 | 28/37 | 82/113 |
| 👮 | Order & Security | — | 0.79 | 2/7 | 5/37 | 34/113 |
| 👷 | Regulatory Enforcement | ▲ | 0.58 | 2/7 | 4/37 | 33/113 |
| ⚖️ | Civil Justice | — | 0.63 | 2/7 | 5/37 | 35/113 |
| 🏛️ | Criminal Justice | — | 0.59 | 2/7 | 4/37 | 33/113 |

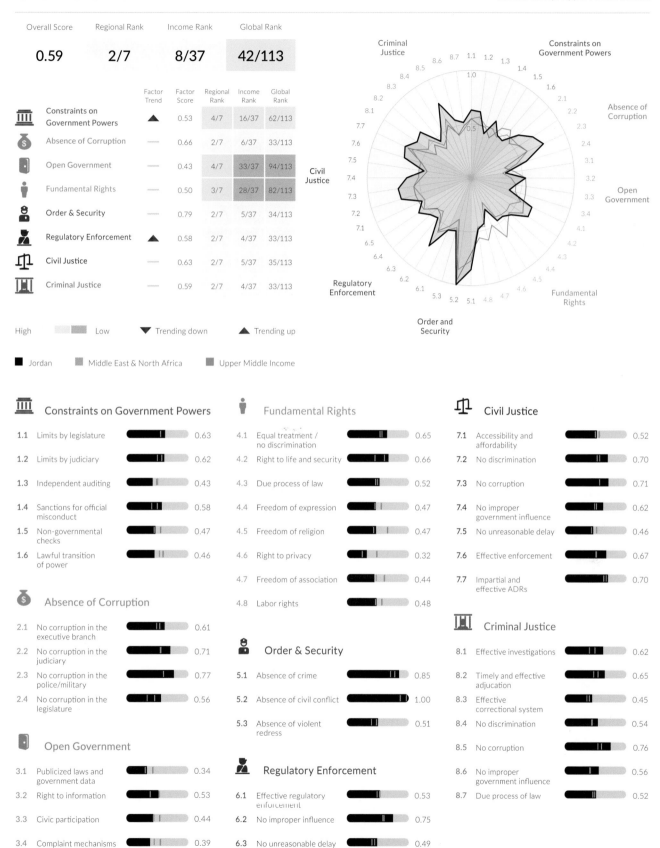

High ▬▬▬ Low   ▼ Trending down   ▲ Trending up

■ Jordan   ▨ Middle East & North Africa   ▪ Upper Middle Income

## 🏛️ Constraints on Government Powers

| | | |
|---|---|---:|
| 1.1 | Limits by legislature | 0.63 |
| 1.2 | Limits by judiciary | 0.62 |
| 1.3 | Independent auditing | 0.43 |
| 1.4 | Sanctions for official misconduct | 0.58 |
| 1.5 | Non-governmental checks | 0.47 |
| 1.6 | Lawful transition of power | 0.46 |

## 💰 Absence of Corruption

| | | |
|---|---|---:|
| 2.1 | No corruption in the executive branch | 0.61 |
| 2.2 | No corruption in the judiciary | 0.71 |
| 2.3 | No corruption in the police/military | 0.77 |
| 2.4 | No corruption in the legislature | 0.56 |

## 📱 Open Government

| | | |
|---|---|---:|
| 3.1 | Publicized laws and government data | 0.34 |
| 3.2 | Right to information | 0.53 |
| 3.3 | Civic participation | 0.44 |
| 3.4 | Complaint mechanisms | 0.39 |

## 👤 Fundamental Rights

| | | |
|---|---|---:|
| 4.1 | Equal treatment / no discrimination | 0.65 |
| 4.2 | Right to life and security | 0.66 |
| 4.3 | Due process of law | 0.52 |
| 4.4 | Freedom of expression | 0.47 |
| 4.5 | Freedom of religion | 0.47 |
| 4.6 | Right to privacy | 0.32 |
| 4.7 | Freedom of association | 0.44 |
| 4.8 | Labor rights | 0.48 |

## 👮 Order & Security

| | | |
|---|---|---:|
| 5.1 | Absence of crime | 0.85 |
| 5.2 | Absence of civil conflict | 1.00 |
| 5.3 | Absence of violent redress | 0.51 |

## 👷 Regulatory Enforcement

| | | |
|---|---|---:|
| 6.1 | Effective regulatory enforcement | 0.53 |
| 6.2 | No improper influence | 0.75 |
| 6.3 | No unreasonable delay | 0.49 |
| 6.4 | Respect for due process | 0.52 |
| 6.5 | No expropriation w/out adequate compensation | 0.60 |

## ⚖️ Civil Justice

| | | |
|---|---|---:|
| 7.1 | Accessibility and affordability | 0.52 |
| 7.2 | No discrimination | 0.70 |
| 7.3 | No corruption | 0.71 |
| 7.4 | No improper government influence | 0.62 |
| 7.5 | No unreasonable delay | 0.46 |
| 7.6 | Effective enforcement | 0.67 |
| 7.7 | Impartial and effective ADRs | 0.70 |

## 🏛️ Criminal Justice

| | | |
|---|---|---:|
| 8.1 | Effective investigations | 0.62 |
| 8.2 | Timely and effective adjudication | 0.65 |
| 8.3 | Effective correctional system | 0.45 |
| 8.4 | No discrimination | 0.54 |
| 8.5 | No corruption | 0.76 |
| 8.6 | No improper government influence | 0.56 |
| 8.7 | Due process of law | 0.52 |

# Kazakhstan

**Region:** Eastern Europe & Central Asia
**Income Group:** Upper Middle Income

| | Overall Score | Regional Rank | Income Rank | Global Rank |
|---|---|---|---|---|
| | 0.50 | 6/13 | 25/37 | 73/113 |

| | | Factor Trend | Factor Score | Regional Rank | Income Rank | Global Rank |
|---|---|---|---|---|---|---|
| 🏛 | Constraints on Government Powers | — | 0.44 | 7/13 | 28/37 | 91/113 |
| 💰 | Absence of Corruption | — | 0.43 | 5/13 | 25/37 | 71/113 |
| 🚪 | Open Government | — | 0.48 | 9/13 | 24/37 | 73/113 |
| 🧍 | Fundamental Rights | — | 0.45 | 10/13 | 31/37 | 92/113 |
| 👤 | Order & Security | — | 0.76 | 5/13 | 7/37 | 40/113 |
| 👷 | Regulatory Enforcement | — | 0.50 | 3/13 | 18/37 | 57/113 |
| ⚖ | Civil Justice | — | 0.55 | 4/13 | 17/37 | 53/113 |
| 🏛 | Criminal Justice | — | 0.41 | 7/13 | 23/37 | 73/113 |

High ▢▢ Low   ▼ Trending down   ▲ Trending up

■ Kazakhstan   ▨ Eastern Europe & Central Asia   ▨ Upper Middle Income

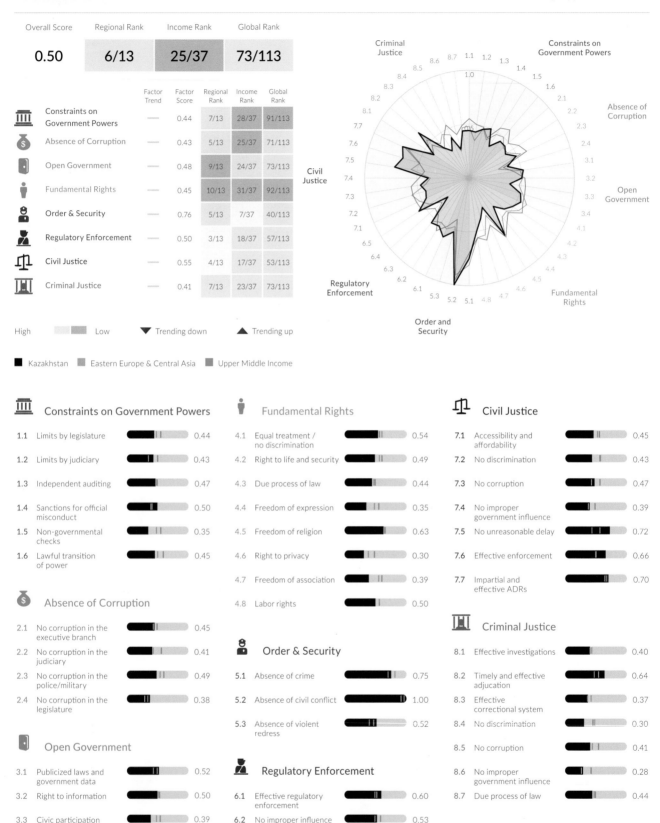

## 🏛 Constraints on Government Powers

| | | |
|---|---|---|
| 1.1 | Limits by legislature | 0.44 |
| 1.2 | Limits by judiciary | 0.43 |
| 1.3 | Independent auditing | 0.47 |
| 1.4 | Sanctions for official misconduct | 0.50 |
| 1.5 | Non-governmental checks | 0.35 |
| 1.6 | Lawful transition of power | 0.45 |

## 💰 Absence of Corruption

| | | |
|---|---|---|
| 2.1 | No corruption in the executive branch | 0.45 |
| 2.2 | No corruption in the judiciary | 0.41 |
| 2.3 | No corruption in the police/military | 0.49 |
| 2.4 | No corruption in the legislature | 0.38 |

## 🚪 Open Government

| | | |
|---|---|---|
| 3.1 | Publicized laws and government data | 0.52 |
| 3.2 | Right to information | 0.50 |
| 3.3 | Civic participation | 0.39 |
| 3.4 | Complaint mechanisms | 0.51 |

## 🧍 Fundamental Rights

| | | |
|---|---|---|
| 4.1 | Equal treatment / no discrimination | 0.54 |
| 4.2 | Right to life and security | 0.49 |
| 4.3 | Due process of law | 0.44 |
| 4.4 | Freedom of expression | 0.35 |
| 4.5 | Freedom of religion | 0.63 |
| 4.6 | Right to privacy | 0.30 |
| 4.7 | Freedom of association | 0.39 |
| 4.8 | Labor rights | 0.50 |

## 👤 Order & Security

| | | |
|---|---|---|
| 5.1 | Absence of crime | 0.75 |
| 5.2 | Absence of civil conflict | 1.00 |
| 5.3 | Absence of violent redress | 0.52 |

## 👷 Regulatory Enforcement

| | | |
|---|---|---|
| 6.1 | Effective regulatory enforcement | 0.60 |
| 6.2 | No improper influence | 0.53 |
| 6.3 | No unreasonable delay | 0.55 |
| 6.4 | Respect for due process | 0.27 |
| 6.5 | No expropriation w/out adequate compensation | 0.57 |

## ⚖ Civil Justice

| | | |
|---|---|---|
| 7.1 | Accessibility and affordability | 0.45 |
| 7.2 | No discrimination | 0.43 |
| 7.3 | No corruption | 0.47 |
| 7.4 | No improper government influence | 0.39 |
| 7.5 | No unreasonable delay | 0.72 |
| 7.6 | Effective enforcement | 0.66 |
| 7.7 | Impartial and effective ADRs | 0.70 |

## 🏛 Criminal Justice

| | | |
|---|---|---|
| 8.1 | Effective investigations | 0.40 |
| 8.2 | Timely and effective adjudication | 0.64 |
| 8.3 | Effective correctional system | 0.37 |
| 8.4 | No discrimination | 0.30 |
| 8.5 | No corruption | 0.41 |
| 8.6 | No improper government influence | 0.28 |
| 8.7 | Due process of law | 0.44 |

# Kenya

| | Overall Score | Regional Rank | Income Rank | Global Rank |
|---|---|---|---|---|
| | 0.43 | 14/18 | 20/28 | 100/113 |

| | | Factor Trend | Factor Score | Regional Rank | Income Rank | Global Rank |
|---|---|---|---|---|---|---|
| 🏛 | Constraints on Government Powers | ▼ | 0.50 | 10/18 | 15/28 | 77/113 |
| 💰 | Absence of Corruption | — | 0.26 | 16/18 | 26/28 | 108/113 |
| 📱 | Open Government | — | 0.49 | 6/18 | 11/28 | 70/113 |
| 👤 | Fundamental Rights | — | 0.47 | 11/18 | 15/28 | 87/113 |
| 👮 | Order & Security | — | 0.51 | 16/18 | 24/28 | 107/113 |
| 👷 | Regulatory Enforcement | — | 0.43 | 10/18 | 18/28 | 92/113 |
| ⚖ | Civil Justice | — | 0.43 | 13/18 | 14/28 | 91/113 |
| 🏛 | Criminal Justice | — | 0.35 | 14/18 | 18/28 | 88/113 |

High ▢▢▢ Low    ▼ Trending down    ▲ Trending up

■ Kenya    ▦ Sub-Saharan Africa    ▦ Lower Middle Income

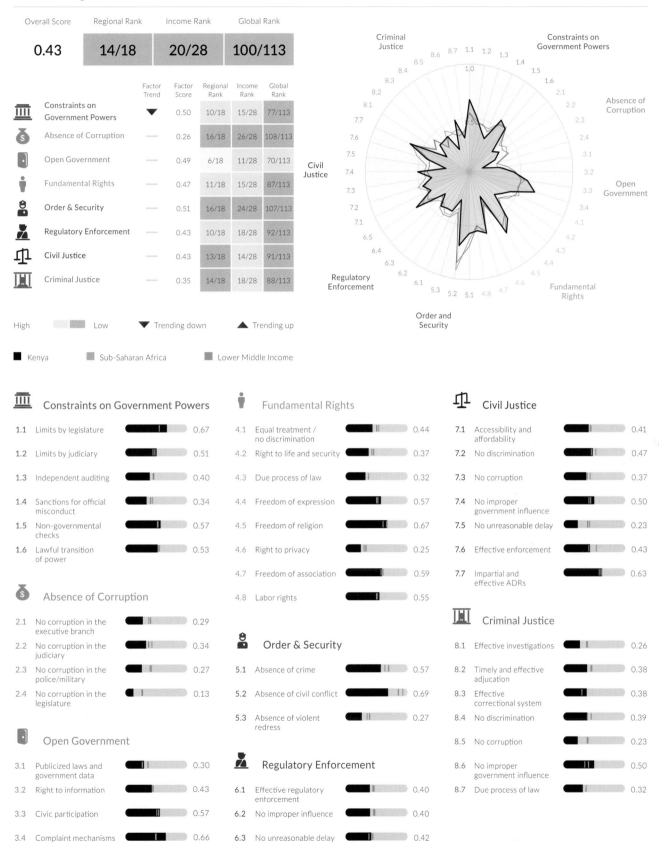

## 🏛 Constraints on Government Powers

| | | |
|---|---|---|
| 1.1 | Limits by legislature | 0.67 |
| 1.2 | Limits by judiciary | 0.51 |
| 1.3 | Independent auditing | 0.40 |
| 1.4 | Sanctions for official misconduct | 0.34 |
| 1.5 | Non-governmental checks | 0.57 |
| 1.6 | Lawful transition of power | 0.53 |

## 💰 Absence of Corruption

| | | |
|---|---|---|
| 2.1 | No corruption in the executive branch | 0.29 |
| 2.2 | No corruption in the judiciary | 0.34 |
| 2.3 | No corruption in the police/military | 0.27 |
| 2.4 | No corruption in the legislature | 0.13 |

## 📱 Open Government

| | | |
|---|---|---|
| 3.1 | Publicized laws and government data | 0.30 |
| 3.2 | Right to information | 0.43 |
| 3.3 | Civic participation | 0.57 |
| 3.4 | Complaint mechanisms | 0.66 |

## 👤 Fundamental Rights

| | | |
|---|---|---|
| 4.1 | Equal treatment / no discrimination | 0.44 |
| 4.2 | Right to life and security | 0.37 |
| 4.3 | Due process of law | 0.32 |
| 4.4 | Freedom of expression | 0.57 |
| 4.5 | Freedom of religion | 0.67 |
| 4.6 | Right to privacy | 0.25 |
| 4.7 | Freedom of association | 0.59 |
| 4.8 | Labor rights | 0.55 |

## 👮 Order & Security

| | | |
|---|---|---|
| 5.1 | Absence of crime | 0.57 |
| 5.2 | Absence of civil conflict | 0.69 |
| 5.3 | Absence of violent redress | 0.27 |

## 👷 Regulatory Enforcement

| | | |
|---|---|---|
| 6.1 | Effective regulatory enforcement | 0.40 |
| 6.2 | No improper influence | 0.40 |
| 6.3 | No unreasonable delay | 0.42 |
| 6.4 | Respect for due process | 0.31 |
| 6.5 | No expropriation w/out adequate compensation | 0.61 |

## ⚖ Civil Justice

| | | |
|---|---|---|
| 7.1 | Accessibility and affordability | 0.41 |
| 7.2 | No discrimination | 0.47 |
| 7.3 | No corruption | 0.37 |
| 7.4 | No improper government influence | 0.50 |
| 7.5 | No unreasonable delay | 0.23 |
| 7.6 | Effective enforcement | 0.43 |
| 7.7 | Impartial and effective ADRs | 0.63 |

## 🏛 Criminal Justice

| | | |
|---|---|---|
| 8.1 | Effective investigations | 0.26 |
| 8.2 | Timely and effective adjucation | 0.38 |
| 8.3 | Effective correctional system | 0.38 |
| 8.4 | No discrimination | 0.39 |
| 8.5 | No corruption | 0.23 |
| 8.6 | No improper government influence | 0.50 |
| 8.7 | Due process of law | 0.32 |

# Kyrgyzstan

| | Overall Score | Regional Rank | Income Rank | Global Rank |
|---|---|---|---|---|
| | 0.47 | 10/13 | 14/28 | 83/113 |

| | | Factor Trend | Factor Score | Regional Rank | Income Rank | Global Rank |
|---|---|---|---|---|---|---|
| 🏛 | Constraints on Government Powers | — | 0.50 | 4/13 | 13/28 | 75/113 |
| 💰 | Absence of Corruption | — | 0.28 | 13/13 | 25/28 | 106/113 |
| 📱 | Open Government | — | 0.55 | 5/13 | 4/28 | 49/113 |
| 👤 | Fundamental Rights | — | 0.54 | 8/13 | 9/28 | 69/113 |
| 👮 | Order & Security | — | 0.75 | 7/13 | 5/28 | 46/113 |
| 👷 | Regulatory Enforcement | — | 0.38 | 13/13 | 25/28 | 104/113 |
| ⚖ | Civil Justice | — | 0.43 | 13/13 | 17/28 | 94/113 |
| 🏛 | Criminal Justice | — | 0.33 | 12/13 | 20/28 | 96/113 |

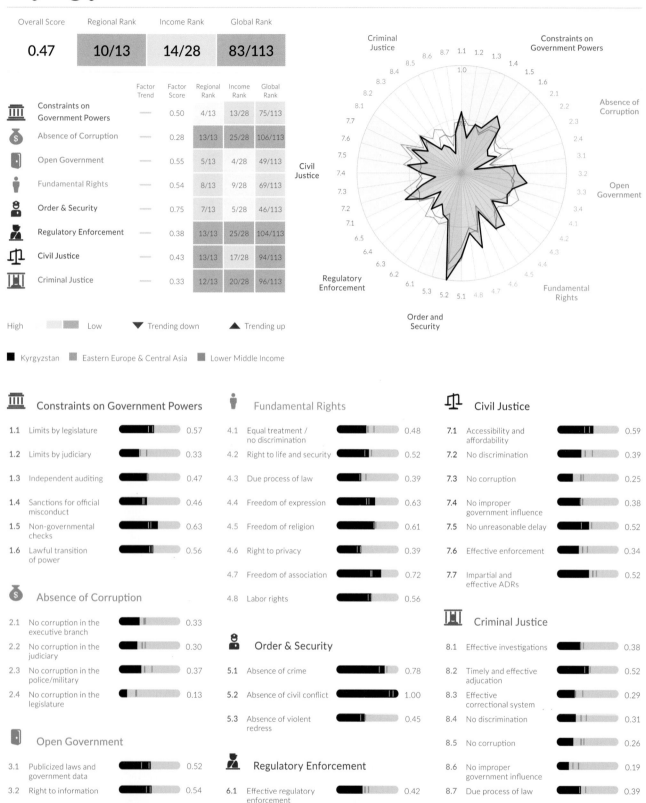

High ▬▬▬ Low     ▼ Trending down     ▲ Trending up

■ Kyrgyzstan     ■ Eastern Europe & Central Asia     ■ Lower Middle Income

## 🏛 Constraints on Government Powers

| | | |
|---|---|---|
| 1.1 | Limits by legislature | 0.57 |
| 1.2 | Limits by judiciary | 0.33 |
| 1.3 | Independent auditing | 0.47 |
| 1.4 | Sanctions for official misconduct | 0.46 |
| 1.5 | Non-governmental checks | 0.63 |
| 1.6 | Lawful transition of power | 0.56 |

## 💰 Absence of Corruption

| | | |
|---|---|---|
| 2.1 | No corruption in the executive branch | 0.33 |
| 2.2 | No corruption in the judiciary | 0.30 |
| 2.3 | No corruption in the police/military | 0.37 |
| 2.4 | No corruption in the legislature | 0.13 |

## 📱 Open Government

| | | |
|---|---|---|
| 3.1 | Publicized laws and government data | 0.52 |
| 3.2 | Right to information | 0.54 |
| 3.3 | Civic participation | 0.63 |
| 3.4 | Complaint mechanisms | 0.51 |

## 👤 Fundamental Rights

| | | |
|---|---|---|
| 4.1 | Equal treatment / no discrimination | 0.48 |
| 4.2 | Right to life and security | 0.52 |
| 4.3 | Due process of law | 0.39 |
| 4.4 | Freedom of expression | 0.63 |
| 4.5 | Freedom of religion | 0.61 |
| 4.6 | Right to privacy | 0.39 |
| 4.7 | Freedom of association | 0.72 |
| 4.8 | Labor rights | 0.56 |

## 👮 Order & Security

| | | |
|---|---|---|
| 5.1 | Absence of crime | 0.78 |
| 5.2 | Absence of civil conflict | 1.00 |
| 5.3 | Absence of violent redress | 0.45 |

## 👷 Regulatory Enforcement

| | | |
|---|---|---|
| 6.1 | Effective regulatory enforcement | 0.42 |
| 6.2 | No improper influence | 0.34 |
| 6.3 | No unreasonable delay | 0.44 |
| 6.4 | Respect for due process | 0.26 |
| 6.5 | No expropriation w/out adequate compensation | 0.44 |

## ⚖ Civil Justice

| | | |
|---|---|---|
| 7.1 | Accessibility and affordability | 0.59 |
| 7.2 | No discrimination | 0.39 |
| 7.3 | No corruption | 0.25 |
| 7.4 | No improper government influence | 0.38 |
| 7.5 | No unreasonable delay | 0.52 |
| 7.6 | Effective enforcement | 0.34 |
| 7.7 | Impartial and effective ADRs | 0.52 |

## 🏛 Criminal Justice

| | | |
|---|---|---|
| 8.1 | Effective investigations | 0.38 |
| 8.2 | Timely and effective adjudication | 0.52 |
| 8.3 | Effective correctional system | 0.29 |
| 8.4 | No discrimination | 0.31 |
| 8.5 | No corruption | 0.26 |
| 8.6 | No improper government influence | 0.19 |
| 8.7 | Due process of law | 0.39 |

# Lebanon

**Region:** Middle East & North Africa
**Income Group:** Upper Middle Income

| Overall Score | Regional Rank | Income Rank | Global Rank |
|---|---|---|---|
| 0.46 | 6/7 | 33/37 | 89/113 |

| | | Factor Trend | Factor Score | Regional Rank | Income Rank | Global Rank |
|---|---|---|---|---|---|---|
| 🏛 | Constraints on Government Powers | ▼ | 0.51 | 5/7 | 21/37 | 73/113 |
| 💰 | Absence of Corruption | — | 0.36 | 7/7 | 32/37 | 88/113 |
| 📱 | Open Government | — | 0.43 | 3/7 | 32/37 | 93/113 |
| 👤 | Fundamental Rights | — | 0.51 | 2/7 | 25/37 | 77/113 |
| 🧑 | Order & Security | — | 0.64 | 5/7 | 24/37 | 83/113 |
| 👮 | Regulatory Enforcement | — | 0.41 | 6/7 | 36/37 | 96/113 |
| ⚖ | Civil Justice | — | 0.48 | 6/7 | 29/37 | 77/113 |
| 🏛 | Criminal Justice | — | 0.31 | 7/7 | 34/37 | 103/113 |

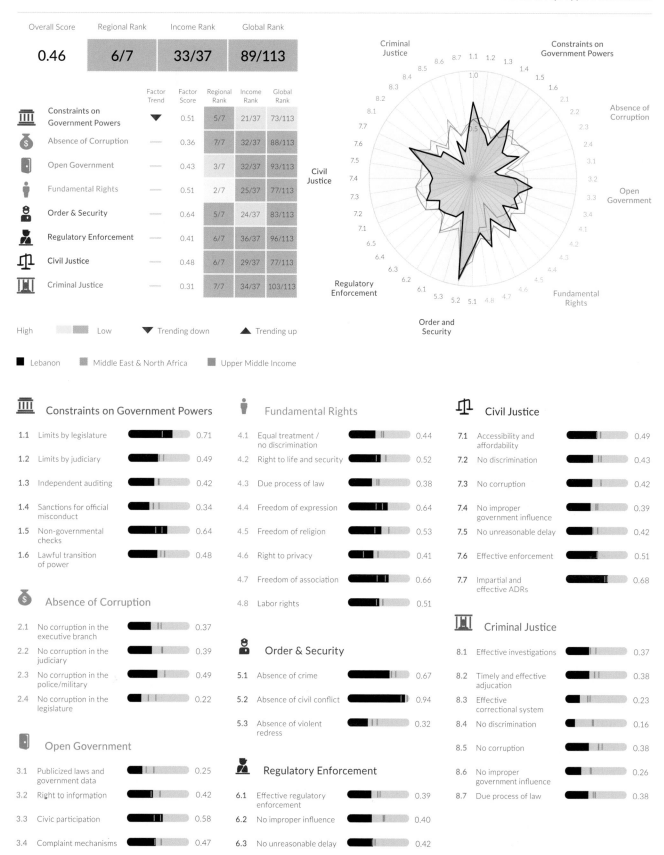

High ▢ Low    ▼ Trending down    ▲ Trending up

■ Lebanon    ▨ Middle East & North Africa    ▨ Upper Middle Income

## 🏛 Constraints on Government Powers

| | | |
|---|---|---|
| 1.1 | Limits by legislature | 0.71 |
| 1.2 | Limits by judiciary | 0.49 |
| 1.3 | Independent auditing | 0.42 |
| 1.4 | Sanctions for official misconduct | 0.34 |
| 1.5 | Non-governmental checks | 0.64 |
| 1.6 | Lawful transition of power | 0.48 |

## 💰 Absence of Corruption

| | | |
|---|---|---|
| 2.1 | No corruption in the executive branch | 0.37 |
| 2.2 | No corruption in the judiciary | 0.39 |
| 2.3 | No corruption in the police/military | 0.49 |
| 2.4 | No corruption in the legislature | 0.22 |

## 📱 Open Government

| | | |
|---|---|---|
| 3.1 | Publicized laws and government data | 0.25 |
| 3.2 | Right to information | 0.42 |
| 3.3 | Civic participation | 0.58 |
| 3.4 | Complaint mechanisms | 0.47 |

## 👤 Fundamental Rights

| | | |
|---|---|---|
| 4.1 | Equal treatment / no discrimination | 0.44 |
| 4.2 | Right to life and security | 0.52 |
| 4.3 | Due process of law | 0.38 |
| 4.4 | Freedom of expression | 0.64 |
| 4.5 | Freedom of religion | 0.53 |
| 4.6 | Right to privacy | 0.41 |
| 4.7 | Freedom of association | 0.66 |
| 4.8 | Labor rights | 0.51 |

## 🧑 Order & Security

| | | |
|---|---|---|
| 5.1 | Absence of crime | 0.67 |
| 5.2 | Absence of civil conflict | 0.94 |
| 5.3 | Absence of violent redress | 0.32 |

## 👮 Regulatory Enforcement

| | | |
|---|---|---|
| 6.1 | Effective regulatory enforcement | 0.39 |
| 6.2 | No improper influence | 0.40 |
| 6.3 | No unreasonable delay | 0.42 |
| 6.4 | Respect for due process | 0.43 |
| 6.5 | No expropriation w/out adequate compensation | 0.38 |

## ⚖ Civil Justice

| | | |
|---|---|---|
| 7.1 | Accessibility and affordability | 0.49 |
| 7.2 | No discrimination | 0.43 |
| 7.3 | No corruption | 0.42 |
| 7.4 | No improper government influence | 0.39 |
| 7.5 | No unreasonable delay | 0.42 |
| 7.6 | Effective enforcement | 0.51 |
| 7.7 | Impartial and effective ADRs | 0.68 |

## 🏛 Criminal Justice

| | | |
|---|---|---|
| 8.1 | Effective investigations | 0.37 |
| 8.2 | Timely and effective adjucation | 0.38 |
| 8.3 | Effective correctional system | 0.23 |
| 8.4 | No discrimination | 0.16 |
| 8.5 | No corruption | 0.38 |
| 8.6 | No improper government influence | 0.26 |
| 8.7 | Due process of law | 0.38 |

# Liberia

**Region:** Sub-Saharan Africa
**Income Group:** Low Income

| Overall Score | Regional Rank | Income Rank | Global Rank |
|:---:|:---:|:---:|:---:|
| 0.45 | 11/18 | 7/12 | 94/113 |

| | Factor Trend | Factor Score | Regional Rank | Income Rank | Global Rank |
|---|:---:|:---:|:---:|:---:|:---:|
| Constraints on Government Powers | — | 0.56 | 5/18 | 4/12 | 58/113 |
| Absence of Corruption | — | 0.26 | 17/18 | 11/12 | 109/113 |
| Open Government | — | 0.48 | 7/18 | 4/12 | 72/113 |
| Fundamental Rights | — | 0.56 | 7/18 | 5/12 | 64/113 |
| Order & Security | — | 0.61 | 14/18 | 10/12 | 96/113 |
| Regulatory Enforcement | — | 0.41 | 12/18 | 6/12 | 98/113 |
| Civil Justice | — | 0.45 | 12/18 | 6/12 | 88/113 |
| Criminal Justice | — | 0.26 | 18/18 | 12/12 | 110/113 |

High ▢ Low   ▼ Trending down   ▲ Trending up

■ Liberia   ■ Sub-Saharan Africa   ▢ Low Income

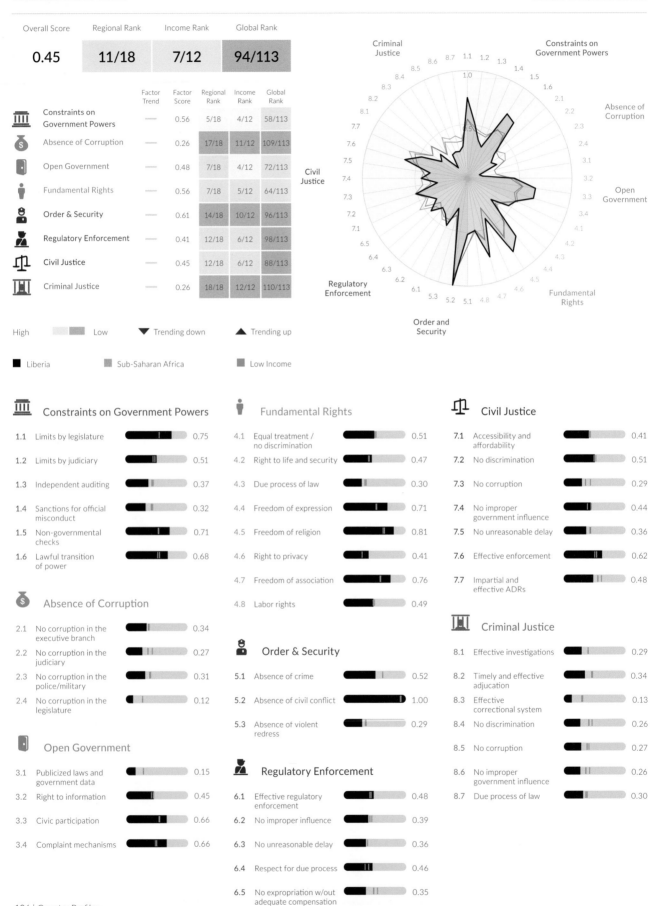

## Constraints on Government Powers

| | | |
|---|---|---|
| 1.1 | Limits by legislature | 0.75 |
| 1.2 | Limits by judiciary | 0.51 |
| 1.3 | Independent auditing | 0.37 |
| 1.4 | Sanctions for official misconduct | 0.32 |
| 1.5 | Non-governmental checks | 0.71 |
| 1.6 | Lawful transition of power | 0.68 |

## Absence of Corruption

| | | |
|---|---|---|
| 2.1 | No corruption in the executive branch | 0.34 |
| 2.2 | No corruption in the judiciary | 0.27 |
| 2.3 | No corruption in the police/military | 0.31 |
| 2.4 | No corruption in the legislature | 0.12 |

## Open Government

| | | |
|---|---|---|
| 3.1 | Publicized laws and government data | 0.15 |
| 3.2 | Right to information | 0.45 |
| 3.3 | Civic participation | 0.66 |
| 3.4 | Complaint mechanisms | 0.66 |

## Fundamental Rights

| | | |
|---|---|---|
| 4.1 | Equal treatment / no discrimination | 0.51 |
| 4.2 | Right to life and security | 0.47 |
| 4.3 | Due process of law | 0.30 |
| 4.4 | Freedom of expression | 0.71 |
| 4.5 | Freedom of religion | 0.81 |
| 4.6 | Right to privacy | 0.41 |
| 4.7 | Freedom of association | 0.76 |
| 4.8 | Labor rights | 0.49 |

## Order & Security

| | | |
|---|---|---|
| 5.1 | Absence of crime | 0.52 |
| 5.2 | Absence of civil conflict | 1.00 |
| 5.3 | Absence of violent redress | 0.29 |

## Regulatory Enforcement

| | | |
|---|---|---|
| 6.1 | Effective regulatory enforcement | 0.48 |
| 6.2 | No improper influence | 0.39 |
| 6.3 | No unreasonable delay | 0.36 |
| 6.4 | Respect for due process | 0.46 |
| 6.5 | No expropriation w/out adequate compensation | 0.35 |

## Civil Justice

| | | |
|---|---|---|
| 7.1 | Accessibility and affordability | 0.41 |
| 7.2 | No discrimination | 0.51 |
| 7.3 | No corruption | 0.29 |
| 7.4 | No improper government influence | 0.44 |
| 7.5 | No unreasonable delay | 0.36 |
| 7.6 | Effective enforcement | 0.62 |
| 7.7 | Impartial and effective ADRs | 0.48 |

## Criminal Justice

| | | |
|---|---|---|
| 8.1 | Effective investigations | 0.29 |
| 8.2 | Timely and effective adjudication | 0.34 |
| 8.3 | Effective correctional system | 0.13 |
| 8.4 | No discrimination | 0.26 |
| 8.5 | No corruption | 0.27 |
| 8.6 | No improper government influence | 0.26 |
| 8.7 | Due process of law | 0.30 |

# Macedonia, FYR

**Region:** Eastern Europe & Central Asia
**Income Group:** Upper Middle Income

| | Overall Score | Regional Rank | Income Rank | Global Rank |
|---|---|---|---|---|
| | 0.54 | 3/13 | 16/37 | 54/113 |

| | | Factor Trend | Factor Score | Regional Rank | Income Rank | Global Rank |
|---|---|---|---|---|---|---|
| 🏛 | Constraints on Government Powers | — | 0.43 | 9/13 | 31/37 | 96/113 |
| 💰 | Absence of Corruption | — | 0.50 | 3/13 | 17/37 | 55/113 |
| 📱 | Open Government | — | 0.56 | 4/13 | 13/37 | 45/113 |
| 👤 | Fundamental Rights | — | 0.54 | 7/13 | 20/37 | 67/113 |
| 👥 | Order & Security | — | 0.74 | 8/13 | 13/37 | 48/113 |
| 👷 | Regulatory Enforcement | — | 0.47 | 5/13 | 24/37 | 70/113 |
| ⚖ | Civil Justice | — | 0.56 | 3/13 | 15/37 | 51/113 |
| 🏛 | Criminal Justice | — | 0.51 | 3/13 | 14/37 | 48/113 |

High ▢▢ Low   ▼ Trending down   ▲ Trending up

■ Macedonia, FYR   ▦ Eastern Europe & Central Asia   ▦ Upper Middle Income

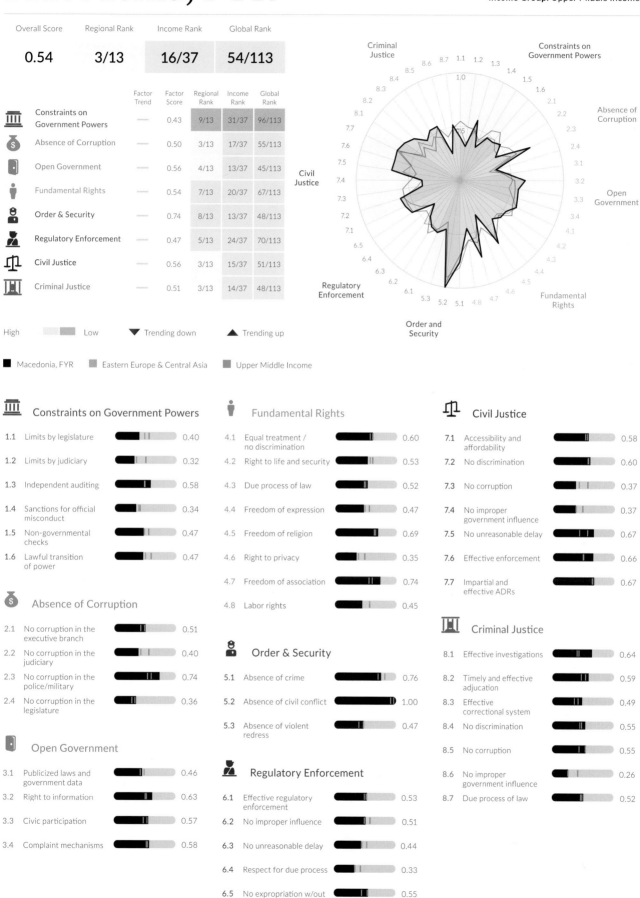

## 🏛 Constraints on Government Powers

| | | |
|---|---|---|
| 1.1 | Limits by legislature | 0.40 |
| 1.2 | Limits by judiciary | 0.32 |
| 1.3 | Independent auditing | 0.58 |
| 1.4 | Sanctions for official misconduct | 0.34 |
| 1.5 | Non-governmental checks | 0.47 |
| 1.6 | Lawful transition of power | 0.47 |

## 💰 Absence of Corruption

| | | |
|---|---|---|
| 2.1 | No corruption in the executive branch | 0.51 |
| 2.2 | No corruption in the judiciary | 0.40 |
| 2.3 | No corruption in the police/military | 0.74 |
| 2.4 | No corruption in the legislature | 0.36 |

## 📱 Open Government

| | | |
|---|---|---|
| 3.1 | Publicized laws and government data | 0.46 |
| 3.2 | Right to information | 0.63 |
| 3.3 | Civic participation | 0.57 |
| 3.4 | Complaint mechanisms | 0.58 |

## 👤 Fundamental Rights

| | | |
|---|---|---|
| 4.1 | Equal treatment / no discrimination | 0.60 |
| 4.2 | Right to life and security | 0.53 |
| 4.3 | Due process of law | 0.52 |
| 4.4 | Freedom of expression | 0.47 |
| 4.5 | Freedom of religion | 0.69 |
| 4.6 | Right to privacy | 0.35 |
| 4.7 | Freedom of association | 0.74 |
| 4.8 | Labor rights | 0.45 |

## 👥 Order & Security

| | | |
|---|---|---|
| 5.1 | Absence of crime | 0.76 |
| 5.2 | Absence of civil conflict | 1.00 |
| 5.3 | Absence of violent redress | 0.47 |

## 👷 Regulatory Enforcement

| | | |
|---|---|---|
| 6.1 | Effective regulatory enforcement | 0.53 |
| 6.2 | No improper influence | 0.51 |
| 6.3 | No unreasonable delay | 0.44 |
| 6.4 | Respect for due process | 0.33 |
| 6.5 | No expropriation w/out adequate compensation | 0.55 |

## ⚖ Civil Justice

| | | |
|---|---|---|
| 7.1 | Accessibility and affordability | 0.58 |
| 7.2 | No discrimination | 0.60 |
| 7.3 | No corruption | 0.37 |
| 7.4 | No improper government influence | 0.37 |
| 7.5 | No unreasonable delay | 0.67 |
| 7.6 | Effective enforcement | 0.66 |
| 7.7 | Impartial and effective ADRs | 0.67 |

## 🏛 Criminal Justice

| | | |
|---|---|---|
| 8.1 | Effective investigations | 0.64 |
| 8.2 | Timely and effective adjucation | 0.59 |
| 8.3 | Effective correctional system | 0.49 |
| 8.4 | No discrimination | 0.55 |
| 8.5 | No corruption | 0.55 |
| 8.6 | No improper government influence | 0.26 |
| 8.7 | Due process of law | 0.52 |

# Madagascar

| | Overall Score | Regional Rank | Income Rank | Global Rank |
|---|---|---|---|---|
| | 0.45 | 10/18 | 6/12 | 90/113 |

| | Factor Trend | Factor Score | Regional Rank | Income Rank | Global Rank |
|---|---|---|---|---|---|
| Constraints on Government Powers | — | 0.46 | 13/18 | 8/12 | 86/113 |
| Absence of Corruption | — | 0.30 | 13/18 | 8/12 | 102/113 |
| Open Government | — | 0.46 | 8/18 | 5/12 | 80/113 |
| Fundamental Rights | — | 0.49 | 9/18 | 7/12 | 84/113 |
| Order & Security | — | 0.73 | 1/18 | 2/12 | 51/113 |
| Regulatory Enforcement | — | 0.38 | 13/18 | 7/12 | 102/113 |
| Civil Justice | — | 0.41 | 15/18 | 9/12 | 100/113 |
| Criminal Justice | — | 0.40 | 10/18 | 6/12 | 76/113 |

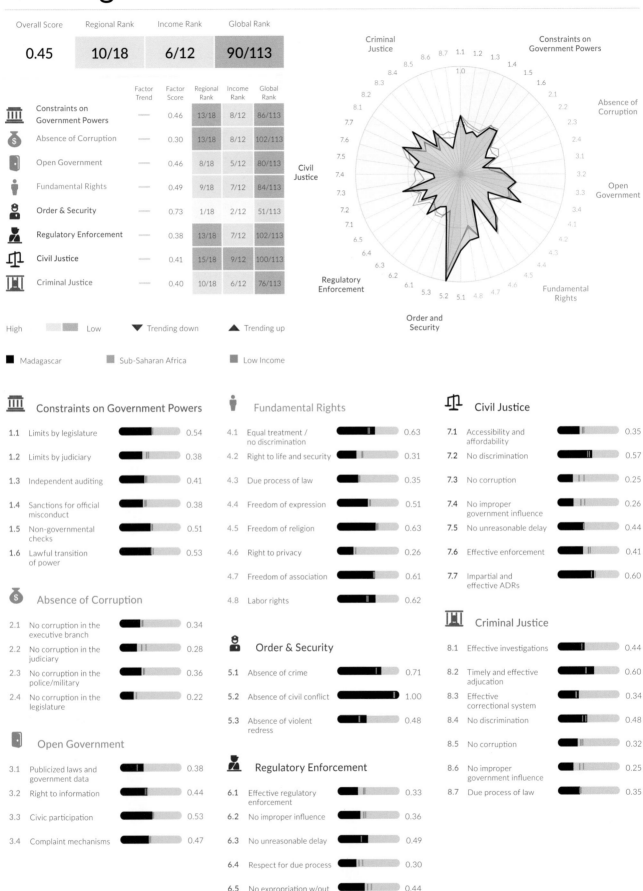

High ▢ Low     ▼ Trending down     ▲ Trending up

■ Madagascar     ▨ Sub-Saharan Africa     ▢ Low Income

## 🏛 Constraints on Government Powers

| | | |
|---|---|---|
| 1.1 | Limits by legislature | 0.54 |
| 1.2 | Limits by judiciary | 0.38 |
| 1.3 | Independent auditing | 0.41 |
| 1.4 | Sanctions for official misconduct | 0.38 |
| 1.5 | Non-governmental checks | 0.51 |
| 1.6 | Lawful transition of power | 0.53 |

## 💰 Absence of Corruption

| | | |
|---|---|---|
| 2.1 | No corruption in the executive branch | 0.34 |
| 2.2 | No corruption in the judiciary | 0.28 |
| 2.3 | No corruption in the police/military | 0.36 |
| 2.4 | No corruption in the legislature | 0.22 |

## 📱 Open Government

| | | |
|---|---|---|
| 3.1 | Publicized laws and government data | 0.38 |
| 3.2 | Right to information | 0.44 |
| 3.3 | Civic participation | 0.53 |
| 3.4 | Complaint mechanisms | 0.47 |

## 👤 Fundamental Rights

| | | |
|---|---|---|
| 4.1 | Equal treatment / no discrimination | 0.63 |
| 4.2 | Right to life and security | 0.31 |
| 4.3 | Due process of law | 0.35 |
| 4.4 | Freedom of expression | 0.51 |
| 4.5 | Freedom of religion | 0.63 |
| 4.6 | Right to privacy | 0.26 |
| 4.7 | Freedom of association | 0.61 |
| 4.8 | Labor rights | 0.62 |

## 👮 Order & Security

| | | |
|---|---|---|
| 5.1 | Absence of crime | 0.71 |
| 5.2 | Absence of civil conflict | 1.00 |
| 5.3 | Absence of violent redress | 0.48 |

## 🛠 Regulatory Enforcement

| | | |
|---|---|---|
| 6.1 | Effective regulatory enforcement | 0.33 |
| 6.2 | No improper influence | 0.36 |
| 6.3 | No unreasonable delay | 0.49 |
| 6.4 | Respect for due process | 0.30 |
| 6.5 | No expropriation w/out adequate compensation | 0.44 |

## ⚖ Civil Justice

| | | |
|---|---|---|
| 7.1 | Accessibility and affordability | 0.35 |
| 7.2 | No discrimination | 0.57 |
| 7.3 | No corruption | 0.25 |
| 7.4 | No improper government influence | 0.26 |
| 7.5 | No unreasonable delay | 0.44 |
| 7.6 | Effective enforcement | 0.41 |
| 7.7 | Impartial and effective ADRs | 0.60 |

## ⚖ Criminal Justice

| | | |
|---|---|---|
| 8.1 | Effective investigations | 0.44 |
| 8.2 | Timely and effective adjucation | 0.60 |
| 8.3 | Effective correctional system | 0.34 |
| 8.4 | No discrimination | 0.48 |
| 8.5 | No corruption | 0.32 |
| 8.6 | No improper government influence | 0.25 |
| 8.7 | Due process of law | 0.35 |

# Malawi

**Region:** Sub-Saharan Africa
**Income Group:** Low Income

| | Overall Score | Regional Rank | Income Rank | Global Rank |
|---|---|---|---|---|
| | 0.51 | 5/18 | 3/12 | 69/113 |

| | | Factor Trend | Factor Score | Regional Rank | Income Rank | Global Rank |
|---|---|---|---|---|---|---|
| 🏛 | Constraints on Government Powers | — | 0.57 | 4/18 | 3/12 | 57/113 |
| 💰 | Absence of Corruption | — | 0.36 | 10/18 | 6/12 | 90/113 |
| 📱 | Open Government | — | 0.50 | 4/18 | 3/12 | 64/113 |
| 👤 | Fundamental Rights | — | 0.58 | 4/18 | 2/12 | 58/113 |
| 👮 | Order & Security | — | 0.62 | 13/18 | 9/12 | 92/113 |
| 👷 | Regulatory Enforcement | — | 0.45 | 6/18 | 3/12 | 79/113 |
| ⚖ | Civil Justice | — | 0.54 | 5/18 | 2/12 | 56/113 |
| ⚖ | Criminal Justice | — | 0.44 | 4/18 | 2/12 | 61/113 |

High ▓ Low  ▼ Trending down  ▲ Trending up

■ Malawi    ▓ Sub-Saharan Africa    ▓ Low Income

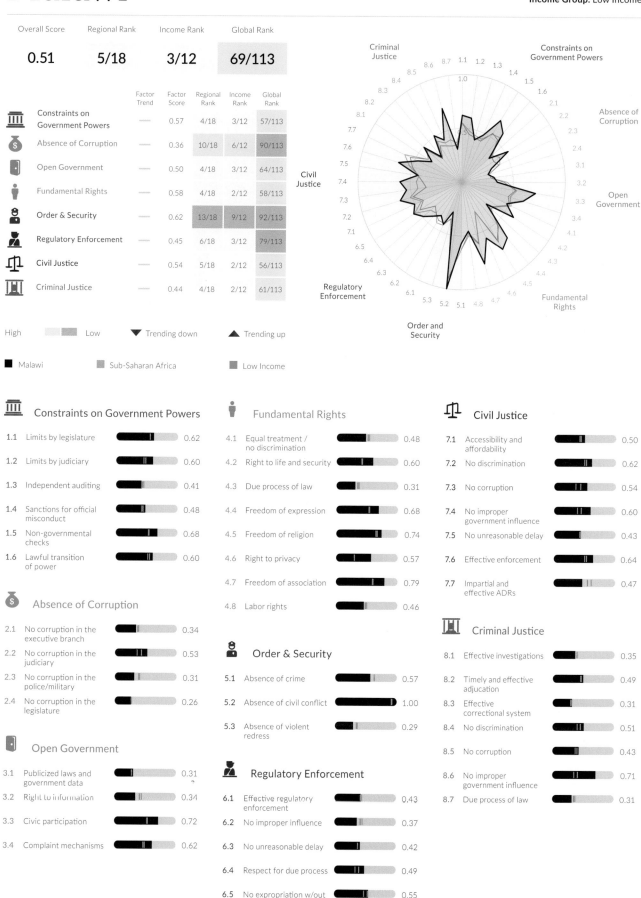

## 🏛 Constraints on Government Powers

| | | |
|---|---|---|
| 1.1 | Limits by legislature | 0.62 |
| 1.2 | Limits by judiciary | 0.60 |
| 1.3 | Independent auditing | 0.41 |
| 1.4 | Sanctions for official misconduct | 0.48 |
| 1.5 | Non-governmental checks | 0.68 |
| 1.6 | Lawful transition of power | 0.60 |

## 💰 Absence of Corruption

| | | |
|---|---|---|
| 2.1 | No corruption in the executive branch | 0.34 |
| 2.2 | No corruption in the judiciary | 0.53 |
| 2.3 | No corruption in the police/military | 0.31 |
| 2.4 | No corruption in the legislature | 0.26 |

## 📱 Open Government

| | | |
|---|---|---|
| 3.1 | Publicized laws and government data | 0.31 |
| 3.2 | Right to information | 0.34 |
| 3.3 | Civic participation | 0.72 |
| 3.4 | Complaint mechanisms | 0.62 |

## 👤 Fundamental Rights

| | | |
|---|---|---|
| 4.1 | Equal treatment / no discrimination | 0.48 |
| 4.2 | Right to life and security | 0.60 |
| 4.3 | Due process of law | 0.31 |
| 4.4 | Freedom of expression | 0.68 |
| 4.5 | Freedom of religion | 0.74 |
| 4.6 | Right to privacy | 0.57 |
| 4.7 | Freedom of association | 0.79 |
| 4.8 | Labor rights | 0.46 |

## 👮 Order & Security

| | | |
|---|---|---|
| 5.1 | Absence of crime | 0.57 |
| 5.2 | Absence of civil conflict | 1.00 |
| 5.3 | Absence of violent redress | 0.29 |

## 👷 Regulatory Enforcement

| | | |
|---|---|---|
| 6.1 | Effective regulatory enforcement | 0.43 |
| 6.2 | No improper influence | 0.37 |
| 6.3 | No unreasonable delay | 0.42 |
| 6.4 | Respect for due process | 0.49 |
| 6.5 | No expropriation w/out adequate compensation | 0.55 |

## ⚖ Civil Justice

| | | |
|---|---|---|
| 7.1 | Accessibility and affordability | 0.50 |
| 7.2 | No discrimination | 0.62 |
| 7.3 | No corruption | 0.54 |
| 7.4 | No improper government influence | 0.60 |
| 7.5 | No unreasonable delay | 0.43 |
| 7.6 | Effective enforcement | 0.64 |
| 7.7 | Impartial and effective ADRs | 0.47 |

## ⚖ Criminal Justice

| | | |
|---|---|---|
| 8.1 | Effective investigations | 0.35 |
| 8.2 | Timely and effective adjucation | 0.49 |
| 8.3 | Effective correctional system | 0.31 |
| 8.4 | No discrimination | 0.51 |
| 8.5 | No corruption | 0.43 |
| 8.6 | No improper government influence | 0.71 |
| 8.7 | Due process of law | 0.31 |

# Malaysia

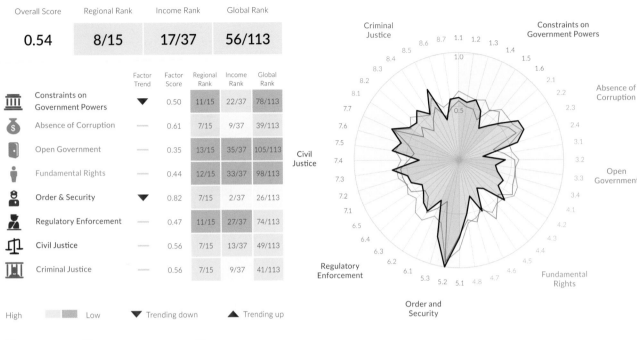

| | | Factor Trend | Factor Score | Regional Rank | Income Rank | Global Rank |
|---|---|---|---|---|---|---|
| 🏛 | Constraints on Government Powers | ▼ | 0.50 | 11/15 | 22/37 | 78/113 |
| 💰 | Absence of Corruption | — | 0.61 | 7/15 | 9/37 | 39/113 |
| 🚪 | Open Government | — | 0.35 | 13/15 | 35/37 | 105/113 |
| 👤 | Fundamental Rights | — | 0.44 | 12/15 | 33/37 | 98/113 |
| 👮 | Order & Security | ▼ | 0.82 | 7/15 | 2/37 | 26/113 |
| 👨‍💼 | Regulatory Enforcement | — | 0.47 | 11/15 | 27/37 | 74/113 |
| ⚖ | Civil Justice | — | 0.56 | 7/15 | 13/37 | 49/113 |
| 🏛 | Criminal Justice | — | 0.56 | 7/15 | 9/37 | 41/113 |

**Overall Score** 0.54 | **Regional Rank** 8/15 | **Income Rank** 17/37 | **Global Rank** 56/113

High ▢▢▢ Low ▼ Trending down ▲ Trending up

■ Malaysia ▢ East Asia & Pacific ▢ Upper Middle Income

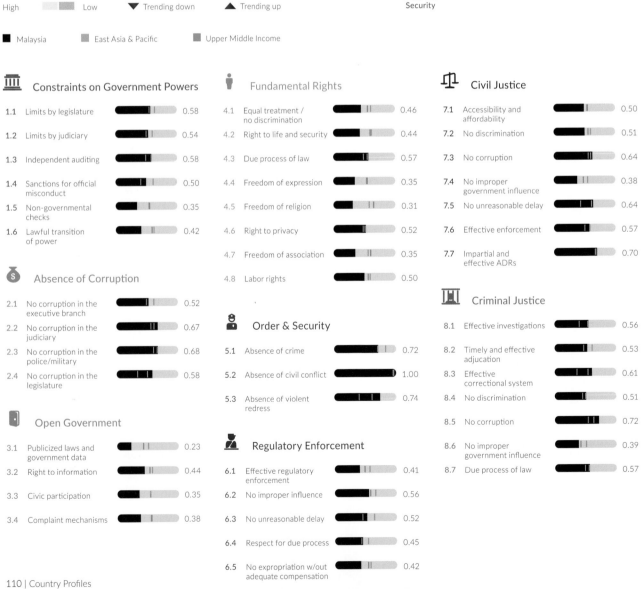

## 🏛 Constraints on Government Powers

| 1.1 | Limits by legislature | 0.58 |
|---|---|---|
| 1.2 | Limits by judiciary | 0.54 |
| 1.3 | Independent auditing | 0.58 |
| 1.4 | Sanctions for official misconduct | 0.50 |
| 1.5 | Non-governmental checks | 0.35 |
| 1.6 | Lawful transition of power | 0.42 |

## 💰 Absence of Corruption

| 2.1 | No corruption in the executive branch | 0.52 |
|---|---|---|
| 2.2 | No corruption in the judiciary | 0.67 |
| 2.3 | No corruption in the police/military | 0.68 |
| 2.4 | No corruption in the legislature | 0.58 |

## 🚪 Open Government

| 3.1 | Publicized laws and government data | 0.23 |
|---|---|---|
| 3.2 | Right to information | 0.44 |
| 3.3 | Civic participation | 0.35 |
| 3.4 | Complaint mechanisms | 0.38 |

## 👤 Fundamental Rights

| 4.1 | Equal treatment / no discrimination | 0.46 |
|---|---|---|
| 4.2 | Right to life and security | 0.44 |
| 4.3 | Due process of law | 0.57 |
| 4.4 | Freedom of expression | 0.35 |
| 4.5 | Freedom of religion | 0.31 |
| 4.6 | Right to privacy | 0.52 |
| 4.7 | Freedom of association | 0.35 |
| 4.8 | Labor rights | 0.50 |

## 👮 Order & Security

| 5.1 | Absence of crime | 0.72 |
|---|---|---|
| 5.2 | Absence of civil conflict | 1.00 |
| 5.3 | Absence of violent redress | 0.74 |

## 👨‍💼 Regulatory Enforcement

| 6.1 | Effective regulatory enforcement | 0.41 |
|---|---|---|
| 6.2 | No improper influence | 0.56 |
| 6.3 | No unreasonable delay | 0.52 |
| 6.4 | Respect for due process | 0.45 |
| 6.5 | No expropriation w/out adequate compensation | 0.42 |

## ⚖ Civil Justice

| 7.1 | Accessibility and affordability | 0.50 |
|---|---|---|
| 7.2 | No discrimination | 0.51 |
| 7.3 | No corruption | 0.64 |
| 7.4 | No improper government influence | 0.38 |
| 7.5 | No unreasonable delay | 0.64 |
| 7.6 | Effective enforcement | 0.57 |
| 7.7 | Impartial and effective ADRs | 0.70 |

## 🏛 Criminal Justice

| 8.1 | Effective investigations | 0.56 |
|---|---|---|
| 8.2 | Timely and effective adjucation | 0.53 |
| 8.3 | Effective correctional system | 0.61 |
| 8.4 | No discrimination | 0.51 |
| 8.5 | No corruption | 0.72 |
| 8.6 | No improper government influence | 0.39 |
| 8.7 | Due process of law | 0.57 |

# Mexico

**Region:** Latin America & Caribbean
**Income Group:** Upper Middle Income

| | Overall Score | Regional Rank | Income Rank | Global Rank |
|---|---|---|---|---|
| | 0.46 | 24/30 | 32/37 | 88/113 |

| | Factor Trend | Factor Score | Regional Rank | Income Rank | Global Rank |
|---|---|---|---|---|---|
| Constraints on Government Powers | ▼ | 0.47 | 23/30 | 25/37 | 83/113 |
| Absence of Corruption | — | 0.32 | 28/30 | 36/37 | 99/113 |
| Open Government | ▲ | 0.61 | 6/30 | 6/37 | 34/113 |
| Fundamental Rights | ▼ | 0.51 | 24/30 | 23/37 | 75/113 |
| Order & Security | — | 0.61 | 23/30 | 31/37 | 94/113 |
| Regulatory Enforcement | — | 0.44 | 24/30 | 32/37 | 85/113 |
| Civil Justice | — | 0.41 | 26/30 | 36/37 | 101/113 |
| Criminal Justice | — | 0.29 | 27/30 | 36/37 | 108/113 |

High ▬ Low ▼ Trending down ▲ Trending up

■ Mexico ■ Latin America & Caribbean ■ Upper Middle Income

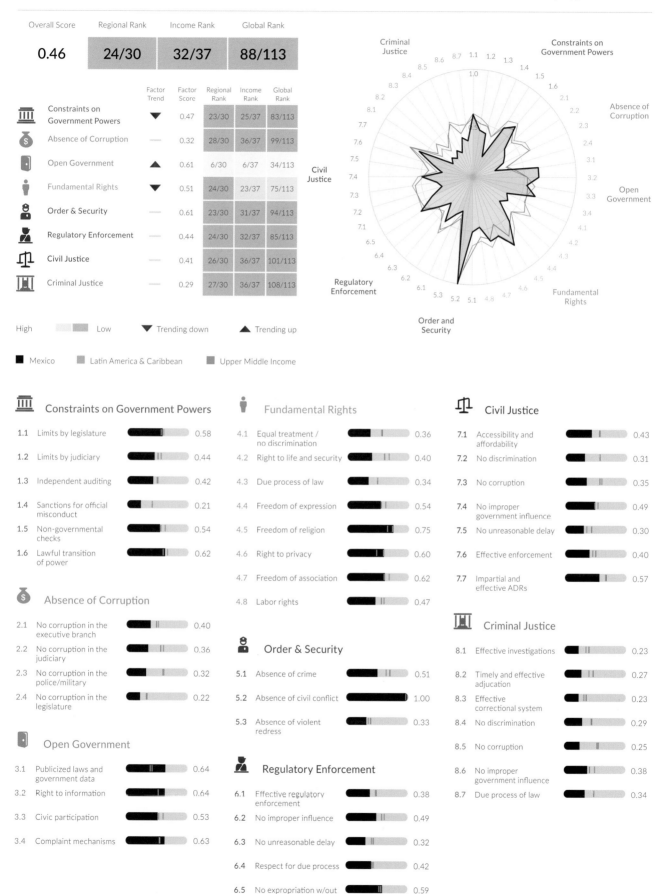

## Constraints on Government Powers

| | | |
|---|---|---|
| 1.1 | Limits by legislature | 0.58 |
| 1.2 | Limits by judiciary | 0.44 |
| 1.3 | Independent auditing | 0.42 |
| 1.4 | Sanctions for official misconduct | 0.21 |
| 1.5 | Non-governmental checks | 0.54 |
| 1.6 | Lawful transition of power | 0.62 |

## Absence of Corruption

| | | |
|---|---|---|
| 2.1 | No corruption in the executive branch | 0.40 |
| 2.2 | No corruption in the judiciary | 0.36 |
| 2.3 | No corruption in the police/military | 0.32 |
| 2.4 | No corruption in the legislature | 0.22 |

## Open Government

| | | |
|---|---|---|
| 3.1 | Publicized laws and government data | 0.64 |
| 3.2 | Right to information | 0.64 |
| 3.3 | Civic participation | 0.53 |
| 3.4 | Complaint mechanisms | 0.63 |

## Fundamental Rights

| | | |
|---|---|---|
| 4.1 | Equal treatment / no discrimination | 0.36 |
| 4.2 | Right to life and security | 0.40 |
| 4.3 | Due process of law | 0.34 |
| 4.4 | Freedom of expression | 0.54 |
| 4.5 | Freedom of religion | 0.75 |
| 4.6 | Right to privacy | 0.60 |
| 4.7 | Freedom of association | 0.62 |
| 4.8 | Labor rights | 0.47 |

## Order & Security

| | | |
|---|---|---|
| 5.1 | Absence of crime | 0.51 |
| 5.2 | Absence of civil conflict | 1.00 |
| 5.3 | Absence of violent redress | 0.33 |

## Regulatory Enforcement

| | | |
|---|---|---|
| 6.1 | Effective regulatory enforcement | 0.38 |
| 6.2 | No improper influence | 0.49 |
| 6.3 | No unreasonable delay | 0.32 |
| 6.4 | Respect for due process | 0.42 |
| 6.5 | No expropriation w/out adequate compensation | 0.59 |

## Civil Justice

| | | |
|---|---|---|
| 7.1 | Accessibility and affordability | 0.43 |
| 7.2 | No discrimination | 0.31 |
| 7.3 | No corruption | 0.35 |
| 7.4 | No improper government influence | 0.49 |
| 7.5 | No unreasonable delay | 0.30 |
| 7.6 | Effective enforcement | 0.40 |
| 7.7 | Impartial and effective ADRs | 0.57 |

## Criminal Justice

| | | |
|---|---|---|
| 8.1 | Effective investigations | 0.23 |
| 8.2 | Timely and effective adjucation | 0.27 |
| 8.3 | Effective correctional system | 0.23 |
| 8.4 | No discrimination | 0.29 |
| 8.5 | No corruption | 0.25 |
| 8.6 | No improper government influence | 0.38 |
| 8.7 | Due process of law | 0.34 |

# Moldova

| | Overall Score | Regional Rank | Income Rank | Global Rank |
|---|---|---|---|---|
| | 0.49 | 8/13 | 11/28 | 77/113 |

| | | Factor Trend | Factor Score | Regional Rank | Income Rank | Global Rank |
|---|---|---|---|---|---|---|
| 🏛 | Constraints on Government Powers | — | 0.43 | 8/13 | 21/28 | 95/113 |
| 💰 | Absence of Corruption | — | 0.28 | 12/13 | 24/28 | 105/113 |
| 📱 | Open Government | — | 0.58 | 2/13 | 3/28 | 38/113 |
| 🧍 | Fundamental Rights | — | 0.58 | 6/13 | 4/28 | 59/113 |
| 👤 | Order & Security | — | 0.81 | 3/13 | 2/28 | 30/113 |
| 👷 | Regulatory Enforcement | — | 0.41 | 11/13 | 20/28 | 97/113 |
| ⚖ | Civil Justice | — | 0.46 | 10/13 | 12/28 | 82/113 |
| 🏛 | Criminal Justice | — | 0.38 | 10/13 | 12/28 | 79/113 |

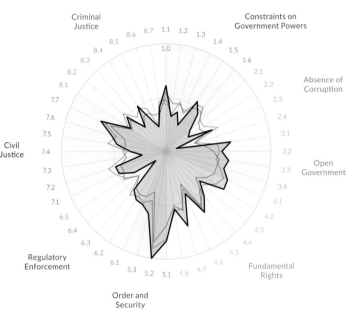

High ▢▢▢ Low   ▼ Trending down   ▲ Trending up

■ Moldova   ■ Eastern Europe & Central Asia   ■ Lower Middle Income

## 🏛 Constraints on Government Powers

| | | |
|---|---|---|
| 1.1 | Limits by legislature | 0.61 |
| 1.2 | Limits by judiciary | 0.33 |
| 1.3 | Independent auditing | 0.38 |
| 1.4 | Sanctions for official misconduct | 0.27 |
| 1.5 | Non-governmental checks | 0.55 |
| 1.6 | Lawful transition of power | 0.46 |

## 💰 Absence of Corruption

| | | |
|---|---|---|
| 2.1 | No corruption in the executive branch | 0.30 |
| 2.2 | No corruption in the judiciary | 0.25 |
| 2.3 | No corruption in the police/military | 0.48 |
| 2.4 | No corruption in the legislature | 0.10 |

## 📱 Open Government

| | | |
|---|---|---|
| 3.1 | Publicized laws and government data | 0.62 |
| 3.2 | Right to information | 0.53 |
| 3.3 | Civic participation | 0.60 |
| 3.4 | Complaint mechanisms | 0.57 |

## 🧍 Fundamental Rights

| | | |
|---|---|---|
| 4.1 | Equal treatment / no discrimination | 0.64 |
| 4.2 | Right to life and security | 0.65 |
| 4.3 | Due process of law | 0.42 |
| 4.4 | Freedom of expression | 0.55 |
| 4.5 | Freedom of religion | 0.67 |
| 4.6 | Right to privacy | 0.43 |
| 4.7 | Freedom of association | 0.72 |
| 4.8 | Labor rights | 0.54 |

## 👤 Order & Security

| | | |
|---|---|---|
| 5.1 | Absence of crime | 0.83 |
| 5.2 | Absence of civil conflict | 1.00 |
| 5.3 | Absence of violent redress | 0.60 |

## 👷 Regulatory Enforcement

| | | |
|---|---|---|
| 6.1 | Effective regulatory enforcement | 0.54 |
| 6.2 | No improper influence | 0.53 |
| 6.3 | No unreasonable delay | 0.47 |
| 6.4 | Respect for due process | 0.13 |
| 6.5 | No expropriation w/out adequate compensation | 0.36 |

## ⚖ Civil Justice

| | | |
|---|---|---|
| 7.1 | Accessibility and affordability | 0.49 |
| 7.2 | No discrimination | 0.50 |
| 7.3 | No corruption | 0.23 |
| 7.4 | No improper government influence | 0.34 |
| 7.5 | No unreasonable delay | 0.47 |
| 7.6 | Effective enforcement | 0.54 |
| 7.7 | Impartial and effective ADRs | 0.68 |

## 🏛 Criminal Justice

| | | |
|---|---|---|
| 8.1 | Effective investigations | 0.40 |
| 8.2 | Timely and effective adjucation | 0.49 |
| 8.3 | Effective correctional system | 0.30 |
| 8.4 | No discrimination | 0.50 |
| 8.5 | No corruption | 0.32 |
| 8.6 | No improper government influence | 0.24 |
| 8.7 | Due process of law | 0.42 |

# Mongolia

**Region:** East Asia & Pacific
**Income Group:** Lower Middle Income

| | Overall Score | Regional Rank | Income Rank | Global Rank |
|---|---|---|---|---|
| | 0.54 | 7/15 | 2/28 | 55/113 |

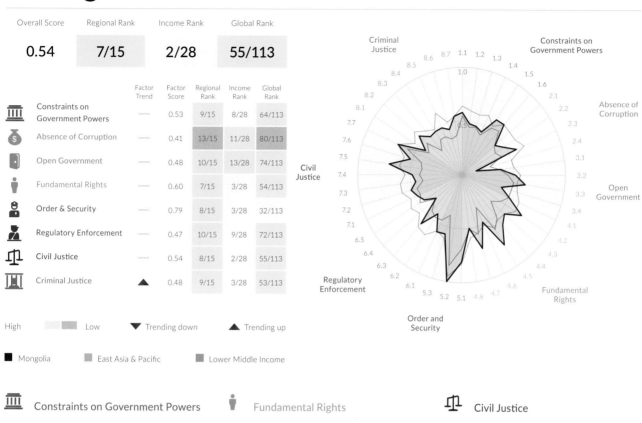

| | Factor Trend | Factor Score | Regional Rank | Income Rank | Global Rank |
|---|---|---|---|---|---|
| Constraints on Government Powers | — | 0.53 | 9/15 | 8/28 | 64/113 |
| Absence of Corruption | — | 0.41 | 13/15 | 11/28 | 80/113 |
| Open Government | — | 0.48 | 10/15 | 13/28 | 74/113 |
| Fundamental Rights | — | 0.60 | 7/15 | 3/28 | 54/113 |
| Order & Security | — | 0.79 | 8/15 | 3/28 | 32/113 |
| Regulatory Enforcement | — | 0.47 | 10/15 | 9/28 | 72/113 |
| Civil Justice | — | 0.54 | 8/15 | 2/28 | 55/113 |
| Criminal Justice | ▲ | 0.48 | 9/15 | 3/28 | 53/113 |

High ▨ Low   ▼ Trending down   ▲ Trending up

■ Mongolia   ▨ East Asia & Pacific   ▨ Lower Middle Income

## Constraints on Government Powers

| | | |
|---|---|---|
| 1.1 | Limits by legislature | 0.58 |
| 1.2 | Limits by judiciary | 0.48 |
| 1.3 | Independent auditing | 0.47 |
| 1.4 | Sanctions for official misconduct | 0.44 |
| 1.5 | Non-governmental checks | 0.61 |
| 1.6 | Lawful transition of power | 0.62 |

## Absence of Corruption

| | | |
|---|---|---|
| 2.1 | No corruption in the executive branch | 0.42 |
| 2.2 | No corruption in the judiciary | 0.48 |
| 2.3 | No corruption in the police/military | 0.58 |
| 2.4 | No corruption in the legislature | 0.14 |

## Open Government

| | | |
|---|---|---|
| 3.1 | Publicized laws and government data | 0.38 |
| 3.2 | Right to information | 0.52 |
| 3.3 | Civic participation | 0.62 |
| 3.4 | Complaint mechanisms | 0.40 |

## Fundamental Rights

| | | |
|---|---|---|
| 4.1 | Equal treatment / no discrimination | 0.51 |
| 4.2 | Right to life and security | 0.69 |
| 4.3 | Due process of law | 0.55 |
| 4.4 | Freedom of expression | 0.61 |
| 4.5 | Freedom of religion | 0.77 |
| 4.6 | Right to privacy | 0.48 |
| 4.7 | Freedom of association | 0.71 |
| 4.8 | Labor rights | 0.50 |

## Order & Security

| | | |
|---|---|---|
| 5.1 | Absence of crime | 0.81 |
| 5.2 | Absence of civil conflict | 1.00 |
| 5.3 | Absence of violent redress | 0.57 |

## Regulatory Enforcement

| | | |
|---|---|---|
| 6.1 | Effective regulatory enforcement | 0.58 |
| 6.2 | No improper influence | 0.43 |
| 6.3 | No unreasonable delay | 0.60 |
| 6.4 | Respect for due process | 0.33 |
| 6.5 | No expropriation w/out adequate compensation | 0.43 |

## Civil Justice

| | | |
|---|---|---|
| 7.1 | Accessibility and affordability | 0.47 |
| 7.2 | No discrimination | 0.51 |
| 7.3 | No corruption | 0.45 |
| 7.4 | No improper government influence | 0.48 |
| 7.5 | No unreasonable delay | 0.71 |
| 7.6 | Effective enforcement | 0.52 |
| 7.7 | Impartial and effective ADRs | 0.68 |

## Criminal Justice

| | | |
|---|---|---|
| 8.1 | Effective investigations | 0.42 |
| 8.2 | Timely and effective adjudication | 0.55 |
| 8.3 | Effective correctional system | 0.47 |
| 8.4 | No discrimination | 0.48 |
| 8.5 | No corruption | 0.48 |
| 8.6 | No improper government influence | 0.44 |
| 8.7 | Due process of law | 0.55 |

# Morocco

**Region:** Middle East & North Africa
**Income Group:** Lower Middle Income

| | Overall Score | Regional Rank | Income Rank | Global Rank |
|---|---|---|---|---|
| | 0.53 | 4/7 | 4/28 | 60/113 |

| | | Factor Trend | Factor Score | Regional Rank | Income Rank | Global Rank |
|---|---|---|---|---|---|---|
| 🏛 | Constraints on Government Powers | — | 0.57 | 3/7 | 6/28 | 53/113 |
| 💰 | Absence of Corruption | ▲ | 0.54 | 3/7 | 1/28 | 50/113 |
| 📱 | Open Government | ▼ | 0.47 | 2/7 | 14/28 | 76/113 |
| 🧍 | Fundamental Rights | — | 0.45 | 5/7 | 17/28 | 91/113 |
| 👤 | Order & Security | — | 0.73 | 3/7 | 6/28 | 50/113 |
| ⚖ | Regulatory Enforcement | — | 0.54 | 3/7 | 2/28 | 41/113 |
| ⚖ | Civil Justice | — | 0.53 | 4/7 | 3/28 | 57/113 |
| ⚖ | Criminal Justice | — | 0.37 | 6/7 | 15/28 | 82/113 |

High ▢▢ Low    ▼ Trending down    ▲ Trending up

■ Morocco    ■ Middle East & North Africa    ■ Lower Middle Income

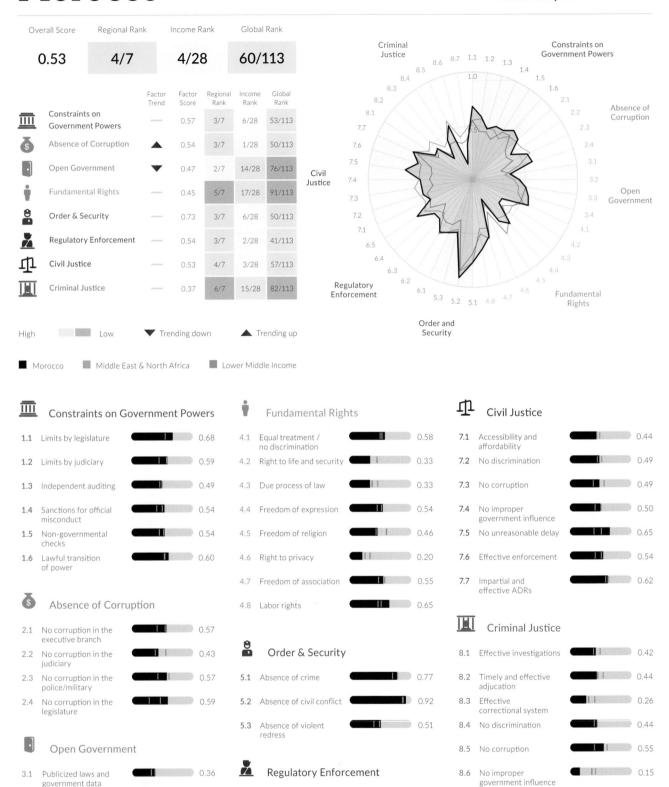

## 🏛 Constraints on Government Powers

| | | |
|---|---|---|
| 1.1 | Limits by legislature | 0.68 |
| 1.2 | Limits by judiciary | 0.59 |
| 1.3 | Independent auditing | 0.49 |
| 1.4 | Sanctions for official misconduct | 0.54 |
| 1.5 | Non-governmental checks | 0.54 |
| 1.6 | Lawful transition of power | 0.60 |

## 💰 Absence of Corruption

| | | |
|---|---|---|
| 2.1 | No corruption in the executive branch | 0.57 |
| 2.2 | No corruption in the judiciary | 0.43 |
| 2.3 | No corruption in the police/military | 0.57 |
| 2.4 | No corruption in the legislature | 0.59 |

## 📱 Open Government

| | | |
|---|---|---|
| 3.1 | Publicized laws and government data | 0.36 |
| 3.2 | Right to information | 0.44 |
| 3.3 | Civic participation | 0.51 |
| 3.4 | Complaint mechanisms | 0.55 |

## 🧍 Fundamental Rights

| | | |
|---|---|---|
| 4.1 | Equal treatment / no discrimination | 0.58 |
| 4.2 | Right to life and security | 0.33 |
| 4.3 | Due process of law | 0.33 |
| 4.4 | Freedom of expression | 0.54 |
| 4.5 | Freedom of religion | 0.46 |
| 4.6 | Right to privacy | 0.20 |
| 4.7 | Freedom of association | 0.55 |
| 4.8 | Labor rights | 0.65 |

## 👤 Order & Security

| | | |
|---|---|---|
| 5.1 | Absence of crime | 0.77 |
| 5.2 | Absence of civil conflict | 0.92 |
| 5.3 | Absence of violent redress | 0.51 |

## ⚖ Regulatory Enforcement

| | | |
|---|---|---|
| 6.1 | Effective regulatory enforcement | 0.54 |
| 6.2 | No improper influence | 0.58 |
| 6.3 | No unreasonable delay | 0.48 |
| 6.4 | Respect for due process | 0.48 |
| 6.5 | No expropriation w/out adequate compensation | 0.63 |

## ⚖ Civil Justice

| | | |
|---|---|---|
| 7.1 | Accessibility and affordability | 0.44 |
| 7.2 | No discrimination | 0.49 |
| 7.3 | No corruption | 0.49 |
| 7.4 | No improper government influence | 0.50 |
| 7.5 | No unreasonable delay | 0.65 |
| 7.6 | Effective enforcement | 0.54 |
| 7.7 | Impartial and effective ADRs | 0.62 |

## ⚖ Criminal Justice

| | | |
|---|---|---|
| 8.1 | Effective investigations | 0.42 |
| 8.2 | Timely and effective adjudication | 0.44 |
| 8.3 | Effective correctional system | 0.26 |
| 8.4 | No discrimination | 0.44 |
| 8.5 | No corruption | 0.55 |
| 8.6 | No improper government influence | 0.15 |
| 8.7 | Due process of law | 0.33 |

# Myanmar

**Region:** East Asia & Pacific
**Income Group:** Lower Middle Income

| | Overall Score | Regional Rank | Income Rank | Global Rank |
|---|---|---|---|---|
| | 0.43 | 14/15 | 19/28 | 98/113 |

| | | Factor Trend | Factor Score | Regional Rank | Income Rank | Global Rank |
|---|---|---|---|---|---|---|
| 🏛 | Constraints on Government Powers | ▲ | 0.50 | 10/15 | 14/28 | 76/113 |
| 💰 | Absence of Corruption | — | 0.44 | 12/15 | 8/28 | 70/113 |
| 📱 | Open Government | — | 0.33 | 14/15 | 25/28 | 107/113 |
| 👤 | Fundamental Rights | — | 0.30 | 15/15 | 27/28 | 109/113 |
| 👮 | Order & Security | — | 0.73 | 11/15 | 7/28 | 53/113 |
| 🧑‍⚖️ | Regulatory Enforcement | — | 0.44 | 13/15 | 14/28 | 87/113 |
| ⚖️ | Civil Justice | — | 0.42 | 14/15 | 20/28 | 98/113 |
| 🏛 | Criminal Justice | — | 0.32 | 14/15 | 22/28 | 101/113 |

High ▢ Low    ▼ Trending down    ▲ Trending up

■ Myanmar    ▨ East Asia & Pacific    ▨ Lower Middle Income

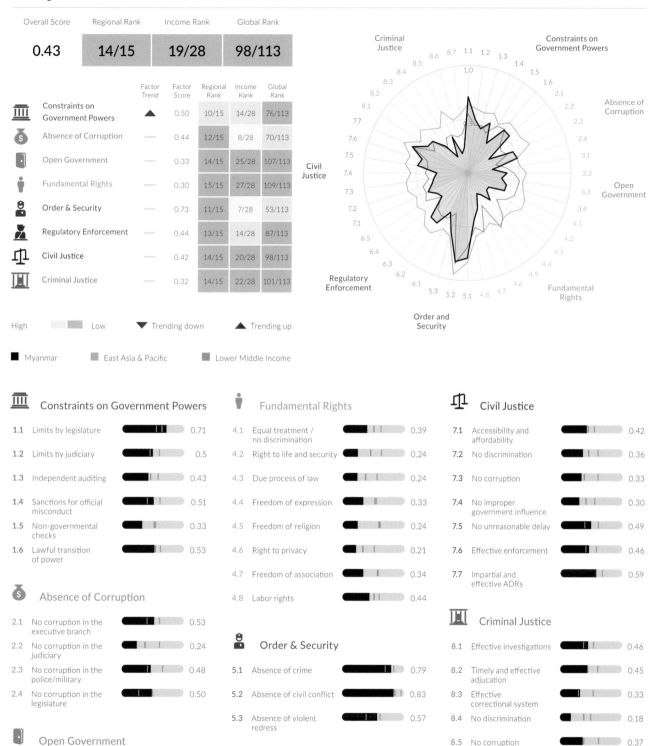

## 🏛 Constraints on Government Powers

| 1.1 | Limits by legislature | 0.71 |
|---|---|---|
| 1.2 | Limits by judiciary | 0.5 |
| 1.3 | Independent auditing | 0.43 |
| 1.4 | Sanctions for official misconduct | 0.51 |
| 1.5 | Non-governmental checks | 0.33 |
| 1.6 | Lawful transition of power | 0.53 |

## 💰 Absence of Corruption

| 2.1 | No corruption in the executive branch | 0.53 |
|---|---|---|
| 2.2 | No corruption in the judiciary | 0.24 |
| 2.3 | No corruption in the police/military | 0.48 |
| 2.4 | No corruption in the legislature | 0.50 |

## 📱 Open Government

| 3.1 | Publicized laws and government data | 0.24 |
|---|---|---|
| 3.2 | Right to information | 0.38 |
| 3.3 | Civic participation | 0.33 |
| 3.4 | Complaint mechanisms | 0.39 |

## 👤 Fundamental Rights

| 4.1 | Equal treatment / no discrimination | 0.39 |
|---|---|---|
| 4.2 | Right to life and security | 0.24 |
| 4.3 | Due process of law | 0.24 |
| 4.4 | Freedom of expression | 0.33 |
| 4.5 | Freedom of religion | 0.24 |
| 4.6 | Right to privacy | 0.21 |
| 4.7 | Freedom of association | 0.34 |
| 4.8 | Labor rights | 0.44 |

## 👮 Order & Security

| 5.1 | Absence of crime | 0.79 |
|---|---|---|
| 5.2 | Absence of civil conflict | 0.83 |
| 5.3 | Absence of violent redress | 0.57 |

## 🧑‍⚖️ Regulatory Enforcement

| 6.1 | Effective regulatory enforcement | 0.40 |
|---|---|---|
| 6.2 | No improper influence | 0.55 |
| 6.3 | No unreasonable delay | 0.54 |
| 6.4 | Respect for due process | 0.33 |
| 6.5 | No expropriation w/out adequate compensation | 0.35 |

## ⚖️ Civil Justice

| 7.1 | Accessibility and affordability | 0.42 |
|---|---|---|
| 7.2 | No discrimination | 0.36 |
| 7.3 | No corruption | 0.33 |
| 7.4 | No improper government influence | 0.30 |
| 7.5 | No unreasonable delay | 0.49 |
| 7.6 | Effective enforcement | 0.46 |
| 7.7 | Impartial and effective ADRs | 0.59 |

## 🏛 Criminal Justice

| 8.1 | Effective investigations | 0.46 |
|---|---|---|
| 8.2 | Timely and effective adjudication | 0.45 |
| 8.3 | Effective correctional system | 0.33 |
| 8.4 | No discrimination | 0.18 |
| 8.5 | No corruption | 0.37 |
| 8.6 | No improper government influence | 0.19 |
| 8.7 | Due process of law | 0.24 |

# Nepal

| | Overall Score | Regional Rank | Income Rank | Global Rank |
|---|---|---|---|---|
| | 0.52 | 1/6 | 2/12 | 63/113 |

| | | Factor Trend | Factor Score | Regional Rank | Income Rank | Global Rank |
|---|---|---|---|---|---|---|
| 🏛 | Constraints on Government Powers | — | 0.63 | 2/6 | 2/12 | 40/113 |
| 💰 | Absence of Corruption | — | 0.38 | 3/6 | 4/12 | 83/113 |
| 🚪 | Open Government | — | 0.54 | 2/6 | 1/12 | 52/113 |
| 🧍 | Fundamental Rights | — | 0.53 | 1/6 | 6/12 | 72/113 |
| 👮 | Order & Security | ▼ | 0.74 | 1/6 | 1/12 | 49/113 |
| 👷 | Regulatory Enforcement | — | 0.48 | 2/6 | 2/12 | 67/113 |
| ⚖ | Civil Justice | — | 0.41 | 3/6 | 8/12 | 99/113 |
| 🏛 | Criminal Justice | — | 0.44 | 2/6 | 1/12 | 60/113 |

High ▒▒▒ Low     ▼ Trending down     ▲ Trending up

■ Nepal     ■ South Asia     ■ Low Income

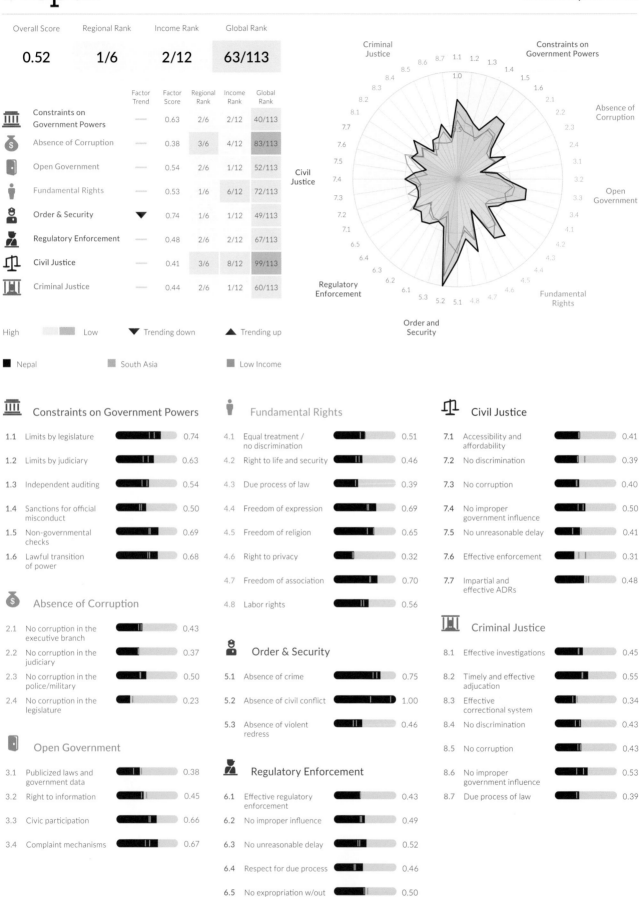

## 🏛 Constraints on Government Powers

| | | | |
|---|---|---|---|
| 1.1 | Limits by legislature | | 0.74 |
| 1.2 | Limits by judiciary | | 0.63 |
| 1.3 | Independent auditing | | 0.54 |
| 1.4 | Sanctions for official misconduct | | 0.50 |
| 1.5 | Non-governmental checks | | 0.69 |
| 1.6 | Lawful transition of power | | 0.68 |

## 💰 Absence of Corruption

| | | | |
|---|---|---|---|
| 2.1 | No corruption in the executive branch | | 0.43 |
| 2.2 | No corruption in the judiciary | | 0.37 |
| 2.3 | No corruption in the police/military | | 0.50 |
| 2.4 | No corruption in the legislature | | 0.23 |

## 🚪 Open Government

| | | | |
|---|---|---|---|
| 3.1 | Publicized laws and government data | | 0.38 |
| 3.2 | Right to information | | 0.45 |
| 3.3 | Civic participation | | 0.66 |
| 3.4 | Complaint mechanisms | | 0.67 |

## 🧍 Fundamental Rights

| | | | |
|---|---|---|---|
| 4.1 | Equal treatment / no discrimination | | 0.51 |
| 4.2 | Right to life and security | | 0.46 |
| 4.3 | Due process of law | | 0.39 |
| 4.4 | Freedom of expression | | 0.69 |
| 4.5 | Freedom of religion | | 0.65 |
| 4.6 | Right to privacy | | 0.32 |
| 4.7 | Freedom of association | | 0.70 |
| 4.8 | Labor rights | | 0.56 |

## 👮 Order & Security

| | | | |
|---|---|---|---|
| 5.1 | Absence of crime | | 0.75 |
| 5.2 | Absence of civil conflict | | 1.00 |
| 5.3 | Absence of violent redress | | 0.46 |

## 👷 Regulatory Enforcement

| | | | |
|---|---|---|---|
| 6.1 | Effective regulatory enforcement | | 0.43 |
| 6.2 | No improper influence | | 0.49 |
| 6.3 | No unreasonable delay | | 0.52 |
| 6.4 | Respect for due process | | 0.46 |
| 6.5 | No expropriation w/out adequate compensation | | 0.50 |

## ⚖ Civil Justice

| | | | |
|---|---|---|---|
| 7.1 | Accessibility and affordability | | 0.41 |
| 7.2 | No discrimination | | 0.39 |
| 7.3 | No corruption | | 0.40 |
| 7.4 | No improper government influence | | 0.50 |
| 7.5 | No unreasonable delay | | 0.41 |
| 7.6 | Effective enforcement | | 0.31 |
| 7.7 | Impartial and effective ADRs | | 0.48 |

## 🏛 Criminal Justice

| | | | |
|---|---|---|---|
| 8.1 | Effective investigations | | 0.45 |
| 8.2 | Timely and effective adjucation | | 0.55 |
| 8.3 | Effective correctional system | | 0.34 |
| 8.4 | No discrimination | | 0.43 |
| 8.5 | No corruption | | 0.43 |
| 8.6 | No improper government influence | | 0.53 |
| 8.7 | Due process of law | | 0.39 |

# Netherlands

**Region:** EU & EFTA & North America
**Income Group:** High Income

| | Overall Score | Regional Rank | Income Rank | Global Rank |
|---|---|---|---|---|
| | 0.86 | 5/24 | 5/36 | 5/113 |

| | | Factor Trend | Factor Score | Regional Rank | Income Rank | Global Rank |
|---|---|---|---|---|---|---|
| 🏛 | Constraints on Government Powers | — | 0.89 | 4/24 | 4/36 | 4/113 |
| 💰 | Absence of Corruption | — | 0.88 | 5/24 | 7/36 | 7/113 |
| 🚪 | Open Government | — | 0.85 | 4/24 | 4/36 | 4/113 |
| 👤 | Fundamental Rights | — | 0.86 | 6/24 | 6/36 | 6/113 |
| 👤 | Order & Security | — | 0.85 | 13/24 | 19/36 | 20/113 |
| 🛡 | Regulatory Enforcement | — | 0.88 | 1/24 | 2/36 | 2/113 |
| ⚖ | Civil Justice | — | 0.88 | 1/24 | 1/36 | 1/113 |
| 🏛 | Criminal Justice | — | 0.80 | 5/24 | 7/36 | 7/113 |

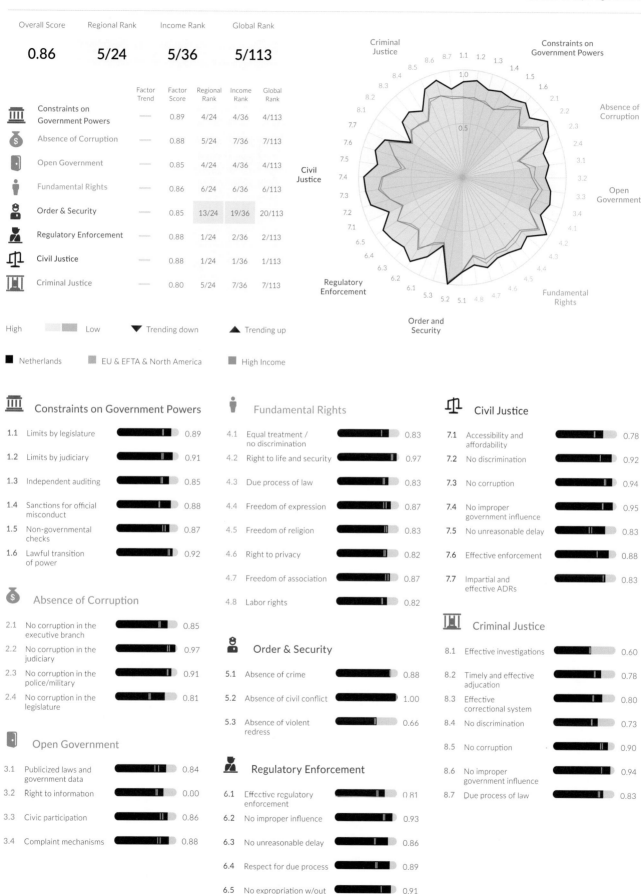

High ▨ Low   ▼ Trending down   ▲ Trending up

■ Netherlands   ▨ EU & EFTA & North America   ▨ High Income

## 🏛 Constraints on Government Powers

| | | |
|---|---|---|
| 1.1 | Limits by legislature | 0.89 |
| 1.2 | Limits by judiciary | 0.91 |
| 1.3 | Independent auditing | 0.85 |
| 1.4 | Sanctions for official misconduct | 0.88 |
| 1.5 | Non-governmental checks | 0.87 |
| 1.6 | Lawful transition of power | 0.92 |

## 💰 Absence of Corruption

| | | |
|---|---|---|
| 2.1 | No corruption in the executive branch | 0.85 |
| 2.2 | No corruption in the judiciary | 0.97 |
| 2.3 | No corruption in the police/military | 0.91 |
| 2.4 | No corruption in the legislature | 0.81 |

## 🚪 Open Government

| | | |
|---|---|---|
| 3.1 | Publicized laws and government data | 0.84 |
| 3.2 | Right to information | 0.00 |
| 3.3 | Civic participation | 0.86 |
| 3.4 | Complaint mechanisms | 0.88 |

## 👤 Fundamental Rights

| | | |
|---|---|---|
| 4.1 | Equal treatment / no discrimination | 0.83 |
| 4.2 | Right to life and security | 0.97 |
| 4.3 | Due process of law | 0.83 |
| 4.4 | Freedom of expression | 0.87 |
| 4.5 | Freedom of religion | 0.83 |
| 4.6 | Right to privacy | 0.82 |
| 4.7 | Freedom of association | 0.87 |
| 4.8 | Labor rights | 0.82 |

## 👤 Order & Security

| | | |
|---|---|---|
| 5.1 | Absence of crime | 0.88 |
| 5.2 | Absence of civil conflict | 1.00 |
| 5.3 | Absence of violent redress | 0.66 |

## 🛡 Regulatory Enforcement

| | | |
|---|---|---|
| 6.1 | Effective regulatory enforcement | 0.81 |
| 6.2 | No improper influence | 0.93 |
| 6.3 | No unreasonable delay | 0.86 |
| 6.4 | Respect for due process | 0.89 |
| 6.5 | No expropriation w/out adequate compensation | 0.91 |

## ⚖ Civil Justice

| | | |
|---|---|---|
| 7.1 | Accessibility and affordability | 0.78 |
| 7.2 | No discrimination | 0.92 |
| 7.3 | No corruption | 0.94 |
| 7.4 | No improper government influence | 0.95 |
| 7.5 | No unreasonable delay | 0.83 |
| 7.6 | Effective enforcement | 0.88 |
| 7.7 | Impartial and effective ADRs | 0.83 |

## 🏛 Criminal Justice

| | | |
|---|---|---|
| 8.1 | Effective investigations | 0.60 |
| 8.2 | Timely and effective adjudication | 0.78 |
| 8.3 | Effective correctional system | 0.80 |
| 8.4 | No discrimination | 0.73 |
| 8.5 | No corruption | 0.90 |
| 8.6 | No improper government influence | 0.94 |
| 8.7 | Due process of law | 0.83 |

# New Zealand

**Region:** East Asia & Pacific
**Income Group:** High Income

| Overall Score | Regional Rank | Income Rank | Global Rank |
|---|---|---|---|
| 0.83 | 1/15 | 8/36 | 8/113 |

| | Factor Trend | Factor Score | Regional Rank | Income Rank | Global Rank |
|---|---|---|---|---|---|
| Constraints on Government Powers | — | 0.86 | 1/15 | 6/36 | 6/113 |
| Absence of Corruption | — | 0.90 | 2/15 | 6/36 | 6/113 |
| Open Government | — | 0.84 | 1/15 | 6/36 | 6/113 |
| Fundamental Rights | — | 0.82 | 1/15 | 10/36 | 10/113 |
| Order & Security | — | 0.86 | 5/15 | 14/36 | 15/113 |
| Regulatory Enforcement | — | 0.82 | 2/15 | 8/36 | 8/113 |
| Civil Justice | — | 0.78 | 4/15 | 11/36 | 11/113 |
| Criminal Justice | — | 0.75 | 4/15 | 13/36 | 13/113 |

High Low ▼ Trending down ▲ Trending up

■ New Zealand ■ East Asia & Pacific ■ High Income

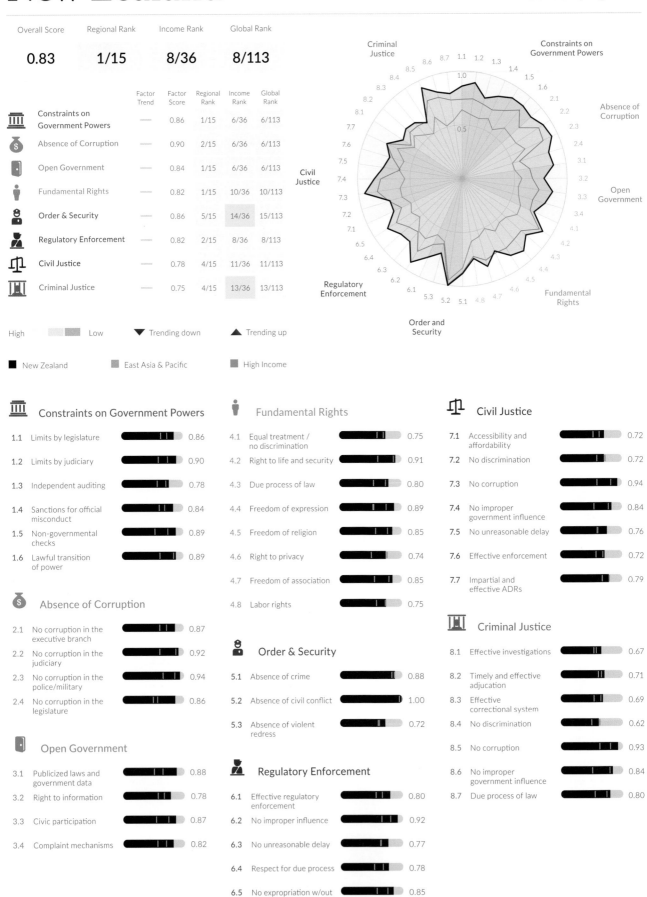

## Constraints on Government Powers

| | | |
|---|---|---|
| 1.1 | Limits by legislature | 0.86 |
| 1.2 | Limits by judiciary | 0.90 |
| 1.3 | Independent auditing | 0.78 |
| 1.4 | Sanctions for official misconduct | 0.84 |
| 1.5 | Non-governmental checks | 0.89 |
| 1.6 | Lawful transition of power | 0.89 |

## Absence of Corruption

| | | |
|---|---|---|
| 2.1 | No corruption in the executive branch | 0.87 |
| 2.2 | No corruption in the judiciary | 0.92 |
| 2.3 | No corruption in the police/military | 0.94 |
| 2.4 | No corruption in the legislature | 0.86 |

## Open Government

| | | |
|---|---|---|
| 3.1 | Publicized laws and government data | 0.88 |
| 3.2 | Right to information | 0.78 |
| 3.3 | Civic participation | 0.87 |
| 3.4 | Complaint mechanisms | 0.82 |

## Fundamental Rights

| | | |
|---|---|---|
| 4.1 | Equal treatment / no discrimination | 0.75 |
| 4.2 | Right to life and security | 0.91 |
| 4.3 | Due process of law | 0.80 |
| 4.4 | Freedom of expression | 0.89 |
| 4.5 | Freedom of religion | 0.85 |
| 4.6 | Right to privacy | 0.74 |
| 4.7 | Freedom of association | 0.85 |
| 4.8 | Labor rights | 0.75 |

## Order & Security

| | | |
|---|---|---|
| 5.1 | Absence of crime | 0.88 |
| 5.2 | Absence of civil conflict | 1.00 |
| 5.3 | Absence of violent redress | 0.72 |

## Regulatory Enforcement

| | | |
|---|---|---|
| 6.1 | Effective regulatory enforcement | 0.80 |
| 6.2 | No improper influence | 0.92 |
| 6.3 | No unreasonable delay | 0.77 |
| 6.4 | Respect for due process | 0.78 |
| 6.5 | No expropriation w/out adequate compensation | 0.85 |

## Civil Justice

| | | |
|---|---|---|
| 7.1 | Accessibility and affordability | 0.72 |
| 7.2 | No discrimination | 0.72 |
| 7.3 | No corruption | 0.94 |
| 7.4 | No improper government influence | 0.84 |
| 7.5 | No unreasonable delay | 0.76 |
| 7.6 | Effective enforcement | 0.72 |
| 7.7 | Impartial and effective ADRs | 0.79 |

## Criminal Justice

| | | |
|---|---|---|
| 8.1 | Effective investigations | 0.67 |
| 8.2 | Timely and effective adjucation | 0.71 |
| 8.3 | Effective correctional system | 0.69 |
| 8.4 | No discrimination | 0.62 |
| 8.5 | No corruption | 0.93 |
| 8.6 | No improper government influence | 0.84 |
| 8.7 | Due process of law | 0.80 |

# Nicaragua

**Region:** Latin America & Caribbean
**Income Group:** Lower Middle Income

| Overall Score | Regional Rank | Income Rank | Global Rank |
|:---:|:---:|:---:|:---:|
| 0.42 | 27/30 | 21/28 | 101/113 |

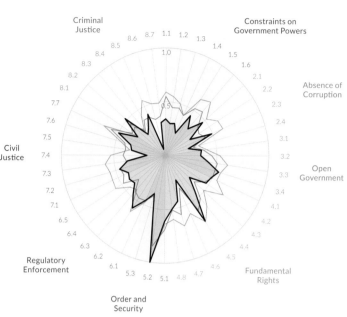

| | Factor Trend | Factor Score | Regional Rank | Income Rank | Global Rank |
|---|:---:|:---:|:---:|:---:|:---:|
| Constraints on Government Powers | — | 0.32 | 29/30 | 25/28 | 107/113 |
| Absence of Corruption | — | 0.37 | 23/30 | 15/28 | 87/113 |
| Open Government | — | 0.41 | 29/30 | 22/28 | 97/113 |
| Fundamental Rights | — | 0.45 | 28/30 | 18/28 | 93/113 |
| Order & Security | — | 0.66 | 16/30 | 14/28 | 79/113 |
| Regulatory Enforcement | — | 0.46 | 22/30 | 10/28 | 75/113 |
| Civil Justice | — | 0.37 | 27/30 | 24/28 | 107/113 |
| Criminal Justice | — | 0.32 | 24/30 | 23/28 | 102/113 |

High ▢ Low   ▼ Trending down   ▲ Trending up

■ Nicaragua   ▨ Latin America & Caribbean   ▨ Lower Middle Income

## Constraints on Government Powers

| | | |
|---|---|---|
| 1.1 | Limits by legislature | 0.34 |
| 1.2 | Limits by judiciary | 0.30 |
| 1.3 | Independent auditing | 0.31 |
| 1.4 | Sanctions for official misconduct | 0.23 |
| 1.5 | Non-governmental checks | 0.44 |
| 1.6 | Lawful transition of power | 0.33 |

## Absence of Corruption

| | | |
|---|---|---|
| 2.1 | No corruption in the executive branch | 0.47 |
| 2.2 | No corruption in the judiciary | 0.28 |
| 2.3 | No corruption in the police/military | 0.49 |
| 2.4 | No corruption in the legislature | 0.23 |

## Open Government

| | | |
|---|---|---|
| 3.1 | Publicized laws and government data | 0.35 |
| 3.2 | Right to information | 0.34 |
| 3.3 | Civic participation | 0.42 |
| 3.4 | Complaint mechanisms | 0.54 |

## Fundamental Rights

| | | |
|---|---|---|
| 4.1 | Equal treatment / no discrimination | 0.49 |
| 4.2 | Right to life and security | 0.47 |
| 4.3 | Due process of law | 0.31 |
| 4.4 | Freedom of expression | 0.44 |
| 4.5 | Freedom of religion | 0.72 |
| 4.6 | Right to privacy | 0.25 |
| 4.7 | Freedom of association | 0.44 |
| 4.8 | Labor rights | 0.50 |

## Order & Security

| | | |
|---|---|---|
| 5.1 | Absence of crime | 0.61 |
| 5.2 | Absence of civil conflict | 1.00 |
| 5.3 | Absence of violent redress | 0.37 |

## Regulatory Enforcement

| | | |
|---|---|---|
| 6.1 | Effective regulatory enforcement | 0.46 |
| 6.2 | No improper influence | 0.58 |
| 6.3 | No unreasonable delay | 0.47 |
| 6.4 | Respect for due process | 0.39 |
| 6.5 | No expropriation w/out adequate compensation | 0.41 |

## Civil Justice

| | | |
|---|---|---|
| 7.1 | Accessibility and affordability | 0.39 |
| 7.2 | No discrimination | 0.46 |
| 7.3 | No corruption | 0.37 |
| 7.4 | No improper government influence | 0.18 |
| 7.5 | No unreasonable delay | 0.33 |
| 7.6 | Effective enforcement | 0.35 |
| 7.7 | Impartial and effective ADRs | 0.50 |

## Criminal Justice

| | | |
|---|---|---|
| 8.1 | Effective investigations | 0.32 |
| 8.2 | Timely and effective adjucation | 0.52 |
| 8.3 | Effective correctional system | 0.26 |
| 8.4 | No discrimination | 0.31 |
| 8.5 | No corruption | 0.42 |
| 8.6 | No improper government influence | 0.06 |
| 8.7 | Due process of law | 0.31 |

# Nigeria

| Overall Score | Regional Rank | Income Rank | Global Rank |
|:---:|:---:|:---:|:---:|
| 0.44 | 13/18 | 17/28 | 96/113 |

| | | Factor Trend | Factor Score | Regional Rank | Income Rank | Global Rank |
|---|---|:---:|:---:|:---:|:---:|:---:|
| 🏛 | Constraints on Government Powers | ▲ | 0.54 | 7/18 | 7/28 | 61/113 |
| 💰 | Absence of Corruption | ▲ | 0.30 | 11/18 | 22/28 | 100/113 |
| 📱 | Open Government | — | 0.43 | 11/18 | 21/28 | 95/113 |
| 👤 | Fundamental Rights | — | 0.46 | 12/18 | 16/28 | 89/113 |
| 👥 | Order & Security | — | 0.48 | 17/18 | 26/28 | 109/113 |
| 👷 | Regulatory Enforcement | — | 0.43 | 9/18 | 15/28 | 89/113 |
| ⚖ | Civil Justice | — | 0.48 | 9/18 | 8/28 | 75/113 |
| 🏛 | Criminal Justice | ▲ | 0.42 | 7/18 | 8/28 | 68/113 |

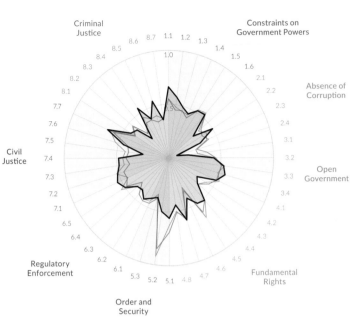

High ▢▢▢ Low    ▼ Trending down    ▲ Trending up

■ Nigeria    ■ Sub-Saharan Africa    ■ Lower Middle Income

---

## 🏛 Constraints on Government Powers

| | | | |
|---|---|---|---:|
| 1.1 | Limits by legislature | ▰▰▰ | 0.66 |
| 1.2 | Limits by judiciary | ▰▰▰ | 0.57 |
| 1.3 | Independent auditing | ▰▰▰ | 0.49 |
| 1.4 | Sanctions for official misconduct | ▰▰▰ | 0.45 |
| 1.5 | Non-governmental checks | ▰▰▰ | 0.52 |
| 1.6 | Lawful transition of power | ▰▰▰ | 0.53 |

## 💰 Absence of Corruption

| | | | |
|---|---|---|---:|
| 2.1 | No corruption in the executive branch | ▰▰▰ | 0.31 |
| 2.2 | No corruption in the judiciary | ▰▰▰ | 0.50 |
| 2.3 | No corruption in the police/military | ▰▰▰ | 0.33 |
| 2.4 | No corruption in the legislature | ▰▰▰ | 0.08 |

## 📱 Open Government

| | | | |
|---|---|---|---:|
| 3.1 | Publicized laws and government data | ▰▰▰ | 0.19 |
| 3.2 | Right to information | ▰▰▰ | 0.43 |
| 3.3 | Civic participation | ▰▰▰ | 0.53 |
| 3.4 | Complaint mechanisms | ▰▰▰ | 0.56 |

## 👤 Fundamental Rights

| | | | |
|---|---|---|---:|
| 4.1 | Equal treatment / no discrimination | ▰▰▰ | 0.50 |
| 4.2 | Right to life and security | ▰▰▰ | 0.32 |
| 4.3 | Due process of law | ▰▰▰ | 0.36 |
| 4.4 | Freedom of expression | ▰▰▰ | 0.52 |
| 4.5 | Freedom of religion | ▰▰▰ | 0.50 |
| 4.6 | Right to privacy | ▰▰▰ | 0.41 |
| 4.7 | Freedom of association | ▰▰▰ | 0.6 |
| 4.8 | Labor rights | ▰▰▰ | 0.44 |

## 👥 Order & Security

| | | | |
|---|---|---|---:|
| 5.1 | Absence of crime | ▰▰▰ | 0.56 |
| 5.2 | Absence of civil conflict | ▰▰▰ | 0.50 |
| 5.3 | Absence of violent redress | ▰▰▰ | 0.38 |

## 👷 Regulatory Enforcement

| | | | |
|---|---|---|---:|
| 6.1 | Effective regulatory enforcement | ▰▰▰ | 0.41 |
| 6.2 | No improper influence | ▰▰▰ | 0.45 |
| 6.3 | No unreasonable delay | ▰▰▰ | 0.39 |
| 6.4 | Respect for due process | ▰▰▰ | 0.40 |
| 6.5 | No expropriation w/out adequate compensation | ▰▰▰ | 0.50 |

## ⚖ Civil Justice

| | | | |
|---|---|---|---:|
| 7.1 | Accessibility and affordability | ▰▰▰ | 0.54 |
| 7.2 | No discrimination | ▰▰▰ | 0.51 |
| 7.3 | No corruption | ▰▰▰ | 0.48 |
| 7.4 | No improper government influence | ▰▰▰ | 0.48 |
| 7.5 | No unreasonable delay | ▰▰▰ | 0.25 |
| 7.6 | Effective enforcement | ▰▰▰ | 0.45 |
| 7.7 | Impartial and effective ADRs | ▰▰▰ | 0.64 |

## 🏛 Criminal Justice

| | | | |
|---|---|---|---:|
| 8.1 | Effective investigations | ▰▰▰ | 0.43 |
| 8.2 | Timely and effective adjudication | ▰▰▰ | 0.40 |
| 8.3 | Effective correctional system | ▰▰▰ | 0.24 |
| 8.4 | No discrimination | ▰▰▰ | 0.55 |
| 8.5 | No corruption | ▰▰▰ | 0.40 |
| 8.6 | No improper government influence | ▰▰▰ | 0.55 |
| 8.7 | Due process of law | ▰▰▰ | 0.36 |

# Norway

| | Overall Score | Regional Rank | Income Rank | Global Rank |
|---|---|---|---|---|
| | 0.88 | 2/24 | 2/36 | 2/113 |

| | | Factor Trend | Factor Score | Regional Rank | Income Rank | Global Rank |
|---|---|---|---|---|---|---|
| 🏛 | Constraints on Government Powers | — | 0.91 | 2/24 | 2/36 | 2/113 |
| 💰 | Absence of Corruption | — | 0.92 | 2/24 | 3/36 | 3/113 |
| ▯ | Open Government | — | 0.87 | 1/24 | 1/36 | 1/113 |
| 👤 | Fundamental Rights | — | 0.89 | 3/24 | 3/36 | 3/113 |
| 👮 | Order & Security | — | 0.9 | 6/24 | 7/36 | 8/113 |
| 👷 | Regulatory Enforcement | — | 0.86 | 2/24 | 3/36 | 3/113 |
| ⚖ | Civil Justice | — | 0.85 | 3/24 | 3/36 | 3/113 |
| ⚖ | Criminal Justice | — | 0.83 | 2/24 | 2/36 | 2/113 |

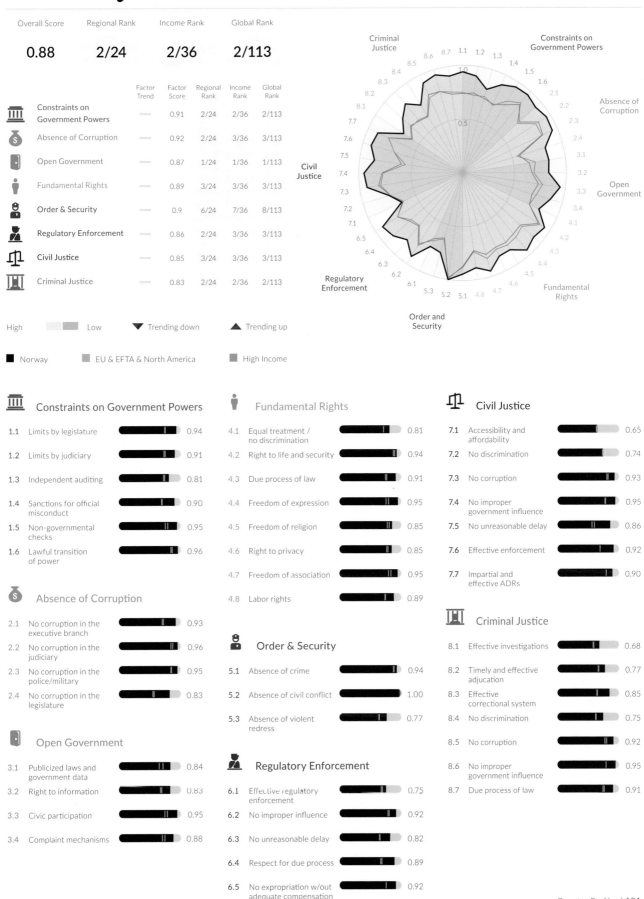

High ▢▢ Low   ▼ Trending down   ▲ Trending up

■ Norway   ▨ EU & EFTA & North America   ▨ High Income

## 🏛 Constraints on Government Powers

| 1.1 | Limits by legislature | 0.94 |
|---|---|---|
| 1.2 | Limits by judiciary | 0.91 |
| 1.3 | Independent auditing | 0.81 |
| 1.4 | Sanctions for official misconduct | 0.90 |
| 1.5 | Non-governmental checks | 0.95 |
| 1.6 | Lawful transition of power | 0.96 |

## 💰 Absence of Corruption

| 2.1 | No corruption in the executive branch | 0.93 |
|---|---|---|
| 2.2 | No corruption in the judiciary | 0.96 |
| 2.3 | No corruption in the police/military | 0.95 |
| 2.4 | No corruption in the legislature | 0.83 |

## ▯ Open Government

| 3.1 | Publicized laws and government data | 0.84 |
|---|---|---|
| 3.2 | Right to information | 0.83 |
| 3.3 | Civic participation | 0.95 |
| 3.4 | Complaint mechanisms | 0.88 |

## 👤 Fundamental Rights

| 4.1 | Equal treatment / no discrimination | 0.81 |
|---|---|---|
| 4.2 | Right to life and security | 0.94 |
| 4.3 | Due process of law | 0.91 |
| 4.4 | Freedom of expression | 0.95 |
| 4.5 | Freedom of religion | 0.85 |
| 4.6 | Right to privacy | 0.85 |
| 4.7 | Freedom of association | 0.95 |
| 4.8 | Labor rights | 0.89 |

## 👮 Order & Security

| 5.1 | Absence of crime | 0.94 |
|---|---|---|
| 5.2 | Absence of civil conflict | 1.00 |
| 5.3 | Absence of violent redress | 0.77 |

## 👷 Regulatory Enforcement

| 6.1 | Effective regulatory enforcement | 0.75 |
|---|---|---|
| 6.2 | No improper influence | 0.92 |
| 6.3 | No unreasonable delay | 0.82 |
| 6.4 | Respect for due process | 0.89 |
| 6.5 | No expropriation w/out adequate compensation | 0.92 |

## ⚖ Civil Justice

| 7.1 | Accessibility and affordability | 0.65 |
|---|---|---|
| 7.2 | No discrimination | 0.74 |
| 7.3 | No corruption | 0.93 |
| 7.4 | No improper government influence | 0.95 |
| 7.5 | No unreasonable delay | 0.86 |
| 7.6 | Effective enforcement | 0.92 |
| 7.7 | Impartial and effective ADRs | 0.90 |

## ⚖ Criminal Justice

| 8.1 | Effective investigations | 0.68 |
|---|---|---|
| 8.2 | Timely and effective adjudication | 0.77 |
| 8.3 | Effective correctional system | 0.85 |
| 8.4 | No discrimination | 0.75 |
| 8.5 | No corruption | 0.92 |
| 8.6 | No improper government influence | 0.95 |
| 8.7 | Due process of law | 0.91 |

# Pakistan

| | Overall Score | Regional Rank | Income Rank | Global Rank |
|---|---|---|---|---|
| | 0.38 | 5/6 | 25/28 | 106/113 |

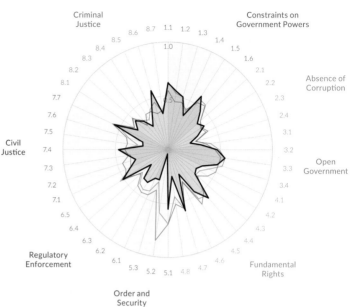

| | Factor Trend | Factor Score | Regional Rank | Income Rank | Global Rank |
|---|---|---|---|---|---|
| Constraints on Government Powers | — | 0.52 | 4/6 | 11/28 | 72/113 |
| Absence of Corruption | — | 0.33 | 5/6 | 21/28 | 97/113 |
| Open Government | — | 0.46 | 4/6 | 16/28 | 79/113 |
| Fundamental Rights | — | 0.39 | 5/6 | 23/28 | 101/113 |
| Order & Security | — | 0.29 | 6/6 | 28/28 | 113/113 |
| Regulatory Enforcement | — | 0.34 | 6/6 | 26/28 | 109/113 |
| Civil Justice | — | 0.37 | 5/6 | 23/28 | 106/113 |
| Criminal Justice | — | 0.38 | 4/6 | 14/28 | 81/113 |

High ▢▢ Low   ▼ Trending down   ▲ Trending up

■ Pakistan   ■ South Asia   ■ Lower Middle Income

## Constraints on Government Powers

| | | |
|---|---|---|
| 1.1 | Limits by legislature | 0.62 |
| 1.2 | Limits by judiciary | 0.55 |
| 1.3 | Independent auditing | 0.51 |
| 1.4 | Sanctions for official misconduct | 0.35 |
| 1.5 | Non-governmental checks | 0.59 |
| 1.6 | Lawful transition of power | 0.47 |

## Absence of Corruption

| | | |
|---|---|---|
| 2.1 | No corruption in the executive branch | 0.37 |
| 2.2 | No corruption in the judiciary | 0.41 |
| 2.3 | No corruption in the police/military | 0.31 |
| 2.4 | No corruption in the legislature | 0.22 |

## Open Government

| | | |
|---|---|---|
| 3.1 | Publicized laws and government data | 0.32 |
| 3.2 | Right to information | 0.47 |
| 3.3 | Civic participation | 0.55 |
| 3.4 | Complaint mechanisms | 0.49 |

## Fundamental Rights

| | | |
|---|---|---|
| 4.1 | Equal treatment / no discrimination | 0.36 |
| 4.2 | Right to life and security | 0.32 |
| 4.3 | Due process of law | 0.34 |
| 4.4 | Freedom of expression | 0.59 |
| 4.5 | Freedom of religion | 0.46 |
| 4.6 | Right to privacy | 0.25 |
| 4.7 | Freedom of association | 0.59 |
| 4.8 | Labor rights | 0.25 |

## Order & Security

| | | |
|---|---|---|
| 5.1 | Absence of crime | 0.55 |
| 5.2 | Absence of civil conflict | 0.04 |
| 5.3 | Absence of violent redress | 0.29 |

## Regulatory Enforcement

| | | |
|---|---|---|
| 6.1 | Effective regulatory enforcement | 0.29 |
| 6.2 | No improper influence | 0.36 |
| 6.3 | No unreasonable delay | 0.35 |
| 6.4 | Respect for due process | 0.21 |
| 6.5 | No expropriation w/out adequate compensation | 0.51 |

## Civil Justice

| | | |
|---|---|---|
| 7.1 | Accessibility and affordability | 0.39 |
| 7.2 | No discrimination | 0.32 |
| 7.3 | No corruption | 0.38 |
| 7.4 | No improper government influence | 0.47 |
| 7.5 | No unreasonable delay | 0.24 |
| 7.6 | Effective enforcement | 0.25 |
| 7.7 | Impartial and effective ADRs | 0.56 |

## Criminal Justice

| | | |
|---|---|---|
| 8.1 | Effective investigations | 0.34 |
| 8.2 | Timely and effective adjudication | 0.41 |
| 8.3 | Effective correctional system | 0.35 |
| 8.4 | No discrimination | 0.26 |
| 8.5 | No corruption | 0.36 |
| 8.6 | No improper government influence | 0.57 |
| 8.7 | Due process of law | 0.34 |

# Panama

| Overall Score | Regional Rank | Income Rank | Global Rank |
|---|---|---|---|
| 0.52 | 17/30 | 20/37 | 62/113 |

| | | Factor Trend | Factor Score | Regional Rank | Income Rank | Global Rank |
|---|---|---|---|---|---|---|
| 🏛 | Constraints on Government Powers | — | 0.56 | 17/30 | 14/37 | 59/113 |
| 💰 | Absence of Corruption | ▼ | 0.45 | 19/30 | 24/37 | 65/113 |
| 📱 | Open Government | — | 0.58 | 8/30 | 10/37 | 41/113 |
| 👤 | Fundamental Rights | — | 0.63 | 15/30 | 14/37 | 49/113 |
| 👮 | Order & Security | — | 0.67 | 14/30 | 22/37 | 73/113 |
| 👷 | Regulatory Enforcement | — | 0.52 | 13/30 | 13/37 | 49/113 |
| ⚖ | Civil Justice | — | 0.48 | 18/30 | 26/37 | 72/113 |
| 🏛 | Criminal Justice | — | 0.29 | 26/30 | 35/37 | 107/113 |

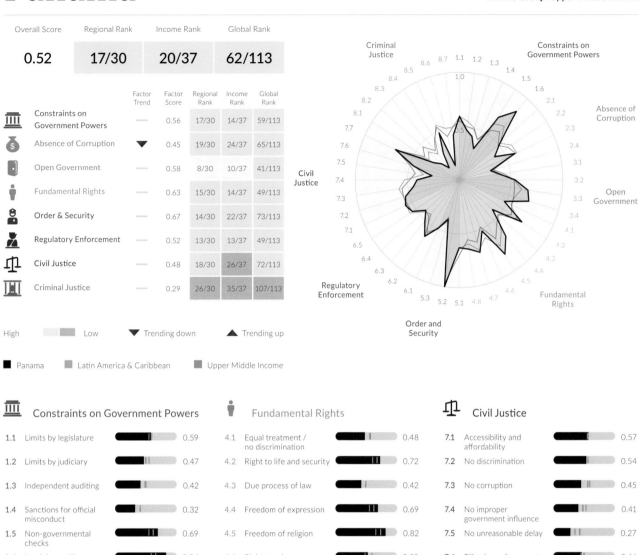

High ▢▢ Low    ▼ Trending down    ▲ Trending up

■ Panama    ▨ Latin America & Caribbean    ▨ Upper Middle Income

## 🏛 Constraints on Government Powers

| | | |
|---|---|---|
| 1.1 | Limits by legislature | 0.59 |
| 1.2 | Limits by judiciary | 0.47 |
| 1.3 | Independent auditing | 0.42 |
| 1.4 | Sanctions for official misconduct | 0.32 |
| 1.5 | Non-governmental checks | 0.69 |
| 1.6 | Lawful transition of power | 0.84 |

## 💰 Absence of Corruption

| | | |
|---|---|---|
| 2.1 | No corruption in the executive branch | 0.51 |
| 2.2 | No corruption in the judiciary | 0.40 |
| 2.3 | No corruption in the police/military | 0.59 |
| 2.4 | No corruption in the legislature | 0.31 |

## 📱 Open Government

| | | |
|---|---|---|
| 3.1 | Publicized laws and government data | 0.39 |
| 3.2 | Right to information | 0.54 |
| 3.3 | Civic participation | 0.67 |
| 3.4 | Complaint mechanisms | 0.70 |

## 👤 Fundamental Rights

| | | |
|---|---|---|
| 4.1 | Equal treatment / no discrimination | 0.48 |
| 4.2 | Right to life and security | 0.72 |
| 4.3 | Due process of law | 0.42 |
| 4.4 | Freedom of expression | 0.69 |
| 4.5 | Freedom of religion | 0.82 |
| 4.6 | Right to privacy | 0.52 |
| 4.7 | Freedom of association | 0.70 |
| 4.8 | Labor rights | 0.65 |

## 👮 Order & Security

| | | |
|---|---|---|
| 5.1 | Absence of crime | 0.63 |
| 5.2 | Absence of civil conflict | 1.00 |
| 5.3 | Absence of violent redress | 0.38 |

## 👷 Regulatory Enforcement

| | | |
|---|---|---|
| 6.1 | Effective regulatory enforcement | 0.49 |
| 6.2 | No improper influence | 0.62 |
| 6.3 | No unreasonable delay | 0.51 |
| 6.4 | Respect for due process | 0.43 |
| 6.5 | No expropriation w/out adequate compensation | 0.54 |

## ⚖ Civil Justice

| | | |
|---|---|---|
| 7.1 | Accessibility and affordability | 0.57 |
| 7.2 | No discrimination | 0.54 |
| 7.3 | No corruption | 0.45 |
| 7.4 | No improper government influence | 0.41 |
| 7.5 | No unreasonable delay | 0.27 |
| 7.6 | Effective enforcement | 0.46 |
| 7.7 | Impartial and effective ADRs | 0.68 |

## 🏛 Criminal Justice

| | | |
|---|---|---|
| 8.1 | Effective investigations | 0.30 |
| 8.2 | Timely and effective adjucation | 0.23 |
| 8.3 | Effective correctional system | 0.15 |
| 8.4 | No discrimination | 0.29 |
| 8.5 | No corruption | 0.48 |
| 8.6 | No improper government influence | 0.14 |
| 8.7 | Due process of law | 0.42 |

# Peru

**Region:** Latin America & Caribbean
**Income Group:** Upper Middle Income

| Overall Score | Regional Rank | Income Rank | Global Rank |
|:---:|:---:|:---:|:---:|
| 0.51 | 18/30 | 22/37 | 65/113 |

| | Factor Trend | Factor Score | Regional Rank | Income Rank | Global Rank |
|---|:---:|:---:|:---:|:---:|:---:|
| Constraints on Government Powers | — | 0.63 | 10/30 | 6/37 | 42/113 |
| Absence of Corruption | — | 0.36 | 24/30 | 33/37 | 91/113 |
| Open Government | — | 0.56 | 10/30 | 14/37 | 46/113 |
| Fundamental Rights | ▲ | 0.64 | 13/30 | 10/37 | 44/113 |
| Order & Security | — | 0.64 | 17/30 | 25/37 | 84/113 |
| Regulatory Enforcement | — | 0.5 | 16/30 | 21/37 | 62/113 |
| Civil Justice | — | 0.44 | 24/30 | 35/37 | 90/113 |
| Criminal Justice | — | 0.34 | 19/30 | 28/37 | 90/113 |

High ▓ Low  ▼ Trending down  ▲ Trending up

■ Peru   ▨ Latin America & Caribbean   ▨ Upper Middle Income

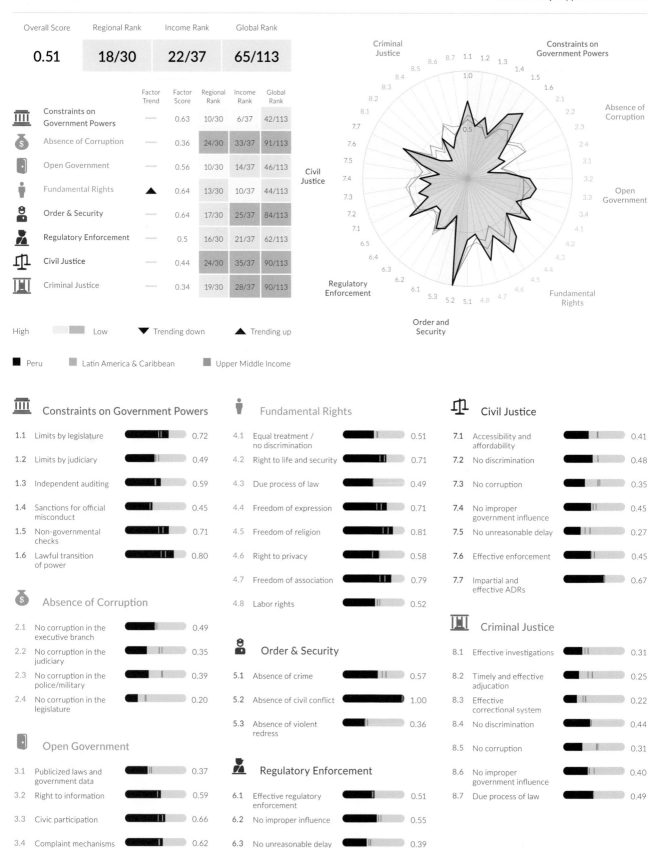

## Constraints on Government Powers

| | | |
|---|---|---:|
| 1.1 | Limits by legislature | 0.72 |
| 1.2 | Limits by judiciary | 0.49 |
| 1.3 | Independent auditing | 0.59 |
| 1.4 | Sanctions for official misconduct | 0.45 |
| 1.5 | Non-governmental checks | 0.71 |
| 1.6 | Lawful transition of power | 0.80 |

## Absence of Corruption

| | | |
|---|---|---:|
| 2.1 | No corruption in the executive branch | 0.49 |
| 2.2 | No corruption in the judiciary | 0.35 |
| 2.3 | No corruption in the police/military | 0.39 |
| 2.4 | No corruption in the legislature | 0.20 |

## Open Government

| | | |
|---|---|---:|
| 3.1 | Publicized laws and government data | 0.37 |
| 3.2 | Right to information | 0.59 |
| 3.3 | Civic participation | 0.66 |
| 3.4 | Complaint mechanisms | 0.62 |

## Fundamental Rights

| | | |
|---|---|---:|
| 4.1 | Equal treatment / no discrimination | 0.51 |
| 4.2 | Right to life and security | 0.71 |
| 4.3 | Due process of law | 0.49 |
| 4.4 | Freedom of expression | 0.71 |
| 4.5 | Freedom of religion | 0.81 |
| 4.6 | Right to privacy | 0.58 |
| 4.7 | Freedom of association | 0.79 |
| 4.8 | Labor rights | 0.52 |

## Order & Security

| | | |
|---|---|---:|
| 5.1 | Absence of crime | 0.57 |
| 5.2 | Absence of civil conflict | 1.00 |
| 5.3 | Absence of violent redress | 0.36 |

## Regulatory Enforcement

| | | |
|---|---|---:|
| 6.1 | Effective regulatory enforcement | 0.51 |
| 6.2 | No improper influence | 0.55 |
| 6.3 | No unreasonable delay | 0.39 |
| 6.4 | Respect for due process | 0.39 |
| 6.5 | No expropriation w/out adequate compensation | 0.65 |

## Civil Justice

| | | |
|---|---|---:|
| 7.1 | Accessibility and affordability | 0.41 |
| 7.2 | No discrimination | 0.48 |
| 7.3 | No corruption | 0.35 |
| 7.4 | No improper government influence | 0.45 |
| 7.5 | No unreasonable delay | 0.27 |
| 7.6 | Effective enforcement | 0.45 |
| 7.7 | Impartial and effective ADRs | 0.67 |

## Criminal Justice

| | | |
|---|---|---:|
| 8.1 | Effective investigations | 0.31 |
| 8.2 | Timely and effective adjudication | 0.25 |
| 8.3 | Effective correctional system | 0.22 |
| 8.4 | No discrimination | 0.44 |
| 8.5 | No corruption | 0.31 |
| 8.6 | No improper government influence | 0.40 |
| 8.7 | Due process of law | 0.49 |

# Philippines

**Region:** East Asia & Pacific
**Income Group:** Lower Middle Income

| Overall Score | Regional Rank | Income Rank | Global Rank |
|---|---|---|---|
| 0.51 | 12/15 | 9/28 | 70/113 |

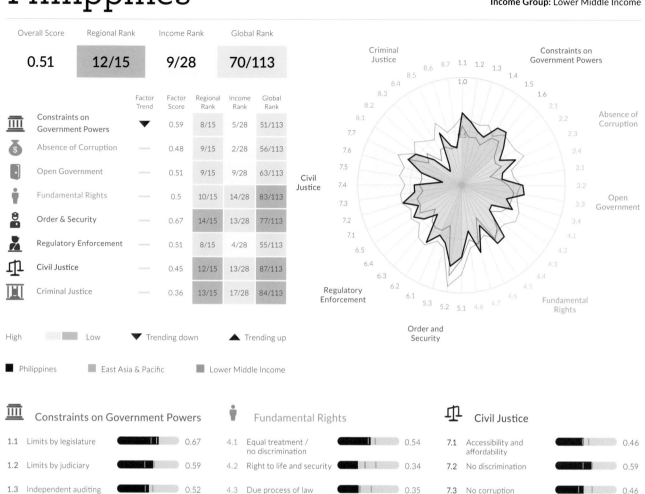

| | Factor Trend | Factor Score | Regional Rank | Income Rank | Global Rank |
|---|---|---|---|---|---|
| Constraints on Government Powers | ▼ | 0.59 | 8/15 | 5/28 | 51/113 |
| Absence of Corruption | — | 0.48 | 9/15 | 2/28 | 56/113 |
| Open Government | — | 0.51 | 9/15 | 9/28 | 63/113 |
| Fundamental Rights | — | 0.5 | 10/15 | 14/28 | 83/113 |
| Order & Security | — | 0.67 | 14/15 | 13/28 | 77/113 |
| Regulatory Enforcement | — | 0.51 | 8/15 | 4/28 | 55/113 |
| Civil Justice | — | 0.45 | 12/15 | 13/28 | 87/113 |
| Criminal Justice | — | 0.36 | 13/15 | 17/28 | 84/113 |

High ▨ Low    ▼ Trending down    ▲ Trending up

■ Philippines    ▨ East Asia & Pacific    ▨ Lower Middle Income

---

## 🏛 Constraints on Government Powers

| | | |
|---|---|---|
| 1.1 | Limits by legislature | 0.67 |
| 1.2 | Limits by judiciary | 0.59 |
| 1.3 | Independent auditing | 0.52 |
| 1.4 | Sanctions for official misconduct | 0.49 |
| 1.5 | Non-governmental checks | 0.63 |
| 1.6 | Lawful transition of power | 0.65 |

## 💰 Absence of Corruption

| | | |
|---|---|---|
| 2.1 | No corruption in the executive branch | 0.53 |
| 2.2 | No corruption in the judiciary | 0.43 |
| 2.3 | No corruption in the police/military | 0.57 |
| 2.4 | No corruption in the legislature | 0.41 |

## 📱 Open Government

| | | |
|---|---|---|
| 3.1 | Publicized laws and government data | 0.39 |
| 3.2 | Right to information | 0.59 |
| 3.3 | Civic participation | 0.61 |
| 3.4 | Complaint mechanisms | 0.45 |

## 🧍 Fundamental Rights

| | | |
|---|---|---|
| 4.1 | Equal treatment / no discrimination | 0.54 |
| 4.2 | Right to life and security | 0.34 |
| 4.3 | Due process of law | 0.35 |
| 4.4 | Freedom of expression | 0.63 |
| 4.5 | Freedom of religion | 0.64 |
| 4.6 | Right to privacy | 0.41 |
| 4.7 | Freedom of association | 0.65 |
| 4.8 | Labor rights | 0.43 |

## 🧑‍💼 Order & Security

| | | |
|---|---|---|
| 5.1 | Absence of crime | 0.67 |
| 5.2 | Absence of civil conflict | 0.76 |
| 5.3 | Absence of violent redress | 0.56 |

## 👷 Regulatory Enforcement

| | | |
|---|---|---|
| 6.1 | Effective regulatory enforcement | 0.51 |
| 6.2 | No improper influence | 0.63 |
| 6.3 | No unreasonable delay | 0.36 |
| 6.4 | Respect for due process | 0.48 |
| 6.5 | No expropriation w/out adequate compensation | 0.55 |

## ⚖ Civil Justice

| | | |
|---|---|---|
| 7.1 | Accessibility and affordability | 0.46 |
| 7.2 | No discrimination | 0.59 |
| 7.3 | No corruption | 0.46 |
| 7.4 | No improper government influence | 0.46 |
| 7.5 | No unreasonable delay | 0.19 |
| 7.6 | Effective enforcement | 0.41 |
| 7.7 | Impartial and effective ADRs | 0.57 |

## 🏛 Criminal Justice

| | | |
|---|---|---|
| 8.1 | Effective investigations | 0.53 |
| 8.2 | Timely and effective adjucation | 0.36 |
| 8.3 | Effective correctional system | 0.17 |
| 8.4 | No discrimination | 0.23 |
| 8.5 | No corruption | 0.53 |
| 8.6 | No improper government influence | 0.38 |
| 8.7 | Due process of law | 0.35 |

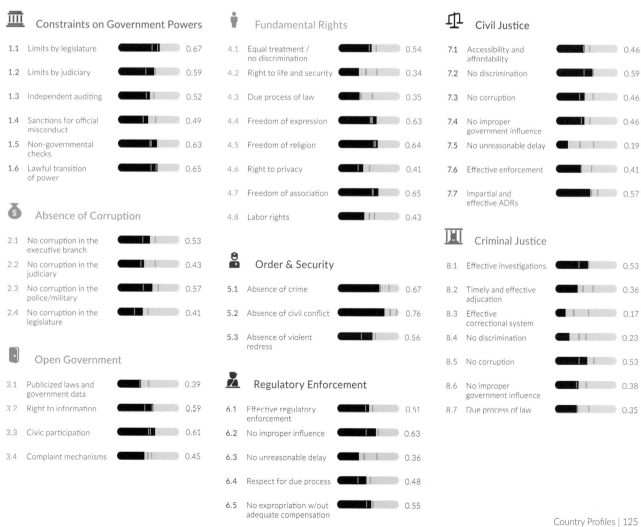

# Poland

**Region:** EU & EFTA & North America
**Income Group:** High Income

| Overall Score | Regional Rank | Income Rank | Global Rank |
|---|---|---|---|
| 0.71 | 15/24 | 22/36 | 22/113 |

| | | Factor Trend | Factor Score | Regional Rank | Income Rank | Global Rank |
|---|---|---|---|---|---|---|
| 🏛 | Constraints on Government Powers | ▼ | 0.68 | 19/24 | 26/36 | 28/113 |
| 💰 | Absence of Corruption | — | 0.73 | 14/24 | 21/36 | 21/113 |
| 📱 | Open Government | — | 0.72 | 14/24 | 16/36 | 16/113 |
| 👤 | Fundamental Rights | — | 0.74 | 18/24 | 25/36 | 26/113 |
| 👮 | Order & Security | — | 0.85 | 12/24 | 18/36 | 19/113 |
| 👷 | Regulatory Enforcement | — | 0.62 | 16/24 | 26/36 | 27/113 |
| ⚖ | Civil Justice | — | 0.66 | 15/24 | 26/36 | 27/113 |
| ⚖ | Criminal Justice | — | 0.69 | 13/24 | 20/36 | 20/113 |

High ▢ Low     ▼ Trending down     ▲ Trending up

■ Poland     ■ EU & EFTA & North America     ■ High Income

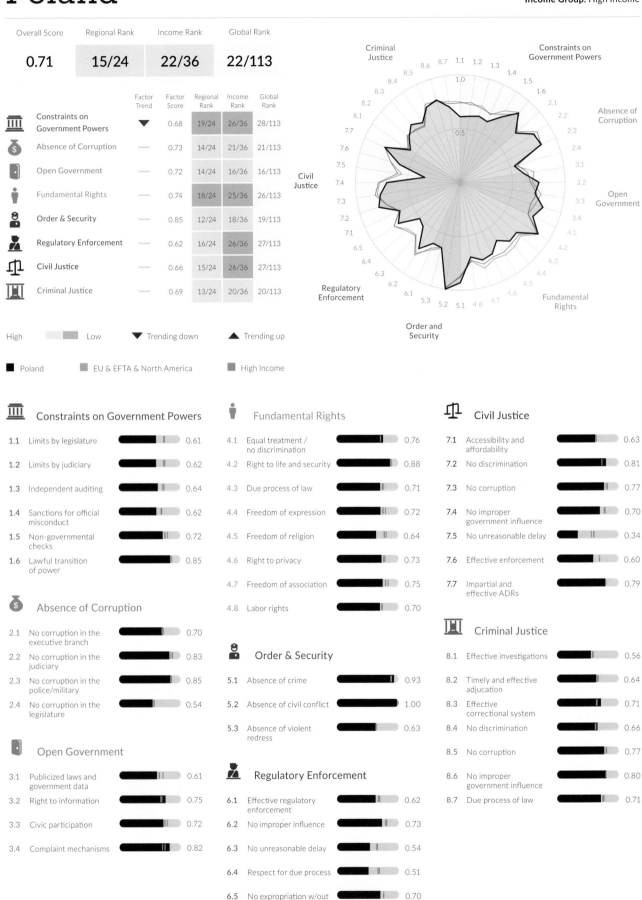

## 🏛 Constraints on Government Powers

| | | |
|---|---|---|
| 1.1 | Limits by legislature | 0.61 |
| 1.2 | Limits by judiciary | 0.62 |
| 1.3 | Independent auditing | 0.64 |
| 1.4 | Sanctions for official misconduct | 0.62 |
| 1.5 | Non-governmental checks | 0.72 |
| 1.6 | Lawful transition of power | 0.85 |

## 💰 Absence of Corruption

| | | |
|---|---|---|
| 2.1 | No corruption in the executive branch | 0.70 |
| 2.2 | No corruption in the judiciary | 0.83 |
| 2.3 | No corruption in the police/military | 0.85 |
| 2.4 | No corruption in the legislature | 0.54 |

## 📱 Open Government

| | | |
|---|---|---|
| 3.1 | Publicized laws and government data | 0.61 |
| 3.2 | Right to information | 0.75 |
| 3.3 | Civic participation | 0.72 |
| 3.4 | Complaint mechanisms | 0.82 |

## 👤 Fundamental Rights

| | | |
|---|---|---|
| 4.1 | Equal treatment / no discrimination | 0.76 |
| 4.2 | Right to life and security | 0.88 |
| 4.3 | Due process of law | 0.71 |
| 4.4 | Freedom of expression | 0.72 |
| 4.5 | Freedom of religion | 0.64 |
| 4.6 | Right to privacy | 0.73 |
| 4.7 | Freedom of association | 0.75 |
| 4.8 | Labor rights | 0.70 |

## 👮 Order & Security

| | | |
|---|---|---|
| 5.1 | Absence of crime | 0.93 |
| 5.2 | Absence of civil conflict | 1.00 |
| 5.3 | Absence of violent redress | 0.63 |

## 👷 Regulatory Enforcement

| | | |
|---|---|---|
| 6.1 | Effective regulatory enforcement | 0.62 |
| 6.2 | No improper influence | 0.73 |
| 6.3 | No unreasonable delay | 0.54 |
| 6.4 | Respect for due process | 0.51 |
| 6.5 | No expropriation w/out adequate compensation | 0.70 |

## ⚖ Civil Justice

| | | |
|---|---|---|
| 7.1 | Accessibility and affordability | 0.63 |
| 7.2 | No discrimination | 0.81 |
| 7.3 | No corruption | 0.77 |
| 7.4 | No improper government influence | 0.70 |
| 7.5 | No unreasonable delay | 0.34 |
| 7.6 | Effective enforcement | 0.60 |
| 7.7 | Impartial and effective ADRs | 0.79 |

## ⚖ Criminal Justice

| | | |
|---|---|---|
| 8.1 | Effective investigations | 0.56 |
| 8.2 | Timely and effective adjucation | 0.64 |
| 8.3 | Effective correctional system | 0.71 |
| 8.4 | No discrimination | 0.66 |
| 8.5 | No corruption | 0.77 |
| 8.6 | No improper government influence | 0.80 |
| 8.7 | Due process of law | 0.71 |

# Portugal

| | Overall Score | Regional Rank | Income Rank | Global Rank |
|---|---|---|---|---|
| | 0.71 | 16/24 | 23/36 | 23/113 |

| | Factor Trend | Factor Score | Regional Rank | Income Rank | Global Rank |
|---|---|---|---|---|---|
| Constraints on Government Powers | — | 0.80 | 12/24 | 14/36 | 14/113 |
| Absence of Corruption | — | 0.72 | 15/24 | 22/36 | 23/113 |
| Open Government | — | 0.67 | 18/24 | 24/36 | 26/113 |
| Fundamental Rights | — | 0.79 | 13/24 | 17/36 | 18/113 |
| Order & Security | — | 0.77 | 20/24 | 29/36 | 39/113 |
| Regulatory Enforcement | — | 0.60 | 18/24 | 29/36 | 31/113 |
| Civil Justice | — | 0.66 | 14/24 | 25/36 | 26/113 |
| Criminal Justice | — | 0.67 | 15/24 | 24/36 | 24/113 |

High ▢▢ Low   ▼ Trending down   ▲ Trending up

■ Portugal   ▨ EU & EFTA & North America   ▨ High Income

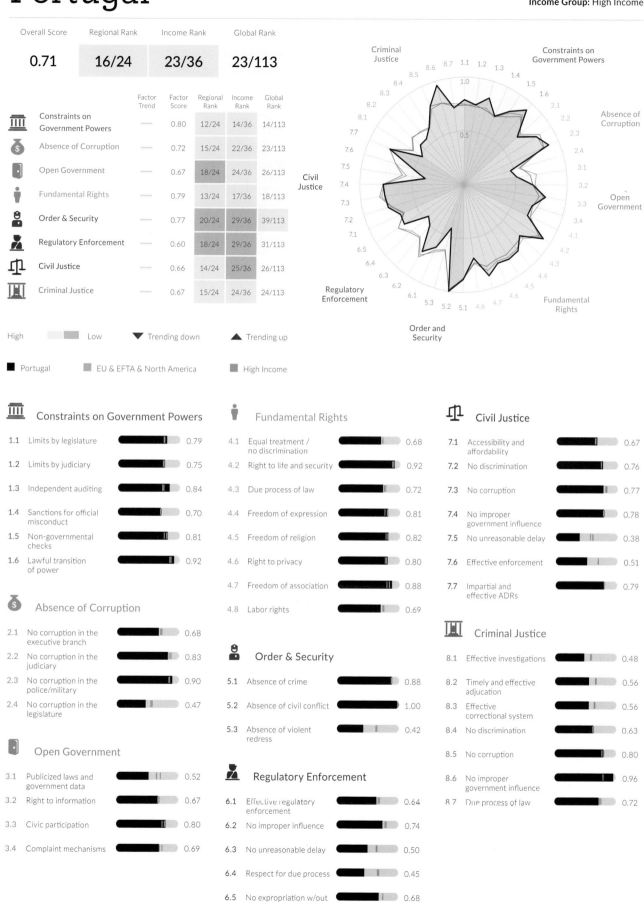

## Constraints on Government Powers

| | | |
|---|---|---|
| 1.1 | Limits by legislature | 0.79 |
| 1.2 | Limits by judiciary | 0.75 |
| 1.3 | Independent auditing | 0.84 |
| 1.4 | Sanctions for official misconduct | 0.70 |
| 1.5 | Non-governmental checks | 0.81 |
| 1.6 | Lawful transition of power | 0.92 |

## Absence of Corruption

| | | |
|---|---|---|
| 2.1 | No corruption in the executive branch | 0.68 |
| 2.2 | No corruption in the judiciary | 0.83 |
| 2.3 | No corruption in the police/military | 0.90 |
| 2.4 | No corruption in the legislature | 0.47 |

## Open Government

| | | |
|---|---|---|
| 3.1 | Publicized laws and government data | 0.52 |
| 3.2 | Right to information | 0.67 |
| 3.3 | Civic participation | 0.80 |
| 3.4 | Complaint mechanisms | 0.69 |

## Fundamental Rights

| | | |
|---|---|---|
| 4.1 | Equal treatment / no discrimination | 0.68 |
| 4.2 | Right to life and security | 0.92 |
| 4.3 | Due process of law | 0.72 |
| 4.4 | Freedom of expression | 0.81 |
| 4.5 | Freedom of religion | 0.82 |
| 4.6 | Right to privacy | 0.80 |
| 4.7 | Freedom of association | 0.88 |
| 4.8 | Labor rights | 0.69 |

## Order & Security

| | | |
|---|---|---|
| 5.1 | Absence of crime | 0.88 |
| 5.2 | Absence of civil conflict | 1.00 |
| 5.3 | Absence of violent redress | 0.42 |

## Regulatory Enforcement

| | | |
|---|---|---|
| 6.1 | Effective regulatory enforcement | 0.64 |
| 6.2 | No improper influence | 0.74 |
| 6.3 | No unreasonable delay | 0.50 |
| 6.4 | Respect for due process | 0.45 |
| 6.5 | No expropriation w/out adequate compensation | 0.68 |

## Civil Justice

| | | |
|---|---|---|
| 7.1 | Accessibility and affordability | 0.67 |
| 7.2 | No discrimination | 0.76 |
| 7.3 | No corruption | 0.77 |
| 7.4 | No improper government influence | 0.78 |
| 7.5 | No unreasonable delay | 0.38 |
| 7.6 | Effective enforcement | 0.51 |
| 7.7 | Impartial and effective ADRs | 0.79 |

## Criminal Justice

| | | |
|---|---|---|
| 8.1 | Effective investigations | 0.48 |
| 8.2 | Timely and effective adjucation | 0.56 |
| 8.3 | Effective correctional system | 0.56 |
| 8.4 | No discrimination | 0.63 |
| 8.5 | No corruption | 0.80 |
| 8.6 | No improper government influence | 0.96 |
| 8.7 | Due process of law | 0.72 |

# Republic of Korea

**Region:** East Asia & Pacific
**Income Group:** High Income

| | Overall Score | Regional Rank | Income Rank | Global Rank |
|---|---|---|---|---|
| | 0.73 | 6/15 | 19/36 | 19/113 |

| | | Factor Trend | Factor Score | Regional Rank | Income Rank | Global Rank |
|---|---|---|---|---|---|---|
| 🏛 | Constraints on Government Powers | ▼ | 0.68 | 6/15 | 25/36 | 27/113 |
| 💲 | Absence of Corruption | ▼ | 0.65 | 6/15 | 29/36 | 35/113 |
| 📱 | Open Government | ▼ | 0.68 | 4/15 | 21/36 | 22/113 |
| 👤 | Fundamental Rights | — | 0.70 | 4/15 | 28/36 | 32/113 |
| 👨‍💼 | Order & Security | — | 0.83 | 6/15 | 21/36 | 23/113 |
| 👷 | Regulatory Enforcement | — | 0.75 | 6/15 | 17/36 | 17/113 |
| ⚖ | Civil Justice | — | 0.81 | 3/15 | 8/36 | 8/113 |
| 🏛 | Criminal Justice | — | 0.71 | 5/15 | 17/36 | 17/113 |

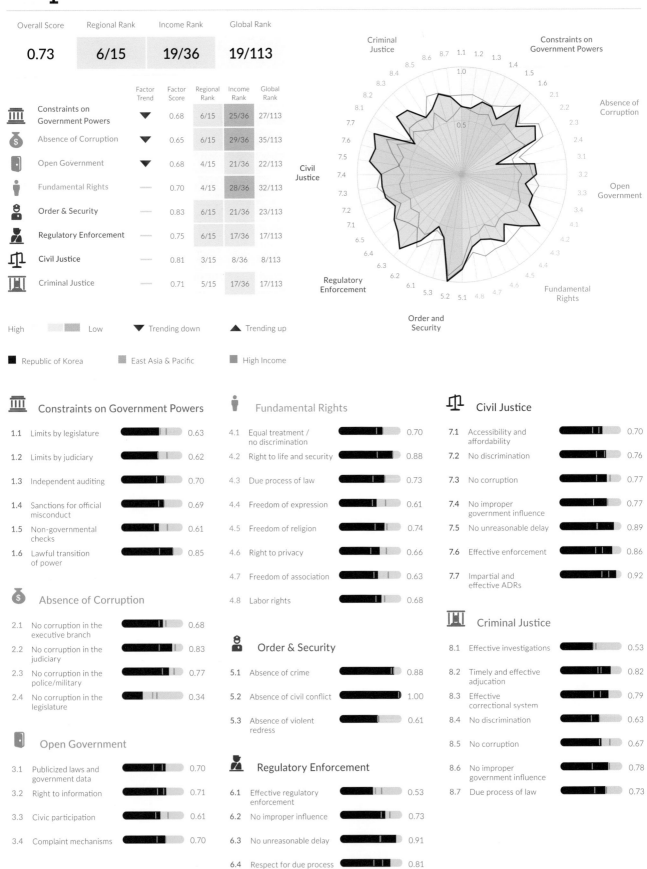

High ▬▬▬ Low      ▼ Trending down      ▲ Trending up

■ Republic of Korea      ■ East Asia & Pacific      ■ High Income

## 🏛 Constraints on Government Powers

| | | |
|---|---|---|
| 1.1 | Limits by legislature | 0.63 |
| 1.2 | Limits by judiciary | 0.62 |
| 1.3 | Independent auditing | 0.70 |
| 1.4 | Sanctions for official misconduct | 0.69 |
| 1.5 | Non-governmental checks | 0.61 |
| 1.6 | Lawful transition of power | 0.85 |

## 💲 Absence of Corruption

| | | |
|---|---|---|
| 2.1 | No corruption in the executive branch | 0.68 |
| 2.2 | No corruption in the judiciary | 0.83 |
| 2.3 | No corruption in the police/military | 0.77 |
| 2.4 | No corruption in the legislature | 0.34 |

## 📱 Open Government

| | | |
|---|---|---|
| 3.1 | Publicized laws and government data | 0.70 |
| 3.2 | Right to information | 0.71 |
| 3.3 | Civic participation | 0.61 |
| 3.4 | Complaint mechanisms | 0.70 |

## 👤 Fundamental Rights

| | | |
|---|---|---|
| 4.1 | Equal treatment / no discrimination | 0.70 |
| 4.2 | Right to life and security | 0.88 |
| 4.3 | Due process of law | 0.73 |
| 4.4 | Freedom of expression | 0.61 |
| 4.5 | Freedom of religion | 0.74 |
| 4.6 | Right to privacy | 0.66 |
| 4.7 | Freedom of association | 0.63 |
| 4.8 | Labor rights | 0.68 |

## 👨‍💼 Order & Security

| | | |
|---|---|---|
| 5.1 | Absence of crime | 0.88 |
| 5.2 | Absence of civil conflict | 1.00 |
| 5.3 | Absence of violent redress | 0.61 |

## 👷 Regulatory Enforcement

| | | |
|---|---|---|
| 6.1 | Effective regulatory enforcement | 0.53 |
| 6.2 | No improper influence | 0.73 |
| 6.3 | No unreasonable delay | 0.91 |
| 6.4 | Respect for due process | 0.81 |
| 6.5 | No expropriation w/out adequate compensation | 0.77 |

## ⚖ Civil Justice

| | | |
|---|---|---|
| 7.1 | Accessibility and affordability | 0.70 |
| 7.2 | No discrimination | 0.76 |
| 7.3 | No corruption | 0.77 |
| 7.4 | No improper government influence | 0.77 |
| 7.5 | No unreasonable delay | 0.89 |
| 7.6 | Effective enforcement | 0.86 |
| 7.7 | Impartial and effective ADRs | 0.92 |

## 🏛 Criminal Justice

| | | |
|---|---|---|
| 8.1 | Effective investigations | 0.53 |
| 8.2 | Timely and effective adjudication | 0.82 |
| 8.3 | Effective correctional system | 0.79 |
| 8.4 | No discrimination | 0.63 |
| 8.5 | No corruption | 0.67 |
| 8.6 | No improper government influence | 0.78 |
| 8.7 | Due process of law | 0.73 |

# Romania

**Region:** EU & EFTA & North America
**Income Group:** Upper Middle Income

| Overall Score | Regional Rank | Income Rank | Global Rank |
|---|---|---|---|
| 0.66 | 19/24 | 3/37 | 32/113 |

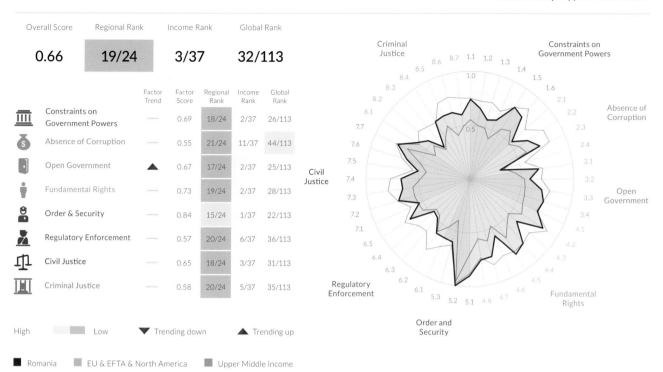

| | | Factor Trend | Factor Score | Regional Rank | Income Rank | Global Rank |
|---|---|---|---|---|---|---|
| 🏛 | Constraints on Government Powers | — | 0.69 | 18/24 | 2/37 | 26/113 |
| 💰 | Absence of Corruption | — | 0.55 | 21/24 | 11/37 | 44/113 |
| 🚪 | Open Government | ▲ | 0.67 | 17/24 | 2/37 | 25/113 |
| 🧍 | Fundamental Rights | — | 0.73 | 19/24 | 2/37 | 28/113 |
| 👤 | Order & Security | — | 0.84 | 15/24 | 1/37 | 22/113 |
| 🧑‍⚖ | Regulatory Enforcement | — | 0.57 | 20/24 | 6/37 | 36/113 |
| ⚖ | Civil Justice | — | 0.65 | 18/24 | 3/37 | 31/113 |
| 🏛 | Criminal Justice | — | 0.58 | 20/24 | 5/37 | 35/113 |

High ▮▮▮ Low   ▼ Trending down   ▲ Trending up

■ Romania   ▨ EU & EFTA & North America   ▨ Upper Middle Income

## 🏛 Constraints on Government Powers

| | | |
|---|---|---|
| 1.1 | Limits by legislature | 0.74 |
| 1.2 | Limits by judiciary | 0.66 |
| 1.3 | Independent auditing | 0.57 |
| 1.4 | Sanctions for official misconduct | 0.60 |
| 1.5 | Non-governmental checks | 0.79 |
| 1.6 | Lawful transition of power | 0.76 |

## 💰 Absence of Corruption

| | | |
|---|---|---|
| 2.1 | No corruption in the executive branch | 0.53 |
| 2.2 | No corruption in the judiciary | 0.66 |
| 2.3 | No corruption in the police/military | 0.74 |
| 2.4 | No corruption in the legislature | 0.30 |

## 🚪 Open Government

| | | |
|---|---|---|
| 3.1 | Publicized laws and government data | 0.67 |
| 3.2 | Right to information | 0.58 |
| 3.3 | Civic participation | 0.70 |
| 3.4 | Complaint mechanisms | 0.74 |

## 🧍 Fundamental Rights

| | | |
|---|---|---|
| 4.1 | Equal treatment / no discrimination | 0.72 |
| 4.2 | Right to life and security | 0.84 |
| 4.3 | Due process of law | 0.60 |
| 4.4 | Freedom of expression | 0.79 |
| 4.5 | Freedom of religion | 0.83 |
| 4.6 | Right to privacy | 0.58 |
| 4.7 | Freedom of association | 0.75 |
| 4.8 | Labor rights | 0.76 |

## 👤 Order & Security

| | | |
|---|---|---|
| 5.1 | Absence of crime | 0.90 |
| 5.2 | Absence of civil conflict | 1.00 |
| 5.3 | Absence of violent redress | 0.61 |

## 🧑‍⚖ Regulatory Enforcement

| | | |
|---|---|---|
| 6.1 | Effective regulatory enforcement | 0.60 |
| 6.2 | No improper influence | 0.60 |
| 6.3 | No unreasonable delay | 0.48 |
| 6.4 | Respect for due process | 0.46 |
| 6.5 | No expropriation w/out adequate compensation | 0.69 |

## ⚖ Civil Justice

| | | |
|---|---|---|
| 7.1 | Accessibility and affordability | 0.54 |
| 7.2 | No discrimination | 0.72 |
| 7.3 | No corruption | 0.66 |
| 7.4 | No improper government influence | 0.67 |
| 7.5 | No unreasonable delay | 0.51 |
| 7.6 | Effective enforcement | 0.64 |
| 7.7 | Impartial and effective ADRs | 0.77 |

## 🏛 Criminal Justice

| | | |
|---|---|---|
| 8.1 | Effective investigations | 0.62 |
| 8.2 | Timely and effective adjudication | 0.54 |
| 8.3 | Effective correctional system | 0.39 |
| 8.4 | No discrimination | 0.63 |
| 8.5 | No corruption | 0.64 |
| 8.6 | No improper government influence | 0.64 |
| 8.7 | Due process of law | 0.60 |

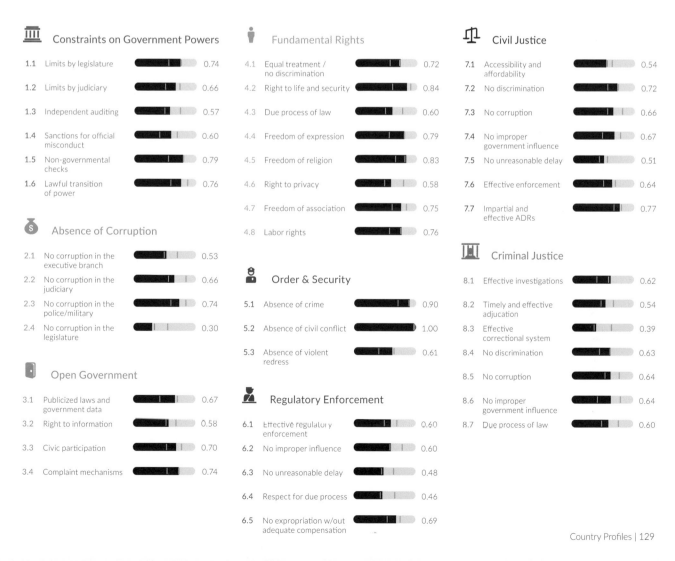

# Russia

| | Overall Score | Regional Rank | Income Rank | Global Rank |
|---|---|---|---|---|
| | 0.45 | 11/13 | 35/37 | 92/113 |

| | Factor Trend | Factor Score | Regional Rank | Income Rank | Global Rank |
|---|---|---|---|---|---|
| 🏛 Constraints on Government Powers | — | 0.40 | 10/13 | 32/37 | 100/113 |
| 💰 Absence of Corruption | — | 0.41 | 8/13 | 30/37 | 78/113 |
| 📱 Open Government | — | 0.49 | 8/13 | 21/37 | 67/113 |
| 👤 Fundamental Rights | — | 0.44 | 11/13 | 32/37 | 97/113 |
| 👮 Order & Security | ▼ | 0.56 | 13/13 | 35/37 | 102/113 |
| 👷 Regulatory Enforcement | — | 0.47 | 6/13 | 25/37 | 71/113 |
| ⚖ Civil Justice | — | 0.52 | 5/13 | 22/37 | 63/113 |
| 🏛 Criminal Justice | — | 0.33 | 13/13 | 32/37 | 98/113 |

High ▨ Low   ▼ Trending down   ▲ Trending up

■ Russia   ▨ Eastern Europe & Central Asia   ▨ Upper Middle Income

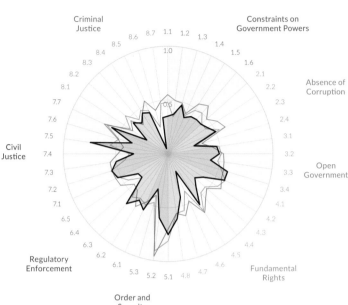

## 🏛 Constraints on Government Powers

| 1.1 | Limits by legislature | 0.35 |
|---|---|---|
| 1.2 | Limits by judiciary | 0.37 |
| 1.3 | Independent auditing | 0.47 |
| 1.4 | Sanctions for official misconduct | 0.37 |
| 1.5 | Non-governmental checks | 0.41 |
| 1.6 | Lawful transition of power | 0.42 |

## 💰 Absence of Corruption

| 2.1 | No corruption in the executive branch | 0.42 |
|---|---|---|
| 2.2 | No corruption in the judiciary | 0.45 |
| 2.3 | No corruption in the police/military | 0.50 |
| 2.4 | No corruption in the legislature | 0.26 |

## 📱 Open Government

| 3.1 | Publicized laws and government data | 0.47 |
|---|---|---|
| 3.2 | Right to information | 0.49 |
| 3.3 | Civic participation | 0.41 |
| 3.4 | Complaint mechanisms | 0.59 |

## 👤 Fundamental Rights

| 4.1 | Equal treatment / no discrimination | 0.59 |
|---|---|---|
| 4.2 | Right to life and security | 0.40 |
| 4.3 | Due process of law | 0.34 |
| 4.4 | Freedom of expression | 0.41 |
| 4.5 | Freedom of religion | 0.56 |
| 4.6 | Right to privacy | 0.18 |
| 4.7 | Freedom of association | 0.42 |
| 4.8 | Labor rights | 0.61 |

## 👮 Order & Security

| 5.1 | Absence of crime | 0.75 |
|---|---|---|
| 5.2 | Absence of civil conflict | 0.60 |
| 5.3 | Absence of violent redress | 0.34 |

## 👷 Regulatory Enforcement

| 6.1 | Effective regulatory enforcement | 0.57 |
|---|---|---|
| 6.2 | No improper influence | 0.51 |
| 6.3 | No unreasonable delay | 0.61 |
| 6.4 | Respect for due process | 0.33 |
| 6.5 | No expropriation w/out adequate compensation | 0.34 |

## ⚖ Civil Justice

| 7.1 | Accessibility and affordability | 0.53 |
|---|---|---|
| 7.2 | No discrimination | 0.56 |
| 7.3 | No corruption | 0.50 |
| 7.4 | No improper government influence | 0.33 |
| 7.5 | No unreasonable delay | 0.75 |
| 7.6 | Effective enforcement | 0.36 |
| 7.7 | Impartial and effective ADRs | 0.59 |

## 🏛 Criminal Justice

| 8.1 | Effective investigations | 0.24 |
|---|---|---|
| 8.2 | Timely and effective adjucation | 0.44 |
| 8.3 | Effective correctional system | 0.38 |
| 8.4 | No discrimination | 0.45 |
| 8.5 | No corruption | 0.42 |
| 8.6 | No improper government influence | 0.05 |
| 8.7 | Due process of law | 0.34 |

# Senegal

**Region:** Sub-Saharan Africa
**Income Group:** Low Income

| | Overall Score | Regional Rank | Income Rank | Global Rank |
|---|---|---|---|---|
| | 0.57 | 4/18 | 1/12 | 46/113 |

| | Factor Trend | Factor Score | Regional Rank | Income Rank | Global Rank |
|---|---|---|---|---|---|
| Constraints on Government Powers | — | 0.67 | 2/18 | 1/12 | 30/113 |
| Absence of Corruption | — | 0.55 | 3/18 | 1/12 | 48/113 |
| Open Government | — | 0.52 | 3/18 | 2/12 | 58/113 |
| Fundamental Rights | — | 0.62 | 3/18 | 1/12 | 51/113 |
| Order & Security | — | 0.67 | 8/18 | 5/12 | 74/113 |
| Regulatory Enforcement | — | 0.56 | 2/18 | 1/12 | 38/113 |
| Civil Justice | — | 0.57 | 4/18 | 1/12 | 47/113 |
| Criminal Justice | — | 0.43 | 6/18 | 4/12 | 66/113 |

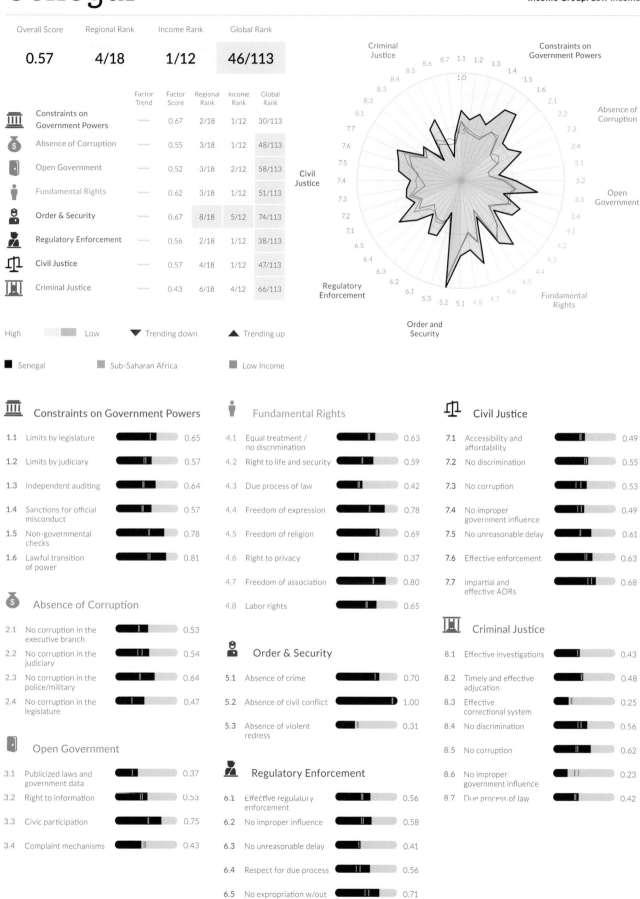

High ▢ Low     ▼ Trending down     ▲ Trending up

■ Senegal     ▨ Sub-Saharan Africa     ▨ Low Income

## Constraints on Government Powers

| | | |
|---|---|---|
| 1.1 | Limits by legislature | 0.65 |
| 1.2 | Limits by judiciary | 0.57 |
| 1.3 | Independent auditing | 0.64 |
| 1.4 | Sanctions for official misconduct | 0.57 |
| 1.5 | Non-governmental checks | 0.78 |
| 1.6 | Lawful transition of power | 0.81 |

## Absence of Corruption

| | | |
|---|---|---|
| 2.1 | No corruption in the executive branch | 0.53 |
| 2.2 | No corruption in the judiciary | 0.54 |
| 2.3 | No corruption in the police/military | 0.64 |
| 2.4 | No corruption in the legislature | 0.47 |

## Open Government

| | | |
|---|---|---|
| 3.1 | Publicized laws and government data | 0.37 |
| 3.2 | Right to information | 0.53 |
| 3.3 | Civic participation | 0.75 |
| 3.4 | Complaint mechanisms | 0.43 |

## Fundamental Rights

| | | |
|---|---|---|
| 4.1 | Equal treatment / no discrimination | 0.63 |
| 4.2 | Right to life and security | 0.59 |
| 4.3 | Due process of law | 0.42 |
| 4.4 | Freedom of expression | 0.78 |
| 4.5 | Freedom of religion | 0.69 |
| 4.6 | Right to privacy | 0.37 |
| 4.7 | Freedom of association | 0.80 |
| 4.8 | Labor rights | 0.65 |

## Order & Security

| | | |
|---|---|---|
| 5.1 | Absence of crime | 0.70 |
| 5.2 | Absence of civil conflict | 1.00 |
| 5.3 | Absence of violent redress | 0.31 |

## Regulatory Enforcement

| | | |
|---|---|---|
| 6.1 | Effective regulatory enforcement | 0.56 |
| 6.2 | No improper influence | 0.58 |
| 6.3 | No unreasonable delay | 0.41 |
| 6.4 | Respect for due process | 0.56 |
| 6.5 | No expropriation w/out adequate compensation | 0.71 |

## Civil Justice

| | | |
|---|---|---|
| 7.1 | Accessibility and affordability | 0.49 |
| 7.2 | No discrimination | 0.55 |
| 7.3 | No corruption | 0.53 |
| 7.4 | No improper government influence | 0.49 |
| 7.5 | No unreasonable delay | 0.61 |
| 7.6 | Effective enforcement | 0.63 |
| 7.7 | Impartial and effective ADRs | 0.68 |

## Criminal Justice

| | | |
|---|---|---|
| 8.1 | Effective investigations | 0.43 |
| 8.2 | Timely and effective adjudication | 0.48 |
| 8.3 | Effective correctional system | 0.25 |
| 8.4 | No discrimination | 0.56 |
| 8.5 | No corruption | 0.62 |
| 8.6 | No improper government influence | 0.23 |
| 8.7 | Due process of law | 0.42 |

# Serbia

**Region:** Eastern Europe & Central Asia
**Income Group:** Upper Middle Income

| Overall Score | Regional Rank | Income Rank | Global Rank |
|---|---|---|---|
| 0.50 | 7/13 | 26/37 | 74/113 |

| | Factor Trend | Factor Score | Regional Rank | Income Rank | Global Rank |
|---|---|---|---|---|---|
| Constraints on Government Powers | — | 0.46 | 5/13 | 26/37 | 84/113 |
| Absence of Corruption | — | 0.41 | 7/13 | 28/37 | 75/113 |
| Open Government | — | 0.56 | 3/13 | 12/37 | 44/113 |
| Fundamental Rights | — | 0.58 | 5/13 | 18/37 | 57/113 |
| Order & Security | — | 0.73 | 9/13 | 14/37 | 54/113 |
| Regulatory Enforcement | — | 0.46 | 7/13 | 29/37 | 78/113 |
| Civil Justice | — | 0.46 | 11/13 | 31/37 | 83/113 |
| Criminal Justice | — | 0.34 | 11/13 | 30/37 | 92/113 |

High Low ▼ Trending down ▲ Trending up

■ Serbia ■ Eastern Europe & Central Asia ■ Upper Middle Income

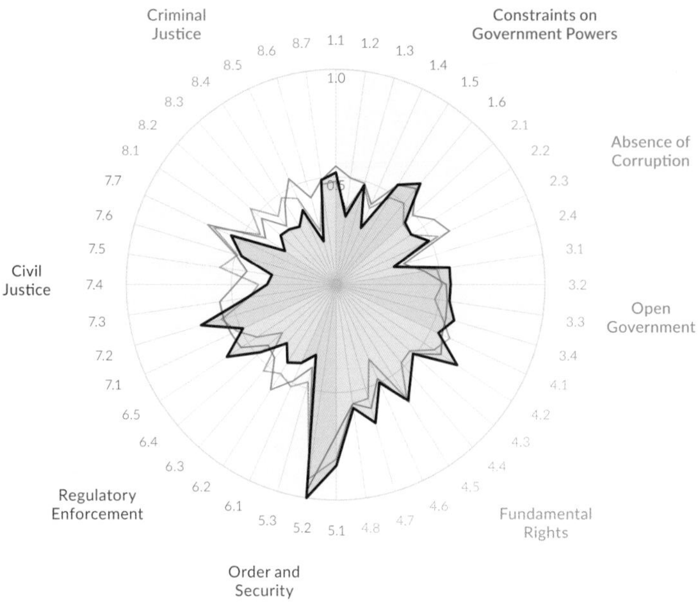


## Constraints on Government Powers

| | | |
|---|---|---|
| 1.1 | Limits by legislature | 0.52 |
| 1.2 | Limits by judiciary | 0.32 |
| 1.3 | Independent auditing | 0.48 |
| 1.4 | Sanctions for official misconduct | 0.29 |
| 1.5 | Non-governmental checks | 0.55 |
| 1.6 | Lawful transition of power | 0.62 |

## Absence of Corruption

| | | |
|---|---|---|
| 2.1 | No corruption in the executive branch | 0.44 |
| 2.2 | No corruption in the judiciary | 0.43 |
| 2.3 | No corruption in the police/military | 0.49 |
| 2.4 | No corruption in the legislature | 0.29 |

## Open Government

| | | |
|---|---|---|
| 3.1 | Publicized laws and government data | 0.55 |
| 3.2 | Right to information | 0.55 |
| 3.3 | Civic participation | 0.55 |
| 3.4 | Complaint mechanisms | 0.59 |

## Fundamental Rights

| | | |
|---|---|---|
| 4.1 | Equal treatment / no discrimination | 0.54 |
| 4.2 | Right to life and security | 0.69 |
| 4.3 | Due process of law | 0.49 |
| 4.4 | Freedom of expression | 0.55 |
| 4.5 | Freedom of religion | 0.64 |
| 4.6 | Right to privacy | 0.50 |
| 4.7 | Freedom of association | 0.67 |
| 4.8 | Labor rights | 0.58 |

## Order & Security

| | | |
|---|---|---|
| 5.1 | Absence of crime | 0.84 |
| 5.2 | Absence of civil conflict | 1.00 |
| 5.3 | Absence of violent redress | 0.34 |

## Regulatory Enforcement

| | | |
|---|---|---|
| 6.1 | Effective regulatory enforcement | 0.40 |
| 6.2 | No improper influence | 0.43 |
| 6.3 | No unreasonable delay | 0.36 |
| 6.4 | Respect for due process | 0.48 |
| 6.5 | No expropriation w/out adequate compensation | 0.62 |

## Civil Justice

| | | |
|---|---|---|
| 7.1 | Accessibility and affordability | 0.49 |
| 7.2 | No discrimination | 0.67 |
| 7.3 | No corruption | 0.43 |
| 7.4 | No improper government influence | 0.33 |
| 7.5 | No unreasonable delay | 0.31 |
| 7.6 | Effective enforcement | 0.47 |
| 7.7 | Impartial and effective ADRs | 0.55 |

## Criminal Justice

| | | |
|---|---|---|
| 8.1 | Effective investigations | 0.29 |
| 8.2 | Timely and effective adjudication | 0.35 |
| 8.3 | Effective correctional system | 0.34 |
| 8.4 | No discrimination | 0.32 |
| 8.5 | No corruption | 0.38 |
| 8.6 | No improper government influence | 0.21 |
| 8.7 | Due process of law | 0.49 |

# Sierra Leone

**Region:** Sub-Saharan Africa
**Income Group:** Low Income

| Overall Score | Regional Rank | Income Rank | Global Rank |
|---|---|---|---|
| 0.45 | 12/18 | 8/12 | 95/113 |

| | Factor Trend | Factor Score | Regional Rank | Income Rank | Global Rank |
|---|---|---|---|---|---|
| Constraints on Government Powers | — | 0.52 | 8/18 | 5/12 | 70/113 |
| Absence of Corruption | — | 0.30 | 12/18 | 7/12 | 101/113 |
| Open Government | — | 0.40 | 12/18 | 7/12 | 98/113 |
| Fundamental Rights | — | 0.57 | 5/18 | 3/12 | 61/113 |
| Order & Security | — | 0.66 | 10/18 | 7/12 | 78/113 |
| Regulatory Enforcement | — | 0.35 | 16/18 | 10/12 | 107/113 |
| Civil Justice | — | 0.40 | 16/18 | 10/12 | 102/113 |
| Criminal Justice | — | 0.36 | 13/18 | 8/12 | 87/v113 |

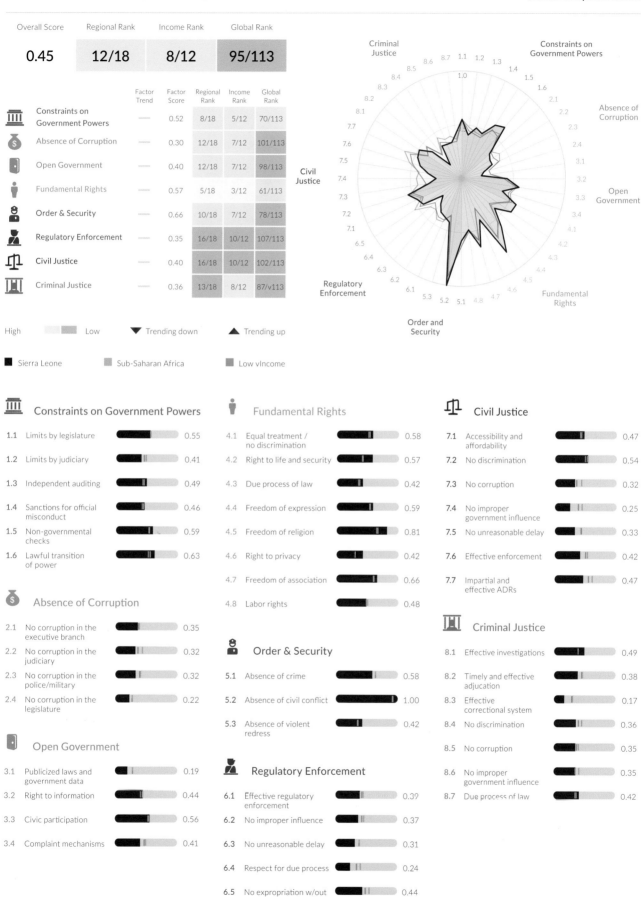

High ▢ Low      ▼ Trending down      ▲ Trending up

■ Sierra Leone      ▨ Sub-Saharan Africa      ▨ Low vIncome

## Constraints on Government Powers

| 1.1 | Limits by legislature | 0.55 |
|---|---|---|
| 1.2 | Limits by judiciary | 0.41 |
| 1.3 | Independent auditing | 0.49 |
| 1.4 | Sanctions for official misconduct | 0.46 |
| 1.5 | Non-governmental checks | 0.59 |
| 1.6 | Lawful transition of power | 0.63 |

## Absence of Corruption

| 2.1 | No corruption in the executive branch | 0.35 |
|---|---|---|
| 2.2 | No corruption in the judiciary | 0.32 |
| 2.3 | No corruption in the police/military | 0.32 |
| 2.4 | No corruption in the legislature | 0.22 |

## Open Government

| 3.1 | Publicized laws and government data | 0.19 |
|---|---|---|
| 3.2 | Right to information | 0.44 |
| 3.3 | Civic participation | 0.56 |
| 3.4 | Complaint mechanisms | 0.41 |

## Fundamental Rights

| 4.1 | Equal treatment / no discrimination | 0.58 |
|---|---|---|
| 4.2 | Right to life and security | 0.57 |
| 4.3 | Due process of law | 0.42 |
| 4.4 | Freedom of expression | 0.59 |
| 4.5 | Freedom of religion | 0.81 |
| 4.6 | Right to privacy | 0.42 |
| 4.7 | Freedom of association | 0.66 |
| 4.8 | Labor rights | 0.48 |

## Order & Security

| 5.1 | Absence of crime | 0.58 |
|---|---|---|
| 5.2 | Absence of civil conflict | 1.00 |
| 5.3 | Absence of violent redress | 0.42 |

## Regulatory Enforcement

| 6.1 | Effective regulatory enforcement | 0.39 |
|---|---|---|
| 6.2 | No improper influence | 0.37 |
| 6.3 | No unreasonable delay | 0.31 |
| 6.4 | Respect for due process | 0.24 |
| 6.5 | No expropriation w/out adequate compensation | 0.44 |

## Civil Justice

| 7.1 | Accessibility and affordability | 0.47 |
|---|---|---|
| 7.2 | No discrimination | 0.54 |
| 7.3 | No corruption | 0.32 |
| 7.4 | No improper government influence | 0.25 |
| 7.5 | No unreasonable delay | 0.33 |
| 7.6 | Effective enforcement | 0.42 |
| 7.7 | Impartial and effective ADRs | 0.47 |

## Criminal Justice

| 8.1 | Effective investigations | 0.49 |
|---|---|---|
| 8.2 | Timely and effective adjucation | 0.38 |
| 8.3 | Effective correctional system | 0.17 |
| 8.4 | No discrimination | 0.36 |
| 8.5 | No corruption | 0.35 |
| 8.6 | No improper government influence | 0.35 |
| 8.7 | Due process of law | 0.42 |

# Singapore

| | Overall Score | Regional Rank | Income Rank | Global Rank |
|---|---|---|---|---|
| | 0.82 | 2/15 | 9/36 | 9/113 |

| | | Factor Trend | Factor Score | Regional Rank | Income Rank | Global Rank |
|---|---|---|---|---|---|---|
| 🏛 | Constraints on Government Powers | — | 0.75 | 3/15 | 19/36 | 20/113 |
| 💰 | Absence of Corruption | — | 0.93 | 1/15 | 2/36 | 2/113 |
| 📱 | Open Government | — | 0.67 | 5/15 | 23/36 | 24/113 |
| 👤 | Fundamental Rights | — | 0.69 | 6/15 | 31/36 | 36/113 |
| 👮 | Order & Security | — | 0.93 | 1/15 | 1/36 | 1/113 |
| 💂 | Regulatory Enforcement | — | 0.90 | 1/15 | 1/36 | 1/113 |
| ⚖ | Civil Justice | — | 0.85 | 1/15 | 4/36 | 4/113 |
| ⏳ | Criminal Justice | — | 0.83 | 1/15 | 4/36 | 4/113 |

High ▢ Low     ▼ Trending down     ▲ Trending up

■ Singapore     ■ East Asia & Pacific     ■ High Income

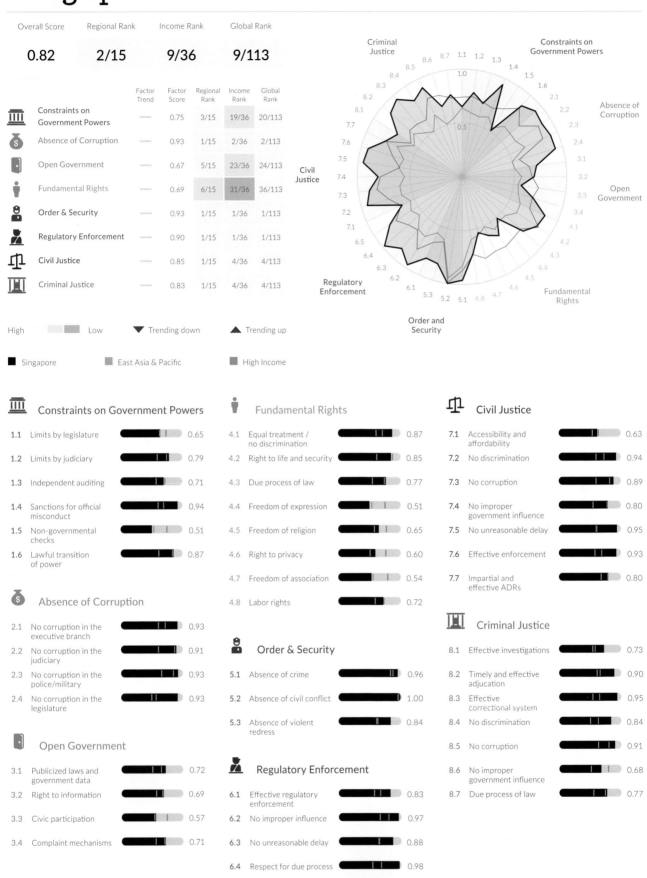

## 🏛 Constraints on Government Powers

| | | |
|---|---|---|
| 1.1 | Limits by legislature | 0.65 |
| 1.2 | Limits by judiciary | 0.79 |
| 1.3 | Independent auditing | 0.71 |
| 1.4 | Sanctions for official misconduct | 0.94 |
| 1.5 | Non-governmental checks | 0.51 |
| 1.6 | Lawful transition of power | 0.87 |

## 💰 Absence of Corruption

| | | |
|---|---|---|
| 2.1 | No corruption in the executive branch | 0.93 |
| 2.2 | No corruption in the judiciary | 0.91 |
| 2.3 | No corruption in the police/military | 0.93 |
| 2.4 | No corruption in the legislature | 0.93 |

## 📱 Open Government

| | | |
|---|---|---|
| 3.1 | Publicized laws and government data | 0.72 |
| 3.2 | Right to information | 0.69 |
| 3.3 | Civic participation | 0.57 |
| 3.4 | Complaint mechanisms | 0.71 |

## 👤 Fundamental Rights

| | | |
|---|---|---|
| 4.1 | Equal treatment / no discrimination | 0.87 |
| 4.2 | Right to life and security | 0.85 |
| 4.3 | Due process of law | 0.77 |
| 4.4 | Freedom of expression | 0.51 |
| 4.5 | Freedom of religion | 0.65 |
| 4.6 | Right to privacy | 0.60 |
| 4.7 | Freedom of association | 0.54 |
| 4.8 | Labor rights | 0.72 |

## 👮 Order & Security

| | | |
|---|---|---|
| 5.1 | Absence of crime | 0.96 |
| 5.2 | Absence of civil conflict | 1.00 |
| 5.3 | Absence of violent redress | 0.84 |

## 💂 Regulatory Enforcement

| | | |
|---|---|---|
| 6.1 | Effective regulatory enforcement | 0.83 |
| 6.2 | No improper influence | 0.97 |
| 6.3 | No unreasonable delay | 0.88 |
| 6.4 | Respect for due process | 0.98 |
| 6.5 | No expropriation w/out adequate compensation | 0.82 |

## ⚖ Civil Justice

| | | |
|---|---|---|
| 7.1 | Accessibility and affordability | 0.63 |
| 7.2 | No discrimination | 0.94 |
| 7.3 | No corruption | 0.89 |
| 7.4 | No improper government influence | 0.80 |
| 7.5 | No unreasonable delay | 0.95 |
| 7.6 | Effective enforcement | 0.93 |
| 7.7 | Impartial and effective ADRs | 0.80 |

## ⏳ Criminal Justice

| | | |
|---|---|---|
| 8.1 | Effective investigations | 0.73 |
| 8.2 | Timely and effective adjucation | 0.90 |
| 8.3 | Effective correctional system | 0.95 |
| 8.4 | No discrimination | 0.84 |
| 8.5 | No corruption | 0.91 |
| 8.6 | No improper government influence | 0.68 |
| 8.7 | Due process of law | 0.77 |

# Slovenia

| Overall Score | Regional Rank | Income Rank | Global Rank |
|---|---|---|---|
| 0.67 | 18/24 | 26/36 | 27/113 |

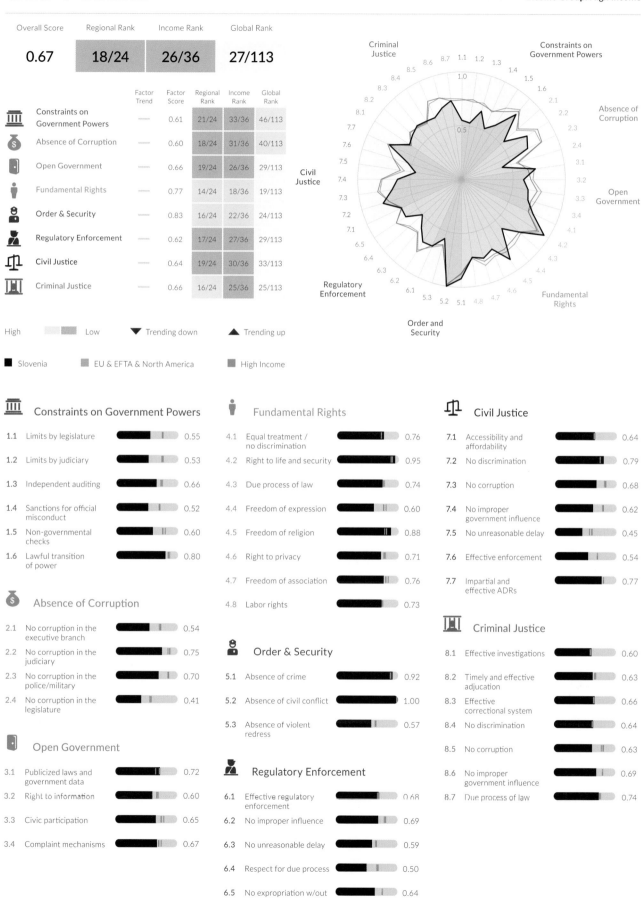

| | Factor Trend | Factor Score | Regional Rank | Income Rank | Global Rank |
|---|---|---|---|---|---|
| 🏛 Constraints on Government Powers | — | 0.61 | 21/24 | 33/36 | 46/113 |
| 💰 Absence of Corruption | — | 0.60 | 18/24 | 31/36 | 40/113 |
| 📱 Open Government | — | 0.66 | 19/24 | 26/36 | 29/113 |
| 👤 Fundamental Rights | — | 0.77 | 14/24 | 18/36 | 19/113 |
| 👨 Order & Security | — | 0.83 | 16/24 | 22/36 | 24/113 |
| 👷 Regulatory Enforcement | — | 0.62 | 17/24 | 27/36 | 29/113 |
| ⚖ Civil Justice | — | 0.64 | 19/24 | 30/36 | 33/113 |
| 🏛 Criminal Justice | — | 0.66 | 16/24 | 25/36 | 25/113 |

High ▭▭ Low   ▼ Trending down   ▲ Trending up

■ Slovenia   ▨ EU & EFTA & North America   ■ High Income

## 🏛 Constraints on Government Powers

| | | |
|---|---|---|
| 1.1 | Limits by legislature | 0.55 |
| 1.2 | Limits by judiciary | 0.53 |
| 1.3 | Independent auditing | 0.66 |
| 1.4 | Sanctions for official misconduct | 0.52 |
| 1.5 | Non-governmental checks | 0.60 |
| 1.6 | Lawful transition of power | 0.80 |

## 💰 Absence of Corruption

| | | |
|---|---|---|
| 2.1 | No corruption in the executive branch | 0.54 |
| 2.2 | No corruption in the judiciary | 0.75 |
| 2.3 | No corruption in the police/military | 0.70 |
| 2.4 | No corruption in the legislature | 0.41 |

## 📱 Open Government

| | | |
|---|---|---|
| 3.1 | Publicized laws and government data | 0.72 |
| 3.2 | Right to information | 0.60 |
| 3.3 | Civic participation | 0.65 |
| 3.4 | Complaint mechanisms | 0.67 |

## 👤 Fundamental Rights

| | | |
|---|---|---|
| 4.1 | Equal treatment / no discrimination | 0.76 |
| 4.2 | Right to life and security | 0.95 |
| 4.3 | Due process of law | 0.74 |
| 4.4 | Freedom of expression | 0.60 |
| 4.5 | Freedom of religion | 0.88 |
| 4.6 | Right to privacy | 0.71 |
| 4.7 | Freedom of association | 0.76 |
| 4.8 | Labor rights | 0.73 |

## 👨 Order & Security

| | | |
|---|---|---|
| 5.1 | Absence of crime | 0.92 |
| 5.2 | Absence of civil conflict | 1.00 |
| 5.3 | Absence of violent redress | 0.57 |

## 👷 Regulatory Enforcement

| | | |
|---|---|---|
| 6.1 | Effective regulatory enforcement | 0.68 |
| 6.2 | No improper influence | 0.69 |
| 6.3 | No unreasonable delay | 0.59 |
| 6.4 | Respect for due process | 0.50 |
| 6.5 | No expropriation w/out adequate compensation | 0.64 |

## ⚖ Civil Justice

| | | |
|---|---|---|
| 7.1 | Accessibility and affordability | 0.64 |
| 7.2 | No discrimination | 0.79 |
| 7.3 | No corruption | 0.68 |
| 7.4 | No improper government influence | 0.62 |
| 7.5 | No unreasonable delay | 0.45 |
| 7.6 | Effective enforcement | 0.54 |
| 7.7 | Impartial and effective ADRs | 0.77 |

## 🏛 Criminal Justice

| | | |
|---|---|---|
| 8.1 | Effective investigations | 0.60 |
| 8.2 | Timely and effective adjucation | 0.63 |
| 8.3 | Effective correctional system | 0.66 |
| 8.4 | No discrimination | 0.64 |
| 8.5 | No corruption | 0.63 |
| 8.6 | No improper government influence | 0.69 |
| 8.7 | Due process of law | 0.74 |

# South Africa

**Region:** Sub-Saharan Africa
**Income Group:** Upper Middle Income

| | Overall Score | Regional Rank | Income Rank | Global Rank |
|---|---|---|---|---|
| | 0.59 | 1/18 | 9/37 | 43/113 |

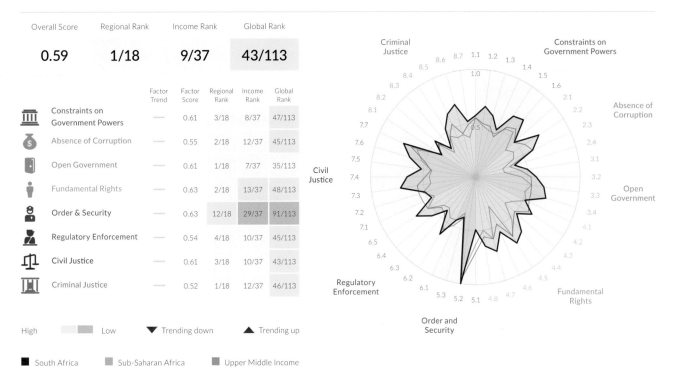

| | Factor Trend | Factor Score | Regional Rank | Income Rank | Global Rank |
|---|---|---|---|---|---|
| Constraints on Government Powers | — | 0.61 | 3/18 | 8/37 | 47/113 |
| Absence of Corruption | — | 0.55 | 2/18 | 12/37 | 45/113 |
| Open Government | — | 0.61 | 1/18 | 7/37 | 35/113 |
| Fundamental Rights | — | 0.63 | 2/18 | 13/37 | 48/113 |
| Order & Security | — | 0.63 | 12/18 | 29/37 | 91/113 |
| Regulatory Enforcement | — | 0.54 | 4/18 | 10/37 | 45/113 |
| Civil Justice | — | 0.61 | 3/18 | 10/37 | 43/113 |
| Criminal Justice | — | 0.52 | 1/18 | 12/37 | 46/113 |

High ▨▨ Low ▼ Trending down ▲ Trending up

■ South Africa ▨ Sub-Saharan Africa ▨ Upper Middle Income

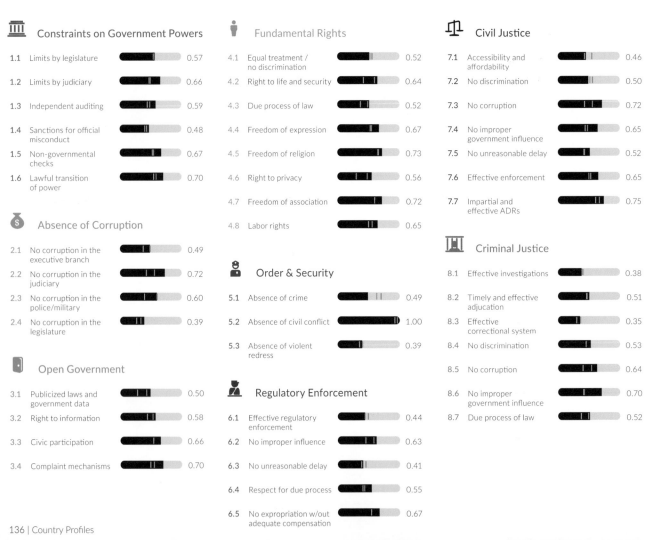

## Constraints on Government Powers

| | | |
|---|---|---|
| 1.1 | Limits by legislature | 0.57 |
| 1.2 | Limits by judiciary | 0.66 |
| 1.3 | Independent auditing | 0.59 |
| 1.4 | Sanctions for official misconduct | 0.48 |
| 1.5 | Non-governmental checks | 0.67 |
| 1.6 | Lawful transition of power | 0.70 |

## Absence of Corruption

| | | |
|---|---|---|
| 2.1 | No corruption in the executive branch | 0.49 |
| 2.2 | No corruption in the judiciary | 0.72 |
| 2.3 | No corruption in the police/military | 0.60 |
| 2.4 | No corruption in the legislature | 0.39 |

## Open Government

| | | |
|---|---|---|
| 3.1 | Publicized laws and government data | 0.50 |
| 3.2 | Right to information | 0.58 |
| 3.3 | Civic participation | 0.66 |
| 3.4 | Complaint mechanisms | 0.70 |

## Fundamental Rights

| | | |
|---|---|---|
| 4.1 | Equal treatment / no discrimination | 0.52 |
| 4.2 | Right to life and security | 0.64 |
| 4.3 | Due process of law | 0.52 |
| 4.4 | Freedom of expression | 0.67 |
| 4.5 | Freedom of religion | 0.73 |
| 4.6 | Right to privacy | 0.56 |
| 4.7 | Freedom of association | 0.72 |
| 4.8 | Labor rights | 0.65 |

## Order & Security

| | | |
|---|---|---|
| 5.1 | Absence of crime | 0.49 |
| 5.2 | Absence of civil conflict | 1.00 |
| 5.3 | Absence of violent redress | 0.39 |

## Regulatory Enforcement

| | | |
|---|---|---|
| 6.1 | Effective regulatory enforcement | 0.44 |
| 6.2 | No improper influence | 0.63 |
| 6.3 | No unreasonable delay | 0.41 |
| 6.4 | Respect for due process | 0.55 |
| 6.5 | No expropriation w/out adequate compensation | 0.67 |

## Civil Justice

| | | |
|---|---|---|
| 7.1 | Accessibility and affordability | 0.46 |
| 7.2 | No discrimination | 0.50 |
| 7.3 | No corruption | 0.72 |
| 7.4 | No improper government influence | 0.65 |
| 7.5 | No unreasonable delay | 0.52 |
| 7.6 | Effective enforcement | 0.65 |
| 7.7 | Impartial and effective ADRs | 0.75 |

## Criminal Justice

| | | |
|---|---|---|
| 8.1 | Effective investigations | 0.38 |
| 8.2 | Timely and effective adjucation | 0.51 |
| 8.3 | Effective correctional system | 0.35 |
| 8.4 | No discrimination | 0.53 |
| 8.5 | No corruption | 0.64 |
| 8.6 | No improper government influence | 0.70 |
| 8.7 | Due process of law | 0.52 |

# Spain

**Region:** EU & EFTA & North America
**Income Group:** High Income

| | Overall Score | Regional Rank | Income Rank | Global Rank |
|---|---|---|---|---|
| | 0.70 | 17/24 | 24/36 | 24/113 |

| | Factor Trend | Factor Score | Regional Rank | Income Rank | Global Rank |
|---|---|---|---|---|---|
| 🏛 Constraints on Government Powers | — | 0.70 | 16/24 | 22/36 | 23/113 |
| 💰 Absence of Corruption | — | 0.69 | 16/24 | 25/36 | 28/113 |
| 📱 Open Government | — | 0.68 | 16/24 | 22/36 | 23/113 |
| 👤 Fundamental Rights | — | 0.77 | 15/24 | 19/36 | 20/113 |
| 👮 Order & Security | — | 0.79 | 19/24 | 27/36 | 36/113 |
| 🧑‍🏭 Regulatory Enforcement | — | 0.67 | 15/24 | 23/36 | 24/113 |
| ⚖ Civil Justice | — | 0.65 | 17/24 | 28/36 | 29/113 |
| 🏛 Criminal Justice | — | 0.63 | 19/24 | 28/36 | 30/113 |

High ▬▬ Low   ▼ Trending down   ▲ Trending up

■ Spain   ■ EU & EFTA & North America   ■ High Income

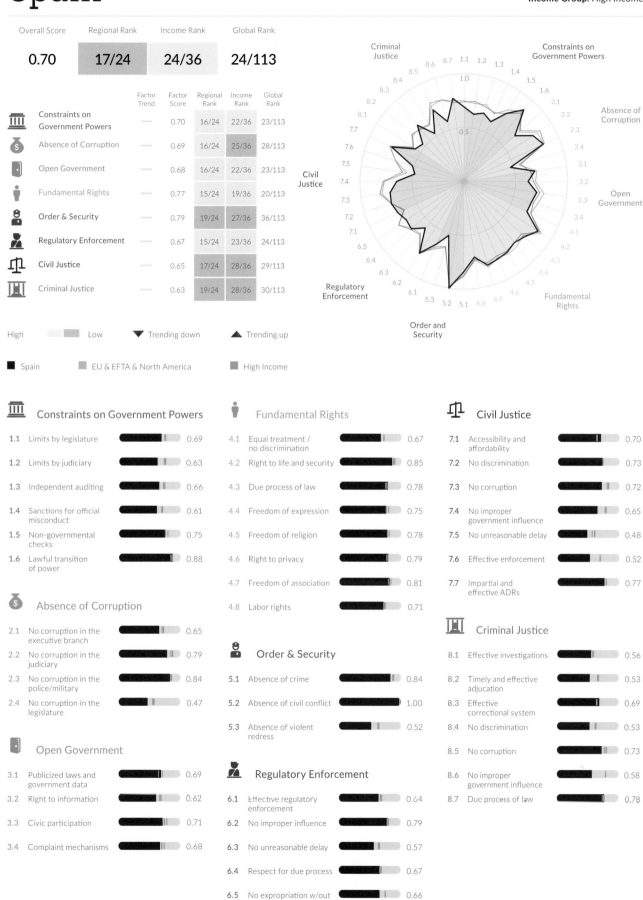

## 🏛 Constraints on Government Powers

| 1.1 | Limits by legislature | 0.69 |
|---|---|---|
| 1.2 | Limits by judiciary | 0.63 |
| 1.3 | Independent auditing | 0.66 |
| 1.4 | Sanctions for official misconduct | 0.61 |
| 1.5 | Non-governmental checks | 0.75 |
| 1.6 | Lawful transition of power | 0.88 |

## 💰 Absence of Corruption

| 2.1 | No corruption in the executive branch | 0.65 |
|---|---|---|
| 2.2 | No corruption in the judiciary | 0.79 |
| 2.3 | No corruption in the police/military | 0.84 |
| 2.4 | No corruption in the legislature | 0.47 |

## 📱 Open Government

| 3.1 | Publicized laws and government data | 0.69 |
|---|---|---|
| 3.2 | Right to information | 0.62 |
| 3.3 | Civic participation | 0.71 |
| 3.4 | Complaint mechanisms | 0.68 |

## 👤 Fundamental Rights

| 4.1 | Equal treatment / no discrimination | 0.67 |
|---|---|---|
| 4.2 | Right to life and security | 0.85 |
| 4.3 | Due process of law | 0.78 |
| 4.4 | Freedom of expression | 0.75 |
| 4.5 | Freedom of religion | 0.78 |
| 4.6 | Right to privacy | 0.79 |
| 4.7 | Freedom of association | 0.81 |
| 4.8 | Labor rights | 0.71 |

## 👮 Order & Security

| 5.1 | Absence of crime | 0.84 |
|---|---|---|
| 5.2 | Absence of civil conflict | 1.00 |
| 5.3 | Absence of violent redress | 0.52 |

## 🧑‍🏭 Regulatory Enforcement

| 6.1 | Effective regulatory enforcement | 0.64 |
|---|---|---|
| 6.2 | No improper influence | 0.79 |
| 6.3 | No unreasonable delay | 0.57 |
| 6.4 | Respect for due process | 0.67 |
| 6.5 | No expropriation w/out adequate compensation | 0.66 |

## ⚖ Civil Justice

| 7.1 | Accessibility and affordability | 0.70 |
|---|---|---|
| 7.2 | No discrimination | 0.73 |
| 7.3 | No corruption | 0.72 |
| 7.4 | No improper government influence | 0.65 |
| 7.5 | No unreasonable delay | 0.48 |
| 7.6 | Effective enforcement | 0.52 |
| 7.7 | Impartial and effective ADRs | 0.77 |

## 🏛 Criminal Justice

| 8.1 | Effective investigations | 0.56 |
|---|---|---|
| 8.2 | Timely and effective adjudication | 0.53 |
| 8.3 | Effective correctional system | 0.69 |
| 8.4 | No discrimination | 0.53 |
| 8.5 | No corruption | 0.73 |
| 8.6 | No improper government influence | 0.58 |
| 8.7 | Due process of law | 0.78 |

# Sri Lanka

**Region:** South Asia
**Income Group:** Lower Middle Income

| Overall Score | Regional Rank | Income Rank | Global Rank |
|---|---|---|---|
| 0.51 | 3/6 | 8/28 | 68/113 |

| | Factor Trend | Factor Score | Regional Rank | Income Rank | Global Rank |
|---|---|---|---|---|---|
| Constraints on Government Powers | — | 0.53 | 3/6 | 10/28 | 66/113 |
| Absence of Corruption | — | 0.45 | 1/6 | 4/28 | 64/113 |
| Open Government | — | 0.48 | 3/6 | 12/28 | 71/113 |
| Fundamental Rights | — | 0.52 | 2/6 | 10/28 | 73/113 |
| Order & Security | — | 0.68 | 2/6 | 11/28 | 68/113 |
| Regulatory Enforcement | — | 0.5 | 1/6 | 5/28 | 58/113 |
| Civil Justice | — | 0.42 | 2/6 | 19/28 | 96/113 |
| Criminal Justice | — | 0.49 | 1/6 | 2/28 | 52/113 |

High ▮▮ Low    ▼ Trending down    ▲ Trending up

■ Sri Lanka    ■ South Asia    ■ Lower Middle Income

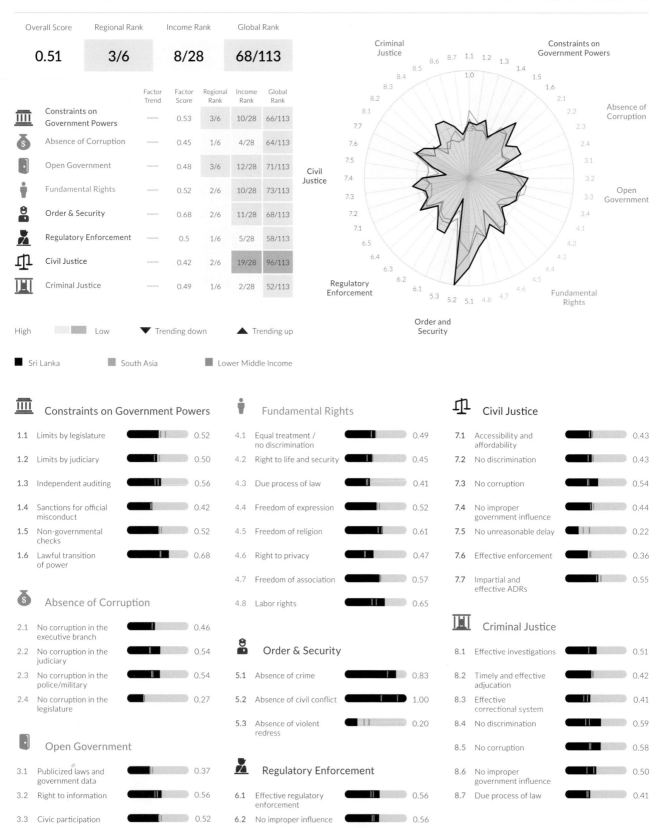

## Constraints on Government Powers

| 1.1 | Limits by legislature | 0.52 |
|---|---|---|
| 1.2 | Limits by judiciary | 0.50 |
| 1.3 | Independent auditing | 0.56 |
| 1.4 | Sanctions for official misconduct | 0.42 |
| 1.5 | Non-governmental checks | 0.52 |
| 1.6 | Lawful transition of power | 0.68 |

## Absence of Corruption

| 2.1 | No corruption in the executive branch | 0.46 |
|---|---|---|
| 2.2 | No corruption in the judiciary | 0.54 |
| 2.3 | No corruption in the police/military | 0.54 |
| 2.4 | No corruption in the legislature | 0.27 |

## Open Government

| 3.1 | Publicized laws and government data | 0.37 |
|---|---|---|
| 3.2 | Right to information | 0.56 |
| 3.3 | Civic participation | 0.52 |
| 3.4 | Complaint mechanisms | 0.48 |

## Fundamental Rights

| 4.1 | Equal treatment / no discrimination | 0.49 |
|---|---|---|
| 4.2 | Right to life and security | 0.45 |
| 4.3 | Due process of law | 0.41 |
| 4.4 | Freedom of expression | 0.52 |
| 4.5 | Freedom of religion | 0.61 |
| 4.6 | Right to privacy | 0.47 |
| 4.7 | Freedom of association | 0.57 |
| 4.8 | Labor rights | 0.65 |

## Order & Security

| 5.1 | Absence of crime | 0.83 |
|---|---|---|
| 5.2 | Absence of civil conflict | 1.00 |
| 5.3 | Absence of violent redress | 0.20 |

## Regulatory Enforcement

| 6.1 | Effective regulatory enforcement | 0.56 |
|---|---|---|
| 6.2 | No improper influence | 0.56 |
| 6.3 | No unreasonable delay | 0.45 |
| 6.4 | Respect for due process | 0.39 |
| 6.5 | No expropriation w/out adequate compensation | 0.55 |

## Civil Justice

| 7.1 | Accessibility and affordability | 0.43 |
|---|---|---|
| 7.2 | No discrimination | 0.43 |
| 7.3 | No corruption | 0.54 |
| 7.4 | No improper government influence | 0.44 |
| 7.5 | No unreasonable delay | 0.22 |
| 7.6 | Effective enforcement | 0.36 |
| 7.7 | Impartial and effective ADRs | 0.55 |

## Criminal Justice

| 8.1 | Effective investigations | 0.51 |
|---|---|---|
| 8.2 | Timely and effective adjudication | 0.42 |
| 8.3 | Effective correctional system | 0.41 |
| 8.4 | No discrimination | 0.59 |
| 8.5 | No corruption | 0.58 |
| 8.6 | No improper government influence | 0.50 |
| 8.7 | Due process of law | 0.41 |

# St. Kitts & Nevis

**Region:** Latin America & Caribbean
**Income Group:** High Income

| | Overall Score | Regional Rank | Income Rank | Global Rank |
|---|---|---|---|---|
| | 0.66 | 6/30 | 29/36 | 30/113 |

| | Factor Trend | Factor Score | Regional Rank | Income Rank | Global Rank |
|---|---|---|---|---|---|
| 🏛 Constraints on Government Powers | — | 0.67 | 4/30 | 27/36 | 31/113 |
| 💰 Absence of Corruption | — | 0.68 | 7/30 | 27/36 | 31/113 |
| 📱 Open Government | — | 0.46 | 23/30 | 34/36 | 78/113 |
| 👤 Fundamental Rights | — | 0.74 | 6/30 | 26/36 | 27/113 |
| 👮 Order & Security | — | 0.82 | 1/30 | 24/36 | 27/113 |
| 💼 Regulatory Enforcement | — | 0.66 | 3/30 | 24/36 | 25/113 |
| ⚖ Civil Justice | — | 0.71 | 4/30 | 21/36 | 22/113 |
| 🏛 Criminal Justice | — | 0.58 | 8/30 | 31/36 | 36/113 |

High ▢ Low   ▼ Trending down   ▲ Trending up

■ St. Kitts & Nevis   ▨ Latin America & Caribbean   ▨ High Income

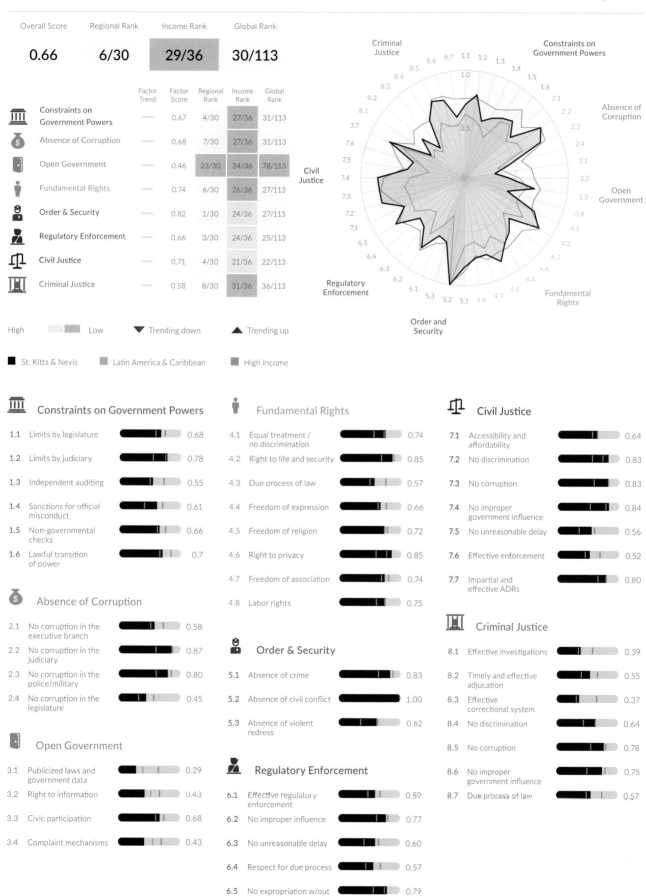

## 🏛 Constraints on Government Powers

| | | |
|---|---|---|
| 1.1 | Limits by legislature | 0.68 |
| 1.2 | Limits by judiciary | 0.78 |
| 1.3 | Independent auditing | 0.55 |
| 1.4 | Sanctions for official misconduct | 0.61 |
| 1.5 | Non-governmental checks | 0.66 |
| 1.6 | Lawful transition of power | 0.7 |

## 💰 Absence of Corruption

| | | |
|---|---|---|
| 2.1 | No corruption in the executive branch | 0.58 |
| 2.2 | No corruption in the judiciary | 0.87 |
| 2.3 | No corruption in the police/military | 0.80 |
| 2.4 | No corruption in the legislature | 0.45 |

## 📱 Open Government

| | | |
|---|---|---|
| 3.1 | Publicized laws and government data | 0.29 |
| 3.2 | Right to information | 0.43 |
| 3.3 | Civic participation | 0.68 |
| 3.4 | Complaint mechanisms | 0.43 |

## 👤 Fundamental Rights

| | | |
|---|---|---|
| 4.1 | Equal treatment / no discrimination | 0.74 |
| 4.2 | Right to life and security | 0.85 |
| 4.3 | Due process of law | 0.57 |
| 4.4 | Freedom of expression | 0.66 |
| 4.5 | Freedom of religion | 0.72 |
| 4.6 | Right to privacy | 0.85 |
| 4.7 | Freedom of association | 0.74 |
| 4.8 | Labor rights | 0.75 |

## 👮 Order & Security

| | | |
|---|---|---|
| 5.1 | Absence of crime | 0.83 |
| 5.2 | Absence of civil conflict | 1.00 |
| 5.3 | Absence of violent redress | 0.62 |

## 💼 Regulatory Enforcement

| | | |
|---|---|---|
| 6.1 | Effective regulatory enforcement | 0.59 |
| 6.2 | No improper influence | 0.77 |
| 6.3 | No unreasonable delay | 0.60 |
| 6.4 | Respect for due process | 0.57 |
| 6.5 | No expropriation w/out adequate compensation | 0.79 |

## ⚖ Civil Justice

| | | |
|---|---|---|
| 7.1 | Accessibility and affordability | 0.64 |
| 7.2 | No discrimination | 0.83 |
| 7.3 | No corruption | 0.83 |
| 7.4 | No improper government influence | 0.84 |
| 7.5 | No unreasonable delay | 0.56 |
| 7.6 | Effective enforcement | 0.52 |
| 7.7 | Impartial and effective ADRs | 0.80 |

## 🏛 Criminal Justice

| | | |
|---|---|---|
| 8.1 | Effective investigations | 0.39 |
| 8.2 | Timely and effective adjucation | 0.55 |
| 8.3 | Effective correctional system | 0.37 |
| 8.4 | No discrimination | 0.64 |
| 8.5 | No corruption | 0.78 |
| 8.6 | No improper government influence | 0.75 |
| 8.7 | Due process of law | 0.57 |

# St. Lucia

**Region:** Latin America & Caribbean
**Income Group:** Upper Middle Income

| | Overall Score | Regional Rank | Income Rank | Global Rank |
|---|---|---|---|---|
| | 0.64 | 8/30 | 5/37 | 36/113 |

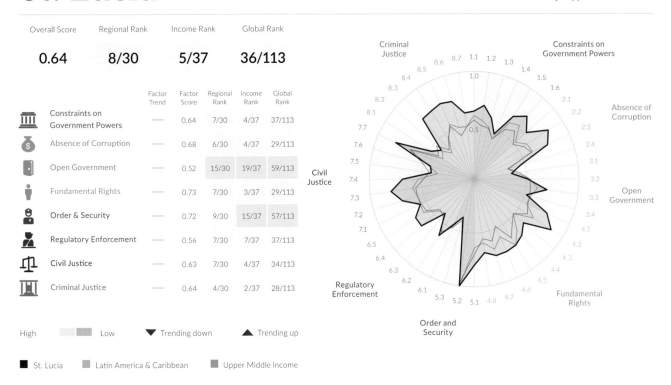

| | | Factor Trend | Factor Score | Regional Rank | Income Rank | Global Rank |
|---|---|---|---|---|---|---|
| 🏛 | Constraints on Government Powers | — | 0.64 | 7/30 | 4/37 | 37/113 |
| 💰 | Absence of Corruption | — | 0.68 | 6/30 | 4/37 | 29/113 |
| 📱 | Open Government | — | 0.52 | 15/30 | 19/37 | 59/113 |
| 👤 | Fundamental Rights | — | 0.73 | 7/30 | 3/37 | 29/113 |
| 👮 | Order & Security | — | 0.72 | 9/30 | 15/37 | 57/113 |
| 👷 | Regulatory Enforcement | — | 0.56 | 7/30 | 7/37 | 37/113 |
| ⚖ | Civil Justice | — | 0.63 | 7/30 | 4/37 | 34/113 |
| 🏛 | Criminal Justice | — | 0.64 | 4/30 | 2/37 | 28/113 |

High ▢▢▢ Low   ▼ Trending down   ▲ Trending up

■ St. Lucia   ▨ Latin America & Caribbean   ▨ Upper Middle Income

## 🏛 Constraints on Government Powers

| | | |
|---|---|---|
| 1.1 | Limits by legislature | 0.63 |
| 1.2 | Limits by judiciary | 0.69 |
| 1.3 | Independent auditing | 0.59 |
| 1.4 | Sanctions for official misconduct | 0.46 |
| 1.5 | Non-governmental checks | 0.69 |
| 1.6 | Lawful transition of power | 0.77 |

## 💰 Absence of Corruption

| | | |
|---|---|---|
| 2.1 | No corruption in the executive branch | 0.66 |
| 2.2 | No corruption in the judiciary | 0.84 |
| 2.3 | No corruption in the police/military | 0.77 |
| 2.4 | No corruption in the legislature | 0.46 |

## 📱 Open Government

| | | |
|---|---|---|
| 3.1 | Publicized laws and government data | 0.36 |
| 3.2 | Right to information | 0.51 |
| 3.3 | Civic participation | 0.70 |
| 3.4 | Complaint mechanisms | 0.52 |

## 👤 Fundamental Rights

| | | |
|---|---|---|
| 4.1 | Equal treatment / no discrimination | 0.76 |
| 4.2 | Right to life and security | 0.87 |
| 4.3 | Due process of law | 0.62 |
| 4.4 | Freedom of expression | 0.69 |
| 4.5 | Freedom of religion | 0.73 |
| 4.6 | Right to privacy | 0.74 |
| 4.7 | Freedom of association | 0.74 |
| 4.8 | Labor rights | 0.69 |

## 👮 Order & Security

| | | |
|---|---|---|
| 5.1 | Absence of crime | 0.80 |
| 5.2 | Absence of civil conflict | 1.00 |
| 5.3 | Absence of violent redress | 0.37 |

## 👷 Regulatory Enforcement

| | | |
|---|---|---|
| 6.1 | Effective regulatory enforcement | 0.46 |
| 6.2 | No improper influence | 0.62 |
| 6.3 | No unreasonable delay | 0.42 |
| 6.4 | Respect for due process | 0.66 |
| 6.5 | No expropriation w/out adequate compensation | 0.66 |

## ⚖ Civil Justice

| | | |
|---|---|---|
| 7.1 | Accessibility and affordability | 0.56 |
| 7.2 | No discrimination | 0.71 |
| 7.3 | No corruption | 0.80 |
| 7.4 | No improper government influence | 0.68 |
| 7.5 | No unreasonable delay | 0.41 |
| 7.6 | Effective enforcement | 0.43 |
| 7.7 | Impartial and effective ADRs | 0.82 |

## 🏛 Criminal Justice

| | | |
|---|---|---|
| 8.1 | Effective investigations | 0.48 |
| 8.2 | Timely and effective adjudication | 0.41 |
| 8.3 | Effective correctional system | 0.74 |
| 8.4 | No discrimination | 0.75 |
| 8.5 | No corruption | 0.77 |
| 8.6 | No improper government influence | 0.75 |
| 8.7 | Due process of law | 0.62 |

# St. Vincent & the Grenadines

**Region:** Latin America & Caribbean
**Income Group:** Upper Middle Income

| Overall Score | Regional Rank | Income Rank | Global Rank |
|:---:|:---:|:---:|:---:|
| 0.61 | 9/30 | 6/37 | 37/113 |

| | | Factor Trend | Factor Score | Regional Rank | Income Rank | Global Rank |
|---|---|:---:|:---:|:---:|:---:|:---:|
| 🏛 | Constraints on Government Powers | — | 0.57 | 15/30 | 11/37 | 54/113 |
| 💰 | Absence of Corruption | — | 0.67 | 8/30 | 5/37 | 32/113 |
| 📱 | Open Government | — | 0.49 | 20/30 | 23/37 | 69/113 |
| 👤 | Fundamental Rights | — | 0.71 | 8/30 | 4/37 | 31/113 |
| 👥 | Order & Security | — | 0.75 | 6/30 | 11/37 | 45/113 |
| 👷 | Regulatory Enforcement | — | 0.54 | 10/30 | 9/37 | 44/113 |
| ⚖ | Civil Justice | — | 0.56 | 13/30 | 14/37 | 50/113 |
| 🏛 | Criminal Justice | — | 0.62 | 5/30 | 3/37 | 31/113 |

High ▢ Low     ▼ Trending down     ▲ Trending up

■ St. Vincent & the Grenadines     ▨ Latin America & Caribbean     ▨ Upper Middle Income

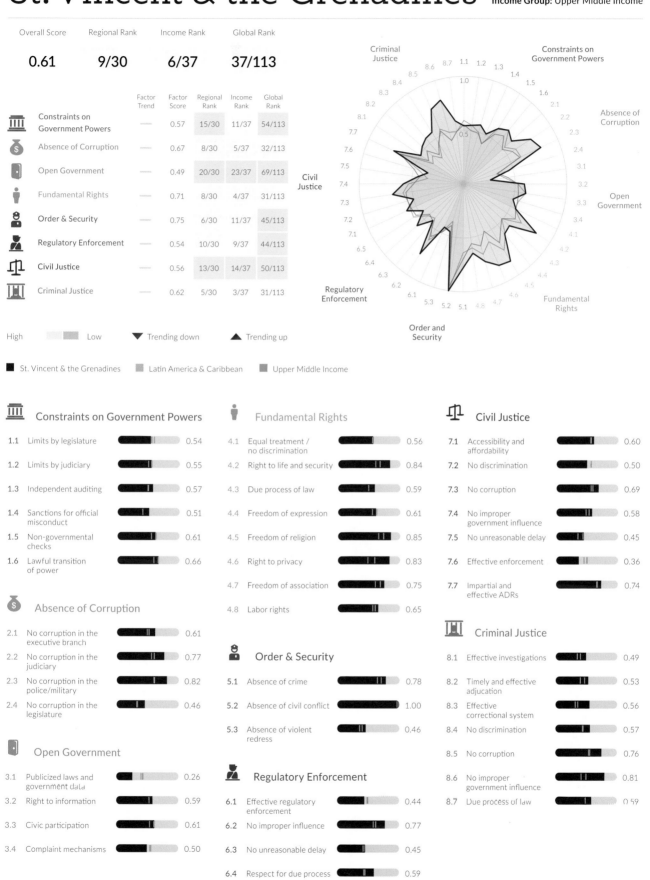

## 🏛 Constraints on Government Powers

| | | |
|---|---|---|
| 1.1 | Limits by legislature | 0.54 |
| 1.2 | Limits by judiciary | 0.55 |
| 1.3 | Independent auditing | 0.57 |
| 1.4 | Sanctions for official misconduct | 0.51 |
| 1.5 | Non-governmental checks | 0.61 |
| 1.6 | Lawful transition of power | 0.66 |

## 💰 Absence of Corruption

| | | |
|---|---|---|
| 2.1 | No corruption in the executive branch | 0.61 |
| 2.2 | No corruption in the judiciary | 0.77 |
| 2.3 | No corruption in the police/military | 0.82 |
| 2.4 | No corruption in the legislature | 0.46 |

## 📱 Open Government

| | | |
|---|---|---|
| 3.1 | Publicized laws and government data | 0.26 |
| 3.2 | Right to information | 0.59 |
| 3.3 | Civic participation | 0.61 |
| 3.4 | Complaint mechanisms | 0.50 |

## 👤 Fundamental Rights

| | | |
|---|---|---|
| 4.1 | Equal treatment / no discrimination | 0.56 |
| 4.2 | Right to life and security | 0.84 |
| 4.3 | Due process of law | 0.59 |
| 4.4 | Freedom of expression | 0.61 |
| 4.5 | Freedom of religion | 0.85 |
| 4.6 | Right to privacy | 0.83 |
| 4.7 | Freedom of association | 0.75 |
| 4.8 | Labor rights | 0.65 |

## 👥 Order & Security

| | | |
|---|---|---|
| 5.1 | Absence of crime | 0.78 |
| 5.2 | Absence of civil conflict | 1.00 |
| 5.3 | Absence of violent redress | 0.46 |

## 👷 Regulatory Enforcement

| | | |
|---|---|---|
| 6.1 | Effective regulatory enforcement | 0.44 |
| 6.2 | No improper influence | 0.77 |
| 6.3 | No unreasonable delay | 0.45 |
| 6.4 | Respect for due process | 0.59 |
| 6.5 | No expropriation w/out adequate compensation | 0.46 |

## ⚖ Civil Justice

| | | |
|---|---|---|
| 7.1 | Accessibility and affordability | 0.60 |
| 7.2 | No discrimination | 0.50 |
| 7.3 | No corruption | 0.69 |
| 7.4 | No improper government influence | 0.58 |
| 7.5 | No unreasonable delay | 0.45 |
| 7.6 | Effective enforcement | 0.36 |
| 7.7 | Impartial and effective ADRs | 0.74 |

## 🏛 Criminal Justice

| | | |
|---|---|---|
| 8.1 | Effective investigations | 0.49 |
| 8.2 | Timely and effective adjucation | 0.53 |
| 8.3 | Effective correctional system | 0.56 |
| 8.4 | No discrimination | 0.57 |
| 8.5 | No corruption | 0.76 |
| 8.6 | No improper government influence | 0.81 |
| 8.7 | Due process of law | 0.59 |

# Suriname

| Overall Score | Regional Rank | Income Rank | Global Rank |
|---|---|---|---|
| 0.53 | 16/30 | 19/37 | 59/113 |

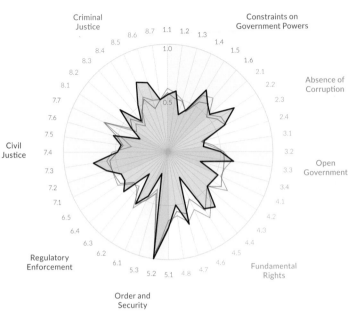

| | | Factor Trend | Factor Score | Regional Rank | Income Rank | Global Rank |
|---|---|---|---|---|---|---|
| 🏛 | Constraints on Government Powers | — | 0.52 | 21/30 | 20/37 | 69/113 |
| 💰 | Absence of Corruption | — | 0.56 | 12/30 | 10/37 | 43/113 |
| 📱 | Open Government | — | 0.45 | 26/30 | 28/37 | 86/113 |
| 🧍 | Fundamental Rights | — | 0.53 | 23/30 | 22/37 | 71/113 |
| 👤 | Order & Security | — | 0.64 | 18/30 | 26/37 | 85/113 |
| 👨‍💼 | Regulatory Enforcement | — | 0.47 | 21/30 | 26/37 | 73/113 |
| ⚖ | Civil Justice | — | 0.51 | 16/30 | 23/37 | 65/113 |
| 🏛 | Criminal Justice | — | 0.54 | 12/30 | 11/37 | 44/113 |

High ▢▢ Low    ▼ Trending down    ▲ Trending up

■ Suriname    ▪ Latin America & Caribbean    ▪ Upper Middle Income

## 🏛 Constraints on Government Powers

| | | |
|---|---|---|
| 1.1 | Limits by legislature | 0.53 |
| 1.2 | Limits by judiciary | 0.57 |
| 1.3 | Independent auditing | 0.36 |
| 1.4 | Sanctions for official misconduct | 0.43 |
| 1.5 | Non-governmental checks | 0.68 |
| 1.6 | Lawful transition of power | 0.58 |

## 💰 Absence of Corruption

| | | |
|---|---|---|
| 2.1 | No corruption in the executive branch | 0.53 |
| 2.2 | No corruption in the judiciary | 0.75 |
| 2.3 | No corruption in the police/military | 0.59 |
| 2.4 | No corruption in the legislature | 0.36 |

## 📱 Open Government

| | | |
|---|---|---|
| 3.1 | Publicized laws and government data | 0.34 |
| 3.2 | Right to information | 0.50 |
| 3.3 | Civic participation | 0.63 |
| 3.4 | Complaint mechanisms | 0.32 |

## 🧍 Fundamental Rights

| | | |
|---|---|---|
| 4.1 | Equal treatment / no discrimination | 0.52 |
| 4.2 | Right to life and security | 0.50 |
| 4.3 | Due process of law | 0.49 |
| 4.4 | Freedom of expression | 0.68 |
| 4.5 | Freedom of religion | 0.63 |
| 4.6 | Right to privacy | 0.26 |
| 4.7 | Freedom of association | 0.70 |
| 4.8 | Labor rights | 0.50 |

## 👤 Order & Security

| | | |
|---|---|---|
| 5.1 | Absence of crime | 0.71 |
| 5.2 | Absence of civil conflict | 1.00 |
| 5.3 | Absence of violent redress | 0.21 |

## 👨‍💼 Regulatory Enforcement

| | | |
|---|---|---|
| 6.1 | Effective regulatory enforcement | 0.45 |
| 6.2 | No improper influence | 0.57 |
| 6.3 | No unreasonable delay | 0.27 |
| 6.4 | Respect for due process | 0.56 |
| 6.5 | No expropriation w/out adequate compensation | 0.49 |

## ⚖ Civil Justice

| | | |
|---|---|---|
| 7.1 | Accessibility and affordability | 0.49 |
| 7.2 | No discrimination | 0.61 |
| 7.3 | No corruption | 0.72 |
| 7.4 | No improper government influence | 0.48 |
| 7.5 | No unreasonable delay | 0.45 |
| 7.6 | Effective enforcement | 0.54 |
| 7.7 | Impartial and effective ADRs | 0.29 |

## 🏛 Criminal Justice

| | | |
|---|---|---|
| 8.1 | Effective investigations | 0.41 |
| 8.2 | Timely and effective adjucation | 0.60 |
| 8.3 | Effective correctional system | 0.38 |
| 8.4 | No discrimination | 0.52 |
| 8.5 | No corruption | 0.71 |
| 8.6 | No improper government influence | 0.67 |
| 8.7 | Due process of law | 0.49 |

# Sweden

**Region:** EU & EFTA & North America
**Income Group:** High Income

| | Overall Score | Regional Rank | Income Rank | Global Rank |
|---|---|---|---|---|
| | 0.86 | 4/24 | 4/36 | 4/113 |

| | | Factor Trend | Factor Score | Regional Rank | Income Rank | Global Rank |
|---|---|---|---|---|---|---|
| 🏛 | Constraints on Government Powers | — | 0.88 | 5/24 | 5/36 | 5/113 |
| 💰 | Absence of Corruption | — | 0.91 | 4/24 | 5/36 | 5/113 |
| 📱 | Open Government | — | 0.84 | 5/24 | 5/36 | 5/113 |
| 👤 | Fundamental Rights | — | 0.88 | 5/24 | 5/36 | 5/113 |
| 👮 | Order & Security | — | 0.92 | 2/24 | 3/36 | 3/113 |
| 👷 | Regulatory Enforcement | — | 0.85 | 3/24 | 4/36 | 4/113 |
| ⚖ | Civil Justice | — | 0.81 | 5/24 | 7/36 | 7/113 |
| ⚖ | Criminal Justice | — | 0.79 | 6/24 | 8/36 | 8/113 |

High ▢ Low    ▼ Trending down    ▲ Trending up

■ Sweden    ▨ EU & EFTA & North America    ■ High Income

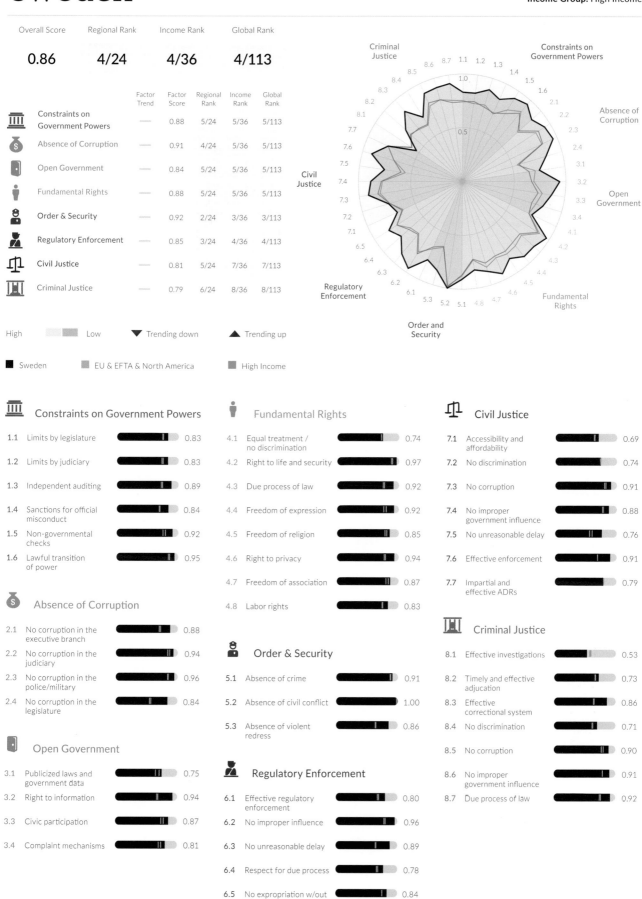

## 🏛 Constraints on Government Powers

| | | |
|---|---|---|
| 1.1 | Limits by legislature | 0.83 |
| 1.2 | Limits by judiciary | 0.83 |
| 1.3 | Independent auditing | 0.89 |
| 1.4 | Sanctions for official misconduct | 0.84 |
| 1.5 | Non-governmental checks | 0.92 |
| 1.6 | Lawful transition of power | 0.95 |

## 💰 Absence of Corruption

| | | |
|---|---|---|
| 2.1 | No corruption in the executive branch | 0.88 |
| 2.2 | No corruption in the judiciary | 0.94 |
| 2.3 | No corruption in the police/military | 0.96 |
| 2.4 | No corruption in the legislature | 0.84 |

## 📱 Open Government

| | | |
|---|---|---|
| 3.1 | Publicized laws and government data | 0.75 |
| 3.2 | Right to information | 0.94 |
| 3.3 | Civic participation | 0.87 |
| 3.4 | Complaint mechanisms | 0.81 |

## 👤 Fundamental Rights

| | | |
|---|---|---|
| 4.1 | Equal treatment / no discrimination | 0.74 |
| 4.2 | Right to life and security | 0.97 |
| 4.3 | Due process of law | 0.92 |
| 4.4 | Freedom of expression | 0.92 |
| 4.5 | Freedom of religion | 0.85 |
| 4.6 | Right to privacy | 0.94 |
| 4.7 | Freedom of association | 0.87 |
| 4.8 | Labor rights | 0.83 |

## 👮 Order & Security

| | | |
|---|---|---|
| 5.1 | Absence of crime | 0.91 |
| 5.2 | Absence of civil conflict | 1.00 |
| 5.3 | Absence of violent redress | 0.86 |

## 👷 Regulatory Enforcement

| | | |
|---|---|---|
| 6.1 | Effective regulatory enforcement | 0.80 |
| 6.2 | No improper influence | 0.96 |
| 6.3 | No unreasonable delay | 0.89 |
| 6.4 | Respect for due process | 0.78 |
| 6.5 | No expropriation w/out adequate compensation | 0.84 |

## ⚖ Civil Justice

| | | |
|---|---|---|
| 7.1 | Accessibility and affordability | 0.69 |
| 7.2 | No discrimination | 0.74 |
| 7.3 | No corruption | 0.91 |
| 7.4 | No improper government influence | 0.88 |
| 7.5 | No unreasonable delay | 0.76 |
| 7.6 | Effective enforcement | 0.91 |
| 7.7 | Impartial and effective ADRs | 0.79 |

## ⚖ Criminal Justice

| | | |
|---|---|---|
| 8.1 | Effective investigations | 0.53 |
| 8.2 | Timely and effective adjucation | 0.73 |
| 8.3 | Effective correctional system | 0.86 |
| 8.4 | No discrimination | 0.71 |
| 8.5 | No corruption | 0.90 |
| 8.6 | No improper government influence | 0.91 |
| 8.7 | Due process of law | 0.92 |

# Tanzania

**Region:** Sub-Saharan Africa
**Income Group:** Low Income

| | Overall Score | Regional Rank | Income Rank | Global Rank |
|---|---|---|---|---|
| | 0.47 | 8/18 | 5/12 | 84/113 |

| | | Factor Trend | Factor Score | Regional Rank | Income Rank | Global Rank |
|---|---|---|---|---|---|---|
| 🏛️ | Constraints on Government Powers | — | 0.52 | 9/18 | 6/12 | 71/113 |
| 💰 | Absence of Corruption | — | 0.39 | 7/18 | 3/12 | 82/113 |
| 📱 | Open Government | ▼ | 0.39 | 14/18 | 10/12 | 101/113 |
| 🧍 | Fundamental Rights | — | 0.48 | 10/18 | 8/12 | 86/113 |
| 👤 | Order & Security | — | 0.64 | 11/18 | 8/12 | 82/113 |
| 👷 | Regulatory Enforcement | — | 0.42 | 11/18 | 5/12 | 93/113 |
| ⚖️ | Civil Justice | — | 0.50 | 8/18 | 3/12 | 68/113 |
| 🏛️ | Criminal Justice | — | 0.41 | 9/18 | 5/12 | 72/113 |

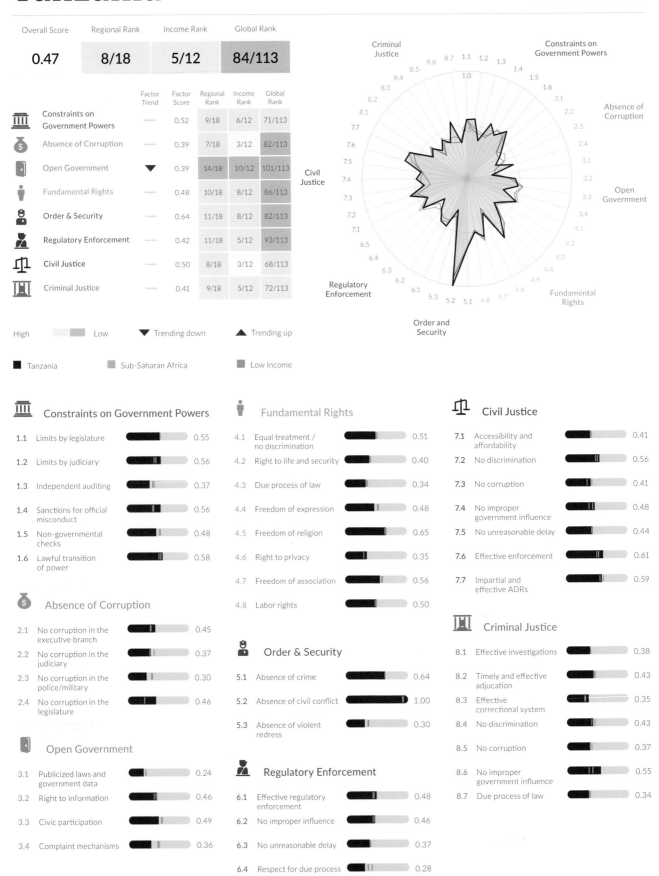

High ▢ Low    ▼ Trending down    ▲ Trending up

■ Tanzania    ■ Sub-Saharan Africa    ■ Low Income

## 🏛️ Constraints on Government Powers

| | | |
|---|---|---|
| 1.1 | Limits by legislature | 0.55 |
| 1.2 | Limits by judiciary | 0.56 |
| 1.3 | Independent auditing | 0.37 |
| 1.4 | Sanctions for official misconduct | 0.56 |
| 1.5 | Non-governmental checks | 0.48 |
| 1.6 | Lawful transition of power | 0.58 |

## 💰 Absence of Corruption

| | | |
|---|---|---|
| 2.1 | No corruption in the executive branch | 0.45 |
| 2.2 | No corruption in the judiciary | 0.37 |
| 2.3 | No corruption in the police/military | 0.30 |
| 2.4 | No corruption in the legislature | 0.46 |

## 📱 Open Government

| | | |
|---|---|---|
| 3.1 | Publicized laws and government data | 0.24 |
| 3.2 | Right to information | 0.46 |
| 3.3 | Civic participation | 0.49 |
| 3.4 | Complaint mechanisms | 0.36 |

## 🧍 Fundamental Rights

| | | |
|---|---|---|
| 4.1 | Equal treatment / no discrimination | 0.51 |
| 4.2 | Right to life and security | 0.40 |
| 4.3 | Due process of law | 0.34 |
| 4.4 | Freedom of expression | 0.48 |
| 4.5 | Freedom of religion | 0.65 |
| 4.6 | Right to privacy | 0.35 |
| 4.7 | Freedom of association | 0.56 |
| 4.8 | Labor rights | 0.50 |

## 👤 Order & Security

| | | |
|---|---|---|
| 5.1 | Absence of crime | 0.64 |
| 5.2 | Absence of civil conflict | 1.00 |
| 5.3 | Absence of violent redress | 0.30 |

## 👷 Regulatory Enforcement

| | | |
|---|---|---|
| 6.1 | Effective regulatory enforcement | 0.48 |
| 6.2 | No improper influence | 0.46 |
| 6.3 | No unreasonable delay | 0.37 |
| 6.4 | Respect for due process | 0.28 |
| 6.5 | No expropriation w/out adequate compensation | 0.50 |

## ⚖️ Civil Justice

| | | |
|---|---|---|
| 7.1 | Accessibility and affordability | 0.41 |
| 7.2 | No discrimination | 0.56 |
| 7.3 | No corruption | 0.41 |
| 7.4 | No improper government influence | 0.48 |
| 7.5 | No unreasonable delay | 0.44 |
| 7.6 | Effective enforcement | 0.61 |
| 7.7 | Impartial and effective ADRs | 0.59 |

## 🏛️ Criminal Justice

| | | |
|---|---|---|
| 8.1 | Effective investigations | 0.38 |
| 8.2 | Timely and effective adjudication | 0.43 |
| 8.3 | Effective correctional system | 0.35 |
| 8.4 | No discrimination | 0.43 |
| 8.5 | No corruption | 0.37 |
| 8.6 | No improper government influence | 0.55 |
| 8.7 | Due process of law | 0.34 |

# Thailand

**Region:** East Asia & Pacific
**Income Group:** Upper Middle Income

| Overall Score | Regional Rank | Income Rank | Global Rank |
|:---:|:---:|:---:|:---:|
| 0.51 | 10/15 | 21/37 | 64/113 |

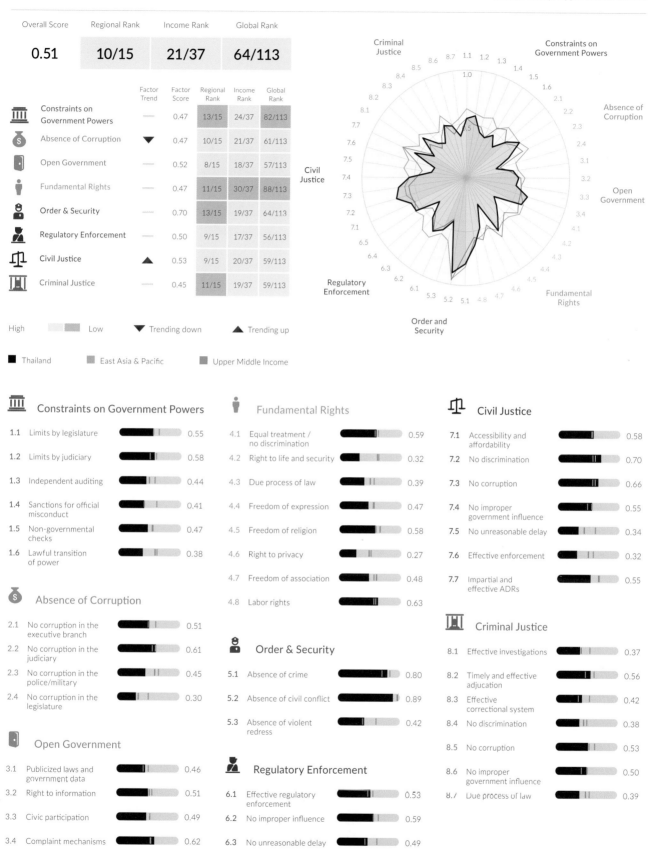

| | | Factor Trend | Factor Score | Regional Rank | Income Rank | Global Rank |
|---|---|:---:|:---:|:---:|:---:|:---:|
| 🏛 | Constraints on Government Powers | — | 0.47 | 13/15 | 24/37 | 82/113 |
| 💰 | Absence of Corruption | ▼ | 0.47 | 10/15 | 21/37 | 61/113 |
| 📱 | Open Government | — | 0.52 | 8/15 | 18/37 | 57/113 |
| 👤 | Fundamental Rights | — | 0.47 | 11/15 | 30/37 | 88/113 |
| 👮 | Order & Security | — | 0.70 | 13/15 | 19/37 | 64/113 |
| 👷 | Regulatory Enforcement | — | 0.50 | 9/15 | 17/37 | 56/113 |
| ⚖ | Civil Justice | ▲ | 0.53 | 9/15 | 20/37 | 59/113 |
| 🏛 | Criminal Justice | — | 0.45 | 11/15 | 19/37 | 59/113 |

High ▮▮ Low    ▼ Trending down    ▲ Trending up

■ Thailand    ▨ East Asia & Pacific    ▨ Upper Middle Income

## 🏛 Constraints on Government Powers

| | | |
|---|---|---:|
| 1.1 | Limits by legislature | 0.55 |
| 1.2 | Limits by judiciary | 0.58 |
| 1.3 | Independent auditing | 0.44 |
| 1.4 | Sanctions for official misconduct | 0.41 |
| 1.5 | Non-governmental checks | 0.47 |
| 1.6 | Lawful transition of power | 0.38 |

## 💰 Absence of Corruption

| | | |
|---|---|---:|
| 2.1 | No corruption in the executive branch | 0.51 |
| 2.2 | No corruption in the judiciary | 0.61 |
| 2.3 | No corruption in the police/military | 0.45 |
| 2.4 | No corruption in the legislature | 0.30 |

## 📱 Open Government

| | | |
|---|---|---:|
| 3.1 | Publicized laws and government data | 0.46 |
| 3.2 | Right to information | 0.51 |
| 3.3 | Civic participation | 0.49 |
| 3.4 | Complaint mechanisms | 0.62 |

## 👤 Fundamental Rights

| | | |
|---|---|---:|
| 4.1 | Equal treatment / no discrimination | 0.59 |
| 4.2 | Right to life and security | 0.32 |
| 4.3 | Due process of law | 0.39 |
| 4.4 | Freedom of expression | 0.47 |
| 4.5 | Freedom of religion | 0.58 |
| 4.6 | Right to privacy | 0.27 |
| 4.7 | Freedom of association | 0.48 |
| 4.8 | Labor rights | 0.63 |

## 👮 Order & Security

| | | |
|---|---|---:|
| 5.1 | Absence of crime | 0.80 |
| 5.2 | Absence of civil conflict | 0.89 |
| 5.3 | Absence of violent redress | 0.42 |

## 👷 Regulatory Enforcement

| | | |
|---|---|---:|
| 6.1 | Effective regulatory enforcement | 0.53 |
| 6.2 | No improper influence | 0.59 |
| 6.3 | No unreasonable delay | 0.49 |
| 6.4 | Respect for due process | 0.34 |
| 6.5 | No expropriation w/out adequate compensation | 0.57 |

## ⚖ Civil Justice

| | | |
|---|---|---:|
| 7.1 | Accessibility and affordability | 0.58 |
| 7.2 | No discrimination | 0.70 |
| 7.3 | No corruption | 0.66 |
| 7.4 | No improper government influence | 0.55 |
| 7.5 | No unreasonable delay | 0.34 |
| 7.6 | Effective enforcement | 0.32 |
| 7.7 | Impartial and effective ADRs | 0.55 |

## 🏛 Criminal Justice

| | | |
|---|---|---:|
| 8.1 | Effective investigations | 0.37 |
| 8.2 | Timely and effective adjucation | 0.56 |
| 8.3 | Effective correctional system | 0.42 |
| 8.4 | No discrimination | 0.38 |
| 8.5 | No corruption | 0.53 |
| 8.6 | No improper government influence | 0.50 |
| 8.7 | Due process of law | 0.39 |

# Trinidad & Tobago

| | Overall Score | Regional Rank | Income Rank | Global Rank |
|---|---|---|---|---|
| | 0.57 | 13/30 | 35/36 | 48/113 |

| | | Factor Trend | Factor Score | Regional Rank | Income Rank | Global Rank |
|---|---|---|---|---|---|---|
| 🏛 | Constraints on Government Powers | — | 0.62 | 11/30 | 31/36 | 44/113 |
| 💰 | Absence of Corruption | — | 0.54 | 14/30 | 35/36 | 49/113 |
| 📱 | Open Government | — | 0.55 | 12/30 | 30/36 | 48/113 |
| 👤 | Fundamental Rights | — | 0.61 | 17/30 | 35/36 | 53/113 |
| 👥 | Order & Security | — | 0.67 | 13/30 | 35/36 | 72/113 |
| 👷 | Regulatory Enforcement | — | 0.54 | 9/30 | 32/36 | 43/113 |
| ⚖ | Civil Justice | — | 0.61 | 11/30 | 32/36 | 42/113 |
| 🏛 | Criminal Justice | — | 0.40 | 15/30 | 36/36 | 74/113 |

High ▬▬ Low     ▼ Trending down     ▲ Trending up

■ Trinidad & Tobago     ▨ Latin America & Caribbean     ▨ High Income

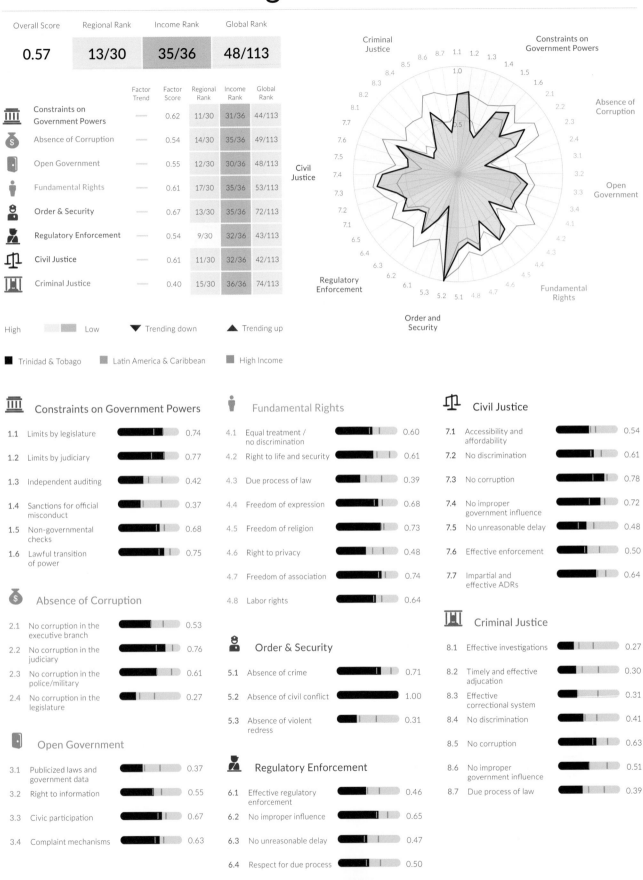

## 🏛 Constraints on Government Powers

| | | |
|---|---|---|
| 1.1 | Limits by legislature | 0.74 |
| 1.2 | Limits by judiciary | 0.77 |
| 1.3 | Independent auditing | 0.42 |
| 1.4 | Sanctions for official misconduct | 0.37 |
| 1.5 | Non-governmental checks | 0.68 |
| 1.6 | Lawful transition of power | 0.75 |

## 💰 Absence of Corruption

| | | |
|---|---|---|
| 2.1 | No corruption in the executive branch | 0.53 |
| 2.2 | No corruption in the judiciary | 0.76 |
| 2.3 | No corruption in the police/military | 0.61 |
| 2.4 | No corruption in the legislature | 0.27 |

## 📱 Open Government

| | | |
|---|---|---|
| 3.1 | Publicized laws and government data | 0.37 |
| 3.2 | Right to information | 0.55 |
| 3.3 | Civic participation | 0.67 |
| 3.4 | Complaint mechanisms | 0.63 |

## 👤 Fundamental Rights

| | | |
|---|---|---|
| 4.1 | Equal treatment / no discrimination | 0.60 |
| 4.2 | Right to life and security | 0.61 |
| 4.3 | Due process of law | 0.39 |
| 4.4 | Freedom of expression | 0.68 |
| 4.5 | Freedom of religion | 0.73 |
| 4.6 | Right to privacy | 0.48 |
| 4.7 | Freedom of association | 0.74 |
| 4.8 | Labor rights | 0.64 |

## 👥 Order & Security

| | | |
|---|---|---|
| 5.1 | Absence of crime | 0.71 |
| 5.2 | Absence of civil conflict | 1.00 |
| 5.3 | Absence of violent redress | 0.31 |

## 👷 Regulatory Enforcement

| | | |
|---|---|---|
| 6.1 | Effective regulatory enforcement | 0.46 |
| 6.2 | No improper influence | 0.65 |
| 6.3 | No unreasonable delay | 0.47 |
| 6.4 | Respect for due process | 0.50 |
| 6.5 | No expropriation w/out adequate compensation | 0.63 |

## ⚖ Civil Justice

| | | |
|---|---|---|
| 7.1 | Accessibility and affordability | 0.54 |
| 7.2 | No discrimination | 0.61 |
| 7.3 | No corruption | 0.78 |
| 7.4 | No improper government influence | 0.72 |
| 7.5 | No unreasonable delay | 0.48 |
| 7.6 | Effective enforcement | 0.50 |
| 7.7 | Impartial and effective ADRs | 0.64 |

## 🏛 Criminal Justice

| | | |
|---|---|---|
| 8.1 | Effective investigations | 0.27 |
| 8.2 | Timely and effective adjucation | 0.30 |
| 8.3 | Effective correctional system | 0.31 |
| 8.4 | No discrimination | 0.41 |
| 8.5 | No corruption | 0.63 |
| 8.6 | No improper government influence | 0.51 |
| 8.7 | Due process of law | 0.39 |

# Tunisia

**Region:** Middle East & North Africa
**Income Group:** Lower Middle Income

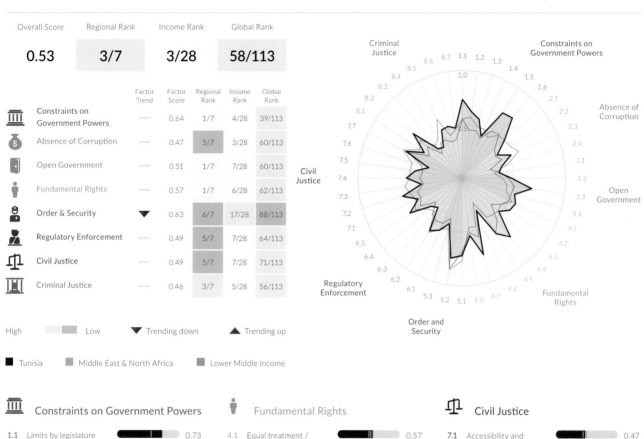

| | Overall Score | Regional Rank | Income Rank | Global Rank |
|---|---|---|---|---|
| | 0.53 | 3/7 | 3/28 | 58/113 |

| | Factor Trend | Factor Score | Regional Rank | Income Rank | Global Rank |
|---|---|---|---|---|---|
| Constraints on Government Powers | — | 0.64 | 1/7 | 4/28 | 39/113 |
| Absence of Corruption | — | 0.47 | 5/7 | 3/28 | 60/113 |
| Open Government | — | 0.51 | 1/7 | 7/28 | 60/113 |
| Fundamental Rights | — | 0.57 | 1/7 | 6/28 | 62/113 |
| Order & Security | ▼ | 0.63 | 6/7 | 17/28 | 88/113 |
| Regulatory Enforcement | — | 0.49 | 5/7 | 7/28 | 64/113 |
| Civil Justice | — | 0.49 | 5/7 | 7/28 | 71/113 |
| Criminal Justice | — | 0.46 | 3/7 | 5/28 | 56/113 |

High ▢ Low    ▼ Trending down    ▲ Trending up

■ Tunisia    ▨ Middle East & North Africa    ▨ Lower Middle Income

## 🏛 Constraints on Government Powers

| | | |
|---|---|---|
| 1.1 | Limits by legislature | 0.73 |
| 1.2 | Limits by judiciary | 0.62 |
| 1.3 | Independent auditing | 0.57 |
| 1.4 | Sanctions for official misconduct | 0.43 |
| 1.5 | Non-governmental checks | 0.72 |
| 1.6 | Lawful transition of power | 0.74 |

## 💰 Absence of Corruption

| | | |
|---|---|---|
| 2.1 | No corruption in the executive branch | 0.54 |
| 2.2 | No corruption in the judiciary | 0.40 |
| 2.3 | No corruption in the police/military | 0.52 |
| 2.4 | No corruption in the legislature | 0.40 |

## 🚪 Open Government

| | | |
|---|---|---|
| 3.1 | Publicized laws and government data | 0.36 |
| 3.2 | Right to information | 0.48 |
| 3.3 | Civic participation | 0.68 |
| 3.4 | Complaint mechanisms | 0.53 |

## 👤 Fundamental Rights

| | | |
|---|---|---|
| 4.1 | Equal treatment / no discrimination | 0.57 |
| 4.2 | Right to life and security | 0.55 |
| 4.3 | Due process of law | 0.47 |
| 4.4 | Freedom of expression | 0.72 |
| 4.5 | Freedom of religion | 0.61 |
| 4.6 | Right to privacy | 0.33 |
| 4.7 | Freedom of association | 0.74 |
| 4.8 | Labor rights | 0.54 |

## 👮 Order & Security

| | | |
|---|---|---|
| 5.1 | Absence of crime | 0.72 |
| 5.2 | Absence of civil conflict | 0.75 |
| 5.3 | Absence of violent redress | 0.44 |

## 👷 Regulatory Enforcement

| | | |
|---|---|---|
| 6.1 | Effective regulatory enforcement | 0.53 |
| 6.2 | No improper influence | 0.58 |
| 6.3 | No unreasonable delay | 0.36 |
| 6.4 | Respect for due process | 0.40 |
| 6.5 | No expropriation w/out adequate compensation | 0.60 |

## ⚖ Civil Justice

| | | |
|---|---|---|
| 7.1 | Accessibility and affordability | 0.47 |
| 7.2 | No discrimination | 0.60 |
| 7.3 | No corruption | 0.40 |
| 7.4 | No improper government influence | 0.54 |
| 7.5 | No unreasonable delay | 0.46 |
| 7.6 | Effective enforcement | 0.34 |
| 7.7 | Impartial and effective ADRs | 0.60 |

## 🏛 Criminal Justice

| | | |
|---|---|---|
| 8.1 | Effective investigations | 0.44 |
| 8.2 | Timely and effective adjudication | 0.63 |
| 8.3 | Effective correctional system | 0.36 |
| 8.4 | No discrimination | 0.34 |
| 8.5 | No corruption | 0.49 |
| 8.6 | No improper government influence | 0.50 |
| 8.7 | Due process of law | 0.47 |

# Turkey

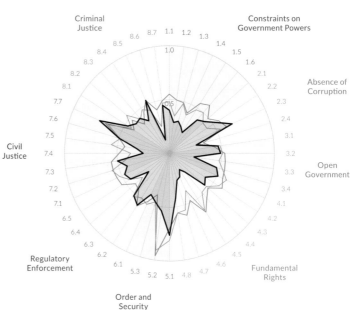

| | Overall Score | Regional Rank | Income Rank | Global Rank |
|---|---|---|---|---|
| | 0.43 | 13/13 | 36/37 | 99/113 |

| | | Factor Trend | Factor Score | Regional Rank | Income Rank | Global Rank |
|---|---|---|---|---|---|---|
| 🏛 | Constraints on Government Powers | — | 0.32 | 12/13 | 36/37 | 108/113 |
| 💰 | Absence of Corruption | — | 0.48 | 4/13 | 19/37 | 58/113 |
| 📱 | Open Government | — | 0.42 | 12/13 | 34/37 | 96/113 |
| 👤 | Fundamental Rights | — | 0.34 | 13/13 | 34/37 | 105/113 |
| 👥 | Order & Security | ▼ | 0.59 | 12/13 | 34/37 | 98/113 |
| 👷 | Regulatory Enforcement | ▼ | 0.44 | 9/13 | 31/37 | 84/113 |
| ⚖ | Civil Justice | — | 0.46 | 12/13 | 33/37 | 86/113 |
| 🏛 | Criminal Justice | — | 0.40 | 8/13 | 24/37 | 75/113 |

High ▢▢ Low      ▼ Trending down      ▲ Trending up

■ Turkey      ▨ Eastern Europe & Central Asia      ▨ Upper Middle Income

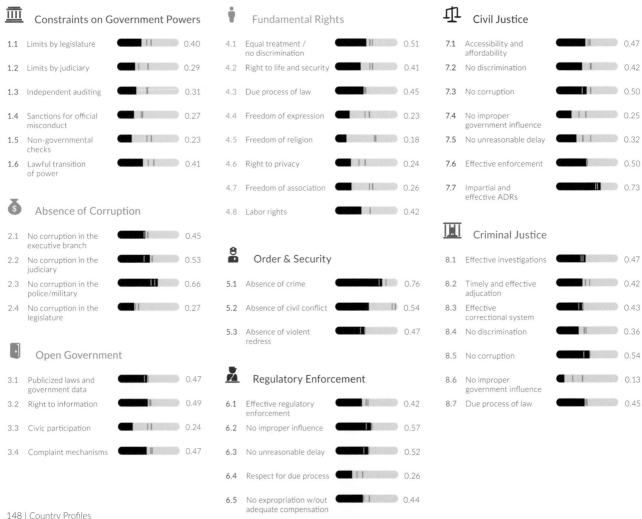

## 🏛 Constraints on Government Powers

| | | |
|---|---|---|
| 1.1 | Limits by legislature | 0.40 |
| 1.2 | Limits by judiciary | 0.29 |
| 1.3 | Independent auditing | 0.31 |
| 1.4 | Sanctions for official misconduct | 0.27 |
| 1.5 | Non-governmental checks | 0.23 |
| 1.6 | Lawful transition of power | 0.41 |

## 💰 Absence of Corruption

| | | |
|---|---|---|
| 2.1 | No corruption in the executive branch | 0.45 |
| 2.2 | No corruption in the judiciary | 0.53 |
| 2.3 | No corruption in the police/military | 0.66 |
| 2.4 | No corruption in the legislature | 0.27 |

## 📱 Open Government

| | | |
|---|---|---|
| 3.1 | Publicized laws and government data | 0.47 |
| 3.2 | Right to information | 0.49 |
| 3.3 | Civic participation | 0.24 |
| 3.4 | Complaint mechanisms | 0.47 |

## 👤 Fundamental Rights

| | | |
|---|---|---|
| 4.1 | Equal treatment / no discrimination | 0.51 |
| 4.2 | Right to life and security | 0.41 |
| 4.3 | Due process of law | 0.45 |
| 4.4 | Freedom of expression | 0.23 |
| 4.5 | Freedom of religion | 0.18 |
| 4.6 | Right to privacy | 0.24 |
| 4.7 | Freedom of association | 0.26 |
| 4.8 | Labor rights | 0.42 |

## 👥 Order & Security

| | | |
|---|---|---|
| 5.1 | Absence of crime | 0.76 |
| 5.2 | Absence of civil conflict | 0.54 |
| 5.3 | Absence of violent redress | 0.47 |

## 👷 Regulatory Enforcement

| | | |
|---|---|---|
| 6.1 | Effective regulatory enforcement | 0.42 |
| 6.2 | No improper influence | 0.57 |
| 6.3 | No unreasonable delay | 0.52 |
| 6.4 | Respect for due process | 0.26 |
| 6.5 | No expropriation w/out adequate compensation | 0.44 |

## ⚖ Civil Justice

| | | |
|---|---|---|
| 7.1 | Accessibility and affordability | 0.47 |
| 7.2 | No discrimination | 0.42 |
| 7.3 | No corruption | 0.50 |
| 7.4 | No improper government influence | 0.25 |
| 7.5 | No unreasonable delay | 0.32 |
| 7.6 | Effective enforcement | 0.50 |
| 7.7 | Impartial and effective ADRs | 0.73 |

## 🏛 Criminal Justice

| | | |
|---|---|---|
| 8.1 | Effective investigations | 0.47 |
| 8.2 | Timely and effective adjudication | 0.42 |
| 8.3 | Effective correctional system | 0.43 |
| 8.4 | No discrimination | 0.36 |
| 8.5 | No corruption | 0.54 |
| 8.6 | No improper government influence | 0.13 |
| 8.7 | Due process of law | 0.45 |

# Uganda

**Region:** Sub-Saharan Africa
**Income Group:** Low Income

| | Overall Score | Regional Rank | Income Rank | Global Rank |
|---|---|---|---|---|
| | 0.39 | 15/18 | 9/12 | 105/113 |

| | Factor Trend | Factor Score | Regional Rank | Income Rank | Global Rank |
|---|---|---|---|---|---|
| Constraints on Government Powers | — | 0.40 | 16/18 | 10/12 | 101/113 |
| Absence of Corruption | — | 0.27 | 15/18 | 10/12 | 107/113 |
| Open Government | — | 0.39 | 13/18 | 9/12 | 100/113 |
| Fundamental Rights | — | 0.39 | 16/18 | 10/12 | 102/113 |
| Order & Security | — | 0.56 | 15/18 | 11/12 | 105/113 |
| Regulatory Enforcement | — | 0.37 | 15/18 | 8/12 | 105/113 |
| Civil Justice | — | 0.42 | 14/18 | 7/12 | 97/113 |
| Criminal Justice | — | 0.34 | 15/18 | 9/12 | 93/113 |

High ▬▬ Low　▼ Trending down　▲ Trending up

■ Uganda　■ Sub-Saharan Africa　■ Low Income

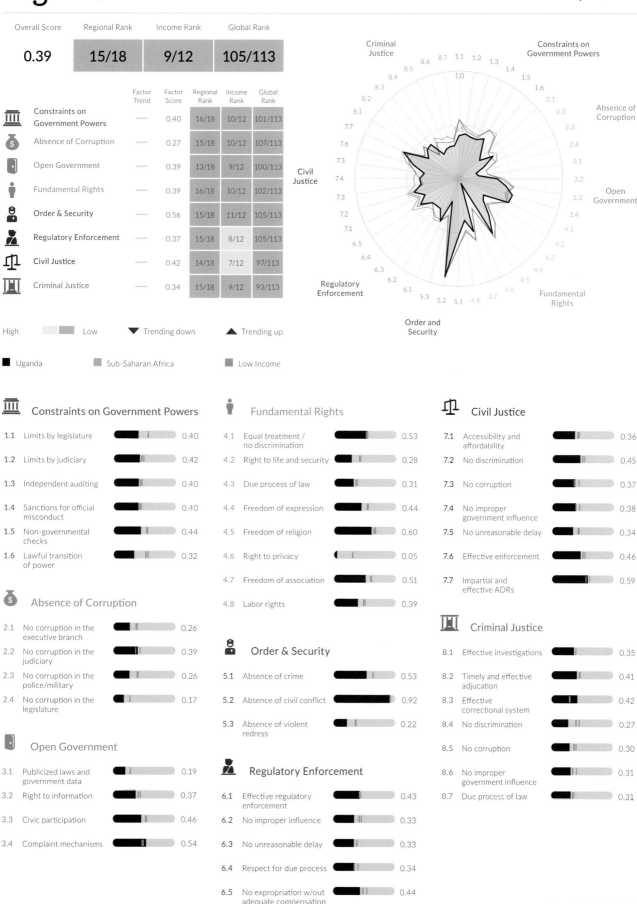

## Constraints on Government Powers

| | | |
|---|---|---|
| 1.1 | Limits by legislature | 0.40 |
| 1.2 | Limits by judiciary | 0.42 |
| 1.3 | Independent auditing | 0.40 |
| 1.4 | Sanctions for official misconduct | 0.40 |
| 1.5 | Non-governmental checks | 0.44 |
| 1.6 | Lawful transition of power | 0.32 |

## Absence of Corruption

| | | |
|---|---|---|
| 2.1 | No corruption in the executive branch | 0.26 |
| 2.2 | No corruption in the judiciary | 0.39 |
| 2.3 | No corruption in the police/military | 0.26 |
| 2.4 | No corruption in the legislature | 0.17 |

## Open Government

| | | |
|---|---|---|
| 3.1 | Publicized laws and government data | 0.19 |
| 3.2 | Right to information | 0.37 |
| 3.3 | Civic participation | 0.46 |
| 3.4 | Complaint mechanisms | 0.54 |

## Fundamental Rights

| | | |
|---|---|---|
| 4.1 | Equal treatment / no discrimination | 0.53 |
| 4.2 | Right to life and security | 0.28 |
| 4.3 | Due process of law | 0.31 |
| 4.4 | Freedom of expression | 0.44 |
| 4.5 | Freedom of religion | 0.60 |
| 4.6 | Right to privacy | 0.05 |
| 4.7 | Freedom of association | 0.51 |
| 4.8 | Labor rights | 0.39 |

## Order & Security

| | | |
|---|---|---|
| 5.1 | Absence of crime | 0.53 |
| 5.2 | Absence of civil conflict | 0.92 |
| 5.3 | Absence of violent redress | 0.22 |

## Regulatory Enforcement

| | | |
|---|---|---|
| 6.1 | Effective regulatory enforcement | 0.43 |
| 6.2 | No improper influence | 0.33 |
| 6.3 | No unreasonable delay | 0.33 |
| 6.4 | Respect for due process | 0.34 |
| 6.5 | No expropriation w/out adequate compensation | 0.44 |

## Civil Justice

| | | |
|---|---|---|
| 7.1 | Accessibility and affordability | 0.36 |
| 7.2 | No discrimination | 0.45 |
| 7.3 | No corruption | 0.37 |
| 7.4 | No improper government influence | 0.38 |
| 7.5 | No unreasonable delay | 0.34 |
| 7.6 | Effective enforcement | 0.46 |
| 7.7 | Impartial and effective ADRs | 0.59 |

## Criminal Justice

| | | |
|---|---|---|
| 8.1 | Effective investigations | 0.35 |
| 8.2 | Timely and effective adjucation | 0.41 |
| 8.3 | Effective correctional system | 0.42 |
| 8.4 | No discrimination | 0.27 |
| 8.5 | No corruption | 0.30 |
| 8.6 | No improper government influence | 0.31 |
| 8.7 | Due process of law | 0.31 |

# Ukraine

**Region:** Eastern Europe & Central Asia
**Income Group:** Lower Middle Income

| | Overall Score | Regional Rank | Income Rank | Global Rank |
|---|---|---|---|---|
| | 0.49 | 9/13 | 12/28 | 78/113 |

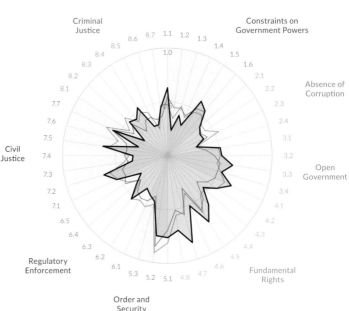

| | Factor Trend | Factor Score | Regional Rank | Income Rank | Global Rank |
|---|---|---|---|---|---|
| Constraints on Government Powers | — | 0.45 | 6/13 | 18/28 | 88/113 |
| Absence of Corruption | — | 0.36 | 9/13 | 16/28 | 89/113 |
| Open Government | — | 0.55 | 6/13 | 5/28 | 50/113 |
| Fundamental Rights | — | 0.63 | 3/13 | 2/28 | 47/113 |
| Order & Security | — | 0.65 | 11/13 | 15/28 | 80/113 |
| Regulatory Enforcement | — | 0.40 | 12/13 | 22/28 | 100/113 |
| Civil Justice | — | 0.47 | 9/13 | 10/28 | 78/113 |
| Criminal Justice | ▲ | 0.40 | 9/13 | 11/28 | 77/113 |

High ▮▮▮ Low   ▼ Trending down   ▲ Trending up

■ Ukraine   ▦ Eastern Europe & Central Asia   ▦ Lower Middle Income

## 🏛 Constraints on Government Powers

| | | |
|---|---|---|
| 1.1 | Limits by legislature | 0.63 |
| 1.2 | Limits by judiciary | 0.24 |
| 1.3 | Independent auditing | 0.39 |
| 1.4 | Sanctions for official misconduct | 0.31 |
| 1.5 | Non-governmental checks | 0.60 |
| 1.6 | Lawful transition of power | 0.55 |

## 💰 Absence of Corruption

| | | |
|---|---|---|
| 2.1 | No corruption in the executive branch | 0.41 |
| 2.2 | No corruption in the judiciary | 0.37 |
| 2.3 | No corruption in the police/military | 0.38 |
| 2.4 | No corruption in the legislature | 0.29 |

## 📱 Open Government

| | | |
|---|---|---|
| 3.1 | Publicized laws and government data | 0.51 |
| 3.2 | Right to information | 0.52 |
| 3.3 | Civic participation | 0.63 |
| 3.4 | Complaint mechanisms | 0.54 |

## 🧍 Fundamental Rights

| | | |
|---|---|---|
| 4.1 | Equal treatment / no discrimination | 0.67 |
| 4.2 | Right to life and security | 0.56 |
| 4.3 | Due process of law | 0.45 |
| 4.4 | Freedom of expression | 0.60 |
| 4.5 | Freedom of religion | 0.73 |
| 4.6 | Right to privacy | 0.51 |
| 4.7 | Freedom of association | 0.84 |
| 4.8 | Labor rights | 0.7 |

## 🧑‍✈️ Order & Security

| | | |
|---|---|---|
| 5.1 | Absence of crime | 0.76 |
| 5.2 | Absence of civil conflict | 0.75 |
| 5.3 | Absence of violent redress | 0.44 |

## 💼 Regulatory Enforcement

| | | |
|---|---|---|
| 6.1 | Effective regulatory enforcement | 0.40 |
| 6.2 | No improper influence | 0.36 |
| 6.3 | No unreasonable delay | 0.53 |
| 6.4 | Respect for due process | 0.39 |
| 6.5 | No expropriation w/out adequate compensation | 0.30 |

## ⚖ Civil Justice

| | | |
|---|---|---|
| 7.1 | Accessibility and affordability | 0.53 |
| 7.2 | No discrimination | 0.63 |
| 7.3 | No corruption | 0.34 |
| 7.4 | No improper government influence | 0.33 |
| 7.5 | No unreasonable delay | 0.62 |
| 7.6 | Effective enforcement | 0.29 |
| 7.7 | Impartial and effective ADRs | 0.57 |

## 🏛 Criminal Justice

| | | |
|---|---|---|
| 8.1 | Effective investigations | 0.26 |
| 8.2 | Timely and effective adjucation | 0.48 |
| 8.3 | Effective correctional system | 0.45 |
| 8.4 | No discrimination | 0.53 |
| 8.5 | No corruption | 0.30 |
| 8.6 | No improper government influence | 0.30 |
| 8.7 | Due process of law | 0.45 |

# United Arab Emirates

| | Overall Score | Regional Rank | Income Rank | Global Rank |
|---|---|---|---|---|
| | 0.66 | 1/7 | 30/36 | 33/113 |

| | | Factor Trend | Factor Score | Regional Rank | Income Rank | Global Rank |
|---|---|---|---|---|---|---|
| 🏛️ | Constraints on Government Powers | — | 0.61 | 2/7 | 32/36 | 45/113 |
| 💰 | Absence of Corruption | — | 0.80 | 1/7 | 15/36 | 15/113 |
| 📱 | Open Government | — | 0.39 | 5/7 | 36/36 | 102/113 |
| 🧍 | Fundamental Rights | — | 0.46 | 4/7 | 36/36 | 90/113 |
| 👤 | Order & Security | — | 0.89 | 1/7 | 11/36 | 12/113 |
| 👷 | Regulatory Enforcement | — | 0.68 | 1/7 | 21/36 | 21/113 |
| ⚖️ | Civil Justice | — | 0.68 | 1/7 | 24/36 | 25/113 |
| 🏛️ | Criminal Justice | — | 0.74 | 1/7 | 14/36 | 14/113 |

High ▬▬ Low     ▼ Trending down     ▲ Trending up

■ United Arab Emirates   ■ Middle East & North Africa   ■ High Income

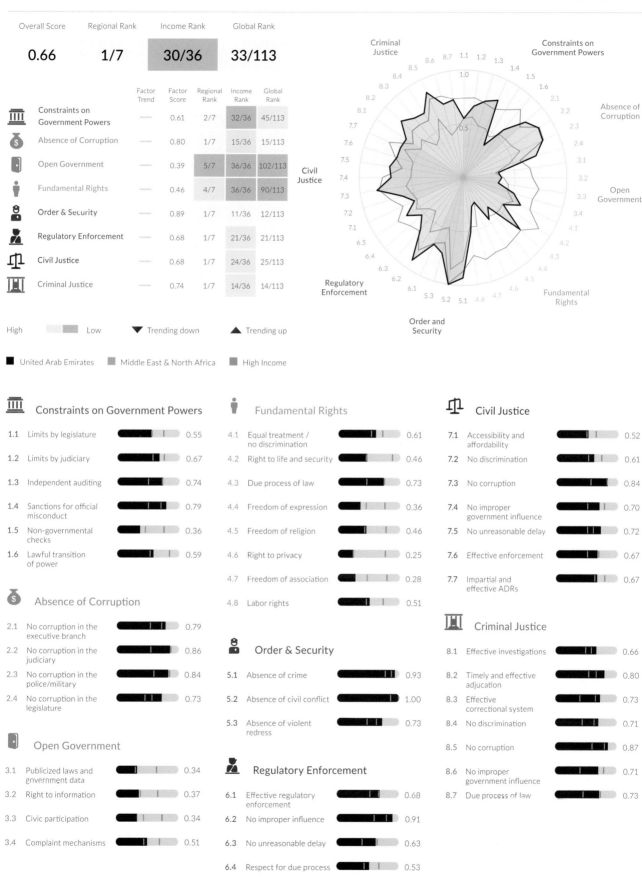

---

## 🏛️ Constraints on Government Powers

| | | |
|---|---|---|
| 1.1 | Limits by legislature | 0.55 |
| 1.2 | Limits by judiciary | 0.67 |
| 1.3 | Independent auditing | 0.74 |
| 1.4 | Sanctions for official misconduct | 0.79 |
| 1.5 | Non-governmental checks | 0.36 |
| 1.6 | Lawful transition of power | 0.59 |

## 💰 Absence of Corruption

| | | |
|---|---|---|
| 2.1 | No corruption in the executive branch | 0.79 |
| 2.2 | No corruption in the judiciary | 0.86 |
| 2.3 | No corruption in the police/military | 0.84 |
| 2.4 | No corruption in the legislature | 0.73 |

## 📱 Open Government

| | | |
|---|---|---|
| 3.1 | Publicized laws and government data | 0.34 |
| 3.2 | Right to information | 0.37 |
| 3.3 | Civic participation | 0.34 |
| 3.4 | Complaint mechanisms | 0.51 |

## 🧍 Fundamental Rights

| | | |
|---|---|---|
| 4.1 | Equal treatment / no discrimination | 0.61 |
| 4.2 | Right to life and security | 0.46 |
| 4.3 | Due process of law | 0.73 |
| 4.4 | Freedom of expression | 0.36 |
| 4.5 | Freedom of religion | 0.46 |
| 4.6 | Right to privacy | 0.25 |
| 4.7 | Freedom of association | 0.28 |
| 4.8 | Labor rights | 0.51 |

## 👤 Order & Security

| | | |
|---|---|---|
| 5.1 | Absence of crime | 0.93 |
| 5.2 | Absence of civil conflict | 1.00 |
| 5.3 | Absence of violent redress | 0.73 |

## 👷 Regulatory Enforcement

| | | |
|---|---|---|
| 6.1 | Effective regulatory enforcement | 0.68 |
| 6.2 | No improper influence | 0.91 |
| 6.3 | No unreasonable delay | 0.63 |
| 6.4 | Respect for due process | 0.53 |
| 6.5 | No expropriation w/out adequate compensation | 0.65 |

## ⚖️ Civil Justice

| | | |
|---|---|---|
| 7.1 | Accessibility and affordability | 0.52 |
| 7.2 | No discrimination | 0.61 |
| 7.3 | No corruption | 0.84 |
| 7.4 | No improper government influence | 0.70 |
| 7.5 | No unreasonable delay | 0.72 |
| 7.6 | Effective enforcement | 0.67 |
| 7.7 | Impartial and effective ADRs | 0.67 |

## 🏛️ Criminal Justice

| | | |
|---|---|---|
| 8.1 | Effective investigations | 0.66 |
| 8.2 | Timely and effective adjudication | 0.80 |
| 8.3 | Effective correctional system | 0.73 |
| 8.4 | No discrimination | 0.71 |
| 8.5 | No corruption | 0.87 |
| 8.6 | No improper government influence | 0.71 |
| 8.7 | Due process of law | 0.73 |

# United Kingdom

**Region:** EU & EFTA & North America
**Income Group:** High Income

| | Overall Score | Regional Rank | Income Rank | Global Rank |
|---|---|---|---|---|
| | 0.81 | 8/24 | 10/36 | 10/113 |

| | Factor Trend | Factor Score | Regional Rank | Income Rank | Global Rank |
|---|---|---|---|---|---|
| 🏛 Constraints on Government Powers | — | 0.85 | 7/24 | 8/36 | 8/113 |
| 💰 Absence of Corruption | — | 0.82 | 9/24 | 14/36 | 14/113 |
| 🚪 Open Government | — | 0.84 | 6/24 | 7/36 | 7/113 |
| 🧍 Fundamental Rights | — | 0.81 | 11/24 | 12/36 | 12/113 |
| 👤 Order & Security | — | 0.85 | 10/24 | 16/36 | 17/113 |
| 💂 Regulatory Enforcement | — | 0.79 | 9/24 | 14/36 | 14/113 |
| ⚖ Civil Justice | — | 0.75 | 10/24 | 16/36 | 16/113 |
| ⚜ Criminal Justice | — | 0.76 | 8/24 | 10/36 | 10/113 |

High ▢ Low ▼ Trending down ▲ Trending up

■ United Kingdom   ▨ EU & EFTA & North America   ▨ High Income

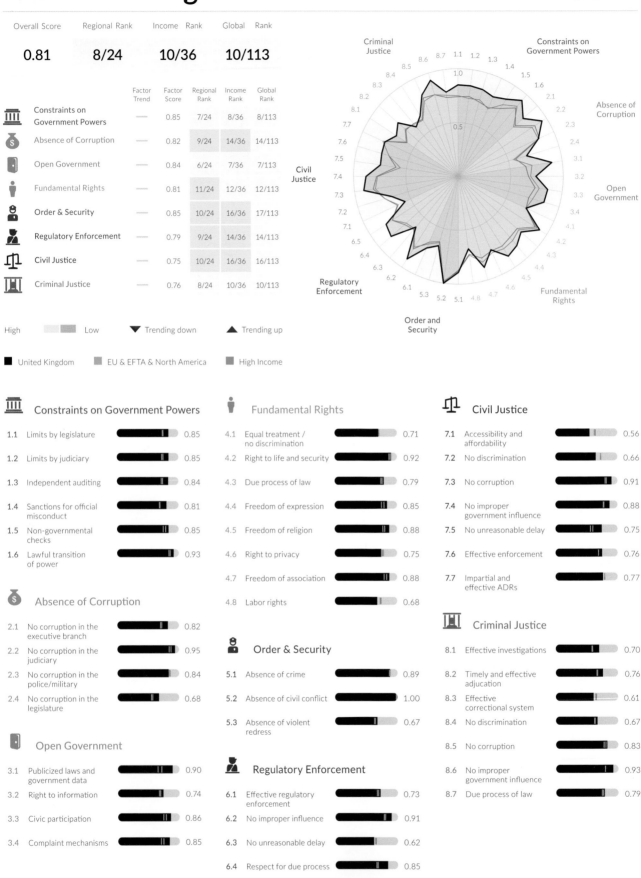

## 🏛 Constraints on Government Powers

| | | |
|---|---|---|
| 1.1 | Limits by legislature | 0.85 |
| 1.2 | Limits by judiciary | 0.85 |
| 1.3 | Independent auditing | 0.84 |
| 1.4 | Sanctions for official misconduct | 0.81 |
| 1.5 | Non-governmental checks | 0.85 |
| 1.6 | Lawful transition of power | 0.93 |

## 💰 Absence of Corruption

| | | |
|---|---|---|
| 2.1 | No corruption in the executive branch | 0.82 |
| 2.2 | No corruption in the judiciary | 0.95 |
| 2.3 | No corruption in the police/military | 0.84 |
| 2.4 | No corruption in the legislature | 0.68 |

## 🚪 Open Government

| | | |
|---|---|---|
| 3.1 | Publicized laws and government data | 0.90 |
| 3.2 | Right to information | 0.74 |
| 3.3 | Civic participation | 0.86 |
| 3.4 | Complaint mechanisms | 0.85 |

## 🧍 Fundamental Rights

| | | |
|---|---|---|
| 4.1 | Equal treatment / no discrimination | 0.71 |
| 4.2 | Right to life and security | 0.92 |
| 4.3 | Due process of law | 0.79 |
| 4.4 | Freedom of expression | 0.85 |
| 4.5 | Freedom of religion | 0.88 |
| 4.6 | Right to privacy | 0.75 |
| 4.7 | Freedom of association | 0.88 |
| 4.8 | Labor rights | 0.68 |

## 👤 Order & Security

| | | |
|---|---|---|
| 5.1 | Absence of crime | 0.89 |
| 5.2 | Absence of civil conflict | 1.00 |
| 5.3 | Absence of violent redress | 0.67 |

## 💂 Regulatory Enforcement

| | | |
|---|---|---|
| 6.1 | Effective regulatory enforcement | 0.73 |
| 6.2 | No improper influence | 0.91 |
| 6.3 | No unreasonable delay | 0.62 |
| 6.4 | Respect for due process | 0.85 |
| 6.5 | No expropriation w/out adequate compensation | 0.82 |

## ⚖ Civil Justice

| | | |
|---|---|---|
| 7.1 | Accessibility and affordability | 0.56 |
| 7.2 | No discrimination | 0.66 |
| 7.3 | No corruption | 0.91 |
| 7.4 | No improper government influence | 0.88 |
| 7.5 | No unreasonable delay | 0.75 |
| 7.6 | Effective enforcement | 0.76 |
| 7.7 | Impartial and effective ADRs | 0.77 |

## ⚜ Criminal Justice

| | | |
|---|---|---|
| 8.1 | Effective investigations | 0.70 |
| 8.2 | Timely and effective adjucation | 0.76 |
| 8.3 | Effective correctional system | 0.61 |
| 8.4 | No discrimination | 0.67 |
| 8.5 | No corruption | 0.83 |
| 8.6 | No improper government influence | 0.93 |
| 8.7 | Due process of law | 0.79 |

# United States

| | Overall Score | Regional Rank | Income Rank | Global Rank |
|---|---|---|---|---|
| | 0.74 | 13/24 | 18/36 | 18/113 |

| | Factor Trend | Factor Score | Regional Rank | Income Rank | Global Rank |
|---|---|---|---|---|---|
| Constraints on Government Powers | — | 0.81 | 11/24 | 13/36 | 13/113 |
| Absence of Corruption | — | 0.73 | 13/24 | 20/36 | 20/113 |
| Open Government | — | 0.78 | 10/24 | 12/36 | 12/113 |
| Fundamental Rights | — | 0.75 | 16/24 | 20/36 | 21/113 |
| Order & Security | — | 0.80 | 18/24 | 26/36 | 31/113 |
| Regulatory Enforcement | — | 0.71 | 13/24 | 19/36 | 19/113 |
| Civil Justice | - | 0.65 | 16/24 | 27/36 | 28/113 |
| Criminal Justice | — | 0.68 | 14/24 | 22/36 | 22/113 |

High ▢▢ Low    ▼ Trending down    ▲ Trending up

■ United States    ▨ EU & EFTA & North America    ▨ High Income

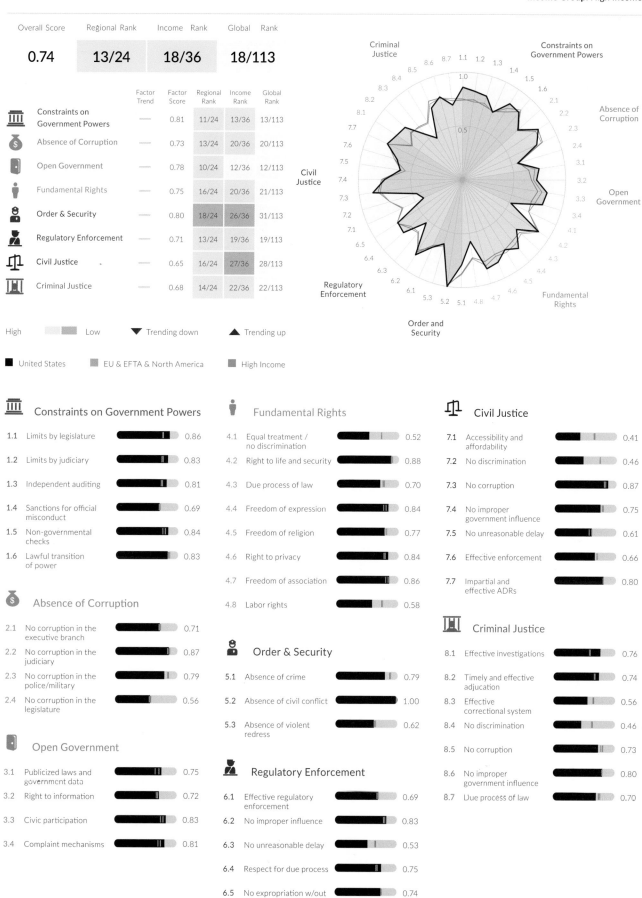

## Constraints on Government Powers

| | | |
|---|---|---|
| 1.1 | Limits by legislature | 0.86 |
| 1.2 | Limits by judiciary | 0.83 |
| 1.3 | Independent auditing | 0.81 |
| 1.4 | Sanctions for official misconduct | 0.69 |
| 1.5 | Non-governmental checks | 0.84 |
| 1.6 | Lawful transition of power | 0.83 |

## Absence of Corruption

| | | |
|---|---|---|
| 2.1 | No corruption in the executive branch | 0.71 |
| 2.2 | No corruption in the judiciary | 0.87 |
| 2.3 | No corruption in the police/military | 0.79 |
| 2.4 | No corruption in the legislature | 0.56 |

## Open Government

| | | |
|---|---|---|
| 3.1 | Publicized laws and government data | 0.75 |
| 3.2 | Right to information | 0.72 |
| 3.3 | Civic participation | 0.83 |
| 3.4 | Complaint mechanisms | 0.81 |

## Fundamental Rights

| | | |
|---|---|---|
| 4.1 | Equal treatment / no discrimination | 0.52 |
| 4.2 | Right to life and security | 0.88 |
| 4.3 | Due process of law | 0.70 |
| 4.4 | Freedom of expression | 0.84 |
| 4.5 | Freedom of religion | 0.77 |
| 4.6 | Right to privacy | 0.84 |
| 4.7 | Freedom of association | 0.86 |
| 4.8 | Labor rights | 0.58 |

## Order & Security

| | | |
|---|---|---|
| 5.1 | Absence of crime | 0.79 |
| 5.2 | Absence of civil conflict | 1.00 |
| 5.3 | Absence of violent redress | 0.62 |

## Regulatory Enforcement

| | | |
|---|---|---|
| 6.1 | Effective regulatory enforcement | 0.69 |
| 6.2 | No improper influence | 0.83 |
| 6.3 | No unreasonable delay | 0.53 |
| 6.4 | Respect for due process | 0.75 |
| 6.5 | No expropriation w/out adequate compensation | 0.74 |

## Civil Justice

| | | |
|---|---|---|
| 7.1 | Accessibility and affordability | 0.41 |
| 7.2 | No discrimination | 0.46 |
| 7.3 | No corruption | 0.87 |
| 7.4 | No improper government influence | 0.75 |
| 7.5 | No unreasonable delay | 0.61 |
| 7.6 | Effective enforcement | 0.66 |
| 7.7 | Impartial and effective ADRs | 0.80 |

## Criminal Justice

| | | |
|---|---|---|
| 8.1 | Effective investigations | 0.76 |
| 8.2 | Timely and effective adjucation | 0.74 |
| 8.3 | Effective correctional system | 0.56 |
| 8.4 | No discrimination | 0.46 |
| 8.5 | No corruption | 0.73 |
| 8.6 | No improper government influence | 0.80 |
| 8.7 | Due process of law | 0.70 |

# Uruguay

**Region:** Latin America & Caribbean
**Income Group:** High Income

| | Overall Score | Regional Rank | Income Rank | Global Rank |
|---|---|---|---|---|
| | 0.72 | 1/30 | 20/36 | 20/113 |

| | | Factor Trend | Factor Score | Regional Rank | Income Rank | Global Rank |
|---|---|---|---|---|---|---|
| 🏛️ | Constraints on Government Powers | — | 0.79 | 1/30 | 16/36 | 16/113 |
| 💰 | Absence of Corruption | — | 0.77 | 1/30 | 18/36 | 18/113 |
| 📱 | Open Government | — | 0.70 | 2/30 | 18/36 | 18/113 |
| 👤 | Fundamental Rights | — | 0.80 | 1/30 | 14/36 | 14/113 |
| 👮 | Order & Security | — | 0.73 | 7/30 | 31/36 | 52/113 |
| 👷 | Regulatory Enforcement | — | 0.69 | 1/30 | 20/36 | 20/113 |
| ⚖️ | Civil Justice | — | 0.73 | 1/30 | 17/36 | 17/113 |
| 🏛️ | Criminal Justice | — | 0.58 | 7/30 | 30/36 | 34/113 |

High ▢ Low   ▼ Trending down   ▲ Trending up

■ Uruguay   ■ Latin America & Caribbean   ■ High Income

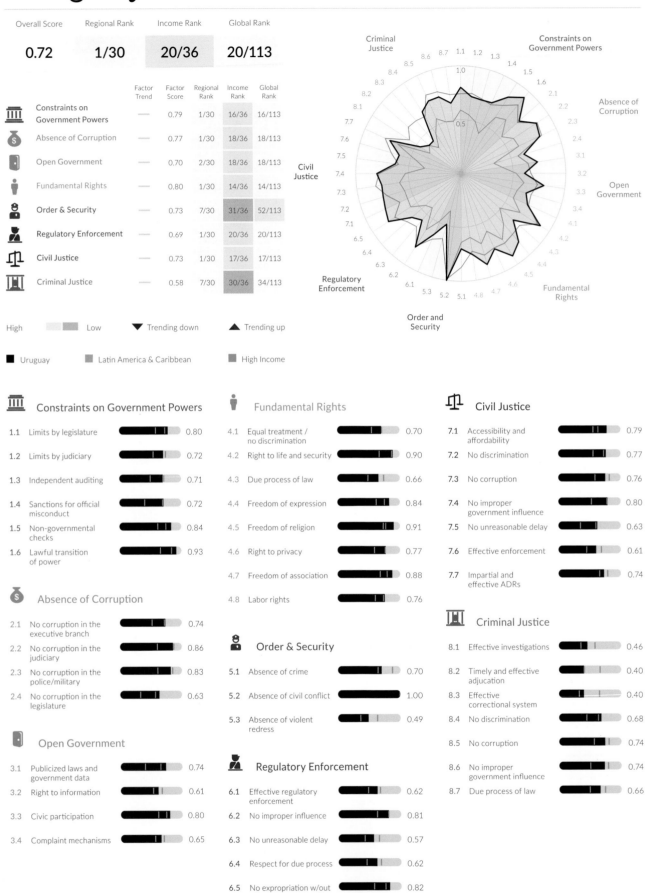

## 🏛️ Constraints on Government Powers

| | | |
|---|---|---|
| 1.1 | Limits by legislature | 0.80 |
| 1.2 | Limits by judiciary | 0.72 |
| 1.3 | Independent auditing | 0.71 |
| 1.4 | Sanctions for official misconduct | 0.72 |
| 1.5 | Non-governmental checks | 0.84 |
| 1.6 | Lawful transition of power | 0.93 |

## 💰 Absence of Corruption

| | | |
|---|---|---|
| 2.1 | No corruption in the executive branch | 0.74 |
| 2.2 | No corruption in the judiciary | 0.86 |
| 2.3 | No corruption in the police/military | 0.83 |
| 2.4 | No corruption in the legislature | 0.63 |

## 📱 Open Government

| | | |
|---|---|---|
| 3.1 | Publicized laws and government data | 0.74 |
| 3.2 | Right to information | 0.61 |
| 3.3 | Civic participation | 0.80 |
| 3.4 | Complaint mechanisms | 0.65 |

## 👤 Fundamental Rights

| | | |
|---|---|---|
| 4.1 | Equal treatment / no discrimination | 0.70 |
| 4.2 | Right to life and security | 0.90 |
| 4.3 | Due process of law | 0.66 |
| 4.4 | Freedom of expression | 0.84 |
| 4.5 | Freedom of religion | 0.91 |
| 4.6 | Right to privacy | 0.77 |
| 4.7 | Freedom of association | 0.88 |
| 4.8 | Labor rights | 0.76 |

## 👮 Order & Security

| | | |
|---|---|---|
| 5.1 | Absence of crime | 0.70 |
| 5.2 | Absence of civil conflict | 1.00 |
| 5.3 | Absence of violent redress | 0.49 |

## 👷 Regulatory Enforcement

| | | |
|---|---|---|
| 6.1 | Effective regulatory enforcement | 0.62 |
| 6.2 | No improper influence | 0.81 |
| 6.3 | No unreasonable delay | 0.57 |
| 6.4 | Respect for due process | 0.62 |
| 6.5 | No expropriation w/out adequate compensation | 0.82 |

## ⚖️ Civil Justice

| | | |
|---|---|---|
| 7.1 | Accessibility and affordability | 0.79 |
| 7.2 | No discrimination | 0.77 |
| 7.3 | No corruption | 0.76 |
| 7.4 | No improper government influence | 0.80 |
| 7.5 | No unreasonable delay | 0.63 |
| 7.6 | Effective enforcement | 0.61 |
| 7.7 | Impartial and effective ADRs | 0.74 |

## 🏛️ Criminal Justice

| | | |
|---|---|---|
| 8.1 | Effective investigations | 0.46 |
| 8.2 | Timely and effective adjudication | 0.40 |
| 8.3 | Effective correctional system | 0.40 |
| 8.4 | No discrimination | 0.68 |
| 8.5 | No corruption | 0.74 |
| 8.6 | No improper government influence | 0.74 |
| 8.7 | Due process of law | 0.66 |

# Uzbekistan

**Region:** Eastern Europe & Central Asia
**Income Group:** Lower Middle Income

| | Overall Score | Regional Rank | Income Rank | Global Rank |
|---|---|---|---|---|
| | 0.45 | 12/13 | 16/28 | 93/113 |

| | Factor Trend | Factor Score | Regional Rank | Income Rank | Global Rank |
|---|---|---|---|---|---|
| Constraints on Government Powers | — | 0.30 | 13/13 | 28/28 | 111/113 |
| Absence of Corruption | — | 0.33 | 10/13 | 20/28 | 96/113 |
| Open Government | — | 0.31 | 13/13 | 26/28 | 109/113 |
| Fundamental Rights | — | 0.36 | 12/13 | 25/28 | 104/113 |
| Order & Security | | 0.91 | 1/13 | 1/28 | 5/113 |
| Regulatory Enforcement | — | 0.45 | 8/13 | 12/28 | 81/113 |
| Civil Justice | — | 0.51 | 6/13 | 4/28 | 64/113 |
| Criminal Justice | — | 0.44 | 6/13 | 6/28 | 62/113 |

High ▮▮ Low      ▼ Trending down      ▲ Trending up

■ Uzbekistan   ▮ Eastern Europe & Central Asia   ▮ Lower Middle Income

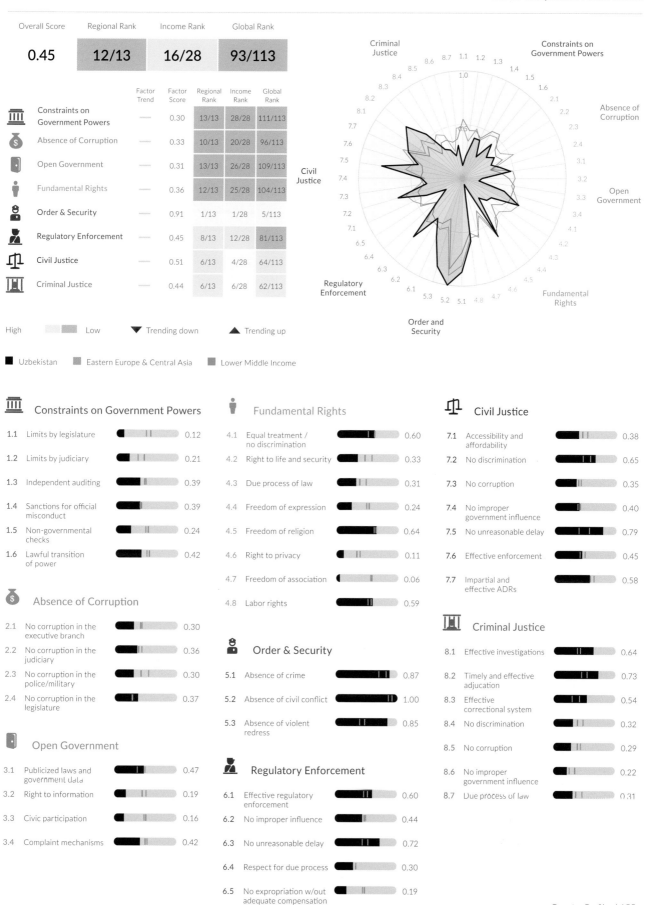

## Constraints on Government Powers

| 1.1 | Limits by legislature | 0.12 |
|---|---|---|
| 1.2 | Limits by judiciary | 0.21 |
| 1.3 | Independent auditing | 0.39 |
| 1.4 | Sanctions for official misconduct | 0.39 |
| 1.5 | Non-governmental checks | 0.24 |
| 1.6 | Lawful transition of power | 0.42 |

## Absence of Corruption

| 2.1 | No corruption in the executive branch | 0.30 |
|---|---|---|
| 2.2 | No corruption in the judiciary | 0.36 |
| 2.3 | No corruption in the police/military | 0.30 |
| 2.4 | No corruption in the legislature | 0.37 |

## Open Government

| 3.1 | Publicized laws and government data | 0.47 |
|---|---|---|
| 3.2 | Right to information | 0.19 |
| 3.3 | Civic participation | 0.16 |
| 3.4 | Complaint mechanisms | 0.42 |

## Fundamental Rights

| 4.1 | Equal treatment / no discrimination | 0.60 |
|---|---|---|
| 4.2 | Right to life and security | 0.33 |
| 4.3 | Due process of law | 0.31 |
| 4.4 | Freedom of expression | 0.24 |
| 4.5 | Freedom of religion | 0.64 |
| 4.6 | Right to privacy | 0.11 |
| 4.7 | Freedom of association | 0.06 |
| 4.8 | Labor rights | 0.59 |

## Order & Security

| 5.1 | Absence of crime | 0.87 |
|---|---|---|
| 5.2 | Absence of civil conflict | 1.00 |
| 5.3 | Absence of violent redress | 0.85 |

## Regulatory Enforcement

| 6.1 | Effective regulatory enforcement | 0.60 |
|---|---|---|
| 6.2 | No improper influence | 0.44 |
| 6.3 | No unreasonable delay | 0.72 |
| 6.4 | Respect for due process | 0.30 |
| 6.5 | No expropriation w/out adequate compensation | 0.19 |

## Civil Justice

| 7.1 | Accessibility and affordability | 0.38 |
|---|---|---|
| 7.2 | No discrimination | 0.65 |
| 7.3 | No corruption | 0.35 |
| 7.4 | No improper government influence | 0.40 |
| 7.5 | No unreasonable delay | 0.79 |
| 7.6 | Effective enforcement | 0.45 |
| 7.7 | Impartial and effective ADRs | 0.58 |

## Criminal Justice

| 8.1 | Effective investigations | 0.64 |
|---|---|---|
| 8.2 | Timely and effective adjudication | 0.73 |
| 8.3 | Effective correctional system | 0.54 |
| 8.4 | No discrimination | 0.32 |
| 8.5 | No corruption | 0.29 |
| 8.6 | No improper government influence | 0.22 |
| 8.7 | Due process of law | 0.31 |

# Venezuela

**Region:** Latin America & Caribbean
**Income Group:** Upper Middle Income

| | Overall Score | Regional Rank | Income Rank | Global Rank |
|---|---|---|---|---|
| | 0.28 | 30/30 | 37/37 | 113/113 |

| | | Factor Trend | Factor Score | Regional Rank | Income Rank | Global Rank |
|---|---|---|---|---|---|---|
| 🏛 | Constraints on Government Powers | — | 0.18 | 30/30 | 37/37 | 113/113 |
| 💰 | Absence of Corruption | ▼ | 0.25 | 30/30 | 37/37 | 110/113 |
| 🚪 | Open Government | — | 0.32 | 30/30 | 37/37 | 108/113 |
| 👤 | Fundamental Rights | ▼ | 0.33 | 30/30 | 35/37 | 107/113 |
| 👮 | Order & Security | — | 0.48 | 30/30 | 37/37 | 110/113 |
| 👷 | Regulatory Enforcement | — | 0.21 | 30/30 | 37/37 | 113/113 |
| ⚖ | Civil Justice | ▼ | 0.29 | 30/30 | 37/37 | 112/113 |
| 🏛 | Criminal Justice | — | 0.13 | 30/30 | 37/37 | 113/113 |

High ▬▬▬ Low      ▼ Trending down      ▲ Trending up

■ Venezuela    ▦ Latin America & Caribbean    ▦ Upper Middle Income

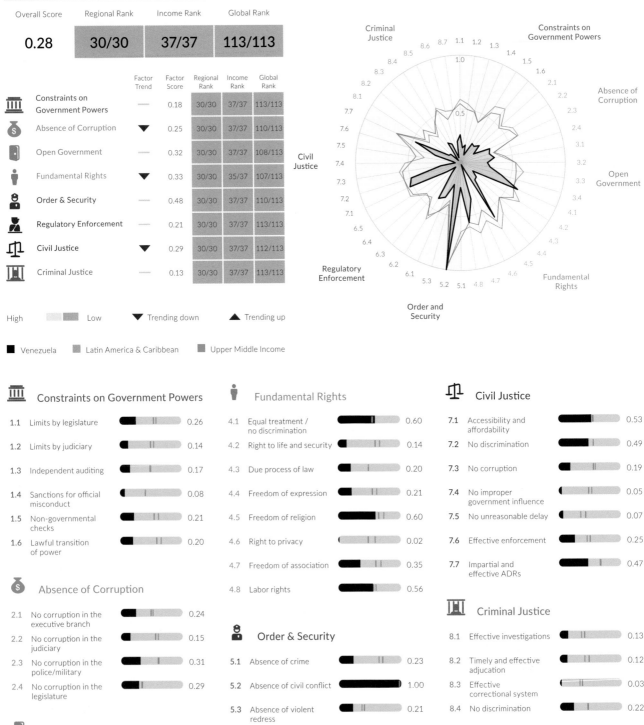

## 🏛 Constraints on Government Powers

| | | |
|---|---|---|
| 1.1 | Limits by legislature | 0.26 |
| 1.2 | Limits by judiciary | 0.14 |
| 1.3 | Independent auditing | 0.17 |
| 1.4 | Sanctions for official misconduct | 0.08 |
| 1.5 | Non-governmental checks | 0.21 |
| 1.6 | Lawful transition of power | 0.20 |

## 💰 Absence of Corruption

| | | |
|---|---|---|
| 2.1 | No corruption in the executive branch | 0.24 |
| 2.2 | No corruption in the judiciary | 0.15 |
| 2.3 | No corruption in the police/military | 0.31 |
| 2.4 | No corruption in the legislature | 0.29 |

## 🚪 Open Government

| | | |
|---|---|---|
| 3.1 | Publicized laws and government data | 0.33 |
| 3.2 | Right to information | 0.26 |
| 3.3 | Civic participation | 0.29 |
| 3.4 | Complaint mechanisms | 0.41 |

## 👤 Fundamental Rights

| | | |
|---|---|---|
| 4.1 | Equal treatment / no discrimination | 0.60 |
| 4.2 | Right to life and security | 0.14 |
| 4.3 | Due process of law | 0.20 |
| 4.4 | Freedom of expression | 0.21 |
| 4.5 | Freedom of religion | 0.60 |
| 4.6 | Right to privacy | 0.02 |
| 4.7 | Freedom of association | 0.35 |
| 4.8 | Labor rights | 0.56 |

## 👮 Order & Security

| | | |
|---|---|---|
| 5.1 | Absence of crime | 0.23 |
| 5.2 | Absence of civil conflict | 1.00 |
| 5.3 | Absence of violent redress | 0.21 |

## 👷 Regulatory Enforcement

| | | |
|---|---|---|
| 6.1 | Effective regulatory enforcement | 0.35 |
| 6.2 | No improper influence | 0.39 |
| 6.3 | No unreasonable delay | 0.13 |
| 6.4 | Respect for due process | 0.06 |
| 6.5 | No expropriation w/out adequate compensation | 0.15 |

## ⚖ Civil Justice

| | | |
|---|---|---|
| 7.1 | Accessibility and affordability | 0.53 |
| 7.2 | No discrimination | 0.49 |
| 7.3 | No corruption | 0.19 |
| 7.4 | No improper government influence | 0.05 |
| 7.5 | No unreasonable delay | 0.07 |
| 7.6 | Effective enforcement | 0.25 |
| 7.7 | Impartial and effective ADRs | 0.47 |

## 🏛 Criminal Justice

| | | |
|---|---|---|
| 8.1 | Effective investigations | 0.13 |
| 8.2 | Timely and effective adjudication | 0.12 |
| 8.3 | Effective correctional system | 0.03 |
| 8.4 | No discrimination | 0.22 |
| 8.5 | No corruption | 0.19 |
| 8.6 | No improper government influence | 0.05 |
| 8.7 | Due process of law | 0.20 |

# Vietnam

**Region:** East Asia & Pacific
**Income Group:** Lower Middle Income

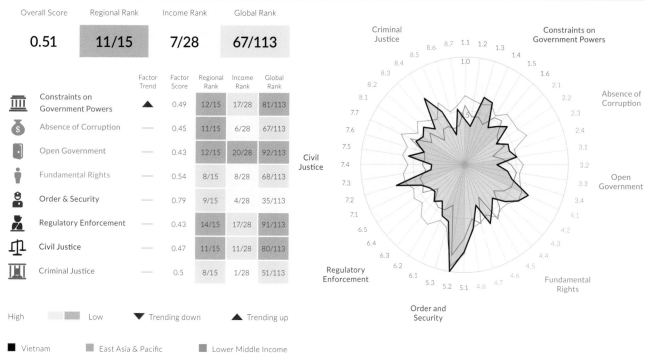

| | Overall Score | Regional Rank | Income Rank | Global Rank |
|---|---|---|---|---|
| | 0.51 | 11/15 | 7/28 | 67/113 |

| | | Factor Trend | Factor Score | Regional Rank | Income Rank | Global Rank |
|---|---|---|---|---|---|---|
| 🏛 | Constraints on Government Powers | ▲ | 0.49 | 12/15 | 17/28 | 81/113 |
| 💰 | Absence of Corruption | — | 0.45 | 11/15 | 6/28 | 67/113 |
| 🚪 | Open Government | — | 0.43 | 12/15 | 20/28 | 92/113 |
| 👤 | Fundamental Rights | — | 0.54 | 8/15 | 8/28 | 68/113 |
| 👤 | Order & Security | — | 0.79 | 9/15 | 4/28 | 35/113 |
| 👮 | Regulatory Enforcement | — | 0.43 | 14/15 | 17/28 | 91/113 |
| ⚖ | Civil Justice | — | 0.47 | 11/15 | 11/28 | 80/113 |
| ⚖ | Criminal Justice | — | 0.5 | 8/15 | 1/28 | 51/113 |

High ▢▢ Low    ▼ Trending down    ▲ Trending up

■ Vietnam    ▪ East Asia & Pacific    ▪ Lower Middle Income

## 🏛 Constraints on Government Powers

| | | |
|---|---|---|
| 1.1 | Limits by legislature | 0.42 |
| 1.2 | Limits by judiciary | 0.36 |
| 1.3 | Independent auditing | 0.65 |
| 1.4 | Sanctions for official misconduct | 0.63 |
| 1.5 | Non-governmental checks | 0.41 |
| 1.6 | Lawful transition of power | 0.47 |

## 💰 Absence of Corruption

| | | |
|---|---|---|
| 2.1 | No corruption in the executive branch | 0.54 |
| 2.2 | No corruption in the judiciary | 0.36 |
| 2.3 | No corruption in the police/military | 0.46 |
| 2.4 | No corruption in the legislature | 0.45 |

## 🚪 Open Government

| | | |
|---|---|---|
| 3.1 | Publicized laws and government data | 0.51 |
| 3.2 | Right to information | 0.31 |
| 3.3 | Civic participation | 0.42 |
| 3.4 | Complaint mechanisms | 0.48 |

## 👤 Fundamental Rights

| | | |
|---|---|---|
| 4.1 | Equal treatment / no discrimination | 0.68 |
| 4.2 | Right to life and security | 0.62 |
| 4.3 | Due process of law | 0.52 |
| 4.4 | Freedom of expression | 0.41 |
| 4.5 | Freedom of religion | 0.49 |
| 4.6 | Right to privacy | 0.60 |
| 4.7 | Freedom of association | 0.39 |
| 4.8 | Labor rights | 0.60 |

## 👤 Order & Security

| | | |
|---|---|---|
| 5.1 | Absence of crime | 0.81 |
| 5.2 | Absence of civil conflict | 1.00 |
| 5.3 | Absence of violent redress | 0.55 |

## 👮 Regulatory Enforcement

| | | |
|---|---|---|
| 6.1 | Effective regulatory enforcement | 0.52 |
| 6.2 | No improper influence | 0.40 |
| 6.3 | No unreasonable delay | 0.45 |
| 6.4 | Respect for due process | 0.38 |
| 6.5 | No expropriation w/out adequate compensation | 0.40 |

## ⚖ Civil Justice

| | | |
|---|---|---|
| 7.1 | Accessibility and affordability | 0.46 |
| 7.2 | No discrimination | 0.69 |
| 7.3 | No corruption | 0.33 |
| 7.4 | No improper government influence | 0.32 |
| 7.5 | No unreasonable delay | 0.55 |
| 7.6 | Effective enforcement | 0.41 |
| 7.7 | Impartial and effective ADRs | 0.52 |

## ⚖ Criminal Justice

| | | |
|---|---|---|
| 8.1 | Effective investigations | 0.48 |
| 8.2 | Timely and effective adjucation | 0.53 |
| 8.3 | Effective correctional system | 0.44 |
| 8.4 | No discrimination | 0.73 |
| 8.5 | No corruption | 0.54 |
| 8.6 | No improper government influence | 0.29 |
| 8.7 | Due process of law | 0.52 |

# Zambia

**Region:** Sub-Saharan Africa
**Income Group:** Lower Middle Income

| | Overall Score | Regional Rank | Income Rank | Global Rank |
|---|---|---|---|---|
| | 0.48 | 7/18 | 13/28 | 81/113 |

| | Factor Trend | Factor Score | Regional Rank | Income Rank | Global Rank |
|---|---|---|---|---|---|
| 🏛 Constraints on Government Powers | — | 0.50 | 11/18 | 16/28 | 79/113 |
| 💰 Absence of Corruption | — | 0.40 | 6/18 | 12/28 | 81/113 |
| 🚪 Open Government | — | 0.43 | 10/18 | 19/28 | 91/113 |
| 🧍 Fundamental Rights | — | 0.45 | 14/18 | 20/28 | 95/113 |
| 👤 Order & Security | — | 0.67 | 6/18 | 12/28 | 70/113 |
| 👷 Regulatory Enforcement | — | 0.45 | 8/18 | 13/28 | 83/113 |
| ⚖ Civil Justice | — | 0.50 | 7/18 | 6/28 | 67/113 |
| ⚖ Criminal Justice | — | 0.42 | 8/18 | 9/28 | 69/113 |

High ▬▬ Low    ▼ Trending down    ▲ Trending up

■ Zambia   ■ Sub-Saharan Africa   ■ Lower Middle Income

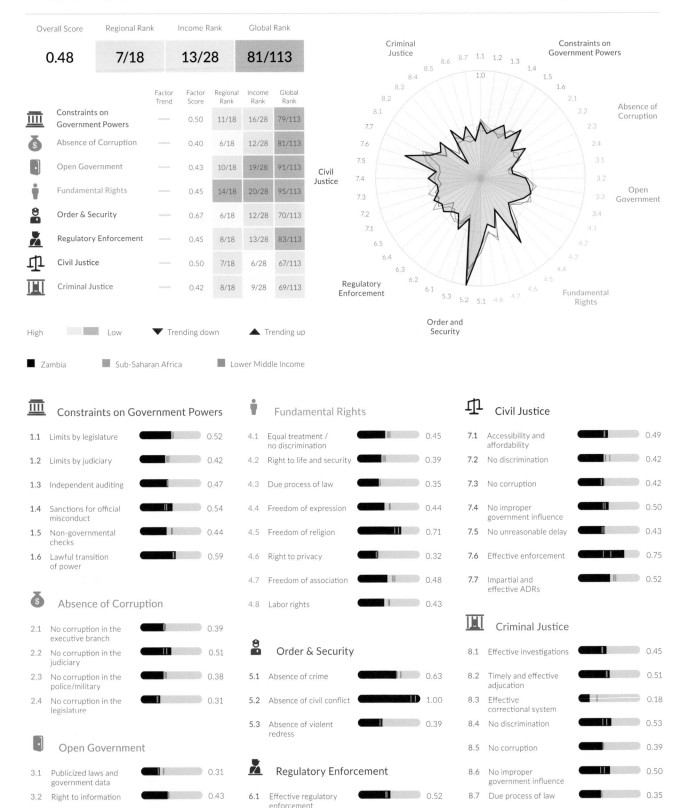

## 🏛 Constraints on Government Powers

| | | |
|---|---|---|
| 1.1 | Limits by legislature | 0.52 |
| 1.2 | Limits by judiciary | 0.42 |
| 1.3 | Independent auditing | 0.47 |
| 1.4 | Sanctions for official misconduct | 0.54 |
| 1.5 | Non-governmental checks | 0.44 |
| 1.6 | Lawful transition of power | 0.59 |

## 💰 Absence of Corruption

| | | |
|---|---|---|
| 2.1 | No corruption in the executive branch | 0.39 |
| 2.2 | No corruption in the judiciary | 0.51 |
| 2.3 | No corruption in the police/military | 0.38 |
| 2.4 | No corruption in the legislature | 0.31 |

## 🚪 Open Government

| | | |
|---|---|---|
| 3.1 | Publicized laws and government data | 0.31 |
| 3.2 | Right to information | 0.43 |
| 3.3 | Civic participation | 0.47 |
| 3.4 | Complaint mechanisms | 0.50 |

## 🧍 Fundamental Rights

| | | |
|---|---|---|
| 4.1 | Equal treatment / no discrimination | 0.45 |
| 4.2 | Right to life and security | 0.39 |
| 4.3 | Due process of law | 0.35 |
| 4.4 | Freedom of expression | 0.44 |
| 4.5 | Freedom of religion | 0.71 |
| 4.6 | Right to privacy | 0.32 |
| 4.7 | Freedom of association | 0.48 |
| 4.8 | Labor rights | 0.43 |

## 👤 Order & Security

| | | |
|---|---|---|
| 5.1 | Absence of crime | 0.63 |
| 5.2 | Absence of civil conflict | 1.00 |
| 5.3 | Absence of violent redress | 0.39 |

## 👷 Regulatory Enforcement

| | | |
|---|---|---|
| 6.1 | Effective regulatory enforcement | 0.52 |
| 6.2 | No improper influence | 0.39 |
| 6.3 | No unreasonable delay | 0.41 |
| 6.4 | Respect for due process | 0.47 |
| 6.5 | No expropriation w/out adequate compensation | 0.44 |

## ⚖ Civil Justice

| | | |
|---|---|---|
| 7.1 | Accessibility and affordability | 0.49 |
| 7.2 | No discrimination | 0.42 |
| 7.3 | No corruption | 0.42 |
| 7.4 | No improper government influence | 0.50 |
| 7.5 | No unreasonable delay | 0.43 |
| 7.6 | Effective enforcement | 0.75 |
| 7.7 | Impartial and effective ADRs | 0.52 |

## ⚖ Criminal Justice

| | | |
|---|---|---|
| 8.1 | Effective investigations | 0.45 |
| 8.2 | Timely and effective adjudication | 0.51 |
| 8.3 | Effective correctional system | 0.18 |
| 8.4 | No discrimination | 0.53 |
| 8.5 | No corruption | 0.39 |
| 8.6 | No improper government influence | 0.50 |
| 8.7 | Due process of law | 0.35 |

# Zimbabwe

| | Overall Score | Regional Rank | Income Rank | Global Rank |
|---|---|---|---|---|
| | 0.37 | 17/18 | 11/12 | 108/113 |

| | Factor Trend | Factor Score | Regional Rank | Income Rank | Global Rank |
|---|---|---|---|---|---|
| 🏛 Constraints on Government Powers | — | 0.26 | 18/18 | 12/12 | 112/113 |
| 💰 Absence of Corruption | — | 0.29 | 14/18 | 9/12 | 104/113 |
| 📗 Open Government | — | 0.30 | 17/18 | 11/12 | 110/113 |
| 👤 Fundamental Rights | — | 0.28 | 18/18 | 12/12 | 113/113 |
| 👤 Order & Security | — | 0.67 | 7/18 | 4/12 | 71/113 |
| 👷 Regulatory Enforcement | — | 0.35 | 17/18 | 11/12 | 108/113 |
| ⚖ Civil Justice | — | 0.46 | 11/18 | 5/12 | 84/113 |
| ⚖ Criminal Justice | — | 0.36 | 12/18 | 7/12 | 85/113 |

High ▢▢ Low   ▼ Trending down   ▲ Trending up

■ Zimbabwe   ▨ Sub-Saharan Africa   ▨ Low Income

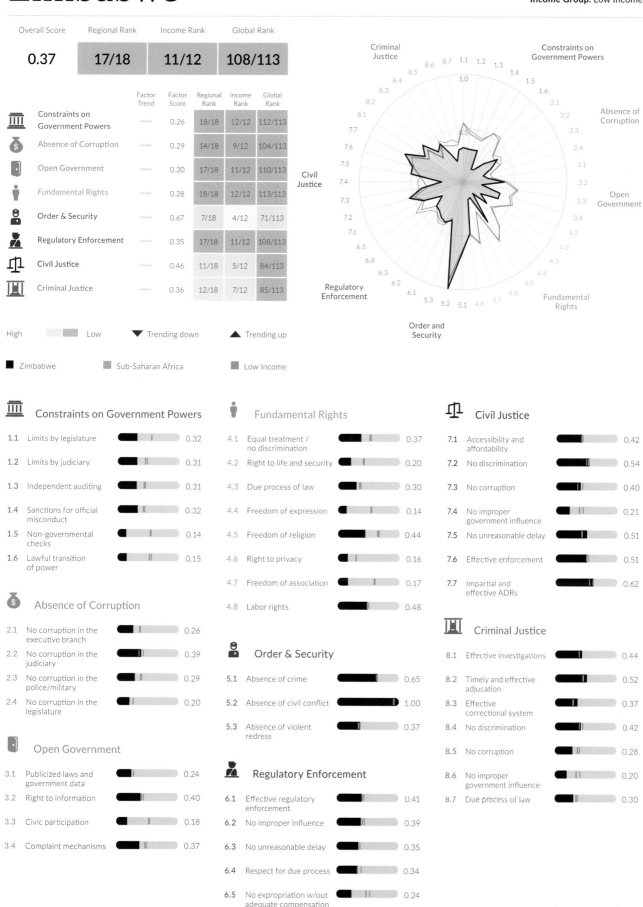

## 🏛 Constraints on Government Powers

| | | |
|---|---|---|
| 1.1 | Limits by legislature | 0.32 |
| 1.2 | Limits by judiciary | 0.31 |
| 1.3 | Independent auditing | 0.31 |
| 1.4 | Sanctions for official misconduct | 0.32 |
| 1.5 | Non-governmental checks | 0.14 |
| 1.6 | Lawful transition of power | 0.15 |

## 💰 Absence of Corruption

| | | |
|---|---|---|
| 2.1 | No corruption in the executive branch | 0.26 |
| 2.2 | No corruption in the judiciary | 0.39 |
| 2.3 | No corruption in the police/military | 0.29 |
| 2.4 | No corruption in the legislature | 0.20 |

## 📗 Open Government

| | | |
|---|---|---|
| 3.1 | Publicized laws and government data | 0.24 |
| 3.2 | Right to information | 0.40 |
| 3.3 | Civic participation | 0.18 |
| 3.4 | Complaint mechanisms | 0.37 |

## 👤 Fundamental Rights

| | | |
|---|---|---|
| 4.1 | Equal treatment / no discrimination | 0.37 |
| 4.2 | Right to life and security | 0.20 |
| 4.3 | Due process of law | 0.30 |
| 4.4 | Freedom of expression | 0.14 |
| 4.5 | Freedom of religion | 0.44 |
| 4.6 | Right to privacy | 0.16 |
| 4.7 | Freedom of association | 0.17 |
| 4.8 | Labor rights | 0.48 |

## 👤 Order & Security

| | | |
|---|---|---|
| 5.1 | Absence of crime | 0.65 |
| 5.2 | Absence of civil conflict | 1.00 |
| 5.3 | Absence of violent redress | 0.37 |

## 👷 Regulatory Enforcement

| | | |
|---|---|---|
| 6.1 | Effective regulatory enforcement | 0.41 |
| 6.2 | No improper influence | 0.39 |
| 6.3 | No unreasonable delay | 0.35 |
| 6.4 | Respect for due process | 0.34 |
| 6.5 | No expropriation w/out adequate compensation | 0.24 |

## ⚖ Civil Justice

| | | |
|---|---|---|
| 7.1 | Accessibility and affordability | 0.42 |
| 7.2 | No discrimination | 0.54 |
| 7.3 | No corruption | 0.40 |
| 7.4 | No improper government influence | 0.21 |
| 7.5 | No unreasonable delay | 0.51 |
| 7.6 | Effective enforcement | 0.51 |
| 7.7 | Impartial and effective ADRs | 0.62 |

## ⚖ Criminal Justice

| | | |
|---|---|---|
| 8.1 | Effective investigations | 0.44 |
| 8.2 | Timely and effective adjucation | 0.52 |
| 8.3 | Effective correctional system | 0.37 |
| 8.4 | No discrimination | 0.42 |
| 8.5 | No corruption | 0.28 |
| 8.6 | No improper government influence | 0.20 |
| 8.7 | Due process of law | 0.30 |

# Methodology

# Methodology

The *WJP Rule of Law Index* is the first attempt to systematically and comprehensively quantify the rule of law around the world, and remains unique in its operationalization of rule of law dimensions into concrete questions.

The *WJP Rule of Law Index 2016* report presents information on eight composite factors that are further disaggregated into 44 specific sub-factors. An outline of these factors and sub-factors begins on the next page. Factor 9, informal justice, is included in the framework, but has been excluded from the aggregated scores and rankings in order to provide meaningful cross-country comparisons. In attempting to present an image that accurately portrays the rule of law as experienced by ordinary people, each score of the *Index* is calculated using a large number of questions drawn from two original data sources collected by the World Justice Project in each country: a General Population Poll (GPP) and a series of Qualified Respondents' Questionnaires (QRQs).

These two data sources collect up-to-date firsthand information that is not available at the global level, and constitute the world's most comprehensive dataset of its kind. They capture the experiences and perceptions of ordinary citizens and in-country professionals concerning the performance of the state and its agents and the actual operation of the legal framework in their country. The country scores and rankings presented in this report are built from more than 500 variables drawn from the assessments of more than 110,000 citizens and 2,700 legal experts in 113 countries and jurisdictions, making it the most accurate portrayal of the factors that contribute to shaping the rule of law in a nation.

# The Indicators of the World Justice Project's Rule of Law Index®

The *World Justice Project's Rule of Law Index* comprises 44 sub-factors organized around eight aggregated factors. The following table presents a summary of the concepts underlying each of these sub-factors. A full map of the variables used to calculate the *Index* scores is available in the "Methodology" section of the *WJP Rule of Law Index* website.

## Factor 1: Constraints on Government Powers

**1.1 Government powers are effectively limited by the legislature**
Measures whether legislative bodies have the ability in practice to exercise effective checks and oversight of the government.

**1.2 Government powers are effectively limited by the judiciary**
Measures whether the judiciary has the independence and the ability in practice to exercise effective checks on the government.

**1.3 Government powers are effectively limited by independent auditing and review**
Measures whether comptrollers or auditors, as well as national human rights ombudsman agencies, have sufficient independence and the ability to exercise effective checks and oversight of the government.

**1.4 Government officials are sanctioned for misconduct**
Measures whether government officials in the executive, legislature, judiciary, and the police are investigated, prosecuted, and punished for official misconduct and other violations.

**1.5 Government powers are subject to non-governmental checks**
Measures whether an independent media, civil society organizations, political parties, and individuals are free to report and comment on government policies without fear of retaliation.

**1.6 Transition of power is subject to the law**
Measures whether government officials are elected or appointed in accordance with the rules and procedures set forth in the constitution. Where elections take place, it also measures the integrity of the electoral process, including access to the ballot, the absence of intimidation, and public scrutiny of election results.

## Factor 2: Absence of Corruption

**2.1 Government officials in the executive branch do not use public office for private gain**
Measures the prevalence of bribery, informal payments, and other inducements in the delivery of public services and the enforcement of regulations. It also measures whether government procurement and public works contracts are awarded through an open and competitive bidding process, and whether government officials at various levels of the executive branch refrain from embezzling public funds.

**2.2 Government officials in the judicial branch do not use public office for private gain**
Measures whether judges and judicial officials refrain from soliciting and accepting bribes to perform duties or expedite processes, and whether the judiciary and judicial rulings are free of improper influence by the government, private interests, and criminal organizations.

**2.3 Government officials in the police and the military do not use public office for private gain**
Measures whether police officers and criminal investigators refrain from soliciting and accepting bribes to perform basic police services or to investigate crimes, and whether government officials in the police and the military are free of improper influence by private interests or criminal organizations.

**2.4 Government officials in the legislative branch do not use public office for private gain**
Measures whether members of the legislature refrain from soliciting or accepting bribes or other inducements in exchange for political favors or favorable votes on legislation.

## Factor 3: Open Government

**3.1  Publicized laws and government data**
Measures whether basic laws and information on legal rights are publicly available, presented in plain language, and are made accessible in all languages. It also measures the quality and accessibility of information published by the government in print or online, and whether administrative regulations, drafts of legislation, and high court decisions are made accessible to the public in a timely manner.

**3.2  Right to information**
Measures whether requests for information held by a government agency are granted, whether these requests are granted within a reasonable time period, if the information provided is pertinent and complete, and if requests for information are granted at a reasonable cost and without having to pay a bribe. It also measures whether people are aware of their right to information, and whether relevant records are accessible to the public upon request.

**3.3  Civic participation**
Measures the effectiveness of civic participation mechanisms, including the protection of the freedoms of opinion and expression, assembly and association, and the right to petition the government. It also measures whether people can voice concerns to various government officers, and whether government officials provide sufficient information and notice about decisions affecting the community.

**3.4  Complaint mechanisms**
Measures whether people are able to bring specific complaints to the government about the provision of public services or the performance of government officers in carrying out their legal duties in practice, and how government officials respond to such complaints.

## Factor 4: Fundamental Rights

**4.1  Equal treatment and absence of discrimination**
Measures whether individuals are free from discrimination - based on socio-economic status, gender, ethnicity, religion, national origin, or sexual orientation, or gender identity - including with respect to public services, employment, court proceedings, and the justice system.

**4.2  The right to life and security of the person is effectively guaranteed**
Measures whether the police inflict physical harm upon criminal suspects during arrest and interrogation, and whether political dissidents or members of the media are subjected to unreasonable searches or to arrest, dentention, imprisonment, threats, abusive treatment or violence.

**4.3  Due process of law and rights of the accused**
Measures whether the basic rights of criminal suspects are respected, including the presumption of innocence and the freedom from arbitrary arrest and unreasonable pre-trial detention. It also measures whether criminal suspects are able to access and challenge evidence used against them, whether they are subject to abusive treatment, and whether they are provided with adequate legal assistance. In addition, it also measures whether the basic rights of prisoners are respected once they have been convicted of a crime.

**4.4  Freedom of opinion and expression is effectively guaranteed**
Measures whether an independent media, civil society organizations, political parties, and individuals are free to report and comment on government policies without fear of retaliation.

**4.5  Freedom of belief and religion is effectively guaranteed**
Measures whether members of religious minorities can worship and conduct religious practices freely and publicly, and whether non-adherents are protected from having to submit to religious laws.

**4.6 Freedom from arbitrary interference with privacy is effectively guaranteed**
Measures whether the police or other government officials conduct physical searches without warrants, or intercept electronic communications of private individuals without judicial authorization.

**4.7 Freedom of assembly and association is effectively guaranteed**
Measures whether people can freely attend community meetings, join political organizations, hold peaceful public demonstrations, sign petitions, and express opinions against government policies and actions without fear of retaliation.

**4.8 Fundamental labor rights are effectively guaranteed**
Measures the effective enforcement of fundamental labor rights, including freedom of association and the right to collective bargaining, the absence of discrimination with respect to employment, and freedom from forced labor and child labor.

## Factor 5: Order & Security

**5.1 Crime is effectively controlled**
Measures the prevalence of common crimes, including homicide, kidnapping, burglary and theft, armed robbery, and extortion, as well as people's general perceptions of safety in their communities.

**5.2 Civil conflict is effectively limited**
Measures whether people are effectively protected from armed conflict and terrorism.

**5.3 People do not resort to violence to redress personal grievances**
Measures whether people resort to intimidation or violence to resolve civil disputes amongst themselves, or to seek redress from the government, and whether people are free from mob violence.

## Factor 6: Regulatory Enforcement

**6.1 Government regulations are effectively enforced**
Measures whether government regulations, such as labor, environmental, public health, commercial, and consumer protection regulations, are effectively enforced.

**6.2 Government regulations are applied and enforced without improper influence**
Measures whether the enforcement of regulations is subject to bribery or improper influence by private interests, and whether public services, such as the issuance of permits and licenses and the administration of public health services, are provided without bribery or other inducements.

**6.3 Administrative proceedings are conducted without unreasonable delay**
Measures whether administrative proceedings at the national and local levels are conducted without unreasonable delay.

**6.4 Due process is respected in administrative proceedings**
Measures whether the due process of law is respected in administrative proceedings conducted by national and local authorities, including in such areas as the environment, taxes, and labor.

**6.5 The government does not expropriate without lawful process and adequate compensation**
Measures whether the government respects the property rights of people and corporations, refrains from the illegal seizure of private property, and provides adequate compensation when property is legally expropriated.

## Factor 7: Civil Justice

**7.1 People can access and afford civil justice**
Measures the accessibility and affordability of civil courts, including whether people are aware of available remedies, can access and afford legal advice and representation, and can access the court system without incurring unreasonable fees, encountering unreasonable procedural hurdles, or experiencing physical or linguistic barriers.

**7.2 Civil justice is free of discrimination**
Measures whether the civil justice system discriminates in practice based on socio-economic status, gender, ethnicity, religion, national origin, sexual orientation, or gender identity.

**7.3 Civil justice is free of corruption**
Measures whether the civil justice system is free of bribery and improper influence by private interests.

**7.4 Civil justice is free of improper government influence**
Measures whether the civil justice system is free of improper government or political influence.

**7.5 Civil justice is not subject to unreasonable delay**
Measures whether civil justice proceedings are conducted and judgments are produced in a timely manner without unreasonable delay.

**7.6 Civil justice is effectively enforced**
Measures the effectiveness and timeliness of the enforcement of civil justice decisions and judgments in practice.

**7.7 Alternative dispute resolution mechanisms are accessible, impartial, and effective**
Measures whether alternative dispute resolution mechanisms (ADRs) are affordable, efficient, enforceable, and free from corruption.

## Factor 8: Criminal Justice

**8.1 Criminal investigative system is effective**
Measures whether perpetrators of crimes are effectively apprehended and charged. It also measures whether police, investigators, and prosecutors have adequate resources, are free of corruption, and perform their duties competently.

**8.2 Criminal adjudiciation system is timely and effective**
Measures whether perpetrators of crimes are effectively prosecuted and punished. It also measures whether criminal judges and other judicial officers are competent and produce speedy decisions.

**8.3 Correctional system is effective in reducing criminal behavior**
Measures whether correctional institutions are secure, respect prisoners' rights, and are effective in preventing recidivism.

**8.4 Criminal system is impartial**
Measures whether the police and criminal judges are impartial and whether they discriminate in practice based on socio-economic status, gender, ethnicity, religion, national origin, sexual orientation, or gender identity.

**8.5 Criminal system is free of corruption**
Measures whether the police, prosecutors, and judges are free from bribery and improper influence from criminal organizations.

**8.6 Criminal justice is free of improper government influence**
Measures whether the criminal justice system is independent from government or political influence.

**8.7 Due process of law and rights of the accused**
Measures whether the basic rights of criminal suspects are respected, including the presumption of innocence and the freedom from arbitrary arrest and unreasonable pre-trial detention. It also measures whether criminal suspects are able to access and challenge evidence used against them, whether they are subject to abusive treatment, and whether they are provided with adequate legal assistance. In addition, it measures whether the basic rights of prisoners are respected once they have been convicted of a crime.

## Data Sources

Every year the WJP collects data from representative samples of the general public (the General Population Polls or GPPs) and legal professionals (the Qualified Respondents' Questionnaires or QRQs) to compute the *Index* scores and rankings. The GPP surveys provide firsthand information on the experiences and the perceptions of ordinary people regarding a range of pertinent rule of law information, including their dealings with the government, the ease of interacting with state bureaucracy, the extent of bribery and corruption, the availability of dispute resolution systems, and the prevalence of common crimes to which they are exposed. The GPP questionnaire includes 101 perception-based questions and 106 experience-based questions, along with socio-demographic information on all respondents. The questionnaire is translated into local languages, adapted to common expressions, and administered by leading local polling companies using a probability sample of 1,000 respondents in the three largest cities of each country.[1] Depending on the particular situation of each country, three different polling methodologies are used: face-to-face, telephone, or online. The GPPs are carried out in each country every other year. The polling data used in this year's report were collected during the fall of 2013 (for 1 country), the fall of 2014 (for 51 countries), and the summer of 2016 (for 61 countries). Detailed information regarding the cities covered, the polling companies contracted to administer the questionnaire, and the polling methodology employed in each of the 113 countries is presented on page 168.

The QRQs complement the polling data with assessments from in-country professionals with expertise in civil and commercial law, criminal justice, labor law, and public health. These questionnaires gather timely input from practitioners who frequently interact with state institutions, including information on the efficacy of courts, the strength of regulatory enforcement, and the reliability of accountability mechanisms. The questionnaires contain close-ended perception questions and several hypothetical scenarios with highly detailed factual assumptions aimed at ensuring comparability across countries. The QRQ surveys are conducted annually, and the questionnaires are completed by respondents selected from directories of law firms, universities and colleges, research organizations, and non-governmental organizations, as well as through referrals from the WJP global network of practitioners, and vetted by WJP staff based on their expertise. The expert surveys are administered in three languages: English, French, and Spanish. The QRQ data for this report include over 2,700 surveys, representing an average of 24 respondents per country. These data were collected from May through September 2016.

## Data Cleaning and Score Computation

Once collected, the data are carefully processed to arrive at country-level scores. As a first step, the respondent-level data are edited to exclude partially-completed surveys, suspicious data, and outliers (which are detected using the Z-score method). Individual answers are then mapped onto the 44 sub-factors of the *Index* (or onto the intermediate categories that make up each sub-factor), codified so that all values fall between 0 (least rule of law) and 1 (most rule of law), and aggregated at the country level using the simple (or unweighted) average of all respondents.

To allow for an easier comparison across years, the 2016 scores have been normalized using the Min-Max method with a base year of 2015. These normalized scores were then successively aggregated from the variable level all the way up to the factor level to produce the final country scores and rankings. In most cases, the GPP and QRQ questions are equally weighted in the calculation of the scores of the intermediate categories (sub-factors and sub-sub-factors). A full picture of how questions are mapped onto indicators and how they are weighted is presented in the WJP website.

## Data Validation

As a final step, data are validated and cross-checked against qualitative and quantitative third-party sources to provide an additional layer of analysis and to identify possible mistakes or inconsistencies within the data. The third-party data sources used to cross-check the *Index* scores are described in Botero and Ponce (2011).

---

[1] This year, the WJP added 11 Latin American and Caribbean countries to the *Index*. Due to the small populations of many of these countries and the difficulties of meeting the sample quotas in the three largest cities, the sampling plan was adjusted in some cases. One adjustment was to decrease the sample size to 500 respondents. A second was to conduct a nationally representative poll that covered a larger portion of the country. For more information on the specific countries and sample sizes, see page 168 on city coverage and polling methodology.

# City Coverage and Polling Methodology in the 113 Indexed Countries & Jurisdictions

| COUNTRY/ JURISDICTION | CITIES COVERED | POLLING COMPANY | METHODOLOGY | SAMPLE | YEAR |
|---|---|---|---|---|---|
| Afghanistan | Kabul, Kandahar, Herat | ACSOR Surveys, a subsidiary of D3 Systems, Inc. | Face-to-face | 1005 | 2016 |
| Albania | Tirana, Durres, Fier | IDRA Research & Consulting | Face-to-face | 1000 | 2016 |
| Antigua & Barbuda | Nationally representative sample | Mercaplan | Face-to-face | 510 | 2016 |
| Argentina | Buenos Aires, Cordoba, Rosario | Statmark Group | Face-to-face | 1006 | 2016 |
| Australia | Sydney, Melbourne, Brisbane | Survey Sampling International | Online | 1000 | 2016 |
| Austria | Vienna, Graz, Linz | Survey Sampling International | Online | 1008 | 2014 |
| Bahamas | Nassau, Freeport, Lucaya | CID-Gallup Latin America | Face-to-face | 504 | 2016 |
| Bangladesh | Dhaka, Chittagong, Khulna | Org-Quest Research | Face-to-face | 1000 | 2016 |
| Barbados | Nationally representative sample | Mercaplan | Face-to-face | 506 | 2016 |
| Belarus | Minsk, Gomel, Mogilev | Market Research & Polls - EURASIA (MRP-EURASIA) | Face-to-face | 1000 | 2014 |
| Belgium | Brussels, Antwerp, Liège | YouGov | Online | 1001 | 2016 |
| Belize | Belize City, San Ignacio, Belmopan | CID-Gallup Latin America | Face-to-face | 1020 | 2014 |
| Bolivia | La Paz, Santa Cruz, Cochabamba | CAPTURA Consulting SRL | Face-to-face | 1000 | 2016 |
| Bosnia & Herzegovina | Sarajevo, Tuzla, Banja Luka | Market Research & Polls - EURASIA (MRP-EURASIA) | Face-to-face | 1000 | 2014 |
| Botswana | Molepolole, Gaborone, Francistown | Intraspace Market Consultancy Ltd. | Face-to-face | 1000 | 2016 |
| Brazil | Rio de Janeiro, Salvador, Sao Paolo | IBOPE Market Research | Face-to-face | 1000 | 2014 |
| Bulgaria | Sofia, Plovdiv, Varna | Alpha Research | Face-to-face | 1001 | 2016 |
| Burkina Faso | Ouagadougou, Bobo Dioulasso, Dédougou | TNS-RMS Cameroon | Face-to-face | 1000 | 2014 |
| Cambodia | Phnom Penh, Battambang, Kampong Cham | Indochina Research | Face-to-face | 1000 | 2014 |
| Cameroon | Douala, Yaoundé, Bamenda | Liaison Marketing | Face-to-face | 1000 | 2016 |
| Canada | Toronto, Montreal, Vancouver | Survey Sampling International | Online | 920 | 2014 |
| Chile | Santiago, Valparaiso, Concepcion | D3 Systems, Inc. | Face-to-face | 1000 | 2014 |
| China | Shanghai, Beijing, Chongqing | WJP in collaboration with local partner | Face-to-face | 1014 | 2016 |
| Colombia | Bogotá, Medellín, Cali | Tempo Group | Face-to-face | 1007 | 2016 |
| Costa Rica | San Jose, Alajuela, Cartago | CID-Gallup Latin America | Face-to-face | 1020 | 2014 |
| Cote d'Ivoire | Abidjan, San Pedro, Bouake | TNS-RMS Cameroon | Face-to-face | 1000 | 2014 |
| Croatia | Zagreb, Split, Rijeka | Ipsos d.o.o. | Face-to-face | 1000 | 2016 |
| Czech Republic | Prague, Brno, Ostrava | Survey Sampling International | Online | 997 | 2014 |
| Denmark | Copenhagen, Arhus, Odense | SIS International Research | Online | 1050 | 2014 |
| Dominica | Nationally representative sample | Statmark Group | Face-to-face | 500 | 2016 |
| Dominican Republic | Santo Domingo, Santiago, La Romana | CID-Gallup Latin America | Face-to-face | 1018 | 2016 |
| Ecuador | Quito, Guayaquil, Cuenca | Statmark Group | Face-to-face | 1000 | 2014 |
| Egypt | Cairo, Alexandria, Giza | D3 Systems, Inc./WJP in collaboration with local partner | Phone/Face-to-face | 300/1000 | 2014/2012 |
| El Salvador | San Salvador, Santa Ana, San Miguel | CID-Gallup Latin America | Face-to-face | 1004 | 2016 |

| COUNTRY/ JURISDICTION | CITIES COVERED | POLLING COMPANY | METHODOLOGY | SAMPLE | YEAR |
|---|---|---|---|---|---|
| Estonia | Tallinn, Tartu, Narva | Norstat | Online | 800 | 2014 |
| Ethiopia | Addis Ababa | Infinite Insight | Face-to-face | 570 | 2014 |
| Finland | Helsinki, Espoo, Tampere | SIS International Research | Online | 1050 | 2014 |
| France | Paris, Lyon, Marseille | YouGov | Online | 1011 | 2016 |
| Georgia | Tbilisi, Kutaisi, Batumi | ACT | Face-to-face | 1000 | 2014 |
| Germany | Berlin, Hamburg, Munich | YouGov | Online | 1012 | 2016 |
| Ghana | Accra, Kumasi, Sekondi-Takoradi | FACTS International Ghana Limited | Face-to-face | 1016 | 2016 |
| Greece | Athens, Thessaloniki, Patras | Survey Sampling International | Online | 1000 | 2014 |
| Grenada | Nationally representative sample | Mercaplan | Face-to-face | 510 | 2016 |
| Guatemala | Guatemala City, Villa Nueva, Mixco | CID-Gallup Latin America | Face-to-face | 1036 | 2016 |
| Guyana | Georgetown, Linden, New Amsterdam | CID-Gallup Latin America | Face-to-face | 506 | 2016 |
| Honduras | Tegucigalpa, San Pedro Sula, La Ceiba | CID-Gallup Latin America | Face-to-face | 1020 | 2014 |
| Hong Kong SAR, China | Hong Kong | IBI Partners | Face-to-face | 1010 | 2014 |
| Hungary | Budapest, Debrecen, Szeged | Market Research & Polls - EURASIA (MRP-EURASIA) | Face-to-face | 1000 | 2014 |
| India | Mumbai, Delhi, Bangalore | DataPrompt International Pvt. Ltd. | Face-to-face | 1002 | 2016 |
| Indonesia | Jakarta, Surabaya, Bandung | MRI-Marketing Research Indonesia | Face-to-face | 1011 | 2014 |
| Iran | Tehran, Mashhad, Isfahan | Ipsos Public Affairs | Telephone | 1005 | 2016 |
| Italy | Rome, Milan, Naples | Survey Sampling International | Online | 1000 | 2014 |
| Jamaica | Kingston & St. Andrew, St. Catherine, St. James | Statmark Group | Face-to-face | 1000 | 2014 |
| Japan | Tokyo, Osaka, Nagoya | Survey Sampling International | Online | 1000 | 2016 |
| Jordan | Amman, Irbid, Zarqa | WJP in collaboration with local partner | Face-to-face | 1000 | 2016 |
| Kazakhstan | Almaty, Astana, Shymkent | WJP in collaboration with local partner | Face-to-face | 1000 | 2016 |
| Kenya | Nairobi, Mombasa, Nakuru | Infinite Insight | Face-to-face | 1085 | 2016 |
| Kyrgyzstan | Bishkek, Osh, Jalalabad | WJP in collaboration with local partner | Face-to-face | 1000 | 2016 |
| Lebanon | Beirut, Tripoli, Sidon | IIACSS | Face-to-face | 1003 | 2014 |
| Liberia | Monrovia, Gbarnga, Kakata | FACTS International Ghana Limited | Face-to-face | 1008 | 2016 |
| Macedonia, FYR | Skopje, Kumanovo, Bitola | Market Research & Polls - EURASIA (MRP-EURASIA) | Face-to-face | 1000 | 2014 |
| Madagascar | Antananarivo, Antsirabe, Toamasina | DCDM Research | Face-to-face | 1000 | 2014 |
| Malawi | Blantyre, Lilongwe, Mzuzu | Consumer Options Ltd. | Face-to-face | 997 | 2014 |
| Malaysia | Kuala Lumpur, Johor Bahru, Ipoh | IBI Partners | Face-to-face | 1011 | 2014 |
| Mexico | Mexico City, Guadalajara, Monterrey | Data Opinion Publica y Mercados | Face-to-face | 1005 | 2014 |
| Moldova | Chisinau, Balti, Cahul | Market Research & Polls - EURASIA (MRP-EURASIA) | Face-to-face | 1000 | 2014 |
| Mongolia | Ulaanbaatar, Darkhan, Erdenet | Sant Maral | Face-to-face | 1000 | 2014 |
| Morocco | Casablanca, Rabat, Marrakesh | Ipsos Public Affairs | Face-to-face | 1000 | 2013 |

| COUNTRY/ JURISDICTION | CITIES COVERED | POLLING COMPANY | METHODOLOGY | SAMPLE | YEAR |
|---|---|---|---|---|---|
| Myanmar | Mandalay, Naypyidaw, Yangon | APMI Partners | Face-to-face | 1008 | 2016 |
| Nepal | Kathmandu, Pokhara, Biratnagar | Solutions Consultant | Face-to-face | 1000 | 2014 |
| Netherlands | Amsterdam, Rotterdam, The Hague | YouGov | Online | 1017 | 2016 |
| New Zealand | Auckland, Wellington, Christchurch | IBI Partners | Telephone | 1003 | 2014 |
| Nicaragua | Managua, Masaya, Leon | CID-Gallup Latin America | Face-to-face | 1020 | 2014 |
| Nigeria | Lagos, Oyo, Kano | Marketing Support Consultancy | Face-to-face | 1000 | 2016 |
| Norway | Oslo, Bergen, Trondheim | SIS International Research | Online | 1050 | 2014 |
| Pakistan | Karachi, Lahore, Faisalabad | Gallup Pakistan (affiliated with Gallup International) | Face-to-face | 1920 | 2016 |
| Panama | Panama City, San Miguelito, David | CID-Gallup Latin America | Face-to-face | 1020 | 2014 |
| Peru | Lima, Arequipa, Trujillo | Datum Internacional S.A. | Face-to-face | 1007 | 2016 |
| Philippines | Manila, Davao, Cebu | APMI Partners | Face-to-face | 1008 | 2016 |
| Poland | Warsaw, Lodz, Krakow | IQS Sp. z o.o. | Face-to-face | 1000 | 2016 |
| Portugal | Lisbon, Villa Nova de Gaia, Sintra | Survey Sampling International | Online | 1001 | 2014 |
| Republic of Korea | Seoul, Busan, Incheon | Survey Sampling International | Online | 1025 | 2016 |
| Romania | Bucharest, Cluj-Napoca, Timisoara | Ipsos S.R.L. | Face-to-face | 1000 | 2016 |
| Russia | Moscow, Saint Petersburg, Novosibirsk | WJP in collaboration with local partner | Face-to-face | 1000 | 2016 |
| Senegal | Dakar, Thiès, Saint-Louis | Liaison Marketing | Face-to-face | 1001 | 2014 |
| Serbia | Belgrade, Novi Sad, Nis | Market Research & Polls - EURASIA (MRP-EURASIA) | Face-to-face | 1000 | 2014 |
| Sierra Leone | Freetown, Bo, Kenema | Liaison Marketing | Face-to-face | 1000 | 2016 |
| Singapore | Singapore | Survey Sampling International | Online | 1000 | 2014 |
| Slovenia | Ljubljana, Maribor, Oelje | Market Research & Polls - EURASIA (MRP-EURASIA) | Face-to-face | 1000 | 2014 |
| South Africa | Johannesburg, Cape Town, Durban | Quest Research Services | Face-to-face | 1000 | 2016 |
| Spain | Madrid, Barcelona, Valencia | YouGov | Online | 1005 | 2016 |
| Sri Lanka | Colombo, Negombo, Kandy | PepperCube Consultants | Face-to-face | 1030 | 2014 |
| St. Kitts & Nevis | Basseterre, St. Peter, St. Thomas Middle Island | UNIMER | Face-to-face | 508 | 2016 |
| St. Lucia | Castries, Micoud, Vieux Fort | Statmark Group | Face-to-face | 1004 | 2016 |
| St. Vincent & the Grenadines | Calliaqua, Kingstown, Kingstown Park | UNIMER | Face-to-face | 501 | 2016 |
| Suriname | Paramaribo, Lelydrop, Brokopondo | CID-Gallup Latin America | Face-to-face | 504 | 2016 |
| Sweden | Stockholm, Gothenburg, Malmo | YouGov | Online | 1002 | 2016 |
| Tanzania | Mwanza, Dar es Salaam, Zanzibar | Consumer Options Ltd. | Face-to-face | 1017 | 2016 |
| Thailand | Bangkok, Udon Thani, Nakhon Ratchasima | Infosearch Limited | Face-to-face | 1005 | 2016 |
| Trinidad & Tobago | Port of Spain, Chaguanas, San Fernando | CID-Gallup Latin America | Face-to-face | 1008 | 2016 |
| Tunisia | Tunis, Sfax, Sousse | BJKA Consulting (BJ Group) | Face-to-face | 1000 | 2014 |
| Turkey | Istanbul, Ankara, Izmir | TNS Turkey | Face-to-face | 1011 | 2016 |
| Uganda | Kampala, Kira, Mbarara | TNS-RMS Cameroon | Face-to-face | 1078 | 2016 |
| Ukraine | Kiev, Kharkiv, Odesa | Market Research & Polls - EURASIA (MRP-EURASIA) | Face-to-face | 1000 | 2014 |

| COUNTRY/ JURISDICTION | CITIES COVERED | POLLING COMPANY | METHODOLOGY | SAMPLE | YEAR |
|---|---|---|---|---|---|
| United Arab Emirates | Dubai, Sharjah, Abu Dhabi | Dolfin Market Research & Consultancy (DolfinX) | Face-to-face | 1610 | 2014 |
| United Kingdom | London, Birmingham, Manchester | YouGov | Online | 1024 | 2016 |
| United States | New York, Los Angeles, Chicago | YouGov | Online | 1018 | 2016 |
| Uruguay | Montevideo, Salto, Paysandú | Datum Internacional S.A. | Face-to-face | 1000 | 2016 |
| Uzbekistan | Tashkent, Samarkand, Fergana | Market Research & Polls - EURASIA (MRP-EURASIA) | Face-to-face | 1000 | 2014 |
| Venezuela | Caracas, Maracaibo, Barquisimeto | WJP in collaboration with local partner | Face-to-face | 1000 | 2016 |
| Vietnam | Hanoi, Haiphong, Ho Chi Minh City | Indochina Research | Face-to-face | 1000 | 2014 |
| Zambia | Lusaka, Ndola, Kitwe | Quest Research Services | Face-to-face | 1000 | 2014 |
| Zimbabwe | Harare, Bulawayo, Chitungwiza | Intraspace Market Consultancy Ltd. | Face-to-face | 1008 | 2016 |

## Methodological Changes to this Year's Report

Every year, the WJP reviews the methods of data collection to ensure that the information produced is valid, useful, and continues to capture the status of the rule of law in the world. To maintain consistency with previous editions and to facilitate tracking changes over time, this year's questionnaires and data maps are closely aligned with those administered in the past.

In order to improve the accuracy of the QRQ results and reduce respondent burden, pro-active dependent interviewing techniques were used to remind respondents who participated in last year's survey of their responses in the previous year.

This year, a few changes were made to some of the indicators and questions of the *Index*. The most important changes occurred in sub-factors 3.1, 3.2, 3.3, 5.1, and 6.4. As a result, the scores of these sub-factors cannot be compared across years. Overall, 94% of questions remained the same between 2015 and 2016.

1.  In the construction of sub-factor 3.1 "Publicized laws and government data," eight questions were dropped and the Open Data Index was added. Sub-factor 3.1 now has 10 questions, and is broken down into two components: publicized laws and the Open Data Index. The Open Data Index is produced by Open Knowledge International and measures the state of open data in countries around the world from the perspective of citizens. In the construction of sub-factor 3.2 "Right to information," six questions were dropped, two questions were added, and one question was replaced. Sub-factor 3.2 now contains 22 questions. In the construction of sub-factor 3.3 "Civic participation," three questions were dropped and two questions were added. Sub-factor 3.3 now contains 30 questions.

2.  In the construction of sub-factor 5.1 "Crime is effectively controlled," two questions were dropped. In addition, the Kidnap Threat Rating, collected by NYA International, was added to sub-factor 5.1 to replace the previous kidnapping indicator. Sub-factor 5.1 now contains eight questions.

3.  In the construction of sub-factor 6.4 "Due process is respected in administrative proceedings," one question was dropped. Sub-factor 6.4 now contains four questions.

## Tracking Changes Over Time

This year's report includes a measure to illustrate whether the rule of law in a country, as measured through the factors of the *WJP Rule of Law Index*, changed over the course of the past year. This measure is presented in the form of arrows and represents a summary of rigorous statistical testing based on the use of bootstrapping procedures. For each factor, this measure takes the value of zero (no arrow) if there was no statistically significant change in the score since last year, a positive value (upward arrow) if there was a change leading to a statistically significant improvement in the score, and a negative value (downward arrow) if there was a change leading to a statistically significant deterioration in the score. This measure complements the numerical scores and rankings presented in this report, which benchmark each country's current performance on the factors and sub-factors of the *Index* against that of other countries.

The measure of change over time is constructed in three steps:

1.  First, last year's scores are subtracted from this year's to obtain, for each country and each factor, the annual difference in scores.
2.  To test whether the annual changes are statistically significant, a bootstrapping procedure is used to estimate standard errors. To calculate these errors, 100 samples of respondent-level observations (of equal size to the original sample) are randomly selected with replacement for each country from the pooled set of respondents for last year and this year. These samples are used to produce a set of 100 country-level scores for each factor and each country, which are utilized to calculate the final standard errors. These errors — which measure the uncertainty associated with picking a particular sample of respondents — are then employed to conduct pairwise t-tests for each country and each factor.
3.  Finally, to illustrate the annual change, a measure of change over time is produced based on the value of the annual difference and its statistical significance (at the 95 percent level).

## Strengths and Limitations

The *Index* methodology displays both strengths and limitations. Among its strengths is the inclusion of both expert and household surveys to ensure that the findings reflect the conditions experienced by the population. Another strength is that it approaches the measurement of rule of law from various angles by triangulating information across data sources and types of questions. This approach not only enables accounting for different perspectives on the rule of law, but it also helps to reduce possible bias that might be introduced by any other particular data collection method. Finally, it relies on statistical testing to determine the significance of the changes in the factor scores over the last year.

With the aforementioned methodological strengths come a number of limitations. First, the data shed light on rule of law dimensions that appear comparatively strong or weak, but are not specific enough to establish causation. Thus, it will be necessary to use the *Index* in combination with other analytical tools to provide a full picture of causes and possible solutions. Second, the methodology has been applied only in three major urban areas in each of the indexed countries. The WJP is therefore piloting the application of the methodology to rural areas. Third, given the rapid changes occurring in some countries, scores for some countries may be sensitive to the specific points in time when the data were collected. To address this, the WJP is piloting test methods of moving averages to account for short-term fluctuations. Fourth, the QRQ data may be subject to problems of measurement error due to the limited number of experts in some countries, resulting in less precise estimates. To address this, the WJP works constantly to expand its network of in-country academic and practitioner experts who contribute their time and expertise to this endeavor. Finally, due to the limited number of experts in some countries (which implies higher standard errors) and the fact that the GPPs are carried out in each country every other year (which implies that for some countries, some variables do not change from one year to another). It is possible that the test described above fails to detect small changes in a country's situation over time.

## Other Methodological Considerations

A detailed presentation of the methodology, including a table and description of the more than 500 variables used to construct the *Index* scores is available at worldjusticeproject.org and in Botero, J. and Ponce, A. (2011) "Measuring the Rule of Law:" WJP Working Paper No.1, available at worldjusticeproject.org/publications.

# Contributing Experts

The *WJP Rule of Law Index® 2016* was made possible by the generous contributions of academics and practitioners who contributed their time and expertise. The names of those experts wishing to be acknowledged individually are listed in the following pages.

This report was also made possible by the work of the polling companies who conducted fieldwork, and the thousands of individuals who have responded to the General Population Poll around the world.

## Afghanistan

**A.R. Rahimghiyasa**
*Law Offices of
A. Rahman Rahimghiyasa*

**Ahmad Nabil Shariq**
*Shajjan & Associates*

**Amanullah Nuristani**
*Afghan Anti-Corruption
Network*

**Baryalai Hakimi**
*Kabul University*

**Belquis Ahmadi**
*USIP*

**Hashmat Khalil Nadirpor**
*LESPA*

**Jürgen Baumann**
*GIZ Strengthening
the Rule of Law*

**Kai Schwiegelshohn**
*GIZ German Development
Cooperation*

**Khalid C. Sekander**
*International
Legal Consultant*

**Khalid Massoudi**
*Masnad Legal Consultancy*

**Mohammad
Shafiq Hamdam**
*Afghan Anti-Corruption
Network*

**Mohammad Tareq Eqtedary**

**Rahmanullah Shahab**
*Afghan Anglo Legal*

**Saeeq Shajjan**
*Shajjan & Associates*

**Sanzar Kakar**
*Afghanistan Holding Group*

**Sayed Ramiz Husaini**

**Shamsi Maqsoudi**
*Shajjan & Associates*

**Zabihullah**
*CAHPO*

**Anonymous Contributors**

## Albania

**Dorant Ekmekçiu**
*Hoxha, Memi & Hoxha*

**Drini Hakorja**

**Enida Zeneli & Artan Bozo**
*BOZO & Associates*

**Eris Hoxha**
*Hoxha, Memi & Hoxha*

**Esa Hala**
*Tonucci & Partners Albania*

**Flavia Xhafo**
*Kalo & Associates*

**Gentiana Agim Tirana**
*Tirana Law Firm*

**Gjergji Gjika**
*Gjika & Associates*

**Jonida Braja Melani**

**Kristaq Profkola**
*Wolf Theiss*

**Mitat Dautaj**
*Catholic University of Our
Lady of Good Counsel*

**Oltjan Hoxholli**
*Legal and Professional
Services Albania*

**Renan Berati**
*Legal and Professional
Services Albania*

**Shirli Gorenca**
*Kalo & Associates*

**Anonymous Contributors**

## Antigua & Barbuda

**David Dorsett**
*Watt, Dorsett & Company*

**Loy L. A. Weste**
*Thomas, John & Co.*

**Megan Samuel-Fields**
*SamuelFields Consulting
Group Ltd*

**Sandy Khouly**
*Richards and Company, St.
John's Antigua*

**Tracy Benn-Roberts**
*TBR Conflict Management &
Legal Services*

**Anonymous Contributors**

## Argentina

**Adrián Goldin**
*Facultad de Derecho de la
Universidad de Buenos Aires*

**Adrián R. Tellas**

**Alberto F. Garay**
*Carrió & Garay Abogados*

**Alberto Gonzalez Torres**
*Baker & McKenzie*

**Alberto Justo Giles**
*Federación de Colegios de
Abogados de la República
Argentina*

**Analía Durán**
*Allende & Brea*

**Carlos Aurelio Cecchetti**
*Hospital Nacional Prof.
Alejandro Posadas*

**Carlos María Ferrer Deheza**
*Estudio Ferrer Deheza*

**Carlos Martínez Sagasta**
*Universidad del Salvador*

**Claudio Jesús Santagati**
*Defensoría General de Lomas
de Zamora,. Buenos Aires
Argentina*

**Dante Omat Graña**
*Fundación Avedis
Donabedian Argentina*

**Diego Silva Ortiz**
*Silva Ortiz, Alfonso,
Pavic & Louge*

**Enrique Alberto López
Zamora**

**Enrique Marian Stile**
*Marval, O'Farrell & Mairal*

**Federico A. Borzi Cirilli**
*Defensas Penales*

**Federico Morgenstern**
*Poder Judicial de la Nación*

**Francisco A. Clucellas**

**Gabriel Martoglio**
*Estudio Martoglio &
Asociados*

**Humberto Federico Rios**
*Fundación Etica y Economia*

**Joaquin Emilio Zappa**
*JP O´Farrell Abogados*

**José Sebastián Elias**
*Universidad de San Andrés*

**Julio Ainstein**
*Universidad Isalud;
Universidad de Buenos Aires*

**Luis Daniel Crovi**

**María Paola Trigiani**
*Alfaro Abogados*

**Martin A. Bello**
*Pirovano & Bello Abogados*

**Martín Langsam**
*Universidad Isalud*

**Matthias Kleinhempel**
*IAE Business School*

**Maximo J. Fonrouge**
*Asociación de Abogados
Sera Justicia*

**Mercedes Balado
Bevilacqua**
*MBB Balado Bevilacqua
Abogados*

**Ómar Eidelstein**
*LKEC*

**P. Eugenio Aramburu**
*PAGBAM*

**Pablo Alejandro Pirovano**
*Pirovano & Bello Abogados*

**Pablo Tornielli**
*Independiente*

**Sandra Guillan**
*De Dios & Goyena Abogados
Consultores*

**Santiago Legarre**
*Pontificia Universidad
Católica Argentina*

**Walter Fernando Godoy**

**Anonymous Contributors**

## Australia

**Alex Cuthbertson**
*Allens*

**Breen Creighton**
*RMIT University*

**Daniel Williams**
*Minter Ellison*

**Esther Stern**
*Flinders University of
South Australia*

**Fiona McDonald**
*Queensland
University of Technology*

**George Williams**
*University of
New South Wales*

**Greg Patmore**
*University of Sydney*

**Hedy Cray**
*Clayton Utz*

**James A. Gillespie**
*University of Sydney*

**John Denton**
*Corrs Chambers Westgarth*

**Kate Burns**
*University of
New South Wales*

**Kate Eastman**
*Six St. James Hall Chambers*

**Manoj Narsey**
*Hewlett Packard Enterprise*

**Mary Anne Noone**
*La Trobe University Australia*

**Mary Crock**
*University of Sydney*

**Merrilyn Walton**
*University of Sydney*

**Michael Sparks**
*International Union for Health
Promotion and Education*

**Nicholas Cowdery**
*University of Sydney*

**Nick Boymal**
*Hewlett Packard Enterprise*

**Peter Cashman**
*University of Sydney*

**Peter Sainsbury**

**Roy Baker**
*Macquarie University*

**Sarah Joseph**
*Monash University*

**Simon Rice**
*Australian National University*

**Sonia Allan**
*Macquarie University*

**Thomas Faunce**
*Australian National University*

**Anonymous Contributors**

## Austria

**Christoph Konrath**
*Austrian Parliamentary
Administration*

**Claudia Habl**
*Austrian Public Health
Institute GÖG*

**Clemens Egermann**
*Barnert Egermann Illigasch
Rechtsanwälte*

**Gerhard Jarosch**
*International Association
of Prosecutors*

**Ivo Greiter**
*Greiter Pegger Kofler &
Partners*

**Johann Brunner**
*Johannes Kepler University
Linz*

**Karl Stöger**
*University of Graz*

**Magdalena Ziembicka**
*Barnert Egermann Illigasch
Rechtsanwälte*

**Manfred Ketzer**
*Hausmaninger Kletter*

**Martin Reinisch**
*Brauneis Klauser Prändl
Rechtsanwälte*

**Martin Risak**
*University of Vienna*

**Thomas Frad**
*KWR Karasek Wietrzyk
Rechtsanwälte GmbH*

**Thomas Hofmann**
*PALLAS Rechtsanwälte
Partnerschaft*

**Walter Rabl**
*Medical University
of Innsbruck*

**Anonymous Contributors**

## Bahamas

**Gavin D. Cassar**
*Cassar & Co.*

**Vann P. Gaitor**
*Higgs & Johnson*

**Wayne R. Munroe**
*Munroe & Associates*

**Anonymous Contributors**

## Bangladesh

**A.H.M. Belal Chowdhury**
*FM Consulting International*

**Abdul Awal**
*SUPRO*

**Al Amin Rahman**
*FM Associates*

**Ashraful Hadi**
*Supreme Court of Bangladesh*

**ASM Alamgir**
*Institute of Epidemiology, Disease Control and Research*

**Badiul Alam Majumdar**
*SHUJAN-Citizens for Good Governance*

**Bilqis Amin Hoque**
*Environment and Population Research Centre*

**Gazi Md Rokib Bin Hossain**
*The Legal Circle*

**Imteaz I. Mannan**
*Save the Children*

**K.A.R. Sayeed**
*Sir Salimullah Medical College and Hospital*

**Mir Shamsur Rahman**
*University of Asia Pacific*

**Mohammad Rafiqul Islam Chowdhury**
*M.R.I. Chowdhury & Associates*

**Rizwanul Islam**
*BRAC Univeristy*

**Saira Rahman Khan**
*BRAC University*

**Sayed Rubayet**
*Save the Children*

**Sultana Kamal**

**Tanim Hussain Shawon**
*Supreme Court of Bangladesh*

**Taslima Yasmin**
*University of Dhaka*

**Anonymous Contributors**

## Barbados

**Andrew C. Ferreira**
*Chancery Chambers LLP*

**Dale D. Marshall**
*George Walton Payne & Co.*

**Jill St. George**
*University of the West Indies, Cave Hill Campus*

**Lalu Hanuman**
*Synagogue Law Chambers*

**Tom Durbin**
*University of the West Indies*

**Anonymous Contributors**

## Belarus

**Aleksey Daryin**
*REVERA*

**Alexander Botian**
*Borovtsov & Salei*

**Anastasia Byckowskaya**
*Stepanovski, Papakul and Partners*

**Andrei Famenka**
*Republic of Belarus State Service of Legal Medicine*

**Andrei Vashkevich**
*Stepanovski, Papakul and Partners*

**Artsemyeu Siarhei**
*Belarusian State University*

**Dmitry Kovalchik**
*Stepanovski, Papakul and Partners*

**Dmitry Semashko**
*Stepanovski, Papakul and Partners*

**Illia Salei**
*Borovtsov & Salei*

**Kirill Tomashevski**
*International University "MITSO"*

**Vadzim Samaryn**
*Belarusian State University*

**Valentina Ogarkova**
*Stepanovski, Papakul and Partners*

**Anonymous Contributors**

## Belgium

**Andrée Puttemans**
*Université Libre de Bruxelles*

**Anna Gibello**
*DBB*

**Bruno Blanpain**
*Marx Van Ranst Vermeersch & Partners*

**Damien Gerard**
*Université Catholique de Louvain*

**Daniel Cuypers**
*University of Antwerp*

**Edoardo Agliata**

**Henry**
*Ordre des barreaux francophones et germanophones de Belgique*

**Michel De Wolf**
*Université Catholique de Louvain*

**Michel Leroy**
*Conseil d'État*

**Nicolas Cariat**
*Université Catholique de Louvain*

**Olivier de Witte**
*Hopital Erasme*

**Papart Patrick**
*Université de Liège*

**Patrick Goffaux**
*Université Libre de Bruxelles*

**Valerie Flohimont**
*Université de Namur*

**Anonymous Contributors**

## Belize

**Anthony G. Sylvestre**
*Musa & Balderamos LLP, Belize City*

**Melissa Balderamos Mahler**
*Balderamos Arthurs LLP*

**VMD Lizarraga**

**Anonymous Contributors**

## Bolivia

**Ariel Morales Vasquez**
*C.R. & F. Rojas - Abogados*

**Asdruval Columba Jofré**
*Asdruval Columba - Consultores Legales*

**Carlos Gerke Siles**
*Estudio Jurídico Gerke, Soc. Civ.*

**Cesar Burgoa Rodriguez**
*Bufete Burgoa*

**Ivan Lima Magne**
*Tribunal Supremo de Justicia*

**Jaime Araujo Camacho & Dafnee Puttkamer Gutiérrez**
*Araujo & Forgues S.C.*

**Javier Mir Peña**
*Mir & Asociados Abogados*

**Jorge Luis Inchauste**
*Guevara & Gutiérrez S.C.*

**Juan Carlos Urenda**
*Urenda Abogados S.C.*

**Juan José Lima Magne**
*Lima & Asociados*

**Juan Pablo Alvarez Belmonte**
*Lima & Asociados*

**Julio Cesar Landivar Castro**
*Guevara & Gutiérrez S.C.*

**Manuel Urenda**
*Urenda Abogados S.C.*

**Marco P. Lazo de la Vega**
*Lazo de la Vega - Abogados S.C.*

**Mostajo & Toro S.C. Firma Legal**

**Nicolas Soliz Peinado**
*Salazar & Asociados*

**Raul A. Baldivia**
*Baldivia Unzaga & Asociados*

**Rene Soria-Saucedo**
*University of Florida*

**Rodrigo Jiménez Cusicanqui**
*Salazar & Asociados*

**Rosario Baptista Canedo**

**Sandra Salinas**
*C.R. & F. Rojas - Abogados*

**Victor Hugo Lima Carreño**

**Victor Vargas Montaño**
*Herrera & Abogados S.C.*

**Anonymous Contributors**

## Bosnia & Herzegovina

**Adis Arapović**
*Centres for Civic Initiatives (CCI)*

**Adisa Omerbegovic Arapovic**
*Sarajevo School of Science and Technology*

**Adnan Duraković**
*University of Zenica*

**Boris Stojanović**
*Boris Stojanović Law Office*

**Denis Pajić**
*University Džemal Bijedić of Mostar*

**Esad Oruc**
*International Burch University*

**Hajrija Sijercic Colic**
*University of Sarajevo*

**Hana Korać**
*International University of Novi Pazar*

**Haris Hojkuric**
*International University of Sarajevo*

**Lana Bubalo**
*University Džemal Bijedić of Mostar*

**Law Office Ruzica Topic, Nebojsa Makaric & Sasa Topic**

**Mehmed Ganic**
*International University of Sarajevo*

**Mehmed Spaho**
*Spaho Law Office*

**Milorad Sladojevic**
*Basic Court Bugojno*

**Miodrag N. Simović**
*Constitutional Court of Bosnia and Herzegovina*

**Mirjana Šarkinović**

**Natasa Krejic**
*Law Firm SAJIC*

**Samil Ramić**
*Municipal Court of Bugojno*

**Selma Spaho**
*Spaho Law Office*

**Slaven Dizdar**
*Marić & Co Law Firm LLC*

**Zijad Dzafic**
*University of Tuzla*

**Anonymous Contributors**

## Botswana

**Ame Rebecca Chimbombi**

**Bonolo Ramadi Dinokopila**
*University of Botswana*

**Dick Bayford**
*Bayford & Associates*

**Gosego Rockfall Lekgowe**
*Dinokopila Lekgowe Attorneys*

**Jaloni Pansiri**
*University of Botswana*

**Jeffrey Bookbinder**
*Bookbinder Business Law*

**Kagiso Jani**
*Tshekiso Ditiro & Jani Legal Practice*

**Mboki Mbakiso Chilisa**
*Collins Chilisa Consultants*

**Motsomi Ndala Marobela**
*University of Botswana*

**Munyaka Wadaira Makuyana**
*Makuyana Legal Practice*

**Patrick Akhiwu**
*Pakmed Pty Ltd.*

**Piyush Sharma**
*Piyush Sharma Attorneys & Co.*

Tshekiso Tshekiso
*Tshekiso Ditiro & Jani Legal Practice*

Tumalano Sekoto
*Botswana Harvard AIDS Institute Partnership*

Anonymous Contributors

## Brazil

André de Melo Ribeiro
*Dias Carneiro Advogados*

Andre Fonseca
*Koury Lopes Advogados*

Caio Scheunemann Longhi
*Uber*

Camila Magalhães Silveira
*University of São Paulo*

Carlos Ayres
*Trench, Rossi e Watanabe Advogados*

Carlos Rebolo
*Hewlett Packard Enterprise*

Carolina G. F. Korbage de Castro
*Korbage de Castro*

Clara Iglesias Keller
*Universidade do Estado do Rio de Janeiro*

Cynthia Lessa da Costa
*Universidade Federal de Juiz de Fora*

Daniel Bushatsky
*Advocacia Bushatsky*

David Braga Junior
*Hospital Premier*

Elival da Silva Ramos
*Universidade de São Paulo*

Fabio Queiroz Pereira
*Universidade Federal de Minas Gerais*

Fábio Ulhoa Coelho
*Advogados Associados*

Felipe Asensi
*Universidade do Estado do Rio de Janeiro*

Fernanda Vargas Terrazas
*Conselho Nacional de Secretarias Municipais de Saúde*

Fernando Alth
*University of São Paulo*

Gabriel Alves da Costa
*Shell Brasil*

Heloisa Estellita
*FGV Direito, Sao Paulo*

Igor Parente
*Shell Brasil*

Isabel Franco
*Koury Lopes Advogados*

Joaquim Falcão

José Carlos Wahle
*Veirano Advogados*

José Ricardo dos Santos Luz Júnior
*Duarte Garcia, Caselli Guimarães e Terra Advogados*

Juliana Cesario Alvim Gomes
*Clínica UERJ Direitos*

Leandro Bonini Farias
*Coutinho e Farias Sociedade de Advogados*

Luciano Feldens
*Pontifícia Universidade Católica do Rio Grande do Sul*

Luiz Guilherme Primos
*Primos e Primos Advogados*

Luiz Gustavo Ribeiro Augusto
*Tribunal Regional do Trabalho da 2ª Região*

Maria Celina Bodin de Moraes
*Pontifical Catholic University of Rio de Janeiro; Universidade do Estado do Rio de Janeiro*

Maria Fernanda Tourinho Peres
*University of São Paulo*

Maria-Valeria Junho Penna
*Universidade Federal do Rio de Janeiro*

Marília Othero
*Hospital Premier*

Marina Croce
*Webedia Group*

Matheus Cherulli Alcantara Viana
*Alcantara Viana, Ristow e Azevedo Advogados*

Mauricio Faragone
*Faragone Advogados Associados*

Michael Freitas Mohallem
*FGV Law School, Rio de Janeiro*

Ordélio Azevedo Sette
*Azevedo Sette Advogados*

Oscar Vilhena Vieira
*FGV Law School, Sao Paulo*

Paulo R. Sehn
*Trench, Rossi e Watanabe Advogados*

Pedro Augusto Gravatá Nicoli
*Universidade Federal de Minas Gerais*

Rachelle Balbinot
*IMED*

Rafael Villac Vicente de Carvalho
*Peixoto & Cury Advogados*

Renato Poltronieri
*Mackenzie University*

Rodrigo Giordano de Castro
*Peixoto & Cury Advogados*

Rodrigo Infantozzi
*LTA Advogados*

Rogerio Fernando Taffarello
*Brazilian Institute for Criminal Sciences*

Sergio Cruz Arenhart
*Ministério Público Federal*

Sergio Mannheimer

Sueli Gandolfi Dallari
*University of São Paulo*

Thiago Bottino
*FGV Direito, Rio de Janeiro*

Thomaz Pereira
*FGV Direito, Rio de Janeiro*

Ulisses Terto Neto
*Order of Brazilian Lawyers Human Rights Commission*

Victor Hugo Criscuolo Boson
*Universidade Federal de Minas Gerais*

Anonymous Contributors

## Bulgaria

Assen Vassilev
*Center for Economic Strategy and Competitiveness*

Bojidar Danev
*Bulgarian Industrial Association*

Darina Baltadjieva
*CMS Sofia*

Desislava Anastasova
*CMS Reich-Rohrwig Hainz Sofia*

Desislava Todorova
*CMS Sofia*

Gergana Ilieva
*Kolcheva, Smilenov, Koev & Partners*

Delchev & Partners

Jean F. Crombois
*American University in Bulgaria*

Jenia Dimitrova
*CMS Sofia*

Lachezar Raichev
*Penkov, Markov & Partners*

Lidia Georgieva
*Medical University - Sofia*

Momiana Guneva
*Burgas Free University*

Nikolai Hristov
*Medical University - Sofia*

Pavel Petkov

Petko Salchev
*National Center of Public Health and Analyses*

Stanislav Hristov
*Stanislav Hristov and Partners*

Anonymous Contributors

## Burkina Faso

Ali Neya
*Cabinet d'Avocat Ali Neya*

Belem Soumaïla
*Cabinet Oumarou Ouedraogo*

Bobson Coulibaly

Boubacar Nacro
*Centre Hôspitalier Universitaire Sourou Sanou*

Edasso Rodrigue Bayala

Guitanga Samuel Ibrahim
*Barreau du Burkina Faso*

Joachimson Kyélem de Tambèla
*Barreau du Burkina Faso*

Lalogo Julien
*Barreau du Burkina Faso*

Maliki Derra
*Cabinet d'Avocat Maliki Derra*

Toure Boubakar
*Université Ouaga I Pr Joseph Ki-Zerbo*

Anonymous Contributors

## Cambodia

Alex Larkin
*DFDL*

Billy Chia-Lung Tai

Chak Sopheap
*Cambodian Center for Human Rights*

Chum Narin
*Community Legal Education Center*

IM Sophea

Jhelum Chowdhury
*Crystal Global Holdings Ltd.*

Kem Ley
*Advance Research Consultant Team*

NY Chandy

Run Saray
*Legal Aid of Cambodia (LAC)*

Sek Sophorn
*Rights & Business Law Office*

Thida Khus
*SILAKA*

Vichuta Ly
*LSCW*

Anonymous Contributors

## Cameroon

Abane Stanley
*The Abeng Law Firm*

Alain Bruno Woumbou Nzetchie
*Cabinet d'Avocats Josette Kadji*

Barthelemy Tchepnang
*Centre d'Appui à la Justice et d'Animation au Développement*

Dorcas Nkongme

Guy Alain Tougoua Djokouale
*Tougoua Law Firm & Co.*

Jean Aimé Kounga
*The Abeng Law Firm*

John Esandua Morfaw
*Strategic Development Initiatives*

Joyce Ngwe Nyamboli
*Destiny Chambers*

Marie-José Essi
*University of Yaoundé I*

Ngoupayo
*HEREG Yaoundé*

Njini Futrih N. Rose
*Bamenda Regional Hospital*

Oscar Alegba
*The Abeng Law Firm*

Roland Abeng
*The Abeng Law Firm*

Tanyi Joseph Mbi
*Tanyi Mbi & Partners*

Tarh Besong Frambo
*The Global Citizens' Initative*

Tentienu Njifack Justin
*Standard Law Firm*

Zakariaou Njoumemi
*HEREG Yaoundé; University of Yaoundé I*

Anonymous Contributors

## Canada

**Adam Dodek**
*University of Ottawa*

**Anne McGillivray**
*University of Manitoba*

**Brian Langille**
*University of Toronto*

**Chuck Harrison**
*Fasken Martineau DuMoulin LLP*

**Daniel M. Campbell**
*Cox & Palmer*

**Del W. Atwood**
*Provincial Court of Nova Scotia*

**Fabien Gélinas**
*McGill University*

**Finn Makela**
*Université de Sherbrooke*

**Frédéric Bachand**
*McGill University*

**Gaynor Roger**
*Shibley Righton LLP*

**Glen Luther**
*University of Saskatchewan*

**Hoi Kong**
*McGill University*

**Jabeur Fathally**
*University of Ottawa*

**Jamie Telfer**
*Hewlett Packard Enterprise*

**Jim Vibert**
*Hewlett Packard Enterprise*

**John Buhlman**
*WeirFoulds LLP*

**Jula Hughes**
*University of New Brunswick*

**Karen Busby**
*University of Manitoba*

**Katherine Lippel**
*University of Ottawa*

**Lise Desmarais**
*Université de Sherbrooke*

**Patrick Essiminy**
*Stikeman Elliott LLP*

**Rick Molz**
*Concordia University*

**Sonny Goldstein**
*Goldstein Financial Consultants*

**William Goodridge**
*Supreme Court of Newfoundland and Labrador*

**Anonymous Contributors**

## Chile

**Alberto Alcalde H.**
*Puga & Ortiz*

**Alfonso Canales Undurraga**
*UH&C Abogados*

**Andrea Abascal**
*Jara del Favero Abogados*

**Andrés Milano García**
*Casado, Milano & Zapata Abogados*

**Carla Robledo M.**
*RC Abogados*

**Carlos Maturana T.**
*Universidad de Concepción*

**Carlos Ossandon Salas**
*Eluchans y Compañia Abogados*

**Carolina Alliende Kravetz**
*Estudio Hoyl Alliende & Abogados*

**Catalina Salem Gesell**
*Pontificia Universidad Católica de Chile*

**Claudio Feller Schleyer**
*Grasty Quintana Majlis y Cia.*

**Cristián Muga Aitken**
*Universidad Diego Portales, Escuela Derecho*

**Cristián Fabres Ruiz**
*Estudio Jurídico Ried Fabres*

**Daniela Horvitz Lennon**
*H&H Abogados; Asociación de Abogados de Familia*

**Domingo Eyzaguirre**
*Della Maggiora Eyzaguirre Abogados*

**Ester Valenzuela**
*Universidad Diego Portales*

**Fabio Jordan**
*Poder Judicial Chile*

**Fernando Lolas**
*Universidad de Chile*

**Fernando Maturana Crino**
*Eyzaguirre & Cia*

**Germán Ovalle Madrid**
*Universidad de Chile*

**Gonzalo Eyzaguirre**
*Eyzaguirre & Cía*

**Gonzalo Hoyl Moreno**
*Hoyl, Alliende & Cía. Abogados*

**Humberto Sánchez Pacheco**
*Defensoría Penal Pública*

**Ignacio Rivadeneira H.**
*Rivadeneira, Colombara y Zegers Abogados*

**Irene Rojas Miño**
*Universidad de Talca*

**Jorge Bofill**
*Bofill Escobar Abogados*

**Jorge Canales G.**
*Peralta, Gutiérrez & Asociados*

**Jorge Wahl**

**José Luis Lara Arroyo**
*Philippi, Prietocarrizosa, Ferrero DU & Uría*

**Juan Enrique Vargas**
*Universidad Diego Portales*

**Juan Pablo Cox Leixelard**
*Universidad Adolfo Ibáñez*

**Juan Pablo Olmedo**
*Fundación Pro Acceso*

**Lizandro Godoy Araneda**
*De la Fuente, Godoy y Abogados*

**Luis Eugenio García-Huidobro**
*Philippi, Prietocarrizosa, Ferrero DU & Uría*

**Luis Eugenio Ubilla Grandi**
*Universidad Católica de la Santísima Concepción*

**Luis Felipe Hubner**
*UH&C Abogados*

**Luis Parada**
*Bahamondez, Alvarez & Zegers*

**Manuel Jiménez Pfingsthorn**
*Jara del Favero Abogados*

**Marcelo Soto Ulloa**
*Universidad de los Andes*

**María Elena Santibáñez Torres**
*Pontificia Universidad Católica de Chile*

**María Isabel Cornejo Plaza**
*Universidad de Chile*

**María Norma Oliva Lagos**
*Corporación de Asistencia Judicial del Bio Bio*

**Mariana Viera**
*Alessandri Abogados*

**Martín Besio Hernández**
*Rivadeneira, Colombara y Zegers Abogados*

**Matías Donoso Lamas**
*Urenda & Cia.*

**Michele Daroch Sagredo**
*Abdala & Cía. Abogados*

**Nicolás Casado Núñez**
*Casado, Milano & Zapata Abogados*

**Omar Morales**
*Montt y Cía Abogados*

**Orlando Palominos**
*Estudio Jurídico - Morales & Besa*

**Patricio Morales Aguirre**
*Estudio Jurídico Pérez Donoso y Cia.*

**Paulo Larrain**
*Noguera Larrain & Dulanto Abogados*

**Roberto Guerrero del Río**
*Guerrero Olivos, Abogados*

**Roberto Guerrero V.**
*Guerrero Olivos, Abogados*

**Rodolfo Fuenzalida S.**
*GFSU Abogados*

**Rodrigo Zegers Reyes**
*Rivadeneira, Colombara y Zegers Abogados*

**Zarko Luksic Sandoval**
*Socio AMLV Abogados*

**Anonymous Contributors**

## China

**Jonathan Isaacs**
*Baker & McKenzie*

**Liu Kaiming**
*Institute of Contemporary Observation*

**Liu Xin**
*China University of Political Science and Law*

**Matthew Murphy**
*MMLC Group*

**Xia Yu**
*MMLC Group*

**Anonymous Contributors**

## Colombia

**Abelardo de la Espriella**
*De la Espriella Lawyers Enterprise*

**Ana Liliana Rios Garcia**
*Universidad del Norte*

**Ana María Muñoz S.**
*Universidad de los Andes*

**Angela María Ruiz Sternberg**
*Universidad del Rosario*

**Aquiles Arrieta**
*Corte Constitucional de Colombia*

**Carlos Álvarez-Moreno**
*Universidad Nacional de Colombia*

**Carlos Andrés Gómez González**
*Universidad Jorge Tadeo Lozano*

**Carlos Mario Molina Arrubla**
*Molina Díaz & Abogados*

**Carolina Posada Isaacs**
*Posse Herrera Ruiz*

**Catalina Herrera von Norden**
*ARI Consulting Group SAS*

**David Fernando Varela S.**
*Pontificia Universidad Javeriana*

**Diego Felipe Valdivieso Rueda**
*VS+M Abogados*

**Eduardo Cárdenas**
*Dentons Cárdenas & Cárdenas*

**Enrique Alvarez**
*Lloreda Camacho & Co.*

**Felipe Aristizabal**
*Nieto & Chalela Abogados*

**Guillermo Hernando Bayona Combariza**

**Ignacio Santamaria**
*Lloreda Camacho & Co.*

**Joe Bonilla Gálvez**
*Muñoz Tamayo & Asociados*

**Jorge Acosta-Reyes**
*Universidad del Norte*

**Jorge Diaz-Cardenas**
*Diaz-Cardenas Abogados*

**Jorge Enrique Galvis Tovar**
*Lloreda Camacho & Co.*

**Jorge Lara Urbaneja**
*ALBP Abogados SAS*

**Juan David Riveros Barragán**
*Sampedro & Riveros Consultores*

**Lucas Fajardo Gutiérrez**
*Brigard & Urrutia Abogados*

**Luis Alberto Tafur Calderón**
*Universidad del Valle*

**Luis Fernando Ramírez Contreras**
*Tribunal Superior de Bogotá*

**Manuel Fernando Quinche Ramírez**
*Universidad del Rosario*

**Marcela Castro-Ruiz**
*Universidad de los Andes*

Mario Alonso Pérez T.
*Philippi, Prietocarrizosa, Ferrero DU & Uría*

Mauricio A. Bello-Galindo
*Baker & McKenzie*

Patricia Moncada Roa
*Universidad de los Andes*

Rafael Tuesca Molina
*Universidad del Norte*

Raúl Alberto Suárez Arcila
*Suárez Arcila & Abogados Asociados*

Ricardo Posada Maya
*Universidad de los Andes*

Sandra Catalina Charris Rebellón
*Sandra Charris Asesoria Legal & Solución de Controversias*

Santiago Gutiérrez-Borda
*Lloreda Camacho & Co.*

Anonymous Contributors

## Costa Rica

Armando Guardia
*Guardia & Cubero Abogados y Notarios*

Arturo Blanco Paez
*Jurexlaw*

Arturo Herrera Barquero
*Caja Costarricense de Seguro Social*

Carlos Góngora Fuentes
*Poder Judicial; Universidad Latina de Costa Rica*

Carlos J. Valerio Monge
*Asociación de Derecho Médico de Costa Rica*

César Hines Céspedes
*Econojuris Abogados*

Emilia Saborio Pozuelo
*Bufete Soley, Saborio & Asociados*

Equipo de LEXINCORP Costa Rica
*LEXINCORP Bufete Centroamericano*

Fátima Porras Moya
*Martínez & Porras Abogados*

Francisco José Aguilar Urbina
*Chairman Emeritus, UN Human Rights Comittee*

Gloriana Valladares Navas
*Navas & Navas Abogados*

Gonzalo Gutierrez A.
*AG Legal*

J. Federico Campos Calderón
*LEXPENAL Abogados*

Juan Marcos Rivero S.
*Bufete Rivero & Asociados. PenalCorp.*

Luis Aangel Sanchez Montero
*Bufete Facio & Cañas*

Luis-Alberto Cordero
*Nassar Abogados Centroamérica*

Marco Durante
*BDS Asesores*

María del Rocío Quirós Arroyo
*AG Legal*

María Paula Solórzano V.
*Pacheco Coto Abogados*

Melissa Mata A.
*AG Legal*

Nicholas V. Chen
*Pamir Law Group*

Rafael Angel Rodriguez Salazar
*La Firma de Abogados*

Roger Guevara Vega
*Batalla Salto Luna*

Sergio Amador
*Batalla Salto Luna*

Silvia Alvarado Quijano
*AG Legal*

Thelma Petrucci
*BLP*

Wilberth Montenegro Reyes
*AG Legal*

Anonymous Contributors

## Côte d'Ivoire

Abauleth Raphael

Abbé Yao
*SCPA Dogué-Abbé Yao & Associés; Société d'Avocats au Barreau de Côte-d'Ivoire*

Affoum Armand Lambert
*Cabinet d'Avocat Affoum*

Alexandre Bairo
*KSK Société d'Avocats*

Arsene Dable
*SCPA Dogué-Abbé Yao & Associés*

Françoise Angeline Assi Kaudjhis-Offoumou
*Association Internationale pour la Démocratie*

Kakou G. Jean

Louis Penali
*Comité National d'Ethique de la Recherche*

Simone Assa-Akoh
*Association des Femmes Juristes de Côte d'Ivoire*

Souleymane Sakho
*SCPA Sakho-Yapobi-Fofana*

Yabasse Lucien Abouya
*Africa Health System Improvement Organization*

Youan G. Joules
*ONG Amepouh*

Anonymous Contributors

## Croatia

Alan Soric
*Law Office Soric & Tomekovic Dunda*

Ana Stavljenic-Rukavina
*DIU Libertas International University*

Andrej Matijević
*Matijević Law Office*

Anita Krizmanic
*Macesic & Partners Law Offices LLC*

Arsen Bačić
*University of Split*

Boris Kozjak
*Kozjak Law Firm*

Božidar Feldman
*Matic, Feldman & Herman Law Firm*

Darko Jurišić
*General Hospital "Dr.Josip Benčević"*

Eleonora Katić

Floriana Bulić-Jakuš
*University of Zagreb School of Medicine*

Ivan Kos
*PETOŠEVIĆ*

Ivana Manovelo
*Macesic & Partners Law Offices LLC*

Ivo Grga

Jasminka Vrbanović
*Law firm Vrbanović & Štefičić*

Jelena Zjacic
*Macesic & Partners Law Offices LLC*

Višnja Drenski-Lasan
*Law Firm Drenski Lasan*

Zoran Vujasin
*Law Firm Vujasin*

Anonymous Contributors

## Czech Republic

Eva Ondrejova

Jan Hurdík
*Okresní soud v Třebíči*

Jan Poláček

Lukáš Prudil
*AK Prudil a Spol., S.R.O.*

Michal Peškar

Ondřej Dušek
*Peterka & Partners*

Pavel Holec
*Holec, Zuska & Partners*

Simona Stočesová
*University of West Bohemia*

Stepan Holub
*Holubová Advokáti S.R.O.*

Tomas Cihula
*Kinstellar*

Tomas Matějovský
*CMS Legal Services*

Vojtech Steininger
*Hartmanová & Steininger, Advokáti*

Anonymous Contributors

## Denmark

Anette Storgaard
*Aarhus University*

Anne Brandt Christensen
*Advokatfirmaet Brandt Christensen*

Anne Skjold Qvortrup
*Gorrissen Federspiel*

Arja R. Aro
*University of Southern Denmark*

Hans Henrik Edlund
*Aarhus University*

Jacob Schall Holberg
*Bech-Bruun Law Firm*

Jakob S. Johnsen
*HjulmandKaptain Law Firm*

Jens Rye-Andersen
*Advokatfirmaet Jens Rye-Andersen*

Lars Lindencrone Petersen
*Bech-Bruun Law Firm*

Marianne Granhøj
*Kromann Reumert*

Morten Broberg
*University of Copenhagen*

Per Andersen
*Aarhus University*

Poul Hvilsted
*Horten Law Firm*

Anonymous Contributors

## Dominica

Ernette C.J. Kangal
*Caribbean Commercial & IP Law Practitioners, LLP*

Rose-Anne Charles

Anonymous Contributors

## Dominican Republic

Alfredo Lachapel
*Lachapel Toribio - Abogados*

Ana Isabel Cáceres
*Troncoso y Cáceres*

Arturo Figuereo Camarena
*Fiallo-Billini Scanlon Abogados & Consultores*

Arturo J. Ramirez
*Ibert, Ramirez & Asociados*

Camilo A. Caraballo Gómez
*Troncoso y Cáceres*

Carlos R. Hernández
*Hernández Contreras & Herrera Abogados*

Carmen L. Martinez Coss
*Espaillat Matos Martinez Coss*

Domingo Suzaña Abreu
*Abogados Suzaña & Asociados*

Edwin Espinal Hernández
*Pontificia Universidad Católica Madre y Maestra*

Edwin Grandel Capellán
*Grandel & Asociados*

Fabiola Medina Garnes
*Medina Garrigó Abogados*

Fernando Roedán
*Ortiz & Hernández, Abogados Asociados*

Francisco Alvarez Valdez
*Participación Ciudadana*

Georges Santoni Recio
*Russin Vecchi & Heredia Bonetti*

Henry Montás
*Templaris Cobranzas, S.R.L.*

Jesus Francos Rodriguez
*Madeina Garrigo Abogados*

José Cruz Campillo
*Jiménez Cruz Peña*

Juan Carlos Ortiz Abreu
*Oficina Ortiz & Comprés*

Loraine Maldonado
*Mesa & Mesa Abogados*

Luz Díaz Rodríguez
*Medina Garrigó Abogados*

María Elena Gratereaux
*Gratereaux Delva & Asociados*

María Esther Fernández Alvarez De Pou
*Russin Vecchi & Heredia Bonetti*

Mary Fernández
*Headrick, Rizik, Alvarez & Fernández*

Miguel Angel Reyes Taveras
*Fundación Justicia y Transparencia*

Richard A. Benoit Domínguez
*Pina Méndez & Asociados*

Rodolfo Mesa
*Mesa & Mesa Abogados*

Rosa Díaz Abreu
*Jiménez Cruz Peña*

Stalin Ciprian Arriaga
*Ciprian Arriaga y Asociados*

Ulises Morlas Pérez
*Cabral & Díaz Abogados*

Vilma Veras-Terrero
*Jiménez Cruz Peña*

Virgilio A. Mendez Amaro
*Mendez & Asociados*

Yamil Musri C.

Anonymous Contributors

## Ecuador

Alfredo G. Brito
*Brito & Pinto*

Ana Belén Posso Fernández
*Ontaneda & Posso Abogados*

Carlos Carrasco Yepez
*A/C Abogados & Consultores*

Carlos Solines Coronel

Cesar Coronel Jones
*Coronel & Perez Abogados*

Ciro Pazmiño Zurita
*P&P Abogados Litigantes*

Clementina Pomar Anta
*Bustamante & Bustamante Law Firm*

David Albarran Pacheco
*A/C Abogados & Consultores*

Diego Almeida Guzmán
*Almeida Guzmán & Asociados*

Diego Ordoñez

Edgar Neira Orellana
*Gallegos, Valarezo & Neira*

Edmundo René Bodero Cali
*Estudio JurÍdico Bodero & Bodero*

Francisco Dávalos Morán
*González Peñaherrera & Asociados*

Gabriel Pinto Navarrete
*Estudio JurÍdico Prado*

Gerardo Aguirre Vallejo

James Pilco Luzuriaga
*Universidad del Azuay*

José Luis Tapia

Jose Ontaneda Andrade
*Ontaneda & Posso Abogados*

Juan Carlos Riofrío Martínez-Villalba
*Universidad de Los Hemisferios*

Juan Jose Campana del Castillo
*Estudio JurÍdico SMARTFLEX*

Leonardo Sempertegui Vallejo
*Sempertegui Ontaneda Abogados*

María Lorena Correa Crespo
*ILP, Gallegos, Valarezo & Neira*

María Sol Sevilla
*Sempertegui Ontaneda Abogados*

Mario I. Armendáriz Y.
*Armendáriz & Asociados Law Office*

Santiago Solines
*Solines & Asociados*

Sebastian Saa - Tamayo
*Almeida Guzmán & Asociados*

Simon Davalos Ochoa
*González Peñaherrera & Asociados*

Anonymous Contributors

## Egypt

Ibrahim Ahmad Ibrahim
*Arab Chamber of Conciliation and Arbitration*

Khaled El Shalakany
*Shalakany Law Office*

Laila El Baradei
*The American University in Cairo*

Mohamed Abdelaal
*Alexandria University*

Mohamed Hanafi Mahmoud
*Egypt High Criminal Court*

Somaya Hosny
*Suez Canal University*

Anonymous Contributors

## El Salvador

Ana Yesenia Granillo de Tobar
*Escuela Superior de Economía y Negocios*

Benjamin Valdez Iraheta
*Benjamin Valdez & Asociados*

Carlos Enrique Castillo
*Romero Pineda & Asociados*

Daniel A. Joya
*Joya & Asociados, Abogados y Notarios de El Salvador*

David Ernesto Claros Flores
*García y Bodán*

David Osvaldo Toledo
*Universidad Católica de El Salvador*

Delmer Edmundo Rodríguez Cruz
*Escuela Superior de Economía y Negocios*

Guillermo Alexander Parada Gámez
*Universidad Centroamericana*

Harold C. Lantan

José Eduardo Barrientos Aguirre
*I&D Consulting*

José Eduardo Tomasino Hurtado
*El Salvador Legal Limitada de Capital Variable - Consortium Legal*

José Freddy Zometa Segovia
*Romero Pineda & Asociados*

Juan José Planas Carías
*Escuela Superior de Economía y Negocios*

Laura Urrutia
*Laboratorios Vijosa*

Mardoqueo Josafat Tóchez Molina
*Lawyers Corp, Tóchez & Asociados*

Marta Celina de Parada

Oscar Samour
*Consortium Legal*

Piero Antonio Rusconi
*Central Law*

Porfirio Diaz Fuentes
*DLM, Abogados, Notarios & Consultores*

Rebeca Atanacio de Basagoitia
*Escalon & Atanacio*

Ricardo A. Cevallos
*BLP*

Rommell Sandoval
*I&D Consulting; SBA Firma Legal*

Teresa Beatriz Merino Benítez
*Romero Pineda & Asociados*

Yudy Aracely Jimenez Rivera
*Firma de Abogados Gold Service*

Anonymous Contributors

## Estonia

Aare Märtson
*University of Tartu*

Andres Parmas
*Tallinn Circuit Court*

Andres Vutt
*University of Tartu*

Anneli Soo
*University of Tartu*

Birgit Sisask
*Law Office Valge & Uiga*

Gaabriel Tavits
*University of Tartu*

Kaja Põlluste
*University of Tartu*

Kari Käsper
*Estonian Human Rights Centre*

Maksim Greinoman
*Advokaadibüroo Greinoman & Co*

Margit Vutt
*Supreme Court of Estonia*

Merle Erikson
*University of Tartu*

Tanel Kerikmäe
*Tallinn University of Technology*

Anonymous Contributors

## Ethiopia

Aberra Degefa Nagawo
*Addis Ababa University*

Alemu M. Negash

Endalkachew Geremew Negash

Girma Kassa Kumsa
*Adama University*

Guadie Sharew Wondimagegn
*Bahir Dar University*

Hiruy Wubie Gebreegziabher
*Monash University*

Mehari Redae
*Addis Ababa University School of Law*

Misganaw Gashaw
*Debre Markos University School of Law*

Simeneh Kiros Assefa
*Addis Ababa Universty*

Tameru Wondm Agegnehu

Tamrat Assefa
*Tamrat Assefa Liban Law Office*

Zemenu Tarekegn Yimenu
*Debre Markos University*

Anonymous Contributors

## Finland

Ari Miettinen
*Fimlab Laboratories Ltd.*

Hannu Honka
*Åbo Akademi University*

Iikka Sainio
*Eversheds Attorneys Ltd.*

Jukka Peltonen
*Asianajotoimisto DLA Piper Finland Oy*

Jussi Tapani
*University of Turku*

Matti Ilmari Niemi
*University of Eastern Finland*

Matti Tolvanen
*University of Eastern Finland*

Mika J. Lehtimaki
*Attorneys-at-Law Trust*

Mika Launiala
*University of Eastern Finland*

Nina Isokorpi
*Roschier, Attorneys Ltd.*

Patrick Lindgren
*ADVOCARE Law Office*

Raimo Isoaho
*University of Turku*

Sanna Leisti
*Rule of Law Finland*

Anonymous Contributors

## France

Denfer Samira

Francis Tartour
*Conseiller Prud'hommes*

Francois Cantier
*Avocats sans Frontières France*

Gauthier Chassang
*Inserm*

Grabli Elisabeth

Jacques Delga
*ESSEC*

Levy David
*Barreau de Paris*

Mahir Idris Albana
*American University in the Emirates*

Marie-Christine Cimadevilla
*Cimadevilla Avocats*

Nataline Fleury
*Ashurst LLP*

Nicolas Mathieu
*Skadden, Arps, Slate, Meagher and Flom LLP*

Nicole Stolowy
*HEC Paris*

Patrice Le Maigat
*Université de Rennes*

Philippe Marin
*Société IMAVOCATS*

SCPA IKT et Associés

Sébastien Ducamp
*Winston & Strawn*

Thierry Berland
*Berland & Sevin Avocats*

Anonymous Contributors

## Georgia

George Gotsadze
*Curatio International Foundation*

George Nanobashvili

Gocha Svanidze
*Law Firm Svanidze and The Partners*

Grigol Gagnidze
*Georgian Barristers & Lawyers International Observatory*

Imeda Dvalidze

Ivdity Chikovani
*Curatio International Foundation*

Ketevan Krialashvili
*Economic Education and Strategic Research Center*

Ketevan Sakhiashvili
*Legal Room LLC*

Lasha Gogiberidze
*BGI Legal*

Revaz Beridze
*Eristavi & Partners, LLC*

Vera Doborjginidze
*Lexpert Group Law Firm*

Zurab Makhuradze
*Legal and Business Consulting LLC*

Anonymous Contributors

## Germany

Alexander Putz
*Steuerberater & Rechtsanwalt*

Andreas M. Michaeli
*Rechtsanwaltssozietät BORN*

Anna Lindenberg

Annegret Berne

Annette Krause
*Rechtsanwälte Krause & Krause*

Baur

Bernhard Trappehl
*Baker & McKenzie*

Burkhard Hess
*Max Planck Institute for Procedural Law*

Burkhard Klüver
*Ahlers & Vogel Rechtsanwälte PartG mbB*

Carsten Momsen
*Freie Universität Berlin*

Christian Wolff
*Schock Rechtsanwälte*

Christof Kerwer
*Universität Würzburg*

Christoph Hexel
*Heuking Kühn Lüer Wojtek PartGmbB*

Christoph Lindner

Dirk Vielhuber
*BG BAU Munich*

Dominik Steiger
*Universität Leipzig*

Friederike Lemme

Gernot A. Warmuth
*Scheiber & Partners*

Gregor Dornbusch
*Baker & McKenzie*

Hauke Hagena

Helmuth Jordan
*Jordan & Wagner Rechtsanwalts-GmbH*

Hermann Bietz

Ingo Friedrich
*International Understanding and Peace*

Ingo Klaus Wamser
*Rechtsanwälte Wamser*

Jessica Jacobi
*Kliemt & Vollstaedt*

Juergen Nazarek

Kathrein Knetsch
*Advovox Rechtsanwalts GmbH*

Lars Nitzsche
*Kanzlei Lederle, Kehl, Germany*

Lars Rieck
*IPCL Rieck & Partner Rechtsanwälte*

Markus Eric Allner
*ALLNER MENGES Rechtsanwälte*

Martin Reufels
*Heuking Kühn Lüer Wojtek*

Martin Sträßer
*Sträßer Rehm Barfield, Chemnitz*

Matthias Nodorf

Michael Zoebisch
*rwzh Rechtsanwälte*

Oliver Bolthausen
*DWF Germany*

Oliver Schellbach
*Schellbach Rechtsanwälte*

Othmar K. Traber
*Ahlers & Vogel Rechtsanwälte PartG mbB*

R. Kunz-Hallstein

Rain Sabine Barth
*Dostal & Sozien Rechtsanwalt*

Rainer M. Hofmann
*Kanzlei im Hofhaus*

Reinhard Arndts
*Mittelstein Rechtsanwälte*

Roland Gross
*Gross::Rechtsanwaelte*

Rudolf du Mesnil de Rochemont

S. Beckmann-Koßmann

Sebastian Reinsch
*Janke & Reinsch Rechtsanwälte*

Stefan Huster
*Ruhr-University Bochum*

Stefan Sasse
*Rechtsanwälte Göhmann*

Stephan Sander
*Kanzlei Sander Berlin*

Thomas Feltes
*Ruhr-University Bochum*

Thomas Jürgens
*Jürgens Rechtsanwaltsgesellschaft mbH*

Tobias Singelnstein
*Freie Universität Berlin*

Tobias Thiedemann
*HP Deutschland GmbH*

Ulrich Keil
*Westfälische Wilhelms Universität Münster*

Ulrike Köllner

Werner Kessing
*Kessing - Hespe - Dr. Steenken*

Wibke Köppler
*Oelmüller & Partner Rechtsanwälte*

Wolf Stahl
*Kanzlei fuer Wirtschaftsrecht*

Wolfgang Hau
*University of Passau*

Anonymous Contributors

## Ghana

Abena Ntrakwah-Mensah
*Ntrakwah & Co.*

Azanne Kofi Akainyah
*A & A Law Consult*

Clement Kojo Akapame
*Ghana Institute of Management and Public Administration*

Dinah Baah-Odoom
*Ghana Health Service*

Emmanuel Maurice Ankrah
*Ghana Health Service*

Felix Ntrakwah
*Ntrakwah & Co.*

Kwame Owusu Agyeman
*University of Cape Coast*

Nana Tawiah Okyir
*Ghana Institute of Management and Public Administration*

Nii Nortey Hanson-Nortey
*Ghana Health Service*

Reuben Kwasi Esena
*University of Ghana School of Public Health*

Richmond Aryeetey
*University of Ghana School of Public Health*

Sam Okudzeto
*Sam Okudzeto & Associates*

Sam Poku
*Business Council for Africa; IMANI Ghana*

Tobias Singelnstein

Shirley Somuah
*Ntrakwah & Co.*

Anonymous Contributors

## Greece

Ada Alamanou
*KLIMAKA NGO*

Anna Damaskou
*Transparency International Greece*

Anthony Mavrides
*Ballas, Pelecanos & Associates LPC*

Avagianou Melina
*KLIMAKA NGO*

Christina Papadopoulou
*IRCT*

Dionysia Kallinikou
*National and Kapodistrian University of Athens Law School*

Dionyssis Balourdos

Fotini N. Skopouli
*Harokopio University*

George Ballas
*Ballas, Pelecanos & Associates LPC*

Grace Katsoulis
*Ballas, Pelecanos & Associates LPC*

Ilias Anagnostopoulos
*Anagnostopoulos Law Firm*

Ioanna Argyraki
*Rokas Law Firm*

Konstantinos Apostolopoulos
*Apostolopoulos Patras Limassol Law*

Konstantinos Valmas-Vloutis

Kostoula Mazaraki
*Nomos Law Firm*

Magda Kapoti-Tazedaki

Moratis Passas Law Firm

Nigel Bowen-Morris
*Stephenson Harwood*

Nikolaos Kondylis
*N. Kondylis & Partners Law Office*

Panagiotis Gioulakos

Panayotis Karydakis
*P.N. Karydakis Law Firm*

Stavros Karageorgiou
*Karageorgiou & Associates Law Firm*

Stefanos Tsimikalis
*Tsimikalis Kalonarou Law Firm*

Themis Tosounidis
*KPAG Law Firm*

Theodoropoulou Virgninia
*Panteion University*

Yota Kremmida
*Hewlett Packard Enterprise*

Anonymous Contributors

## Grenada

Afi Ventour & Co.

Darshan Ramdhani
*Law Offices of Ramdhani & Associates*

Karen M. Samuel
*Samuel Phillip & Associates*

Yurana Phillip
*Afi Ventour & Co.*

Anonymous Contributors

## Guatemala

Alfredo Rodríguez Mahuad
*Consortium Legal - Guatemala*

Alvaro Castellanos Howell
*Consortium Legal - Guatemala*

Alvaro R. Cordon
*Cordón, Ovalle & Asociados*

Ana Gisela Castillo A.
*Saravia y Muñoz*

Andrés Dubón Ruiz
*Comte & Font - Legalsa*

Astrid Carolina Domínguez Méndez
*Consortium Legal - Guatemala*

Carlos A. Flores Cano
*Despacho Flores Cano*

Carlos Roberto Cordón Krumme
*Cordón, Ovalle & Asociados*

David Erales Jop
*Consortium Legal - Guatemala*

David Ernesto Chacón Estrada
*Universidad de San Carlos de Guatemala*

Diana Paola De Mata Ruiz
*Consortium Legal - Guatemala*

Diego Alejos Rivera
*Consortium Legal - Guatemala*

Edson López
*Integrum Law Firm*

Elías Arriaza
*Consortium Legal - Guatemala*

Emanuel Callejas A.
*Carrillo & Asociados*

Enrique Möller
*EY Law*

Erick Wong
*Cordón, Ovalle & Asociados*

Estuardo Mata Palmieri
*QIL+4 Abogados*

Gabriel Arturo Muadi Garcia
*Muadi, Murga y Jimenez*

Harvey Pacay

Jesse Omar García Muñoz
*Grupo Interamericana*

Juan José Porras Castillo
*Palomo & Porras*

Julio Roberto García-Merlos García
*Universidad Francisco Marroquín*

Luis Pablo Cóbar Benard
*Integrum Law Firm*

Marco Antonio Palacios López
*Palacios & Asociados*

Marcos Palma
*Integrum Law Firm*

Mario Roberto Guadrón Rouanet
*Palomo & Porras*

Ninoshka Urrutia
*Consortium Legal - Guatemala*

Pedro Mendoza Montano
*Iurisconsulti Abogados y Notarios*

Rafael Fernando Mendizábal de la Riva
*Universidad de San Carlos de Guatemala*

Rodolfo Alegría
*Carrillo & Asociados*

Rodolfo Estuardo Salazar
*Arenales & Skinner Klee*

Rodrigo Callejas
*Carrillo & Asociados*

Ruby María Asturias Castillo
*Pacheco Coto Abogados*

Tanya Fernández Batres

Vilma Judith Chavez
*Universidad Galileo*

Anonymous Contributors

## Guyana

Esther Sam
*Attorney General's Chambers*

Eusi Anderson
*Law Office of Eusi Anderson Esq.*

Joann Alexis Bond
*Attorney General's Chambers*

Kelly-Ann Payne-Hercules
*Ministry of Education*

Mirza Ahmad Sahadat
*Sahadat Law Office*

Stephen Roberts
*Hughes, Fields and Stoby*

Vonetta Atwell-Singh
*Attorney General's Chambers*

Anonymous Contributors

## Honduras

Jose Alvarez
*BLP*

Juan Diego Lacayo González
*Aguilar Castillo Love*

Juan José Alcerro Milla
*Aguilar Castillo Love*

Leobildo Cabrera Cabrera
*Colegio de Abogados de Honduras*

Miguel Joaquín Melgar Guevara
*García y Bodán*

Milton Carcamo

Ruben A. Rodezno Sandoval
*Bufete Danzilo & Asociados (HONDURASLAW)*

Vanessa Oquelí
*García y Bodán*

Anonymous Contributors

## Hong Kong SAR, China

Charles Kwong
*The Open University of Hong Kong*

David C. Donald
*The Chinese University of Hong Kong*

Farzana Aslam
*University of Hong Kong*

Ho Lok Sang
*Lingnan University*

Ho Sai Yin Daniel
*University of Hong Kong*

IP Shing Hing

James A. Rice
*Lingnan University*

James L.W. Wong
*Century Chambers*

Michael Chai
*Bernacchi Chambers*

Michael Vidler
*Vidler & Co. Solicitors*

Navin Babani

Pui Yin Lo
*Gilt Chambers*

Rick Glofcheski
*University of Hong Kong*

Susan Kendall
*Baker & McKenzie*

Tam Yat Hung
*University of Hong Kong*

Yun Zhao
*University of Hong Kong*

Anonymous Contributors

## Hungary

András Jakab
*Pázmány Péter Catholic University*

Daniel Szabo
*Hewlett Packard Enterprise Hungary*

Gábor Baruch
*Baruch Law Firm*

Gabor Papp
*Papp D Gabor Ugyvedi iroda*

Petra Bárd
*National Institute of Criminology*

Viktor Lorincz
*Hungarian Academy of Sciences*

Zsolt Zengodi

Anonymous Contributors

## India

A. Nagarathna
*National Law School of India University*

Abhimanyu Shandilya
*Hewlett Packard Enterprise*

Anil Paleri
*Institute of Palliative Medicine*

Ashok Ramgir
*Harsh Impex*

Bontha Veerraju Babu
*Indian Council of Medical Research*

Damodhar Padmanabha
*Hewlett Packard Enterprise*

E. N. Thambi Durai

I. C. Dwivedi
*National Election Watch*

J. L. N. Murthy
*Jonnalagadda LLP*

Lalit Bhasin
*Bhasin & Co., Advocates*

Nirmal Kanti Chakrabarti
*KIIT University School of Law*

Pramod Singh
*Lux Veritas, Advocates & Solicitors*

Puneet Misra
*AIIMS*

Rajas Kasbekar
*Little & Co., Advocates and Solicitors*

Ruchi Sinha
*TISS*

Sankaran Ramakrishnan

Saurabh Misra
*Saurabh Misra & Associates*

Shankar Das
*Tata Institute of Social Sciences, Mumbai*

Shivani Bhardwaj
*Sathi All For Partnerships*

Subhash Bhatnagar
*Indian Institute of Management*

Vipender Mann
*KNM & Partners*

Yadlapalli S. Kusuma
*All India Institute of Medical Sciences*

Yashomati Ghosh
*National Law School of India University*

Anonymous Contributors

## Indonesia

Alamo D. Laiman
*Legisperitus Lawyers*

Andrew I. Sriro
*Dyah Ersita & Partners*

Anne Hyre
*Johns Hopkins University/ Jhpiego*

Erpan Faryadi
*ILC Asia*

Hanim Hamzah
*Roosdiono & Partners (ZICOlaw)*

Immanuel A. Indrawan
*Indrawan Darsyah Santoso Attorneys at Law*

Mardjono Reksodiputro
*University of Indonesia*

Sartono
*Hanafiah Ponggawa &
Partners*

Sianti Candra
*Roosdiono & Partners
(ZICOlaw)*

Sunardjo Sumargono
*Law Office of Semar
Suryakencana Cipta
Justiceindo*

Tauvik M. Soeherman
*Paramadina Graduate School
of Diplomacy and Strategic
International Policies*

Todung Mulya Lubis
*Lubis, Santosa & Maramis
Law Firm*

Tony Budidjaja
*Budidjaja & Associates*

Tristam Pascal Moeliono
*Catholic University of
Parahyangan*

Anonymous Contributors

## Iran

Abolfazl Shirazi
*Avicenna Research Institute*

Arash Izadi
*Izadi Law Firm*

Ehsan Hosseinzadeh
*Educated Lawyers Law Firm*

Encyeh Seyed Sadr
*Bayan Emrooz Law Firm*

Hamid Bagherzadeh
*Iranian Bar Assosiation*

Mohammad Rahmani
*Bayan Emrooz Law Firm*

Nasim Gheidi &
Amirhossein Tanhaei
*Gheidi & Associates Law
Office*

Nima Nasrollahi Shahri
*APP Lawfirm (Dentons)*

Parviz Azadfallah
*Tarbiat Modares University*

Soroosh Falahati
*Bayan Emrooz Law Firm*

Yahya Rayegani
*PraeLegal Iran*

Anonymous Contributors

## Italy

Alberto Fantini
*Studio Legale Tonucci &
Partners*

Alessio Di Amato
*Astolfo Di Amato e Associati*

Anna Mastromarino
*University of Turin*

Anna Simonati
*University of Trento*

Antonella Antonucci
*Università degli Studi di Bari
Aldo Moro*

Antonio Cassatella
*University of Trento*

Antonio Viscomi
*Università Magna Grecia di
Catanzaro*

Astolfo di Amato
*Astolfo Di Amato e Associati*

Daniele Geronzi & Chiara
Lunetti
*Legance - Avvocati Associati*

Davide Cacchioli
*Pedersoli e Associati*

Emanele Cortesi
*CMA Law Firm*

Emanuele Scafato
*Società Italiana di Alcologia*

Enrico Maria Mancuso
*Università Cattolica del sacro
Cuore, Milano*

Enzo Balboni
*Università Cattolica del sacro
Cuore, Milano*

Francesco Maria Avato
*University of Ferrara*

Gian Luigi Gatta
*Università degli Studi di
Milano*

Giuseppe Lorenzo Rosa

Giuseppe Scassellati
Sforzolini

Lorenzo Zoppoli
*University of
Naples Federico II*

Luigi Mori
*Biolato, Longo, Ridola & Mori*

Manuela Cavallo
*Portolano Cavallo*

Marco Esposito
*Parthenope
University of Naples*

Mariano Cingolani
*University of Macerata*

Massimiliano Delfino
*University of Naples
Federico II*

Patrizio Ivo D'Andrea
*University of Ferrara*

Pauline R. Rosa

Pierpaolo Martucci
*University of Trieste*

Pietro Faraguna
*LUISS Guido Carli University*

Riccardo Del Punta
*University of Florence*

Roberto Caranta
*University of Turin*

Roberto Rosapepe

Roberto Toniatti
*University of Trento*

Rocchina Staiano
*Università di Teramo*

Serena Forlati
*University of Ferrara*

Valerio De Stefano
*Bocconi University*

Anonymous Contributors

## Jamaica

Althea Bailey
*Community Health &
Psychiatry*

Anthony Clayton
*University of the West Indies*

Antoinette Barton-Gooden
*University of the West Indies*

Audrey Brown

Cynthia Pearl Pitter
*University of the West Indies*

David Smith
*University of the West Indies*

Emile G.R. Leiba
*DunnCox, Attorneys-at-law*

Eris Schoburgh
*University of the West Indies*

J. Peter Figueroa
*University of the West Indies*

Joanne Wood Rattray
*DunnCox, Attorneys-at-law*

Kevin O. Powell
*Hylton Powell,
Attorneys-at-Law*

Lester O. Shields
*University of the West Indies*

Marie Freckleton
*University of the West Indies*

Narda Graham
*DunnCox, Attorneys-at-law*

Nicola Satchell
*University of the West Indies*

Paul D. Brown
*University of the West Indies*

Rachael Irving
*University of the West Indies*

Samantha Burke
*Lex Caribbean,
Attorneys-at-Law*

Sharon Neil Smith
*Patterson Mair Hamilton*

Sharon White
*University of the West Indies*

Sonia D. Gatchair
*University of the West Indies*

Sylvia Mitchell
*University of the West Indies*

Verona Henry Ferguson
*University of the West Indies*

Anonymous Contributors

## Japan

Hiroshi Nishihara
*Waseda University*

Masanori Iwasa
*The Law Office of
Takashi Takano*

Masanori Tanabe
*Sakai Law Office*

Naohiro Yashiro
*Showa Women's University*

Shigeji Ishiguro
*Oguri & Ishiguro Law Office*

Toshiaki Higashi
*University of Occupational
and Environmental Health*

Yasuhiro Fujii
*Law Office of Yasuhiro Fujii*

Anonymous Contributors

## Jordan

Al-Nawayseh Abdulellah
*Mutah University*

Anwar Mahmoud Batieha
*Jordan University of
Science and Technology*

George Hazboun
*International Consolidated for
Legal Consultations*

Mahmoud Ali Quteishat

Rasha Laswi
*Zalloum and Laswi Law Firm*

Tamara Al Rawwad
*University of Houston*

Thaer Najdawi
*A & T Najdawi Law Office*

Anonymous Contributors

## Kazakhstan

Aidos Kussainov
*Sayat Zholshy & Partners
Law Firm*

Assel Kulisheva
*Michael Wilson &
Partners Ltd.*

Dmitriy Chumakov
*Sayat Zholshy & Partners
Law Firm*

Larissa Orlova
*Michael Wilson &
Partners Ltd.*

Nurzhan Albanov
*Dentons Kazakhstan*

Sergei Vataev
*Dechert Kazakhstan Ltd.*

Sofia Zhylkaidarova
*SIGNUM Law Firm*

Yerjanov Timur
*Kazakh National University*

Yerzhan Yessimkhanov
*GRATA International*

Zhanat Alimanov
*KIMEP University*

Anonymous Contributors

## Kenya

Angela Waweru
*Kaplan & Stratton Advocates*

Dennis Mung'ata
*Gichimu Mung'ata Advocates*

Edward Bett
*D.K Korir & Associates
Advocates*

Jacqueline Kamau

James Mang'erere
*Mang'erere J. and Co.,
Advocates*

John Mudegu Vulule
*Kenya Medical Research
Institute*

Kamau Karori
*IKM Advocates*

Kiingati Ndirangu
*Kairu Mbuthia & Kiingati
Advocates*

Laila Abdul Latif
*George & Lydeen Advocates*

Leonard Samson Opundo

Milly Odongo

Thomas N. Maosa
*Maosa & Co., Advocates and Attorneys*

Wilfred Nderitu
*Nderitu & Partners Advocates*

Anonymous Contributors

## Kyrgyzstan

Aikanysh Jeenbaeva
*Academy of Public Administration*

Akbar Suvanbekov
*Ministry of Health*

Albanova Aizhan

Azamat Kerimbaev
*ABA ROLI*

Elena Babitskaya
*VERITAS Law Agency*

Ermek Mamaev
*Kalikova & Associates Law Firm*

Jenishbek Arzymatov

Jyldyz Tagaeva
*Kalikova & Associates Law Firm*

Nadejda Prigoda
*Kyrgyz-Russian Slavic University*

Saltanat Moldoisaeva
*Ministry of Health*

Zhanyl Abdrakhmanova
*Centil Law*

Anonymous Contributors

## Lebanon

Abel F. Mourad
*Al-Manar University of Tripoli*

Antoine G. Ghafari

Elias Chalhoub
*Arab Center for the Development of the Rule of Law and Integrity*

Elias Matar
*Abou Jaoude & Associates Law Firm*

Jean E. Akl
*Akl Law Practice*

Jihad Irani
*University of Balamand*

Joelle Choueifati

Khatoun Haidar
*Synergy - Takamol*

Mohamad Ramadan
*Elaref International Law Office*

Pierre Obeid
*University of Balamand*

Rany Sader
*Sader Legal Publishing*

Roula Zayat
*Arab Center for the Development of the Rule of Law and Integrity*

Salah Mattar
*Mattar Law Firm*

Souraya Machnouk
*Abou Jaoude & Associates Law Firm*

Tony Zreik
*Lebanese American University*

Wissam Kabbara
*Lebanese American University*

Anonymous Contributors

## Liberia

Alfred Hill
*International Development Law Organization*

Cecil Griffiths
*Liberia National Law Enforcement Association*

Hannan J. Karnley-Bestman

James C.R. Flomo
*Public Defenders' Program of Liberia*

Kula L. Jackson
*Heritage Partners & Associates Inc.*

Lorma Baysah
*Rural Human Rights Activists Programme*

Robert N. Gbarbea
*The Carter Center*

T. Debey Sayndee
*Kofi Annan Institute, University of Liberia*

Anonymous Contributors

## Macedonia

Aleksandar Godjo
*Godzo, Kiceec & Novakovski*

Aleksandar Ickovski

Aleksandra Baleva Grozdanova
*Godzo, Kiceec & Novakovski*

Besa Arifi
*South East European University*

Biljana Chavkoska

Dance Gudeva Nikovska
*Ss. Cyril and Methodius University*

Darko Nikodinovski
*Trpenoski Law Firm*

Deljo Kadiev

Doncho Donev
*Ss. Cyril and Methodius University*

Dori Kimova
*Kimova Law Office*

Ilija Nedelkoski
*Cakmakova Advocates*

Katerina Lazareska

Leonid Trpenoski
*Trpenoski Law Firm*

Ljupka Noveska Andonova

Maja Jakimovska
*Cakmakova Advocates*

Maja Risteska
*AD Insurance Policy*

Neda Milevska Kostova
*Studiorum Centre for Regional Policy Research and Cooperation*

Sinisha Dimitrovski
*Law Firm TEMIS SB*

Stefan Chichevaliev
*Studiorum Centre for Regional Policy Research and Cooperation*

Strashko Stojanovski
*Goce Delchev University*

Svetlana Veljanovska

Anonymous Contributors

## Madagascar

Andry Michaël Rajaoharison
*Etude Rajaoharison Andry Michaël*

Antsa L. Ramiakajato
*Cabinet d'Avocats Willy Razafinjatovo*

Bakoly Razaiarisolo Rakotomalala

Ketakandriana Rafitoson
*Wake Up Madagascar*

Lala Ratsiharovala

Léonard Velozandry
*Barreau de Madagascar*

Njara Andrianasoavina
*Cabinet d'Avocats*

Rajerison Alexandra
*Barreau de Madagascar*

Rajerison Olivia Alberte
*Cabinet Rajerison*

Rakotomanantsoa
*John W Ffooks & Co. Law Firm*

Ralambondrainy Rakotobe Nelly
*Cour Suprême de Madagascar*

Rapelanoro Rabenja Fahafahantsoa
*Université Antananrivo*

Rasolonanahary Vololoniaina

Raymond Rakotomanga
*Jhpiego Maternal and Childhood Survival Program*

Riki Joselito Rakotobe
*Cabinet d'Avocat Associés*

Anonymous Contributors

## Malawi

Adamson S. Muula
*University of Malawi*

Allan Hans Muhome
*Malawi Law Society*

Annabel Mtalimanja
*High Court of Malawi*

Charles Mangani
*Malawi College of Medicine*

Gabriel Kambale
*G.K. Associates*

George Naphambo
*Naphambo and Company*

Gift Nankhuni
*G. Nankhuni & Partners*

Jack N'riva
*Malawi Judiciary*

James A.P. Mwaisemba
*Sanctuary Dental Clinic*

Jean Kayira
*Malawi Judiciary*

Madalitso M'meta
*M&M Global Law Consultants*

Martha Kaukonde
*Competition and Fair Trading Commission*

Patrice C. Nkhono
*Mbendera & Nkhono Associates*

Remmie Ng'omba
*Wilson and Morgan*

Sosten Chilumpha

Anonymous Contributors

## Malaysia

Ashgar Ali Ali Mohamed

Chew Phye Keat
*Raja, Darryl & Loh*

Dato' Azmi Mohd Ali
*Azmi & Associates*

Faridah Jalil
*Universiti Kebangsaan Malaysia*

Loong Caesar
*Raslan Loong*

Rizal Rahman
*Universiti Kebangsaan Malaysia*

S. B. Cheah
*S. B. Cheah & Associates*

Sharon Kaur
*University of Malaya*

Vijayan Venugopal
*Shearn Delamore & Co.*

Anonymous Contributors

## Mexico

Alejandra Moreno Altamirano
*Universidad Nacional Autónoma de México*

Alfonso Rodriguez Arana
*Legalmex S.C.*

Alfredo Kupfer-Domínguez
*Sanchez Devanny, Eseverri, S.C.*

Alonso González-Villalobos

Aurea Esther Grijalva Eternod
*Universidad de Guadalajara*

Carlos de Buen Unna
*Bufete de Buen, S.C.*

Carlos Enrique Burguete Medina
*Lazo, Villa, Moel y García, S.C.*

Cinthya Castillero Vera
*Universidad Nacional Autónoma de México; Gerbera Capital Asesores, S.C.*

Daniel Carrancá de la Mora
*Instituto Mexicano para la Justicia*

Elias Huerta Psihas
*Asociación Nacional de Doctores en Derecho*

Emiliano Baidenbaum
*Hewlett Packard Enterprise*

Enrique Camarena Domínguez
*Maqueo, De Garay y Aguilar, S.C.*

Esteban Maqueo Barnetche
*Maqueo, De Garay y Aguilar, S.C.*

Franz Oberarzbacher
*ITAM*

Gilberto Miguel Valle Zulbarán
*Basham Ringe & Correa, S.C.*

Guillermo A. Gatt Corona
*ITESO y Universidad Panamericana*

Guillermo Piecarchic
*PMC GROUP*

Héctor González Schmal

Hugo Hernández-Ojeda Alvírez
*Hogan Lovells BSTL, S.C.*

Iván García Gárate
*Borde Jurídico*

Jorge Luis Silva Méndez
*Banco Mundial*

José Alberto Campos Vargas
*Sanchez Devanny, Eseverri, S.C.*

José Antonio Sadurní González
*AA&R*

José Arturo Granados Cosme
*Universidad Autónoma Metropolitana*

José Fernández de Cevallos y Torres
*Asociación Nacional de Doctores en Derecho*

José Rodrigo Moreno Rodríguez
*Medina y Rodríguez Abogados, S.C.*

Juan Carlos Tornel
*Hewlett Packard Enterprise*

Juan Francisco Torres Landa R.
*Hogan Lovells*

Juan Manuel Juarez Mesa
*Contramar Abogados*

L. Alberto Balderas Fernández
*Jáuregui y Del Valle, S.C.*

Luciano Mendoza Cruz
*Universidad Nacional Autónoma de México*

Mario Alberto Rocha
*PricewaterhouseCoopers*

Monica Schiaffino
*Littler Mexico*

Oliva López Arellano
*Universidad Autónoma Metropolitana*

Pablo Medina Magallanes
*Medina y Rodríguez Abogados, S.C.*

Rodrigo Lazo
*Lazo, Villa, Moel y García, S.C.*

Sergio López Moreno
*Universidad Autónoma Metropolitana*

Teresa Carmona

Victor Manuel Ortega Gonzalez
*Fundación Civitas Firma, A.C.*

Anonymous Contributors

## Moldova

Adrian Belii
*Nicolae Testemitanu State University of Medicine and Pharmacy*

Alexandru Cuznetov
*Moldova State University*

Alexei Croitor

Daniel Martin
*BAA ACI Partners*

Graur Eugeniu
*NGO Certitudine*

Iulia Furtuna
*Turcan Cazac Law Firm*

Marica Dumitrasco
*Academy of Sciences of Moldova*

Vitalie Zama

Anonymous Contributors

## Mongolia

B. Enkhbat
*MDS & KhanLex LLP*

Badamragchaa Purevdorj
*Open Society Forum of Mongolia*

Batbayar Ganbayar
*Batbayar and Partners LLP*

Bayar Budragchaa
*ELC Advocates LLP*

David C. Buxbaum
*Anderson & Anderson LLP*

Erdenebalsuren Damdin
*Supreme Court of Mongolia*

Erdenebat Ganbat
*General Prosecutors Office*

G. Batjargal
*MDS & KhanLex LLP*

Ganbat Byambaa
*Ulaanbaatar City Health Department*

Indermohan S. Narula
*Global Fund*

Khishigsaikhan Batchuluun
*Open Society Forum of Mongolia*

Munkhdorj Badral
*Mongol Advocates LLP*

Munkhjargal Ragchaakhuu
*BNP LLP*

Nomingerel Khuyag

Saranchimeg Byamba
*National Registration and Statistical Office*

Sunjid Dugar
*Civic Engagement Project*

Zanaa Jurmed
*Center for Citizens' Alliance*

Anonymous Contributors

## Morocco

Abdelaziz Amraoui

Abdellah Bakkali
*Bakkali Law Firm*

Ali Lachgar Essahili
*Lachgar Essahili Law Firm*

Azzedine Kettani
*Kettani Law Firm*

Badi Ali
*Centre Marocain des Droits de l'Homme*

Lhassan M'Barki
*Southern for Studies and Sustainable Development*

M. S. Briou
*BriouLaw*

Mimoun Charqi
*Charqi Lex Consulting*

Mohamed Aakinou

Mohamed Baske Manar
*Université Cadi Ayyad*

Mohamed El Mernissi
*FIGES*

Mohamed Salmi
*Comité des droits de l'Homme*

Nesrine Roudane
*NERO Boutique Law Firm*

Richard D. Cantin
*NERO Boutique Law Firm*

S. Fenjiro

Saad Moummi

Tarik Mossadek
*Université Hassan I. Settat*

Zineb Idrissia Hamzi
*Hamzi Law Firm*

Anonymous Contributors

## Myanmar

Cho Cho Myint
*Interactive Co., Ltd.*

Kyaw Kyaw Han

Min Thein
*Rajah & Tann NK Legal Co. Ltd.*

Myint Aung
*Aids Support Group*

Nickey Diamond
*Fortify Rights*

Tin Sein
*Polastri Wint & Partners Legal Services Ltd.*

U Mya Thein
*U Mya Thein & Legal Group*

Win Naing
*Supreme Court of Myanmar*

Wint Thandar Oo
*Polastri Wint & Partners Legal Services Ltd.*

Anonymous Contributors

## Nepal

Bijaya Prasad Mishra
*Kalyan Law Firm*

Bishnu Luitel
*BG Law Foundation*

Budhi Karki
*Constitutional Litigation & Consultancy Services*

Gourish K. Kharel
*Kto Inc.*

Madhab Raj Ghimire
*PSM Global Consultants P. Ltd*

Narayan P. Ghimire
*Pradhan, Ghimire & Associates*

Nil Mani Upadhyay

Rabin Subedi
*Public Interest Law, Advocacy and Litigation Nepal*

Rup Narayan Shrestha
*Avenue Law Firm*

Sangha Ratna Bajracharya
*Institute of Medicine*

Shankar Limbu
*Lawyers' Association for Human Rights of Nepalese Indigenous Peoples*

Shiva Prasad Rijal
*Pioneer Law Associates Ltd.*

Subarna K. Khatry
*Nepal Nutrition Intervention Project - Sarlahi*

Sudeep Gautam
*Center for Legal Research and Resource Development*

Sudha Kafle

Anonymous Contributors

## Netherlands

A.A. Bloemberg
*Mesland & Vroegh Advocaten*

Agnes C. Gebhard
*KNCV TB Foundation*

Arnold Versteeg
*Macro & Versteeg Advocaten*

Eugenie Nunes
*Boekel*

G. den Hertog
*Galavazi Den Hertog*

Hans J. Hoegen Dijkhof
*Hoegen Dijkhof Attorneys & Tax Counsellors*

Hansko Broeksteeg
*Radboud University*

JAC Meeuwissen
*Trimbos Institute, Institute of Mental Health and Addiction*

Jacqueline van den Bosch
*IVY Corporate Defence & Investigations*

Jasper van Hulst
*Höcker Advocaten*

Joost Italianer
*NautaDutilh N.V.*

M.E. van den Akker
*Hewlett Packard Enterprise*

M.J. de Heer
*Vakbond De Unie*

Marcel Willems
*Kennedy Van der Laan NV*

Petrus C. van Duyne
*Tilburg University*

S.F.H. Jellinghaus
*Tilburg University; De Voort Advocaten*

Theo de Roos
*Tilburg University*

Anonymous Contributors

## New Zealand

**Aaron Lloyd**
*Minter Ellison Rudd Watts*

**Alan Knowsley**
*Rainey Collins Lawyers*

**Alberto Costi**
*Victoria University of Wellington*

**Andrew Geddis**
*University of Otago*

**Andrew Schulte**
*Cavell Leitch*

**Austin Forbes**

**Brian Keene**

**Campbell Roberts**
*The Salvation Army Social Policy and Parliamentary Unit*

**Cheryl Simes**
*Kiwilaw*

**Chris Noonan**
*University of Auckland*

**D. J. Lyon**
*Lyon O'Neale Arnold*

**Danny Jacobson**
*D. Jacobson & T. Marshall Employment Lawyers*

**David V. Williams**
*University of Auckland*

**Dean Kilpatrick**
*Anthony Harper Lawyers*

**Denise Arnold**
*Lyon O'Neale Arnold*

**Erich Bachmann**
*Hesketh Henry*

**Gay Morgan**
*University of Waikato*

**Geoff Hall**
*University of Otago*

**Gordon Anderson**
*Victoria University of Wellington*

**Grace Haden**
*Transparency New Zealand, Ltd.*

**Jyostana Haria**
*Justitia Chambers*

**Kathryn Guise**
*Brown Partners Lawyers*

**Kevin J. Riordan**
*Office of the Judge Advocate General*

**M. B. Rodriguez Ferrere**
*University of Otago*

**Malcolm Rabson**

**Marie Bismark**
*University of Melbourne*

**Marie Grills**
*RPB Law*

**Mark Bennett**
*Victoria University of Wellington*

**Mark Winger**
*Holmden Horrocks*

**Mary-Rose Russell**

**Matt Berkahn**
*Massey University*

**Michael Bott**

**Mike French**
*Auckland University of Technology*

**Nick Crang**
*Duncan Cotterill*

**Nicola Wheen**
*University of Otago*

**Nigel Hampton**

**Paul Michalik**

**Paul Roth**
*University of Otago*

**Penny Bright**

**Peter Watts**
*University of Auckland*

**Petra Butler**
*Victoria University of Wellington*

**Simon Ladd**
*Bell Gully*

**Sonja M. Cooper**
*Cooper Legal*

**Stephen Eliot Smith**
*University of Otago*

**Stephen Franks**
*Franks Ogilvie*

**Steven Zindel**
*Zindels*

**Trevor Daya-Winterbottom**
*University of Waikato*

**W. John Hopkins**
*University of Canterbury*

**W. M. Thomson**
*University of Otago*

**William Akel**
*Simpson Grierson*

**Anonymous Contributors**

## Nicaragua

**Ana Carolina Álvarez Gil**
*Consortium Legal - Nicaragua*

**Angélica María Toruño García**
*Universidad Evangélica Martin Luther King Jr.*

**David José Sánchez Soza**
*Consortium Legal - Nicaragua*

**John L. Minnella**
*Minnella Romano y Asociados*

**Luis Manuel Perezalonso Lanzas**
*Bufete Jurídico Perezalonso*

**Ramiro Rodríguez Urcuyo**
*INTERPROLAW*

**Samantha Aguilar Beteta**
*Consortium Legal - Nicaragua*

**Urania Ruiz Condega**

**Víctor Jesús Méndez Dussán**
*Asociación Nicaragüense de Salud Pública*

**Anonymous Contributors**

## Nigeria

**Abdulfattah Adewale Bakre**
*Legal Aid Council of Nigeria*

**Abdulhamid Abdullahi Bagara**
*Community Health and Research Initiative - Kano*

**Adamu M. Usman**
*F.O. Akinrele & Co.*

**Adedolapo Akinrele**
*F.O. Akinrele & Co.*

**Adewale Akande**
*Auxilium Attorneys*

**Agu Ezetah**
*Law Agu Ezetah & Co.*

**Aniekan Ukpanah**
*Udo Udoma & Belo-Osagie*

**Bisi Bright**
*LiveWell Initiative*

**Bolanle O. Jibogun**
*Legal Aid Council of Nigeria*

**Chioma Kanu Agomo**
*University of Lagos*

**Chudi Nelson Ojukwu**
*LC&N*

**Chukwuemeka Castro Nwabuzor**
*Nigerian Institute of Advanced Legal Studies*

**Chukwunweike Ogbuabor**
*University of Nigeria*

**Dolapo Akinrele**
*F.O. Akinrele & Co.*

**Eno Ebong**
*Hewlett Packard Enterprise*

**Enoch Mozong Azariah**
*Legal Aid Council of Nigeria*

**Felicia Nwanne Monye**
*University of Nigeria*

**Festus Okechukwu Ukwueze**
*University of Nigeria*

**Festus Onyia**
*Udo Udoma & Belo-Osagie*

**Funmilola OlaOlorun**
*University of Ibadan College of Medecine*

**Gbenga Odusola**
*Gbenga Odusola & Co.*

**Godwin Etim**
*AELEX*

**Godwin O. Obla**

**Innocent Abidoye**
*Nnenna Ejekam Associates*

**Joseph E. O. Abugu**
*Abugu & Co.*

**Jumoke Fajemirokun**
*Advisory Legal Consultants*

**Michael Abayomi Bisade Alliyu**
*Chief Yomi Alliyu & Co.*

**Michael C. Asuzu**
*University of Ibadan College of Medecine*

**Morenikeji Osilaja**
*Sofunde Osakwe Ogundipe & Belgore*

**Nelson Ogbuanya**
*Nocs Consults*

**Nkadi Anthony**
*F.O. Akinrele & Co.*

**Obiajulu Nnamuchi**
*University of Nigeria*

**Oghogho Makinde**
*Aluko & Oyebode*

**Oladejo Justus Olowu**
*American University of Nigeria School of Law*

**Olasupo Olaibi**
*Supo Olaibi & Company*

**Olubunmi Fayokun**
*Aluko & Oyebode*

**Olumide Aju**
*F.O. Akinrele & Co.*

**Olumide Ekisola**
*Adejumo & Ekisola: Legal Practitioners*

**Oluwadamilare Yomi-Alliyu**
*Chief Yomi Alliyu & Co.*

**Onjefu Adoga**
*Brooke Chambers Law Firm*

**Ozofu Olatunde Ogiemudia**
*Udo Udoma & Belo-Osagie*

**Pontian N. Okoli**
*University of Dundee*

**Precious Aderemi**
*Babalakin & Co., Nigeria*

**Terrumun Z. Swende**
*Benue State University College of Health Sciences*

**Yomi Dare**
*Yomi Dare & Co.*

**Yusuf Ali San**
*Yusuf Ali & Co.*

**Anonymous Contributors**

## Norway

**Arild Vaktskjold**
*Sjukehuset i Innlandet og Høgskulen i Hedmark*

**Bent Endresen**
*EBT Advocates*

**Erik Keiserud**
*Advokatfirmaet Hjort DA*

**Erlig Lind**
*Advokatfirmaet Wiersholm*

**Harald B. Ciarlo**

**Ivar Alvik**
*University of Oslo*

**Jan Frich**
*University of Oslo*

**Jan Fridthjof Bernt**
*University of Bergen*

**Jon T. Johnsen**
*University of Oslo*

**Karl Harald Søvig**
*University of Bergen*

**Magne Strandberg**
*University of Bergen*

**Magnus Ødegaard**
*Bing Hodneland Advokatselskap DA*

**Niels R. Kiær**
*Rime Advokatfirma DA*

**Stella M. Tuft**
*Microsoft*

**Terje Einarsen**
*University of Bergen*

**Tor Vale**

**Ulf Stridbeck**
*University of Oslo*

**Anonymous Contributors**

## Pakistan

**Abdul Ghaffar Khan**
*Fazleghani Advocates*

**Asma Balal**
*Marie Stopes Society*

**Asma Jahangir**
*AGHS Legal Aid Cell*

**Faiza Muzaffar**
*Legis Inn Attorneys &
Corporate Consultants*

**Hasan Hameed Bhatti**
*Lahore Waste
Management Company*

**Iftikhar Ahmad Tarar**
*Punjab University Law College*

**Karamat Ali**
*PILER*

**Kausar S. Khan**
*Aga Khan University*

**Mohammad Akmal Wasim**
*Legal Rights Forum*

**Mohammad Zakaria**

**Muhammad Nouman Shams**
*Qazi Law Associates,
Advocates &
Legal Consultants*

**Muzaffar Islam**
*Legis Inn Attorneys &
Corporate Consultants*

**Qasim Ali Bhatti**

**Rubina Ali**

**Saqib Jillani**
*Jillani & Co.*

**Shams ul Haque Joiya**
*Right Law Company*

**Sohail Bawani**
*Aga Khan University*

**Tariq Rahim**
*Tariq Rahim Law Associates*

**Umer Farooq**
*Ayub Medical College*

**Xaher Gul**
*Marie Stopes Society*

**Anonymous Contributors**

## Panama

**Alcides Gabriel
Castillo Rivera**
*Acabogadopty*

**Ibis Sánchez-Serrano**
*The Core Model
Corporation, SA*

**Mario A. Rognoni H.**
*Arosemena, Noriega &
Contreras*

**Tomás Humberto
Herrera Díaz**
*Movimiento I
nstitucionalidad y Justicia*

**Anonymous Contributors**

## Peru

**Alberto Varillas C.**
*García Sayán Abogados*

**Alfredo Gastañeta Alayza**
*García Sayán Abogados*

**Arturo Gárate Salazar**
*Universidad Federico
Villarreal*

**Cecilia Ma Cardenas**

**César Puntriano Rosas**
*Pontificia Universidad
Católica del Perú*

**Danilo Sanchez Coronel**
*Universidad Cesar Vallejo*

**Dennis Oswaldo
Vílchez Ramírez**
*Estudio Ghersi Abogados*

**Elena Timoteo Quispe**

**German Jimenez Borra**
*Estudio Muñiz, Ramirez, Perez
Taiman & Olaya Abogados*

**Glenn Alberto
Lozano Zanelly**
*Universidad Inca Garcilaso
de la Vega*

**Gonzalo Garcia
Calderon Moreyra**
*Estudio Garcia Calderon*

**Grover Jonny
Arangurí Carranza**
*Seguro Social del Perú*

**Gustavo de los Ríos Woolls**
*Rey & de los Ríos - Abogados*

**Ismael Cornejo-Rosello
Dianderas**
*Gerencia Regional
de Salud Arequipa*

**Jean Paul Borit**
*Hewlett Packard Enterprise*

**José Luis Velarde Lazarte**
*Estudio Olaechea*

**Julio Espinoza Jiménez**
*Universidad Federico
Villarreal*

**Karla Zuta Palacios**

**Marco Alarcon**
*Estudio Echecopar*

**Marcos Ricardo
Revatta Salas**
*Universidad Nacional San Luis
Gonzaga de Ica*

**María del Pilar Pozo García**
*Hospital Central Fuerza
Aérea del Perú*

**Nelson Ramirez Jiménez**

**Orlando De Las Casas**
*Estudio Yori Abogados*

**Raquel Cancino**
*Universidad Peruana
Cayetano Heredia*

**Ricardo Antonio
Pauli Montewnegro**

**Rosa Maria
Velasco Valderas**
*Instituto Nacional de
Ciencias Neurológicas*

**Rossana Maccera**

**Anonymous Contributors**

## Philippines

**Afdal B. Kunting**
*Zamboanga City
Medical Center*

**Carmelita Gopez Nuqui**
*Development Action for
Women Network*

**Cesar L. Villanueva**
*Governance Commission
for GOCCs*

**Emerico O. De Guzman**
*ACCRALAW*

**Enriquito J. Mendoza**
*Romulo Mabanta
Buenaventura Sayoc & de los
Angeles*

**Francis Tom Temprosa**
*Ateneo de Manila University
School of Law*

**Jesusito G. Morallos**
*Follosco Morallos & Herce*

**Joanna Maries Narvaez**

**Joanne B. Babon**
*Follosco Morallos & Herce*

**Jonathan Sale**

**Jose Cochingyan III**
*Cochingyan & Peralta
l aw Offices*

**Karen Gomez Dumpit**
*Commission on Human Rights
of the Philippines*

**Ma. Louisa Viloria-Yap**
*The Law Firm of Garcia Inigo
& Partners*

**Maita Chan-Gonzaga**
*Ateneo de Manila University
School of Law*

**Marizen Santos**
*Commission on Human Rights
of the Philippines*

**Nancy Joan Javier**
*Javier Law*

**Oliver Pantaleon**
*ACCRALAW*

**Reginald A. Tongol**
*Regie Tongol Law and
Communications Firm*

**Reynald Trillana**
*Philippine Center for Civic
Education and Democracy*

**Ronahlee A. Asuncion**
*SOLAIR, University of the
Philippines Diliman*

**Anonymous Contributors**

## Poland

**Adam Morawski**
*Morawski & Partners
Law Firm*

**Agnieszka Helsztyńska**
*Kancelaria Adwokacka
Agnieszka Helsztyńska*

**Andrzej Brodziak**
*Institute of
Occupational Medicine and
Environmental Health*

**Jacek Wierciński**
*Warsaw University*

**Janusz Bojarski**
*Nicolaus Copernicus
University*

**Joanna
Kosińska-Wiercińska**

**Krzysztof Kowalczyk**
*BSJP*

**Krzysztof Rastawicki**
*Rastawicki Mianowski
Sawicki sp.k.*

**Krzysztof Wierzbowski**
*Wierzbowski Eversheds*

**Małgorzata Grzelak**
*Squire Patton Boggs*

**Paweł Lipski**
*Wierzbowski Eversheds*

**Piotr Jakub Rastawicki**
*Rastawicki Mianowski
Sawicki sp.k.*

**Piotr Sadownik**
*Gide Loyrette Nouel*

**Radoslaw T. Skowron**
*KKPW Law Office*

**Stefan Jaworski**

**Tomasz Trojanowski**
*Przychodnia Wassowskiego*

**Anonymous Contributors**

## Portugal

**Anja Bothe**
*Universidade Autónoma
Lisbon*

**António José Casa Nova**
*Escola Superior de Saúde de
Portalegre*

**Carlos Lopes Ribeiro**
*CR - Advogados*

**Carolina Boullosa Gonzalez**
*ACE - Sociedade de
Advogados, RL*

**Eduardo Buisson Loureiro**

**Eduardo Correia
de Azevedo**
*Chaves, Roquette, Matos,
Azevedo & Asociados*

**Fernando Antas da Cunha**
*Antas da Cunha & Asociados*

**Inês Reis**
*PBBR - Sociedade de
Advogados*

**Joana Barrilaro Ruas**
*Ferreira da Conceição,
Menezes & Associados*

**José Alves do Carmo**
*AVM Advogados*

**Libertário Teixeira**
*LTCF Law Firm*

**Luis Brito Correia**
*Luis Brito Correia, Advogados*

**Luis Miguel Amaral**
*Luis Miguel Amaral -
Advogados*

**Margarida Lucas Rodrigues**
*ACE - Sociedade de
Advogados*

**Maria do Rosário Anjos**
*Anjos, Martins & Asociados*

**Miguel Andrade**
*Miguel Andrade Lawyers*

**Miguel Reis**
*MRA Lawyers*

**Pedro Pinto**
*PBBR  Sociedade de
Advogados*

**Rui Tavares Correia**
*Abreu & Marques*

**Sandrine Bisson Marvao**
*Bisson Marvao*

Teresa Anselmo Vaz
*Anselmo Vaz, Afra & Asociados*

Tiago Melo Alves
*Melo Alves - Advogados*

Anonymous Contributors

## Republic of Korea

Bok Ki Hong
*Yonsei University School of Law*

Charles Choo
*Jehyun Law*

Duk Yeon Lee
*Yonsei University School of Law*

Haksoo Ko
*Seoul National University School of Law*

Hwang Lee
*Korea University School of Law*

Jaeseop Song
*Shin & Kim*

Jeongeun Choi
*Yoon & Yang*

Jeongoh Kim
*Yonsei University*

Jiyong Park
*Yonsei University*

Junsok Yang
*The Catholic University of Korea*

Sang Won Lee
*Seoul National University*

Sangbong Lee
*Hwang Mok Park, PC*

Seungwoo Lee
*Kim & Chang*

Anonymous Contributors

## Romania

Alexandru Moldoveanu
*Țuca Zbârcea & Asociații*

Anca Albulescu
*bpv Grigorescu Stefanica*

Andrei Danciu
*SCA Cataniciu & Asociații*

Andrei Mircea Zamfirescu
*Gilescu, Valeanu, Nathanzon & Partners - CHSH*

Aura Campeanu
*PETOŠEVIĆ*

Aurora Ciuca
*Iasi Bar of Barristers; Stefan cel Mare University*

Bogdan C. Stoica
*Popovici Nitu Stoica & Asociatii*

Catalin Micu
*Zamfirescu Racoti & Partners*

Christian Bogaru
*Bogaru, Braun Noviello & Associates*

Cornescu Oana Lucia
*Țuca Zbârcea & Asociații*

Cosmin Flavius Costaş
*Costaş, Negru & Asociații - Societate Civilă de Avocați*

Cristina Alexe
*ACEADVISOR, Attorneys at Law*

Dan Curiciuc
*SCA Zamfirescu Racoti & Partners*

Dan Oancea
*Dan Oancea Law Office*

Daniel Nitu
*Babes-Bolyai University; Iordachescu & Associates Law Firm*

Dariescu Cosmin
*Alexandru Ioan Cuza University of Iași*

Diana Botau
*Babes-Bolyai University*

Dragos Daghie
*Daghie & Asociații*

Felicia Rosioru
*Babes-Bolyai University*

Flavius A. Baias
*University of Bucharest*

Gheorghe Piperea
*Piperea & Asociații*

Gherdan Sergiu
*Gherdan Law Office*

Iulian Patrascanu
*Fine Law - Patrascanu & Associates*

Larion Alina Paula
*Stefan cel Mare University*

Lazăr Ioan
*Baroul Alba*

Lazar Laura
*Babes-Bolyai University*

Lucian Bondoc
*Bondoc & Asociații, SCA*

Marius Balan
*Alexandru Ioan Cuza University of Iași*

Maxim Mihaela Liliana
*Țuca Zbârcea & Asociații*

Mihai Dunea
*Alexandru Ioan Cuza University of Iași*

Mihail Romeo Nicolescu
*Romeo Nicolescu Law Office*

Miloiu Ciprian

Nicolae-Bogdan Bulai
*University of Bucharest*

Ovidiu Podaru
*Babes-Bolyai University*

Panainte Vasile Septimiu
*Alexandru Ioan Cuza University of Iași*

Radu Rizoiu
*Rizoiu & Asociații, SCA*

Roxana Iordachescu
*Iordachescu & Associates Law Firm*

Serban Paslaru
*Țuca Zbârcea & Asociații*

Sergiu Golub
*Babes-Bolyai University*

Stoia Iulian Aleander
*Bucharest Bar Association*

Valeriu M. Ciuca
*Alexandru Ioan Cuza University of Iași*

Veronica Dobozi
*Stoica & Asociații*

Anonymous Contributors

## Russia

Alexander Romanov
*RANEPA*

Andrey Neznamov
*Dentons*

Anton Iuzhanin
*Russin & Vecchi, LLC*

Eduard Margulyan
*Moscow Legal Bureau of Margulyan & Kovalev*

Natalia G. Prisekina
*Russin & Vecchi, LLC*

Natalya Morozova
*Vinson & Elkins, LLP*

Nikolai Kostenko
*Moscow Helsinki Group*

Vladimir Yarkov
*Urals State Law University*

Zhanna Iosivna Ovsepyan
*South Federal University*

Anonymous Contributors

## Saint Kitts & Nevis

Charles Wilkin
*Kelsick, Wilkin, and Ferdinand*

Dia Forrester
*Daniel Brantley Attorneys at Law*

Gyan Robinson
*Daniel Brantley Attorneys at Law*

Jan Dash
*Liburd and Dash, LP*

Lenora Walwyn
*WalwynLaw*

Michella Adrien
*Michella Adrien Law Offices*

Rayana Dowden
*WEBSTER*

Anonymous Contributors

## Saint Lucia

Leandra Gabrielle Verneuil
*Jennifer Remy & Associates*

Paulette Francis
*Paulette Francis Chambers*

Trudy O. Glasgow
*Trudy O. Glasgow & Associates*

Virginia Joseph
*Spartan Health Science University*

Anonymous Contributors

## Saint Vincent & the Grenadines

Heidi Badenock
*UNILAC*

Israel R. Bruce
*Bruce Law Chambers*

Michaela Ambrose
*Baptiste & Co. Law Firm, Inc.*

Mikhail Charles
*Baptiste & Co. Law Firm, Inc.*

Moureeze Franklyn
*Baptiste & Co. Law Firm, Inc.*

Patricia P. Marks-Minors
*The Law Firm of Marks & Marks*

S. C. Fraser
*Sentinel Law*

Shirlan Barnwell
*LegalEase SVG Inc.*

Anonymous Contributors

## Senegal

Akanni
*Université Cheikh Anta Diop de Dakar*

Ameth Ba
*SCP Ba & Tandian*

Bocar Balde
*GENI & KEBE Law Firm*

Boubacar Borgho Diakite
*GENI & KEBE Law Firm*

Christian Faye
*Christian Faye & Associés*

Cire Cledor Ly
*Avocat du Barreau de Dakar*

Diène Kolly Ousseynou Diouf
*Université Assane Seck de Ziguinchor*

El Hadji Mame Gning
*EMG-Avocats Sénégal*

Ibrahima-Baidy Niane
*Avocats Sans Frontières Sénégal*

Mamadou Ba
*USADF Sénégal*

Mansour Gningue
*GENI & KEBE Law Firm*

Moussa Mbacke

Moussa Sarr
*SCP Mame Adama Gueye et Associés*

Moustapha Ndoye et ses collaborateurs

Ndiaye Semou
*Université Cheikh Anta Diop de Dakar*

Samba Cor Sarr
*Ministère de la Santé et de l'Action sociale*

Anonymous Contributors

## Serbia

Danilo Curcic
*YUCOM Lawyers' Committee for Human Rights*

Djordje Djurisic
*Law Office of Djordje Djurisic*

Dragan Psodorov
*Joksovic, Stojanovic & Partners*

Dusan S. Dimitrijevic
*Dimitrijevic Law Office*

Dušan Stojković
*Stojković Law Office*

Ivan Kovacevic
*Lalin Law Office*

Nadica Figar

Nebojsa Stankovic
*Stankovic & Partners*

Petar Stojanovic
*Joksovic, Stojanovic & Partners*

Simonida Sladojevic-Stanimirovic

Vladimir Marinkov
*Guberina-Marinkov Law Office*

Zeljko Kuvizic
*Kuvizic & Tadic Law Office*

Anonymous Contributors

## Sierra Leone

Africanus Sorie Sesay
*Tanner Legal Advisory*

Augustine Sorie-Sengbe Marrah
*Yada Williams and Associates*

Editayo Pabs-Garnon

Lornard Taylor
*Taylor & Associates*

Anonymous Contributors

## Singapore

Chia Boon Teck
*Chia Wong LLP*

Dan W. Puchniak
*National University of Singapore*

Elizabeth Siew-Kuan Ng
*National University of Singapore*

Eric Tin Keng Seng
*Donaldson & Burkinshaw LLP*

Foo Cheow Ming

Gregory Chan C.T.
*The Occupational and Diving Medicine Centre*

Jaclyn L. Neo
*National University of Singapore*

K.H. Mak
*Gleneagles Medical Centre*

Michael Ewing-Chow
*National University of Singapore*

Simon Chesterman
*National University of Singapore*

Stefanie Yuen Thio
*TSMP Law Corporation*

Anonymous Contributors

## Slovenia

Andrej Bukovnik
*PETOŠEVIĆ*

Anton Gradišek
*Dagra D.O.O.*

Grega Strban
*University of Ljubljana*

Jorg Sladič
*University of Maribor*

Josip Sever

Matija Repolusk
*Repolusk Law Firm*

Matjaz Jan
*ODI Law Firm*

Peter Kos

Primož Rožman
*Blood Transfusion Centre of Slovenia*

Suzana Kraljić
*University of Maribor*

Tilen Tacol
*Law Firm Ilić & Partners LLP*

Tine Mišic
*ODI Law Firm*

Anonymous Contributors

## South Africa

Altair Richards
*ENSafrica*

Bart Willems
*Stellenbosch University*

Bernadine Benson
*University of South Africa*

Boitumelo Mmusinyane
*University of South Africa*

Chantelle Feldhaus
*North-West University*

Christa Rautenbach
*North-West University*

D. A. Hellenberg
*University of Cape Town School of Public Health & Family Medicine*

Fawzia Cassim
*University of South Africa*

Francois Venter
*North-West University*

Funmilola Abioye
*University of South Africa*

Gerhard Kemp
*Stellenbosch University*

Graham Damant
*Bowman Gilfillan*

Gusha Xolani Ngantweni
*University of South Africa*

Hanneretha Kruger
*University of South Africa*

Henry Ngcobo
*Bowmans*

Johann Kriegler
*Freedom UnderLaw*

John Ataguba
*University of Cape Town School of Public Health & Family Medicine*

John Brand
*Bowman Gilfillan*

John Faris
*Institute for Dispute Resolution in Africa, University of South Africa*

Jonathan Klaaren
*University of the Witwatersrand*

Kelly Phelps
*University of Cape Town*

Leon M. Louw
*Free Market Foundation*

Lindiwe Maqutu
*University of KwaZulu-Natal*

M. A. Du Plessis
*University of the Witwatersrand*

M. Budeli-Nemakonde
*University of South Africa*

Mark Lazarus
*Hewlett Packard Enterprise*

Marlize I. van Jaarsveld
*Fairleigh Dickinson University*

Martin Brassey

Michael Evans
*Webber Wentzel*

Milton Seligson
*Cape Bar*

N. A. Cameron
*Stellenbosch University*

N. G. Mtshali
*University of KwaZulu-Natal*

Peter Jordi
*Wits Law Clinic*

Pieter du Toit
*North-West University*

R. S. Green
*Cox Yeats*

Rolien Roos
*North-West University*

Rudolph Zinn
*University of South Africa*

S. S. Terblanche
*University of South Africa*

Tamara Cohen
*University of KwaZulu-Natal*

Tana Pistorius
*University of South Africa*

Thulani Nkosi
*Wits Law Clinic*

Victoria Bronstein
*University of the Witwatersrand*

Yousuf A. Vawda
*University of KwaZulu-Natal School of Law*

Anonymous Contributors

## Spain

Alfonso Pedrajas Herrero
*Abdón Pedrajas & Molero Abogados & Asesores Tributarios*

Alfonso Trallero
*Bajo & Trallero Abogados*

Álvaro Torres Lana
*Universidad de La Laguna*

Andrea Macía Morillo
*Universidad Autónoma de Madrid*

Antonio Pedrajas Quiles
*Abdón Pedrajas Abogados, SLP*

Araceli Peláez
*De Castro Gabinete Jurídico*

AuxMundus
*AuxMundus Abogados Internacionales*

Carles García Roqueta
*Mallart & Garcia Roqueta Abogados*

Carlos Alvarez Dardet
*Universidad de Alicante*

Carlos Campillo-Artero
*Universitat Pompeu Fabra*

Carlos Gómez de la Escalera

Carmen Sáez Lara
*Universidad de Córdoba*

César Aguado Renedo
*Universidad Autónoma de Madrid*

Christian Herrera Petrus
*Herrera Advocats*

Daniel Marín Moreno
*Gómez-Acebo & Pombo*

Diego Gómez Iniesta
*Universidad de Castilla-La Mancha*

Elena Espinosa
*Servicio Canario de Salud*

Emilio Díaz Ruiz
*Universidad Complutense de Madrid*

Esther Fernández Molina
*Universidad de Castilla-La Mancha*

Esther Mercado Garcia
*Universidad de Castilla-La Mancha*

Federico Durán López
*Catedráticos Universidad de Córdoba*

Federico Rodríguez Morata
*Universidad de Castilla-La Mancha*

Fernando Alberich Arjona
*De Castro Gabinete Jurídico*

Fernando Bondía Román
*Universidad Carlos III de Madrid*

Fernando Escorza Muñoz
*Dirección General de Salud Pública y Consumo*

Gustavo de las Heras
*Universidad de Castilla-La Mancha*

Gustavo López-Muñoz Larraz
*López-Muñoz y Larraz & Associados*

Jacobo Dopico Gómez-Aller
*Universidad Carlos III de Madrid*

Javier Melero
*Melero & Gené Advocats*

Javier Ramirez Iglesias
*Hewlett Packard; IE Law School*

Jesús Padilla Gálvez
*Universidad de Castilla-La Mancha*

Joan R. Villalbí
*Agència de Salut Pública de Barcelona*

Jorge Sirvent García
*Universidad Carlos III de Madrid*

José Cid
*Universidad Autónoma de Barcelona*

Jose Dominguez Ortega
*Cremades y Calvo Sotelo Abogados*

José Fernández-Rañada
*J & A Garrigues, SLP*

Jose Luis Cebrian Gutierrez
*J & A Garrigues, SLP*

José Luis Cembrano Reder
*Asociación Española de Abogados de Familia (AEAFA)*

Jose Luis de Peray
*Fundación de Religiosos para la Salud*

José Luis Goñi Sein
*Catedrático de Derecho del Trabajo de la Universidad Pública de Navarra*

José Mª Ordóñez Iriarte
*Sociedad Española de Sanidad Ambiental*

José María Labeaga Azcona
*Universidad Nacional de Educación a Distancia*

José Vte. Martí-Boscà
*Universitat de Valencia*

Josefa Cantero Martinez
*Universidad de Castilla-La Mancha*

Juan Alberto Díaz López
*J. A. Díaz - Litigación Penal*

Juan Antonio Lascuraín
*Universidad Autónoma de Madrid*

Juan Francisco Aguiar Rodriguez
*Servicio Canario de Salud*

Juan Ignacio Marcos González
*Despacho de abogados Marcos Abogados Bilbao*

Juan M. Terradillos
*Universidad de Cádiz*

Juan Oliva
*Universidad de Castilla-La Mancha*

Juana María Serrano García
*Universidad de Castilla-La Mancha*

Luis Gaite
*Hospital Universitario Marques de Valdecilla*

Manuel Alvarez Feijoo
*Uría Ménendez Abogados, SLP*

Manuel Ángel De las Heras García
*Universidad de Alicante*

Manuel García-Villarrubia
*Uría Menéndez Abogados*

Mar Carrasco Andrino
*Universidad de Alicante*

Margarita Isabel Ramos Quintana
*Universidad de La Laguna*

María Acale Sánchez
*Universidad de Cádiz*

María Barberá Riera
*Sociedad Española de Sanidad Ambiental*

María Cristina Pumar Atrio
*Rambla Abogados & Asesores*

Marina Lorente Lara
*J & A Garrigues, SLP*

Mario Ibáñez López

Martín Godino
*Asociación Nacional de Laboralistas*

Mercedes Pérez Manzano
*Universidad Autónoma de Madrid*

Orlanda Díaz-García
*Universidad de Castilla-La Mancha*

Paz Mercedes de la Cuesta Aguado
*Universidad de Cantabria*

Rafael Ortiz Cervello
*Garrigues Abogados*

Rebeca Benarroch
*Benarroch*

Remedios Menéndez Calvo
*Universidad de Alcalá*

Roberto Mazorriaga Las Hayas
*Rambla Abogados & Asesores*

Rosa Zarza Jimeno
*Garrigues Abogados*

Rosario Vicente Martínez
*Universidad de Castilla-La Mancha*

Santiago Fernández Redondo
*Hospital Universitario La Princesa*

Teresa Martín Zuriaga
*Gobierno de Aragon*

Teresa Rodriguez Montañés
*Universidad de Alcalá*

Anonymous Contributors

## Sri Lanka

Anusha Wickramasinghe

Chrishantha Abeysena
*University of Kelaniya*

Gamini Perera
*International Law Chambers*

John Wilson
*John Wilson Partners*

Kandiah Neelakandan
*Neelakandan & Neelakandan*

Madhawa Lokusooriya

N. Sivarajah
*University of Jaffna*

Savantha De Saram
*D. L. & F. De Saram*

Anonymous Contributors

## Suriname

Anne-Marel M. Linger
*4 Justice Advocaten*

Eloa Fanita van der Hilst
*4 Justice Advocaten*

Humphrey Richinel Schurman
*Schurman Advocaten*

Susil G. R. Khoenkhoen
*S.G.R. Khoenkhoen Law Firm*

Anonymous Contributors

## Sweden

Amanda Humell
*Hewlett Packard Enterprise*

Åsa Esbjörnson Carlberg
*HP PPS Sverige AB*

Bengt Lundell
*Lund University*

Birgitta Nyström
*Lund University*

Björn Ohde
*Advokataktiebolaget Roslagen*

Boel Flodgren
*Lund University*

Catherine Lions
*Umea University*

Christer Thordson
*Legal Edge*

Christian Diesen
*Stockholm University*

Claes Sandgren
*Stockholm University*

Göran Millqvist
*Stockholm University*

Gunilla Lindmark
*University of Uppsala*

Gustaf Sjöberg
*Stockholm University*

Jack Ågren
*Stockholm University*

Jessika van der Sluijs
*Stockholm University*

Johan Sangborn
*Swedish Bar Association*

Karl-Arne Olsson
*Wesslau Söderqvist Advokatbyrå*

Karol Nowak
*Lund University*

Katrin Lainpelto
*Stockholm University*

Laura Carlson
*Stockholm University*

Magnus Stenbeck
*Karolinska Institutet*

Mats Hellström
*Hellström Law Firm*

Mauro Zamboni
*Stockholm University*

Mikael Johansson
*Raoul Wallenberg Institute of Human Rights and Humanitarian Law*

Nils Gottfries
*University of Uppsala*

Ola Zetterquist
*Gothenburg University*

Olle Mårsäter
*University of Uppsala*

Petter Holm
*Front Advokater*

Reinhold Fahlbeck
*Lund University*

Sverker Jönsson
*Lund University*

Ulf Maunsbach
*Lund University*

Vilhelm Persson
*Lund University*

Anonymous Contributors

## Tanzania

Abdallah Juma
*AJM Solicitors and Advocates Chambers*

Anne H. Outwater
*Muhimbili University of Health and Allied Sciences*

Asina-Emmy Omari
*University of Dar es Salaam*

Doreen Fariji Mwamlangala
*The Open Univeristy of Tanzania*

Eliud Kitime
*The Open Univeristy of Tanzania*

Eliud Wandwalo
*MUKIKUTE*

Emmanuel C. Moshi
*University of Dodoma*

Eustard Athance Ngatale
*Ngatale & Company Advocates*

Gervas E. Yeyeye
*The Open Univeristy of Tanzania*

Grace Kamugisha Kazoba
*Institute of Finance Management*

Patricia Boshe
*The Open Univeristy of Tanzania*

Samuel V. G. Karua
*Karua and Company Advocates*

Anonymous Contributors

## Thailand

Anant Akanisthaphichat
*Thai Law Firm*

Chanvit Tharathep
*Thailand Ministry of Public Health*

Chulapong Yukate
*ZICOlaw*

Jeeranun Klaewkla
*Mahidol University*

Premprecha Dibbayawan
*Jural Law Office*

Ugrid Milintangkul
*Thailand National Health Commission*

Wonpen Kaewpan

Anonymous Contributors

## Trinidad & Tobago

Afiya B. France
*University of the West Indies*

Asaf Hosein

Bellina Barrow

Christopher Sieuchand
*M.G. Daly & Partners*

Gerard Hutchinson
*University of the West Indies*

Glenn Hamel-Smith
*M. Hamel-Smith & Co.*

Gregory Pantin
*M. Hamel-Smith & Co.*

Hasine Shaikh
*Regius Chambers*

Keri A. Kitson

Linda A. Greene
*Penco Courts Law Chambers*

Mark Ramkerrysingh
*Fitzwilliam, Stone,
Furness-Smith, and Morgan*

Martin Anthony George
*Martin Anthony George & Co.*

Matthew Gayle
*University of Birmingham*

Michelle T. Ramnarine

Nisha K. Persad
*N. K. Persad & Co.*

Rishi P. A. Dass
*Victoria Chambers*

Rose-Marie Belle Antoine
*University of the West Indies*

Tamara Avita Jackson

Timothy Hamel-Smith
*M. Hamel-Smith & Co.*

Anonymous Contributors

## Tunisia

Abdelwahab Hechiche
*University of South Florida*

Amel Gorbej

Amine Hamdi
*Zaanouni & Associates
Law Firm*

Hamza Wajdi
*Hamza Wajdi Avocats*

Imed Oussaifi
*Cabinet Maître Oussaifi*

Karim Ben Hamida
*Karim Ben Hamida Law Firm*

Nadhir Ben Ammou

Radhouane Elaiba
*Elaiba & Associés*

Ridha Mezghani
*R. Mezghani Law Office*

Zied Lejmi
*Zaanouni & Associates
Law Firm*

Anonymous Contributors

## Turkey

Altan Liman
*Aydaş Liman Kurman
Attorneys at Law*

Berrin Gökçek Yılmaz
*Anadolu University*

Cagatay Yilmaz
*Yilmaz Law Offices*

Esenyel Barak Bal
*Cailliau & Colakel Law Firm*

Eser Tekeli Soylu

Fatih Selim Yurdakul
*Yurdakul Law Office*

Levent Aydaş
*Aydas Liman Kurman
Attorneys at Law*

Mahmut Kaçan
*MK Law Firm*

Murat Volkan Dülger
*Dulger Law Office*

Nuray Gökçek Karaca
*Anadolu University*

Onur Demirci

Osman Hayran
*Istanbul Medipol University*

R. Murat Önok
*Koç University;
Turkish Press Council*

Sinan Aslan
*Aslan Hukuk
Danışmanlık Bürosu*

Teoman Akünal
*Akunal Law Office*

Ufuk Aydin
*Anadolu University*

Anonymous Contributors

## Uganda

Augustine Kaheeru
Bahemuka
*Kahuma, Khalayi &
Kaheeru Advocates*

Birungyi Cephas Kagyenda
*Birungyi, Barata & Associates*

Brigitte Kusiima
Byarugaba Sendi
*Shonubi,
Musoke & Co. Advocates*

Busingye Kabumba
*Development Law Associates;
Makerere University
School of Law*

Charles Kallu Kalumiya
*Kampala
Associated Advocates*

Diana Prida Praff
*Platform for Labour Action*

Emmanuel Luyirika
*African Palliative
Care Association*

Francis Opedun
*EVAMOR
International Limited*

George Omunyokol
*GP Advocates and Solicitors*

J. B. Rwakimari
*Abt Associates, Inc.*

Laura Nyirinkindi
*Pro Initiatives Agency*

Lilian Keene-Mugerwa
*Platform for Labour Action*

Monica T. Kirya
*Independent Law &
Development Specialist*

Mulalira Faisal Umar
*Nabukenya,
Mulalira & Co. Advocates*

Namusobya Salima
*Initiative for Social and
Economic Rights*

Nicholas Opiyo
*Chapter Four Uganda*

Ronald Mutalya
*Mutalya & Co. Advocates*

Anonymous Contributors

## Ukraine

Andrey Tarasov
*Tarasov & Partners*

Andrii Gorbatenko
*Legal Alliance Law Company*

Gatseliuk Vitalii
*Koretsky Institute of
State and Law*

Igor Svechkar
*Asters Law Firm*

Iryna Kalnytska
*GOLAW*

Iryna Shevchuk
*EnGarde Attorneys
at Law, LLC*

Ivan Horodyskyy
*Ukrainian Catholic University*

Karchevskiy Nikolay
*Lugansk State University of
Internal Affairs*

Lyubomyr Drozdovskyy
*Khasin & Drozdovskyy
Barristers Association*

Mariia Taras
*Ukrainian Catholic University
Rule of Law Center*

Markian Malskyy
*Arzinger Law Firm*

Oleksandr Bodnaruk
*Yuriy Fedkovych Chernivtsi
National University*

Oleksandr Skliarenko
*Skliarenko,
Sydorenko and Partners*

Pavlo Lukomskyi
*Salkom Law Firm*

Scott E. Brown
*Frishberg & Partners*

Sergei Konnov
*Konnov & Sozanovsky*

Sergiy Oberkovych
*GOLAW*

Taras Tsymbrivskyy
*Ukrainian Catholic University*

Valentyn Gvozdiy
*GOLAW*

Valeriia Gudiy
*Ilyashev & Partners Law Firm*

Yaroslav Ognevyuk
*Doubinsky & Osharova*

Anonymous Contributors

## United Arab Emirates

Amer Saadeddin
*Health Bay Holistic Center*

Christopher Williams
*Bracewell LLP*

Eman Al Amari
*Art of Marriage and Family
Therapy Center*

Ibrahim Elsadig
*Dentons*

Mirza R. Baig
*Dubai Pharmacy College*

Mohammed R. Alsuwaidi
*Alsuwaidi and Company*

Nazanin Aleyaseen
*K & L Gates LLP*

Rami Olwan
*University of Sharjah*

Stuart Paterson

Tarek Nakkach
*Hewlett Packard Enterprise*

Zeyad Jaffal
*Al Ain University of
Science and Technology*

Anonymous Contributors

## United Kingdom

Adam Winchester
*Lancaster University*

Alan J. Masson W.S.
*Anderson Strathern LLP*

Amy Holcroft
*Hewlett Packard Enterprise*

Anne Bradshaw
*Imperial College
Healthcare NHS Trust*

Charlotte Peterson
*Hewlett Packard Enterprise*

Christopher May
*Lancaster University*

Eleanor Kearon
*Hewlett Packard Enterprise*

Fernne Brennan
*University of Essex*

Georgina Firth
*Lancaster University*

J. S. Nguyen-Van-Tam
*University of Nottingham*

James Bell
*Slater and Gordon LLP*

Jan van Zyl Smit
*Bingham Centre for
the Rule of Law*

Jill Stavert
*Edinburgh Napier University*

Julian Cox
*Hewlett Packard Enterprise*

Kiron Reid
*University of Liverpool*

Lawrence McNamara
*Bingham Centre for
the Rule of Law*

Lord Woolf
*House of Lords*

Mark Lubbock
*Ashurst LLP*

Michael Jefferson
*University of Sheffield
School of Law*

Nigel Duncan
*City Law School*

Peter Hungerford-Welch
*City, University of London*

Peter McTigue
*Nottingham Trent University*

Richard Ashcroft
*Queen Mary University of
London School of Law*

Richard W. Whitecross
*Edinburgh Napier University*

Sara Fovargue
*Lancaster University
Law School*

Simon Honeyball
*University of Exeter*

Tony Ward
*Northumbria University*

Anonymous Contributors

## United States

A. Renee Pobjecky
*Pobjecky & Pobjecky, LLP*

Alan Houseman
*National Equal Justice Library*

Andrew D. Kaizer
*Calhoun & Lawrence, LLP*

Arthur Hunter, Jr.
*Orleans Parish Criminal
District Court*

Barbara J. Fick
*University of Notre Dame
Law School*

Bruce P. Frohnen
*Ohio Northern University
College of Law*

Bryan A. Liang
*University of California
San Diego - Global Health
Policy Institute*

Christopher R. Kelley
*University of Arkansas
School of Law*

Claudia Rast
*Butzel Long*

David Birenbaum
*Fried Frank*

Deborah Klein Walker
*Abt Associates*

Earl Johnson, Jr.
*Western Center on
Law and Poverty*

Earl V. Brown Jr.
*AFL-CIO Solidarity Center*

Elise Groulx Diggs
*Doughty Street Chambers*

H. David Kelly, Jr.
*Beins, Axelrod, P.C.*

Ian Gray
*Hewlett Packard Enterprise*

James H. Pietsch
*University of Hawaii*

Jason Coates
*American Public
Health Association*

Jeffrey Aresty
*InternetBar.org Institute, Inc.*

John Hummel
*Deschutes County Oregon
District Attorney*

John Pollock
*National Coalition for a Civil
Right to Counsel*

John R. LaBar
*Henry, McCord, Bean, Miller,
Gabriel & LaBar, P.L.L.C.*

Ken Scott
*Stanford University*

Kenneth W. Goodman
*University of Miami Miller
School of Medicine*

Kepler B. Funk
*Funk, Szachacz &
Diamond, LLC*

Kevin D. Williams
*Berkeley Youth Alternatives*

Laurel Bellows

Len Sandler
*University of Iowa
College of Law*

Leslie L. Davidson
*Columbia University Mailman
School of Public Health*

Mark Hauswald
*University of New Mexico*

Mary A. Carnell
*John Snow Inc.*

Maryellen Reynolds
*Attorneys Judicial Mediation
Consulting Team*

Matthew Keck
*Hewlett Packard Enterprise*

Michael A. Lodzinski
*Hewlett Packard Enterprise*

Michele Forzley
*Forzley & Associates*

Patrick Del Duca
*Zuber Lawler & Del Duca LLP*

Paul Bender
*Arizona State University*

Peter Edelman
*Georgetown University
Law Center*

Peter W. Zinober
*Greenberg Traurig, PA*

Rayford H. Taylor
*Gilson Athans PC*

Renaldy J. Gutierrez
*Gutierrez & Associates*

Renee M. Landers
*Suffolk University Law School*

Reynolds, Johnson, Crouse,
Anderson, Arnld
*Attorneys Judicial Military
Consulting Team*

Ricks Frazier

Robert Brown
*Hewlett Packard Enterprise*

Robert J. Collins
*University of Pennsylvania*

Sherman L. Cohn
*Georgetown University
Law Center*

Sonia Srivastava
*Hewlett Packard Enterprise*

Stephen A. Saltzburg
*The George Washington
University Law School*

Thomas Y. Mandler
*Hinshaw & Culbertson*

Timothy E. Dolan
*Policy Foresight*

Timothy Mackey
*University of California San
Diego - School of Medicine*

Vernellia Randall
*University of Dayton School
of Law*

Anonymous Contributors

## Uruguay

Amalia Laborde

Andrés Fuentes
*Arcia Storace Fuentes
Medina Abogados*

Beatriz Murguía
*Murguía - Aguirre*

Camilo Martínez Blanco
*Universidad de Montevideo*

Enrique Moller Mendez
*ALS Global Law & Accounting*

Escandor El Ters
*Hospital Público, Jefe de
Cirugía Oncológica*

Gonzalo Gari
Irureta Goyena
*Posadas, Posadas & Vecino*

Héctor Ferreira
*Hughes & Hughes*

Julio Iribarne Pla
*Ferrere Abogados*

Martín Fridman
*Ferrere Abogados*

Martín Risso Ferrand
*Universidad
Católica del Uruguay*

Ricardo Mezzera
*Mezzera Abogados*

Santiago Pereira Campos
*Rueda Abadi Pereira*

Anonymous Contributors

## Uzbekistan

Scott Radnitz
*University of Washington*

Shukhrat Khudayshukurov
*Advokat-Himoya Law Office*

Anonymous Contributors

## Venezuela

Alberto Jurado
*ALC Penal*

Alexis E. Aguirre S.
*ARAQEREYNA*

Álvaro Badell Madrid
*Badell & Grau*

Andreina Peláez Escalante
*Badell & Grau*

Andres Hernandez Lossada

Andrés L. Halvorssen
*Raffalli, de Lemos, Halvorssen,
Ortega y Ortiz Abogados*

Antonio Canova
*Un Estado de Derecho*

Carlos Alberto
Henríquez Salazar

Carlos H. Ramones Noriega
*Global Criminal Law Office*

Carlos Simón Bello Rengifo
*Universidad
Central de Venezuela*

Catherina Gallardo
*Gallardo Vaudo & Asociados*

Fernando M. Fernández
*Universidad
Central de Venezuela*

Gilberto A. Guerrero-Rocca
*Florida International
University College of Law*

Gonzalo Himiob Santomé
*Foro Penal Venezolano*

Jaime Martínez Estévez
*Rodner, Martínez & Asociados*

Jesus Escudero
*Torres, Plaz & Araujo*

José Alberto Ramirez
*Hoet, Pelaez,
Castillo & Duque*

José Manuel Ortega P.
*Palacios, Ortega y Asociados*

Juan Carlos
Garantón-Blanco
*Universidad Católica
Andrés Bello*

Juan Carlos Torcat
*ONG Orpanac*

Juan Korody

Juan M. Raffalli
*Raffalli, de Lemos, Halvorssen,
Ortega y Ortiz Abogados*

Luis Gonzalo Monteverde
*Torres, Plaz & Araujo*

Luis Ortiz Alvarez

Manuel A. Gomez
*Florida International
University College of Law*

Nathalie Emperatriz
González Pérez
*Rodriguez & Mendoza*

Ramon Jose Medina
*Torres, Plaz & Araujo*

Ricardo J. Cruz Rincón
*Escritorio Chumaceiro-
González Rubio*

Rosa Virginia Superlano

Anonymous Contributors

## Vietnam

Kent Wong
*VCI Legal*

Kieu Anh Vu
*Le Nguyen Law Office*

Ngo Huu Nhi
*Thien An Law Office*

Nguyen Huu Phuoc
*Phuoc & Partners Law Firm*

Nguyen Thu Hang
*VN CONSULT Law Firm*

Pham Tri Dung
*Hanoi School of Public Health*

Pham Van Phat
*An Phat Pham Law Firm*

Quang Nguyen Nhan

Vo Dinh Duc
*P&P Law Firm*

Vu Dzung
*YKVN*

Anonymous Contributors

## Zambia

Anne Namakando-Phiri
*University of Zambia*

Arthur Mazimba

Fares Florence Phiri
*Nodi Trust School*

Melvin L. M. Mbao
*North-West University*

Mulopa Ndalameta
*Musa Dudhia & Co.*

Naomy Lintini
*RayBeam Enterprises*

Pamela Sibanda Mumbi

Tiziana Marietta
*Sharpe & Howard
Legal Practitioners*

Anonymous Contributors

## Zimbabwe

**Andrew Makoni**
*Mbidzo, Muchadehama &
Makoni Legal Practitioners*

**Bellinda Chinowawa**
*Zimbabwe Lawyers for
Human Rights*

**Brighton Mahuni**
*Scanlen &
Holderness Solicitors*

**Casper Pound**
*Family Aids Support
Organisation*

**Chido Mashanyare**
*Dube, Manikai & Hwacha
Legal Practitioners*

**Godman Chingoma**
*Dube, Manikai & Hwacha
Legal Practitioners*

**Isiah Mureriwa**
*Scanlen &
Holderness Solicitors*

**John T. Burombo**
*Maja & Associates*

**Mordecai Pilate Mahlangu**
*Gill, Godlonton & Gerrans*

**Simplicio Bhebhe**
*Kantor & Immerman
Legal Practitioners*

**Tawanda Tandi**
*Kantor & Immerman
Legal Practitioners*

**Tendai F. Mataba**
*Wintertons Legal Practitioners*

**Tinoziva Bere**
*Bere Brothers
Legal Practitioners*

**Wadzanai Vudzijena**
*Coghlan, Welsh &
Guest Legal Practitioners*

**Zanudeen Makorie**
*Coghlan, Welsh &
Guest Legal Practitioners*

**Anonymous Contributors**

# Acknowledgements

# Acknowledgements

The World Justice Project's Honorary Chairs, Directors, Officers, Staff, Financial Supporters, and Sponsoring Organizations are listed in the last section of this report.

Polling companies, research organizations, and contributing experts are listed in the "Methodology" section of this report.

## Academic Advisors

Mark David Agrast, American Society of International Law; Jose M. Alonso, World Wide Web Foundation; Rolf Alter, OECD; Eduardo Barajas, Universidad del Rosario; Maurits Barendrecht, Tilburg University; Tonu Basu, Open Government Partnership; Christina Biebesheimer, The World Bank; Tim Besley, London School of Economics; Paul Brest, Stanford University; Jose Caballero, IMD Business School; David Caron, Kings College, London; Thomas Carothers, Carnegie Endowment; Marcela Castro, Universidad de los Andes; Peter Chapman, Open Society Justice Initiative (OSJI); Eduardo Cifuentes, Universidad de los Andes; Sherman Cohn, Georgetown University; Christine M. Cole, Crime & Justice Institute; Mariano-Florentino Cuellar, Stanford University; Helen Darbishire, Access Info Europe; Nicolas Dassen, Inter-American Development Bank; Larry Diamond, Stanford University; Claudia J. Dumas, Transparency International USA; Sandra Elena, Ministerio de Justicia y Derechos Humanos; Brad Epperly, University of South Carolina; Julio Faundez, Warwick University; Hazel Feigenblatt, Global Integrity; Todd Foglesong, Munk School of Global Affairs at the University of Toronto; Tom Ginsburg, University of Chicago; Joseph Foti, Open Government Partnership; James Goldston, Open Society Justice Initiative (OSJI); Jorge Gonzalez, Universidad Javeriana; Alejandro Gonzalez-Arriola, Open Government Partnership; Jon Gould, American University; Martin Gramatikov, HiiL; Brendan Halloran, Transparency and Accountability Initiative; Linn Hammergren; Tim Hanstad, Landesa; Wassim Harb, Arab Center for the Development of Rule of Law and Integrity; Nathaniel Heller, Open Government Partnership; Vanessa Herringshaw, Transparency and Accountability Initiative; Susan Hirsch, George Mason University; Ronald Janse, University of Amsterdam Law School;

Erik G. Jensen, Stanford University; Haroon Khadim, PAE; Rachel Kleinfeld, Carnegie Endowment; Jack Knight, Duke University; Harold H. Koh, Yale University; Margaret Levi, Stanford University; Iris Litt, Stanford University; Clare Lockhart, The Institute for State Effectiveness; Zsuzsanna Lonti, OECD; Diego Lopez, Universidad de los Andes; William T. Loris, Loyola University; Lauren E. Loveland, National Democratic Institute (NDI); Paul Maassen, Open Government Partnership; Beatriz Magaloni, Stanford University; Jenny S. Martinez, Stanford University; Toby McIntosh, FreedomInfo.org; Toby Mendel, Centre for Law and Democracy; Nicholas Menzies, The World Bank; Ghada Moussa, Cairo University; Sam Muller, HiiL; Robert L. Nelson, American Bar Foundation and Northwestern University; Alfonsina Peñaloza, Hewlett Foundation; Harris Pastides, University of South Carolina; Randal Peerenboom, La Trobe University and Oxford University; Angela Pinzon, Universidad del Rosario; Shannon Portillo, George Mason University; Michael H. Posner, New York University; Roy L. Prosterman, University of Washington; Anita Ramasastry, University of Washington; Mor Rubinstein, Open Knowledge Foundation; Angela Ruiz, Universidad del Rosario; Audrey Sacks, The World Bank; Lutforahman Saeed, Kabul University; Michaela Saisana, EU-JRC; Andrea Saltelli, EU-JRC; Moises Sanchez, Alianza Regional por la Libertad de Expresion; Andrei Shleifer, Harvard University; Jorge Luis Silva, The World Bank; Gordon Smith, University of South Carolina; Christopher Stone, Open Society Foundations; Rene Uruena, Universidad de los Andes; Stefan Voigt, University of Hamburg; Barry Weingast, Stanford University; Michael Woolcock, The World Bank.

Roland Abeng; Lukman Abdul-Rahim; Mame Adjei; Priya Agarwal-Harding; Mariam Ahmed; Lina Alameddine; Sarah Alexander; Erica Jaye Ames; Rose Karikari Anang; Evelyn Ankumah; Jassim Alshamsi; Ekaterina Baksanova;

Hamud M. Balfas; Laila El Baradei; Sophie Barral; April Baskin; Ivan Batishchev; Rachael Beitler; Laurel Bellows; Ayzada Bengel; Dounia Bennani; Clever Bere; Rindala Beydoun; Karan K. Bhatia; Eric C. Black; Cherie Blair; Rob Boone; Juan Manuel Botero; Oussama Bouchebti; Raúl Izurieta Mora Bowen; Ariel Braunstein; Kathleen A. Bresnahan; Michael Brown; Susanna Brown; William R. Brownfield; David Bruscino; Carolina Cabrera; Ted Carrol; Javier Castro De León; John Catalfamo; Fahima Charaffeddine; David Cheyette; Nabiha Chowdhury; Jose Cochingyan, III; Kate Coffey; Sonkita Conteh; Barbara Cooperman; Hans Corell; Adriana Cosgriff; Ana Victoria Cruz; Alexander E. Davis; Beth Davis; Bryce de Flamand; James P. DeHart; Brackett B. Denniston, III; Russell C. Deyo; Surya Dhungel; Adama Dieng; Andrew Domingoes; Killian Dorier; Alyssa Dougherty; Sandra Elena; Roger El Khoury; Sanal Enkhbaatar; Adele Ewan; Fatima Fettar; Steve Fisher; Eric Florenz; Abderrahim Foukara; Kristina Fridman; Morly Frishman; Viorel Furdui; Minoru Furuyama; William H. Gates, Sr.; Anna Gardner; Dorothy Garcia; Sophie Gebreselassie; Dwight Gee; Sujith George; Adam Gerstenmier; Jacqueline Gichinga; Suzanne E. Gilbert; Brian Gitau; Travis Glynn; Arturo Gomez; Nengak Daniel Gondyi; Lindsey Graham; Deweh Gray; Michael S. Greco; Elise Groulx; Paula F. Guevara; Heena Gupta; Arkady Gutnikov; Karen Hall; Margaret Halpin; Kunio Hamada; Leila Hanafi; Sana Hawamdeh; Kate Helms; Alvaro Herrero; Sheila Hollis; Michael Holston; R. William Ide, III; Murtaza Jaffer; Chelsea Jaeztold; Hassan Bubacar Jallow; Sunil Kumar Joshi; Marie-Therese Julita; Megan Kabre; Jessica Kane; Rashvin Kaur; Anne Kelley; Howard Kenison; Junaid Khalid; Elsa Khwaja; Se Hwan Kim; Stuti Kokkalera; Laurie Kontopidis; Simeon Koroma; Steven H. Kraft; Larry D. Kramer; Jack Krumholtz; Lianne Labossiere; Samantha Liberman; Joanna Lim; Deborah Lindholm; Hongxia Liu; Annie Livingston; Jeanne L. Long; Clarissa Lopez-Diarte; Stephen Lurie; Biola Macaulay; Ahna B. Machan; Maha Mahmoud; Biawakant Mainali; Andrew Makoni; Dijana Malbaša; Frank Mantero; Madison Marks; Roger Martella; Vivek Maru; John Mason; Elisa Massimino; Hiroshi Matsuo; Michael Maya; Bethany McGann; Matthew Mead; Sindi Medar-Gould; Nathan Menon; Ellen Mignoni; Aisha Minhas; Claros Morean; Liliana Moreno; Junichi Morioka; Carrie Moore; Katrina Moore; Marion Muller; Xavier Muller; Jenny Murphy; Rose Murray; Norhayati Mustapha; Reinford Mwangonde; Doreen Ndishabandi; Ilija Nedelkoski; Layda Negrete; Patricia van Nispen; Daniel Nitu; Elida Nogoibaeva; Victoria Norelid; Justin Nyekan; Sean O'Brien; Peggy Ochanderena; Bolaji Olaniran; Joy Olson; Mohamed Olwan; Gustavo Alanis Ortega; Bolaji Owasanoye; Kedar Patel; Angeles Melano Paz; Karina Pena; Valentina Pérez Botero;

Ronen Plechnin; Kamal Pokhrel; John Pollock; Cynthia Powell; Nathalie Rakotomalia; Javier Ramirez; Eduardo Ramos-Gómez; Daniela Rampani; Richard Randerson; Claudia Rast; Yahya Rayegani; Nick Rehmus; Adrian F. Revilla; Ludmila Mendonça; Lopes Ribeiro; Kelly Roberts; Nigel H. Roberts; Amir Ron; Maria Rosales; Liz Ross; Steve Ross; Patricia Ruiz de Vergara; Irma Russell; Bruce Sewell; Humberto Prado Sifontes; Uli Parmlian Sihombing; Hajrija Sijerčić-Čolić; William Sinnott; Lumba Siyanga; Brad Smith; Leslie Solís; Joshua Steele; Lourdes Stein; Thomas M. Susman; Elizabeth Thomas-Hope; Jinni Tran; Laurence Tribe; Christina Vachon; Robert Varenik; Jessica Villegas; Maria Vinot; Raymond Webster; Robin Weiss; Dorothee Wildt; Jennifer Wilmore; Jason Wilks; Malin Winbom; Russom Woldezghi; Stephen Zack; Keyvan Zamani; Jorge Zapp-Glauser; Roula Zayat; Fanny Zhao.

Altus Global Alliance; APCO Worldwide; Fleishman-Hillard; The Center for Advanced Study in the Behavioral Sciences, Stanford University; The Center on Democracy, Development, and the Rule of Law, Stanford University; The German Bar Association in Brussels; Governance Data Alliance; Google Inc.; The Hague Institute for the Internationalisation of Law (HiiL); The Legal Department of Hewlett-Packard Limited; The Legal Department of Microsoft Corporation; The Whitney and Betty MacMillan Center for International and Area Studies, Yale University; Rule of Law Collaborative, University of South Carolina; The University of Chicago Law School; Vera Institute of Justice.

# About the World Justice Project

# About the World Justice Project

The World Justice Project® (WJP) is an independent, multidisciplinary organization working to advance the rule of law around the world.

Effective rule of law reduces corruption, combats poverty and disease, and protects people from injustices large and small. It is the foundation for communities of peace, opportunity, and equity—underpinning development, accountable government, and respect for fundamental rights.

Founded by William H. Neukom in 2006 as a presidential initiative of the American Bar Association (ABA), and with the initial support of 21 other strategic partners, the World Justice Project transitioned into an independent 501(c)(3) non-profit organization in 2009. Its offices are located in Washington, DC, and Seattle, WA, USA.

## Our Approach

The World Justice Project (WJP) engages citizens and leaders from across the globe and from multiple work disciplines to advance the rule of law. Our work is founded on two premises: 1) the rule of law is the foundation of communities of peace, opportunity, and equity, and 2) multidisciplinary collaboration is the most effective way to advance the rule of law. Based on this, WJP's mutually-reinforcing lines of business employ a multidisciplinary, multi-layered approach through original research and data, an active and global network, and practical, on-the-ground programs to advance the rule of law.

## Research and Scholarship

The WJP's Research & Scholarship work supports research about the meaning and measurement of the rule of law, and how it matters for economic, socio-political, and human development. The Rule of Law Research Consortium (RLRC) is a community of leading scholars from a variety of fields harnessing diverse methods and approaches to produce research on the rule of law and its effects on society.

## WJP Rule of Law Index®

The WJP Rule of Law Index provides original, impartial data on how the rule of law is experienced in everyday life in 113 countries around the globe. It is the most comprehensive index of its kind. To date, more than 270,000 citizens and experts have been interviewed worldwide. Index findings have been referenced by heads of state, chief justices, business leaders, public officials, and the press, including media outlets in over 125 countries worldwide.

## Engagement

Engagement efforts include connecting and developing a global network, organizing strategic convenings, and fostering practical, on-the-ground programs. At our biennial World Justice Forum, regional conferences, and single-country engagements, citizens and leaders come together to learn about the rule of law, build their networks, and design pragmatic solutions to local rule of law challenges. In addition, the World Justice Challenge provides seed grants to support practical, on-the-ground programs addressing discrimination, corruption, violence, and more.

## Honorary Chairs

The World Justice Project has the support of outstanding leaders representing a range of disciplines around the world. The Honorary Chairs of the World Justice Project are:

Madeleine Albright; Giuliano Amato; Robert Badinter; James A. Baker III; Cherie Blair; Stephen G. Breyer; Sharan Burrow; David Byrne; Jimmy Carter; Maria Livanos Cattaui; Arthur Chaskalson;* Hans Corell; Hilario G. Davide, Jr.; Hernando de Soto; Adama Dieng; William H. Gates, Sr.; Ruth Bader Ginsburg; Richard J. Goldstone; Kunio Hamada; Lee H. Hamilton; Mohamed Ibrahim; Hassan Bubacar Jallow; Tassaduq Hussain Jillani; Anthony M. Kennedy; Beverley McLachlin; George J. Mitchell; John Edwin Mroz;* Indra Nooyi; Sandra Day O'Connor; Ana Palacio; Colin L. Powell; Roy L. Prosterman; Richard W. Riley; Mary Robinson; Petar Stoyanov; Richard Trumka; Desmond Tutu; Antonio Vitorino; Paul A. Volcker; Harold Woolf; Andrew Young; Zhelyu Zhelev.*

## Board of Directors

Sheikha Abdulla Al-Misnad; Emil Constantinescu; William C. Hubbard; Suet-Fern Lee; Mondli Makhanya; William H. Neukom; Ellen Grace Northfleet; James R. Silkenat.

## Directors Emeritus

President Dr. Ashraf Ghani Ahmadzai

## Officers and Staff

William C. Hubbard, *Chairman of the Board*; William H. Neukom, *Founder and CEO*; Deborah Enix-Ross, *Vice President*; James R. Silkenat, *Director and Vice President*; Lawrence B. Bailey, *Treasurer*; Gerold W. Libby, *General Counsel and Secretary*.

**Staff:** Juan Carlos Botero, *Executive Director*; Alejandro Ponce, *Chief Research Officer*; Rebecca Billings; Josiah Byers; Alicia Evangelides; Radha Friedman; Amy Gryskiewicz; Camilo Gutiérrez Patiño; Matthew Harman; Roberto Hernández; Clara Jiang; Jeremy Levine-Drizin; Sarah Chamness Long; Debby Manley; Joel Martinez; Nikki Ngbichi-Moore; Afua Ofosu-Barko; Christine Pratt; Gerard Vinluan; Nancy Ward; Hunter Zachwieja.

## Financial Supporters

**Foundations:** Allen & Overy Foundation; Bill & Melinda Gates Foundation; Carnegie Corporation of New York; Chase Family Philanthropic Fund; The Edward John and Patricia Rosenwald Foundation; Ewing Marion Kauffman Foundation; Ford Foundation; GE Foundation; Gordon and Betty Moore Foundation; National Endowment for Democracy; Neukom Family Foundation; North Ridge Foundation; Oak Foundation; Pinnacle Gardens Foundation; Salesforce Foundation; The Stanley S. Langendorf Foundation Judson Family Fund at The Seattle Foundation; The William and Flora Hewlett Foundation.

**Corporations:** AmazonSmile; Anonymous, Apple, Inc.; The Boeing Company; E.I. DuPont de Nemours & Company; Google, Inc.; General Electric Company; Hewlett-Packard Company; Intel Corporation; Invest In Law Ltd; Johnson & Johnson; LexisNexis; McKinsey & Company, Inc.; Merck & Co., Inc.; Microsoft Corporation; Nike, Inc.; PepsiCo; Texas Instruments, Inc.; Viacom International, Inc.; WalMart Stores, Inc.

**Law Firms:** Allen & Overy LLP; Boies, Schiller & Flexner, LLP; Cochingyan & Peralta Law Offices; Drinker Biddle & Reath LLP; Fulbright & Jaworski; Garrigues LLP; Gómez-Acebo & Pombo; Haynes and Boone, LLP; Holland & Knight LLP; Hunton & Williams; K&L Gates; Mason, Hayes+Curran; Nelson Mullins Riley & Scarborough LLP; Roca Junyent; Sullivan & Cromwell LLP; SyCip Salazar Hernandez & Gatmaitan; Troutman Sanders LLP; Turner Freeman Lawyers; Uría Menéndez; White & Case LLP; Winston & Strawn LLP.

**Governments:** Irish Aid; Singapore Ministry of Law; U.S. Department of State.

**Professional Firms and Trade Associations:** American Bar Association (ABA); ABA Section of Administrative Law and Regulatory Practice; ABA Section of Antitrust Law; ABA Business Law Section; ABA Criminal Justice Section; ABA Section of Dispute Resolution; ABA Section of Environment, Energy, and Resources;

* Deceased

ABA Health Law Section; ABA Section of Individual Rights & Responsibilities; ABA Section of Intellectual Property Law; ABA Section of International Law; ABA Judicial Division; ABA Section of Labor and Employment Law; ABA Section of Litigation; ABA Section of Real Property, Trust and Estate Law; ABA Section of State and Local Government Law; ABA Section of Taxation; Major, Lindsey & Africa; Union of Turkish Bar Associations; United States Chamber of Commerce & Related Entities; Welsh, Carson, Andersen & Stowe.

**Institutions:** Eastminister Presbyterian Church; Society of the Cincinnati.

**Individual Donors:** Mark Agrast; Randy J. Aliment; H. William Allen; William and Kay Allen; David and Helen Andrews; Anonymous; Keith A. Ashmus; Kirk Baert; Robert Badinter; Lawrence B. Bailey; Martha Barnett; Richard R. Barnett, Sr.; Jonathan Barstow; April Baskin; David Billings; Juan Carlos Botero; Pamela A. Bresnahan; Toby Bright; Colin Brooks; Jack Brooms; Richard D. Catenacci; Maren Christensen; Valerie Colb; Lee and Joy Cooper; Russell C. Deyo; Sandra Disner; Mark S. Ellis; Deborah Enix-Ross; Matthew and Valerie Evans; William and Janet Falsgraf; Jonathan Fine; Malcolm Fleming; William Forney; Steven Fredman; Phillip Galgiani; Suzanne Gilbert; Tom Ginsberg; Jamie S. Gorelick; Lynn T. Gunnoe; Margaret Halpin; Harry Hardin; Joshua Harkins-Finn; Norman E. Harned; Albert C. Harvey; Judith Hatcher; Thomas Z. Hayward, Jr.; Benjamin H. Hill, III; |Claire Suzanne Holland; Kathleen Hopkins; Avery Horne; R. Thomas Howell, Jr.; William C. and Kappy Hubbard; R. William Ide; Marina Jacks; Patricia Jarman; Elias Jonsson; George E. Kapke; Peter  E. Halle and Carolyn Lamm; Suet Fern Lee; Myron and Renee Leskiw; Margaret Levi; Gerold Libby; Paul M. Liebenson; Iris Litt; Hongxia Liu; Roderick and Karla Mathews; Lucile and Gerald McCarthy; Sandy McDade; Brian McDonald; M. Margaret McKeown; James Michel; Leslie Miller; William R. Moller; Liliana Moreno; Nelson Murphy; Justin Nelson; Robert Nelson; William H. Neukom; Jitesh Parikh; Scott Partridge; J. Anthony Patterson Jr.; Lucian T. Pera; Maury and Lorraine Poscover; David Price; Llewelyn G. Pritchard; Michael Reed; Joan and Wm. T Robinson III; Daniel Rockmore; Rachel Rose; Robert Sampson; Erik A. Schilbred; Judy Schulze; James R. Silkenat; Rhonda Singer; Thomas Smegal; Ann and Ted Swett; Joan Phillips Timbers; Kathleen Vermillion; Nancy Ward; H. Thomas Wells; Dwight Gee and Barbara Wright.

**Strategic Partners**

American Bar Association; American Public Health Association; American Society of Civil Engineers; Arab Center for the Development of the Rule of Law and Integrity; Avocats Sans Frontières; Canadian Bar Association; Club of Madrid; Hague Institute for the Internationalisation of Law; Human Rights First; Human Rights Watch; Inter-American Bar Association; International Bar Association; International Chamber of Commerce; International Institute for Applied Systems Analysis; International Organization of Employers; International Trade Union Confederation; Inter-Pacific Bar Association; Karamah: Muslim Women Lawyers for Human Rights; Landesa; NAFSA: Association of International Educators; Norwegian Bar Association; People to People International; Transparency International USA; Union Internationale des Avocats; Union of Turkish Bar Associations; U.S. Chamber of Commerce; The World Council of Religious Leaders; World Federation of Engineering Organisations; World Federation of Public Health Associations.

"Laws of justice which Hammurabi, the wise king, established... That the strong might not injure the weak, in order to protect the widows and orphans..., in order to declare justice in the land, to settle all disputes, and heal all injuries."
**-Codex Hammurabi**

"I could adjudicate lawsuits as well as anyone. But I would prefer to make lawsuits unnecessary."
**-Analects of Confucius**

"It is more proper that law should govern than any one of the citizens."
**- Aristotle, Politics (350 BCE)**

"If someone disobeys the law, even if he is (otherwise) worthy, he must be punished. If someone meets the standard, even if he is (otherwise) unworthy, he must be found innocent. Thus the Way of the public good will be opened up, and that of private interest will be blocked."
**- The Huainanzi 139 BCE (Han Dynasty, China)**

"We are all servants of the laws in order that we may be free."
**- Cicero (106 BCE - 43 BCE)**

"The Law of Nations, however, is common to the entire human race, for all nations have established for themselves certain regulations exacted by custom and human necessity."
**-Corpus Juris Civilis**

"Treat the people equally in your court and give them equal attention, so that the noble shall not aspire to your partiality, nor the humble despair of your justice."
**-Judicial Guidelines from 'Umar Bin Al-Khattab, The Second Khalifa of Islam'**

"No freeman is to be taken or imprisoned or disseised of his free tenement or of his liberties or free customs, or outlawed or exiled or in any way ruined, nor will we go against such a man or send against him save by lawful judgement of his peers or by the law of the land. To no-one will we sell or deny or delay right or justice."
**-Magna Carta**

"Where-ever law ends, tyranny begins."
**- John Locke, Two Treatises of Government (1689)**

"Good civil laws are the greatest good that men can give and receive. They are the source of morals, the palladium of property, and the guarantee of all public and private peace. If they are not the foundation of government, they are its supports; they moderate power and help ensure respect for it, as though power were justice itself."
**-Jean-Étienne-Marie Portalis. Discours Préliminaire du Premier Projet de Code Civil**

"All human beings are born free and equal in dignity and rights... Everyone is entitled to all the rights and freedoms set forth in this Declaration, without distinction of any kind, such as race, colour, sex, language, religion, political or other opinion, national or social origin, property, birth or other status."
**-Universal Declaration of Human Rights**